THE READER OVER YOUR SHOULDER

The READER OVER YOUR SHOULDER

A Handbook for Writers of English Prose

by

ROBERT GRAVES

B.Litt., Oxon, once Professor of English Literature at the Royal Egyptian University

&

ALAN HODGE

B.A., Oxon

Authors of The Long Week End

COLLIER BOOKS, NEW YORK

First Collier Books Edition 1966

Second Printing 1967

The Macmillan Company, New York

PRINTED IN THE UNITED STATES OF AMERICA

CONTENTS

PART I

THE READER OVER YOUR SHOULDER

PART II

EXAMINATIONS AND FAIR COPIES

CONTENTS

ACKNOWLEDGEMENTS

We thank all those writers who have allowed us to make critical use of the passages from their books which we quote in Part II, p. 207; we have asked (and been granted) permission wherever the material used seemed to exceed in length or importance the critic's legitimate allowance. The following publishers have asked us to make formal acknowledgements to them: Messrs. George Allen and Unwin on behalf of Mr. Aldous Huxley, Messrs. Ernest Benn on behalf of Mr. J. W. N. Sullivan and Sir Leonard Woolley, Messrs. Blackwell and Mott on behalf of Mr. C. Day Lewis, Cambridge University Press on behalf of Sir Arthur Eddington, Sir James Jeans, Professors Bertrand Russell and A. N. Whitehead, Messrs. Chatto and Windus on behalf of Dr. F. R. Leavis, The National Council for Civil Liberties on behalf of Sir Norman Angell, Messrs. John Murray on behalf of Sir Cyril Norwood, Oxford University Press on behalf of Mr. J. Middleton Murry, Messrs. George Routledge on behalf of Professor I. A. Richards.

Finally we thank our friends Norman Cameron, Patricia Carey, Clifford Dalton, John Dennis, Margaret Frame, John Graves, Francis Hemming, Basil Liddell Hart, Colin McFadyean, Thomas Matthews, James Reeves, Darcy Sullivan, Virginia Wimperis and Gilbert Yates for various assistance in preparing this book.

To

JENNY NICHOLSON

PART I
THE READER OVER YOUR SHOULDER

★

CHAPTER ONE
THE PECULIAR QUALITIES OF ENGLISH

THE most ancient European languages — those that have longest avoided infiltration by other languages — are the most complicated in their grammar and syntax. The age of a language can be roughly guessed by a count of its declensions, conjugations, moods, tenses, voices, cases, genders and numbers. Latin is clearly less ancient than Greek, since it has no 'middle voice', no 'dual number' and no 'optative mood'[1] — thus in Latin at least seven words are needed to express the sentence 'If only you two thieves had drowned yourselves', but in Greek only four. French is clearly less ancient than Latin, since it has no separate neuter gender and does not decline its nouns; also, its conjugations are far simpler. English is clearly less ancient than French: except for its pronouns, it is free of gender differentiation.

Grammatical simplicity is the mark of a vernacular. The word 'vernacular', formed from the Roman historian Varro's phrase *vernacula verba*, 'unliterary expressions used by slaves or serfs', has often since been used loosely to mean 'the native language of a peasantry'; but few of Varro's slaves can have been native Italians — they may have been Greeks, Bithynians, Africans or Germans — and the language they spoke among themselves was a mixed lingo, sometimes called 'camp Latin', which later developed in Italy into modern Italian, in Spain into Spanish, in France into French. Properly speaking, then, a vernacular is a lingo, or language of domestic convenience, compounded of the languages spoken by master and alien slave. It has a less complicated grammar and syntax than the languages from which it springs, but rapidly accumulates words as the slaves become freedmen, and their children are born as freemen, and finally their great-grandchildren, marrying into their masters' families, are

[1] These denote respectively: action done for oneself (between the active and passive *voices*); reference to two people (between the singular and plural *numbers*); expression of a wish (supplementing the indicative and subjunctive *moods*).

accepted as cultured people with full rights as citizens. The historical origins of German, which is not very primitive in structure, are obscure; modern German, however, is not a vernacular in Varro's sense, but a late artificial compound of several kindred dialects, with a far smaller vocabulary of early borrowings from the Latin and Greek than the other languages of Western Europe.

English is a vernacular of vernaculars. It began in the eleventh century as the lingo used between the Norman-French conquerors and their Anglo-Saxon serfs, and though it became a literary language in the fourteenth century has never crystallized in the way that Italian, French and Spanish have done. A proof of this is that no writer of English would be credited with a perfect literary style merely because he had exactly modelled himself on some native paragon – say, Addison in England, or Emerson in the United States – as Italians, Spaniards and Frenchmen might be after modelling themselves, respectively, on Boccaccio, Cervantes and Bossuet. To write English well, it is generally agreed, is not to imitate, but to evolve a style peculiarly suited to one's own temperament, environment and purposes. English has never been jealously watched over by a learned Academy, as French has been since the seventeenth century; nor protected against innovations either by literary professionalism, as with Italian, or, as with Spanish, by the natural decorum of the greater part of those who use it. It is, indeed, an immense, formless aggregate not merely of foreign assimilations and local dialects but of occupational and household dialects and personal eccentricities.

The general European view is that English is an illogical, chaotic language, unsuited for clear thinking; and it is easy to understand this view, for no other European language admits of such shoddy treatment. Yet, on the other hand, none other admits of such poetic exquisiteness, and often the apparent chaos is only the untidiness of a workshop in which a great deal of repair and other work is in progress: the benches are crowded, the corners piled with lumber, but the old workman can lay his hand on whatever spare parts or accessories he needs or at least on the right tools and materials for improvising them. French is a language of fixed models: it has none of this workshop untidiness and few facilities for improvisation. In French, one chooses the finished phrase nearest to one's purpose and, if there is nothing that can be 'made to do', a long time is spent getting the Works – the Academy – to supply or approve a new model. Each method has its own advantages. The English method tends to ambiguity and obscurity of expression in any but the most careful writing; the French to limitation of thought. The late Sir Henry Head was once preparing an address on neurology for a learned society in Paris.

He wrote it in what he hoped was French, but took the precaution of asking a French professor to see that it was correctly phrased. The manuscript was returned marked: '*pas français, pas français, pas français*', with suggested alterations; but almost every '*pas français*' could be matched with a '*pas vrai*', because the amendments in *français* impaired the force of the argument.

As for the view that English is illogical: it certainly differs greatly in character from French, Italian, Spanish and German, which are claimed to be logical languages. These are all able codifications of as much racial experience as can be translated into speech: theoretically, each separate object, process or quality is given a registered label and ever afterwards recognized by label rather than by individual quality. Logical languages are therefore also rhetorical languages, rhetoric being the emotionally persuasive use of labels, with little concern for the things to which they are tied. English has always tended to be a language of 'conceits': that is, except for the purely syntactical parts of speech, which are in general colourless, the vocabulary is not fully dissociated from the imagery out of which it has developed – words are pictures rather than hieroglyphs.

Matthew Arnold, who as a critic did insufficient justice to the peculiar genius of the English language, suggested in his essay on the 'Influence of Literary Academies' (1875) that:

> 'The power of French Literature is in its prose-writers, the power of English Literature in its poets. While the fame of many poets of France depends on the qualities of intelligence they exhibit, qualities which are the distinctive support of prose, many of the prose-writers . . . depend wholly for their fame on the imaginative qualities they exhibit, which are the distinctive support of poetry.'

The truth is, that the French are not plagued by their metaphors tending to get out of hand and hamper the argument; whereas English writers of prose or poetry find that, so soon as a gust of natural feeling snatches away the merely verbal disguise in which their phrases are dressed, the pictorial images stand out sharply and either enliven and enforce the argument or desert it and go on a digressive ramble. English writers seldom have any feeling for purity of literary form in the Classical sense: it is both their strength and their weakness that imaginative exuberance breaks down literary restraint.

'Fixed' English, which may be dated from Dr. Johnson's *Dictionary*, completed in 1755, fulfils the need of a safer, less ambitious language arranged on the same system and dedicated to the same uses as French – a language of agreed preconceptions. 'Fixed' English makes possible a

French-English, English-French, or a German-English, English-German dictionary. Each foreign label has its English counterpart: 'Glory' is matched (not very satisfactorily) with '*la gloire*' and *der Ruhm*; '*le matelot*' and *der Matrose* with 'sailor'. 'Fixed' English compares well enough with other languages, but is often more mechanically, and therefore more correctly, employed by foreigners than by those whose mother-tongue it is and who are always inclined to slip back into free English. 'Fixed' English is an easy language to learn, like colloquial Arabic; but of free English, as of scholarly Arabic, no wise person will ever claim final mastery — there is no discovered end to either language. 'Fixed' English is never more than momentarily fixed. The conventional, hotel-manager English that foreigners learn is always a little stilted and a little out of date by the time that the book from which they learn it is published; and twenty years later the book will read very quaintly.

English, whether 'fixed' or 'free', has certain unusual advantages in structure. In the first place, it is almost uninflected and has no genders. The Romance and Germanic languages, not having had occasion to simplify themselves to the same degree, still retain their genders and inflections. There is no logical justification for genders. They are a decorative survival from a primitive time when the supposed sex of all concepts — trees, diseases, cooking implements — had to be considered for the sake of religious convention or taboo. Yet even new scientific words have to decide, so soon as coined, on their hypothetical sex. Writers of the Romance and Germanic languages have an aesthetic objection to a genderless language. But when a language is used for international exchange of ideas the practical disadvantages of gender are generally admitted to outweigh its decorative qualities. Gender is illogical, in being used partly to express actual sex, e.g. *le garçon*, *la femme*, and partly to dress words up, e.g. *la masculinité*, *le féminisme*; *le festin*, *la fête*. If one does wish to give sex-characteristics to concrete objects or abstractions (as, for example, masculinity to 'sword' and 'pen' and femininity to 'Parliament'), the existing gender is an actual hindrance to any such renewal of mythology. An inflected tense has a certain beauty from which writers in these languages refuse to be parted; but, for merely practical uses, an inflected tense such as *je serai*, *tu seras*, *il sera*, *nous serons*, *vous serez*, *ils seront* seems unnecessary to Britons and Americans, particularly since the French have dropped noun and adjective inflections almost as completely as they have.

The eventual disappearance of Norman-French from England after the Conquest was never in doubt once Anglo-Saxon had been simplified to meet the needs of the French-speaking invaders. Anglo-Saxon was deficient in words to fit the new methods of trade and government, and these had to be borrowed from French, which had a closer connexion with Rome, the source of all contemporary civilization Passing the stage of Broken Saxon the new vernacular developed an easy grammar and syntax, a modification of Anglo-Saxon, but with French turns whereever a legal or literary subtlety was needed. The vocabulary, though enormously enriched with Norman-French and Latin words of advanced culture, remained Anglo-Saxon in foundation: English words of Anglo-Saxon origin, though not half so numerous as Romance words, are used about five times as often. One feature of the happy-go-lucky development of English was that adjectives were made to do service for nouns, nouns for verbs, and so on; until by Elizabethan times it could be said that all parts of speech in English were interchangeable.

This interchangeability is a great help to accurate expression; for example, where an adjective formed in the usual way from a noun has wandered slightly from its original sense. If one wishes to discuss the inflections of a verb and does not wish to write 'verbal inflections', because 'verbal' means 'of a word' rather than 'of a verb', one is free to write 'verb inflections', using a noun for an adjective.

Further gains to English in this early period were: the wide choice of prefixes and suffixes which the pooling of the wealth of both languages gave, the use of auxiliary words to help out the verb tenses, and the new freedom won by prepositions. There is a greater richness of prepositions in English than in any other language of Western Europe: for instance, the French *de* has to bear the whole burden of the English prepositions 'of', 'from', 'out', and *à* of 'at', 'to', 'till', while German has no separation between 'of' and 'from'; 'into' and 'out of' are double prepositions with no equivalent in either French or German.

The British have long been conscious of the extreme subtlety of their language. James Clarence Mangan, in his humorous essay *My Bugle and How I Blow It*, published in the early 1830's, wrote about one use of the preposition 'in':

> 'I am the Man in the Cloak. In other words, I am by no manner of means the Man *of* the Cloak or the Man *under* the Cloak. The Germans call me "*Der Mensch mit dem Mantel*", the Man with the Cloak. This is a deplorable error in the nomenclature of that otherwise intelligent people: because my cloak is not part and parcel of myself. The cloak is outside and the man is inside, but each is a distinct entity. I admit you may say, "The Man with the Greasy Countenance", thus also Slawken-Bergius (*vide* "Tristram Shandy") calls his hero "The Stranger with the Nose", for, however long, the nose was an integral

part of the individual. With me the case is a horse of a different colour. I do not put my cloak on and off, I grant, but I can do so when I please: and therefore it is obvious to the meanest capacity that I am the Man *in* the Cloak and no mistake.'

Mangan's objection to the German idiom could have been strengthened by an opposite objection to the French '*l'homme à la redingote*', where greater emphasis is laid on the cloak than on the man. Mangan, as he says, is not 'the Man *of* the Cloak'; yet, '*l'homme dans la redingote*' is no more French than '*Der Mensch in dem Mantel*' is German. And nearly three centuries before Mangan Sir Philip Sidney had written in his *Apology for Poetry*:

'English giveth us great occasion to the right use of matter and manner, being indeed capable of any excellent exercising of it. I know some will say that it is a mingled language. And why not so much the better, taking the best of both the other? Another will say it wanteth Grammar. Nay, truly it hath that praise, that it wanteth not Grammar, for Grammar it might have, but it needs not; being so easy of itself and so void of those cumbersome differences of Cases, Genders, Moods, and Tenses, which I think was a piece of the Tower of Babylon's curse, that a man should be put to school to lean his mother tongue. But for the uttering sweetly and properly the conceits of the mind, which is the end of speech, that it hath equally with any other tongue in the world: and is particularly happy in compositions of two or three words together, near the Greek, far beyond the Latin: which is one of the greatest beauties can be in a language.'

The growth of English as a common language of conqueror and conquered had one great disadvantage: the slowness with which it arrived at a common convention for the pronunciation and spelling of words. Neither the French nor the Anglo-Saxons could form their mouths properly for the management of the others' language, particularly of the vowels; yet the French scribes had to write Saxon words in their legal records, and the Saxon scribes in submitting accounts in writing had to adopt a convention of spelling which their masters would understand. Each district, too, had its different dialect. East Midland finally became the dominant one, but words were brought into it from other dialects with different spelling conventions; when at last a general convention was agreed upon, it was (and remains) a tissue of inconsistencies – the most serious handicap to English as a language for international use.

The termination *-ough*, for instance, occurs in words as differently sounded as 'rough', 'bough', 'cough', 'thorough', 'though', 'through' and 'hiccough': the *gh* represents what was once an Anglo-Saxon guttural corresponding with the Greek letter *chi.* This guttural the Norman-French could not, or would not, pronounce: either they made an *f* sound of it or they sounded the vowel and left out the consonant altogether. It is probable that this habit became fashionable among people of Saxon blood who wished to pass as members of the ruling caste, and except in the North, where it lasted much later and still survives in many dialect words, the *gh* passed out of the spoken language and, in the written, remains merely as an historic relic. To the different pronunciation of vowels in different parts of the country, these -ough words are sufficient witnesses; as is the *ch* in 'Church', 'Christian', 'chivalry' and 'pibroch' to the inconsistency of the spelling convention. The trouble was that the scribes had only twenty-six letters (of which x, k, and q were redundant) to express forty-three common sounds. They tried various methods, such as doubling a consonant to show that the vowel which came before was short, e.g. 'batter', and putting a final 'e' after a consonant to show that the vowel was long, e.g. 'bone'. None of these methods could be used consistently while the pronunciation was still so various; and the scribes did as well as could be expected, short of inventing a new alphabet.

Spelling conventions have changed continually ever since and are not yet stabilized. The word 'mutton', before its spelling was thus fixed early in the reign of James I, had been spelt: 'moltoun', 'motoun', 'motone', 'motene', 'motonne', 'motton', 'mouton', 'muton', 'muttoun', 'mutown' and 'mutten'. 'Button', stabilized at about the same time, had had a still greater range of spelling variations including 'botheum' and 'buttowne'. Yet even after this newly borrowed Romance words in '*-on*' were not similarly Englished as '-on': *balon*, *marron*, *musqueton*, *salon*, were spelt 'balloon', 'marroon', 'musketoon', 'saloon'. This 'oo', which also represented the narrow vowel in the word 'good', was then confused with the broader 'oo' sound as in 'food' and 'moon'. In more recent times the English have either spelt and pronounced the newly borrowed words in *-on* in the French way, if they are words of limited use, such as *soupçon* and *raison d'être*; or, if they are words capable of popular use, they have Englished them much as they did the words first borrowed. So *bâton*, as in 'conductor's baton', is made to rhyme with *fatten*; and on the barrack-square *échelon* has come to rhyme with 'stretch along'. However, on the whole the English-speaking peoples have become more willing to pronounce and spell foreign words as they are spelt and pronounced in their countries of origin. Broadcasting assists this tendency: for example, 'garridge' for 'garage' would have become general in Britain but for the French pronunciation insisted on by the B.B.C. This new respect for accuracy of pronunciation has made things rather worse than before. For instance, the Irish word 'lough', not long borrowed, has added one more pitfall to the pronunciation of words in '-ough'. Conscientious English travellers to Ireland try to manage the sound, but the dictionaries compromise by directing that it shall be pronounced 'lok' — 'k' is at any rate a guttural and nearer to the original sound than 'f'.

Certain advantages have been derived even from these confusions. Where there has been more than one pronunciation of a word, it has very often been split into two words, each devoted to a different sense and usually spelt differently. 'Through' and 'thorough' provide an instance of differentiation both of spelling and pronunciation; 'flower' 'flour' 'gest' and 'jest' of differentiation in spelling only. It sometimes happens that the same word is borrowed more than once from the same language, the first borrowing having already changed in sense. Thus the second borrowing becomes a new English word and, the spelling convention having meanwhile also changed, is easily distinguished from the early borrowing. The word 'saloon' was the eighteenth-century English equivalent of the French *salon*, meaning a reception-room in a palace or great house. In early Victorian times it began to be vulgarized, and now has come to mean merely a large room in a commercial establishment. *Salon*, borrowed again, means the reception room of a lady of fashion, where wits and notabilities assemble for mutual entertainment. Similarly, 'antick', with its more modern forms 'antic' and 'antique', present very different views of things antiquated.

In accepting English, one must accept the inconsistent spelling cheerfully, not only for the practical service it has given in the differentiation of meaning, but on its own account, as one learns to accept and even love the irregularities of a friend's face. There is to the English eye something distasteful in phonetic spelling. Attempts to force it upon the language, though supported by all the logic in the world, are unavailing — 'because of the ugly look the words have — too much "k" and "z" and "ay".' One would have less objection to phonetic or 'simplified' spelling if it could be introduced retrospectively in one's grandfather's days; but nobody likes to make such sacrifices for the sake of his grandchildren.

As the regularizing of spelling and pronunciation on a rational basis has never succeeded, so the permanent limiting of particular words to particular senses, the fixing of English, has never come to much. There have been professorial panjandrums who have undertaken the reformation of the language as their life's task; there have even been short periods, usually after a time of national disturbance, when the governing classes have had fits of tidiness and thought about putting the dictionary into better order. But English has always resisted attempts to cramp its growth.

Alexander Gil (Headmaster of St. Paul's School when Milton was a pupil) wrote in 1619 in his *Logonomia Anglica* to complain of the 'new mange in speaking and writing', for which he held Chaucer originally responsible.

> 'O harsh lips! I now hear all around me such words as *common, vices, envy, malice*, even *virtue, study, justice, pity, mercy, compassion, profit, commodity, colour, grace, favour, acceptance*. But whither, I pray in all the world, have you banished those words which our forefathers used for these new-fangled ones? Are our words to be exiled like our citizens? Is the new barbaric invasion to extirpate the English tongue? O ye Englishmen, on you, I say, I call in whose veins that blood flows, retain, retain what yet remains of our native speech, and whatever vestiges of our forefathers are yet to be seen, on these plant your footsteps.'

He was not heeded, nor were the literary oligarchs of the early and middle eighteenth century who tried to impose 'decorum' permanently on English. We find Jonathan Swift vainly protesting in his *Bickerstaff Papers* (1723) against: the 'abundance of polysyllables introduced by the late war, *speculations, operations, preliminaries, ambassadors, communication, circumvallation, battalions*'; and at the same time against such slang as '*banter, uppish, bamboozle, kidney, mob, sham, bully, shuffling* and *palming*' — just as in October 1941 a Mr. Faning wrote to the *Daily Telegraph*:

> 'Sir — I view with concern the increasing introduction of German words into our language — such words as "blitz", "panzer", "luftwaffe" and others.
>
> Surely it is sad to reflect on the ease with which Germany can invade our language, if not our shores!
>
> If no check is put upon this practice these horrible words will become incorporated into our English vocabulary. German is uncouth and hardly fit for a civilized nation.'

Nobody will ever succeed in annulling the natural right, which every English-speaking person can claim, of borrowing words from foreign languages, coining words, making new distinctions in sense between alternative forms of the same word, resurrecting ancient words, or using whatever grammatical oddities he may please — provided he can satisfy his neighbours, colleagues, or readers, that the coining, the distinction, the borrowing, the resurrection, or the grammatical oddity is necessary. The proof of necessity will be that they adopt the form themselves.

The practice of making new words by declaration is of long standing. For example, the word 'mumpsimus', meaning 'an erroneous doctrinal view obstinately adhered to', was first put into currency by Henry VIII, in a speech from the throne in 1545. He remarked, 'Some be too stiff in their old mumpsimus, others be too busy and curious in their sumpsimus.' He was referring to the familiar story of a priest who, on being reproved for reading in the Mass '*quod in ore mumpsimus*' instead of '*quod in ore sumpsimus*' ('which we have taken in our mouths'), his Missal being mis-copied, replied that he had read it with an *m* for forty years, 'and I will not change my old mumpsimus for your new sumpsimus.' The word has held its own since, though the doctrinal sense has lost its importance compared with the scholastic sense: it now means 'an established manuscript-reading which, though obviously incorrect, is retained blindly by old-fashioned scholars'.

In several countries the declaration of an individual is not enough to settle a word, even though this is built up regularly from native material or correctly formed from Latin or Greek. The declaration has to be endorsed by the Ministry of Fine Arts or the recommendation of a university committee or learned society. The English word 'defeatism' is formed from the French word *défaitisme* current in 1915, which is not officially French: that is to say, in the early Twenties Marshal Foch, as a member of the *Académie Française*, vetoed its adoption into the Dictionary, on the ground that it was an un-French concept and intolerable. It appears apologetically, however, in A. Dauzat's *Dictionnaire Etymologique*, 1938, as: '1904, appliqué aux Russes; vulgarisé 1915.'

A passage from Lewis Carroll's *Alice Through the Looking-Glass.*

> 'Humpty-Dumpty said: "There's glory for you." "I don't know what you mean by 'glory,'" Alice said. Humpty-Dumpty smiled contemptuously. "Of course you don't till I tell you. I meant, 'There's a nice knock-down argument for you!'" "But 'glory' doesn't mean 'a nice knock-down argument'," Alice objected. "When *I* use a word," Humpty-Dumpty said in rather a scornful tone, "it means just what I choose it to mean, neither more nor less." "The question is," said Alice, "whether you *can* make words mean so many different things." "The question is," said Humpty Dumpty, "which is to be Master – that's all." Alice was too much puzzled to say anything, so after a minute Humpty-Dumpty began again. "They've a temper, some of them – particularly verbs, they're the proudest – adjectives you can do anything with, but not verbs – however, *I* can manage the whole lot of them! IMPENETRABILITY! That's what I say!"
>
> "Would you tell me, please," said Alice, "what that means?" "Now you talk like a reasonable child," said Humpty-Dumpty, looking very much pleased. "I meant by 'impenetrability' that we've had enough of that subject, and it would be just as well if you'd mention what you mean to do next, as I don't suppose you mean to stop here

> the rest of your life.'' ''That's a great deal to make one word mean,'' Alice said in a thoughtful tone. ''When I make a word do a lot of work like that,'' said Humpty-Dumpty, ''I always pay it extra.'' ''Oh!'' said Alice. She was too much puzzled to make any other remark. ''Ah, you should see 'em come round me of a Saturday night,'' Humpty-Dumpty went on, wagging his head gravely from side to side, ''for to get their wages, you know.'''

Lewis Carroll himself added several words to the language; and not only in the United States, where novelty of expression is widely exploited as a proof of national vigour, but in Great Britain too, enterprising people are every day doing the same. The greater part of their inventions has only a local and temporary currency; but a residue satisfies a national demand and sticks in the general vocabulary. Wars, politics and the popularization of scientific inventions are the chief causes of new words gaining wide currency; often these are forgotten again within the year. (One cannot yet tell whether the word 'quisling' will outlast the Nazi technique of preparing for the invasion of a country by political infiltration.) English dictionaries are collections of precedents, rather than official code-books of meaning.

In the United States, intelligent writers sometimes use a far less rigidly grammatical prose than British-born writers would dare. This is from an article (1941) by Otis Ferguson, about 'The Spirits of Rhythm', a negro orchestra:

> '[First it was] . . . Douglas Daniels and Leo Watson, who sang, played and messed around with their feet down any cab rank in St. Louis, to coax pennies ringing on to the sidewalk. . . .
>
> They started with ukeleles, because at the time of ''Yes, We Have No Bananas'' every kid going to school had about a dollar's worth of ukelele under his arm, whack it every chance he got. They started innocent of music as any kind of exercise and even to-day, as Doug says, there isn't a one of them could read a note as big as that table. But they have an active book of arrangements that can keep them going all night; and while it's all in their heads and something they have got up through playing together, you couldn't start out cold and get a book like that for less than a thousand dollars.
>
> Their act is what the record labels call vocal with inst. accomp., the inst. at present being a guitar, two tipples (a small-size guitar, using only the first four strings) and a double-bass. But that gives you no idea. The truth is, with just the four of them playing along they have more balance, depth and lift than any of the bands they are supposed to ''relieve'' on the stand. . . .
>
> Twenty desks of violins in your local grade-school symphony may

make more noise than the four instruments of the Budapest Quartet without getting the power in music, and a half-acre of Goldman Band can take Nola at around 380 to the minute without getting the sense of motion of one good two-finger piano player doing Lazy. . . .

They picked up Teddy Bunn in Washington. Teddy Bunn is the present guitar player. He is a perfectly terrible man, but has the mostest fun, and seems to be resigned to music, though there was a time when somehow or other he got hold of an electric guitar and he was playing electric all over the place, and those were not happy days. He is one of the most brilliant men in the business, and keep your pockets sewed up.'

This is good English in its unconventional way. Mr. Ferguson is taking the same liberties with prose as 'The Spirits' took with music, just to make his write-up fit the subject — there are negroish conversational inflexions throughout: for example, the abrupt 'whack it every chance he got', the emphatic 'there isn't a one of them', and the swift change of tone in 'and keep your pockèts sewed up.' He admires 'The Spirits' as showing musical genius and 'plays along' with them without finding their racy speech any more comical than their music. Some of these inflexions may one day become incorporated in the main vocabulary of English.

CHAPTER TWO

THE PRESENT CONFUSION OF ENGLISH PROSE

THERE is not, and cannot be, any permanent model of literary English; but there are everywhere obvious differences between written and spoken English. A speaker reinforces his meaning with gestures and vocal inflexions, and if the people he addresses still do not understand they can ask for further explanation; whereas a writer, not enjoying either of these advantages, must formulate and observe certain literary principles if he wishes to be completely understood. Granted, he may not always wish to be so understood: a good deal of play is made in English with deliberate looseness of phrase.[1] But the only relevant standard by which to judge any straightforward piece of prose is the ease with which it conveys its full intended sense to the readers to whom it is addressed, rather than its correctness by the laws of formal English grammar. A disadvantage of English grammar, as taught in schools until recently,[2] is that it is not originally English, nor even Latin. It is Alexandrian-Greek grammar modified to serve a language of altogether different habits; and it is often inadequate to its task – just as formal English prosody (designed on the Greek model) is inadequate to serve English poetry. The vernacular freedom of English allows many meanings, complex and simple, to be struck from the interplay of words, which in Greek or Latin or even French would be ruled out by the formal relationships insisted on by grammatic logic. How could one adequately translate into any of these languages the passage by Otis Ferguson quoted at the end of Chapter One, or the following from E. E. Cummings's carefully written Introduction to his *Collected Poems* (1938)?

> 'The poems to come are for you and for me and are not for mostpeople
>
> – it's no use trying to pretend that most people and ourselves are alike. Mostpeople have less in common with ourselves than the squarerootofminusone. You and I are human beings; mostpeople are snobs. . . .
>
> You and I wear the dangerous looseness of doom and find it becoming.

[1] The Balfour declaration, for example, which promised the Jews a 'National Home in Palestine' may well have been disingenuous rather than merely careless: while not alarming our Arab allies it allowed ardent Zionists to understand the word 'in' as meaning 'consisting of' rather than 'situated within the borders of'.

[2] In modern schools the 'grammar of function' is now taught.

Life, for eternal us, is now; and now is much too busy being a little more than everything to seem anything, catastrophic included.

Life, for mostpeople, simply isn't. Take the socalled standard of living. What do mostpeople mean by "living"? They don't mean living. They mean the latest and closest plural approximation to singular prenatal passivity which science, in its finite but unbounded wisdom, has succeeded in selling their wives. If science could fail, a mountain's a mammal. Mostpeople's wives can spot a genuine delusion of embryonic omnipotence immediately and will accept no substitutes — luckily for us, a mountain is a mammal. The plusorminus movie to end moving, the strictly scientific parlour-game of real unreality, the tyranny conceived in misconception and dedicated to the proposition that every man is a woman and any woman a king, hasn't a wheel to stand on. What their most synthetic not to mention transparent majesty, mrsandmr collective foetus, would improbably call a ghost is walking. He isn't an undream of anaesthetized impersons, or a cosmic comfortstation, or a transcendentally sterilized lookiesoundiefeelietastie-smellie. He is a little more than everything, he is democracy; he is alive: he is ourselves.'

Cummings, it will be noted, has his own typographical conventions and metaphysical vocabulary and, being a true poet, a broad enough mind to reconcile eternal and diurnal terms. But he and Otis Ferguson were alike writing, in the passages quoted, not for 'mostpeople' but for a small special public: each knew the conventional rules of English prose but had something particular to say that he believed could not be said except by breaking them. It is seldom that the passionate necessity arises for writing so peculiarly and, when it does, only a small special public can be expected to understand. Our book concerns English as it should be written for the large general public always, and for a small special public on any but the most unusual occasions.

There is an instinctive mistrust of grammarians in Britain and the United States, and a pride in following one's natural course in writing. Deliberate obscurity is rare. We suggest that whenever anyone sits down to write he should imagine a crowd of his prospective readers (rather than a grammarian in cap and gown) looking over his shoulder. They will be asking such questions as: 'What does this sentence mean?' 'Why do you trouble to tell me that again?' 'Why have you chosen such a ridiculous metaphor?' 'Must I really read this long, limping sentence?' 'Haven't you got your ideas muddled here?' By anticipating and listing as many questions of this sort as possible, the writer will discover certain tests of intelligibility to which he may regularly submit his work before he sends it off to the printer.

No writer should fail to reckon with modern reading habits. As each year until the fall of France more and more reading matter was obtruded on people's notice, they had to protect themselves in some way from having their whole leisure time engrossed by it. How much of the averagely interesting book is actually read nowadays by the averagely interested person? It can only be a small part, and of that small part a good deal is lost because, though the eye goes through the motions of reading, the mind does not necessarily register the sense. Even when a book is being read with the most literal attention—a fair example is proof-reading by the author, his friends and members of the publishing firm and printing house—scores of errors pass by undetected.[1]

It is not that modern people are less intelligent than their grandparents: only that, being busier, they are less careful. They must learn to take short cuts, skimming through the columns of a newspaper, flicking over the pages of a book or magazine, deciding at each new paragraph or page whether to read it either attentively or cursorily, or whether to let it go unread. There is a running commentary in the mind. For example, in reading a *Life of Napoleon*: 'page 9 . . . yes, he is still talking about Napoleon's childhood and the romantic scenery of Corsica . . . something about James Boswell and Corsican independence . . . tradition of banditry . . . now back to the family origins again . . . wait a minute . . . no . . . his mother . . . more about her . . . yes . . . French Revolution . . . page 24, more about the French Revolution . . . still more . . . page 31, not interested . . . ah . . . Chapter 2, now he's at the military school. . . . I can begin here . . . but oughtn't to waste time over this early part . . . in the artillery, was he? . . . but when do we get to the Italian campaign?' And even when the reader does get to the Italian campaign and settles down comfortably to the story, he seldom reads a sentence through, word by word. Usually, he takes it in either with a single comprehensive glance as he would a stream or a field of cows that he was passing in the train, or with a series of glances, four or five words to a glance. And unless he has some special reason for studying the narrative closely, or is in an unusually industrious mood, he will not trouble about any tactical and geographical niceties of the campaign that are not presented with lively emphasis and perfect clarity. And, more serious still from the author's

[1] Why so many well-educated people spell badly is that they were quick-brained as children and learned to take in two or three words at a time, before going to school and learning exceptions to the ordinary spelling rules. Thus they may never, since nursery days, have *read* a word which they habitually mis-spell (though they may come across it twenty times a week); but see it as they think it should be. We have found 'Aircraftman' spelt correctly only once in American journals against the scores of times we have seen it spelt 'Aircraftsman'.

point of view, he will not stop when the eye is checked by some obscurity or fancifulness of language, but will leave the point unresolved and pass on. If there are many such obstructions he will skim over them until his eye alights on a clear passage again.

Imaginative readers rewrite books to suit their own taste, omitting and mentally altering as they read. And most readers automatically correct obvious errors in sense as well as misprints. Such a slip as 'Cain's murder by Abel did not go unavenged' would almost certainly pass unnoticed by every reader who was familiar from childhood with the Bible story: he would read it as 'Cain's murder of Abel' or 'Abel's murder by Cain'. And if some Hebrew scholar perhaps wished to report an alternative legend in which it was Cain, not Abel, who was murdered, this point would have to be underscored emphatically before educated people could be expected to read the story correctly. Writers who use such unfamiliar words as 'aerobat', 'comport', 'dietic', 'sublimination' find them so often altered by typists and printers into 'acrobat', 'comfort', 'dietetic' and 'sublimation' that most readers may be presumed to do the same in their minds. The old catch of asking someone to repeat the verse:

> Tobacco, Tobacco, Tobacco!
> When you're sick it makes you well,
> And it makes you well when you're sick,
> Tobacco, Tobacco, Tobacco!

is to the point here. Nine intelligent people out of ten will reverse the order of the words in the third line, to change the repetition into an antithesis:

> And when you're well it makes you sick.

We do not suggest that writers should indulge busy readers by writing down to them – giving them nothing but short messages simply phrased; but only that sentences and paragraphs should follow one another so easily and inevitably, and with such economy of phrase, that a reader will have no encouragement to skip.

There is a hasty way of writing which is a counterpart to the hasty way of reading. It is becoming more common every year and raising less and less protest. A speech, or an article, has to be written by a certain day; there are the usual interruptions and distractions. The writer is hurried but confident, with a fairly clear notion of what he wants to say. He dashes down or dictates a first draft, reads it through quickly, or has it read back to him, makes a few verbal alterations, calls it done and immediately turns to some other business. The greater the haste in which the draft is written, the closer will it come to his ordinary conversational style; and will therefore have a certain intimate charm of expression, unless of course he has trained himself to think wholly in clichés. But it is likely to contain repetitions, contradictions, muddled sequences of ideas, dropped threads, hastily chosen phrases, irrelevancies, queer variations of tense and case — especially when he is writing on a topic new to him and not merely repeating his own or someone else's remembered phrases. And phrases that seemed good enough to him in his haste — useful stand-ins for the star phrases he could not quite command — will often not only fail to convey a particular meaning to the reader but will make a blank of the whole passage.

It is not only single words and phrases that are used as stand-ins. Someone is asked, perhaps, for an article on the Rebuilding of London, or on God and the War, or on the German National Character. He has probably two or three quite good points to make but feels that an article of this sort needs a general philosophical or historical setting. He is himself neither a philosopher nor a historian and has therefore to vamp out a rhetorical introduction and conclusion. The busy eye, reading such an article, understandingly discounts the stand-in paragraphs and goes straight for the points, which in the popular press are often considerately printed in heavy type; but, in doing so, is liable to miss whatever of importance may be embedded in the rhetoric.

In spoken English haste has been the chief cause of the increasing confusion. People in important positions use a ragged conversational style that in the leisured Eighties would have been attributed to drink, mental decay or vicious upbringing. The rank and file have followed suit. The tempo of life in the United States of America is faster than in Britain and conversational looseness in Congress has been carried further than in the Houses of Parliament. The haywire innovations[1] of conversational English — not merely the slang vocabulary but the logical confusion — have worked their way into literary prose, chiefly because the growing prejudice against academic writing as pompous and sterile of ideas tempts writers to disguise their commonplaces.

Probably the habit of dictation to a typist has been responsible for a good deal of the confusion. Business and official letters and reports were once drafted by the person responsible and then, after careful emendation, given to a junior clerk for copying. They are now dictated to a shorthand typist (whose chief recommendation is usually her speed) and very often are not even read back before they are typed. Few people are capable of

[1] To appreciate the force of 'haywire' one must have seen the confusion caused in an American hayfield when the wire cable, intended to secure a huge stack against tornadoes, has slipped and tangled itself in coils among the fallen hay and the haymakers.

composing a difficult report or letter so that all the sentences of a paragraph are neatly related, unless they write it out for themselves and are able constantly to glance up and down the page, altering and erasing. Sometimes the typist is not only part of the office-equipment but an audience: the employer will wish to give an impression of fluency and infallibility rather than fumble and fuss over words. Though nine letters out of ten write themselves, their subjects being so familiar and their phrasing so formalized, the tenth, which deals with an unusual case, will present a literary problem from which there is no escape even with the business-man's lifebelt 'Comma, on the basis of which' and his breeches-buoy 'Paragraph, under the circumstances, therefore'. The employer blusters through somehow; the efficient typist quickly reduces the muddle to a clear page of typescript; and it then acquires so authoritative a look that it is usually signed and sent off without emendation.

Reluctance to disturb the orderliness of a typewritten or manuscript page is often responsible for clumsy composition. The writer has an afterthought, and instead of recasting his sentence to include it, tags it on at the end. For example:

> '*The pupils at Smith Town Engineering College were negroes* [here he remembers that most of them were too light-coloured to be called negroes] *or rather mulattoes* [but here he remembers two or three of inky blackness] *for the most part;* [here he remembers the staff] *as were also the majority of the teachers, except for a Chinese demonstrator in physics* [here he does not want to suggest that any white men taught] *and some negroes.*'

A neater form of the sentence is:

> 'Most of the pupils, and also of the teachers, at Smith Town Engineering College were mulattoes; the remainder, except for a Chinese demonstrator in physics, were negroes.'

The difference between conversational and written English can be seen from the following statement attributed to Dr. Hugh Dalton, M.P., then Minister of Economic Warfare, at a Press Conference in 1940:

> 'I have here as an emblem of the success of the blockade a portion of a cable which once belonged to a German plane.
>
> Normally this would be made of rubber containing a copper wire. Shortage of rubber is evident from the fact that within a very thin coating of rubber the wire is held within a glass contraption. Glass beads enclose the copper wire.'

No doubt Dr. Dalton made himself clear by passing the piece of cable round for inspection. But a talk, when printed, cannot take the place of descriptive writing. It was legitimate for Dr. Dalton to refer offhandedly to a 'glass contraption', and then, when interest was aroused, to concentrate attention on the glass beads and raise his voice in emphasis; by so doing he avoided the apparent contrast between 'contraption' and 'beads'. But whoever in his Ministry prepared the official 'hand-out' forgot that newspaper readers would not be able to examine the 'emblem'; and that these conversational remarks would therefore not describe it adequately and would fail as propaganda. Newspaper readers would naturally raise the following points:

Within a very thin coating of rubber the wire is held within a glass contraption. Where is the coating of rubber? Between the wire and the glass contraption? Or outside the glass contraption?

Shortage of rubber is evident from the fact that within a very thin coating of rubber the wire is held within a glass contraption. How is it evident? Might not glass be better than rubber for the purpose? To make this quite clear, the purpose of the coating should have been stated.

An emblem of the success of the blockade. The swastika is an emblem. So are: a broken obelisk, a lily, a broad arrow, an olive branch. This piece of cable has no such hieroglyphic character. It is either 'evidence' of the success of the blockade, or a 'token' of it.

Within a very thin coating of rubber the wire is held within a glass contraption. Glass beads enclose the copper wire. If the glass contraption consists of beads, the word is surely not 'coating', because this would mean that each bead was coated, but 'envelope'? Also the reintroduction of the word 'copper' makes an unintentional contrast between the two 'wires'. They are really the same thing.

The wire is held within a glass contraption . . . Glass beads enclose the copper wire. The second statement seems to be an amplification of the first.

Normally this would be made of rubber containing a copper wire. This is like saying that a pond consists of duck-weed and mud with water in the middle. The wire is the cable; the rubber is merely the insulation.

A cable which once belonged to a German plane. 'Once' seems long ago for so immediate a conclusion as Dr. Dalton was drawing. Did the inflexions of his voice convey a further message? The severity of German losses in aircraft?

If Dr. Dalton's Publicity Officer had been doing his work properly this is what the public would have read in the newspapers:

'This piece of cable, taken from a wrecked German plane, is evidence of the success of our blockade. Hitherto the Germans have made their cables of copper wire thickly sheathed with rubber. Now, as you see, they pack the wire in glass beads, held together by a very thin rubber envelope. Only a severe rubber shortage can have reduced them to this insecure insulating device.'

In the Commons debate immediately following the announcement that Great Britain was at war with Germany, Mr. Gallagher, the Communist member, spoke under emotional stress. This is a verbatim report from *Hansard*:

> 'I tried to impress on the House at the time of Munich, and now that disaster is threatening to come on the whole of Europe I want to ask, whether it is possible to get this House, representing as it does the people of the country, seriously to discuss a complete change of Government, in order to get a Government that will seek to save the young manhood of this country, and bring the war to a speedy end, instead of concerning itself with spreading the war.'

People speak like this in moments of passion, and contrive somehow to make themselves understood. Perfection of phrasing is not necessary in public speaking: indeed, Charles James Fox, who was an authority on Parliamentary rhetoric, said that a speech which read well was 'a damned bad one' when spoken. This is how Mr. Gallagher might have amended his speech for *Hansard* before the Library copies were printed:

> 'I asked the House an important question during the crisis which was resolved by the Munich Conference. Now that disaster once more threatens all Europe, I shall repeat it: Can we not, as representatives of the British people, seriously discuss a change of Government? Can we not appoint a Government which will try to preserve the lives of our young manhood, and concern itself rather with smothering war than with spreading war further?'

To haste as a cause of confusion must be added distraction. Normally, except for those who work in the early hours of the morning, or who live up a long country lane, it is almost impossible to avoid being disturbed by incidental noises of traffic, industry, schools, and the wireless, or by the telephone, or by callers. Few people can immediately switch their minds from one complicated subject to another, and presently switch back again, without losing something in the process. Most business men and journalists claim that they are accustomed to noise and can 'work through anything'. But this does not mean that they are not affected by noise: part of the brain must be employed in sorting out the noises and discounting them. The intense concentration achieved when one writes in complete silence, security and leisure, with the mental senses cognizant of every possible aspect of the theme as it develops – this was always rare and is now rarer than ever. Modern conditions of living encourage habitual distraction and, though there are still opportunities for comparative quiet, most people feel that they are not really alive unless they are in close touch with their fellow men — and close touch involves constant disturbance. Hart Crane, a leading American poet of the Nineteen-Twenties, decided that he could not write his best except with a radio or victrola playing jazz at him and street-noises coming up through the open window. He considered that distraction was the chief principle of modern living; he cultivated it, distractedly, and committed suicide in his early thirties.

A third general cause of confusion has been timidity. A fear of feeling definitely committed to any statement that might cause trouble or inconvenience seems to haunt almost everyone in Britain who holds a public position, however unimportant.

A fourth cause of confusion has been dividedness of mind. When people have to write from a point of view which is not really their own, they are apt to betray this by hedging, blustering, an uneasy choice of words, a syntactical looseness. We mean, for example, Cabinet Ministers expressing the view of a Cabinet from which they have often considered resigning; priests, assailed by honest doubt, who must continue to enunciate church dogma; Communists uneasily following the party-line; officials relaying to the public some order from headquarters of which they disapprove; critics borrowing aesthetic standards not properly understood.

British writers excel in straightforward narrative, once they have finished their introductory generalizations and got into their narrative stride. But they tend to be embarrassed by any autobiographical element. What was a rhetorical device in the Classical schools of oratory — *meiosis* or under-emphasis — and came into facetious use in Victorian times (e.g. 'Pedestrianism in November is a matter of not a little unpleasantness'), is now second nature to most Englishmen, and has lost its original ironic purpose. It now means modesty: 'At four thousand I ran into a spot of bother — a couple of Ju.88s who dived at me from a cloud and one of them didn't do my port engine any too much good, but I managed to put paid to him — the crew baled out — and then I watched the other go down in bits and pieces — not a pretty sight — well, I met a passing Messerschmidt on the way home. . . .' Conversationally this style can be charming, but in prose it makes for irrelevancy, material omission, faulty connexion, logical weakness and, eventually, boredom.

There is no natural safeguard in the English language against the faults of haste, distraction, timidity, dividedness of mind, modesty. English does not run on its own rails, like French, with a simply managed mechanism of knobs and levers, so that any army officer or provincial mayor can always, at a minute's notice, glide into a graceful speech in celebration of any local or national event, however unexpected. The fact is, that English has altogether too many resources for the ordinary person, and nobody holds it against him if he speaks or writes badly. The only English dictionary with any pretension to completeness as a collection of literary precedents, the *Oxford English Dictionary*, is of the size and price of an encyclopedia; and pocket-dictionaries do not distinguish sufficiently between shades of meaning in closely associated words: for example, between the adjectives 'silvery', 'silvern', 'silver', 'silvered' 'argent', 'argentine', 'argentic', 'argentous'. Just as all practising lawyers have ready access to a complete legal library, so all professional writers (and every other writer who can afford it) should possess or have ready access to the big *Oxford English Dictionary*. But how many trouble about the real meanings of words? Most of them are content to rub along with a Thesaurus — which lumps words together in groups of so-called synonyms, without definitions — and an octavo dictionary. One would not expect a barrister to prepare a complicated insurance or testamentary case with only *Everyman's Handy Guide to the Law* to help him; and there are very few books which one can write decently without consulting at every few pages a dictionary of at least two quarto volumes — *Webster's*, or the shorter *Oxford English Dictionary* — to make sure of a word's antecedents and meaning.

To write English perfectly is impossible in practice: occasional ambiguities or slight improprieties of phrase are discoverable in every book — there has never been a writer who did not have some blind spot in his reading eye. Even to write it well is difficult. The alternative chosen by those who cannot carry on their daily business without constantly writing reports, demands and orders is a dialect of limited vocabulary with no pretence to the literary graces, designed as a vehicle of restricted meaning. 'Officialese', 'legal English' and 'business English' merge into one another as the general service dialect of impersonality, for use in every case where people are not private individuals but merely (according to the context) the public, the electorate, the parties concerned, age groups, man power, personnel, consumers. We discuss this dialect at length in Chapter Four.

Some of the chief contentions in this chapter are borne out by Mr. H. G. Andrews, poet and English teacher in a West Country school, who writes:

'The presence of the wireless set in eight million English homes makes the job of teaching much harder in these days, especially where the Government system allots only one teacher to forty or fifty children.

The child is so used to a background of noise, mainly vocal, that he has acquired the habit of ignoring its import. . . .

'It is difficult to get boys to grasp the bare essentials of the language, let alone think logically. The standard of good English in these uncertain, disorderly days is imposed by the few on the very many, and the few grow daily more slack and slipshod in their maintenance of the standard. Writers in the Select Press and for the B.B.C. come sprawling arsy versy over the most obvious trip-wires. The increasingly confused state of educated prose has been a chief symptom of the sickness of our wrong-headed civilization during the last twenty years. . . . It is dispiriting to teach the elements of English composition to boys most of whom will not set pen to paper more than a dozen times a year, after they leave school, and then only to sign their names on an indicated dotted line. It would be stupid to teach my boys the analytical syntax that brought a blight on my own boyhood: I teach them such functional grammar as will help them to compose a straightforward, sensible narrative paragraph with the commas and stops in the right places. I do not bother them with any considerations of euphony – as Lewis Carroll's Duchess said to Alice: "Take care of the sense and the sounds will take care of themselves!" '

CHAPTER THREE

WHERE IS GOOD ENGLISH TO BE FOUND?

EXPERTS in every scientific or learned subject communicate with one another in a distinct technical dialect; and when, now and then, one of them is asked for a popular lecture or book on his own subject, it is seldom that he is able to translate his ideas into an English immediately intelligible to his readers. Usually he has only a meagre general vocabulary. The language which, say, a theologian, an electrical engineer and a morbid-psychologist would use amongst themselves if they were thrown into contact would probably be a loose, schoolboy slang — their common dialect before they began to specialize. Three hundred years ago a correspondingly diverse group of experts, whenever they had difficulty in making themselves understood to one another in English, could fall back on Latin. The reason for stabilizing all learned terms in Latin, helped out with a little Greek, was to avoid the looseness of vernacular expression: each plant, planet or physical phenomenon was fixed in the corpus of knowledge by being given a unique and inalienable name. Botanists, with great advantage to themselves, have kept faithfully to a single Latin register of terms; other scientists, including zoologists, have not done so, nor have philosophers, and their subjects are consequently full of overlapping, ambiguous and contradictory terms. A conscientious scientist, historian or philosopher, wishing to master every aspect of his subject, must now learn not merely one language, Latin, but three or four — French, German, Italian, perhaps Russian — often more. Even so, he cannot always be sure that the meaning of a certain word in a foreign language is exactly equivalent to its counterpart in his own. There is no international lexicon of scientific and learned terms, and the international Scientific Congress of 1922 failed to agree even to a proposal for limiting to nine the languages in which scientific works might be written in order to qualify for international recognition.

The recent substitution in most British schools of French and English for Latin has had on the whole a vicious effect on English prose. The pupil in the old-fashioned grammar-school was faced with the problem of finding English equivalents to Latin phrases and so became aware of the peculiar properties of English. The teaching of French does not have the same illuminating effect, either because it is closer in structure and spirit to English than Latin is or because it has been taught without the tradition of scholarly discipline that clings to a long-studied dead language. The clue to the appropriate use of a great many English words is to be found in their Latin originals, which occur in French only in degenerate forms: especially important is a knowledge of the effect of Latin prepositions on the verbs to which they are prefixed. Moreover, Latin, though surpassed by English in richness of vocabulary and flexibility of grammar, did for centuries put a useful check on any literary bad manners in which writers of English might feel inclined to indulge. A useful test of the logic of metaphorical English prose is to translate it into Latin.

The following editorial comment from a leading London weekly (1941) is typical of what will not pass the test:

> 'The next few weeks may decide whether the Easter egg which Matsuoka and Molotoff laid in the Kremlin last Sunday is just a shell, or full of dynamite. Although fresh from the nest, it already emits several displeasing odours.'

The Latin point of view would be that a man cannot lay an egg, still less can two men; that Easter eggs are either real eggs, in which case they contain a yoke and a white, or artificial eggs, in which case they are not 'laid'; that if the egg were just a shell it would not smell, nor would it if it were filled with dynamite; that one egg can only emit one odour, not several. The passage is therefore untranslatable. The Romans, though they had a broad sense of stage humour and enjoyed absurd jokes at the baths and at banquets, kept their prose free from extravagance.

It is unfortunate that English, which has for some time been the most widely used language in the world – the chief language of trade, and the national or administrative language of six hundred million people – should be so difficult a one – and that there should be no short cuts to learning it.[1] There are, however, compensations for this difficulty. Frenchmen who make errors in English are not obliged to feel the same

[1] One well-advertised expedient is 'Basic English' ('British American Scientific International Commercial'), a self-denying restriction of language to a vocabulary of 850 words – carefully selected as serving all international needs and designed to have technical vocabularies built on to it, like a sectional bookcase. This may have its advantages as a simply-learned, artificial language for foreigners to use to foreigners, but it does not help English-speaking people to speak or write English better. They find it extremely difficult to confine themselves to such a meagre ration of words, especially of verbs: to remember that they must say not 'I wrote a letter' but 'I put a letter down on paper'; and not 'I read a letter' but 'I went through a letter'. If there is any virtue in a dialect that dispenses with a number of common words, 'Basic' is outdone by the picturesque trade-English used in West Africa. The Nigerian official who wishes to announce a total eclipse of the sun to his black subordinates says: 'Him kerosene b'long Jesus Christ by'm-by all done, b —— r up, finish.'

embarrassment as Englishmen who, speaking French, mistake the gender of some simple household utensil: for, however strange their accent, they are unlikely to use English more clumsily than a great many people whose mother-tongue it is.

Situations arise in English unparalleled in more rigidly grammatical languages. If an intelligent foreigner were asked to translate into English a simple Latin sentence '*Mala fortuna semper obruet talem qualis ego*', he would probably write: 'Misfortune will always overwhelm such as I', and justify it grammatically by pointing out that 'such' was accusative, the object of the word 'overwhelm', and was followed by an independent clause 'as I', with the word 'am' understood. He would be right; and only wrong if he decided that 'such as me' was ungrammatical – on the ground that in no sane language can nominative and accusative be used alternatively in the same phrase, and that in all Romance and Germanic languages the nominative would be used. However, 'such as me', treated as a declinable compound pronoun, has been used in English since at least the year 1412, when Hoccleve wrote:

> Earthern vessel, to such a man as me,
> Full fitting is. . . .

It may be assumed that, though grammatically there are two alternatives, 'such as I' and 'such as me', one of them will be more suitable than the other to the context. In no book of usages will the foreigner find any ruling upon this. However, a writer sensitive to the emotional logic of English would probably write 'Misfortune will always overwhelm such as me', but (if the sense had to be reversed) 'Misfortune will never overwhelm such as I'. His feeling would be that the phrase 'such as me' bows passively before misfortune, whereas 'such as I' resists it actively and uprightly.

Or, what is the plural of 'formula'? The dictionary allows a choice either of 'formulae' or 'formulas', but suggests no rule for deciding when to use which. Probably most sensitive people would write: 'Professor Brown advised his pupils to memorize a number of thermodynamic formulae,' but 'The Foreign Minister, before signing the pact, was offered a choice of three formulas.' The Latin plural tends to be used in scientific contexts, the English plural in non-scientific ones. Prose-writers, however, meet this sort of problem less frequently than poets, nor are they obliged so often to transcend conventional usage or to coin new words.

One of the differences in English between prose and poetry is that, while the prose writer must nowadays assume his reader to be a busy person whose eye sweeps along the page at a fairly steady rate, seldom pausing long even at key passages, the poet, unless he is a suicidal Hart Crane, still assumes his reader to have perfect leisure and patience for dwelling on each word in a poem and appreciating its relation with every other. Prose, in fact, is expected to reveal its full content at first reading; poetry only at third or fourth. The first glance at a poem takes in its prose sense as a base on which to build up the poetic sense. For example, the following stanza from Keats's *La Belle Dame sans Merci* presents a simple story situation:

> I saw pale kings and princes too,
> Pale warriors, death pale were they all —
> They cried "La Belle Dame Sans Merci
> Hath thee in thrall."

Having grasped so much, one considers the lines in poetic terms. 'What literary context do these pale kings, princes and warriors recall? What force has the repetition of the word 'pale'? And who or what is *La Belle Dame Sans Merci?* Why has she a mediaeval French name?' One is free to interpret her fatal person according to personal experience. To Keats, she seems to have been a mixture of Fanny Brawne, with whom he was hopelessly in love, Consumption, which had carried off his brother Tom and was to kill him too, and the intractable Spirit of Poetry. One notes how the conventional phrase 'She has enthralled you', by being resolved into its original elements, recovers its metaphorical force of 'has you in slavery'; and how the internal rhyme of *merci* with *thee* echoes in the mind and gives 'thee' the force of 'thee too'; and how the variation of vowel-sounds gives iridescence to the lines; and how well-suited to the sense the alliteration is; and what a shiver comes with the word 'warriors'.

Poetic meaning, then, is contained in the complicated correspondence between the words used, regarding both as sense and as sound, and in latent meanings of the words evoked by the rhythmic spell. The unusual juxtaposition of two words may carry a weight of meaning over which a thoughtful reader will spend as much time as over a page or more of prose argument. In ordinary prose one does not look for correspondences of this sort, or for latent meanings. Reading as prose the sentence 'La Belle Dame Sans Merci hath thee in thrall' one would miss the rhyme of *merci* and 'thee' and, mentally accentuating the first syllable of *merci*, would give no greater stress to 'thee' than to 'hath'.

If, therefore, a prose writer has some thought to express that has occurred to him with poetic knottiness, he must either prepare the reader for this knot by unmistakable warnings, and help him slowly to disentangle it by subsequent comment; or he must withhold the knot and provide a prose equivalent instead. It would, for example, be unwise to write in prose: 'Reprisals in war are a mad and vicious spiral', and expect the reader to take this odd metaphor in his stride. Either he would automatically read it as 'a vicious circle'; or his reaction would be 'Why not "vicious circle"? Can a spiral be vicious, in the sense that it always comes back to the same point? Surely it advances as it revolves?' He would read on, mystified and perhaps annoyed. Yet a reader of poetry confronted with the couplet:

War's vicious spiral
Of mad reprisal . . .

would lay his book down for a moment. He would think: 'Yes, if in war both belligerents wage a secondary war of reprisals for some original act of wantonness, a vicious circle results, and not so much a vicious circle as a vicious spiral: as hysteria mounts, the first punishment returns in ever heightened form to the punisher – so that the conflict is prolonged to a point of common exhaustion that could hardly have been reached had either side shown restraint at the outset.' This reflection is the prose equivalent of the poetic couplet.

There should be two main objects in ordinary prose writing: to convey a message, and to include in it nothing that will distract the reader's attention or check his habitual pace of reading – he should feel that he is seated at ease in a taxi, not riding a temperamental horse through traffic. But there is a form of prose called, at different times, 'the conceited style', 'the grand style', 'prose-poetry' and 'aesthetic prose', the aim of which is to divert leisured readers by ingenious or graceful feats with language. It originated in Graeco-Roman schools of forensic oratory where young men learned the art of dressing up an argument for the benefit of a judge or jury so that it might seem stronger than it really was. In this sort of prose, correspondences of sound and meaning are exploited, rhythms are imposed on the sense rather than created naturally by it, and the reader is amused by literary references, witty turns of language and far-fetched metaphors.

There were three sorts of prose in Latin while it was still a living language: the plain, the polished and the florid. Plainness of language was a virtue under the early Republic, but after the conquest of Greece the Romans became embarrassed by their lack of culture and took to polishing their speeches and letters. By the time of the Early Empire, the plain style was held pedestrian and boorish and the polished also had gone out of fashion: Cicero's admired works, which had been composed on careful rhythmic principles, now seemed pompous and boring. Then, as orators and historians found less and less to say, original thinking being dangerous under the Empire, every sort of bright decoration – 'tropes' as they were called in the schools – was used to enliven the safe but threadbare themes. At English universities, where from the Middle Ages until late Victorian times the chief ostensible aim of education was to make the boys fluent public speakers in Latin, the polished and the florid styles were taught. In general, the plain style, as found in the works of Caesar and Sallust, was reserved for grammar-school boys. In the next chapters we shall show how strong an effect oratorical education had on English prose: for several centuries few writers who had been to the University refrained from decorating their work with Senecan flourishes and flowers or from cultivating a sonorous Ciceronian grace.

Rhetoric is meant to be spoken, or at least read with an attentive mental ear. Though speeches and sermons are still publicly delivered and the radio has even enlarged their audiences, no novelist or historian now expects his work to be read aloud as in Classical times. It is obviously futile to use rhetorical devices which are meant for the ear and expect them to catch the eye – especially an eye that reads three times faster than ordinary talking-pace. We are confident that few of our readers noticed a trick played on them on line 12 of page 36, where we introduced into ordinary prose a highly stylized sentence connected by a complex system of interlaced alliterations: they were reading for sense, not style. A company report or a newspaper leader might be published in blank verse and, so long as the lay-out was a prose one, nobody would notice the metre. A sentence in a Victorian mathematical work ran something like this:

> 'It may at first sight seem unlikely that the pull of gravity will depress the centre of a light cord, held horizontally at a high lateral tension; and yet no force, however great, can stretch a cord, however fine, into a horizontal line that shall be absolutely straight.'

It was years before someone discovered that the second part of the sentence was a perfect *In Memoriam* rhymed stanza.

We have no quarrel with rhetoric: it is a legitimate and honoured pastime like acrostics or card-play. But since English by its simplicity of structure permits a greater mobility of thought than other languages, and so can express subtler insinuations and more powerful thrusts of meaning, an English writer with something to say needs no rhetorical art. That the hurry of modern life has put both the florid and the polished styles out of fashion, except for very special audiences, is not to be deplored if this leads to a more general appreciation of the capacity of the plain style. By 'plain' we do not mean bald (as, say, the style of the *Anglo-Saxon Chronicle* is bald), but simple and neat. For example, neither rhythmic repetition, adjectival profusion, nor quaintness of metaphor will convince a reader nearly so easily that such and such a house was disgustingly dirty and its proprietor an old wretch, as a simple, unemphatic anecdote of what happened early one Monday morning between the kitchen and the backdoor.

Towards the end of the nineteenth century Samuel Butler recorded in his notebook as a private eccentricity that, unlike his contemporaries Pater and Ruskin, he had never cultivated his literary style but tried instead to make his handwriting as clear as possible. Nowadays it is difficult to read Pater or Ruskin at all, because the information and ideas (many of them valuable) that they have to offer are so overlaid with painfully cultivated styles as to confuse rather than enchant; whereas Butler, who carried his aim of simple clarity past handwriting into prose, is still a modern.

Where is good English to be found? Not among those who might be expected to write well professionally. Schoolmasters seldom write well: it is difficult for any teacher to avoid either pomposity or, in the effort not to be pompous, a jocular conversational looseness. The clergy suffer from much the same occupational disability: they can seldom decide whether to use 'the language of the market-place' or Biblical rhetoric. Men of letters usually feel impelled to cultivate an individual style — less because they feel sure of themselves as individuals than because they wish to carve a niche for themselves in literature; and nowadays an individual style usually means merely a peculiar range of inaccuracies, ambiguities, logical weaknesses and stylistic extravagancies. Trained journalists use a flat, over-simplified style, based on a study of what sells a paper and what does not, which is inadequate for most literary purposes.

As a rule, the best English is written by people without literary pretentions, who have responsible executive jobs in which the use of official language is not compulsory; and, as a rule, the better at their jobs they are, the better they write. Some command a much larger vocabulary than others, are more eloquent and more aware of historic precedent in the use of words; but faults in English prose derive not so much from lack of knowledge, intelligence or art as from lack of thought, patience or goodwill. Though often letters, speeches and reports must be written in a hurry and, because of the countless considerations that clear writing involves, are bound in some way to fall short of the full intended meaning, conscientious people will always regret this necessity and arrange their affairs as far as possible to avoid it. Arnold Bennett in his *Literary Taste* pointed out that faults of style are largely faults of character.

'How often has it been said that Carlyle's matter is marred by the harshness and eccentricities of his style? But Carlyle's matter is harsh and eccentric to precisely the same degree as his style. His behaviour was frequently ridiculous, if not abominable.'

The writing of good English is thus a moral matter, as the Romans held that the writing of good Latin was. And the British people, though at times it recognizes and applauds the first-rate in art, literature, statesmanship, technical achievement, social conduct and so on, is always over-indulgent of the second-, third- or fourth-rate and often taken in by the simply bad. The national instinct is towards what is good, but there is a long-standing aversion to laying down standards in too final a way – cheats, scoundrels, careerists and dunces have profited greatly from this in politics, business, society, art and literature – and though it is generally assumed that there is good and bad writing in the present, as well as in the past, it is felt that nobody should be either hardy enough to define the difference or ill-mannered enough to make a detailed study of the shortcomings of his fellow-writers. In fact, a leading trait of the British character is not only to suspend judgement on values but never to think further than is absolutely necessary, and to put off radical change of behaviour or policy until compelled by an acute crisis. We regard the present crisis as acute enough to excuse this book.

The short-term view of writing and public speaking held between 1919 and 1939 corresponded closely with the short-term view of clothes, household belongings and vehicles as temporary conveniences, soon out of date, not worth making well enough to last a lifetime. It was argued that almost every speech was wholly forgotten after three weeks and almost every book after three years. 'Why then trouble to write really well? Would anyone but a fool make a motor-car to be admired by posterity? The most economical car is the one built to run well and look smart only for the length of time that a car remains up-to-date mechanically – three to five years. The same is true of books.'

The consequent tendency of English – even of the dignified language spoken in Parliament – to become loose, confused and ungraceful was first officially recognized, and condoned, in 1924. Stanley Baldwin, political leader of the business class which had gradually taken over the direction of national affairs from the impoverished land-owning class, then made a statement of appalling frankness to the Cambridge Union, admitting the anti-literary prejudice of his associates, and even glorying in it:

'If there is one thing which those who have been in any other profession than the Bar distrust more than another, it is the eloquent man.

> In the business world . . . the man who has the power of talking is not the man who gets promotion. To be able to express oneself, in business, is always to be written down as not quite first class . . . it is not necessarily the man most fluent of speech to whom we should entrust the destinies of the country.'

This was a curious reversion to a view which had been held in the Middle Ages by the land-owning class, but was already by Stuart times abandoned in all but a few backward counties. Richard Pace wrote of it in his Latin *De Fructu*, 1517:

> 'One of those whom we call gentlemen, who always carry a horn slung at their backs as though they would hunt during dinner, said: "I swear by God's Body I would rather that my son should hang than study literature. It behoves the sons of gentlemen to blow the horn tunefully, to hunt skilfully, to train a hawk well and carry it elegantly. But the study of literature should be left to rustics." '

When the policies of the anti-literary business party were finally discredited after a few months of the Second World War, and an all-party government was formed, the only Prime Minister acceptable to the Labour leaders was Winston Churchill, who had long been distrusted by the Baldwinian business members and 'written down as being not quite first class' because he was the most Classically eloquent member of the House, and who, shortly after his appointment, expressed his impatience with confused, unfluent business English in a strong memorandum to all Government departments.

Chapters Five to Nine will show the unsteady course followed by English prose through the centuries. Every social and political change was marked by a corresponding change in the character of prose; and it may be assumed that the change in British life which follows the Second World War will be as pronounced as the one that followed the First World War. We hope, but cannot prophesy, that the style of prose best suited to the new conditions will be:

> Cleared of encumbrances for quick reading: that is, without unnecessary ornament, irrelevancy, illogicality, ambiguity, repetition, circumlocution, obscurity of reference.
>
> Properly laid out: that is, with each sentence a single step and each paragraph a complete stage in the argument or narrative; with each idea in its right place in the sequence, and none missing; with all connections properly made.
>
> Written in the first place for silent reading, but with consideration for euphony if read aloud.
>
> Consistent in use of language; considerate of the possible limitations

of the reader's knowledge; with no indulgence of personal caprice nor any attempt to improve on sincere statement by rhetorical artifice.

Such a style has no chance of immediate adoption in public life, even in contexts where it is realized that officialese is unsuitable and that a simpler, more intimate English must be used. The following Government announcement, which appeared in all the London and provincial daily newspapers on June 1st, 1941, and which combines the technique of the politician with that of the advertising man, is an interesting example of the effect on prose of present social and economic conditions.

> 'RATIONING OF CLOTHING, CLOTH AND FOOTWEAR
> FROM JUNE 1ST, 1941
>
> 'There is enough for all if we share and share alike. Rationing is the way to get fair shares. *Fair shares* — when workers are producing bombs and aeroplanes and guns instead of frocks, suits and shoes. *Fair shares* — when ships must run the gauntlet with munitions and food rather than with wool and cotton. *Fair shares* — when movements of population outrun local supplies. Rationing is not the same as shortage. Rationing, or *fair shares*, is the way to *prevent* a shortage without interfering with full war production.
>
> So, from now on (June 1st, 1941) you will have to present coupons to buy clothing, cloth, footwear and knitting-wool. At present the coupons to be used are the Margarine Coupons in your Food Ration Book. (You don't need these for margarine and it is a great saving of paper to use this page for the clothing ration.) There are 26 coupons on the margarine page. The numbers printed on them are to be ignored; each coupon counts 1 only. You will receive 40 more coupons making 66 to last you *for a full year*.'

This is not good prose. Indeed, it caused confusion for a day or two, in some districts. Many people were under the impression that to the 'guns or butter?' choice, which had been semi-officially put before them some months before, a new choice was now added: 'clothing or margarine?' Some clothiers had to explain that they could not give a customer a pair of socks, say, in exchange for three coupons' worth of margarine; and grocers that they were not authorized to give extra margarine to customers who had enough clothing for the whole of the ensuing year. Yet if the advertisement had been written in better prose it would not have served the Government's purpose so well. It was the work of a skilled advertising man, whose business it was to 'sell' the rationing scheme to the public. Advertising men admit that they can rarely afford either to tell the truth or count on the intelligence of the public. The appeal must largely be to the passions. Whether the passions appealed to are mean or generous depends on the nature of the goods advertised; but in either case the style will necessarily be loose.

If the Government had not decided to introduce clothes-rationing gently to the unintelligent masses, but had instead given a practical summary of the situation which made rationing necessary, something like the following might have been issued:

> 'RATIONING OF CLOTHING, CLOTH AND FOOTWEAR
> FROM JUNE 1ST, 1941
>
> 'Many of the ships which once brought us wool, cotton and hides from overseas have been sunk; others are now carrying food and munitions instead. And many of the workers who used these raw materials for making frocks, suits, shoes, etc. have been called up to do more important war work. Far fewer of these goods are therefore being manufactured, which has caused inconvenient local shortages – for example, in country districts crowded with evacuees – and selfish hoarding. Since nobody must go short of these goods while others have more than enough, we have decided to ration them.
>
> So, from to-day, if you want to buy cloth, knitting-wool, clothes, boots, shoes, etc – let us call all this ''Clothing, etc.'' – you will have to give up coupons. The first twenty-six coupons for you to use are those on page 10 of your ration book. They are headed ''Margarine'' and have numbers printed on them. Cross out the word ''Margarine'', writing instead ''Clothing, etc.'', and pay no attention to the numbers, since all the coupons are of the same value and can be used whenever you please. You will continue to get your usual ration of margarine from the coupons on page 11. Later, each of you will be given a sheet of forty more coupons for ''Clothing, etc.'', making 66 in all, to last you until June 1st, 1942.'

In this slightly longer version several important points left out from the original are restored: that some workers are still producing clothing and footwear, and some ships still importing the raw materials; that there is a national shortage, as well as local shortages, of clothing and footwear, the inconveniences of which can be mitigated by rationing; that there has been some hoarding; that the term 'Clothing' includes cloth and footwear; that the so-called 'margarine coupons' are now to be used for clothing, not margarine; that 'this page' means the Margarine Page and not the page of the newspaper on which the advertisement appears; that the margarine ration can be got as usual with the help of another page of coupons; that the numbers printed on the so-called Margarine Coupons do not limit the time during which these can be used for buying 'Clothing, etc.'

Yet, despite its greater clarity as prose, this version would be regarded as 'bad advertising'. The theory of advertising, which has been gradually deduced from a practical analysis of sales-statistics is that most people do not read carefully, and to sell them popular commodities in a competitive world one must take advantage of their carelessness: one must give them, not careful prose, but prose that has the effect of conversational haste and catches the eye with one or two alluring phrases. In this case, the Government copy-writer did his job well enough. He avoided telling unpalatable truths, namely that there was a national clothing shortage, that the evacuation-scheme had caused serious local shortages, that many ships had been sunk, and that there had been hoarding. This would have had a depressing effect, ranged popular feeling against evacuees, and encouraged the hoarding of still uncontrolled goods. He politically refrained from saying even that the Government had decided to ration clothing; to do so might have made people grumble at the Government. He wrote instead in a way suggesting that fate and the public themselves were jointly responsible for the scheme. By the elementary tricks of repeating and italicizing *fair shares*, mentioning the saving of paper, and focusing attention on the ships that gallantly ran the gauntlet, he made his point: that justice, gratitude and economy alike required that the nation should cheerfully submit to further rationing inconveniences. The sketchiness of the instructions about the use of coupons did not matter much: broadcast explanations of the scheme and detailed instructions issued to clothiers and grocers would be sufficient to clear up any serious misunderstanding. By the middle of the week, indeed, even the stupidest people had got the idea into their heads and the scheme was working well.

CHAPTER FOUR

THE USE AND ABUSE OF OFFICIAL ENGLISH

In the course of their work, Government officials have to use the formal phraseology which has been called 'Whitehallese' but is by no means restricted to the Ministries of Whitehall. All the lesser Government establishments use variants of it – post-offices, police-stations, income-tax offices, municipal councils and education authorities. So also do such semi-official bodies as Corporations and Royal Institutes. Nor can any clear distinction be drawn between the Government style and other official styles – any society, club, or trade union that has committee meetings, minutes and memoranda uses an official style in discussing and recording its business. These official styles shade off into the business style. What is generally meant by 'the business style' is the phraseology perpetuated in the signs of Pitman's shorthand – 'We are in receipt of your favour of the 4th ult.' etc. – but such phrases, which are regarded as ungenteel by the Civil Service, cover only the shopping side of business. The management of a large firm has complicated matters of policy to discuss and decide upon. However chatty the preliminary discussions may be, final decisions are always worded officially. The larger the firm, and the more corporation-minded its management, the more official-looking does this language become. There is no great difference of technique between running a huge monopolistic concern and running a Government Department; naturally therefore, there is no great difference of language.

The Civil Service has the most official-looking of styles. When a Principal Assistant-Secretary drafts an official document, it is not he who is supposed to be speaking: it is a Department of the Crown. Or, if the document contains instructions to the public, it is not even a Department speaking, but His Majesty's Government with the backing of the Law and the sanction of Parliament. The style must therefore be dignified and impersonal and in keeping with the formal traditions of Parliamentary and legal language.

Parliament has several traditional languages. One of them is the rhetorical. Mr. Churchill's methods of rousing and persuading his hearers are much the same as those of Gladstone and Burke; and this tradition is likely to hold so long as speeches are delivered in a raised voice across the floor of the House, not spoken conversationally into a microphone, as in some European Parliamentary chambers; and so long as there are survivors of the landed gentry who a generation ago formed the bulk of the British ruling classes. This style is sometimes known as the Republican, because under the Roman Republic the Senate was composed of men closely corresponding in rank, wealth and attainments with members of the British Parliament in the eighteenth and nineteenth centuries, and the procedure and language were strikingly similar. Mr. Churchill seems to think almost habitually in the Republican style, and in his historical writings indulges in such flights as this, from his *World Crisis*:

> 'There is nothing on which policy, however wise, can build; no foothold can be found for virtue or for valour, no authority or impetus for a rescuing genius. The mighty framework of German Imperial Power, which a few days before had overshadowed the nations, shivered suddenly into a thousand individually disintegrating fragments. All her Allies, whom she had so long sustained, fell down, broken and ruined, begging separately for peace. The faithful armies were beaten at the front and demoralized from the rear. The proud, efficient navy mutinied. Revolution exploded in the most disciplined of States. The Supreme War Lord fled.
>
> Such a spectacle appals mankind; and a knell rang in the ears of the victors, even in their hours of triumph.'

But the landed gentry have gradually been ousted from Parliament by Labour representatives and men of business, and the pure Republican style is now attempted by few members. The rest tend to use the official style even in debates where general principles of government are raised. And the greater part of Parliamentary proceedings does not lend itself to rhetorical treatment. When Bills are debated point by point in Committee, or when questions on departmental matters are put to Ministers, this is done in pure Civil Service style. For Question Time, for instance, the question is printed beforehand on the Order Paper for the Day; the answer is then composed by the senior officials of the Government Department concerned and read out by the Minister. A question was asked early in 1941 on the employment, in auxiliary Army services, of aliens from the Balkans. It ran:

> 'In view of the fact that the Bulgarian Government has pursued a course of action very deleterious to this country, ought not applications from Bulgarians to be treated with the greatest reserve?'

The questioner was Philip Noel Baker, an acute critic of Government Departments, yet his question was as well-veiled as any Government statement and there were reasons why it should be so. 'In view of the fact that' is a purposely loose phrase implying that because the Bulgarians have done *x* the British Government should do *y*; but it avoids making

British action hinge too definitely on Bulgarian action. His Majesty's Government is presumed to be above any small-minded policy of reprisals; it moves independently, keeping the facts large-mindedly 'in view', and leaves historians to work out the relationship between them and its course of action – *post hoc* is not necessarily *propter hoc*. 'Pursued a course of action' – a course of action and its pursuit suggests a deliberate purpose: all kinds of sinister calculations are thus politely imputed to the Bulgarians. 'Deleterious' is a euphemism for 'bad for us'; there may be set-backs, difficulties, obstacles, misfortunes, but it is always presumed that the Government is powerful enough to overcome them. Granted, 'deleterious' is originally a very strong word taken over from the Greek ('*deleterios*', destructive), but it has somehow been softened (perhaps by use in advertisements for patent medicines) into meaning 'unfavourable in the long run'. Finally, 'treated with the greatest reserve'. This is the official equivalent of 'not trusted an inch', and has the advantage of concealing beneath the cloak of diplomatic courtesy the most active forms of distrust: it can mean either taking no notice, or giving the lie direct, or even putting through the third degree. It is almost as useful a covering phrase as 'taking the appropriate steps'.

When a supplementary question is tacked on, *ex tempore*, to a tabled question, it is nearly always officially phrased; and is answered, *ex tempore*, in the same style – even by Ministers who in debate are natural orators. Here is Mr. Churchill himself answering a supplementary question by Mr. Alfred Edwards, tacked on to a tabled question about the desirability of taking steps to have all Acts of Parliament translated into Basic English:

> 'Mr. Edwards: Does the Prime Minister not think it would be a great economy of the time of this House and a saving of money if the language of the official draughtsmen, after they have done their best or their worst with Bills, were translated into more understandable English? Will he contemplate the calamity that might befall us if these draughtsmen translated his speeches into official language?
>
> Mr. Churchill: There is a great deal of official jargon, but it is not with a view to causing inconvenience, but because those who are entrusted with expressing the decisions of this House in a statutory form have found that to be the most convenient and precise method. With regard to the idea that we should try to describe everything in Basic English, that is a very fanciful idea. I would call Mr. Edwards's attention to the fact that the word "basic", like its neighbour "basal", are both under great suspicion at the present time – (laughter) – in the way in which they are used.'

It will be noticed that Mr. Churchill, fumbling for his answer, has used several stereotypes of expression, very loosely connected: 'but it is not with a view to', 'with regard to the idea that', 'I would call Mr. Edwards's attention to the fact that'.

The style commonly derided as 'officialese' is really 'legalese'. Parliament passes hundreds of Bills, and Government Departments issue thousands of regulations, all of which have to be phrased in the technical language that gives them currency in courts of law. They are full of back-references to previous laws and to the definitions contained in them, and stylistically they must fit into the existing body of legislation. An Act is an inclusive statement which has to apply to thousands of particular cases, and is characterized by two chief devices: first, the listing of particulars, as in 'any box, chest, case, coffer, casket or other receptacle', and second, the repetition of qualifying clauses. The following is an example of repetition from an Act enabling local authorities to start repairs quickly when buildings are damaged by air-raids:

> 'Where under the said Section One a local authority serves on the person having control of a building a notice of their intention to execute works at the expiration of the period specified in the notice and within that period the said person gives to the authority notice in writing that he does not object to the execution by the authority of the works specified in the notice the authority may execute those works before the expiration of the said period.'

First there are block phrases setting out the circumstance: 'the person having control of a building', 'the intention to execute works', 'at the expiration of the period specified'; then follows the new regulation, the block phrases repeated in order to make quite clear from the legal point of view that everything remains the same in the second context, except the obligation to wait until a formal time-limit has expired. A very small change at a great expense of words. In a recent *London Gazette* a column and a half was used to order a simple decrease of half an inch in the width of a medal-ribbon.

In the lower departments of Ministries and in their branch offices, such as post-offices, labour-exchanges, registry offices, most business is conducted in this legalistic language, with the help of set forms: someone wants to apply for a job, or a pension, or a contract, or a licence; and without a word Form J 16 or 272 A is handed to him to fill in. Where set forms are inadequate to the occasion, stereotyped phrases are fished out from the pool and strung together to suit the context. Thinking comes to be done in the same stereotypes.

Court evidence given by police-officers is an example of such thinking. A constable is not allowed to submit evidence in ordinary English: the desk-sergeant 'gorblimeys' it for him, leaving in their natural state only the words attributed to the accused persons or to witnesses.

> 'On the fifth inst. at nine p.m. approximately, when on duty, I was approaching the western outskirts of Sutton Porcorum, when I observed accused behaving in a suspicious manner in the company of the female witness. There was a light haze at the time. Accused was seated in a squatting posture on a branch of a municipal plane-tree adjoining no. 3 Pelham Place, at about ten feet from ground level, and the female witness, who was in a recumbent position on the municipal bench under the said tree was inciting accused to make an entry into the premises. The words she used were: "Go on, Alf, go on in, have a bit of pluck! No one won't see you." The female witness appeared to be under the influence of drink: she spoke these words in a highly jocular manner. The impression she conveyed was that she was sky-larking.'

The official style in the higher departments of a Ministry is comparatively free from cumbrous legalistic devices, because its ordinary records and announcements are not called into question in courts of law. It is much less complex in structure and correspondingly less definite in meaning. The subjects about which higher Government officials have to write are, for the most part, concerned with policy and the appropriate application of policy. Policy itself is not expressed in legal terms, but kept fluid until particular circumstances crystallize it into precedents. The relationship between various aspects and items of policy is thus undefined until some departmental annalist relates them in retrospect; so the day-to-day style of a Government Department is full of ambiguous phrases and loosely related clauses – nobody can be quite sure how things will turn out and nobody wishes to commit himself. The following are quotations from more than usually vague minutes (1934-7) circulated in a large Ministry:

> 'While the 80% can be used as a guide, other general conditions must be taken into account, and in particular we should not approve allowances for any particular force much in excess of the allowances at present paid in the generality of forces where circumstances are parallel.'

> 'I am rather doubtful whether there is much to be gained by taking these representations too seriously. On the whole I think the next step, if any, might be to make further enquiries.'

> 'This is a border line case, but not, I think, very far over the border: I agree that in this case and in somewhat similar cases an interview at H.O. may save us trouble.'

And here is a peremptory reminder from the Stationery Office:

'Dear Sir,

I have to call attention to communications from this Department of 3.4.34, 17.4.34 (''refer'' and ''hastener'') and 26.5.34 (letter under above reference) respecting . . . in view of the fact that no reply has yet been received to any of them.

The matter is now urgent to the extent pointed out in the third paragraph of my letter of 26th ultimo.

Yours faithfully'

These quotations raise another point: the non-committal timorousness of the official style. A Department does not give away the details of its work: sometimes because they are so complex that no one person fully understands them, sometimes because they are confidential, but more often because of the tradition of anonymous silence observed by the Civil Service in all its contacts with the outside world. Government officials, like members of the British Medical Association, are not allowed to advertise themselves, nor to get into trouble in the newspapers nor to defend themselves if they do. The Minister is briefed to answer for his Department if it is criticized in Parliament and no one else may do so in any other way – except in recent years the Public Relations Officer, who is allowed to write letters to *The Times* in defence of his Department, provided that he does not touch on major matters of policy. One of the effects of this rule is to make officials afraid of publicity. To avoid it they will publish the most indefinite generalities phrased with the most face-saving ingenuity; and when a Department needs to explain something to the public in order to persuade them to some co-operative action, it has to employ professional publicity-men untainted by the habit of official reticence.

In theory His Majesty's Government is One, collectively responsible for the actions of any part of it, and in practice most of its decisions are collectively made, no single person being actually responsible. This constitutional doctrine is applied within Departments and within the departmental committees. The Minister is allowed by courtesy to write 'I have decided', but all departmental officials must use the passive voice: 'it is considered desirable', 'it was felt necessary', 'in this connexion it might be pointed out'. The official always speaks in the name of his Minister, the Minister in the name of the Cabinet, the Cabinet in the name of the King. This ceremonial practice makes for extreme indecisiveness. When a great many officials have to be consulted on a complicated matter the circumstances may have changed entirely before they manage to agree. The delays so caused are fancifully ascribed to 'red tape'. Any interim announcement of such deliberations is sure to be even more indefinite than usual, for the draft of it will have gone through many hands to ensure that all signs of disagreement are well covered up. Even the frankest committee minutes on the most hotly contested questions are rarely more explicit than: 'There appeared to be considerable divergence of opinion regarding the line to be adopted in the event of .....'

The official style is at once humble, polite, curt and disagreeable: it derives partly from that used in Byzantine times by the eunuch slave-secretariat, writing stiffly in the name of His Sacred Majesty, whose confidence they enjoyed, to their fellow-slaves outside the palace-precincts – for the Emperor had summary power over everyone; and partly from the style used by the cleric-bureaucracy of the Middle Ages, writing stiffly in the name of the feudal lords to their serfs and, though cautious of offending their employers, protected from injury by being servants of the Church, not of the Crown, and so subject to canon, not feudal, law. The official style of civil servants, so far as it recalls its Byzantine derivation, is written by slaves to fellow-slaves of a fictitious tyrant; and, so far as it recalls its mediaeval derivation, is written by members of a quasi-ecclesiastical body, on behalf of quasi-feudal ministers (who, being politicians, come under a different code of behaviour from theirs) to a serf-like public. Permanent civil servants are sacrosanct, for they cannot be dismissed from their employment by a Minister of the Crown, but only transferred to another Department; yet they fear his displeasure, if juniors, because of his influence with their departmental chiefs.

Here is a typical official announcement:

> 'As regards the slaughter of sound cattle and sheep it must be recognized that by reason of the inevitable fluctuation in the supplies both from overseas and from home sources and the limited capacity of cold stores the maintenance of the meat ration presents problems of exceptional difficulty, and the Minister of Agriculture is anxious that farmers should do their utmost within the limits imposed by war-time feeding conditions to assist in maintaining a regular supply of fat stock for slaughter.'

This paragraph has suffered from collective authorship; no single person could possibly have written so confusedly by himself. The first phrase is the official way of introducing a new aspect of a subject without stating its connexion with what goes before or follows. After 'as regards' comes 'it must be recognized', a frequent form of official exhortation, put in the passive voice because officials are never quite sure whether they are exhorting themselves, other officials, the public in general, or some unspecified section of the public. Here it appears, but not until the fifth line, that they are exhorting farmers. When 'by reason of' follows such a phrase it can be assumed that the Department is about to offer excuses about the 'difficulties of the present situation', yet carefully avoid blaming anyone in particular. 'Presents problems of exceptional difficulty' is the formula used here. This is how the situation appears to officials who know something of the details that make up the problem; but when addressing the public they forget that some people will know nothing of the details and others will be all too intimately acquainted with them, and that both will be inclined to regard general talk about 'problems' as a cover for muddle and lack of understanding. Now comes the real point, the instructions which farmers are to follow: they are to send their beasts regularly to slaughter. But since the necessary orders for ensuring such regularity would be impossibly complicated and vexatious, recourse is had to the voluntary principle. The farmers are told politely that the Minister is 'anxious' and that they 'should do their utmost to assist in maintaining a regular supply'. The paragraph reads absurdly because the official style, when used in addresses to the public, should be reserved for orders – a plea for co-operation should be written in the simple, catchy style of good advertisement copy. There is no excuse here for such heavily veiled language.

The chief trouble with the official style is that it spreads far beyond the formal contexts to which it is suited. Most civil servants, having learned to write in this way, cannot throw off the habit. The obscurity of their public announcements largely accounts for the disrepute into which Departmental activities have fallen: for the public naturally supposes that Departments are as muddled and stodgy as their announcements.

The habit of obscurity is partly caused by a settled disinclination among public servants to give a definite refusal even where assent is out of the question; or to convey a vigorous rebuke even where, in private correspondence, any person with self-respect would feel bound to do so. This mood is conveyed by a polite and emasculated style – polite because, when writing to a member of the public, the public servant is, in theory at least, addressing one of his collective employers; emasculated because, as a cog in the Government machine, he must make his phrases look as mechanical as possible by stripping them of all personal feeling and opinion. One of the common emasculating devices is to convey decisions in the conditional tense. They are thus translated from the ordinary world of practice into a region of unfulfilled hypothesis:

> 'The suggestion contained in your letter of 10th August regarding the terms of Clause 7 of the   and   (Wartime) Regulations Act has received the fullest consideration, but the Minister would scarcely agree that they might under normal conditions be regarded as in any way offensive in tendency.'

This means that the departmental chief does not consider the wording of Clause 7 to be rude. The correspondent must not be bluntly told so, lest he should think his complaint had not been considered at all, but at the same time he must be gently reproached for having attributed offensive intentions to the authors of the Act. This is achieved by the conditional tense and the subjunctive which follows it; the complaint is thus turned into an hypothesis which, it is implied, should never have been proposed. Another example of this stylistic emasculation: a junior official had written a Minute, the purport of which was 'a byelaw on the subject is not necessary,' but a senior amended it to 'a byelaw on the subject is not in the present circumstances considered necessary'; and so threw doubt on the view expressed, though it was permanently settled.

There are many ways of delicately suggesting that a correspondent should not have troubled His Majesty's Government. For instance:

> 'It would appear, however, that in the conditions prevailing this contention could hardly be regarded as justifiable . . .'

rather than:

> 'No, we disagree. Why don't you trust us? We are in a far better position than you to know all the facts and precedents.'

Or:

> 'The Minister is not aware that any undertaking of this character has been entered into, and for your information I am instructed to remind you that the point in question was made abundantly clear to the satisfaction of all parties in our letter of May 17th, 1939.'

rather than:

> 'We took good care to promise nothing in 1939. Why bring the matter up again, you fools?'

Such cloaked phrasing is not reserved for the negative side of public business: official requests are often as emasculated as refusals or denials:

> 'I am instructed by the Minister to make enquiries with a view to obtaining information as to whether . . .'

'We want to know' would have been simpler; but an official must not stupidly admit to ignorance. He avoids doing so by making 'information' the chief word in the sentence: even officials can legitimately ask for 'information', as general medical practitioners can ask for a 'second opinion', without seeming incompetent. But having got 'information' into the sentence, the official's problem is how to connect it with the machinery of his Department and with the facts he wants to know. Hence 'with a view to obtaining' and 'as to whether': both are valuable means of introducing an appearance of relationship into a difficult succession of abstract nouns.

We have mentioned a disagreeable quality mixed with the politeness of official letters. The official himself often finds it tedious to write such letters, and his tedium is communicated to his style. But a more positive kind of disagreeableness is caused rather by the contradiction inherent in all official writing: the public approaches, or is approached by, temperamental individuals who are paid to disguise themselves as anonymous parts of a vast and unerring mechanism. A member of the public may know that he is in communication with a particular official, but can never identify him if he wishes to call him personally to account. He feels the same fear and distaste as when meeting bats in a dark room – not sure whether they are merely bats or, as their menacingly evasive gyrations suggest, creatures far more powerful and uncanny.

This sense is strengthened by the standing instructions that all letters from the public should be addressed to the Permanent Under-Secretary, and not to any named official. Officials make a habit of signing their names so illegibly that no one can decipher their signature and so be tempted to by-pass the 'proper channels' by starting a personal correspondence. Even announcements of changes in the staff at Ministries are usually made in terms of machinery. A junior official once drafted a public announcement beginning: 'The Minister has decided to appoint a statistical officer.' This was amended by one of his seniors to: 'The Minister has decided to inaugurate a statistical section.' It was then pointed out to the senior by an official more senior still that the appointment of one officer scarcely constituted a section. He wisely concurred and altered the draft again: 'The Minister has decided to inaugurate the nucleus of a statistical section.' The traditions of the machine were thus preserved at the cost of three unnecessary words.

Temporary civil servants, particularly women, feel uncomfortable in their use of the official style. It goes against their consciences to write something which conveys no precise meaning, but only the general impression 'we could say more'. Yet they feel obliged to conform to this style, because they are seldom lawyers and, when applying rules which they do not understand, do not wish to commit themselves to a precise opinion on any doubtful point. Often they have to write a letter like the following:

Dear Madam,

I am directed to refer to your letter no. 1 of the 3rd instant and to state that the circumstances of your case are not covered by any provision in the relevant sub-section of section 10 of the Railway Passengers' Insurance (Consolidation) Act 1918 and that therefore it would appear that you are not entitled to compensation under the Act.

I am, Madam,

your obedient servant

They long to write instead:

Dear Mrs. Smith,

So far as I can make out, the Railway Insurance Act, as it applies to your case, is shamefully unfair; but that is not my fault. I prefer not to go into the exact reasons why we cannot see that you get paid compensation for the damage you suffered from no fault of your own; the fact is, nobody here in this office is quite sure of the legal implications of the various sub-sections which come into question and if I gave you a summary of what *I* think they are, somebody important might read it and disagree and put me on the mat. I feel very badly about your case, really I do, and nothing would give me greater pleasure than to be able to write to you in the same warm way that the Chancellor of the Exchequer uses in the Personal Column of *The Times* when he acknowledges anonymous gifts to the Treasury; but all my letters have to begin "I am directed to refer to your letter no. —— of —— and to state that ——" and that makes too chilly a start for any pleasantness. Anyhow, charity begins at home, and it's as much as my job is worth to press for your getting compensation. So you won't get it. Please don't argue about this, because it will waste hours of your time and ours. Most of the other people in the office agree with me that the wording of the Act is against you; and only Parliament can amend Acts.

Yours sincerely, etc.

It is only very rarely that frankness and humour are admitted into official correspondence; however, they would be likely to occur in a confidential report, supposedly written by the Prime Minister to the King – for example, on the progress of a Government Bill – but in fact drafted by a high Treasury official. It might contain such phrases as:

'It was before a very thin and jaded house that the Bill was presented for its Third Reading – and the Government Whips had some difficulty in keeping sufficient of their flock on the right side of the wicket-gate to assure its passing – truancy was particularly rife in the back benches. . . .'

The official style is generally used in public announcements by business firms and corporations; the only exceptions being occasional announcements in humorous form released by their advertising departments. Even informal announcements addressed vaguely to 'you', instead of beginning 'The public is requested' remain hopelessly official; often with fawning and snarling in the same sentence.

The following is a notice posted in 1940-41 in all the coaches of a West Country Bus Company:

> 'It is our desire to give you good travel service where most needed. If you experience inconvenience especially during the busy summer months we would ask your kind forbearance in the national interest which imposes economy in fuel and man-power. It will be our endeavour, as always, to serve your best interests.'

It will be noticed that the principal subject, the war, is omitted; that the phrase 'we would ask your kind forbearance in the national interest' has the disagreeable implication that it is unpatriotic to complain when buses are late or full; that 'to serve your best interests' is patronizing as well as repetitive; that no apologies are offered. What is probably meant is:

> 'Your interests are still our closest concern, as in peacetime. We will give you the best possible bus-service, consistent with necessary war economies in men and fuel. So please bear patiently the inconveniences which, to our deep regret, you are likely to suffer especially during the busy summer months.'

It would be foolish to quarrel with any of the dialects of officialese. Army officers are privileged to write: 'At the conclusion of the tactical exercise officers, warrant officers and n.c.o's will stand fast; other ranks will proceed in an orderly manner to their respective hutments' – instead of: 'After the manœuvres all private soldiers will return quietly to their huts; the rest of the battalion will stand fast'. And business-men are privileged to write: 'Reference your esteemed advice undated' instead of 'Thank you for this morning's letter.' These are the styles that suit full-dress military uniform or formal business-dress. So long as such an impersonal dialect is written plainly according to its own rules, the only objection that one can raise is to an inappropriate extension of its use. For example, when a business man who has bought a country estate sends round an intimidating circular to a tenantry long accustomed to the direct personal language of generations of squires:

> 'The Loamshire Investment Company Limited wish it to be clearly understood that in future all applications for repair of roofs, window fitments, etc. will be made in writing direct to the Estate office and not communicated by word of mouth to individual employees concerned with such work.'

Or when B.B.C. bulletins containing good news are written in the same flat style that is found serviceable in lessening the impact of bad.

To many business men the official style is a proof-armour that they assume, often ridiculously, in every contact with their subordinates: managing directors of large stores and of public utility corporations are caricatured as using it even to their wives and children. The manager of a large advertising agency was obliged in 1938 to dismiss three of his copy-writers because an important customer-firm had given notice that they were withdrawing their account. He did not wish the reason for his decision to be known and was so nervous and embarrassed when he gave the three copy-writers their notice of dismissal that he forgot himself: he shook hands with one of them and said how sorry he was to lose him.

This encouraged the copy-writer to ask: 'In that case, sir, why are you getting rid of me?'

The manager grew red, fumbled round for a suitable stereotype and finally stammered . . . 'A highly improper question . . . highly improper! Let me remind you of the fact that *this is neither the time nor the place* to ask such a highly improper question!'

The following shrewd and valuable remarks were circulated, about 1930, in one of the larger Ministries by a senior Civil Service official; we have edited them here and there:

> 'I find myself involved in daily drudgery with letters and minutes referred to me, forced to correct glaring errors in spelling, grammar and punctuation. For the most part these errors arise from thoughtlessness rather than miseducation. For example:
>
> A letter begins by "acknowledging" a report received weeks earlier, formal acknowledgement having already been made.
>
> A Municipal Council is "reminded" of an opinion not previously communicated to it, or has something obvious "explained" to it, or has something not obvious introduced to it with the phrase "of course' .
>
> The second sentence of a two-page letter begins with "I am to add" — a phrase which is nearly always needless and only justified when it occurs in the final paragraph.
>
> A careless abbreviation has been used — "Bye-laws concerned with h.w.c." — which the typist misreads as "height of water-closets" when what is meant is "the housing of the working classes".
>
> The Minister is said to "regret" that he cannot intervene in some affair when there is no reason for such regret, and even sometimes when the Courts are dealing with the person so addressed. Regret must not be allowed to creep in as "common form" but should be kept for deserving cases. Or the Minister is said to be "glad" or "happy" to intervene. These words, like "regret", may suggest more than is meant; and it is

therefore better to use colourless but practical words, such as "ready", "prepared" or "willing", or merely "will intervene"—unless any real encouragement is intended.

An Act of Parliament or bye-law is said to be "to the following effect", and then the relevant sub-section is quoted. This suggests that the quotation is merely a paraphrase.

'We must try to write our letters with an eye to the recipient. To take two small examples: we ought to know that the request to "submit" drafts, observations and so on irritates some Local Authorities because of its suggestion that they are in a subservient position—"send" or "show" are shorter and better words. And we ought to know that Local Authorities will be exasperated to have their proposals rejected on the ground that to implement them "would be contrary to the practice of the Department". The tactful phrasing is: "The Minister cannot properly implement these proposals because . . ."

Unless a person who writes to us seems to be asking for a snub by putting on airs or being deliberately rude we must not frame our answer in a way to make him feel that he has made a fool of himself or taken a liberty in writing to us: for example, we must not begin by saying that we do not understand his letter, unless we literally do not. If there is some obscure phrase or reference contained in it, we can ask him, in the second or third sentence, to elucidate this; but must not discourage him by throwing it back at him at the outset.

In writing to outsiders about letters, sent on to us from other Departments of Government, which do not, however, concern us, we must not answer crudely:

" 'I am directed to advert to your letter forwarded from the Board of Trade and to state that the Minister has no jurisdiction . . ."

It will give the recipient a better impression of the Service if we answer:

"Your letter was forwarded to us by the President of the Board of Trade, who has himself no jurisdiction, to ascertain whether the Minister could help you. He regrets, however (if regrets are appropriate), that he is not in a position to do so, and, so far as he is aware, the matter does not fall within the powers of any Department of Government."

I have nothing to say against the old style of drafting letters, clauses, and so on, where the object is to be complete and precise, or (occasionally) when for practical reasons an air of portentousness has to be assumed. But in this style unnecessary words are often used merely from a habit of circumlocution. For example:

"As regards the suggestion in your letter I am to say that the Minister agrees to the course suggested."

Why not: "The Minister agrees to the course suggested in your letter."?

Or: "It is not clear from the terms of your letter whether the Council have had under consideration the question whether the fact that, in pursuance of Section 5, they are required to do A, renders B unnecessary."

Why not: "It is not clear from your letter whether or not the Council have considered, that because Section 5 requires them to do A, it will be unnecessary for them also to do B"?

Or: "With respect to your letter relative to the desirability of the adoption in the case of an urban district of a regulation restricting the fouling of pavements by dogs, I am to state . . ."

Why not: "In answer to your enquiry, whether it is desirable for an urban district to adopt a regulation restricting the fouling of pavements by dogs, I am to state . . ."?

'We must not let a letter be ambiguous because the question it answers has been ambiguously phrased. Recently a Local Authority asked whether an enactment, which they cited, authorised expenditure "in connexion with" a certain object. We answered this loose question with an equally loose answer "Yes", whereas the enactment authorised only certain specified categories of expenditure which, though "in connexion with" the object named, did not fall within the authorised categories; it was challenged and Branch X complained, justly, that we had put them in a difficulty. If we had quoted the enactment this difficulty would never have arisen.'

These remarks are admirable, but there are not many officials who have the knowledge, taste, time and patience to give their subordinates similar lessons in logic and manners. What perhaps is needed in every Department of Government is a trained Minute-master, charged to read through samples of Minutes by junior officials, carefully checking and explaining all infringements of the official decencies. Moreover, an example of discrimination in use of official language should be set by the Civil Service in general. Though the official style may continue in internal use in the Departments, ordinary straightforward English should be used for all external purposes. Similarly, crystallized legal language, though it may be retained for security's sake in the framing of laws and regulations, should not appear in notices posted on the public boards in church porches or in the vestibules of town halls. Or not unless glosses are provided in understandable – and we do not mean Basic – English for all whom they may concern.

CHAPTER FIVE

THE BEGINNINGS OF ENGLISH PROSE

KING ALFRED translated a number of Latin books into Anglo-Saxon, sometimes called Early English. The capacities of Anglo-Saxon will be seen when we compare a Latin passage with his translation of it. Later we will compare Alfred's translation with one of the same passage made five centuries later by the poet Chaucer, who wrote in a language which is more recognizably English. The Latin passage is from the twelfth section of Book III of Boëthius's *Consolation of Philosophy*. Boëthius, the last of the Roman philosophers, was Consul in A.D. 510 under Theodoric the Ostrogoth.

Quae sontes agitant metu
Ultrices scelerum deae
Iam maestae lacrimis madent.
Non Ixionium caput
Velox praecipitat rota
Et longa site perditus
Spernit flumina Tantalus.
Vultur dum satur est modis,
Non traxit Tityi jecur.
Tandem, "Vincimur", arbiter
Umbrarum miserans ait,
"Donamus comitem viro
Emptam carmine conjugem.
Sed lex dona coerceat,
Ne, dum Tartara liquerit,
Fas sit lumina flectere."
Quis legem det amantibus?
Major lex amor est sibi.
Heu, noctis prope terminos
Orpheus Eurydicen suam
Vidit, perdidit, occidit.
Vos haec fabula respicit
Quicumque in superum diem
Mentem ducere quaeritis.
Nam qui Tartareum in specus
Victus lumina flexerit,
Quidquid praecipuum trahit
Perdit, dum videt inferos.

In his translation, made about the year 888, Alfred worked under difficulties: Anglo-Saxon was a limited and clumsy language, and the poem was written in a very cultivated style. His object was to convey as much of the matter and moral as his audience, who knew nothing of Classical myth or of philosophy, could take in. He expanded, condensed, added and omitted as he pleased. This is his version:

'Tha eode he furthur oth he gemette tha graman gydena the folcisce menn hatath *Parcas*, tha hi secgath thaet on nanum menn nyton nane are, ac aelcum menn wrecen be his gewyrhtum; tha hi secgath thaet walden aelces mannes wyrde. Tha ongonn he biddan heora miltse; tha ongunnon hi wepan mid him. Tha eode he furthur, ond him urnon ealle hellwaran ongean, ond laeddon hine to hiora cininge, ond ongunnon ealle sprecan mid him, ond biddan thaes the he baed. Ond thaet unstille hweol the Ixion waes to gebunden, Levita cyning, for his scylde, thaet othstod for his hearpunga, ond Tantalus se cyning, the on thisse worulde ungemetlice gifre waes, ond him thaer thaet ilce yfel fyligde thaere gifernesse, he gestilde. Ond se vultor sceolde forlaetan thaet he ne slat tha lifre Tyties thaes cyninges, the hine aer mid thy witnode; ond eall hellwara witu gestildon, tha hwile the he beforan tham cyninge hearpode. Tha he tha longe ond longe hearpode, tha cleopode se hellwara cyning, ond cwaeth: "Wuton agifan thaem esne his wif, for thaem he hi haefth geearnad mid his hearpunga." Bebead him tha thaet he geare wisse, thaet he hine naefre under baec ne besawe, sithan he thonanweard waere, ond saede, gif he hine under baec besawe, thaet he sceolde forlaetan thaet wif. Ac tha lufe mon maeg swithe uneathe othe na forbeodan: wei la wei! hwaet Orpheus tha laedde his wif mid him, oth the he com on thaet gemaere leohtes ond theostro; tha eode thaet wif aefter him. Tha he forth on thaet leoht com, tha beseah he hine under baec with thaes wifes; tha losade hio him sona. Thas leasan spell laerath gehwylcne monn thara the wilnath helle thiostro to flionne, ond to thaes sothan Godes liohte to cumanne, thaet he hine ne besio to his ealdan yflum, swa thaet he hi eft swa fullice fulfremme, swa he hi aer dyde; for thaem swa hwa swa mid fulle willan his mod went to thaem yflum the he aer forlet, ond hi thonne fullfremeth, ond he him thonne fullice liciath, and he hi naefre forlaetan ne thencth, thonne forlyst he eall his aerran good, buton he hit eft gebete.'

Here is the same version modernized by us for readers who cannot make out the Anglo-Saxon; we have not been able to do justice to Alfred's use of alliteration, which is the principal embellishment of his prose; this was an Anglo-Saxon, not a Latin, device.

'... Then went he further until he met the grim goddesses that men of this earth call the *Parcae* who, they say, are not unwitting of any man and requite every man according to his works and, they say, rule every man's fate. Then began he to ask their mercy; then began they to weep with him. Then went he further and there ran to meet him all the men of Hell and led him to their King and all began to speak with him and pleaded for that which he pleaded. And that unstill wheel to which Ixion was bound, the King of the Levites, for his sin, that stood still at his harping; and Tantalus the King that in this world was boundless greedy and was there beset by the same evil of greed, he was still. And the vulture should cease from tearing the liver of King Tityus, who before pained him therewith; and all pains ceased for the men of Hell the while he harped before their King. Then long and long he harped. Then cried the King of Hell and said: "Let us give back this man his wife, for he has earned her with his harping." He bade him take good care that he should never look behind him when he was going thence, and said that, if he looked behind him, he should lose his wife. But to Love one may hardly indeed forbid things, or not at all: well-a-day! Orpheus led his wife with him until he came to the bourne of light and dark; then went his wife after him. When he came forth into that light, then did he look behind him at his wife; then they lost themselves forthwith. This untrue story teaches every man of those who wish to escape from the darkness of Hell and come to the true light of God, that he should not look back upon his old evils so as often to enter into them again as fully as he did before; for whoever with full intent turns in desire back to the evils which he once left behind and enters into them again, so that they fully please him and he neither leaves them nor thinks of so doing, then that man loses all his former good, unless he makes atonement often.'

Alfred was the best educated layman in England – he had been to school at Rome – and his translation is very good indeed, considering the difficulties of his task. He introduces a dramatic element into the story that is absent from Boëthius's version: Orpheus's steady progress through Hell, the commotion of the shades, their intercession with the Judge, the harping long and long. This is in compensation for the lost lyricism, and he strengthens the effect not only with alliteration but with forceful repetition of key-words. He also does not fail to remedy Boëthius's chief poetic fault, which is the idiomatic but blank *vidit, perdidit* ('he saw, he lost') at the crisis of the poem instead of *respectans ibi perdidit* ('looking back, he lost her there'[1]). But nobody could call this graceful prose. It is a bald succession of events linked up with the words 'then' and 'and'.

[1] The word *Parcae*, a gloss which Alfred has incorporated in the text, is a plain mistake: the Furies, not the Fates, were meant by Boëthius. His making Ixion a King of the Levites (instead of the Lapithae) is deliberate: he is linking the story to popular Biblical knowledge. The death of Orpheus is Boëthius's mistake; Orpheus continued to live, according to the Classical legend.

Only at the end is there any attempt to build up a sentence in the Latin style, and even that would have been pronounced barbarous by Latin orators because of the lame and illogical 'unless he makes atonement often.' Also, at the point where the men of Hell take Orpheus before their King, it is not clear to whom the 'him's refer.

Norman-French had been introduced into England before the Norman Conquest: it was spoken freely at the court of Edward the Confessor. After the Conquest it became the domestic language of the governing class, though Anglo-Saxon was still used by the artisans and peasants. Latin was the language of religion, learning and Canon Law. Both Norman-French and Anglo-Saxon then gradually gave place to English, which (as we point out in Chapter One) was Anglo-Saxon with its rigid grammar loosened and its vocabulary enriched with Norman-French. Very little of the earliest popular work in English is in prose: the common people were illiterate and the only way of getting a wide public for a work of instruction or entertainment was to put it into simple, easily memorized verse. This is why poems as late as the fourteenth century, notably Langland's revolutionary *The Vision of Piers Ploughman*, 1362, were written in a distinctly Anglo-Saxon style – the verse unrhymed, alliterative and measured by a count of stresses, not syllables—whereas prose had shed its Anglo-Saxon crudeness and taken on the gentility of Norman-French.

Most early prose-works in English were translations from popular Latin or French books, the reason being that English had lately displaced Norman-French as the national language, so that English text-books were needed in the schools. The political ties between France and England were still strong and French remained the language of heraldry, feudal law and polite society; but the son of an ordinary well-to-do family learned it at school, not in the home. And now that he had also learned to read and write English, more and more books were written in English prose, the invention of printing in the fifteenth century enormously increasing their circulation.

Chaucer's translation from Boëthius was made in 1374. He kept closely to the text, and his only additions, apart from the glosses, were points that Boethius had perhaps been wrong to omit: that it was for pity, not rage or any other emotion, that the Furies wept; that the penalty for looking back was that Eurydice should be lost; and that Orpheus (this was also corrected by Alfred) did look back.

> 'And the thre goddesses, furiis and vengeresses of felonyes that tormenten and agasten the soules by anoy, woxen sorweful and sory, and wepyn teeris for pite. Tho was nat the heved of Ixion y-tormented by the overthrowynge wheel. And Tantalus, that was destroied by the wood-

nesse of long thurst, despyseth the floodes to drynken. The foul that hyghte voltor, that etith the stomak (or the gyser) of Tycius, is so fulfild of his song that it nil eten ne tiren no more. At the laste the lord and juge of soules was moevid to misericordes, and cryede: "We ben overcomen," quod he; "yeve we to Orpheus his wif to beren hym compaignye; he hath wel y-bought hire by his faire song and his ditee. But we wolen putten a lawe in this and covenaunt in the yifte; that is to seyn that, til he be out of helle, yif he loke behynde hym, that his wyf shal comen ageyn unto us". But what is he that may yeven a lawe to loverys? Love is a grettere lawe and a strengere to hymself thanne any lawe that men mai yyven. Allas! whanne Orpheus and his wyf weren almest at the termes of the nyght (that is to seyn, at the last boundes of helle), Orpheus lokede abakward on Eurudyce his wif, and lost hire, and was deed. This fable apertenith to yow alle, who so evere desireth or seketh to lede his thought into the sovereyn day (that is to seyn, in-to cleernesse of sovereyn good). For who so that evere be so overcomen that he ficche his eien in-to the put of helle (that is to seyn, who so sette his thoughtes in erthly thinges,) al that evere he hath drawen of the noble good celestial he lesith it. . . .'

If the passage is read without the parenthetical glosses (they were for schoolboys and would now be printed as footnotes) it will be found to have a carefully considered rhythm, which is not Latin, through the phrases in the longer sentences are arranged in the logical order of Latin prose; and is not French, though the many French words included, such as 'vengeresses of felonyes, that tormenten', give it a Southern grace; and is not Anglo-Saxon, in spite of the simplicity of language and the occasional heavy alliteration – 'And Tantalus, that was destroied by the woodnesse of long thurst, despyseth the floodes to drynken.' Anglo-Saxon was the language of the belly; Norman-French, that of the heart – the Normans had learned to have hearts since they had settled in France; Latin, that of the brain. English, as Chaucer used it, was a reconciliation of the functions of all these organs. But in Chaucer's as in all the best English prose, the belly rules: English is a practical language. The main purpose of Chaucer's writing was entertainment, and in all his prose, which includes two of the *Canterbury Tales* (1386) and a treatise on the *Astrolabe* (1391), he shows a more careful consideration for the reader's ease than any previous writer of English. His contemporaries, the Lollards, a sect headed by John Wyclif, who had gone from legitimate criticism of Church organization to heretical criticism of Church doctrine, are important as the first to develop the English vocabulary of theological, ecclesiastical and political arguments; but their style is without grace, and keeps close in its phrasing to monkish Latin.

The Travels of Sir John Maundeville, who is supposed to have lived from 1322-1356, was published in England about the year 1400; it may have been translated from the French. *The Travels* is a very wild geographical treatise, in part a guide book for pilgrims to the Holy Land, filled with descriptions of mythical animals, plants, people; the style returns in naiveness almost to that of King Alfred, and far fewer French words are used than by Chaucer. Maundeville (if he was the author of the travels attributed to him) assembles a great many legendary details and links them together, usually by a series of 'and's, without consideration for rhythm or variety of phrasing; and with constant repetitions – 'some men say', 'as men say', 'And men say' – 'form and likeness of a great dragon', 'into the likeness of a dragon', 'in that form of a dragon'.

> 'And some men say that the Isle of Lango is yet the daughter of Hippocrates, in form and likeness of a great dragon, that is a hundred fathom of length, as men say; for I have not seen her. And they of the Isles call her, Lady of the Land. And she lieth in an old castle, in a cave, and showeth twice or thrice a year. And she doth no harm to no man, but if men do her harm. And she was thus changed and transformed, from a fair damsel, into the likeness of a dragon, by a goddess, that was cleped Diana. And men say, that she shall so endure in that form of a dragon, unto the time that a knight come, that is so hardy, that dare come to her and kiss her on the mouth: and then shall she turn again to her own kind and be a woman again.'

Yet there is an element in Maundeville's prose not found in Chaucer's: the Celtic sense of wonder and magic, which appears most purely in the Welsh tales of the *Mabinogion* and the Gaelic legend-cycles of Finn, Oisin and Cuchulain. Celtic themes had already been introduced to English readers: the twelfth-century Welshman, Geoffrey of Monmouth, had put a number of British legends, including those of King Lear and King Arthur, into his much-read Latin '*Chronicles of Britain*'; and an Irish legend about Manannan, the God of the Sea, was the original of a fourteenth-century English alliterative poem *Sir Gawayn and the Green Knight*. But these themes came into England chiefly by way of France. The British legend of King Arthur and the Knights of the Round Table had been used in several French romances, and appealed to Western chivalry as worthily combining vigorous action with fine sentiment; the knights of Brittany, where a language akin to Welsh was spoken, had given the Norman-French a taste for them. French romances were extremely popular with the English educated classes; and Sir Thomas Malory's well-known *Morte d'Arthur*, 1470, one of the first books printed in English, shows the deep influence of French prose.

Here is an extract from Queen Guenevere's speech at her last meeting with her lover, Sir Lancelot:

> 'Through this man and me hath all this war been wrought, and the death of the most noblest knights of the world; for through our love and that we loved together is my most noble lord slain. Therefore, Sir Lancelot, wit thou well that I am set in such a plight to get my soul's health; and yet I trust, through God's grace, that after my death to have a sight of the blessed face of Christ, and at doomsday to sit on his right side, for as sinful as ever I was are saints in heaven. Therefore, Sir Lancelot, I require thee and beseech thee heartily, for all the love that ever was betwixt us, that thou never see me more in the visage; and I command thee on God's behalf, that thou foresake my company, and to thy kingdom thou return again and keep well thy realm from war and wrack. For as well as I have loved thee, mine heart will not serve me to see thee; for through thee and me is the flower of kings and knights destroyed. Therefore, Sir Lancelot, go to thy realm, and there take thee a wife, and live with her with joy and bliss, and I pray thee heartily, pray to our Lord, that I may amend my misliving.'

This is an intricate emotional rhythm, the tone rising with each 'Therefore, Sir Lancelot' and gradually falling again, a little lower each time. But despite his understanding of the language of the heart, Malory did not renounce the belly. He remained English in his preference for short native words wherever they served as well as long foreign ones; and in his use of alliteration in moments of stress – for example, the bitter 'to sit on his right side for as sinful as ever I was are saints in heaven'. This is a work intended to be read aloud at the firesides of great houses on cold winter evenings, and is to be judged as oratory rather than prose: an oratory appealing to the sentiments rather than to the intellect. Nothing is known of Sir Thomas Malory, and his personality is unobtrusive: he is free alike of the clerical habit of distorting history to point some adventitious moral, and of the scholastic habit of surfacing it floridly. The story seems to tell itself.

None of the chroniclers and romance-writers who immediately followed Malory introduced any fresh element into English prose or equalled his command of it. But something new was taking place in English intellectual life: this was the revived study of the Greek and Latin classics.

After the expulsion of the Byzantine armies from Italy in the seventh century Greek had been forgotten in Western Europe; and, because of Church schisms, the Latin West lost contact with the Greek East until the time of the later Crusades. Then, as the western fringe of the Byzantine

Empire was occupied by the Venetians and the remainder gradually overrun by Turkish armies – its capital, Constantinople, was captured in 1453 – Greek scholars migrated into Italy, bringing with them the traditions of classical Greek learning. Greek presently reached the universities of Oxford and Cambridge and the Court of London, by way of Paris and the Low Countries. Twenty years after the publication of the *Morte d'Arthur* the Dutch scholar, Erasmus, was teaching in London, and his friends Dean Colet, Bishop Fisher and Sir Thomas More had become the recognized leaders of English 'New Learning'.

Latin had been the international language of secular as well as of religious learning. Its style was copied not from the Classical orators and historians but from the Christian theologians of three or four centuries later and from monkish translations of Aristotle's principles of Greek logic. Mediaeval education consisted largely in learning how to argue logically in Latin. Scholastic text-books provided students with the exact logical terms in which to develop the themes of their arguments, and it was taken for granted that all arguments were theological. This tradition was broken by the New Learning. Though such scholars as Erasmus and Sir Thomas More continued to write in Latin they despised scholastic theology, and regarded the Greek and Latin classics from the purely literary and moral point of view known as Humanism. In tracing Latin to its Classical sources, they threw off the burden of mediaeval commentary, and without prejudice studied Plato's idealism as well as the precepts of the early Church Fathers, and the pagan love-poems of Catullus as well as the *Rhythm* of St Bernard of Morlaix. A more secular outlook replaced the theological – though one no less Christian and no less concerned with morals; and this freedom from mediaeval habits of thinking gave new scope to writing.

The revival of Greek had in itself little effect on English prose style, Greek not being an eccentric enough language to supply a fashion in novel idioms. The conventions of mediaeval Latin prose remained long after the subject matter of writing had changed. All education, of nobles and courtiers as well as of scholars and clerics, and in Latin as well as in the modern languages, was still based on monastic conventions, though these were reinforced and expanded by a study of the masters of Classical oratory, Cicero and Quinctilian, and continued so until late in the seventeenth century. Out of them grew both the polished and the florid, or 'conceited', styles of Elizabethan writing.

The polished style is seen to most advantage in translations from the Latin by university men who hesitated to add verbal embellishments to the original texts, but felt that to be plain was not enough. William

Adlington's translation, 1566, of *The Golden Ass*, a Latin romance written by Lucius Apuleius, a first-century Roman provincial, is a good example of this polished style. Adlington apologized, in his dedication to the Earl of Sussex, that 'so pleasant and worthy a work' was 'now barbarously and simply framed in English'; but he must have known that he wrote far better English than Apuleius had written Latin. The last sentence of the following passage is admirable for moving in imitation of the magical scene it describes; as the first sentence is for ending with a string of short, jerky words which suggest how the narrator choked. These were still the times when romances were read aloud, and such close suiting of the prose rhythm to the sense must have contributed greatly to the pleasure of the readers:

> 'The other night being at supper with a sort of hungry fellows, while I did greedily put a great morsel of meat in my mouth, that was fried with the flour of cheese and barley, it cleaved so fast in the passage of my throat and stopped my wind in such sort, that I was well nigh choked. And yet at Athens before the porch there called Peale, I saw with these eyes a Juggler that swallowed up a two-hand sword, with a very keen edge, and by and by for a little money, that we that looked on gave him, he devoured a chasing spear with the point downward. And after that he had conveyed the whole spear within the closure of his body, and brought it out again behind, there appeared on the top thereof (which caused us all to marvel) a fair boy pleasant and nimble, winding and turning himself in such sort that you would suppose he had neither bone nor gristle, and verily think that he were the natural Serpent, creeping and sliding on the knotted staff, which the god of Medicine is feigned to bear.'

There was also a plain style, which was a revival of the unpretentious *Anglo-Saxon Chronicle* style; but with its syntax improved by grammar-school and Cathedral-school study of the less stylistic Classical authors, such as Sallust and Caesar, and of the pleasant colloquies of Erasmus. Elizabethan accounts of voyages, travels and adventures, especially when the matter was interesting enough in itself not to require rhetorical improvement, were written in this plain style. Here is a passage from Richard Hakluyt's collection of Elizabethan voyages as reported to him by the masters of the vessels which had taken part in them: it concerns John Hawkins' voyage to the West Indies in 1567:

> 'The most part of the men that were left alive in the *Jesus* made shift and followed the *Minion* in a small boat; the rest, which the little boat was not able to receive, were enforced to abide the mercy of the Spaniards (which I doubt was very little); so with the *Minion* only, and

the *Judith* (a small barque of fifty tons) we escaped, which barque the same night forsook us in our great misery. We were now removed with the *Minion* from the Spanish ships two bow-shots, and there rode all that night. The next morning we recovered an island a mile from the Spaniards, where there took us a North wind, and being left only with two anchors and two cables (for in this conflict we lost three cables and two anchors), we thought always upon death which ever was present; but God preserved us to a longer time.'

This plain style was considered suitable for merchants, artisans, seamen, farmers; the florid and polished styles of rhetoric were reserved for the governing classes. This separation of styles by class distinctions did a great disservice to prose. The habit of making a rigmarole out of sentences that could and should be quite simple, or imposing an artificial pattern on them, is one of which educated writers have never for long broken themselves.

The rhetoricians of the New Learning wrote out prescriptions for adorning any theme, serious or humorous, religious or secular, that a priest, scholar, courtier or politician might care to write upon. A ready and appropriate use of the new conceits, or flowers of speech, both in writing and speaking became the sign of good breeding. But most of the text-books of this rhetorical system were merely expanded editions of those that had been used throughout the Middle Ages for more purely logical studies: they tabulated the stages through which a theme should go. These stages were called 'topics'[1] or 'places', and known by such logical terms as 'definition', 'division', 'etymology', 'cause', 'effect', 'antecedent', 'consequence', 'comparison', 'similitude', 'example', and 'testament of authority'. In mediaeval literature, rhetoric and logic had become inextricably mixed, but the bias had always been toward logic. The bias of humanistic writers was towards rhetoric.

There was a school convention for filling out a rhetorical frame-work with an accumulation of similes, proverbs and moralistic sayings of all kinds. To provide students and writers with plentiful material, anthologies were compiled of the moralistic sentences of Classical and mediaeval authors. Perhaps the most influential of these were the three which Erasmus issued about 1500, the *Adages*, the *Apothegms*, and the *Similes*: they were frequently adapted and translated into English in the course of the sixteenth century.

Richard Taverner put these compilations to typical use, in 1539.

[1] The word 'topics' was derived from the title of Cicero's treatise on oratory, in which he reduced the complicated logic of Aristotle to seventeen main headings, for the benefit of lawyers and politicians who wished to regularize the order of ideas in their speeches.

His method was to write a short English commentary on a Latin proverb, thus:

'Vino vendibili suspensa hedera nihil opus

'Wine that is saleable and good needeth no bush or garland of ivy to be hanged before. Like as men will seek out good wine, though there be no sign at all to direct and appoint them where it is sold, for all good things need no commendation of any outward badge or token. Good merchandise and also pure and substantial things of what kind so ever they be do praise themselves. The English proverb is thus *Good wine needeth no sign.*'

Taverner has amplified the proverb by explaining why the wine needs no bush, and by giving a further example ('good merchandise'), so that it becomes a generalization. He also expands it with 'doublets':

'no bush or garland of ivy'
'to direct and appoint them'
'outward badge or token'

This use of doublets was one of the characteristics of the rhetorical style, and is familiar to Anglicans from the Book of Common Prayer, first published in 1549.

'Dearly beloved brethren, the scripture moveth us in sundry places to *acknowledge and confess* our manifold *sins and wickedness* . . . and that we should not *dissemble nor cloak* them . . .'

Doublets suggest legal phraseology and so give an air of authority to a sentence.

The essay and the 'character' both grew out of this new rhetorical fashion: they dealt at first with single themes, expanded according to the rules of rhetoric and filled out with sententious matter. Bacon's *Essays*, the first book of which appeared in 1597, were composed largely of such themes. Many of the essays are linkings together of a dozen or so aphoristic remarks, under such headings as 'Of Study', 'Of Discourse', 'Of Regiment and Health'. These read as if Bacon had transcribed them with little further thought directly from his Commonplace Book: it was customary for gentlemen, scholars and writers of his time – and for the next two centuries – to keep Commonplace Books, into which they copied sententious phrases that they came across in the course of their reading. The 'character', modelled on the *Characters* of the Greek Theophrastus, was a pithy summary of some human types: 'the cuckold', 'the pander', 'the melancholy man', 'the good steward', 'the sycophant', 'the sanguine man', 'the boastful soldier', 'the devout widow', 'the shrew'.

Many manuals of the new rhetoric were published. One appeared so late as 1660, the year of the Restoration, written by Charles Hoole, a schoolmaster. It describes concisely the methods that schoolboys should follow in amplifying Latin fables:

> 'Let them strive (who can best) to turn the Fable into English prose and adorn and amplify it with fit Epithets, choice Phrases, acute Sentences, witty Apothegms, lively Similitudes, pat Examples, and Proverbial speeches; all agreeing to the matter of morality therein couched.'

How closely essayists kept to the prescribed pattern can be seen in this extract from a typical Elizabethan pamphlet, *The School of Abuse*, written by Stephen Gosson and published in 1579. It is an attack upon the immorality of plays — which were just then becoming popular — and upon the practices of poets in general.

> 'I must confess that poets are the whetstones of wit, notwithstanding that wit is dearly bought: where honey and gall are mixed, it will be hard to sever the one from the other. The deceitful Physician giveth sweet Syrups to make his poison go down the smoother: the Juggler casteth a mist to work the closer: the Sirens' song is the Sailor's wrack: the Fowler's whistle, the Bird's death: the wholesome bait, the Fish's bane: the Harpies have Virgins' faces, and vultures' talents: Hyena speaks like a friend, and devours like a Foe: the Wolf jets in Wether's fells: many good sentences are spoken by Danus, to shadow his knavery: and written by Poets, as ornaments to beautify their thoughts, and set their trumpery to sale without suspect.'

Much of this passage is written in irregular verse, skilfully cross-alliterated:

> The deceitful physician
> Giveth sweet Syrups
> To make his poison
> Go down the smoother:
> The Juggler casteth a mist
> To work the closer.
>
> The Sirens' song
> Is the Sailor's wrack:
> The Fowler's whistle,
> The Birds' death:
> The wholesome bait
> The Fish's bane. . . .

Gosson's judgement on poetry was equally applicable to contemporary prose writing: almost any theme in prose, no matter how trite or stupid, could be presented in the 'trumpery' disguise that he denounced. His own method of ornamentation was to heap illustrations one upon another, all in proverb form, and all, apparently, gathered from contemporary anthologies. Some of his instances contain Classical allusions — the Harpies, the Sirens, Danus — this use of the 'testimony of the ancients' was especially popular. The purpose of introducing so many proverbs and so much other testimony must originally have been to convince readers of the universal truth of an argument; but Gosson and his contemporaries used them simply for the technical pleasure that they gave to the rhetorically trained. Greater admiration for a fertile invention than for a just conclusion was expected from the reader.

Logic had been cultivated in the Christian church so that clerics could readily confute heretics and pagans; and if it had not been for this precaution Christianity might well have gone the way of many other religions that had originated in supernatural revelation. But logic was now being put to frivolous uses: a famous orator would go from university to university showing off his capacity for argument by defending ridiculous paradoxes: for example, James (The Admirable) Crichton of Clunie (1560 1585), a Scottish prodigy, visited the universities of France and Italy, not only challenging the graduates there to contests in horsemanship, fencing and the improvisation of verse, but defending paradoxes against all comers, as many as two thousand at a single session. Such paradoxes were: that the Devil was a woman; that Aaron was a cripple; that mandrakes had immortal souls; that Balaam's ass spoke French; that Eve and her daughters played with dolls together. This game amused the younger wits at Court, who played it with secular instances and plentiful punning. In Shakespeare's *Two Gentlemen of Verona* (1591) Speed and Proteus chop logic with each other as follows:

SPEED. Sir Proteus, save you! Saw you my master?
PRO. But now he parted hence, to embark for Milan.
SPEED. Twenty to one, then, he is shipp'd already,
And I have play'd the sheep,[1] in losing him.
PRO. Indeed, a sheep doth very often stray,
An if the shepherd be a while away.
SPEED. You conclude that my master is a shepherd, then, and I a sheep?
PRO. I do.
SPEED. Why then my horns are his horns,[2] whether I wake or sleep.
PRO. A silly answer, and fitting well a sheep.
SPEED. This proves me still a sheep.

[1] 'Sheep' was pronounced 'ship'. [2] A pun on cuckoldry.

PRO. True, and thy master a shepherd.

SPEED. Nay, that I can deny by a circumstance.

PRO. It shall go hard but I'll prove it by another.

SPEED. The shepherd seeks the sheep, and not the sheep the shepherd; but I seek my master, and my master seeks not me: therefore I am no sheep.

PRO. The sheep for fodder follow the shepherd, the shepherd for food follows not the sheep; thou for wages followest thy master, thy master for wages follows not thee: therefore thou art a sheep.

SPEED. Such another proof will make me cry "baa".

PRO. But dost thou hear? gavest thou my letter to Julia?

SPEED. Ay, sir. I, a lost mutton, gave your letter to her, a laced mutton[1]; and she, a laced mutton, gave me, a lost mutton, nothing for my labour.

PRO. Here's too small a pasture for such store of muttons.

SPEED. If the ground be overcharged, you were best stick her.

PRO. Nay, in that you are astray; 'twere best pound you.

SPEED. Nay, sir, less than a pound shall serve me for carrying your letter.

PRO. You mistake: I mean the pound, – a pinfold.

Shakespeare, being a tradesman's son and neither destined for the priesthood nor the law, had not gone to a university, and was continually satirizing rhetoricians. He wrote no essays or prose trifles himself, but the instructions given by Hamlet to 'Certain Players', apparently written for Shakespeare's own company, are simple, vigorous, and phrased in good grammar-school Latin style.

HAMLET. Speak the speech, I pray you, as I pronounced it to you, trippingly on the tongue; but if you mouth it, as many of your players do, I had as lief the town-crier spoke my lines. Nor do not saw the air too much with your hand, thus; but use all gently: for in the very torrent, tempest, and – as I may say – whirlwind of passion, you must acquire and beget a temperance, that may give it smoothness. O! It offends me to the soul to hear a robustious periwig-pated fellow tear a passion to tatters, to very rags, to split the ears of the groundlings, who for the most part are capable of nothing but inexplicable dumb-shows and noise: I would have such a fellow whipped for o'erdoing Termagant; it out-herods Herod: pray you avoid it.

FIRST PLAY. I warrant your honour.

HAM. Be not too tame neither, but let your own discretion be your tutor: suit the action to the word, the word to the action; with this special observance, that you o'erstep not the modesty of nature; for anything so overdone is from the purpose of playing, whose end,

[1] 'Mutton' was slang for 'prostitute'.

both at the first and now, was and is, to hold, as 'twere, the mirror up to nature; to show virtue her own feature, scorn her own image, and the very age and body of the time his form and pressure.

A successful university defender of paradoxes was named a 'wrangler', a word that long survived at Cambridge in the phrase 'senior wrangler', and wrangling naturally led to a cultivation of personal invective, the *argumentum ad hominem.* Oratorical writers excelled as counsels for the prosecution: defence did not give their talents sufficient scope. They used the same rhetorical apparatus as Gosson used against the poets, to attack rival writers, opposing schools of thought, the prevailing vices of society and the ills of the world in general. Invective naturally made use of crushing words, as fantastical and high-sounding as possible.

Elizabethan writers of courtly romances were similarly bound by the conventions of rhetoric, and reflected in their work the latest fashions of speech from the French and Italian courts. The most popular of these romance-writers was John Lyly, who was also a schoolmaster and a dramatist. His chief prose works were *Euphues, the Anatomy of Wit*, published in 1579, and *Euphues, His England*, published in 1580. The hero of both is a young Athenian of good family who travels first in Italy and afterwards in England. He meets with few adventures, for there is scarcely any 'story'; instead, there are moralistic discourses, exchanges of letters and tourneys of elaborate wit between him and his friends. The carefully pointed style in which the books are written, spangled with proverbs and conceits in the Spanish fashion, has given the word 'Euphuism' to the English language. The vocabulary and composition of Euphuism are simple enough, but its array of rhetorical devices is formidable. The following passage is a sort of one-sided repartee, a moralizing upon Euphues's rejection of good advice offered him by one of his elders:

> 'Here ye may behold, Gentlemen, how lewdly wit standeth in his own light, how he deemed no penny good silver but his own, preferring the blossom before the fruit, the bud before the flower, the green blade before the ripe ear of corn, his own wit before all men's wisdom. Neither is that reason, seeing for the most part it is proper to call those of sharp capacity to esteem themselves as most proper: if one be hard in conceiving, they pronounce him a dolt; if given to study, they pronounce him a dunce; if merry, a jester; if sad, a saint; if full of words, a sot; if without speech, a cipher.'

Euphuists, in fact, scorned plain and direct language, because it gave them no opportunity for the display of what in their days passed for wit and would have revealed many of their thoughts as platitudinous.

In only one of many other romances is the florid, rhetorical style used as elegantly as in *Euphues*: this is Sir Philip Sidney's *Arcadia*, which also appeared in 1580. Though his style is more flowing than Lyly's, his conceits are just as far-fetched: for instance, he refers to the evening as 'About the time that candles begin to inherit the sun's office', and to a country retreat as 'a pleasant refuge from the choleric look of Phoebus'. Such fancifulness was particularly a young man's fashion: neither Lyly nor Sidney had long left the university.

CHAPTER SIX

THE ORNATE AND PLAIN STYLES

OLDER and graver writers were meanwhile working out a new style by imitating the period of Cicero – that is, the long sentence made up of a series of clauses balanced in rhythm and in sense. It was especially suited to writings on such serious subjects as moral theory and ecclesiastical doctrine. Richard Hooker perfected it in his *Ecclesiastical Polity*, the first volumes of which were published in 1594 when he was forty years old, an exposition of the doctrines of the Church of England and a defence of its official status. *Ecclesiastical Polity* has the intonations of a sermon and the periodic structure of Cicero's orations. Two sentences will illustrate its qualities:

> 'As therefore man doth consist of different and distinct parts, every part endued with manifold abilities which all have their several ends and actions thereunto referred; so there is this great variety of duties which belong to men, that dependency and order by means whereof, the lower sustaining always the more excellent, and the higher perfecting the more base, they are in their times and seasons continued with most exquisite correspondence. Labours of bodily and daily toil purchase freedom for actions of religious joy, which benefit these actions requite with the gift of desired rest – a thing most natural and fit to accompany the solemn festival duties of honour which are due to God.'

The rhythm is familiar: many clerics still attempt it. The structure of the sentences is more complex than any we have quoted so far; and yet the complexity is not achieved by the mechanical use of 'topics', nor due either to fancifulness or to an exceptional depth and subtlety of thought. He makes use of the 'doublet' and (similarly suggesting legal phraseology) of plentiful dependent clauses, the points of dependence being emphasized by repetition: 'different and distinct *parts*, every *part* endued with . . .', 'purchase freedom for *actions* of religious joy, which benefit these *actions* requite . . .', 'the gift of desired rest, a *thing* most natural and fit . . .' Balanced explanatory clauses are also frequent: 'the lower sustaining the more excellent, and the higher perfecting the more base'. In this way the arrangement of the thought itself results in a measured rhythm. The devices of rhetoric employed conform with the Ciceronian structure. From this style, a compromise between the polished and the florid, derive all the ornate writings of the seventeenth century and later, including the sonorous treatises of John Milton.

The writers of the first half of the seventeenth century attempted more subjects than the Elizabethans, and expatiated on them more broadly and with more various attitudes of mind. However, rhetorical training and moral purposefulness still imposed a discipline on their styles; so that whatever refinements were devised, in the way of subtle adornments and fine-sounding periodic rhythm, were kept within the bounds of verbal meaning. There was ornateness on the most trivial subjects, but no general slackness in sense.

The Authorized Version of *The Bible* was completed in 1611. It was a careful collation of five earlier renderings of the original Hebrew and Greek – namely, William Tyndale's translation of the *New Testament* in 1525 and the *Pentateuch* in 1530, Miles Coverdale's Bible of 1535, Thomas Matthews' Bible of 1537, and the 'Great Bible' which Coverdale edited in 1539 under the direction of Thomas Cranmer. Its authors drew on the experience of all previous writers of English ecclesiastical prose in order to compound a language of noble ornateness. The Hebrew itself was ornate (especially in the Psalms, the Prophets, the Song of Solomon, the Book of Jonah) with an incantatory device of repetitive phrasing,[1] well suited to the now copious English vocabulary: the Latin of the Vulgate had not done it justice. This example is from the sixtieth chapter of Isaiah:–

> 'Arise, shine; for thy light is come, and the glory of the Lord is risen upon thee. For behold, the darkness shall cover the earth, and gross darkness the people; but the Lord shall arise upon thee, and his glory shall be seen upon thee. And the Gentiles shall come to thy light, and kings to the brightness of thy rising.
>
> The sun shall be no more thy light by day; neither for brightness shall the moon give light unto thee: but the Lord shall be to thee an everlasting light, and thy God thy glory. Thy sun shall no more go down; neither shall thy moon withdraw herself: for the Lord shall be thine everlasting light, and the days of thy mourning shall be ended.'

The force of the prophecy is conveyed by an interlacing of repeated phrases and rhythms. Thus, 'shine; thy *light* is come' is taken up and expanded at the end of the verse in 'the Gentiles shall come to thy *light*, and kings . . . etc.' 'Arise . . . the *glory* of the *Lord* is *risen* upon thee' is taken up by 'the *Lord* shall *arise* upon thee, and his *glory* shall be seen upon thee' (this has the further internal repetition of 'upon thee'); and intervening are the correlative phrases '*darkness* shall cover . . . *gross darkness* the people'. The second verse begins with the theme of the sun no more a light by day nor the moon by night; this is taken up in the second sentence and reversed

[1] In the synagogues of Palestine the first phrase of a pair was sung by the *hassan*, the second by the congregation as a sort of confirmatory echo.

in sense—'Thy sun shall no more go down neither shall thy moon withdraw herself'. Intervening are 'the Lord . . . to thee an everlasting light' and 'thy God thy glory'. The first of these two phrases is almost exactly repeated in the second sentence. The close of the verse sums up the hope implicit in the whole passage: 'the days of thy mourning shall be ended'.

The rhetorical exquisiteness of such writing encouraged those who heard the Bible read in church to read it aloud at home. It cast a religious spell even on listeners who did not understand the sense. Many devotional tracts written in Biblical style were published, and as the conflict between the Puritan (Low Church) and the Arminian (High Church) parties grew increasingly bitter, pamphleteers thundered at one another like major prophets.

Many religious writers practised a less lofty, more intellectual style, full of ingenious word-play, learnèd reference and scholastic conventions. John Donne the poet, who took Holy Orders in 1615 and later became Dean of St. Paul's, had made a close study of mediaeval theology, and demonstrated it in the antithetical logic of his arguments. He examined each text like a lawyer, drawing out its implications with an adroit and exhaustive verbal wit. The following passage is taken from a sermon on Saint Paul's shipwreck at Malta; the text being 'They changed their minds and said that he was a god.'

> 'The first words of our text carry us necessarily so far back as to see from what they changed; and their periods are easily seen: their *terminus a quo* and their *terminus ad quem*, were these; first that he was a murderer, then that he was a god. An error in morality; they censure deeply upon light evidence: an error in divinity; they transfer the name and estimation of a god upon an unknown man. Place both the errors in divinity (as you may justly do); and then there is an error in charity, a hasty and inconsiderate condemning; and an error in faith, a superstitious creating of an imaginary god. Now upon these two general considerations will this exercise consist; first that it is natural logic, and argumentation naturally implanted in man, to argue and conclude thus, great calamities are inflicted, therefore God is greatly provoked. These men of Malta were but natural men, but barbarians (as S. Luke calls them), and yet they argue and conclude so: Here is a judgement executed, therefore here is evidence that God is displeased. And so far they kept within the bounds of humanity and piety too. But when they descended hastily and inconsiderately to particular and personal applications,—This judgement upon this man is an evidence of his guiltiness in this offence, then they transgressed the bounds of charity; that because a viper had seized Paul's hand, therefore Paul must needs be a murderer.'

Donne here speaks of the sermon as an 'exercise', meaning that he is conscious of the neatness of the argument, and of its verbal complexity. It reads easily only if spoken aloud with the dramatic modulations of voice which Donne must have used in the pulpit: then the key-phrases stand out and the verbal pattern is revealed. The fullness of Donne's style was rigidly controlled by his 'metaphysical' mind: he indulged in complex argument, but not in verbal luxury. A more florid style was practised by the writers of the Arminian party in the times of Charles I; especially by Jeremy Taylor, a writer of tracts, the most famous of which are *Holy Living* and *Holy Dying*.

Taylor was born in 1613 and became rector of a village in Rutlandshire; when the Civil War broke out he retired to Wales and lived on the estate of a patron; during the Commonwealth he was imprisoned. After the Restoration he became a bishop; and died in 1667. His style is neither strongly intellectual nor strongly emotional; it is discursive, fanciful, flowing. There is a periodic structure to his sentences, but the subordinate phrases intertwine luxuriously about it, especially when similes drawn from Nature are concerned. Of these he was particularly fond, as of all illustrations to his themes which could be presented with whimsical or pathetic charm. For example:

> 'So we sometimes espy a bright cloud formed into an irregular figure; when it is observed by unskilful and fantastic travellers, it looks like a centaur to some, and as a castle to others; some tell that they saw an army with banners, and it signifies war; but another, wiser than his fellow, says it looks for all the world like a flock of sheep, and foretells plenty; and all the while it is nothing but a shining cloud, by its own mobility and the activity of a wind cast into a contingent and inartificial shape; so it is in this great mystery of our religion, in which some espy strange things which God intended not, and others see not what God has plainly told.'

It was typical of Taylor to make the fanciful elaboration of this simile carry more conviction than the moral to which it points. Even the most controversial and learned of his works were written for pleasant reading rather than for sonorous delivery from the pulpit. In Taylor and his fellows can be observed a slackening of religious purpose: the theological moralist has become a man of letters.

An even more original style was achieved by Sir Thomas Browne (1605 to 1682). Though wealthy enough to lead a leisured life, he studied medicine and practised it in various parts of England before finally settling down in literary retirement at Norwich. His first and most popular book was *Religio Medici*, published in 1643; in it he declared himself a firm believer in the Church of England, but was clearly less interested in its doctrines than in the emotions with which its more elaborate ceremonies inspired him. He was a lover of curiosities, his chief interests being antiquities, ritual, and recondite scholarship. Most of his writings concern these: the *Garden of Cyrus*, for example, is a miscellany of information about the uses of the quincunx (the arrangement of trees in groups of five) and of meditations upon its significance. *Hydriotaphia* or *Urn Burial* is a discourse on the practice of preserving the ashes of the dead, with solemn reflections on the vain shortness of life. It contains some of Browne's most stately and sombre passages, such as this:

> 'What song the Sirens sang, or what name Achilles assumed when he hid himself among women, though puzzling questions, are not beyond all conjecture. What time the persons of these ossuaries entered the famous nations of the dead, and slept with princes and counsellors, might admit a wide solution. But who were the proprietaries of these bones, or what bodies these ashes made up, were a question above antiquarism; not to be resolved by man, nor easily perhaps by spirits, except we consult the provincial guardians, or tutelary observators. Had they made as good provision for their names, as they have done for their relics, they had not so grossly erred in the art of perpetuation. But to subsist in bones, and be but pyramidally extant, is a fallacy of duration. Vain ashes which in the oblivion of names, persons, times, and sexes, have found unto themselves a fruitless continuation and only arise unto late posterity, as emblems of mortal vanities, antidotes against pride, vain-glory and madding vices. Pagan vain-glories which thought the world might last for ever, had encouragement for ambition; and, finding no Atropos unto the immortality of their names, were never dampt with the necessity of oblivion. Even old ambitions had the advantage of ours, in the attempts of their vain-glories, who acting early, and before the probable meridian of time, have by this time found great accomplishment of their designs, whereby the ancient heroes have already out-lasted their monuments, and mechanical preservations. But in this latter scene of time, we cannot expect such mummies unto our memories, when ambition may fear the prophecy of Elias, and Charles the Fifth can never hope to live within two Methusalahs of Hector.'

This is neither fanciful nor argumentative, but inconsequentially reflective. It begins with the vanity of attempts to achieve immortality by means of anonymous urn-burial, and ends with the thought that nowadays the world's comparatively short expectation of life does not warrant such attempts – besides, it is implied, Christian doctrine offers a different and truer kind of immortality. Yet no point is strongly pressed home; each sentence is disjoined in thought from the next one, coherence being provided only by the uniformly resonant rhythm and stately language, and by the sombre quaintness of Browne's imagination.

There are mixed motives in such writing. Browne is ostensibly passing judgement on the foolish desire for physical self-perpetuation, but he is also giving himself pleasure in the exercise of a noble style, and perhaps also aiming at literary immortality. His sentences are always weighty, yet they are not overlong — some, indeed, are almost epigrammatic — and are often enlivened by touches of melancholic wit, such as 'pyramidally extant', 'probable meridian of time' and 'never hope to live within two Methusalahs of Hector'.

At the same time the plain style was coming into wider use. Francis Bacon in the more scientific parts of his work had subordinated the pattern of rhetoric to the plain courses of inductive reasoning. Early science dealt in simple experiments which demanded simple narrative treatment. The more complicated forms of rhetoric were also sometimes abandoned even in subjects where they had been considered essential. For example, Ben Jonson's *Discoveries*, 1630, a series of judgements upon literature and behaviour which he put together in his old age, have the same dramatic vigour and clarity as the prose of his plays. Here is a paragraph upon the Corruption of Morals:

> 'There cannot be one colour of the mind, another of the wit. If the mind be staid, grave, and composed, the wit is so; that vitiated, the the other is blown and deflowered. Do we not see, if the mind languish, the members are dull? Look upon an effeminate person, his very gait confesseth him. If a man be fiery, his motion is so; if angry, 'tis troubled and violent. So that we may conclude wheresoever manners and fashions are corrupted, language is. It imitates the public riot. The excess of feasts and apparel are the notes of a sick state; and the wantonness of language of a sick mind.'

The button-holing of the reader in 'Do we not see, if the mind languish, the members are dull? Look upon the effeminate person . . .' is a device not to be found in ornate writing. Jonson, the son of an artisan, had served in the Army before he became a fashionable dramatist and writer of court masques. He had the same critical attitude towards rhetoric, and the same native eloquence, as Shakespeare. It was natural that his unambiguous moral judgements should be expressed in a firm and lucid style. Writers who have something original to say tend to cast aside rhetorical devices as interfering with the sense. Where they fail to do so, because of hoping to impress as well as to inform, the reader's attention is divided. John Milton's extravagantly Latinized prose-works, of which the best known is his *Areopagitica*, a plea for the freedom of the Press, are instances of this: the reader is distracted from following the argument by wonder at the sustained antique oratory, as it soars into rhapsody or dives boldly into Billingsgate. Here is an example of the Miltonic period from his *Observations on the Articles of Peace between the Earl of Ormond and the Irish*:

> 'And how securely, how smoothly, with how little touch or sense of any commiseration, either princely or so much as human, he hath sold away that justice so oft demanded, and so oft by himself acknowledged to be due for the blood of more than two hundred thousand of his subjects, that never hurt him, never disobeyed him, assassinated and cut in pieces by those Irish barbarians, to give the first promoting, as is more than thought, to his own tyrannical designs in England, will appear by the eighteenth article of his peace; wherein without the least regard of justice to avenge the dead, while he thirsts to be avenged upon the living, to all the murders, massacres, treasons, pyracies, from the very fatal day wherein that rebellion first broke out, he grants an act of oblivion.'

But the letters, despatches, newspaper reports and other unliterary records of the time were written in fairly workmanlike English; and there were political theorists and philosophers, the best known of whom was Thomas Hobbes, who wrote straightforwardly and elegantly – for this was before philosophical thought had become abstruse and transcendental and while it was still for the most part concerned with common-sense questions.

Hobbes's most famous book is his *Leviatian, Or, The Matter, Power and Form of a Commonwealth*, which was first published in 1651, after the closing of the theatres and the temporary triumph of the Puritan party in the Civil Wars had swept away what was left of foppish rhetoric. Hobbes argues in favour of strong centralized government, the necessity for which had been shown by the war. One of the most thoughtful of his other treatises, *Human Nature, Or, The Fundamental Principles of Policy*, had appeared in 1650. The following quotation from it is part of a disquisition on love:

> 'Of love, by which is to be understood the joy man taketh in the fruition of any present good, hath been spoken already in the first section, chapter seven, under which is contained the love men bear to one another or pleasure they take in one another's company: and by which nature men are said to be sociable. But there is another kind of love which the Greeks call Eros, and is that which we mean when we say that a man is in love: forasmuch as the passion cannot be without

diversity of sex, it cannot be denied but that it participateth of that indefinite love mentioned in the former section. But there is a great difference betwixt the desire of a man indefinite and the same desire limited *ad hunc*: and this is that love which is the great theme of poets: but not withstanding their praises, it must be defined by the word "need": for it is a conception man hath of his need of that one person desired. The cause of this passion is not always, nor for the most part, beauty or other quality in the beloved, unless there be withal hope in the person that loveth: which may be gathered from this, that in great difference of persons, the greater have often fallen in love with the meaner, but not the contrary. And from hence it is that for the most part they have much better fortune in love whose hopes are built on something in their person than those that trust to their experiences and service; and they that care less than they that care more: which not perceiving, many men cast away their services as one arrow after another, till, in the end, together with their hopes, they lose their wits.'

Despite the cynical and somewhat flippant conclusion, this analysis has been carefully worked out: Hobbes first defines his terms and then applies them. The sentences are complex; not for the sake of ornateness but because the thought is complex. The language itself is simple; short, plain words for the most part, with little grandiloquence, though 'participateth', for 'partakes', is perhaps intended to recall St Paul's Epistle to the Corinthians in the Authorized Version. The paragraph is good prose because precise thinking.

As soon as the Civil Wars were over there began a struggle between the orthodox Puritans and the combined forces of Independency, or Dissent. The Independents won, because they controlled the Army. Their writing and preaching at its best was direct and homely — though at its worst it was an extraordinary mixture of 'text-splitting' and Old Testament prophetic fury. The most gifted (after Milton) of the Independent writers was John Bunyan, who had served as a common soldier under Cromwell, but repented of his evil life in the ranks and was converted to godliness. In 1655, after having proved his ability as a lay preacher, he was ordained. He spent five years travelling the country, preaching. At the Restoration he was arrested and imprisoned for twelve years in Bedford Gaol, where he wrote *The Pilgrim's Progress*.

Bunyan who seems to have had no Latin education, modelled his literary style on that of the Authorized Version of the Bible; yet, because he was concerned with making his allegories clear and applicable, did not overburden his style with the more elaborate movements of Biblical rhetoric. He had also learned a good deal from John Foxe's simply and quietly written *Book of Martyrs* (1563).

The dialogue of *The Pilgrim's Progress* suggests, in its economy and picturesqueness, the verbatim report of a capable assize-clerk; and in its balanced phrasing, Cranmer's Church Catechism. Christian comes up with Faithful in the course of his journey, and Faithful tells him of his first encounter with Adam the First:

> 'When I came to the foot of the hill called *Difficulty*, I met with a very aged man, who asked me what I was and whither bound. I told him that I am a pilgrim going to the Celestial City. Then said the old man, Thou lookest like an honest fellow; wilt thou be content to dwell with me for the wages that I shall give thee? Then I asked him his name, and where he dwelt. He said his name was *Adam the First*, and that he dwelt in the town of Deceit. I asked him what was his work, and what the wages he would give. He told me that his work was many delights, and his wages that I should be his heir at last. I further asked him what house he kept, and what further servants he had. So he told me that his house was maintained with all the dainties in the world; and that his servants were those of his own begetting. Then I asked him if he had any children. He said that he had but three daughters: *The Lust of the Flesh*, *The Lust of the Eyes*, and *The Pride of Life* and that I should marry them all if I would. Then I asked him how long time he would have me live with him? And he told me, As long as he lived himself.'

Though the plain style continued to gain ground, some admired writers of the late seventeenth century still tended to ornateness. Here is a sentence by Sir William Temple, one of Charles II's ablest diplomats, written about 1680 when a controversy was raging between the partisans of Ancient and of Modern learning. Temple was on the side of the Ancients:

> 'Whether it be that the fierceness of Gothic humours, or noise of their perpetual wars, frighted it away, or that the unequal mixtures of the modern languages would not bear it; certain it is, that the great heights and excellency both of poetry and music fell with the Roman learning and empire, and have never since recovered the admiration and applauses that before attended them.'

The effortless formality of this sentence shows how the periods of Cicero had now become naturalized in the language. The eloquence rises in urbanely modulated tones, through 'whether it be that the fierceness of . . . or noise of . . .', tops the peak at 'certain it is that . . .' and gradually descends to the level of 'admiration and applauses that before attended them'. Temple gives emphasis to the main part of his sentence with reiterated doublets:

'great heights and excellency'
'both of poetry and music'
'Roman learning and empire'
'admiration and applauses'

The chief use of two of these seems to be the filling-out of the rhythm, for there is not much distinction in meaning between 'heights' and 'excellency', or between 'admiration' and 'applauses'.

Since the Court had returned from its exile in France, the elegant correctitude of French manners and writing was much admired and imitated. French was still the language of the heart, but of a dried heart. Wit became more ironical, more satirical, more politely malicious. Florid or ornate rhetoric now went out of fashion: writers were expected to be neat, graceful, amusing, and to use a clarified and moderated style, even for the most serious subjects. The new aim was a natural-seeming ease and a gentlemanly good taste.

Dr. John Eachard, Vice-Chancellor of Cambridge University, published in 1670 his *Grounds and Occasions of the Contempt of the Clergy and Religion Inquired Into*, one of the earliest books to be so free from rhetorical devices that the reader need not put himself into a 'period' frame of mind to enjoy them. It is remarkable as being written by a man so academically distinguished.

'We know, the language that the very learned part of this nation must trust to live by, unless it be to make a bond or prescribe a purge (which possibly may not oblige or work so well in any other language as Latin), is the English. As for Divinity, in this place I shall say no more, but that those usually that have been rope-dancers in the schools, oft-times prove jack-puddings in the pulpit. The world is now, especially in discourse, for one language; and he that has somewhat in his mind of Greek or Latin, is requested nowadays to be civil, and translate it into English for the benefit of the company. And he that has made it his whole business to accomplish himself for the applause of a company of boys, school-masters, and the easiest of country divines, and has been shouldered out of the Cockpit for his wit, when he comes into the world is the most likely person to be kicked out of company for his pedantry, and overweening opinion of himself.

Amongst the first things that seem to be useless may be reckoned the high tossing and swaggering preaching, either mountingly eloquent, or profoundly learned. For there be a sort of divines who, if they do but happen of an unlucky hard word all the week, they think themselves not careful of their flock if they lay it not up till Sunday, and bestow it amongst them in their next preachment.

... If the minister's words be such as the constable uses, his matter plain and practical to such as come to the common market, he may pass possibly for an honest well-meaning man, but by no means for any scholar; whereas, if he springs forth now and then in high raptures towards the uppermost heavens, dashing here and there an all-confounding word; if he soars aloft in unintelligible huffs, preaches points deep and mystical, and delivers them as dark and phantastical: this is the way, say they, of being accounted a most able and learned instructor. This learned way of talking, though for the most part it is done merely out of ostentation, yet sometimes (which makes not the case much better) it is done in compliment and civility to the all-wise patron, or all-understanding justice of the peace in the parish; who, by the common farmers of the town, must be thought to understand the most intricate notions, and the most difficult languages.

I certainly know several of that disposition, who, if they chance to have a man of any learning or understanding, more than the rest of the parish, preach wholly at him, and level most of their discourse at his supposed capacity, and the rest of the good people shall have only a handsome gaze or view of the parson. As if plain words, useful and intelligible instructions, were not as good for an esquire, or one that is in commission from the king, as for him that holds the plough or mends the hedges.'

Samuel Pepys's *Diary*, from 1659-1669, which was not intended for publication, is written in much the same easy style.

CHAPTER SEVEN

CLASSICAL PROSE

AN all-purpose English prose style was emerging, which avoided the excesses both of coarse familiarity and of ornate abstruseness. Dr Eachard quotes typical examples of both sorts of excess. The abstruse sermon that began: 'As Solomon went up six steps to come to the great throne of ivory, so must I ascend six degrees to come to the high top meaning of my text;' and the over-familiar sermon:

> 'A father calls his child to him, saying, Child, pull off this stocking. The child, mightily joyful that it should pull off father's stocking, takes hold of the stocking, and tugs, and pulls, and sweats, but to no purpose; for stocking stirs not, for it is but a child that pulls. Then the father bids the child to rest a little, and try again; so then the child sets on again, tugs again, and pulls again, and sweats again, but no stocking comes; for child is but a child still. Then, at last, the father, taking pity on his child, puts his hand behind, and slips down the stocking, and off comes the stocking. Then how does the child rejoice! for child hath pulled off father's stocking. Alas! poor child! it was not child's strength, it was not child's sweating, that got off the stocking; but it was the father's hand behind that slipped down the stocking. Even so —'

John Dryden, who had vigour and independence of mind, used the new plain, graceful style. He was proud of his severity with words and his thought flowed swiftly, without epigrammatic eddies or ornamental cascades. In this paragraph, from an essay on the *Parallel between Poetry and Painting*, he gives advice on writing which he himself put into practice:

> 'As in the composition of a picture the painter is to take care that nothing enter into it which is not proper or convenient to the subject, so likewise is the poet to reject all incidents which are foreign to his poem and are naturally no part of it; they are wens and other excrescences, which belong not to the body, but to deform it. No person, no incident in the piece or in the play, but must be of use to carry on the main design. All things else are like six fingers to the hand, when nature, which is superfluous in nothing, can do her work with five. A painter must reject all trifling ornaments, so must a poet refuse all tedious and unnecessary descriptions. A role which is too heavy is less an ornament than a burthen.'

What Dryden achieved by severity and self-discipline came more easily to his contemporary, Daniel Defoe, who was educated at a private academy of the sort founded in late Stuart times for boys debarred from the universities because they belonged to Dissenting families. He made his living by writing, but was constantly in debt because of unlucky speculations in trade; and in 1703 was punished for his ironical pamphlet, *The Shortest Way with Dissenters*, by being pilloried, fined 200 marks and imprisoned in Newgate until he could pay the fine. By 1719, when he was sixty, he had published about one hundred and fifty pamphlets on religion, commerce, history, politics, topicalities. Then he wrote *Robinson Crusoe*, the first English novel in the modern sense, and followed it with several more, including *Roxana*, *Moll Flanders* and *Colonel Jack*. These were remarkable for telling credible and exciting stories and for being peopled with characters from real life, a world away from the moralistic puppets of *Euphues* and *Arcadia*.

Defoe was also one of the first English journalists in the modern sense and for several years published a weekly *Review*, most of which he wrote himself. Since he set himself so many varied tasks, and was always working against time, it was natural that he should sometimes make grammatical slips and fall short of graceful expression. But for the most part his style was lucid, vigorous, plain and indicative of a warm heart and sensitive feelings. Here is a passage from the preface to the eighth quarto volume of his *Review*. It will be noted that he does not use doublets or alliterative emphasis; and that the antitheses are not artificial but rise naturally from the strangeness of his experiences.

'To return to my own case: I am a stoic in whatever may be the event of things. . . .

In the school of affliction I have learnt more philosophy than at the academy, and more divinity than from the pulpit; in prison, I have learnt to know that liberty does not consist in open doors, and the free egress and regress of locomotion. I have seen the rough side of the world as well as the smooth; and have, in less than half a year, tasted the difference between the closet of a king and the dungeon of Newgate. I have suffered deeply for cleaving to principles; of which integrity I have lived to say, none but those I suffered for, ever reproached me with it. The immediate causes of my suffering have been the being betrayed by those I trusted, and scorning to betray those who trusted me. To the honour of English gratitude, I have this remarkable truth to leave behind me – that I was never so basely betrayed as by those whose families I had preserved from starving; nor so basely treated as by those I starved my own family to preserve. The same chequer-work of fortune attends me still: the people I have served, and love to serve, cut my throat every day, because I will not cut the throats of those that have served and assisted me.'

Here is an example of his swift narrative style, from the *Journal of the Plague Year*, 1722, an historical reconstruction of the events of 1665, when he had been only five years old.

'Another infected person came and knocked at the door of a citizen's house, where they knew him very well; the servant let him in, and being told the master of the house was above, he ran up, and came into the room to them as the whole family was at supper. They began to rise up a little surprised, not knowing what the matter was; but he bade them sit still, he only came to take his leave of them. They asked him, "Why, Mr ——, where are you going?" "Going," says he, "I have got the sickness and shall die tomorrow night." It is easy to believe, though not to describe, the consternation they were all in; the women and the man's daughters, which were but little girls, were frightened almost to death, and got up, all running out, one at one door and one at another, some downstairs and some upstairs, and getting together as well as they could, locked themselves into their chambers, and screamed out of the window for help, as if they had been frightened out of their wits. The master, more composed than they, though both frighted and provoked, was going to lay hands on him and throw him downstairs, being in a passion; but then considering a little the condition of the man, and the danger of touching him, horror seized his mind, and he stood like one astonished. The poor distempered man, all this while, being, as well, diseased in his mind as in his body, stood still like one amazed; at length he turns round. "Ay," he says, with all the seeming calmness imaginable, "is it so with you all? Are you all disturbed at me? Why, then, I'll e'en go home and die there." And so he goes immediately downstairs. The servant that had let him in goes down after him with a candle, but he was afraid to go past him and open the door, so he stood on the stairs to see what he would do; the man went and opened the door, and went out and flung the door after him.'

The remarkably equable, detached attitude of mind shown in Defoe's handling of this ludicrous and yet terrible story became more common as the eighteenth century advanced. The Earl of Chesterfield was renowned for it, and it usually went with a gracefulness of style which could reconcile the reader to the most controversial theme. For example, it is difficult to quarrel with the misogyny of the following letter of Chesterfield's, written in 1763 to his heir, Arthur Stanhope; though the same subject treated by, say, Stephen Gosson or a Presbyterian pamphleteer of the 1640's would have been odious.

'In answer to the favour of your last letter, in which you desire my opinion concerning your third marriage, I must freely tell you, that in matters of religion and matrimony I never give advice: because I will not have any body's torments in this world or the next laid to my charge. You say, that you find yourself lonely and melancholick at Mansfield, and I believe it: but then the point for your mature consideration is, whether it is not better to be alone than in bad company; which may very probably be your case with a wife. I may possibly be in the wrong, but I tell you very sincerely, with all due regard to the sex, that I never thought a woman good company for a man tête-à-tête, unless for one purpose, which, I presume, is not yours now. You had singular good fortune with your last wife, who has left you two fine children, which are as many as any prudent man would desire. And how would you provide for more? Suppose you should have five or six, what could you do with them?... My brother gave me exactly the same reasons that you do for marrying his third wife. He was weary of being alone, and had by God's good providence found out a young woman of retired disposition, and who had been bred up prudently under an old grandmother in the country; she hated and dreaded a London life, and chose to amuse herself at home with books, her drawing and her music. How this fine prospect turned out I need not tell you.... Upon the whole, you will marry or not marry as you think best: but, to take a wife, merely as an agreeable and rational companion, will commonly be found to be a great mistake. Shakespeare seems to be a good deal of my opinion, when he allows them only this department,

"To suckle fools, and chronicle small beer".'

By the reign of Queen Anne, the strictly didactic and moralistic purpose of writing had disappeared with the old rhetorical conventions: writers now inquired, discoursed, entertained, told stories, but, unless they were divines, seldom preached. It is true that Defoe usually tacked on a chapter of conventional repentance to his pseudo-autobiographical novels of roguery; but that was merely to avoid being censured as encouraging vice. His characters have few qualms of conscience while engaged in their felonies.

The new style was particularly suited to satire and irony. Defoe was one of the first prose-writers to use dry irony for the purpose of ridicule. The rhetorical writers had slapped on their irony with a trowel, introducing it with 'forsooth' or 'in God's name!' But Defoe in his *Shortest Way with Dissenters*, dryly accepting the thesis that religious uniformity was desirable, let the argument take its own unchecked course, the natural conclusion being that half-measures were useless – the stiff-necked rascals must be exterminated without pity.

Jonathan Swift, the Dean of St Patrick's, was sardonical rather than ironical: he used understatement and innuendo with a fierce scorn that made his simple phrases sting. His *Tale of a Tub*, 1704, *Gulliver's Travels*, 1726, and most of his political pamphlets, including the terrible *Modest Proposal for Preventing the Children of Poor People from becoming a Burthen to their Parents, or the Country*, 1729, were written in a quiet unostentatious style but often in a murderous mood. Swift was a disciple of Temple in preferring ancient to modern learning; and there is a strong Latin element in his style which, though very plain, never becomes monotonous, because of the devilish liveliness of his intelligence.

Oliver Goldsmith used the plain style in his novel *The Vicar of Wakefield*, 1766; so did Henry Fielding, a hard-working London magistrate, in his *Joseph Andrews*, 1742, and *Tom Jones*, 1749, the most readable of mid-eighteenth-century adventure novels. His prose has no solemn rhythm, no considered periodic structure, no romantic appeal; but the same compelling ironical quietness as Swift, from whose writings he had learned much – even more quietness, for he was without Swift's passionate hatreds. Here is a paragraph from his *Life of Jonathan Wild the Great*, 1743. The hero is a thief and informer who has been meditating in a tavern on the misfortunes that have lately attended his enterprises:

> 'His soliloquy and his punch concluded together; for he had at every pause comforted himself with a sip. And now it came first into his head that it would be more difficult to pay for it than to swallow it; when, to his great pleasure, he beheld at another corner of the room one of the gentlemen whom he had employed in the attack on Heartfree, and who, he doubted not, would readily lend him a guinea or two; but he had the mortification, on applying to him, to hear that the gaming-table had stript him of all booty which his own generosity had left in his possession. He was, therefore, obliged to pursue his usual method on such occasions: so, cocking his hat fiercely, he marched out of the room without making any excuse, or anyone daring to make the least demand.'

In his second sentence Fielding succeeds with particular skill in distinguishing between the 'him's; and this is one of the sure tests of good narrative writing.

John Hawkesworth's *Voyages*, 1773, though not gracefully written, are typical in their plain readableness of most factual reporting of the time. The following passage is from an account of a leak sprung in Captain Cook's 370-ton barque *Endeavour* during his first voyage of exploration to the South Seas.

> 'Between the inside lining of the ship's bottom, and the outside planking, there is a space of about seventeen or eighteen inches. The man who had hitherto taken the depth of water at the well, had taken

it no farther than the ceiling; but being now relieved by another person, who took the depth to the outside planking, it appeared by this mistake that the leak had suddenly gained upon the pumps, the whole difference between the two plankings. This circumstance deprived them of all hopes, and scarce anyone thought it worth while to labour for the longer preservation of a life which must so soon have a period. But the mistake was soon discovered; and the joy arising from such unexpected good news, inspired the men with so much vigour, that before eight o'clock in the morning, they had pumped out considerably more water than they had shipped. They now talked confidently of getting the ship into some harbour, and set heartily to work to get in their anchors; one of which, and the cable of another, they lost. Having a good breeze from the sea, they got under sail at eleven o'clock, and stood for the land.

As they could not discover the exact situation of the leak, they had no prospect of stopping it within side of the vessel; but the following expedient, which one of the midshipmen had formerly seen tried with success, was adopted. They took an old studding-sail, and having mixed a large quantity of oakum and wool, chopped small, it was stitched down in handfuls on the sail, as light as possible, the dung of their sheep and other filth being spread over it. Thus prepared, the sail was hauled under the ship by ropes, which kept it extended until it came under the leak, when the suction carried in the oakum and wool from the surface of the sail. This experiment succeeded so well, that instead of three pumps, the water was easily kept under with one.'

Two examples of loose grammar will be noticed here. In the second sentence of the passage, 'but being now relieved' should properly be 'but upon his being relieved'; and in the second sentence of the second paragraph 'it was stitched down' should be 'they stitched it down'. But in neither case is any ambiguity caused by this carelessness.

However, the plain style did not long satisfy the London coffee-house wits. They could not return to Euphuism – that was barbarous; or to ornateness – that was old-fashioned. They must achieve a style which would ensure the necessary separation of themselves from the mob. Joseph Addison found one: the elegant style. He was the most admired essayist of his time; and wrote for gentlemanly newspapers, *The Tatler*, *Spectator* and *Guardian*, on such subjects as the foibles of country gentlemen and the social properties of ladies' fans. Dr Samuel Johnson, the leading literary authority of the eighteenth century, considered Addison the best writer of his kind: 'Whoever wishes to attain an English style, familiar but not coarse, and elegant but not ostentatious,' he wrote, 'must give his days and nights to the volumes of Addison.' Johnson also noted: 'He thinks justly, but he thinks faintly.' The scrupulous charm with which Addison invested his faintness can be seen in the following passage:

> 'Nature seems to have taken a particular care to disseminate her blessings among the different regions of the world, with an eye to the mutual intercourse and traffic among mankind, that the natives of several parts of the globe might have a kind of dependence upon one another, and be united together in their common interest. Almost every degree produces something peculiar to it. The food often grows in one country and the sauce in another. The fruits of Portugal are corrected by the products of Barbadoes: the infusion of a China plant sweetened with the pith of an Indian cane. . . .'

This exemplifies the chief characteristics of the elegant style, which soon became standardized among educated people with formal rather than original minds: namely, well-balanced phrases, and periphrasis.

The careful balance of phrases was an old rhetorical obsession. Periphrasis derived from Latin verse – the composition of Latin verses, with the help of a dictionary of poetical phrases, had been a gentleman's accomplishment since the Renaissance – by way of English pastoral verse of the type of Alexander Pope's *Windsor Forest*, 1704. It was a habit of writing and speaking around a subject by using descriptive aliases instead of simple nouns. These aliases were sometimes merely informative, but more often ironical and amusing. *Windsor Forest* contains many lines like the following about the angler (it was a sign of elegance to personify 'the angler' instead of writing generally about anglers or angling):

> With looks unmoved, he hopes the scaly breed,
> And eyes the dancing cork and bending reed.

'Scaly breed' now seems a ridiculous alias for fish, but it does purport to tell the reader something about the properties of fish; 'bending reed' is an alias for a fishing rod but it, too, is pseudo-informative as well as ornamental. The passage just quoted from Addison's essay has four aliases in the last sentence. The 'fruits of Portugal' stand for wine, and the products of Barbadoes' for dessert fruits; the 'infusion of a China plant' stands for tea, the 'pith of an Indian cane' for sugar. In this sort of writing, long expository sentences alternate with short summary ones, usually also epigrammatic, as: 'The food often grows in one country and the sauce in another.' Here a naughty misuse of words constitutes the wit; for food grows, but not sauces except as ingredients. It is in the long sentences that a careful balance of phrase is most marked; here, in the first one it is achieved by the spacing out of varied but simple adjectives: particular care – different regions – mutual intercourse – several parts – common interest. The gently distributed emphasis of these is sharpened in the final doublet of phrases:

> 'might have a kind of dependence one upon another
> and be united together in their common interest.'

The theme being thus firmly fixed, Addison then has the pleasure of illustrating it.

The elegant style could be used for more serious themes than Addison's; but it suited neither original thinking nor strongly expressed feeling. Subsequent writers who originally adopted it as a proof of their gentility modified it when it proved inadequate to their purposes. Dr Johnson himself modified it as he grew surer of his powers. In the first part of his life he had written pamphlets – periodical essays and a novel, *Rasselas*, 1759 – all in a rigid and Latinate variety of the elegant style. He seldom turned out amusing trifles, for he was a middle-class provincial with a conscience, not an easy-going London wit, and was happiest when applying his shrewd but narrow judgement to every topic, serious and light, that presented itself. He is seen at his best in his *Lives of the Poets*, which were published as prefaces to collected editions of the English poets between 1779 and 1781.

This paragraph from the *Life of Swift* is characteristic of Johnson's solid style:

> 'In the poetical works of Swift, there is not much upon which the critic can exercise his powers. They are often humorous, almost always light, and have the qualities which recommend such compositions, easiness and gaiety. They are, for the most part, what their author intended. The diction is correct, the numbers are smooth, and the rhymes exact. There seldom occurs a hard-laboured expression, or a redundant epithet; all his verses exemplify his own definition of a good style; they consist of "proper words in proper places".'

The conversational energy in this is directed solely towards clear statement, with no deviations for the sake of elegance. Though the phrases are balanced with correctitude each is thoughtfully intended and all are essential to the full definition of Swift's style.

> 'They are often humorous
> almost always light,'

This descriptive judgement is followed immediately by a definitive one:

> 'and have the qualities which recommend such compositions,
> easiness and gaiety,'

Then Johnson particularizes:

> 'the diction is correct,
> the numbers are smooth,
> and the rhymes exact
>
> seldom occurs a hard-laboured expression
> or a redundant epithet.'

It is a stylized pattern of statement, yet every item represents the full intent of the author.

At the end of the century the expansive minds of Edward Gibbon and Edmund Burke led them to create expansive styles superficially resembling those of a hundred years before. Their rhetoric, however, was solidly grounded, free from the fanciful discursiveness of the ornate style. The first volume of Gibbon's *Decline and Fall of the Roman Empire* was published in 1776, the last in 1788. Here is the beginning of a long period on the pretensions of the Emperor Constantius:

> 'The protection of the Rhaetian frontier and the persecution of the Catholic Church detained Constantius in Italy about eighteen months after the departure of Julian. Before the Emperor returned into the East, he indulged his pride and curiosity in a visit to the ancient capital. He proceeded from Milan to Rome along the Aemilian and Flaminian ways; and as soon as he approached within forty miles of the city, the march of a prince who had never vanquished a foreign country assumed the appearance of a triumphal procession.'

It will be noticed that words of Anglo-Saxon origin are far fewer in this style of writing than in almost any before or since—alternatives could easily have been found for the words of Latin and French origin that have displaced them—'detained', 'returned', 'indulged', 'proceeded', 'approached', 'vanquished', 'assumed'; 'protection', 'persecution', 'departure', 'appearance', 'procession'. But Gibbon aimed at a solemnity suited to the vastness of the story he presented; and sonorous words also suited his ironical mood when he was treating of mean motives. He had learned mock-solemnity from Addison (with Addison it had been a more obvious mannerism, because the body of his work was light). The device of ironically linking incompatibles had also been Addison's. Here, for instance, Gibbon links the protection of the Rhaetian frontier with the persecution of the Catholic Church, as though his readers would accept them as being on the same moral plane. Another fashionable trick is the sudden conversion of a particular person or object into a generalization: as in 'the march of a prince who . . . .' Gibbon's style in fact contains all the literary devices of the standard elegant style, but transcends it because of his philosophic scepticism and his massive ordering of detail. He became the chief literary model for solid historians for the next hundred years or more.

For politicians, Burke's different but equally weighty style, based on that of Demosthenes, the most famous orator of Athens, has likewise served as a model. Burke, though an oratorical writer, was not a successful speaker in Parliament: when he rose to speak, the House emptied. His liberality of outlook but conservativeness of feeling remain typical of English political life. He belonged to the Whig party, which opposed the personal government of George III and welcomed the theories of liberty which inspired the American War of Independence; but later in life he denounced the French Revolution, which seemed to him to have substituted for orderly government the lawless tyranny of mobs and factions. It is typical of English politics, too, that Burke never tried to co-ordinate his thought into a system, but unfolded it piecemeal in the course of particular controversies. It was not consistently reasoned thought, but impassioned eloquence hinged on a few recurrent axioms. Especially in his *Reflections on the French Revolution*, Burke pleads rather than argues; he tries to convince his readers of the rightness of his beliefs by forensic overstatement:

> 'With a compelled appearance of deliberation they [the French National Convention] vote under the dominance of a stern necessity. They sit in the heart, as it were, of a foreign republic; they have their residence in a city whose constitution has emanated neither from the charter of the king, nor from their legislative power. There they are surrounded by an army not raised either by the authority of their crown, or by their command; and which, if they should order to dissolve itself, would instantly dissolve them. There they sit, after a gang of assassins had driven away some hundreds of their members, whilst those who held some moderate principles, with more patience or better hope, continue every day exposed to outrageous insults and murderous threats. There a majority, sometimes real, sometimes pretended, captive itself, compels a captive king to issue as royal edicts, at third hand, the polluted nonsense of their most licentious and giddy coffee houses.'

The facts were that a majority of the States-General had seized power, proclaimed themselves a National Convention and were using their authority for more and more radical ends. Burke does not say simply that he disapproves of this behaviour in principle. Instead he heaps up scornful items of denunciation: the Convention is acting under compulsion; it has no juridical authority on behalf either of the king, the army or itself; it is a prey to its own wildest factions and these are polluted, licentious and giddy. Burke singles out what is detestable in those who contravene his principles, and by persuading his readers to share his detestation, makes them assent to the principles. This has become the prime method of political rhetoric.

Among new elements introduced into English prose in the eighteenth century were: the sentimental ('sentimental' did not mean, as it usually does now, 'facilely emotional', but 'having one's finer feelings well schooled') and the Gothic, or neo-barbaric elegant-grotesque. Both were fashionable reactions against plain elegance. The sentimental derived from the roguish language of French court intrigue, and the Gothic from the gentry's sudden realization, on the publication of Bishop Percy's *Reliques of English Poetry*, 1765, that there was a certain rugged charm in the 'bold bawdry and open manslaughter' of the mediaeval Border ballads. Both the sentimental and the Gothic later became mixed up with Germanism. The sentimental was first popularized by the Reverend Lawrence Sterne, an Irishman who, like most eighteenth-century clergymen of the Established Church, did not take his Orders very seriously. Here is a typical passage from his *Sentimental Journey through France and Italy*, 1767:

> '*C'est bien comique*, t'is very droll, said the lady smiling, from the reflection that this was the second time we had been left together by a parcel of nonsensical contingencies – *c'est bien comique*, said she – There wants nothing, said I, to make it so, but the comic use which the gallantry of a Frenchman would put it to – to make love the first moment, and the offer of his person the second.
>
> 'T'is their *fort*, replied the lady.
>
> It is supposed so at least – and how it has come to pass, continued I, I know not: but they have certainly got the credit of understanding more of love, and making it better than any other nation on earth: but for my own part, I think them arrant bunglers, and in truth the worst set of marksmen that ever tried Cupid's patience.'

In his *Tristram Shandy* Sterne also popularized the deliberately inconsequential style, to amuse people who were easily bored with the relentless orderly progress of narrative or argument. Here is Tristram Shandy's father reading an absurd German controversy on a philosophical question, 'whether fancy begets the nose, or the nose begets fancy':

> 'The learned suspected *Scroderus* of an indecent sophism in this – and Prignitz cried out aloud in the dispute, that *Scroderus* had shifted the idea upon him – but *Scroderus* went on, maintaining his thesis.
>
> My father was just balancing within himself, which of the two sides he should take in the affair; when *Ambrose Paraeus* decided it in a

moment, and by overthrowing the systems, both of *Prignitz* and *Scroderus*, drove my father out of both sides of the controversy at once.

Be witness –

I don't acquaint the learned reader – in saying it, I mention it only to shew the learned, I know the fact myself –

That this *Ambrose Paraeus* was chief-surgeon and nose-mender to *Francis* the ninth of *France*, and in high credit with him and the two preceding, or succeeding kings (I know not which) – and that, except in the slip he made in his story of *Taliacotius's* noses, and his manner of setting them on – he was esteemed by the whole college of physicians at the time, as more knowing in the matter of noses, than any one who had ever taken them in hand.'

The interest in 'Gothic' was fostered in England by Horace Walpole, a dilettante historian and antiquarian, son of Sir Robert Walpole, the Whig Prime Minister; but his *Castle of Otranto*: *A Gothic Story*, 1765, which started the fashion for neo-Gothic tales, was an elegant and amusing trifle, not one of those dismal, heavily emotional tales of horror, imitated from the German, which were everyone's reading in the early nineteenth century. Here is a quotation from Mrs Ann Radcliffe's *Mysteries of Udolpho*, 1794, a typical work of this kind.

'She leaned pensively on the wall of the rampart, and waited for him. The gloom of twilight sat deep on the surrounding objects, blending in soft confusion the valley, the mountains, and the woods, whose tall heads stirred by the evening breeze gave the only sounds that stole on the silence – except a faint, faint chorus of distant voices that arose from within the castle.

"What voices are those?" said Emily, as she fearfully listened.

"It is only the signor and his guests carousing," replied Annette.

"Good God!" thought Emily, "can this man's heart be so gay when he has made another being so wretched? – if, indeed, my aunt is yet suffered to feel her wretchedness! Oh! whatever are my own sufferings, may my heart never, never be hardened against those of others!"

She looked up with a sensation of horror at the east turret, near which she then stood. A light glimmered through the grates of the lower chamber, but those of the upper one were dark.'

This was the first clear instance of German influence on English literature, and due to the increasing contact between the two countries since the House of Hanover had become the Royal House of England. The 'grand tour of Europe', which since the sixteenth century every young gentleman had made the coping-stone in the arch of his education, no longer included only France, Spain and Italy – it continued through Switzerland to Western Germany. The mediaeval castles on the Rhine, the apostrophic emotionalism of German drama, the antique pageantry of petty German courts, the thorough and daring philosophical researches of Kant and others, the very clumsiness of German diction, had great charm for the young man fresh from the neat, elegant insincerities of Paris and Rome. They reminded him of the Teutonic basis of English: the French and Latin parts seemed only a veneer. So the 'German cousin' sentiment began.

The passionate apostrophe to the reader, the Muse, 'Just Heavens' and so forth, with a revival of the obsolete 'thou' and 'thee', that occurs so frequently in late-eighteenth and early nineteenth-century novels is also German in tone; though the plain apostrophe as an author's aside had been used by Fielding and his contemporaries to provide an occasional relief from narrative. Here is a fairly late example of the apostrophe from *Lavengro*, George Borrow's novel of gipsy life, 1851.

> 'O thou pride of London's east! — mighty mart of old renown! — for thou art not a place of yesterday: long before the Roses red and white battled in fair England, thou didst exist — a place of throng and bustle — a place of gold and silver, perfumes and fine linen. Centuries ago thou couldst extort the praises even of the fiercest foes of England. Fierce bards of Wales, sworn foes of England, sang thy praises centuries ago; and even the fiercest of them all, Red Julius himself, wild Glendower's bard, had a word of praise for London's ''Cheape'', for so the bards of Wales styled thee in flowing odes. Then, if those who were not English, and hated England, and all connected therewith, had yet much to say in thy praise, when thou wast far inferior to what thou art now, why should true-born Englishmen, or those who call themselves so, turn up their noses at thee, and scoff thee at the present day, as I believe they do?'

Another eighteenth-century novelty was the pathetic style. Samuel Richardson, a sentimental printer, exploited it in his novels *Pamela: or Virtue Rewarded*, 1739, *Clarissa*, 1747, and *Sir Charles Grandison*, 1753. It was derived from contemporary French women novelists and reached its most lachrymatory pitch in Victorian times. And there was the mock-heroic originally used in satiric verse — Alexander Pope's *Rape of the Lock* and *Dunciad* are the best known examples — a humorous way of writing about trifling or coarse subjects as if they were important and magnificent. And the luxurious pseudo-Oriental style that originated in France and first became naturalized in English with a novel, *Vathek*, 1786, by William Beckford, a talented and dissipated young millionaire. And the pseudo-Celtic style of James Macpherson who, in 1760, published what purported to be prose translations from the ancient Gaelic epics of Oisin, or Ossian: it was simple, naturalistic, exclamatory and had wide currency in Europe, where it was known to be the favourite reading of the Emperor Napoleon.

CHAPTER EIGHT

ROMANTIC PROSE

IMMENSE changes were taking place in British life: industrial revolution, railway-building, libertarianism, startling increase of population, scientific discovery, popular education. There was far more to write about, far more written, and far more reading done. People began to study English literature as they had once studied the Classics, no longer holding that poetry began with Milton, or at the earliest with Spenser: it was traced back to Skelton, Gower and Chaucer, and their complete poetical works, with those of the Elizabethans, were added to the uniform edition for which Dr Johnson had written his *Lives*. There was also a new awareness of prose styles of the past and thus of the changes of fashion in prose, which became a temptation to create new fashions. Foreign literature was increasingly studied and translated. The early nineteenth century was rich in individual talent, and the French Revolution had so altered European civilization that to maintain eighteenth-century standards of behaviour either in life or literature seemed anachronistic.

The poets and the more literary prose-writers at the turn of the century shared an attitude known as Romanticism, which encouraged the formation of individualistic styles. The poets had turned to Nature for their inspiration, and for their politics to the French Revolutionary doctrines of natural rights and liberty; they disembarrassed themselves of eighteenth-century poetic diction and each contrived a diction of his own. Many of them, such as Samuel Taylor Coleridge, John Keats, Percy Bysshe Shelley, revived antique vocabularies; and this had a greater effect on prose than the prose they themselves wrote, which was on the whole free from archaism, word-coinings or other eccentricities. It was the prose-writers, or the poets who were not able to express themselves completely in poetry, who introduced Romantic, personal, imaginative styles into prose. They abandoned the conventions of Addison and Johnson, and many of them reverted to the ornate seventeenth-century style. They did not, however, revive the moralistic basis of seventeenth-century writing; the models that were most studied being those in which there was least serious moral concern: Jeremy Taylor, Robert Burton (author of *The Anatomy of Melancholy*, 1621), and Sir Thomas Browne. The subjects of Romantic writing were the same in prose as in poetry: warm feelings about Nature, God and Liberty, personal experiences of love, emotional dreams.

The most ornate of the Romantic writers was Thomas de Quincey, who lived from 1785 until 1859, and was for many years a neighbour of William Wordsworth's, at Grasmere. Nearly all his works appeared as essays in periodicals, for he was impatient of long and sustained effort. Like Coleridge, he was addicted to opiates and their influence is to be seen in his dream-fantasies. These are far removed from everyday conversational writing. The following example is taken from his *Suspiria De Profundis*, a work in which the writing is most 'fine'. De Quincey is describing three symbolic sisters, Our Lady of Tears, Our Lady of Sighs, and Our Lady of Darkness:

> 'But the third sister who is also the youngest . . . Hush! whisper while we talk of her. Her kingdom is not large, or else no flesh could live, but within that kingdom all power is hers. Her head, turreted like that of Cybele, rises almost beyond the reach of sight. She droops not; and her eyes, rising so high, might be hidden by distance. But being what they are, they cannot be hidden; through the treble veil of crape that she wears, the fierce light of a blazing misery that rests not for matins or vespers, for noon of day or noon of night, for ebbing or for flowing tide, may be read from the very ground.'

There is an affected quaintness here in the metaphorical language: kingdom, turret, veils of crape, matins and vespers – these are 'Gothic' properties, already used by romance-writers and fetched out again later by the pre-Raphaelites. They are used to suggest a remote and mystical atmosphere of melancholy: but only to suggest, never to define, for little that was definite was admitted into Romantic fantasy. The melancholy was characteristic of much early nineteenth-century work; it derived from Robert Burton and his contemporaries, and from the German Goethe's *Sorrows of Werther* by way of Lord Byron.

Walter Savage Landor, another elaborate writer, lived from 1775 until 1864. His chief prose work is *Imaginary Conversations*, composed between 1825 and 1829 during his residence in Italy. The style has a firm and elegant basis, for Landor never gave himself up to pure rhapsody: he preserved some of the worldly common sense of the eighteenth century. Nevertheless the *Conversations* are so elaborated as not to resemble any kind of spoken English, especially when natural scenery is described. This example is taken from the discourse of Epicurus to two girl pupils:

> 'Fountain I can hardly say there is; but on the left there is a long crevice or chasm, which we have never yet visited, and which we cannot discern until we reach it. This is full of soft mould, very moist, and many high reeds and canes are growing there; and the rock itself too drips with humidity along it, and is covered with more tufted moss and more

variegated lichens. This crevice, with its windings and sinuosities, is above four hundred paces long, and in many places eleven, twelve, thirteen feet wide, but generally six or seven. I shall plant it wholly with lilies of the valley, leaving the irises which occupy the sides as well as the clefts, and also those other flowers of paler purple, from the autumnal cups of which I collect the saffron; and forming a narrow path of such turf as I can find there, or rather following it as it creeps among the bays and hazels and sweet-briar, which have fallen at different times from the summit and are now grown old, with an infinity of primroses at their roots.'

The details of this description are exactly worked out and make it seem much more real than the passage we quoted from de Quincey, for Landor does not indulge in metaphorical fantasy. Yet the greater part of the interest in reading it, and therefore presumably in writing it, lies not in the scene described nor in Epicurus's intentions, but in the rhythmical skill with which the words and phrases are put together. The model is the Latin letter of the type written in the time of Nero by the younger Pliny to his friends, always graceful and practical, yet a literary epistle rather than a letter. (The crevice described by Landor had its original on Pliny's country estate.)

Few of the celebrated writers of the nineteenth century, however, were purely stylists. Landor himself was a man of strong opinions, and did not hesitate to express them. Even de Quincey had judgements to deliver, dream-prompted though most of them were. Charles Lamb, whose essays are charming, whimsical, pathetic and quaint, nevertheless conveys through the mist a personal outlook which is something more than the sum of these qualities. There are ages when writers share a common background, the particular genius of each illuminating a special aspect of it. This was so in the eighteenth century, but not in the nineteenth. De Quincey, Landor and Lamb all had ornate styles, but no common background.

Thomas Carlyle, a dyspeptic Scot with an admiration for German culture, wrote his *History of the French Revolution*, 1837, in a pompous, elegant, somewhat sentimental style; but the style of his *Sartor Resartus*, 1833, and *Heroes and Hero Worship*, 1840, in which his moralistic teaching found more direct expression, was so restless, blurred and cranky that his Romantic admirers decided that he must be a genius. He used the same style later in his histories. Here is a passage from his *History of King Friedrich II of Prussia*, 1858:

' "Admirable feat of Strategy! What a General, this Prince Karl!" exclaimed mankind, — Cause-of-Liberty mankind with special enthusiasm; and took to writing *Lives* of Prince Karl, as well as tar-burning and *te-deum*-ing on an extensive scale. For it had sent the Cause of Liberty bounding up again to the top of things, this of crossing the Rhine, in such fashion. And in effect, the Cause of Liberty, and Prince Karl himself, had risen hereby to their acme or culminating point in World-History; not to continue long at such height, little as they dreamt of that, among their tar-burnings. The feat itself, – contrived by Nadasti, people say, and executed (what was the real difficulty) by Traun, – brought Prince Karl very great renown, this Year; and is praised by Friedrich himself, now and afterwards, as masterly, as Julius Caesar's method, and the proper way of crossing rivers (when executable) in face of the enemy. And indeed Prince Karl, owing to Traun or not, is highly respectable in the way of Generalship at present, and did in these Five Months, from June onward, really considerable things. At his very acme of Life, as well as of Generalship; which, also, soon changed, poor man; never to culminate again.'

For Carlyle, as for Gibbon, history was a branch of literature which presented him with opportunities for dramatic story-telling and personal interpretation: he did not feel obliged to show scholarly caution. In telling his story he is always himself present, directing it, frequently roused to indignation or pity and frequently passing abrupt, downright, one-sided judgement. He ridiculed as 'Professor Dry-as-Dust' the German historian, Leopold von Ranke, who had insisted that history should be regarded as a science, rather than an art, and who is now regarded as the Father of modern history.

Though a few professional writers worked out an individual style suited to their temperament and purposes, ordinary people suffered by no longer having any simple all-purpose style that they could imitate. The elegant style was now reserved for formal use, and was constantly burlesqued: for example by Thomas Love Peacock, whose first satirical novel, *Headlong Hall*, appeared in 1816: he took the more pompous standard devices and treated them facetiously. The Biblical style was now quaint; the atmosphere of the new century was too fanciful for the plain style; French, German and Oriental and mock-antique fashions, though very well for novel-writing, were unsuited for general use. Many writers who had important views to express could therefore find no distinctive style in which to do so: for instance, John Stuart Mill and Charles Darwin. In the eighteenth century their prose would have taken on the inflections of standard elegance and been sustained by it, as was the prose of Hume and Newton. The fact was, that the United Kingdom was tending to become a middle-class commercial democracy. Aristocratic wit no longer set the general literary tone, which was increasingly utilitarian, prudish, tasteless and emotionally unstable. In witness of their confusion of mind the more restless writers of the early nineteenth century began to mix their styles incongruously, in the same book. The effect is that of a variety performance with turns to please all sections of the audience. For example, here are excerpts from different parts of Harriette Wilson's *Memoirs*, published in 1825. She was a Regency adventuress, admitted to high society because of her beauty, her wit and the distinction of the men who competed, and paid, for her favours.

First, the opening paragraph. The conventionally elegant 'Whether it was love, or the severity of my father, the depravity of my own heart, or the winning arts of the noble lord' is a smart mock-heroic foil to the downright: 'It was in fact a dead bore':

> 'I shall not say why and how I became, at the age of fifteen, the mistress of the Earl of Craven. Whether it was love, or the severity of my father, the depravity of my own heart, or the winning arts of the noble lord, which induced me to leave my paternal roof and place myself under his protection, does not much signify now: or if it does, I am not in the humour to gratify curiosity in this matter.
>
> I resided on the Marine Parade, at Brighton; and I remember that Lord Craven used to draw cocoa trees, and his fellows, as he called them, on the best vellum paper, for my amusement. Here stood the enemy, he would say; and here, my love, are my fellows: there the cocoa trees etc. It was, in fact, a dead bore. All these cocoa trees and fellows, at past eleven o'clock at night, could have no peculiar interest for a child like myself, so lately in the habit of retiring early to rest. One night, I recollect, I fell asleep; and, as I often dream, I said, yawning, and half awake, Oh, Lord! Oh, Lord! Craven has got me into the West Indies again.'

Then she attempts an inconsequential style in telling how she went to live with the Duke of Argyle:

> 'It was at that critical period of his life, when his whole and sole possessions appeared to consist in three dozen of ragged lawn shirts, with embroidered collars, well fringed in his service; a threadbare suit of snuff colour, a little old hat with very little binding left, an old horse, an old groom, an old carriage and an old chateau. It was to console himself for all this antiquity, I suppose, that he fixed upon so very young a mistress as myself. Thus, after having gone through all the routine of sighs, vows and rural walks, he, at last, saw me blooming and safe in his dismal chateau in Argyle Street.
>
> Joy produced a palpitation which had, well nigh, been fatal to . . . No matter, to be brief. . . .
>
> A late hour in the morning blushed to find us in the arms of each

other, as Monk Lewis, or somebody else says; but the morning was pale when compared to the red on my cheek – aye, ladies, pure red, when I, the very next day, acquainted Fred Lamb with my pretty, innocent, volatile adventure!'

Then the elegant style without mock-heroics, just to show that she can manage it:

> Characters and feelings, unnaturally stretched on the sentimental bed of torture, must return with violence to their natural tone and dimensions, says a celebrated French writer. The idol of romantic passion, in some unlucky moment of common sense, or common life, is discovered to be the last thing their worshippers would wish the idol to be found – a mere human being! with passions, and infirmities, and wants, utterly unprovided for by the statutes of romance. Soon we find, too, a certain falling off in our own powers of human life, a subjection to common accidents, ill health and indigence, which sicklies o'er the rich colouring of passion with the pale cast of humanity.'

Then the plain style tinged with irony:

> 'I hit upon a new plan of getting rid of Mrs Nesbit, a certain widow lady, now living with her family at Versailles, a relation, I believe, of Lord Bathurst. I will tell you all about it. My being thrown into her honourable society was a mere accident, and I was well disposed to keep my distance, and talk only to the male part of our company. Mrs Nesbit not only put herself forward, and took an active part in our conversation, but she called me My Dear, took me aside, and declared that she had taken a great fancy to me; hoped we should meet in town; detailed to me all the beauties of her young family; and further, to prove her unreserved friendship, took me out of the society of some very pleasant young men, into a cold, dirty bedroom, where she acquainted me with an affliction that had befallen that part of her person, which made it impossible for her to sit down without torture. I was very sorry, and duly condoled with her, of course; but I never saw the lady in my life before, and, if I had, how could I help her tremendous boils, or their very critical situation!'

Then the sentimental style, when she meets Lord Byron for the first time:

> 'The stranger hesitated.
>
> "Don't you understand French?" I inquired.
>
> "Perfectly."
>
> "Well then, take out your watch. In one quarter of an hour you shall be free from all my persecution; but, give me that time, pray do!"
>
> "Agreed," said the stranger smiling, as he gracefully offered me his arm.

"This," said I, pressing the arm I had taken, "this seems, I am sorry to say, to be mere solid flesh and blood. I had fancied – "

"What?"

"Why," continued I, half ashamed of myself, "upon my word and honour, I do confess I thought you something supernatural!"

The stranger's countenance brightened, and he asked me eagerly if I had ever seen him before.'

Then the joking apostrophe:

> 'Oh muse, etc., etc., etc., grant me eloquence to do justice to my subjects on that great and mighty occasion! In the meantime let me conclude, or rather let us proceed to draw these anecdotes into something like the form of a conclusion, because I their writer am tired of them, if you the reader of them are not.'

Then the pathetic style:

> ' "Do you not breathe with rather less pain?" I asked, while I pressed her cold damp hand between my own.
>
> "At all events," answered poor Fanny, "I would rather die here, than in the close apartment I have just quitted. How sweet and refreshing the flowers smelt, as I was carried along the garden! I did not see them, for I could not endure the light. I wish I could," continued Fanny, fixing her clear, still lovely blue eyes on my face beseechingly. "The prospect, I understand, is most beautiful from the room above us; but I shall never see it."
>
> "Do, dearest Fanny," said I, making a violent effort to conceal my tears, lest they should agitate my suffering sister, "let me open one of the shutters a very little. The air is mild and delicious, and the heat no longer oppressive, as it was when you passed through the garden."
>
> The last ray of the setting sun fell on poor Fanny's pale, beautiful features, as I drew back the curtains. It was one of those lovely evenings in the month of June, which often succeed a thunderstorm, and the honeysuckles, which clustered round the windows, emitted a rich and fragrant perfume.'

The book ends with a moralistic vision in which the Gothic, Oriental, pseudo-Celtic, sentimental and elegant styles mix in a purple cloud:

> '. . . Suddenly the atmosphere was impregnated with the odour of the Indian berry, which grew in immense quantities around me. My senses were affected by it, and a voluptuous indolence began to steal over me. . . . I beheld, coming towards me, a being of extraordinary beauty. His age might be near thirty, judging by the strong growth of a beard, which curled in rich abundance over his chin; but his dark blue eyes of fire told him younger.

"I am called Passion," said he. "There lies your road to Peace and Happiness," and he pointed to the height of the mountain. "Misery is here, and, though left of all when you foresake me, I scorn to complain. I deceive none but the weak and the wilful. If this bursting heart, this writhing lip speak not, leave me to the fate I deserve, and which I shall meet undismayed. Misery lies this way," repeated Passion, tearing his luxurious hair in all the frenzy of maddened sensation, while his teeth gnawed his nether lip till the red current disfigured a mouth of unequalled loveliness. He was turning from me with rapidity.

"Stay," said I faintly. He snatched me to his heart in all the wildness of frenzy. His heaving bosom seemed to threaten suffocation. His ardent gaze, and the liquid fire flashing from his eyes, dazzled and bewildered me. They spoke of feelings but guessed at by our softer nature; yet coloured by our sanguine minds even beyond reality. The pulsations of his heart were seen, nay almost heard; and still he curbed the passion which was consuming him; and still he had not pressed the lip, which quivered with delicious expectation.'

A similar ringing of the changes is found in the novels of Captain Marryat, whose plain narrative style in describing events at sea is swift, lively and logical; he becomes involved in melodramatic absurdities when he is describing events ashore; and also uses the facetious style as dramatic relief. Here are contrastive passages from *Rattlin the Reefer*, 1836, by Edward Howard, an imitator of Marryat's—which Marryat edited to make still more like his own work:

'We had now been some time at quarters, and everything was ready for chasing and fighting. But the fun had already begun to the northward. Our second man-of-war brig, the *Curlew*, had closed considerably upon the felucca, which was evidently endeavouring to make the chase a windward one. The brig closed more upon her than she ought. It certainly enabled her to fire broadside after broadside upon her, but, as far as we could perceive, with little or no effect. In a short time the privateer contrived to get in the wind's eye of the man-of-war and away they went. After the four ships had been taken possession of, and which were each making a different course, we sent three of the boats — the barge, yawl and pinnace — under the command of Mr Silva, in order to recapture them, of which there was every prospect, as the breeze was light and would probably not freshen before ten o'clock; for however the captured vessels might steer, their courses must be weather ones, as, if they had attempted to run to leeward, they must have crossed the body of the convoy.'

The following passage is about an Irish usher whose wooden leg is stuck in a bog:

' "But really, now I come to think of it," chimed in the now enraptured widow, "a very serious alarm has seized me. Suppose that the piece of wood, so nicely planted in this damp clay, were to take root and throw out fibres. Gracious me! only suppose that you should begin to vegetate. I do declare that you look quite green about the eyes already!"

"Mercy me!" whispered the wag, "if he should grow up, he'll certainly turn into a plane tree; for really, he is a very plain man."

The wielder of the ruler gave a tremendous wriggle with the whole body, which proved as ineffectual as it was violent. . . .

"What a fine cock-shy he would make!" said Master Blubberlips.

"O, I should so like to see it," said the lady. "It will be the first time he has been made shy in his life." '

Yet the tradition of literary elegance had not suddenly lapsed. Jane Austen, for example, carried it on: although her novels do not deal with the higher reaches of society, they reflect the general refinement of the lesser well-to-do. Among Jane Austen's favourite authors were Richardson, Johnson and Cowper, and the plain polish of her own style owes something to their example. She seems to have perfected it by a method of elimination: anything in the least heavy, artificial, absurd or pathetic was cut out. Her way of observing manners was naturally ironical, and also naturally sincere and true. Here is the first sentence of *Emma*, published in 1816:

'Emma Woodhouse, handsome, clever, and rich, with a comfortable home and a happy disposition, seemed to unite some of the best blessings of existence; and had lived nearly twenty-one years in this world with very little to distress or vex her.'

The use of the three adjectives, 'handsome', 'clever', and 'rich', the balancing of 'comfortable home' with 'happy disposition' and the rounded close of the double verbs, 'to distress or vex her', are devices in the eighteenth-century tradition; yet the spirit in which they are used is distinctive, because Jane Austen was a distinctive person using an established technique for stories drawn from her own experience.

Robert Southey, who became Poet Laureate in 1813, was one of the authors who did not make any violent departure from eighteenth-century elegance. His best known prose work is the *Life of Nelson*, published in the same year. The solid structure of his style is to be seen even in the most impassioned parts – for instance, in a sentence from the last paragraph upon Nelson's death:

'The most triumphant death is that of a martyr; the most awful that of a martyred patriot; the most splendid that of the hero in the hour of victory, and if the chariot and the horses of fire had been vouchsafed for Nelson's translation, he could scarcely have departed in a greater blaze of glory.'

There is the same care here in making generalized distinctions as there is in Johnson, but it is used heavily in a crescendo of praise:

> The death of a martyr is a triumph;
> the martyr who is also a patriot is awe-inspiring;
> the patriot martyr who is also a hero in the hour of victory is not only triumphant and awe-inspiring but most splendid.

To remedy any lack of weight that the word 'splendid' might have, Southey adds the figure of speech drawn from the ascent of Elijah into Heaven. Not much of his work climbs such steeps of rhetoric as this, but all is equally vigorous.

Lord Macaulay was the most fluent writer of his day, and known as 'the book in breeches' because of his phenomenal memory for facts. He balanced his phrases, repeated the same idea in different forms and with different instances, and used all the more emphatic devices of the eighteenth century, but with a force and humourless bias distinctly his own. The following example is taken from his *History of England*, the first volume of which appeared in 1848. He is describing the radical Whig politicians who took refuge in Holland and incited the Duke of Monmouth to rebellion against James II:

> 'These refugees were in general men of fiery temper and weak judgement. They were also under the influence of that peculiar illusion which seems to belong to their situation. A politician driven into banishment by a hostile faction generally sees the society which he has quitted through a false medium. Every object is distorted and discoloured by his regrets, his longings and his resentments. Every little discontent seems to him to portend a revolution. Every riot is a rebellion. He cannot be convinced that his country does not pine for him as much as he pines for his country. He imagines that all his old associates, who still dwell at their homes and enjoy their estates, are tormented by the same feelings which make life a burden to himself. The longer his expatriation, the greater does this hallucination become. The lapse of time which cools the ardour of the friends whom he has left behind inflames his. Every month his impatience to revisit his native land increases: and every month his native land remembers and misses him less.'

There are many epigrammatic effects here: 'men of fiery temper and weak judgement', and the three successive sentences beginning with

'Every', which increase in emphasis as they diminish in length. The sentences lack a close inter-connexion: all amplify the illusions of the exiled politician, all share the continuously sharp rhythm, but each is separate and there is no progressive movement of thought. The whole body of shot is fired at the same still target.

Macaulay was far from dispassionate in his approach to history: he collected his facts with care, but he marshalled them so that they more often supported a special plea than provided an impartial summary.

The elegant, pompous style was still used in official and formal letters, in court proceedings and, curiously enough, in popular journalism. Here, for example, is part of a newspaper account (1828) of the examination of the corpse of Maria Marten, who had been murdered at Polstead, Suffolk, by one William Corder:

> '*Disinterment of the Body*
>
> 'After the remains of Maria Marten had been laid in Polstead Churchyard upwards of five weeks, some circumstances transpired which led to a belief that a supposed defect in the evidence might be supplied, and which had reference to the cause of her death. In consequence of this probability of new light being thrown on the subject, Mr Wayman, the coroner, met several professional gentlemen at the Cock Inn, at Polstead, on the 3rd of June, 1828, where they held a consultation as to the propriety of disinterring the body, and the result of their conference was, that it was agreed that the ashes of Maria Marten should be again removed from their resting-place. This resolution was carried into effect with all secrecy at an early hour on the following morning.'

Here is part of an advertisement which Corder had printed in the *Morning Herald* and *Sunday Times*:

> 'MATRIMONY — A Private Gentleman, aged 24, entirely independent, whose disposition is not to be exceeded, has lately lost the chief of his family by the hand of Providence, which has occasioned discord among the remainder, under circumstances most disagreeable to relate. To any female of respectability, who would study for domestic comfort, and willing to confide her future happiness in one every way qualified to render the marriage state desirable, as the advertiser is in affluence, the lady must have the power of some property, which may remain in her own possession.'

This advertisement was answered by forty-five women, and all but one, who was illiterate, wrote in the same elegant style. Semi-educated people continued to use this style even in family letters until the beginning of the twentieth century, and it also persisted in provincial journals.

The perfectly plain style was extremely rare in the nineteenth century.

It occurred chiefly in court reports of depositions at trials and inquests. Here, for example, is the evidence of Maria Marten's father at the trial of William Corder.

> '*Thomas Marten*, examined by *Mr. Andrews*. — I am a mole-catcher and labourer. I live at Polstead. Maria Marten was my daughter. She was about twenty-six years old when she went away last on the 18th of May, last year. I did not see her that morning because I go out very early. I do not know how long the prisoner and she were on intimate terms, but I believe a year and a half. I did not find out that Maria had gone away till Saturday the 19th. On Sunday, the 20th, I saw Corder at my house, when he told me that he had taken my daughter to Ipswich, and that he was going to be married to her as soon as the license he had got came back from London. He said Maria was with the sister of a gentleman that he (Corder) went to school with at Hadleigh. He told me, when he came to take leave of me in September, that he had purchased a new suit of clothes for the wedding. I have received two letters from him, which I have given to the attorney for the prosecution. I was present at the first examination at Polstead. I searched the Red Barn on the 19th of April, in consequence of what my wife used to say to me. There is a lane goes down by the side of the barn. I examined this bay [points to the model], which was covered with litter and fodder. Mr. Pryke, Mrs. Corder's bailiff, was with me. He raked and I poked into the straw a good while before we found anything, when, raking the straw, I found some large loose stones about the middle of the bay, and there was an appearance of the earth having been disturbed. When I had poked with my mole-spike about four inches, I found something come out with it like flesh. I smelt of it, and it was very disagreeable. We made further search and found that the hole contained a body.'

One of the very few notable writers in the early nineteenth century who used the plain style was William Cobbett. Cobbett was a self-educated man, the son of a Surrey farmer. He served for a while in the Army in Canada, rising to the rank of sergeant-major; taught as a tutor in Philadelphia; farmed in the United States; returned to England and entered political life with his reputation already made as a controversial journalist. The chief objects of his scorn were privilege and jobbery; his chief interest was always agriculture, and in the *Weekly Political Register*, which he founded on his return to England, he combined detailed observations on the state of farming with bitterly partisan comment. He delivered his opinions unhesitatingly, without literary graces, and was so anti-Romantic that he even thought Shakespeare a fraud. In country matters he was at his plainest, since he approached them from the point of view of a practical farmer concerned with existing conditions, improvements and remedies. In contrast to the Romantic writers, his descriptions are always of agricultural, not of natural, scenery. This quotation comes from *Rural Rides*, and is dated April 19th, 1830:

> 'The land in this, which is called the high part of Lincolnshire has generally stone, a solid bed of stone of great depth, at different distances from the surface. In some parts, this stone is of a yellowish colour and in the form of very thick slate; and in these parts the soil is not so good; but, generally speaking, the land is excellent; easily tilled, no surface water; the fields very large; not many trees; but what there are, particularly the ash, very fine and of free growth; and innumerable flocks of those big, long-wooled sheep from one hundred to a thousand in a flock, each having from eight to ten pounds of wool upon his body. One of the finest sights in the world is one of these thirty to forty acre fields, with four or five or six hundred ewes, each with her one or two lambs skipping about upon grass, the most beautiful that can be conceived, and on lands as level as a bowling green. I do not recollect having seen a mole-hill or an ant-hill since I came into the country; and not one acre of wasted land, though I have gone the whole length of the country one way, and am now got nearly half-way back another way.

The rhythm of this is jerky, because of Cobbett's habit of interpolating explanatory and descriptive clauses suddenly as they occur to him. It is also hastily written: words like 'part', 'way', and 'this' are often unnecessarily repeated, and a more careful writer would not, for instance, have allowed to stand uncorrected the duplication in '*one* of the finest sights . . . is *one* of these fields'. These are failings in literary grace, but do not detract from his general straightforwardness.

Few other writers in the nineteenth century wrote about country matters without artifice or sentiment, even naturalists like Richard Jefferies: it was an industrial age, and the country was commonly regarded as a tranquil retreat from business and bustle.

CHAPTER NINE

RECENT PROSE

MIDDLE-CLASS family life was the subject of most early and middle-nineteenth century novels that were not Gothic tales of mystery and horror, or calmer, historical novels of the Sir Walter Scott, Harrison Ainsworth school. Though the novelists often introduced moral teaching and pleas for social reform into their stories, they were chiefly concerned with the delineation of character and the development of plot. This realism was a safeguard against over-elaborate writing, although the plain style was now regarded as 'low' even by the village constable. It was a heavily emotional realism, however, because a new emphasis upon the duty of showing mercy and charity toward the unfortunate had made pathos as highly esteemed as wit had formerly been.

There had been no sudden revolution in England as there had been in France, but successive agitations in favour of particular reforms; and these were usually prompted as much by humanitarian as by political feelings. The new industrial middle classes were enjoying a prudently guarded opulence, and at the same time, in manufacturing districts there was poverty and misery on a scale that had not been known in England since the Black Death. The middle classes felt collectively, though not individually, responsible for this state of affairs, and from their guilty humanitarianism grew numerous movements for piece-meal social reform and numerous minor philanthropic institutions. The equalitarian arguments that had brought about the French Revolution were used, in a modified form, to bring about such reforms as the abolition of slavery under the British flag; but the feelings which made them possible derived rather from the Christian charity insisted on by the Methodists, and other evangelical reformers of the period, than from equalitarianism.

The severity shown by the new religious spirit against idle and lascivious reading, especially on a Sunday, compelled popular novelists to turn humanitarian; and besides the naturally poor and oppressed, their pity had to take in all those who came to moral or financial grief. The strict and sedate code of behaviour that had supervened on the lax and reckless Regency code was two-sided: public opinion first struck down all who failed to meet their social obligations, then pitied them as they lay bleeding. All personal and social problems were seen through a haze of sympathy, which was, however, not allowed to obscure the harshness of moral censure. Women, children and the poor were weaker vessels, particularly liable to sin and misfortune; when they fell, and were hurried away into charitable quarantine, the blame for their miserable fate was conscientiously laid on the defects of social circumstances.

In Thackeray's novels, pathos is usually an undertone, only occasionally rising to a loud throb, as in this passage from *Vanity Fair*, 1848:

> 'She was wrapped in a white morning dress, her hair falling on her shoulders and her large eyes fixed and without light. By way of helping on the preparations for the departure, and showing that she too could be useful at a moment so critical, this poor soul had taken up a sash of George's from the drawers whereon it lay and followed him to and fro, with the sash in her hand, looking on mutely while the packing proceeded. She came out and stood leaning at the wall, holding this sash against her bosom, from which the heavy net of crimson dropped like a large stain of blood.'

Several devices here raise the tone of the passage from sadness to pathos. 'Large eyes fixed and without light' is a sentimental overstatement; 'mutely' instead of 'silently' carries a further suggestion of suffering; with 'this poor soul' Thackeray enters personally on the scene to intercede for the reader's pity; and in the last sentence the simile of the bloodstain is shocking in its poignancy. Similar devices for moving the emotions of their readers, most of whom lived dull and sheltered lives, were used by all the well-known novelists and magazine writers of this period, including George Eliot, George Borrow, Charles Kingsley, Charles Dickens, and the Americans, Edgar Allan Poe, Nathaniel Hawthorne, Herman Melville, Washington Irving. Dickens's stories are never allowed to tell themselves: he forcibly obtrudes his own emotions, often raising the pitch of the style to hysteria. He also tries to heighten the effect of his pathetic passages by a foil of robust facetiousness; as Elizabethan dramatists had heightened their tragic effects by comic relief. Here is a quotation from his *Old Curiosity Shop*:

> 'She was dead. Dear, patient, gentle, noble Nell was dead. Her little bird — a poor slight thing the pressure of a finger would have crushed — was stirring nimbly in its cage; and the strong heart of its child mistress was mute and motionless for ever.
>
> Where were the traces of her early cares, her sufferings, and fatigues? All gone. Sorrow was dead indeed in her, but peace and perfect happiness were born; imaged in her tranquil beauty and profound repose.
>
> And still her former self lay there, unaltered in this change. Yes. The old fireside had smiled upon that same sweet face; it had passed, like a dream, through haunts of misery and care; at the door of the

poor schoolmaster on the summer evening, before the furnace fire on the cold wet night, at the still bedside of the dying boy, there had been the same mild lovely look. So shall we know the angels in their majesty, after death.

The old man held one languid arm in his, and had the small hand tight folded to his breast, for warmth. It was the hand she had stretched out to him with her last smile – the hand that had led him on, through all their wanderings. Ever and anon he pressed it to his lips; then hugged it to his breast again, murmuring that it was warmer now; and, as he said it, he looked, in agony, to those who stood around, as if imploring them to help her.'

And here is another passage from the same book, with death treated facetiously:

' "Then we have nothing for it but resignation," said Mr. Brass; "nothing but resignation, and expectation. It would be a comfort to have his body; it would be a dreary comfort."

"Oh, beyond a doubt," assented Mrs. Jiniwin hastily; "if we once had that, we should be quite sure."

"With regard to the descriptive advertisement," said Sampson Brass, taking up his pen. "It is a melancholy pleasure to recall his traits. Respecting his legs now –?"

"Crooked, certainly," said Mrs. Jiniwin.

"Do you think they *were* crooked?" said Brass, in an insinuating tone. "I think I see them now coming up the street very wide apart, in nankeen pantaloons a little shrunk and without straps. Ah! What a vale of tears we live in. Do we say crooked?"

"I think they were a little so," observed Mrs. Quilp with a sob.

"Legs crooked," said Brass, writing as he spoke. "Large head, short body, legs crooked –"

"Very crooked," suggested Mrs. Jiniwin.

"We'll not say very crooked, ma'am," said Brass piously. "Let us not bear hard upon the weaknesses of the deceased. He is gone, ma'am, to where his legs will never come in question. – We will content ourselves with crooked, Mrs. Jiniwin."

"I thought you wanted the truth," said the old lady. "That's all." '

This is melodrama in novel-form. Versions of most of Dickens's novels were staged during his lifetime. He was a natural orator and actor. He seems to have spoken over to himself, under his breath, every sentence that he wrote; and he toured Britain and the United States, giving public readings from his works. This accounts for much of his popularity in Victorian times, when the example set by the Queen popularized domesticity – the father of the family, instead of spending his evenings drinking and singing at the club as his own father had done, was supposed to stay at home and join a family reading circle. In the *Old Curiosity Shop*, as in all Dickens's novels, each chapter begins with an obvious cue to the reader: 'This should be read by Paterfamilias, in his manly, jolly voice,' or 'This is for the gentle, womanly voice of Materfamilias,' or 'Master John may be trusted with this.'

The popular Victorian novel (which was usually published in fortnightly parts, so that no member of a family could read on to the end, ahead of the rest) cannot be judged by modern solo-reading standards: its pictorial qualities, its frequent changes in atmosphere, the crowdedness that now make it such difficult going, explain themselves if it is read aloud dramatically to a roomful of leisured people of various ages in mid-Victorian costume. The practice of home-reading gradually lapsed at the turn of the century, and virtually ended with the First World War.

Pictorial styles were also used by John Ruskin and Walter Pater, who were not novelists but literary preachers and therefore indulged in even greater complexity of language. When Ruskin confined himself to expounding moral or aesthetic theory his style was fairly straightforward, but this was rare: his elaborate word-painting usually crowded out the precepts it was supposed to illustrate. The following sentence, describing the front of St Mark's Cathedral, is taken from the *Stones of Venice*, 1851-1853:

> 'And well may they fall back, for beyond those troops of ordered arches there rises a vision out of the earth, and all the great square seems to have opened out of it in a kind of awe, that we may see it far away; — a multitude of pillars and white domes, clustered into a low pyramid of coloured light, a treasure-heap, it seems, partly of gold, and partly of opal and mother-of-pearl, hollowed beneath into five great vaulted porches, ceiled with fair mosaic, and beset with sculpture of alabaster, clear as amber, and delicate as ivory, sculpture fantastic and involved, of palm leaves and lilies, and grapes and pomegranates, and birds clinging and fluttering among the branches, all twined together into an endless network of buds and plumes; and, in the midst of it, the solemn forms of angels, sceptred, and robed to the feet, and leaning to each other across the gates, their figures indistinct among the gleaming of the golden ground through the leaves beside them, interrupted and dim like the morning light as it faded back among the branches of Eden, when first its gates were angel-guarded long ago.'

A luxuriant mass of details is given, but with little sense of relation between them. The majestic sweep of the rhythm carries the reader over the details before he has time to assemble them in his mind. Ruskin himself must have formed a general impression of St Mark's and then carefully studied particulars, but does not here present them in such proportion as to explain his impression. It will be noticed how frequently the word 'among' occurs in the last few lines — birds among the branches, figures among the gleaming gold, light among the branches of Eden — all entrancing items in the decoration, but with no precise or essential places in it. This is a misrepresentation of the solid design of St Mark's.

Pater was much more Classical in spirit than Ruskin, in the sense that he was clear and not luxuriant, elaborate and not profuse. But he, too, was trying to convey impressions of indescribable feelings: he wanted to catch and record in print the aesthetic *frissons*, or thrills, which he considered the highest rewards of a cultured existence. This could only be done indirectly by suggestion and parable. His novel, *Marius the Epicurean*, is one long historical parable, and his other works purely suggestive sketches.

Just as Ruskin, in a final effort to communicate his impression of St Mark's, makes use of a conceit about dawn breaking in the Garden of Eden, so Pater has recourse to fancy in trying to describe the feelings with which Leonardo da Vinci's *La Gioconda* inspired him. He imagines the mood of the painter on the day that he added the famous smile. The paragraph is taken from *Studies in the History of the Renaissance*, published in 1873; it was written at Oxford, where Pater was a college tutor, at a time when Ruskin was also lecturing there.

> 'On this day truly no mysterious light, no irresistibly leading hand from afar, reached him; only, the peculiarly tranquil influence of its first hour increased steadily upon him in a manner with which, as he conceived, the aspects of the place he was then visiting had something to do. The air there, air supposed to possess the singular property of restoring the whiteness of ivory, was pure and thin. An even veil of lawn-like white cloud had now drawn over the sky; and under its broad, shadowless light every hue and tone of time came out upon the yellow old temples, the elegant pillared circle of the shrine of the pastoral Sybil, the houses seemingly of a piece with the ancient fundamental rock.'

Pater calculated the pictorial suggestiveness of each word, subordinating its sense to the emotional, vocal and rhythmical context. He did this more precisely than Ruskin because his emotions had greater precision and he was better able to isolate and analyse them. Nevertheless, the repeated rhyme of 'air there, air' reads somewhat affectedly.

Among the exceptional writers who avoided both the pathetic and the pictorial styles were Anthony Trollope and Samuel Butler. Trollope escaped a formal education because of the poverty of his family; but his mother, author of *Domestic Manners of the Americans*, was a shrewd and vigorous writer and he seems to have learnt much from her. He spent most of his life as a Post Office official and hunting man. He published more than twenty long novels, all dealing with middle-class family life, plainly told and with few emotional digressions. Conversation and pure narrative make up the greater part of them, and there is far less descriptive writing than in most nineteenth-century novels from Sir Walter Scott's onwards. The following is a passage from the first chapter of *Orley Farm*, published in 1862:

> 'The whole stood in one line fronting on to a large lawn which fell steeply away from the house into an orchard at the bottom. The lawn was cut in terraces, and here and there upon it there stood apple trees of ancient growth; for here had been the garden of the old farmhouse. They were large, straggling trees, such as do not delight the eyes of modern gardeners; but they produced fruit by the bushel, very sweet to the palate, though probably not so perfectly round, and large, and handsome as those which the horticultural skill of the present day requires.'

Trollope does not refrain from making general comments – for example, this comment on the modern taste in apples – but they are always short and relevant. He does not draw an elaborate 'atmosphere' out of them; the story distills its own atmosphere as it unfolds. Here he has given a brief and factual setting before breaking into the story proper.

Samuel Butler was not primarily a novelist: most of his works were treatises on art, literature, psychology and science; but he wrote a Utopian fantasy in novel form, *Erewhon*, 1872, and twenty years later a sequel, *Erewhon Revisited*, and one domestic novel, *The Way of All Flesh*, written between 1872 and 1884 but not published until after his death in 1903. He is usually described as a satirist, because these novels expose many of the shams of contemporary life, but his satire is very different from Swift's: it is more analytical and more understanding, less witty, more humorous and more original. His style is plain and unemotional, but sharper than Trollope's because his judgements are less conventionally formed. This is from *The Way of All Flesh*:

> 'Some people say that their schooldays were the happiest in their lives. They may be right, but I look with suspicion upon those whom I hear saying this. It is hard enough to know whether one is happy or unhappy now, and still harder to compare the relative happiness or unhappiness of different times of one's life; the utmost that can be said is that we are fairly happy so long as we are not distinctly aware of

> being miserable. As I was talking with Ernest one day not so long since about this, he said he was so happy now that he was sure he had never been happier, and did not wish to be so, but that Cambridge was the first place where he had ever been consciously and continuously happy.'

Butler has not let this piece of analysis get out of hand: his style is equal to it. Excesses and shortcomings in Victorian prose, and in modern prose which derives from it, are usually due to the writer's not knowing just how to reconcile the sense of what he wishes to say with the various literary devices which pride of craftsmanship has impelled him to use. Butler's style is as free from these devices as it is from fanciful emotional colouring. He lived on a small income; published all his books, except *Erewhon*, at a loss; and was generally regarded as a crank because of his refusal to conform with literary and scientific fashions.

Butler died when the twentieth century was just beginning; his own century had bequeathed it no general prose tradition. There were conventions of pathetic writing, of pictorial writing, of ornate historical and political writing, but these were suited only to certain subjects and the achievement of certain effects. Most famous writers of the late nineteenth century had worked out eccentrically individual styles. William Morris revived the mediaeval narrative manner, with a mixture of devices taken from Thomas Malory and the authors of Norse sagas. George Meredith used a complex metaphorical language, the obscure implications of which were a fascinating study for his admirers. There was also the precious and witty style of Oscar Wilde, based on Ruskin and Pater; and, based on French models, the 'sensitive' and lucid style of George Moore. Here is a painfully sensitive passage from George Moore's *Confessions of a Young Man*, 1886:

> 'Then there is a failure – I can do nothing, nothing; my novel I know is worthless; my life is a leaf, it will flutter out of sight. I am weary of everything and wish I were back in Paris. I am weary of reading, there is nothing to read, Flaubert bores me. What nonsense has been talked about him! Impersonal! He is the most personal writer. But his odious pessimism! How weary I am of it, it never ceases, it is lugged in *à tout propos* and the little lyrical phrase with which he winds up every paragraph, how boring it is! Happily, I have "A Rebours" to read, that prodigious book, that beautiful mosaic. Huysmans is quite right, ideas are well enough until you are twenty, afterwards only words are bearable . . . a new idea, what can be more insipid – fit for Members of Parliament. Shall I go to bed? No. I would that I had a volume of Verlaine, or something of Mallarmé's to read – Mallarmé for preference. Huysmans speaks of Mallarmé in "A Rebours",

and in hours like these a page of Huysmans is as a dose of opium, a glass of something exquisite and spirituous.'

In 1878 the rugged-minded Charles Doughty, a poet and physician, went travelling in the deserts of Arabia, disguising neither his Christian distaste for Moslem superstition nor his English dislike for thievish and temperamental Arabs, and wrote a monumental account of his experiences in *Arabia Deserta*, 1888. He had not gone for adventure or for geographical or ethnological reasons, but (as he later told T. E. Lawrence) to 'redeem English from the slough into which it has fallen since the time of Spenser'. Here is an illustration of the way in which he redeemed English from neologisms:

> 'We journeyed in the beaten path towards Gofar; and after going a mile, "Let us wait, quoth Eyâd, and see if this Merjàn be not coming." At length we saw it was he who approached with a bundle on his head, – he brought temmn and dates, which his sister (wedded in the town) had given him. Eyâd drew out a leathern budget, in which was some victual for the way that he had received from the Mothîf, (without my knowledge): it was but a little barley meal and dates of ill kind, in all to the value of about one shilling. We sat down, Merjàn spread out his good dates, and we breakfasted; thus eating together I hoped they might yet be friendly, though only misfortunes could be before me with such unlucky rafîks. . . .
>
> "Nay, said Eyâd, beginning to swagger, the returning shall not be as our coming; I will ride myself." I said no more; and cast thus again into the wilderness I must give them line.'

And Doughty's contemporary, the complex-minded Henry James, an American with strong English sympathies, invented a new way of teasing the sentence with carefully contrived parentheses that delayed but did not confuse the rhythm as it meandered towards a comfortable close. This is from one of his later novels, *The Golden Bowl*, 1905:

> 'Charlotte throned, as who should say, between her hostess and her host, the whole scene having crystallized as soon as she took her place, to the right quiet lustre; the harmony was not less sustained for being superficial, and the only approach to a break in it was while Amerigo remained standing long enough for his father-in-law, vaguely wondering, to appeal to him, invite or address him, and then, in default of any such word, selected for presentation to the other visitor a plate of *petits fours*. Maggie watched her husband – if it now could be called watching – offer this refreshment; she noted the consummate way – for "consummate" was the term she privately applied – in which Charlotte cleared her acceptance, cleared her impersonal smile, of any

betrayal, of any slightest value, of consciousness; and then felt the slow surge of a vision that, at the end of another minute or two, had floated her across the room to where her father stood, looking at a picture, an early Florentine sacred subject, that he had given her on her marriage.'

Many more styles were invented as the twentieth century advanced and since there was keen competition among writers as to who should be 'great' and since it was admitted that 'greatness' was achieved only by a highly individual style, new tricks and new devices multiplied. In this plurality of styles little writers grew confused: they imitated one Master after another – Pater, Morris, James, Moore, Wilde – in the hope of suddenly finding themselves great men in their own right. It did not occur to them that unless they had something to say there was no need to write: most of them expected the ritual of writing to produce the subject.

Robert Louis Stevenson in an essay on literary style recommended imitation. He admitted that:

'Whenever I read a book or a passage that particularly pleased me, in which a thing was said or an effect rendered with propriety, in which there was either some conspicuous force or some happy distinction in the style, I must sit down at once and set myself to ape that quality. In these vain bouts, I got some practice in rhythm, in harmony, in construction, and the co-ordination of parts. I have thus played the sedulous ape to Hazlitt, to Lamb, to Wordsworth, to Sir Thomas Browne, to Defoe, to Hawthorne, to Montaigne, to Baudelaire and to Obermann.'

The effect of this sedulous imitation was to make Stevenson's works seem rather unreal: the negative virtue of faultlessness in an artificial prose style, especially where the writer's chief object is 'to render an effect', can be very disagreeable. A reader feels that he is being written at, not written for. Other writers were neither so industrious nor so expert as Stevenson in their imitations of 'The Masters', and so the Edwardian pudding-stone style began. It is still used by young writers who feel that they cannot be taken seriously until they have read the chief books of ancient and advanced contemporary literature in at least six languages and mastered all the styles and devices. Naturally they do not really read these books, or know the languages; but use crammer-school methods for learning just enough to pass muster. The literary result recalls the old Scottish nonsense story of Sir Gammer Vance who had a famous collection of curiosities and 'lived in a little thumb-bottle just outside his own front door'.

Typical pudding-stone is Sir Arthur Quiller-Couch's style, though he was not a young writer when he adopted it. In his unpretentious popular novels of the 'Eighties and 'Nineties he had been at his best: with simple humorous tales of the West Country and, though avoiding any suspicion of illiteracy, with no thought of setting himself up as an authority on English. He later took up style as a simple evangelist might take up ritual; and was appointed King Edward VII Professor of English Literature at Cambridge University. The following is a quotation from his *On the Art of Writing*, 1916. It is a concoction of styles which the contemporary reader was perhaps expected to taste critically with: 'Ah! a savour of Morris! Ah! a smack of Bunyan! Ah! a touch of Henry James! Ah, oh, ah! a tang, taste, suspicion, whiff, of Burke, Hazlitt, Jeremy Taylor, Washington Irving!'

> 'Seeing that in human discourse, infinitely varied as it is, so much must ever depend on *who* speaks, and to *whom*, in what mood and upon what occasion; and seeing that Literature must needs take account of all manner of writers, audiences, moods, occasions; I hold it a sin against the light to put up a warning against any word that comes to us in the fair way of use and wont (as "wire", for instance, for telegram), even as surely as we should warn off hybrids or deliberately pedantic impostors, such as "anti-body" and "picture-drome", and that, generally, it is better to err on the side of liberty than on the side of the censor: since by the manumitting of new words we infuse new blood into a tongue of which (or we have learnt nothing from Shakespeare's audacity) our first pride should be that it is flexible, alive, capable of responding to new demands of man's untiring quest after knowledge and experience.'

In this passage we see the first clear signs of the breakdown of prose logic that has become so evident since the end of the First World War. Even in late Victorian times, no person of Sir A. Quiller Couch's eminence would have dared to publish a sentence so plainly grotesque as 'By the manumitting of new words we infuse new blood into a tongue which is flexible, alive, capable of responding to new demands of man's untiring quest after knowledge and experience.' When the test of translation into Latin is applied, it fails at every point. No Latin orator would have figured new words as slaves to be manumitted: he would have seen them as barbarians applying for citizenship. Nor would he have figured the act of manumission as infusing new blood into anything: he would have put in the step here left out, namely, that after manumission the former slaves would be permitted to marry into their masters' families. Nor would he have mixed metaphor and realism in the phrase 'infuse new blood into a tongue': for blood is usually infused into the veins of the arm or leg and never into a tongue. Nor would he have written of a *tongue* as 'flexible and alive': he would have known that any human tongue, unless its owner happens to be paralysed, poisoned, or frozen stiff, is flexible and alive. He would therefore have avoided the word *lingua* (which means 'tongue' in the senses both of speech and of the organ of speech) and used instead '*modus loquendi*', a 'manner of speaking'. Nor would he have admitted that a tongue into which new blood has been infused could 'respond to man's demands' as if it were a separate person or animal. Nor would he have mixed his vocabularies—Ennius with Petronius—as is done here: the Elizabethan phrase 'I hold it a sin against the light to put up a warning against any word that comes to us in the fair way of use and wont' mixed with the late-Victorian devotional-scientific phrase 'capable of responding to new demands of man's untiring quest'.

In Victorian times there was a clean separation, in the popular mind, of journalism from literature: journalism was considered vulgar, however well the journalist worked. The favourite debating theme—'Will Kipling *live*?'—was based on a doubt whether anyone whose writing had been formed by journalistic practice could possibly be 'great', rather than on a doubt of Kipling's integrity as an observer and a moralist. It did not occur to anyone that O. Henry, Kipling's American counterpart, could 'live'; he was a mere reporter of the language of the bar and lodging-house and had a prison record. Yet it was felt that Kipling and O. Henry had some quality that Meredith and Henry James lacked; and gradually popular novelists began to simplify their style in imitation. This made a cleavage between popular and literary writers, or, as they became known shortly after the First World War, 'Low-brows and High-brows'. If this had meant a cleavage between the writers who wrote stylistically and those who wrote plainly, it would have been excellent: but journalism then implied grammatical and verbal looseness and, as the influence of American journalism grew, a gradual weakening of logic under self-induced emotional stress. Whether to range oneself with the Low-brows or with the High-brows was a difficult choice.

As the twentieth century advanced, the competition in style became a competition in being modern rather than in being great. Writers in Britain, however, were less affected by the modernist obsession than American writers, especially those who had visited France. Throughout the Victorian era the Americans had looked to Britain to set the literary standard for all departments of writing except the humorous, in which they took the lead under Mark Twain, Artemus Ward, and Gelett Burgess. In other departments they emulated their British contemporaries, and very often surpassed them in grace and clarity of language: for example, Victorian England could not boast of two essayists so judicious and correct as Ralph

W. Emerson and James Russell Lowell. But at the end of the First World War the Americans knew themselves to be the strongest and richest nation of the world, and therefore felt that this cultural dependence on Britain derogated from their national dignity. As in the War of Independence, when British political and military influence had to be shaken off, they turned for help to Paris. Paris had for long been the world-centre of literary, philosophical and artistic fashion. American writers, as would-be spokesmen of the most modern country in the world, needed the most modern of styles to express this feeling adequately; naturally, they went to Paris. For ten years Paris teemed with American literary experimentalists – the franc was low, life was free, there was no Prohibition. They returned finally to the United States in 1930, when the Great Depression deprived them of their incomes, having all served their apprenticeships in one or other of the schools of modernist writing.

The most celebrated American writer in Paris was Gertrude Stein. She had settled there several years before the tide of experimentalists flowed, and stayed for several years after it had ebbed – witnessing the defeat of France in 1940. She had been trained as a neurologist and philosopher and her experiments in writing derived from an assumption that Time and Progress, as nineteenth-century scientists and theologians had understood them, were now irrelevant concepts: in the modern world they were replaced by the simple casual relationships which arise out of mere continuous existence. This assumption was given weight by the findings of the new school of relativity-physicists, published after the First World War.

Gertrude Stein's method consisted in turning to a literary purpose the unreasoned relations of words in people's minds and the disconnection and repetition which are normal in modern conversation. She thus abandoned the tradition of orderly prose narrative – the old kind of story about the things that happened to people, arising out of some given situation and in turn giving rise to further happenings and new situations. For the most part her prose was a simple succession and repetition of words, phrases and sentences, without historical beginning or ending and without logical meaning. It was humorous and exciting, to those interested in new uses of words, but difficult to read. Solemn literary critics and newspaper comedians derided it; but in Paris in the 'Twenties she had a great following among the young American émigrés – who learnt from her how to use the simplest words and the most conversational idioms in new rhythmical movements which would give their work a characteristically American pace.

In the 'Thirties, when she had become an accepted literary figure,

Gertrude Stein was invited to make important lecture-tours in the United States. She then explained what her 'nonsense' meant. Here is a paragraph from a lecture on *Narration*, delivered in 1934. If it is read over with conversational emphasis it makes plain sense, although the thought is most complicated:

> 'When I first began writing really just began writing, I was tremendously impressed by anything by everything having a beginning a middle and an ending. I think one naturally is impressed by anything having a beginning a middle and an ending when one is beginning writing and that is a natural thing because when one is emerging from adolescence, which is really when one first begins writing, one feels that one would not have been one emerging from adolescence if there had not been a beginning and a middle and an ending to anything. So paragraphing is a thing that anyone is enjoying and sentences are less fascinating, but then gradually well if you are an American gradually you find that it is not really necessary that anything that everything has a beginning a middle and an ending and so you struggling with anything as anything has begun and begun does not really mean that begun and thing does not really mean beginning or begun.'

Gertrude Stein solved the logical problem of Time, which she speaks about here, by frequent use of the timeless present participle.

Only one other writer in English carried his experiments in prose so far as Gertrude Stein; and he went in a totally different direction. This was James Joyce, an Irishman, whose Dublin upbringing and Jesuit education provide the constant background to his work. Like the American experimentalists, he spent the greater part of his life on the Continent, in Switzerland, France and Italy. Being out of contact with the mass of his compatriots has always helped the literary innovator. Joyce's first books, *Dubliners* and *Portrait of the Artist as a Young Man*, were straightforward stories in the realistic style of the French-influenced Anglo-Irish school. His next book, *Ulysses*, a long novel describing twenty-four hours in the lives of a group of Dublin people, is made up chiefly of their inconsequential talk and ruminations. Woven into these, by means of word-associations, are recurring Greek and Latin themes – particularly the theme of Ulysses the Wanderer which gives the book its title. *Ulysses* became famous partly because it was banned as obscene by the British and American Customs authorities, partly because it was the most ambitious attempt yet made to use 'the stream of consciousness' in writing: that is, to reveal the private thoughts of characters in all their natural confusion. This manner of writing was founded on psychological researches which had been intended to show that consciousness was a turbid stream of mixed desires and memories: it was thus a psychological assumption rather than a prose style. Many other writers made use of it, with many varying styles.

Ulysses begins in a straightforward manner but soon becomes more complicated, passing, like Harriette Wilson's *Memoirs*, through a series of imitations or parodies of all previous English styles. It is as if Joyce was testing each of them in order and finding all wanting. In his last book, *Finnegan's Wake*, published in 1940, after he had been working on it for fifteen years, he finally invented a comically composite style and language which he could call his own: a super-pudding-stone. In it, ordinary English words are portmanteau'd and deliberately misspelt, others are introduced from many foreign languages, including Hebrew and Sanskrit, and the result is an almost indecipherable system of interlacing puns and verbal associations imposed upon the familiar Irish background. Here is a comparatively easy passage:

> 'What wouldn't I poach — the rent in my riverside my otther shoes, my beavery honest! — for a dace feast of grannom with the finny ones, flashing down the swansway, leaps ahead of the swift mac Eels and the pursewinded carpers, rearin antis rood perches astench of me, or, when I'd like own company best, with the help of a norange and bear, to be reclined by the lasher on my logansome, my g.b.d. in my f.a.c.e., solfanelly in my shellyholders and lov'd latakia the benuvolent, for my nosethrills with jealosomines wilting away to their heart's deelight and the king of saptimber letting down his humely odours for my consternation, dapping my griffen, burning water in the spearlight, or catching trophies of the king's royal college of sturgeons for to bake pike and pie while, O twined me abower in l'Alouette's Tower, all Adelaide's naughtingerls, juckjucking benighth me, I'd tonic my twittynice Dorian blackbudds off my singasongasongapiccolo to pipe musicall airs on numberous fairyaciodes.'

This is a fisherman's idyll spoken by an Irish priest: if it is read aloud, the Irish rhythm can be easily felt, and many familiar Irish properties recognized. If it is studied closely, more and more linguistic detail can be interpreted. This appeals to the reader's vanity of general knowledge and guessing power — 'Ah,' he says, 'by the *naughtingerls* he means also *nightingales* — because the German for nightingale is *Nachtigall* and *nachte* is old English for *naughty*, and 'gal' is 'girl', which in the Middle Ages was also spelt 'gerl'; and *nosethrills* are *nostrils* — the mediaeval spelling was *nosthrils*; and *jealosomines* are *jessamines* because of the old English term *jelsomine* from the Italian *gelsomino*. And *norange* recalls the derivation of 'orange' from the Spanish word *naranja*. And surely '*swansway*', besides meaning the river Liffey, contains a glancing reference to Proust's long, indolent novel, Englished as *Swann's Way*? And *logansome* is a mixture of *lonesome* and *logan-stone*, or rocking stone. . . . etc., etc. In order to understand the whole book the reader would have to disentangle patiently as much more of the snarled detail as he could (a part depends on private associations of Joyce's); then he would have to put together a new book, working out the relations between the details and trying to see what Joyce intended to signify. No writer could, or need, carry stylistic or linguistic experiment further than this.

When Joyce died, shortly after the publication of this book, it was time for writers in search of literary novelty and complex styles of their own to realize that the game was played out. Joyce had caught 'all the trophies of the king's royal college of sturgeons'. Meanwhile, too, Gertrude Stein had analysed conversational speech, taking it to pieces and gradually building it up again with successive studies of the word, the phrase, the sentence, the paragraph; so there was now little more to be learned about conversation. At last writers were at liberty to use prose for simple prose purposes – and not feel behind the times in doing so.

CHAPTER TEN

THE PRINCIPLES OF CLEAR STATEMENT—I

WE here record our own principles for writing prose. They are concerned partly with the secure conveyance of information and partly with its decent, or graceful, conveyance, and have been suggested by our recent examination of a great mass of miscellaneous writing. Our practice was to glance at every book or paper we found lying about and, whenever our reading pace was checked by some difficulty of expression, to note the cause. Eventually we formulated our principles after cataloguing the difficulties under forty-two general headings — twenty-five concerned with clarity of statement, and sixteen with grace of expression.

The ancient Greeks, in working out their principles for prose, found that they could not confine themselves to Orthology (a study of the proper formation of words), Accidence (a study of the grammatical relation of words) and Syntax (a study of the grammatical relation of phrases and sentences): they had to include Logic, which is the study of the proper relation of ideas. We have found the same. Logic concerns the secure conveyance of information: information containing a contradiction or an absurdity is as puzzling to the recipient as one from which relevant facts are omitted or in which ambiguities or grammatical faults occur.

We are aware that the formulation of these principles invites the objection that Principle Nine contains Principles One to Seven (those that apply most practically to the writing of messages and narratives); that Principle Twenty-Three contains Principles Seventeen to Twenty-Five, and that Principle Eight contains the whole series; but look into any carpenter's tool-bag and see how many different hammers, chisels, planes and screw-drivers he keeps there — not for ostentation or luxury, but for different sorts of job.

The twenty-five numbered principles which we formulate for clarity of statement are contained in Chapters Ten, Eleven and Twelve; the sixteen lettered principles which concern the graces of expression are contained in Chapter Thirteen.

PRINCIPLE ONE

It should always be made clear who is addressing whom, and on the subject of whom.

We shall begin with the word 'we'. Throughout this book 'we' means Robert Graves and Alan Hodge, and nobody else. The casual use of 'we' is often extremely confusing. It may mean 'we', members of a nation identifying themselves with their Government or armed forces ('we are doing very well against Italy'); or 'we', the common people protesting against the Government; or 'we', the thinking people ('we can see that this argument is invalidated by etc.'); or 'we', the writer and the particular public he addresses; or 'we', a committee or other collaborative body; or 'we', the participants in certain recorded events; or we, the Editor. Each of these uses is legitimate so long as the 'we' is clearly defined, and remains constant in sense throughout the passage in which it occurs. Every writer should be clear *wha he is* for the purpose of writing – whether himself, or the representative of a point of view, or the spokesman of a particular group. Similarly with 'you'. Every writer should envisage his potential public – which may be twenty people, two hundred, twenty thousand, or the whole wide world – and should write nothing either above or below its supposed capacity.

Religious writers are particularly capricious in their use of 'we'. Sometimes 'we' means the priesthood, sometimes the Church, sometimes sinners. If a preacher says: 'My brethren, we are all worshippers of the Devil and of Mammon,' he obviously expects his congregation to understand this as a formal expression of Christian self-abasement, not as a definition of Church policy; yet in some contexts it is not at all clear whether he is speaking as priest or as sinner.

The following is from an essay on the Elizabethan playwright, John Marston, by T. S. Eliot; he is discussing *The Tragedy of Sophonisba*:

> 'We may be asked to account, in giving this play such high place, for the fact that neither contemporary popularity nor the criticism of posterity yields any support. Well; it may be modestly suggested that in our judgements of Elizabethan plays in general we are very much influenced by Elizabethan standards. The fact that Shakespeare transcended all other poets and dramatists of the time, imposes a Shakespearean standard: whatever is of the same kind of drama as Shakespeare's, whatever may be measured by Shakespeare, however inferior to Shakespeare's it may be, is assumed to be better than whatever is of a different kind. However catholic-minded we may be in general, the moment we enter the Elizabethan period we praise or condemn plays [etc. etc.].'

The first 'we' is Mr Eliot's editorial 'we'; the 'we' in the second sentence and the 'we' in the last means all critics *except* Mr Eliot – who gives high place to *The Tragedy of Sophonisba* because, as he goes on to say, it is not Shakespearean but 'Senecal'.

Many writers avoid the direct attribution of acts or words to their authors, wherever this might possibly cause trouble or heart-burning. This often makes a passage read mysteriously. In a recent 'Sermon on Silence', by the aged Bishop of Norwich (who writes in the overterse style of Seneca), it is not clear who first made the remark about the Silent Column hinted at in the second sentence; who misapprehended or exaggerated the remark; whose good sense subsequently restored proportion; and so on throughout the passage:

> 'We hear little now of the silent column. What was first said seems to have been misapprehended or exaggerated. Good sense has subsequently restored proportion. Such good sense often leads to a wholesome reversal or disuse of formal declarations which came to be felt mistaken or out of place. The practice of law and the formulation of Church system supply examples of discarding the obsolete. No one desires to discountenance thoughtful criticism directed to quicker winning of the war or to silence anyone who has something worth hearing to say. The upshot of the discussion seems to be "Think before you speak". This will protect you from folly and regret.
>
> Once a word has been spoken it is out of control. A plan when disclosed invites criticism and ceases to be the property of the originator. Silence often gives to authority a greater weight than the spoken word. Reserve need involve nothing unfriendly or disagreeable.'

A more outspoken writer would have put:

> 'Mr Duff Cooper, the Minister of Information, who first coined the phrase "The Silent Column" has now perhaps realized that when he recommended the public so urgently to silence he had lost his sense of proportion. Perhaps he has reasoned with himself: "Must people be silenced who have something worth while to say, especially about quicker ways of winning the war than those already tried? – I should not want that to happen." At any rate, we now hear little about the Silent Column; and this is another of the many cases in which Ministerial exhortations have wisely been either withdrawn or allowed to become a dead letter. (Representatives of the Law and the Church frequently do the same thing with obsolete or mistaken formulas.)
>
> My own conclusion about silence is that people ought always to think before they speak and thus avoid saying anything regrettable: for once a word has been spoken, though it may be withdrawn, it cannot be unsaid.
>
> Silence is particularly becoming in a person who is responsible for making important decisions. If he discloses a plan before the proper time he invites criticisms which may prevent its being carried out as he intended. Often, the less a person in authority says, the more respect he earns. A reserved person is not necessarily considered unfriendly or disagreeable.'

A very frequent cause of misunderstanding is careless use of the word 'he'. The convention about 'he' or 'him' is that it refers to the person most recently mentioned, unless this happens to be someone of so little importance in the sentence that the person of most importance is obviously the 'he' in the writer's mind. For example: 'Pankerton picked up the meal sack, which happened to belong to his brother Fred; he staggered with it through the hall and disappeared in the shrubbery.' Obviously the 'he' who staggered out was Pankerton himself, not his brother Fred. But who are the different 'he's' in this passage from a pulp novel?

> 'Dave ruminated. The Lynchburg Kid was up to his old tricks, eh? He would see to it that the district was set ablaze. He couldn't afford to let him get away with that – so there'd be dirty work at the cross-roads before the night was much older.'

The best way out of difficulty would have been to write:

> 'Dave ruminated. He would see to it that the district was set ablaze now that the Lynchburg Kid was up to his old tricks. The Kid couldn't afford to let him get away with that, so there'd be dirty work at the cross-roads before the night was much older.'

Here are two other examples in which a regard for Principle One would have made for clearer prose. H. G. Wells in a newspaper article:

> 'Within recorded time there is no such thing as a complete natural man.
>
> He clips himself, he cuts himself about, he hacks bits off himself. He tattoos himself, and sticks things through his ears and nose, he wraps skins and fabrics about himself.'

Who is this 'he'? Nobody has yet been mentioned except 'a complete natural man', and even his existence has been denied. It cannot even be 'man' in general: Mr Wells' readers, for example, do not stick things through their ears and noses. 'Atticus', the Sunday columnist:

> 'So far none of the offspring of our Premiers have [*sic*] looked like emulating the younger Pitt.'

He goes on to discuss the sons of Bonar Law, Baldwin, Lloyd George, Ramsay MacDonald, but without explaining the Pitt reference. Since he does not mention Miss Megan Lloyd George or Miss Ishbel MacDonald, it may be concluded that by 'offspring' he means 'sons', and since he goes back no further in date than Lloyd George, he probably means 'our recent Premiers', not 'all our Premiers since Pitt'. The sentence would have been clearer if written:

'So far no son of any recent British Premier has looked like succeeding his father, as the younger Pitt succeeded his.'

PRINCIPLE TWO

It should always be made clear which of two or more things already mentioned is being discussed.

The following are examples of a failure to be clear in this sense. From a newspaper short-story:

'Mr Rattray used morosely to couple Charley and young Herb with Hitler and Goering, saying that he did not know which he disliked the more.'

What did Mr Rattray not know? Whether he disliked Charley more than young Herb (or contrariwise)? Or whether he disliked Charley and young Herb as a pair more than Hitler and Goering as a pair (or contrariwise)?

From Roger Coxon's biography, *Chesterfield and his Critics*:

'Criticism at its worst may hinder, and at its best hasten the rejection of a bad or the acceptance of a good trend in art; but beyond this fourfold function in the light of history criticism seems to have done little more, so far as broad movements are concerned.'

Of the eight functions mentioned, which four does he mean? The choice lies between:—the hindering of the rejection of a bad trend; the hastening of the same; the hindering of the acceptance of a good trend; the hastening of the same; the hindering of the acceptance of a bad trend; the hastening of the same; the hindering of the rejection of a good trend; the hastening of the same. One might guess that the four Mr Coxon means are:—the hindering of the rejection of a good trend; the hindering of the acceptance of a bad; the hastening of the acceptance of a good; the hastening of the rejection of a bad. But since he is speaking about the function of criticism in supplying history with movements, not about its moral function, these are not necessarily the correct four.

An interesting example of a writer making an effort to distinguish which from which, and failing in consequence to get things straight, is found in Miss L. Susan Stebbing's critique of political thought, *Thinking to Some Purpose*:

'It is instructive to compare this [analogy of Sir Arthur Eddington's] with the analogy quoted from Professor Andrade at the beginning of this chapter. Eddington does not use his analogy purely for the sake of illustration; he uses it in order to draw conclusions with regard to the nature of the external world and the nature of our knowledge about the external world.'

Miss Stebbing conscientiously repeats 'external world' perhaps because the phrase 'our knowledge about it' (which would be grammatically irreproachable, as referring to the most recently named object) might be misunderstood. She has not been quite conscientious enough. She has left out an element in her argument, by a failure to distinguish between 'knowledge of the external world' (which an animal might have) and 'knowledge of the nature of the external world' (which a thinking person might have). She probably felt, as she wrote, that 'nature of the knowledge of the nature of the external world' was an impossibly cumbersome phrase; so compromised with 'the nature of our knowledge about the external world' which reads more easily, but is not adequate to the context.

An easy way out would have been:

> 'It is instructive to compare this analogy [of Sir Arthur Eddington's] with that quoted from Professor Andrade at the beginning of this chapter. Eddington does not use his analogy for the sake of illustration, so much as for drawing conclusions with regard to the nature of the external world and to that of our knowledge of this nature.'

PRINCIPLE THREE

Every unfamiliar subject or concept should be clearly defined; and neither discussed as if the reader knew all about it already nor stylistically disguised.

It is a common defect of English critical writing that terms are not immediately defined, but alter in meaning during the argument. Art-critics, for example, write about 'significant form' in painting without explaining what the form is supposed to signify, and use it in the same context equally for 'representational' and 'abstract' pictures. They also introduce musical metaphor into their descriptions of painting – 'Mr Duncan Grant's delicious contrapuntal effects', 'the shrill arpeggios of Guevara' – without defining the extremely tenuous relation of music to painting. Literary critics use the word 'romantic' as though it had only one meaning rather than a thousand shades of meaning lying between the concepts 'derived from the Latin' and 'emotional'. Theorists of political economy are equally slipshod: they will, for example, build financial arguments on the assumption that there is only one sort of statistically recognized ton, though actually there are nine or ten. This is done less in ignorance than in self-defence: not to turn a blind eye to the difference between the ton-measure used in various sets of statistics would involve them in so much mathematical drudgery that they would fall behindhand in their theorizing. Similarly, they prefer to use 'value' as though it had a simple, evident, invariable meaning, rather than define the criterion of evaluation in each context.

The evasive use of language in official writing has been commented on in Chapter Four. Such evasion is not confined to official contexts. For example, in the following letter to the Press (1940), the Principal of Webster's College, Aberdeen, seems incapacitated by the official style from stating his case simply; (Or is he using it as a cloak for writing in what might be thought an unrealistic or even 'defeatist' strain?)

> 'Sir—The immediate issue in regard to "reprisals" would appear to be indiscriminate bombing v. objective bombing.... So long as our brave lads are sent out to bomb objectives, and thus cripple the enemy at the source, so long will they perform their duties with zeal and enthusiasm....'

What he probably means is:

> 'Sir: I trust that the Government will not order immoral counter-measures to the recent air raids. So long as our brave Scottish airmen are sent out to cripple the enemy by dropping bombs on military objectives, rather than to take reprisals against his civil population by an indiscriminate bombing of residential districts, they will perform their duties with zeal....'

Modern stylistic disguises of sense are innumerable. They range from the neo-Euphuistic novel-style to the smart-aleck style of football reporting. To take a midway example: a well-informed American professor, Louis Gottschalk, writing in modern academic style on the literary origins of the French Revolution:

> 'As for Raynal, it is Lamartine who is responsible for the statement that Marat was chiefly under his intellectual sway. Lamartine in this case as in others has allowed his poetic imagination to run away with his historical judgement. There is more cause to consider the influence of Beccaria. Though the great Italian criminologist received but scanty mention in the voluminous writings of Marat, the latter's *Plan de Législation Criminelle* resembles the former's *Traitè des Délits et des Peines* to such an extent as to have led to the accusation of plagiarism by later writers—a charge which was nevertheless not justified. But another and perhaps greater source of inspiration and knowledge for this work must certainly have been Montesquieu's *Esprit des Lois.*'

The best schooling for historians of this sort would be to make them write out their paragraphs as if they were to be cabled at a shilling a word, and then put back the 'and's and 'the's and other unimportant but comforting parts of speech. Thus:

'LARMARTINE UNTRUSTWORTHY HISTORIAN WHEN RHETORICAL FIRST STATED MARATS WRITING OVERINFLUENCED BY RAYNAL STOP LATER WRITERS UNJUSTIFIABLY ACCUSE MARAT PLAGIARIZING BECCARIA ITALIAN CRIMINOLOGIST HARDLY MENTIONED IN MARATS WORKS STOP PLAUSIBLE BECAUSE RESEMBLANCE MARATS PLAN LEGISLATION BECCARIAS TRAITE DELITS STOP ANYHOW PLAN OWES MOST MONTESQUIEUS ESPRIT LOIS.'

which would ease out again to:

'It was Lamartine, an untrustworthy historian when he was writing rhetorically, who first said that Marat's work was over-influenced by Raynal. Later writers also accuse Marat of plagiarizing Beccaria, the Italian criminologist, whom he hardly mentions in all his many writings. This is unjustified, though more plausible since there is a certain resemblance between Marat's *Plan de Législation Criminelle* and Beccaria's *Traité des Délits et des Peines*. In any case, Marat's *Plan* owes more to Montesquieu's *Esprit des Lois* than to any other work.'

A common stylistic disguise of sense is irony. Great care should be taken to let the reader know just when the ironical note is sounded and just when it ceases. An example from a letter by an evacuee girl:

'The old cat was on to me yesterday about being careful with my crusts. I bet she's careful enough with hers, the old devil. . . . I don't suppose she'd give one to a beggar-child, not if it was starving. I must waste not and want not and put everything in the savings bank for safety. I must bow down to her as if she was a little tin image. I must get out of this place before I go potty.

The three 'I must's here are not parallel. The first is the reported advice of the Old Cat; the second is the writer's ironical deduction from the tones that the Old Cat has used in giving this advice; the third is the writer's practical decision, given without irony.

Here is an example of the amusing hit-or-miss style used by highly paid columnists, in this case by Viscount Castlerosse (now the Earl of Kenmare):

'After the advertising interlude Dick Daintree returned to his old love, the City, and then when this war broke out he joined the Navy again and served under Captain Vivian, who may or may not, I am not quite sure, have served in the same term as myself at Osborne.'

Of what was Lord Castlerosse not quite sure? Whether it was perhaps a different Captain Vivian? Or whether it was perhaps a different term? Or whether it was perhaps not Osborne, but Sandhurst, or even West Point?

Here is an example of failure to work out a descriptive sentence in sufficient detail for a reader to understand it immediately. It is by Lt.-Col. G. Val Myer, F.R.I.B.A., architect to the B.B.C.:

> '[At the outset it was thought that the ideal arrangement would be to place all the studios on one floor at the top of the building.] The site of Broadcasting House, however, though picturesque in form, is irregular, which fact would have caused the studios so grouped to be of awkward shape.'

The obscurity of the second sentence is due to the following errors in expression:

> 'The site, though picturesque in form. . . .'

A site cannot have picturesque *form*: picturesque form is three-dimensional.

> '. . . though picturesque in form . . . would have caused the studios . . . to be of awkward shape.'

Here a false contrast is suggested between the picturesque form of the site and the awkward shape of the studios.

> '. . . which fact would have caused. . . .'

This is an unnecessary restatement of the subject.

Furthermore, Col. Myer has not made it clear that the studios were to be of a certain size. By building them small enough he could have made them what shape he liked. And even if he had built them of the right size, one or two of them at least could have been made the right shape. He means perhaps:

> [At the outset it was thought that the ideal arrangement would be to place all the studios on one floor at the top of the building.] But though the irregularity of the site suggested a picturesque form for Broadcasting House, it prevented me from fitting enough studios of the right size into a single storey, unless I gave some of them awkward shapes.

PRINCIPLE FOUR

There should never be any doubt left as to where *something happened or is expected to happen.*

A great many generalizations in books and newspapers are untrue because the limited locality to which they refer is not mentioned. For example:

> 'Everyone this autumn is wearing amusing antelope-skin gloves.'

This may have been true in 1934 of every woman, or almost every woman, of a certain income level in certain London districts; elsewhere it was demonstrably untrue. Fashion notes of this sort were not, however, confined to the expensive shiny-paper magazines but appeared in newspapers of the widest circulation; historians will find them most misleading. Or:

> 'Nobody has any confidence left in astrologers'

– a generalization of still more restricted application.

Or:

> 'You will find bee-orchids almost anywhere in Devon'

– meaning perhaps in a few fields in several parishes in the Torbay district of South Devon.

A typical example of failure to make a geographical situation clear occurs in a despatch from the war-correspondent of a London daily paper (March, 1941): –

> 'For over three weeks the armies of the Sudan have been sitting here on the last stretch of the Eritrean plain with what seemed to be an insurmountable obstacle before them. There, confronting them, towered a ridge of solid rock thousands of feet high – a high ridge that rose from the plain at an angle of 90 deg. and was crowned by a succession of arrow-head peaks. The only road up those peaks, and to Keren hidden between them, had been blasted out of existence by the Italians, now expert in the art of demolition. . . .
>
> Under the light of the moon shortly afterwards I moved in with our forward troops, creeping up the last stretch of passable road leading to the escarpment . . . while behind the guns rumbled up the gradients.'

This is a very confused account. We shall comment on it point by point: –

> '. . . a succession of arrow head peaks. The only road up those peaks and to Keren hidden between them. . . .'

Keren may have been hidden from the British forces by a row of peaks; or from the British forces by one row and from the Italian reserves at Asmara by another; or may have lain between two peaks of a row, or of a succession; but could not have been 'hidden between a succession of peaks'. And from where did the road run? Did it merely switchback up and down the peaks of the ridge-top before eventually turning east towards Keren? Probably what is meant is 'up the cliff crowned by those peaks', though 'a succession of peaks' suggests that they were arranged in depth, which would imply a succession of ridges, not one ridge.

'There . . . towered a ridge of rock thousands of feet high. . . .'

The next paragraph makes it clear that where the plain ended an escarpment began. An escarpment is a stretch of high land separated from low by a steep cliff. This cliff may be crowned with a ridge but cannot be a ridge itself, because the nature of an escarpment is that the ground-level on one side is much higher than that on the other; whereas a ridge slopes away more or less equally on both sides.

'. . . a high ridge which rose from the plain at an angle of 90 degrees and was crowned by a succession of . . . peaks. The only road up those peaks . . . had been blasted out of existence by the Italians. . . .'
'. . . creeping up the last stretch of passable road. . . .'
'. . . while behind the guns rumbled up the gradient.'

If, as seems possible, 'up these peaks' means 'up the cliff crowned by the peaks', what about 'blasted away'? The cliff rose vertically from the plain, and since the guns 'rumbled up the gradient' of 'the last stretch of passable road', this must have been cut slantwise up the face of the cliff. The road cannot therefore have been 'blasted out of existence'.

Probably the correspondent meant: –

'For over three weeks our army from the Sudan had been encamped at the edge of the plain from which I write this despatch, with what seemed an insurmountable obstacle towering before them – the buttress of the Eritrean escarpment. It is a cliff of solid rock, thousands of feet high, and in parts sheer precipice, crowned with a row of peaks like stone arrow-heads. These form a ridge behind which lies Keren. The only road to Keren from the plain used to slant across the cliff face (?), but the Italians, experts in demolition, blasted it away some time ago. . . .

A screen of skirmishers began to climb the cliff by moonlight . . . We moved cautiously up the last passable stretch of road that mounted from the plain to the base of the cliff. Behind us rumbled the field artillery.'

PRINCIPLE FIVE

There should never be any doubt left as to when.

History is almost valueless without dates or other indications of time. Historical novelists who begin: 'The Tartar chief quaffed his cup of blue-white *kavasse* and bounded into his saddle' or: 'Petronella knelt by the Western door of St Peter's Cathedral with a cold shaft of golden light slanting upon her white neck' ought to give indications before the first chapter is finished of the approximate year, or at least the century, in which these events are supposed to have taken place.

Even where dates do not much matter the proper sequence of events remains important. Bad reporting or bad detective-story writing consists largely in muddling the sequence of events.

The following are examples of various misleading indications of time.

From a novel by Francis Brett Young:

> 'The cruising liner swayed to her moorings alongside the quay at Naples. For ten days turbines had driven her throbbing hull, with the short respite of calls at Gibraltar and Algiers, out of the Atlantic swell into a paler, glassier sea.'

This suggests that the liner took ten days to go from, say, Cadiz to Algiers; and, to anyone weak in geography, that she met an Atlantic swell off the Algerian coast.

From an article by J. Wentworth Day:

> 'Queen Elizabeth, that wise woman who saw future truths centuries before their birth, said that London was too big.'

If Queen Elizabeth's remark was not true until nearly four centuries later, it was not a wise one. Mr Day probably meant:

> 'Queen Elizabeth, in a fit of petulance, anticipated by nearly four centuries the present complaint: "London is too big." '

From an article (1940) by F. G. S. Salisbury, the war-correspondent:

> 'More intensive bombing of Germany and an increasingly effective discouragement of day and night raiders over this country take us confidently into November – three months after Hitler's advertised conquest of Britain.'

Since this conquest had not taken place, it should have been made plain whether November was three months after the date supposed to have been assigned by Hitler to the conquest of Britain, or three months after the date on which he advertised his intention of conquering it.

From a newspaper article (Nov. 1939):

> 'Tension between states is so great that all are arming to the teeth for a conflict which as has long been known might come at any moment, which really indeed began in Spain in 1936, and has certainly begun now.'

Come, come, when *did* it begin? The sentence probably means: 'International tension had long prepared us for the European war, for which Franco's successful insurrection in Spain was the prelude, and which, with all nations arming to the teeth, has now at last begun in earnest.'

From a recent biography of Earl Granville, by Ethel Colbourn Mayne:

> There is a ballad by Sydney Dobell in which a young man is reminded, over and over again, that he comes of a doomed race: "O Keith of Ravelston, the sorrows of thy line!" Reading the *Private Correspondence of Lord Granville Leveson Gower* (*afterwards Earl Granville*), we seem to hear a kindred refrain, more cheerfully worded indeed but in the early letters no less charged with foreboding. "O Granville Leveson Gower, the glories of thy line!" For though this young man was reminded that his race was illustrious, Granville's family and friends were almost as gloomily presageful as Keith of Ravelston's apostrophist was to be.'

This is very confusing, especially the 'was to be', because it introduces two time levels, the historic and the fictional. Granted, Sydney Dobell was a poet of the Eighteen-Fifties and Earl Granville was a Regency politician; but Dobell's apostrophe was supposed to have been written in mediaeval times, and the reader has perhaps already fixed it hypothetically in the early fifteenth century — for all he knows there may have been a historical Keith of Ravelston.

From 'Parochial Memories' in a West Country newspaper:

> 'A fat man eating whelks at a barrow. An opening window shining with its panes into my eyes. The dull murmur of the sea. The whine of the hurdy-gurdy man. Sand in my shoes. Earlier than 1873, when there was no railway in the little town, manners were simple. Fishing was the main industry and nets were spread where Woolworth's emporium now stands.'

Here the writer should have dated the memories of the first five short sentences, to show whether they go back before the year 1873.

PRINCIPLE SIX

There should never be any doubt left as to how much, *or* how long.

Most recorded quantities and durations are necessarily approximate. English is a tricky language to use for approximations, because illogical conversational usage can be confused with prose usage, which is, or should be, logical. 'Infinitesimal', for example, is an adjective properly applied to the difference between the quantities 99·9 and 100 — even in journalistic prose it should not be applied to the size of a grain of dust that has stopped a watch from ticking; 'microscopic' would also be an exaggeration in this context, for though the watch-mender used a magnifying glass to examine the works, he would probably be able to see the grain without. However, there is a popular scale of emotional approximation (not to be found in any dictionary or table of measures) for estimating the comparative degrees of success in, say, catching a train. It may be legitimately used in prose and goes something like this:

Not nearly, nearly, almost, not quite, all but, just not, within an ace, within a hair's breadth – oh! by the skin of my teeth, *just*, only just, with a bit of a rush, comfortably, easily, with plenty to spare.

It could perhaps be phrased mathematically, with a scale of minutes and seconds – the ideal zero being the half-second at which the coaches begin moving out of the station too fast for even an athlete to scramble into a compartment.

Similarly, there is a popular measure of proportion, with approximate percentages as follows:

'(100 %) Mr. Jordan's fortune consisted wholly of bar-gold.
(99 %) Practically all his fortune consisted of bar-gold.
(95%) His fortune consisted almost entirely of bar-gold.
(90%) Nearly all his fortune consisted of bar-gold.
(80%) By far the greater part of his fortune consisted of bar-gold.
(70%) The greater part of his fortune consisted of bar-gold.
(60%) More than half his fortune consisted of bar-gold.
(55%) Rather more than half his fortune consisted of bar-gold.
(50%) Half his fortune consisted of bar-gold.
(45%) Nearly half his fortune consisted of bar-gold.
(40%) A large part of his fortune consisted of bar-gold.
(35%) Quite a large part of his fortune consisted of bar-gold.
(30%) A considerable part of his fortune consisted of bar-gold.
(25%) Part of his fortune consisted of bar-gold.
(15%) A small part of his fortune consisted of bar-gold.
(10%) Not much of his fortune consisted of bar-gold.
(5%) A very small part of his fortune consisted of bar-gold.
(1%) An inconsiderable part of his fortune consisted of bar-gold.
(0%) None of his fortune consisted of bar-gold.'

This simple, generally accepted, scale is confused by writers who, for dramatic effect, try to make 5% seem more than it is. For example, the late Earl of Birkenhead twice uses the same forensic trick in the following autobiographical passage:

'No inconsiderable part of my reading leisure has been spent in the company of swash-bucklers and pirates. . . . Before I was of age I had read all Scott's novels more than once. I had galloped as often with *The Three Musketeers* from Boulogne, and dived with the Count of Monte Cristo from the Chateau d'If into the midnight sea; and I cannot but believe, in reference to my own career, that no inconsiderable portion of any success which I may have achieved derives from the impulse of these magicians and the example and emulation of their heroes.'

Perhaps he means that 5% of his reading leisure was spent in the company of fictional swashbucklers and pirates, and 2% of his success was derived from his reading of Scott, Dumas and the rest. He has used this negative formula because he cannot in either case conscientiously write 'quite a large part'; and yet, remembering his novel about a swashbuckler named Ralph Rashleigh, is pretty sure that it was more than 1%. Similarly with 'more than once': he is aware that he read very few of the Waverley Novels through more than twice – perhaps only *Ivanhoe*; but 'more than once' sounds far more than 'at least twice'. In the next sentence 'as often as more than once' is a hard quantity to estimate. Perhaps it means simply 'twice'.

The following blurred sentence is from Dr. C. Alington's *A Schoolmaster's Apology.* He is writing about the learning of poems by heart:

> 'We no longer impose on our youth the gigantic tasks which an earlier generation performed with success, and it may well be that the verbal memories of our pupils suffer in proportion.'

If, say, one-third of the gigantic tasks were now imposed, the verbal memories might be said to suffer 'in proportion'. But since these tasks are no longer imposed at all, the verbal memories cannot suffer 'in proportion' – unless by being totally destroyed. The sentence should have run something like this:

> 'We do not impose on the present generation of schoolboys nearly such gigantic tasks as we once successfully performed, and perhaps, therefore, their verbal memories are proportionately weaker than ours.'

PRINCIPLE SEVEN

There should never be any doubt left as to how many.

English has many traditional figures of speech for estimating number, which have now lost their original connotations. From an early level of national experience, a 'legion' seemed a huge number of armed men. But when a speaker now says: 'The mothers who ungrudgingly do without sleep themselves, if their babies are sleepless, are a credit to the country – their name is legion', he means there are 'millions of mothers like that'. Yet a Roman legion consisted of four or five thousand men only. Similarly: 'There are a myriad grains of sand on this beach' – but a myriad is only ten thousand, and probably 'tens of millions' is intended. It is wiser to avoid such rhetorical use of numbers. The phrase 'as the stars of the sky', for example, either may mean ten thousand, which is the approximate number of stars visible to the naked eye of a person with very good sight; or it may mean the hundreds of thousands of stars seen through telescopes or registered at observatories; or it may even mean the many hundreds of millions of stars now computed by advanced physicists to be in existence.

The scale of approximate counting is: 'one or two, two or three, a few, several, a dozen or so, a score or so, a dozen or two, a score or two, a few dozen, dozens, a hundred or so, a few score, scores, a hundred or two, a few hundred, hundreds, a thousand or so, etc.'

If the impression of number is still vaguer, one uses 'many, a good many, a large number' and so on, according to the context. But there are disingenuous measures of number that ought to be avoided in writing: for example, 'handful' when not applied to nuts, blackberries, coffee-beans and similar small objects. Here are three instances of its use. From a newspaper article:

> 'Few as women M.P.s have been — a handful in comparison with their male colleagues — they have often made their mark in the House of Commons.'

If a comparison had here been made between a handful and a bucketful, it would have meant something. As a matter of fact the number of women M.P.s was then fourteen — a number which corresponds pretty well with A. L. Rowse's assessment of 'handful' in a monthly journal:

> 'Pasteur, Debussy, Degas, Pierre Curie, Mallarmé, Bergson, the two Charcots, Alexis Carrel, André Citroën, Blériot, Père de Foucauld, Saint Thérèse of Lisieux, Madame de Noailles, Sarah Bernhardt, Gaston Paris, Littré, Le Corbusier, a handful of names taken almost at random reveals the variety of talents or of genius that modern France has bred or provided a home for.'

But Mr. Rowse's handful is taken from millions, which suggests that for him a handful is not a number proportioned to a total sum as, in the M.P. context, a handful of fourteen was to six hundred. And when Mr. Mallory Browne, European Editorial Manager of the *Christian Science Monitor*, wrote (1940):

> 'Lord Lothian has been in all but a handful of the forty-eight States of the Union . . .'

it was difficult for his readers to guess whether Lord Lothian had missed out merely, say, Montana, Nebraska, and Nevada, or whole sections of the South-West and North-West amounting to twenty States or more.

G. D. H. Cole wrote in the autumn of 1939:

> 'In this spirit, presumably, Mr. Chamberlain gave the unqualified British guarantee to the Polish Government, and one forgets how many other European Governments, which he was powerless to help without Soviet aid.'

The suggestion was that Mr. Chamberlain had given so many guarantees that people lost count. In fact, guarantees were given to three countries only: to Poland, Roumania, and Greece. Mr. Cole was being disingenuous.

From a letter to the Press by John Gielgud, on the subject of Sunday theatres:

> 'Quite apart from the fact that a week of matinee performances might help to balance the Budget and encourage enterprise and employment, it seems a great pity that actors should not be allowed to serve the public at the times when the greatest majority of them are likely to have a little leisure and inclination for the theatre.'

How many is the 'greatest majority' of forty-six million people? Where there is no comparison between recorded majorities, one should say no more than 'the majority' or, by a conversational licence, 'a large majority'.

CHAPTER ELEVEN

THE PRINCIPLES OF CLEAR STATEMENT – II

PRINCIPLE EIGHT

Every word or phrase should be appropriate to its context.

THIS is a counsel of perfection. No writer of English can be sure of using exactly the right words even in a simple context, and even after twenty or thirty years of self-education. But he should at least act on the assumption that there is always an exactly right word, or combination of words, for his purpose – which he will gratefully recognize as such if it happens to occur to him; and that, though he may not always find the right word, he can at least learn by experience to avoid the quite wrong, and even the not quite wrong, ones.

The chief trouble with English is the vastness of the vocabulary, and the lack of a dictionary that, instead of presenting closely related words as roughly synonymous, clearly distinguishes them from one another. Laura Riding has written of the puzzlement of a student who wishes, for example, to find out the meaning of the word 'modify'. The dictionary gives 'alter, change'. He then turns to 'alter' and is told that it means 'change, modify'; and to 'change', and is told that it means 'alter, modify'. Until an authoritative dictionary of related meanings is published, each writer must painfully build one in his own head from his casual experience of words. The big *Oxford English Dictionary* now helps him in this task with the precedents it gives for the usages of words. He will, for instance, gather from it that 'change' is the more general word; that 'modify' is used of change in detail, usually made in answer to some objection; and that 'alter' is a more wholesale form of change than 'modify'. But there has been so much careless writing by well-known, as well as by anonymous and little-known, writers that precedents for almost any stupid choice of words can be found – as it were screw-drivers used for chisels, and contrariwise.

Take, for example, the word 'protagonist'. It first meant, 'the leading actor in a Greek drama'. Originally the Greek *dramatis personae* consisted merely of this leading actor and a 'chorus' with whom he exchanged confidences. After a time a *deuteragonist* (or second actor), a *tritagonist* (or third actor), and so on, were added. The 'protagonist' remained the leading actor. The word was first adopted into English in the seventeenth century and is still a useful one. For example:

> 'In Milton's *Paradise Lost*, as in the classical religious dramas of Spain, the Devil is the protagonist.'

But in the late nineteenth century, perhaps from a misreading of John Morley's much-quoted remark (1877): 'If social equity is not a chimaera, Marie Antoinette was the protagonist of the most execrable of causes', 'protagonist' came to mean 'leading spokesman or spokeswoman'. In the last few years it has come to be used as a pompous equivalent of 'champion':

> 'Miss Christabel Pankhurst will be remembered as one of the leading protagonists of the Women's Suffrage Movement.'

This is absurd, because either she was the protagonist, or else she played a secondary part; but this usage (which would allow twenty Princes of Denmark to appear in *Hamlet*) seems already too firmly established to be shaken. For the blunting of a useful word and the addition of an unnecessary synonym for 'champion' the 'handy dictionaries' are responsible: they give 'leading actor, spokesman', as the meaning of 'protagonist' instead of 'the leading actor or spokesman'.

Prospectuses of some Correspondence Schools of English promise richness of vocabulary, but chiefly in terms of synonyms: students, they say, will learn to speak of a strange event as an 'unusual occurrence', or a 'remarkable happening', or an 'extraordinary incident'. But students are not promised any instruction in the difference between these phrases, or even allowed to suspect that there is any difference.

A great many misuses of words arise from ignorance. An example from a novel by James Hilton:

> 'When he had been at Millstead a little while he would, he decided, import some furniture from home . . . For the immediate present a few photographs on the mantelpiece, Medici prints on the walls, a few cushions, books of course, and his innumerable undergraduate pipes and tobacco-jars, would wreak a sufficiently pleasant transformation.'

Probably Mr. Hilton believed 'wreak' to be the present infinitive of 'wrought'; but the correct form is 'work'. One may wreak harm, wrong, vengeance and similarly unpleasant things, but nothing pleasant at all.

From a novel (1937) by Dr. A. J. Cronin:

> 'The din [of the restaurant] rose and fell like a transpontine college yell.'

By 'transpontine' he probably meant 'American'; and would perhaps have written 'trans-Atlantic' if this had not been too closely associated in his mind with liners – so, as we reconstruct the story, he consulted the Thesaurus and caught at the word 'transpontine'. He evidently thought that, since *pontus* is Latin for 'sea', 'trans-pontine' must mean 'from over the sea'. It does not – it means ' over the bridges', and is derived from *pons* not *pontus.* Its only familiar usage in English is the theatrical one: it means 'on the Surrey side of the Thames from London' and, therefore, from the style of drama in vogue at the Surrey-side theatres in the middle of the nineteenth century, 'melodramatic'.

From an article by an American journalist, Paul Manning:

> 'It's when dinner is over that the real conference of the day begins. Churchill and his key dinner guests sit around in an atmosphere of heavy cigar smoke and beat and mould Britain's policy into a malleable form.'

The dictionary definition of 'malleable' is 'capable of being beaten into shape' (e.g. brass is malleable); it is a companion-word to 'fictile' which means capable of being moulded (e.g. clay is fictile) and 'ductile' which means 'capable of being drawn out thin' (e.g. tin or pure gold is ductile). Since one cannot therefore be said to mould a policy into a malleable form, still less beat it into one, perhaps he means merely 'easily manageable'.

Leading American politicians have added numerous precedents to the language from ignorance of the correct forms. President Harding coined 'normalcy' from ignorance of 'normality'. Wendell Willkie wrote:

> 'My grandparents left Germany ninety years ago, because they were Protestants against autocracy and demanded the right to live as free men.'

– as though a Protestant were one who made a *protest* rather than a *protestation* (or declaration on oath). Senator Gibson of Vermont demanded the

> '. . . expulsion of the diplomatic and consular staff of Germany, Italy, and the French Vichy Government, . . . on the ground that behind the cloak of diplomatic immunity they are conniving for our downfall.'

He apparently thought that 'connivance' was the equivalent of 'conspiracy' – perhaps because a foreman or night-watchman who 'connives', that is to say winks at, a theft or other felony committed on the premises for which he is responsible, is liable to be tried for 'conspiracy'. But to conspire for the downfall of the United States is not to 'connive' for it. Perhaps the Senator meant 'contriving our downfall'.

Thoughtlessness, rather than ignorance, accounts for the following passages. From a parish magazine:

> 'None of us is very perfect, none of us is very Christian. We are all very subject to human errancy, very dead in spirit, very lost to grace.'

The writer should have considered that there are no degrees in perfection, Christianity, subjection, death or loss. He and his fellows may be not nearly perfect, not really Christian, fully subject to errancy, long dead, or hopelessly lost; but not 'very' any of these things.

From an article by Hilaire Belloc:

> 'We see it exemplified in the cumulative effect of raids upon urban populations and of physical destruction, especially in things that cannot be quickly replaced. It is true that a corresponding attrition is going on against the enemy, and particularly in his air army.'

In the first sentence does he mean 'in things' or 'of things'? Can one be said to witness physical destruction *in* things—surely only physical decay or break-down? In the second sentence, can attrition go on *against* the enemy? 'Attrition' is a word like 'erosion'—one could hardly say that erosion was going on against a cliff. And can attrition be said to 'go on in his air army'? Surely only a process of attrition could do so? And what is an air army? Is it air-borne troops, or airmen?

From an article by the Managing Director of *The Farmer and Stockbreeder* (1941):

> 'No industry has worked greater miracles than dairy farming. It emerged from an unusually severe winter with scarcely a ripple in the continuous flow of milk to the consumer . . .'

A ripple does not necessarily imply a snag, and a sluggish stream does not ripple so much as a fast one; so that the absence of ripples does not suggest either that there was no hitch in the milk supply, or that it flowed particularly fast.

There is a class of error that is merely grammatical. Here, for example, is an extract from the minutes of a Parish Council:

> 'Resolved that the Clerk writes to the proprietors as follows: "The Council undertakes that we shall show no disposition to take precipitate action nor to object to them arranging the matter in their own way so long as it has been speedily arranged."'

Here 'writes' should, grammatically, be 'write' (with the word 'shall' understood). And 'we shall' should be 'we will', because the future tense goes: 'I shall, thou wilt, he will, we shall, you will, they will'—except in the case of a resolve, threat or undertaking, in which case it goes: 'I will, thou shalt, he shall, we will, you shall, they shall'. And 'nor' should be 'or', unless the word 'to' is omitted, because a simple alternative ruled by a negative does not need 'nor' for 'or'. And 'object to them arranging the matter' should be 'object to their arranging the matter', the hypothetic objection being not to the people, but to the arrangement. And 'so long as it has been speedily arranged' should be 'so long as it be speedily arranged', because 'so long as' imposes a condition and therefore in formal language demands a present subjunctive – not, in any case, a perfect indicative. And 'the Council undertakes that we' is an absurd change from the third person singular to the first person plural.

Emphatic words natural to conversation often lose their significance in prose. For example, Captain Liddell Hart writes in a newspaper article (November, 1940):

> 'The occupation of Roumania may prove of invaluable help in improving Germany's own petrol supplies.'

'Invaluable help' means help that is powerful or timely but not assessable in terms of financial or other value. The element of doubt in the phrase makes it inappropriate for use after 'may prove', which already denotes doubt. It would have been better to write: 'is likely to prove of great value in improving . . .'

Many words have been so debased by conversational use that they cannot be safely used in serious poetry or prose. Nathaniel Hawthorne could write in 1862, 'however awfully holy the subject'; Thomas Hood in 1845, 'Spring . . . bitter blighter'; and Tennyson in *The Princess*, 1847, 'Wan was her cheek, her blooming mantle torn'. None of these usages would be possible now. One would have to write: 'however awesomely holy the subject', 'Spring . . . bitterly blighting', 'Wan was her cheek, her flowering mantle torn'.

When the word 'dole', as a synonym for 'Unemployment Insurance Benefit', crept into Bank of England publications in the 'Thirties, a sensitive bank-official pointed out to the authorities that this was 'illiterate': 'dole', a catch-word first introduced by the *Daily Mail* in June, 1919, to mean 'Unemployed Insurance Benefit', really denoted 'charitable gifts sparingly dealt out by patrons to clients', and seemed inapplicable to payments made under an insurance scheme. The word 'illiterate' had the desired result: 'dole' was ejected. As a matter of fact, the Bank of England could have made out a good case for 'dole' as originally meaning 'a portion, especially one that belongs by right to the recipient' – in fact, 'a square deal', *deal* and *dole* being originally the same word.

PRINCIPLE NINE

No word or phrase should be ambiguous.

The most frequent cause of lost battles, political strife, and domestic understanding is ambiguity of terms in reports, orders or requests. Recrimination of the following sort has its parallel at General Head-Quarters after most lost battles, and at Party Head-Quarters after most lost elections:

Girl: Why didn't you meet me in the break, as I told you?
Boy: You weren't there, darling.
Girl: I was. I waited five minutes.
Boy: That's funny. Didn't you say outside Woolworth's?
Girl: Yes, and you weren't there.
Boy: But I was.
Girl: What? Don't tell me you were fool enough to stand outside Woolworth's when you knew I was getting my toffees at Littlewood's?
Boy: Well, you said Woolworth's. You've just said you said it. Littlewood's isn't Woolworth's.
Girl: It's the same sort of place and you know I always go there for my toffees, stupid. And if you were there, as you say, why didn't you see me as I came out of the Works? I go right past Woolworth's.
Boy: I don't know. Why didn't *you* see *me*? I was there at eleven o'clock sharp.
Girl: Eleven o'clock — no wonder! What a man!
Boy: But you said you'd nip out in your eleven o'clock.
Girl: Oh, you prize-fool! Haven't I told you and told you that in summer-time we have our eleven-o'clock at ten-thirty?

The disastrous charge of the Light Brigade at Balaclava in the Crimean War was made because of a carelessly worded order to 'charge for the guns' — meaning that some British guns which were in an exposed position should be hauled out of reach of the enemy, not that the Russian batteries should be charged. But even in the calmest times it is often very difficult to compose an English sentence that cannot possibly be misunderstood.

From the Minutes of a Borough Council Meeting:

Councillor Trafford took exception to the proposed notice at the entrance of South Park: 'No dogs must be brought to this Park except on a lead.' He pointed out that this order would not prevent an owner from releasing his pets, or pet, from a lead when once safely inside the Park.

The Chairman (*Colonel Vine*): What alternative wording would you propose, Councillor?

Councillor Trafford: 'Dogs are not allowed in this Park without leads.'

Councillor Hogg: Mr. Chairman, I object. The order should be addressed to the owners, not to the dogs.

Councillor Trafford: That is a nice point. Very well then: 'Owners of dogs are not allowed in this Park unless they keep them on leads.'

Councillor Hogg: Mr. Chairman, I object. Strictly speaking, this would prevent me as a dog-owner from leaving my dog in the back-garden at home and walking with Mrs. Hogg across the Park.

Councillor Trafford: Mr. Chairman, I suggest that our legalistic friend be asked to redraft the notice himself.

Councillor Hogg: Mr. Chairman, since Councillor Trafford finds it so difficult to improve on my original wording, I accept. 'Nobody without his dog on a lead is allowed in this Park.'

Councillor Trafford: Mr. Chairman, I object. Strictly speaking, this notice would prevent me, as a citizen who owns no dog, from walking in the Park without first acquiring one.

Councillor Hogg (with some warmth): Very simply, then: 'Dogs must be led in this Park.'

Councillor Trafford: Mr. Chairman, I object: this reads as if it were a general injunction to the Borough to lead their dogs into the Park.

Councillor Hogg interposed a remark for which he was called to order; upon his withdrawing it, it was directed to be expunged from the Minutes.

The Chairman: Councillor Trafford, Councillor Hogg has had three tries; you have had only two . . .

Councillor Trafford: 'All dogs must be kept on leads in this Park.'

The Chairman: I see Councillor Hogg rising quite rightly to raise another objection. May I anticipate him with another amendment: 'All dogs in this Park must be kept on the lead.'

This draft was put to the vote and carried unanimously, with two abstentions.

From a travel book by Ethel Mannin, 1934:

'The Socialist authorities in Vienna built cheap modern flats for the workers.'

Were they cheap to build? Or cheap to live in? Or both?

From a despatch to a London newspaper:

'An official circular, which fell into the hands of the Polish Government in London, orders the encouragement of improper literature. Dr. Goebbels hopes probably that such literature will help to break morale. It would be rather comic if there were not other methods towards the same goal.'

This probably does not mean 'If someone told me that this was the only way of breaking Polish morale, I should laugh' but 'That is not so comic as it seems at first sight, since the Germans use other, more brutal, means of breaking Polish morale.'

In a country village a certain Mrs. Hill wrote to Mrs. Sanders, a neighbour:

> 'Dear Mrs. Sanders:
> Will you kindly tell my daughter how much water-glass is a lb, as I bought mine last year and I cannot remember, and I am pickling eggs to-night for the Vicarage? And have you any apples?
> Yours
> K. HILL.'

Mrs. Sanders wrote back:

> 'Dear Mrs. Hill:
> A lb of water-glass is about as much as will go into the jam-jar I send you with my little boy. Yes, thank you, I have enough apples to last me through the winter.
> Yours,
> P. SANDERS.'

But what Mrs. Hill had meant was: 'How much does water-glass cost a pound? I have some left over from last year and don't want to charge the Vicarage an unreasonable price. And may I buy some of your apples?' This is the sort of thing that starts a village feud.

Many cases of ambiguity are due to coincidence: words to whose appropriateness in a sentence no objection could otherwise be raised form accidental misalliances with words placed near to them, and so seem to mean something entirely different. Here is an example from a pamphlet by Professor Dennis Saurat, Director of the *Institut Français* in London:

> 'In the animal races those in which the *female bears* in pain give the greater care to their young, and those races in which birth is painless show, as a rule, no affection for their offspring.'

It would have read less grotesquely as: 'the female suffers pain during parturition.'

From a *Countryman's Diary* in a newspaper:

> 'The hedges now seem less bare with the young male catkins already showing palest yellow and the elder coming into leaf.'

Since 'the elder' seems to mean 'the elder male catkins', the word 'elder-bushes' should have been used.

From a newspaper account of Red Cross work:

> Parcels had been sent on several days before this.

This would explain itself if written either as:

> Parcels had been sent on several occasions before this.

or as:

> Parcels had been sent on, several days before this.

Ambiguity occasionally arises from a difficulty, in prose, of rendering vocal inflexions; even italicizing is often insufficient. A house-owner hears the sound of breaking glass and rushes out to catch whoever threw the stone. 'Who threw that stone?' he asks a big boy who is lounging not far off. 'I can't say, Sir', the boy answers. The tone may be offhand and so convey genuine or affected ignorance, or it may be guarded and solemn and so convey an unwillingness to give evidence against another boy. Probably the householder will understand, but there is no typographical device for indicating the different tones in print. Or a girl says to an airman who has just bailed out into her father's garden: 'You may see me again'. There is no typographical device for showing whether she means, 'You have my permission to call again at our house,' or simply, 'Who knows but that we may meet again?' – though the airman will probably understand. This sort of ambiguity occurs occasionally in newspaper reports from police-courts. For example:

> 'Summoned at Tunbridge Wells yesterday for speeding at 53 miles an hour through a main street of the town, John Shorter of Brightlington Road, Crofton Park, S.E.4, wrote: "A clear road and a pretty girl waiting at the other end proved too great a temptation for me."
>
> Shorter, who has since joined the R.A.F., was fined £1, the Mayor (Alderman C. E. Westbrook) remarking: "In the circumstances we cannot be too drastic." '

Since the fine does not appear either very heavy or very light, the reader will not know whether the Mayor meant 'In these atrocious circumstances, even the heaviest fine I might impose would not be undeserved': or, 'So charming an excuse disarms me: I cannot impose so heavy a fine as I usually do.'

PRINCIPLE TEN

Every word or phrase should be in its right place in the sentence.

Perhaps the most frequently misplaced word in English is 'only'. In conversation the speaker's accent would make it perfectly plain, for example, what was meant by:

'The Council are only warned to do their own repairs.'

When this is recorded on paper it may mean either: 'The Council are only warned (not instructed) to do their own repairs' or 'Only the Council (not individual householders) are warned to do their own repairs.' But what it is intended to mean is perhaps: 'The Council are warned to do only their own repairs (not repairs for which they are not legally responsible).'

'Either' is another word frequently misplaced. From a written commentary (1941) by Raymond Gram Swing:

> 'The Atlantic, as far as Iceland, either will be left alone by Axis warships, or the United States will be in the shooting war....'

It should have been:

> 'Either the Atlantic as far as Iceland will be left alone by Axis warships, or the United States will be in the shooting war....'

Here are other miscellaneous examples of misplaced words or phrases.

From a newspaper 'short':

> 'Latest reports show that 28,306 children do not go to school in England. More than 4½ million are getting full-time instruction, 72,505 are receiving part-time schooling.'

Far more than 28,306 children do not go to school in England; but in England 28,306 children do not go to school.

From Captain Arthur Cotterell's *It's Nice to be in the Army:*

> 'About 15 p.c. of men will delay reporting sick too long. Sergeant-majors usually arrive to report sick feet first.'

This means:

> 'About 15 p.c. of men will delay too long before reporting sick. Sergeant-majors usually arrive feet first to report sick.'

From a newspaper leader:

> 'Mussolini accused the Fuehrer of having lost the war by attacking unnecessarily Soviet Russia.'

Was Russia unnecessarily Soviet?

From a despatch to a London newspaper:

> 'Señor Suñer was not convinced that even the German people believed in the success of German arms, but were dejected under the Nazi regime.'

He means:

'Señor Suñer was convinced that even the German people did not believe in the success of German arms and were dejected under the Nazi regime.'

PRINCIPLE ELEVEN

No unintentional contrast between two ideas should be allowed to suggest itself.

Unintentional contrasts are often due to elegant variation of a descriptive phrase.

The following is from a newspaper report:

'Mrs. Gwendolen Foster, a member of the theatrical profession, prayed for the dissolution of her marriage with Mr. Basil Foster, an actor.'

This falsely suggests that Mrs. Foster was not an actress, but a dresser, a programme-girl, a prompter, or the like.

From a despatch by the New York correspondent of a London weekly:

'Writers favouring Mr. Willkie crossed swords with authors who are for Roosevelt.'

Since the word 'author' is somewhat grander than 'writer' the suggestion is that the more successful writers were Democrats.

From an Exchange Telegraph report (1926):

'On entering the Guildhall, Mr. Lloyd George was enthusiastically cheered, while Lord Oxford was accorded a great ovation.'

The reader wonders which of the two received the louder applause.

From a novel by Ernest Raymond:

'Soon Clara Shepherd appeared, but he could not have stated the details of her dress, his awareness of his wife's clothes being always in inverse ratio to his consciousness of his own.'

The apparent contrasts between 'Clara Shepherd' and 'his wife' and between 'awareness' and 'consciousness' could both have been avoided.

'Soon his wife, Clara, appeared, but he could not have described her dress offhand: the more conscious he was of his own clothes the less he always was of hers.'

The phrases 'in inverse ratio to' and 'varying inversely with' are unnecessary and cumbersome in any except mathematical contexts. The rhyme:

> 'A wise old bird sat on an oak;
> The more he heard the less he spoke;
> The less he spoke the more he heard.
> Let us not joke at that old bird'

does not read more precisely when changed to:

> 'Upon an oak sat a wise old bird;
> What he spoke was in inverse ratio to what he heard;
> What he heard varied inversely with what he spoke.
> At that wise bird let us not joke.'

PRINCIPLE TWELVE

Unless for rhetorical emphasis, or necessary recapitulation, no idea should be presented more than once in the same prose passage.

Rhetoricians often use a key-word or phrase three times to make it seem holy, important or indisputably true. But, apart from this hoary device, repetitiveness is nowadays considered a sign of pauperdom in oratory, and of feeble mindedness in narrative.

Undisguised repetition needs no illustration; but here are various examples of concealed repetition. From a published speech by Neville Chamberlain:

> 'We want to see established an international order based upon mutual understanding and mutual confidence, and we cannot build such an order unless it conforms to certain principles which are essential to the establishment of confidence and trust.'

When we remove the repeated ideas, this passage reduces to:

> 'The international order that we wish to establish must conform to certain principles of mutual understanding and trust.'

From an article by J. Wentworth Day, the agricultural expert:

> 'To-day, the difficulties of defending . . . Greater London have taught us the lesson that to defend the Capital, we must go to the lengths and expense of defence and strategy enough to defend a small country, let alone a great city. . . . That is merely one example of many which I could multiply.'

This reduces to:

> 'We have now learned that the defence of Greater London raises strategic and financial problems that suggest a small country rather than a city. . . . I could quote many such examples.'

From a leader (1941) by J. A. Spender:

> 'We are to Russia, as she is to us, one of the imponderables which cannot be weighed in the ordinary diplomatic scales.'

This reduces either to:

> 'Russia is to us, as we are to her, an imponderable diplomatic problem.'

Or to:

> 'Russia cannot weigh us, nor we her, in the ordinary diplomatic scales.'

From '*The Sleeping Beauty* at the London Alhambra', by Sacheverell Sitwell:

> '... But the prospect of five scenes and three hundred dresses by Leon Bakst was in thrilling anticipation for me.'

Here, 'was in thrilling anticipation for me' should have been merely 'thrilled me'.

From a novel by Norah James:

> ' "Yes, sir, I'll see to it," she answered and put another gleaming plate on the pile that was rising at her side in a shining mound.'

This reduces to:

> ' "Yes, sir, I'll see to it." And she added another plate to the gleaming pile at her side.'

From G. K. Chesterton's *Sketch of Dickens*:

> 'But it is true to say that his whole soul was seldom in anything about which he was wholly serious.'

This reduces to:

> 'But he was seldom wholly serious about anything.'

PRINCIPLE THIRTEEN

No statement should be self-evident.

Platitudes, such as 'all flesh is grass'; 'all men are liars'; 'the Law is an ass' – must be distinguished from 'tautological', or self-evident, statements, such as 'every mortal man must die', 'No liars speak the truth', 'Foolish old men often do foolish things'.

A typical example of tautology is a Departmental Minute (1930):

> 'Minutes are not to be written in illegitimate places.'

i.e. 'Minutes must not be written in places where they must not be written'. What was perhaps meant was: 'Minutes are not to be written on odd slips of paper, or anywhere but on the Minute sheets provided.'

From a book-review in a Church newspaper:

> 'In the contents of *Bells and Grass* (Faber, 7s. 6d.) the best of old and new are an expression of spontaneous delight in things that are of inestimable value, but have no price.'

All things with no price in this metaphorical sense are of inestimable value.

PRINCIPLE FOURTEEN

No important detail should be omitted from any phrase, sentence or paragraph.

The common sense or the knowledge of the prospective reader must be accurately gauged. It would not be enough, for example, to tell a semi-educated audience that in 1825 the journey from Rome to Venice took from a week to ten days, without reminding them that railways had not yet been built in Italy. Even an educated audience would expect to be told (or reminded) what was the distance by road from Rome to Venice, what was the normal means of conveyance — coach all the way? or horseback for part of it? — and what natural obstacles lay between the two cities.

The following are miscellaneous examples of the omission of relevant detail, a fault usually due to the writer's impatience to get something down on paper.

From a gardening handbook:

> 'Light soils — i.e. soils light to the spade and not in colour — quickly lose their moisture.'

But soil may be both light to the spade and light in colour. The word 'necessarily' should have been inserted after 'not'.

From a newspaper article:

> 'Fires in workshops and factories operating for the Reich are every-day affairs. By one means or another, the output has been brought down in many cases from 40 to 60 per cent.'

The omission of the word 'by' before '40 to 60 per cent' makes nonsense of the second sentence.

From a novel by Edith Bagnold:

> 'Round and round went the horses, and the rain down Velvet's neck.'

This means: 'and the rain went down Velvet's neck.' The rain did not go round and round down Velvet's neck.

From a statement by Admiral of the Fleet Lord Chatfield (1941):

> 'The longer the war lasts, the more certain it will be that the land forces will be essential for ultimate victory, quite apart from our imperial dangers now.'

This probably means:

> 'We need a strong army now for imperial defence, and the longer the war lasts the more evident it will be that ultimate victory can only be won by attacking the enemy on the Continent of Europe with a very strong army indeed.'

From a newspaper article:

> '... Everywhere the town is a magnet to young people, and the drift from the land in many parts of the world is a problem for farmers and for governments.'

The problem is incompletely stated: 'the drift from the land' is not a problem, but a fact. The problem may be how it is caused, or how it is to be checked, or how many young people who have already drifted away are to be recalled. Such incomplete statements are influenced by newspaper headings: e.g. 'The Drift from the Land – Problem for Farmers'. (Note also the misplaced phrase. The last clause should have run: 'and the drift from the land is a problem for farmers, and for governments, in many parts of the world.')

From a newspaper leader (1940):

> 'The friendly onlooker is confident that whatever they have to endure the British will ... find the way of turning the tables on their enemy. He anticipates what the Prime Minister said on Tuesday.'

This probably means:

> '... He anticipates that the prophecy made by the Prime Minister on Tuesday will be fulfilled.'

From a newspaper item:

> 'Antique lace, much of it of great value and dating back to the early seventeenth century, which has been collected to go to America, was on view in London yesterday. A party is to be given at the British Embassy in Washington in November to show the lace. It will afterwards be sold free of expense in the principal American stores.'

Free of expense to whom? The donors, the stores, or the customers?

PRINCIPLE FIFTEEN

No phrase should be allowed to raise expectations that are not fulfilled.

Writers often begin a sentence with, say, 'Turning to cheese', or 'When we come to consider cheese,' and then, leaving this phrase in the air, continue with 'the protein content varies considerably from sample to sample', or, more grotesquely, with 'Professor Queso has listed over a thousand distinct European varieties of the cream cheese'.

From a fishmonger's letters:

'Referring to your kind enquiry, you may expect the lobsters by the first delivery on the 15th instant.'

and

'Referring to your further kind enquiry, the lobsters will arrive by the first delivery on the 16th instant.'

In the first case, it is the person addressed who seems to be referring to the enquiry; in the second case, it seems to be the lobsters.

From a novel by Somerset Maughan:

'Bathing as they did three or four times a day, he could not get his hair to stay down, and the moment it was dry it spread over his head in unruly curls.'

The 'they' is two boys and a man called Tom. Perhaps what is meant is:

'It is hard for anyone who bathes, as they did, three or four times a day, and has unruly hair, to get it to stay down. Tom couldn't, and the moment it was dry, it spread over his head in curls.'

From a travel pamphlet:

'Kenya is a land of contrasts. On the one hand you meet with the highest refinements of educated English society, and the next moment you find yourself confronted with a picturesque savage whose chief pleasures in life are to hunt lions with a spear and feed on raw flesh.'

Here the reader will not perhaps realize that the contrast has already been made, and will expect an 'On the other hand' in a later sentence.

The following is from Field-Marshal Lord Birdwood's memoirs, *Khaki and Gown*:

'So far from being a stern and unsympathetic man of the kind repellent to children, I well remember how, when our son was a small boy of about five, we were at a Garden Party at Viceregal Lodge in Simla, when suddenly there was a large crash. This frightened Chris, who at once ran up to Lord Kitchener, seizing his hand and standing close to him for protection — a gesture which evidently pleased him enormously at the time.'

Rejecting the possibility that either Lord Birdwood himself or 'our son' is the subject of 'So far from being an unsympathetic man', one reads on, in search of a suitable subject — until the sentence ends disappointingly with 'a large crash'.

Lord Birdwood should have written something of this sort:

'Lord Kitchener was by no means a stern and unsympathetic man of the kind repellent to children, as the following incident proves. At a Garden Party at Viceregal Lodge in Simla, when our son Chris was about five, there was a sudden loud crash . . . etc.'

PRINCIPLE SIXTEEN

No theme should be suddenly abandoned.

We separate this Principle from Principle Fourteen, 'No important detail should be omitted from any phrase, sentence or paragraph', because disappointed anticipation may cause readers who would not baulk at a simple omission to lose track of an argument or narrative.

From a boys' adventure story:

'There were five of us in the long boat — Henri, Allen, Sophocles, Big Otter and myself. Well, I needn't describe myself — you'll soon see the sort of man I was in those days. But at any rate Henri was a big square-jawed argumentative French-Canadian, weighing about two hundred pounds, Sophocles was a fat, greasy little Greek cook with a genius for savoury rice dishes, and Big Otter was a Seminole Indian, the bravest man I ever met. We shipped a lot of water the first day, for the sea was still a bit rough.'

What about Allen? Until the boy reading the story has Allen securely placed he will feel the same sort of discontent as when he knows, by an unsatisfied feeling in his mouth, that he did not quite finish eating his apple and yet cannot remember where he has laid it down.

From a literary article in a provincial paper:

'The change in Foster's mentality is to be seen, as we read these letters of the years 1881-93, both in the literary composition and in the handwriting. The sprawling "a's" and "u's", the grotesque capitals, the hobbledehoy loops to the "g's" and the "y's", give place to a neat and clerkly script, with the capitals modelled exactly on those of contemporary copperplate. In 1894 he married Letitia Fareham.'

What about Foster's literary composition?

CHAPTER TWELVE

THE PRINCIPLES OF CLEAR STATEMENT—III

PRINCIPLE SEVENTEEN

Sentences and paragraphs should be linked together logically and intelligibly.

It should always be clear whether a sentence explains, amplifies or limits the statement that it follows; or whether it introduces either a new subject, or a new heading of the original subject.

From a newspaper feature, *All the Year Round in Your Garden*:

> 'Picking over seed-potatoes in the potting shed is a pleasant job. You will find many with ugly blotches and scabs and not be sure whether they will favour your prospects of a good crop. . . .'

The connection between these two sentences is blurred. Either the second should begin a new paragraph, to show that the gardener's anxieties about his crop do not illustrate the pleasantness of the job; or else it should be introduced with a 'But'.

From memoirs published in a provincial paper:

> 'On leaving the hospital of Saint Antoine, I remember, the Empress Eugénie was carried almost to her carriage by the crowd, who eagerly pressed around her, weeping, kissing her hands and heaping blessings on her head. But the most comical event of the day was when a coal-black negro from Dahomey presented himself at the Palace with a basket of freshly caught fish. . . .'

Here the 'But' is illogical, because it suggests that the simple enthusiasm of the crowd was also comical.

From a book-review by Basil de Sélincourt:

> 'Having loved Ruskin unsubdued, he [Sydney Cockerell] was ready to love and be loved by everybody; as the girl friend who later became a nun wrote to him from her novice cell: "You do seem to have a remarkable capacity for meeting distinguished people." That is it; they are all here; Hardy, Doughty, Lawrence, Blunt, Mrs. Hardy, Lady Burne-Jones, Charlotte Mew. . . .'

The phrase 'as the girl friend wrote' purports to justify the statement that Sydney Cockerell was ready to love and be loved by *everyone*; but all that it provides is a (possibly ironical) reference to his being ready to love and be loved by distinguished people.

Here is part of an article by Admiral C. J. Eyres:

> 'The Germans in the last war, in the use of lethal gas and unrestricted submarine warfare, acted disgracefully and immorally, just because the German Government had formally, by Treaty, denounced their use, and were dishonouring their bond.'

The 'just because' should be 'for' or 'since'. Either of these words would explain why the Admiral considered the Germans to have acted 'disgracefully and immorally'. The 'because' suggests that the motive for the Germans' disgraceful and immoral actions was merely to flout a previous renunciation by their Government of the use of certain weapons. (He probably means 'renounced', not 'denounced'.)

From an address to the University of Oxford by Viscount Halifax, its Chancellor:

> 'What has, for example, been the driving force behind the Nazi movement in Germany? It has been German youth. . . . Their point of view stands in stark opposition to yours. They do not understand your way of thinking. Your ideals mean nothing to them. . . .
>
> The real conflict, therefore, to-day is not between age and youth, but between youth and youth. . . .'

The 'therefore' is illogical, unless Lord Halifax is washing his hands of the conflict on the ground that it is not of his making.

PRINCIPLE EIGHTEEN

Punctuation should be consistent and should denote quality of connexion, rather than length of pause, between sentences or parts of sentences.

There is a widespread ignorance among writers of English as to the use and usages of punctuation. Many of them leave their commas, semi-colons, and the rest of the more difficult signs, to be corrected by their typists, or by the printers. The trouble is that there are two conventions for English punctuation, which contradict each other. The older convention is that punctuation-marks denote duration of pause between parts of a sentence or paragraph. This was stated as follows by J. Mason in his *Elocution* (1748): 'A comma stops the voice while we may privately tell one, a semi-colon, two; a colon three; and a period four.' (Here 'period' means 'full stop'.) The more sensible and more modern convention, which we recommend, is that all punctuation-marks that do not (like the question and the exclamation mark) merely denote tone of voice, show in what relation to one another sentences, or parts of a sentence, are intended by the writer to stand.

The Comma

The original meaning of 'comma' is not the tadpole-like comma-sign, but a distinct part of a sentence, which should be cut off from the other parts by comma-signs. If the part to be cut off comes in the middle of a sentence, as in this one, a pair of comma-signs is put to show how much is being cut off. But a part cut off from the beginning or end of a sentence has only one comma sign, as in this case. The cutting-off of part of a sentence prevents two or more parts from running together in a way that might disturb the sense.

The commonest example of sense being disturbed by the omission of a comma is a sentence containing 'because'. 'I did not go to the party, because I was not wanted' means that I did not go, and that my reason for not going was that I was not wanted. But 'I did not go to the party because I was not wanted' means that I *did* go, but that my reason for going was not that I wished to spite the people there who did not want me to go.

Here is a rather complicated example of a 'because' sentence, taken from J. W. N. Sullivan's *Bases of Modern Science*, 1928:

> 'Our aesthetic and religious experiences need not lose the significance they appear to have merely because they are not taken into account in the scientific scheme.'

This might mean:

> 'Our aesthetic and religious experiences need not have their apparent significance cancelled by the mere failure of Science to include them in its scheme.'

Or, less probably, it might mean:

> 'Our aesthetic and religious experiences need not lose the appearance of significance which is given them by the mere failure of Science to include them in its scheme.'

If Mr. Sullivan, wishing to prevent his readers from taking the second of these two alternatives, had put a comma at 'have', then he would have offered them a third and still more improbable meaning:

> 'Why our religious and aesthetic experiences need not lose their apparent significance is merely that Science has failed to include them in its scheme.'

How, then, should he have punctuated the sentence? He should have written it along the lines of one or the other of our first two alternative versions.

Here is a typical example of under-punctuation from a newspaper:

> 'Harton Miners' Lodge have sent a protest to the Durham Miners' Association because a number of ex-miners transferred a month ago to Harton Collieries from vital war work under the Government back to the pit scheme and since drawing the guaranteed wage of £3 9s. without having any work to do were given fourteen days' notice immediately they were put on the pay-roll.

To help the reader to pick his way through this long but well constructed sentence there should have been commas after 'ex-miners' and 'work to do' and 'back to the pit' should have been 'back-to-the-pit'.

Here is an example of over-punctuation, which is far less often found, from a leader by Edward Hulton in his *Picture Post*:

> 'The world has long, in fact, been, whether we like it or no, not really a series of countries, but one country in a state of grave disharmony.'

Each of these commas can be justified, but when a sentence comes so thickly studded as this it should be rewritten in a simpler way. For example:

> 'Whether we like it or no, the world has in fact long been a single country in a state of grave disharmony, not an aggregate of mutually hostile countries.'

The Long Dash

In some cases, comma-signs are not quite strong enough to mark the cutting-off of part of a sentence from the remainder. Where a very strong separation has to be made between a part and the main body of the sentence, the long dash can be used. Take, for example, the news-item:

> 'Only one house in the row was left standing with all its windows intact.'

The sense of the context in which this sentence occurred proved that it meant:

> 'Only one house in the row was left standing, but this was undamaged: it even had all its windows intact.'

not:

> 'Only one house, of those left standing in the row, had its windows intact.'

A comma after 'standing', in the original version, would not have done justice to this freak occurrence. Instead, a long dash was needed, thus:

> 'Only one house in the row was left standing – with all its windows intact.'

Here is another news item, which at first sight reads mysteriously:

> 'Ex-Sergt. Oliver Brooks, V.C., hero of Loos, who has died at Windsor, aged 51, was decorated by King George V, who was in bed in a train following the accident when he fell from his horse in France.'

No, the train was not following Sergt. Brooks' accidental tumble from his horse in France; neither was King George V. The facts were: that King George was in bed in a hospital train as the result of falling from his horse while reviewing troops in France, and that he called Sergt. Brooks to his bedside for a decoration ceremony. But it would not be enough to put a comma after 'train': a long dash is needed to show that the rest of the sentence is another story tacked on to the account of the bedside decoration.

The long dash is also used to join together short sentences of headings which do not quite deserve a full stop. For example:

> 'I have been in such trouble lately – Mrs. Purdell calling about the little shoes – not done, of course – and then a load of soot falls down the chimney, bang on top of the muffins warming in the grate – how the lodger carried on! – and I lost my wedding ring, washing – it was twenty-two carat gold – and now this!'

The Parenthesis

Another substitute for the comma is the parenthesis. Parenthesis-signs are always used in pairs. They denote an explanatory comment or aside of such a sort that, in speaking, one would naturally lower one's voice slightly to show that the comment was not part of the main argument of the sentence. Where the explanatory comment does not need this lowering of the voice, it is customarily put between long dashes. Thus:

> 'Mr. Hollins (he always seemed "Mr." to me, even when he was an Earl) nodded to us in his friendly way.'

But:

> 'Mr. Hollins – generous, open-hearted Mr. Hollins! – nodded at us in his friendly way.'

Parenthesis-signs are curved, brackets are rectangular. Brackets are used for critical interpolations: that is, for explanatory or corrective remarks inserted by an author in a passage quoted from someone else's work or from previous work of his own. Thus:

> 'Young William Hunter wrote: "It is easy to be a Company man" [this was while the East India Company still ruled in Calcutta] "and yet be superior to the common run; but it is impossible to be first class and fritter your evenings away in walking cuadrills [sic] and consuming ices".'

When one parenthetical remark occurs within another, brackets are sometimes used to prevent the reader getting confused between them; but this practice is not to be recommended, because the brackets then seem to be enclosing a critical interpolation. If one has to put one parenthetical remark within another (for example, in the present – admittedly rather clumsy – instance) it is more safely enclosed between long dashes, as here.

The Full-Stop

A full-stop, also called a 'period', ends a sentence. (If the sentence does not end, what seems to be a full-stop is merely a single dot. We will discuss the dot separately.) There are degrees in the value of full-stops. Sentences end with full-stops; but when paragraphs end with full-stops the rest of the line is left blank – the next paragraph beginning on the following line, after a slight space (or 'indentation') which indicates that this is a new paragraph. A paragraph should concern only one phase of a narrative or argument. This phase may be large or small, but must be self-contained. In a novel, for example, a paragraph may contain either a brief summary of the heroine's early life (or declining years), or merely perhaps a complete account of her reflections as she passed on some occasion from the music-room to the conservatory. In a critical work, it may contain, for example, a concise account of Shakespearean forgeries in the Eighteenth Century, or merely, perhaps, one self-contained part of an argument intended to prove that Ireland, one of the forgers, possessed a copy of the *Hamlet* First Quarto.

The newspaper practice of trying to brighten an article by printing ordinary sentences as if they were paragraphs often confuses the reader: he does not know where one subject ends and another begins. The following is an example of 'false paragraphing' (1941):

> 'According to the Nazi High Command, German forces, driving from Gomel across the Desna River and from the Dnieper on both sides of Kremenchug, have met at a point 130 miles east of Kiev. The Germans say that four Soviet armies have been caught between the arms of these giant pincers.
>
> Even if the German claim is true, it will take them weeks to mop up

the Russians in the huge area enclosed in the pincers. Already their advance has been slow, painful and costly in the extreme.

This is shown in the Berlin admission that at many points the Russians are still launching fierce counter-attacks across the Dnieper and in a Moscow report that a German troop-train with ammunition was blown up by Russian bombers near Dniepropetrovsk.

Meanwhile, Marshal Timoshenko's victories at Yelnva and Yartsevo in the Smolensk region have removed, at least temporarily, the direct German threat to Moscow.

In one sector alone his forces have destroyed 60 Nazi tanks in the last four days, and during eight days fighting the Nazis lost 10,000 dead and wounded.'

The impropriety of the paragraphing here is seen in the fifth sentence. Because it begins a paragraph, 'This is shown' seems at first sight to relate to the prophecy made in the third sentence, that the Germans will take weeks to mop up the Kiev armies — rather than to the historical comment, made in the fourth sentence, that they have been meeting with great difficulties in their Ukraine offensive considered as a whole. With proper paragraphing the passage would have read as follows:

'According to the Nazi High Command, German forces, driving from Gomel across the Desna River and from the Dnieper on both sides of Kremenchug, have met at a point 130 miles east of Kiev. The Germans say that four Soviet armies have been caught between the arms of these giant pincers. Even if their claim is true, it will take weeks to mop up the Russians in the huge area enclosed by the pincers.

Already their general advance in the Ukraine has been slow, painful and costly in the extreme. This is shown in the Berlin admission that at many points the Russians are still launching fierce counter-attacks across to the west bank of the Dnieper, and in a Moscow report that a German troop train with ammunition was blown up by Russian bombers near Dniepropetrovsk.

Meanwhile, Marshal Timoshenko's victories at Yelnya and Yartsevo in the Smolensk region have removed, at least temporarily, the direct German threat to Moscow. In one sector alone his forces have destroyed 60 Nazi tanks in four days and during eight days' fighting the Nazis lost 10,000 dead and wounded.'

It is sometimes said that one should never start a sentence with 'And' or 'But' — that these conjunctions are only for internal use. This is not so. One may start a sentence with 'But' if to tack it on to the previous sentence after a semi-colon would not be appropriate. For example:

'Uther ap Mathonwy was King of Thulë. According to Gandolph the Jongleur he lived in a palace wholly paved with gilt ginger-bread and hard plum-cake. But this is not the Thulë of Heine's ballad: it is situated rather within the confines of fabulous Cockagne.'

Here it would have been wrong to tack on the third sentence to the second, since the 'But' refers back to the first.

Similarly:

> 'Uther died of grief in his palace after the loss of his daughter Reynardine who accidentally swallowed fern-seed and disappeared from mortal gaze. (According to Gandolph, the fern-seed had been brought in on a careless page's hunting-shoes and trodden into the gingerbread and plum-cake.) And that was the end of the Royal House of Thulë.'

Here it would have been wrong to tack the third sentence on to the second, not only because there are already two 'and's' in the last seven words, but because 'And that was the end' refers to Uther's death, not to the page's carelessness. And the word 'And' could not be omitted without a loss of narrative grace. One should not, however, begin a paragraph with an 'And' or a 'But'. If one did, it would mean that the preceding paragraph was not a complete one.

The Asterisk

A row of asterisks implies an omission. It may be an omission that cannot be avoided — as, for example, in the following passage:

> 'The letter as it survived the fire was only decipherable in places. It ran:
>
> Dear Godf * * * have you really broken off * * * coming as it does between the first squalid app * * * but never mind — all will be well, when all is forgotten.
>
> Your loving Sally.
>
> P.S. The kitten swall * * *'

Or it may be a deliberate omission, especially where intimate narrative details are left for the reader to supply. For example:

> ' "It is our marriage-night," he mumbled in confusion.
>
> Very deliberately she came over to him, kissed him dispassionately, sat on the edge of the poor iron bedstead, and began briskly to unlace her shoes.
>
> * * *

The Dot

Single dots are used to mark the end of an abbreviated word, such as 'Mr.', 'etc.', 'Ltd.'. A row of dots has two legitimate significances: either that the person who is supposed to be speaking is hesitating with 'er . . .

um . . . er', or that it would be tedious or irrelvant for the writer to write out the sentence or paragraph in full.

For example:

' "Let me see . . .", Mr. Quennell remarked, "it would be . . . yes . . . seventeen . . . no! exactly eighteen shillings! Thank you, Madam, I'm sure!" '

Or:

'The law provided that: "any person found guilty under the aforesaid Act of killing or maiming any domestic animal, to wit, horse, mare, gelding, mule, hinny . . . hound or dog, shall be mulcted of fifteen marks, unless aforesaid person be a knight of the shire, burgess, pot-walloper . . . or yeoman worth £10, and shall be confined to the stocks for the space of thirty-six hours, where the beadle shall be at pains . . ." '

The Exclamation Mark

Exclamation marks, also called 'notes of admiration', should be sparingly used. Queen Victoria used so many of them in her letters that a sentence by her that ends with a mere full-stop seems hardly worth reading. Exclamation marks do not necessarily close a sentence, as a full stop does. For example:

'And then, horror! in marched Mrs. Blackstone with the little corpse held out accusingly between the pincers of the kitchen fire-tongs!'

The Question Mark

A question mark, similarly, can appear in the middle of a sentence without necessarily ending it. For example:

'That she had asked herself, was he really there? or was she imagining things? now troubled her conscience.'

The Semi-Colon and the Colon

A sentence joined only with commas (or the equivalent of commas in parenthesis-signs, brackets, long dashes and the like) is a single sentence. But sentences are often twins, triplets or even quintuplets, sextuplets and septuplets — semi-colons and colons make them so. A 'colon' originally meant a separate limb of a sentence, as a 'comma' was a piece cut off from the limb or trunk.

In modern usage, a semi-colon is no longer a pause of the time-value of half a colon — or two-thirds, as Mason suggested: it has an entirely different function. The chief modern distinction between a semi-colon and a colon is that parallel statements, if united in the same sentence to show their close connection, are (as in this sentence) separated with a semi-colon; whereas two statements, the second of which is looked forward to by the first, are separated with a colon. Examples:

> 'Mr. Jones went laughing up the hill; Mrs. Jones, in tears, down to the mill-pond. The dew was heavy on the grass of Farmer Turvey's four-acre field; above her head no stars were visible; somewhere an owl hooted. An idea entered Mrs. Jones' puzzled pate: she would refresh herself with a few drops of old and mild. She called out: "Child, child, run home and fetch me a pot of beer!" But it was not a child after all, as it proved: it was only the village pump!'

Care should be taken, when using colons and semi-colons in the same sentence, that the reader understands how far the force of each sign carries. Take, for example, the following sentence:

> 'It was as I anticipated: the *Friendship* came up with the rest of the fleet at about six bells; the privateer then thought better of it and sheered off, lying about two leagues to windward.'

Here the reader would not know whether the narrator had anticipated merely that the *Friendship* would come up with the rest of the fleet, or also that the privateer would then sheer off. A full stop at 'six bells' would make things clear.

A long dash may be put after a colon, for emphasis. For example:

> 'The Captain arose and said: "Come, Antonio, amuse the men, and tell them one of your favourite stories!" Antonio, arose, rolled the quid from side to side in his coarse mouth and, after a pause, began thus:—
>
> "About the year 1874, in Lisbon . . ." '

Commas may do the work of colons and semi-colons in very short sentences. For example:

> 'He ran off, I followed. He stumbled and fell, I overtook him. He cried, "Are you mad?" I assured him, "Certainly I am not."

In each of the first two of these sentences the comma should, strictly, have been a semi-colon; in each of the last three, it should have been a colon. (In German no such relaxation is permitted: the colons and semi-colons would have to be used.)

The Hyphen

The hyphen is used to link words which, if separated, might possibly have some other meaning than the one intended, or confuse the reader's eye.

The following is an example of an obvious lack of hyphens, from an American antique-dealers' journal:

> 'High prices are still paid for pre-Christian Seltzer Pennsylvania Dutch chests, if painted with flowers in the *fractur* style.'

These were not pre-Christian Dutch chests. Christian Seltzer was a late-eighteenth-century painter of chests, fire-boards and such-like for the 'Dutch', or Germans, of Pennsylvania. The sentence should therefore have run:

> 'High prices are still paid for pre-Christian-Seltzer Pennsylvania-Dutch chests, if painted with flowers in the *fractur* style.'

The accidental omission or insertion of a hyphen often makes nonsense of a passage:

> 'In the Southern States slave-owners of property were expected to give their masters a proportion of its yield.'

Here 'slave-owners' should be 'slave owners' – i.e. slaves who were owners of property.

> 'A child photographer yesterday celebrated his silver wedding at Herne Bay: he was Mr. John Tulse, one of the first to specialize in the use of gauze filters.'

Mr. Tulse was really a child-photographer.

Adjectives should not be joined to their nouns with hyphens except in such special cases as blue-book, large-black pig, French-polisher, small-sword – where to omit the hyphen would be to endanger the sense.

PRINCIPLE NINETEEN

The order of ideas in a sentence or paragraph should be such that the reader need not rearrange them in his mind.

The natural arrangement of ideas in critical argument is:

Statement of problem.
Marshalling of evidence, first on main points, then on subsidiary ones – the same sequence kept throughout the argument.
Credibility of evidence examined.
Statement of possible implications of all evidence not wholly rejected.
The weighing of conflicting evidence in the scale of probability.
Verdict.

The natural arrangement of ideas in historical writing is the one recommended in *Alice in Wonderland* by the King of Hearts to the White Rabbit:

> 'Begin at the beginning, and go on till you come to the end: then stop.'

The natural arrangement of ideas in familiar correspondence – unless some all-important news pushes its way forward to the first place – is:

Acknowledgement of previous letter.
Comment on the points raised in it, in order of importance – the recipient's interests being given priority.
New information in order of importance – the recipient's interests being given priority.
Questions.
Postscript.

It would take up too much space to analyse a mishandled argument in full. But readers will be familiar with the sort of argument that, if it ever commits itself to a statement of the problem, does not do so until a mass of jumbled evidence on subsidiary points has been adduced, after which it gives the verdict, and then evidence on the principal point, and then an irrelevant report on 'what the soldier's wife said', and then contradictory statements about evidence on subsidiary points, and then perhaps a reconsideration of the verdict, and then fresh evidence, and finally a restatement of the verdict. Doubts are cast by modern mathematicians on the universal validity of the conclusions reached by Euclid in his propositions; but at least he knew how to handle an argument, and always wound up with 'This conclusion should be tested by practical experiment'.

We shall, however, quote part of a carelessly constructed argument by Major-Gen. Sir Andrew McCulloch. It is from his answer to an editorial question (October 1941): 'Do you think that any form of British invasion of Europe would be possible during the next weeks or months?'

> 'I think it feasible to force an entry into Europe. This opinion, however, is of little value, because I do not know what force is available. If I knew as much as Mr. Churchill or the Chiefs of Staff my views might be of value. As it is, my opinions are in the realm of dreams. For this reason I shall take a purely imaginative situation, and on this premiss shall discuss the relative merits of landing at various places on the coast of Europe.'

The logical order of ideas in this passage is:

1 If I knew as well as Mr. Churchill or the Chiefs of Staff
2 what forces are available

3 my views might be of value;
4 but I do not know,
5 and, when, therefore,
6 after discussing the comparative merits of various landing-places,
7 I pronounce it feasible to force an entry into Europe,
8 my premisses
9 must be recognized as no less imaginative
10 than if I had dreamed them.

The order in the original is 7, 4, 2, 1, 3, 10, 5, 9, 8, 6.

Readers are familiar with the long badly arranged family letter – everything jumbled together so confusedly that they have to read it through several times to find their way about it. No need to quote an example here. We shall, however, quote examples of newspaper reporting in which, because the historic order of events does not correspond with the order of what is held to be their dramatic importance, the reader's sense of what happened is distracted. Here is part of a report by Joan Slocombe of her experiences in Unoccupied France:

'But Vichy is dreary beyond words. I preferred Marseilles. In Vichy there is no plump madame of the green-grocery store for ever remarking on my accent. She asked, "Are you English?" and then drew me into the inner room, where over twenty people were listening to the B.B.C. French broadcast.

That happened to me in a cheerful, sunny little street in Marseilles one evening.'

The natural order of events is:

1 Marseilles was dreary enough
2 But a plump madame who kept a green-grocery store
3 in a cheerful little street
4 was always remarking on my foreign accent and one
5 sunny evening
6 asked me: 'Are you English?'
7 When I said 'Yes' she
8 drew me into an inner room where over twenty people were listening to the B.B.C. French broadcast.
9 There was none like her in Vichy,
10 which is dreary beyond words.

The order in the original is: 10, 1, 9, 2, 4, 6, 8, 3, 5, (with 7 omitted). The length of the two versions is the same.

But confused sequence of ideas is not confined to journalistic writing.

Here is a hasty sentence from Rose Macaulay's essay on Virginia Woolf:

> 'With her conversation was a flashing, many-faceted stream, now running swiftly, now slowing into still pools that shimmered with a hundred changing lights, shades and reflections, wherein sudden coloured fishes continually darted and stirred, now flowing between deep banks, now chuckling over sharp pebbles.'

To suit the antiqueness of 'still pools that shimmered', 'a hundred changing lights', and 'wherein sudden coloured fishes', as well as to show the reader his way about the sentence, a conventional eighteenth-century treatment would have been appropriate here. Miss Macaulay might well have told with antithetical care how the water ran alternately deep and shallow, fast and slow, wide and narrow, through level fields, down rocky inclines. The principal imaginative figure, the pools of coloured fish, should have been placed at the end: this would have avoided the suggestion that the sudden coloured fish chuckled over the pebbles. Thus:

> 'Conversation with her resembled a changeable bright stream that now widening, chuckled over sharp pebbles, and now narrowing, flowed smoothly between steep banks; now it cascaded over rocks; now it lagged and deepened into still pools (shimmering with a hundred reflected lights and shades) wherein coloured fishes suddenly appeared, slowly swimming, and as suddenly darted from view.'

The exact position of subordinate clauses in relation to the main body of a sentence has never been fixed in English. However, there is this difference between modern English and Classical Latin usage: that, in Latin, subordinate clauses are put before the main body of the sentence, though sometimes the first of them may be artfully designed to hold the chief meaning of the sentence – even so complicated a writer as Cicero observes this general rule; whereas in English the rule is exactly reversed. We will show what we mean by rewriting the foregoing sentence in the Latin style:

> 'This, however, that in Latin, exactly in reverse manner to English usage, unless some subordinate clause, being artfully designed to hold the chief meaning of the sentence, comes first, all subordinate clauses – such is the general rule observed by even so complicated a writer as Cicero – are put before the main body of the sentence: this, I say, is a difference between modern English and classical Latin.'

It will be noted that this version recalls the prose of Milton, who tried to impose Latin syntax on English.

PRINCIPLE TWENTY

No unnecessary idea, phrase or word should be included in a sentence.

This does not mean that one should write with as much compression as if one were sending a cable, when short of cash, and scheming how to make one word do the work of three – for the reader will take far longer to get the sense of a skeleton message than that of the same message written out in full: it means that irrelevancies, at least, should be cut out. It is difficult to define what an 'irrelevancy' is in narrative, because most British readers enjoy almost any sort of incidental anecdote or reflection, tacked on to a story with only the feeblest excuse; but there are certain proprieties to be observed. For example, the following sentence from a recent history of Peter the Great of Russia seems to us improper:

> 'In his progress through this province Peter may have passed through the little town where, some two centuries later, his successor the Czar Nicholas II was to be murdered. We wonder what Peter's feelings would have been had he been granted prevision of this dastardly crime! Arrived back at his Capital . . .'

Since it is not even certain that Peter passed through the town, his hypothetic feelings do not seem relevant to the story, especially as the author has made no attempt to reconstruct them.

From a Tobruk despatch by J. H. Hodson, a war correspondent (1941):

> 'After that we breakfasted on sardines, biscuits, and tea in an atmosphere that seemed (fictitiously, no doubt) as peaceful and quiet as a beach in Devon.'

The parenthetic 'fictitiously, no doubt' belongs to some other story – e.g.: 'our hosts told us (fictitiously, no doubt) that they often borrow the enemy's spoons to stir their tea-cups.'

From a novel by James Hilton:

> '. . . sometimes on these delectable Fridays he would cycle for miles along the flat fen roads with the wind behind him, and return in the afternoon by crawling romantic-looking branch-line trains which always managed to remind him of wild animals, so completely had the civilized thing been submerged in the atmosphere of what it had sought to civilize.'

The idea of white men 'going native' in remote savage districts which they came to civilize is irrelevantly superimposed on the idea of domesticated animals that escape from civilization and run wild.

From a newspaper article:

> 'That, plainly, is the only way open to us of dealing with India, or

with any other colony or mandated territory that is capable of looking after its own affairs.'

The word 'other' is irrelevant: India is not either a colony or a mandated territory of Britain.

In the following example, from Sir Walter Citrine's *My Finnish Diary*, the unnecessary words are due to geniality:

'The ice lay in patches somewhere about a dozen feet across in all sorts of shapes. The steamer made easy work of it and soon cut a channel through, guided by the red and green lights which we saw swinging out at us. There was a lighthouse beyond, shooting out its rays through the darkness.'

Since nobody expects ice to stand up on edge or to form in geometrical figures, and since lighthouses do not usually flash in daylight, this boils down to:

'Guided by red and green swinging lights the steamer easily cut a channel through the patches of ice, which measured on an average two or three yards across. Beyond, a lighthouse flashed.'

From an article by the Marquess of Crewe:

'The British Empire is no parvenu creation. The Tudors justly claimed that even then the Crown of England was an Imperial Crown, for it ruled several nations.'

When was the 'even then' time to which the Tudors referred in their claim that the Crown of England was an Imperial one? None has been indicated. If 'even then' is omitted, this problem does not arise.

PRINCIPLE TWENTY-ONE

All antitheses should be true ones.

This means that all antitheses, or contrasts, should be between opposing ideas of the same order. Here is an example of an antithesis between ideas of different orders from Hansard's report of a speech by Mr. Arthur Greenwood, M.P. (Aug. 1939):

'Our spirit has not weakened; our spirit has deepened.'

Here 'has deepened' should have been 'has strengthened'.

An example, from a gardening book, of an antithesis between similar ideas of the same order:

'Good soil deserves digging, bad soil needs it.'

The antithesis should not have been between what bad soil needs and what good soil deserves. Both soils need digging; both deserve digging. The intended antithesis here is perhaps:

> 'Good soil needs digging, to get the best crops out of it; bad soil needs digging, to get any crops out of it at all.'

An example from an article by Negley Farson:

> 'Bevin has just made a startling, yet bold . . . speech when he declared that positions in the Diplomatic Corps should be thrown open to working-class boys.'

Bold speeches are usually startling.

From a book-review by Desmond Macarthy:

> 'Certainly I have never come across a better letter-writer than Lady Wentworth either in envelopes or print.'

He means presumably: 'Certainly, I have seldom come across better letters, published or unpublished, than Lady Wentworth's.'

From a novel by Graham Greene:

> 'Drover was not reading; they spied on him through a little window the size of a postcard in the cell door. He was asleep upright on his chair, clenched hands hanging between his knees. He might have been sitting for his portrait in the grey loose unaccustomed clothes, seen at better advantage than half hidden by a bus's hood, but in his dreams he seemed to be in a bus still; a foot pressed the floor, the hands opened a little and twisted.'

In the last sentence there are four sets of true antitheses telescoped into a single false one. The first is: 'he might have been sitting for his portrait, but he was asleep.' The second is: 'he was wearing grey loose clothes, unlike his busman's uniform.' The third is: 'sitting in this chair his figure showed to advantage; but when he drove a bus he was half hidden by the bus's hood.' The fourth is: 'he was asleep, but in a position suggesting that he was driving a bus in his dreams.'

PRINCIPLE TWENTY-TWO

Over-emphasis of the illogical sort tolerated in conversation should be avoided in prose.

In conversation people say: 'There are dozens of octogenarians in our village' [meaning, nine] 'and hundreds of children who have never seen the sea' [meaning, fifty or sixty] 'and a parson who invariably goes to sleep while preaching' [meaning, 'who openly smothered a yawn last Sunday']. Yet, reading a prose study of *Our Village*, one would take such remarks literally and feel aggrieved if they turned out to be misleading.

Here are examples of conversational emphasis that we consider inadmissible in good prose.

From an editorial of the *British Medical Journal*:

> 'That food is more important in the preservation of health than housing was shown by the late Dr. M'Gonigle at B——, but this is by no means to say that housing is not of the first importance.'

If food is more important than housing, housing cannot be of the first importance.

From a book review by A. G. Macdonell:

> '*The Voyage* seems to be an incomparably better book thán *Sparkenbroke*. Mr. Morgan has cut out almost all the dead-wood which used to encumber his writing and make him so difficult to read. There is still the misty silvery atmosphere of spiritual exaltation which Mr. Morgan can evoke as no one else since Conrad, but now the men and women are clear and vigorous against the mist and silver.'

It was not an incomparably better book – as Mr. Macdonell proved by the comparisons in the two succeeding sentences.

From two newspaper reports:

> 'The route from America is now a more essential artery to us than it have ever been.'

> 'Sir Horace Wilson, head of the Civil Service, has circulated to all departments a demand for man-power economy by the stringent cutting-out of less essential work.'

There are no degrees in essentiality: a thing is either essential or unessential.

Here is a characteristic example of forensic over-emphasis in a newspaper leader:

> 'The outrages committed by the German forces in the present war are almost identical with those they committed in the last except that they are even more atrocious; the excuses with which they are accompanied are exactly similar except that they are even more shameless. Mr. Churchill, in a flash of genius, divined this when he declared the present war to be "a continuation" of the last.'

Here the over-emphatic 'almost identical' and 'exactly similar', by restricting the possible differences between German behaviour in the First World War and the Second, take the wind from the sails of 'even more atrocious' and 'even more shameless'. Also, 'a flash of genius' is praise which leads the reader to expect a satisfyingly original epigram from Mr. Churchill instead of a sensible commonplace.

PRINCIPLE TWENTY-THREE

Ideas should not contradict one another, or otherwise violate logic.

The practice of oratorical disputation in mediaeval schools, though it led to absurd logic-chopping, and though little attempt was made to verify the truth of the facts used in the arguments, did at least make people conscious of the logical consequences of what they said. A modified form of such disputation might usefully be revived in English education. School-children would soon be able to put their finger on logical flaws and would gradually learn to avoid absurdities themselves.

From the Historical Introduction to the *Oxford English Dictionary*:

> 'In this way began the system of voluntary readers, without whose help the material for the Society's Dictionary could never have been collected at all, except at a prohibitive cost of time and money.'

But if the cost had been prohibitive, the material could not have been collected.

From a novel by John Masefield:

> 'Do you see him?
> There went the fox, indeed, a little red flashing thing, looking much smaller than he was, because he was already fully extended.'

If the fox was fully extended, it might possibly look larger than it really was — as a cat does when it puffs out its fur to frighten dogs or as a horse does when it 'goes full out' — but not smaller.

From the autobiography of David Kirkwood, M.P.:

> 'Sir William Joynson-Hicks had made a stupid blunder by instructing a raid on "Arcos", the headquarters in London of the commercial section of the Russian Government, for the purpose of discovering an imaginary document which wasn't there.'

If the police knew that the document was not at 'Arcos' and indeed that it existed only in their imagination, their purpose could not have been to discover it. (But perhaps the passage is ironical.)

PRINCIPLE TWENTY-FOUR

The writer should not, without clear warning, change his standpoint in the course of a sentence or paragraph.

What grammarians call 'false sequence of tenses' (e.g. 'He would not have come if he *saw* me coming too') and 'false concord' (e.g. 'Common-sense and honesty *is* all I ask', or 'I gave the wether *her* feed') are becoming increasingly common in English. The Latin grammarians took a more serious view of false sequence than the Greeks: the famous Greek historian Thucydides, especially when quoting speeches, often started a sentence with one construction and finished it with another. The Latins were right to be strict, for the eye is always delayed by a false sequence or concord.

Here is a typical example of false concord from a notice issued by a Head Warden of 'Rural Areas F. Division'.

> 'A new organization has been formed and is known as the "Fire Guard". The object of this body is to recruit every available person to fight fires in their own homes.
>
> A meeting will be held at the Galmpton Institute on Wednesday September 10th at 8 p.m., when the Chief Officer of the Totnes Rural District Fire Services will attend to fully explain the scheme. It is hoped that everyone who can will attend, even if they are already members of a stirrup-pump party.'

It should have been: '. . . every person to fight fires in his own home', 'everyone will attend, even if he is already a member'.

In English one may legitimately refer to a Council, a firm or a society as either 'they' or 'it' — as one may refer to Great Britain, or Germany, or The Church, or a ship, as either 'she' or 'it' — but whichever form is chosen, should be consistently used. Here are examples of inconsistency.

From a report by the Committee of Convocation (1931):

> 'Further, we would stress the debt of the Church for this provision of some form of worship for her sons scattered over the seven seas in ships and lighthouses, on the Continent, in the Australian back-blocks, in Canadian clearings, in loneliness in tropical Africa, where the Church itself is unable to supply regular ministrations.'

Because of 'her sons' it should be 'the Church herself'.

From a leader by J. A. Spender:

> 'All eyes are on Great Britain, which has announced that she does not recognize partitions of territory carried through by violence in the middle of war.'

It should be 'who has announced', because of the 'she' that follows.

Here are typical examples of false sequence of tenses. From the American news-magazine *Time* – an account of Napoleon's Moscow campaign:

> 'Before his troops marched last week, Hitler may – and very likely did – pause to review this pertinent chapter of history.'

This should be 'may have paused and very likely did'.

From a newspaper article, in which the past and historic-present are improperly mixed:

> 'Now, while Marx's activist theory of knowledge curtailed the view that human beings are continuously changing, when he comes to treat them historically he conceives of them as uniform.'

It should be 'came' . . . 'conceived'.

From *Why Britain is at War*, by the Hon. Harold Nicolson, M.P.:

> 'Would it really mean for us a loss of prestige and power if all our African colonies were placed under the mandatory system and administered in the interests of the natives and of humanity as a whole? That in fact is the system which we are already adopting. We should notice little change.
>
> And in return for this we should achieve a world which is worth fighting for.'

The 'is' in the last sentence may be justified as a Thucydidean usage which gives greater emphasis to the sentence. But, grammatically, 'would be' is correct.

Most changes of standpoint are due to the writer's forgetting how his sentence started. (The grammatic term is 'anacoluthia'.)

From a book-review by Desmond Macarthy:

> 'There are a few things in his letters which Time has made to look more foolish and some more wise than they were when uttered.'

This should have been either:

> 'Time has made a few things in his letters look more foolish, and a few wiser, than when they were first written.'

Or:

> 'Some things in his letters now look more foolish, and some wiser, than when they were first written.'

From an article in a gardening journal:

> 'These markings are caused partly by natural etiolation, sometimes because of frost, but generally from a microscopic pest.'

This should be either 'partly ... partly ... mostly'; or 'sometimes ... sometimes ... most often'; or 'in some cases ... in others ... generally'. In each case it should have been 'by', not 'because of' or 'from'.

From a Ministry of Information advertisement:

> 'To-day, the fanaticism of the Nazis is matched by a faith that is stronger and more enduring than their own, ...'

Either: 'matched with', or 'opposed by'.

From a parish notice:

> 'Scrap metal, tins, paper will be collected the first Monday of every month; refuse will also be collected on alternate Tuesdays of each week.'

Very few of the parishioners noticed anything unusual about this – until Tuesday.

From a novel by Agatha Christie:

> In his mind phrase after phrase succeeded each other.

Either:

> '... phrase succeeded phrase'

Or:

> '... many phrases succeeded one another'

From *The Long Week End*, by Robert Graves and Alan Hodge:

> 'Samuel Butler, a prophet before his time, had suggested in his *Note-Books* ...'

Either 'a shrewd prophet' or 'who was in advance of his time'. Admittedly, many prophets including (so Biblical scholars say) Jeremiah have been prophets after their times – i.e. some of the prophecies credited to them were written after the events to which they referred – but this was not what we meant.

PRINCIPLE TWENTY-FIVE

In each list of people or things all the words used should belong to the same category of ideas.

For example, one does not write: 'Various sorts of animals – carnivorous, herbivorous, fructivorous, marsupial, rodent.' The first three sorts of animals are classified according to their diet, the fourth according to its order in natural history, the fifth according to its family.

An Oxford butcher advertises himself as: 'Family, pork and general butcher.' 'Family' denotes a particular class of custom; 'pork' denotes a range of commodities sold; 'general' may denote either that he butchers all animals fit for human consumption or that he sells to casual buyers as well as to families. The correct description is: 'Family and General Butcher; Specialist in Pork'.

From a B.B.C. news bulletin:

> 'The combined operations in Libya were a notable example of land, air, and naval coöperation.'

This should have been 'land, air and sea coöperation'.

From a local paper:

> 'The hotels have been taken over by the military, the Navy and the R.A.F.'

In popular usage the initials 'R.A.F.' have no counterpart: for 'R.N.' is not used and the Army as a whole has no initials. Since 'the military' is in a category by itself — such forms as 'the naval' and 'the aerial' not being used — this sentence should have read:

> 'The hotels have been taken over by the Navy, Army and Air Force.'

The form 'by the Royal Navy, the Army and the Royal Air Force' calls unnecessary attention to the Army's lack of royal patronage despite its seniority to the Royal Air Force.

CHAPTER THIRTEEN

THE GRACES OF PROSE

THERE is a Debateable Land between the region governed by our numbered principles, those concerned with the secure conveyance of information, and the region governed by our lettered principles, those concerned with its graceful conveyance. For example, most cases of the use of obscure references, discussed under Principle F, also come under Principle 3, which concerns general unintelligibility of expression; and most cases of the circumlocution discussed under Principle G also come under Principle 20, which concerns irrelevancies. That does not trouble us. We have separated the two classes of principles because a failure to conform with the lettered ones is an offence against sensibility, rather than sense; whereas with the numbered ones the offence is against sense, rather than sensibility.

PRINCIPLE A

Metaphors should not be mated in such a way as to confuse or distract the reader.

Metaphors are used more often in English than in most modern European languages, and far more often than in Latin or Greek. A metaphor is a condensed simile. Here are two similes:

> 'Marriage is like a lottery — with a great many blanks and very few prizes.'
>
> 'Our struggle against sin resembles a cricket-match. Just as the batsman strides out to the wicket, armed with pads, gloves and bat, and manfully stands up to demon bowling, with an adversary behind him always ready to stump him or catch him out . . . and when the sun sets, and stumps are drawn, he modestly carries his bat back to the pavilion, amid plaudits. So likewise the Christian . . . And when, finally, safe in the celestial pavilion, he lays aside the bat of the spirit, unbuckles the pads of faith, removes the gloves of doctrine and casts down the cap of sanctity upon the scoring-table, — lo, inside, is the name of The Maker!'

Examples of metaphors derived from these two similes are:

> 'Poor Edwin has indeed drawn a blank in the matrimonial lottery.'
>
> 'St. Paul, that great sportsman, faced the bowling manfully in the struggle against Paganism.'

When two unconnected similes are reduced to metaphors, and these are combined in the same sentence, the effect on the reader is to blur both of the mental pictures which the metaphors call up:

> 'Edwin's matrimonial record deserves our praise rather than our pity: he drew two blanks but on each occasion faced the bowling manfully.'

The mismating of metaphors is justified only in facetious contexts. For example, Mr. R. A. Butler, M.P., remarked in a Commons debate:

> 'The Hon. Member for East Wolverhampton is to be congratulated on producing a very tasty rehash of several questions which have been fully ventilated in this House up to date.'

Here, the unpleasant implications of the word 'ventilated' were sure of a laugh. The columnist 'Atticus' often makes genial use of the mismated metaphor. For example:

> 'Colonel Moore-Brabazon's predecessor, Sir John Reith, continues on his Gulliver's travels, and is now on his way to that distant land, the House of Lords, from whose bourne no traveller returns.'

But there is no facetiousness in this remark by Mr. Arthur Greenwood, M.P. (1939):

> 'While we strive for peace, we are leaving no stone unturned to meet the situation should the fateful blow fall.'

In what conceivable circumstances could anyone turn up a stone to ward off a fateful blow? Mr. Greenwood meant:

> 'We who strive for peace are seeking every means of warding off the fateful blow.'

The Archbishop of Canterbury in a pamphlet (1940):

> 'But just as truly pioneers of that far-off age are those who accept the common obligations of men and strive to live in the spirit of Christ as they discharge them.'

One may be the pioneer of a new route to some far-off land; one may be the herald or harbinger of a new age; one may be the prophet of a far-off age. But 'a pioneer of a far-off age' is a difficult conception.

From a letter to the Press by Eden Philpotts:

> 'Exorcize forever the vision of Germany as a bleeding martyr who calls upon civilization to cut the cancer from her bosom; since Germany is herself the cancer. . . .

She penetrates web and woof, destroying the fabric of human society, pouring her venom through every existing channel of international relations, creating nests and pockets in the healthy tissue of her neighbours, fouling and destroying the forests of human kind that her own fungus breed alone shall inherit the earth and the fulness thereof . . .'

A ready test of the legitimacy of a metaphor is whether it can be illustrated even in fantastic caricature or diagram. Mr. Philpotts fails to pass the test here: it would puzzle the most ingenious and morbid-minded painter alive, even Salvador Dali, to show a seeming cancer in the world's bosom, which is really a fungus, pouring venom through channels in the universal cloth fabric, at the same time creating nests and pockets in the healthy tissues of her neighbour fungus-cancers (?), and destroying forests of mankind.

There are many nearly dead metaphors in English; but they are apt to revive when two or three are included in the same sentence.

From a newspaper article:

'The I.F.S. had held out the olive branch, but nothing of a concrete nature had come out of it.'

PRINCIPLE B

Metaphors should not be piled on top of one another.

Constant change of metaphor is very tiring to the reader: the visualizing of metaphors requires a different sort of mental effort from that required for visualizing facts.

Here is an account from the American magazine *Time* of President Roosevelt's electoral campaign in 1940:

'No ivory tower held Candidate Roosevelt. He knew well that a candidacy should reach its crest on Election Day and not one moment before. But the Gallup Poll, giving him a terrific majority, left no option now but to go ahead and kill off Candidate Willkie, for any slip from that lead might still be fatal in a year as full of loose electricity as 1940. He decided to go ahead full steam.'

It would have been better to write this report in a simple sustained metaphor — for example, that of a boxer who has planned to win a match on points, intending not to go all out until the last round, but getting an unexpected chance to kill off his opponent in an earlier one. In the *Time* version the change from the electricity to the steam metaphor is particularly confusing.

'Atticus' sometimes overdoes his trick of mismating metaphors. An occasional mismating may be good fun, but an orgy disgusts.

> 'After a series of punishing defeats the Premier's son, Mr. Randolph Churchill, has won a bloodless victory and will now join the gallant six hundred at Westminster. No doubt he will have mellowed since the days when as a young politician he not only rode ahead of the hounds but in front of the fox.'

H. G. Wells is being solemn, not facetious, in this sentence from a newspaper article:

> 'And the raw material, that hairy ape, is so made over that it is only in some moment of crazy lust, panic, rage or bestial vitality that we realize he is still the core, the blood injection at the root of us all.'

Mr. Wells tends to take a scientific view of language—that words are tools, and those with the strongest pictorial associations have the keenest cutting edge: if he wishes to express himself trenchantly why should he not use 'hairy ape', 'the core', 'blood injection', 'at the root of us all'? Because it is dangerous to play with edged tools.

Readers would understand and accept Mr. Wells's meaning far better if he had written:

> 'And the passionate material of which we all are made has been so carefully processed in the factory of our social habits that it is only an occasional crazy moment of lust, rage, or panic that suddenly recalls our bestial origin.'

PRINCIPLE C

Metaphors should not be used in such close association with unmetaphorical language as to produce absurdity or confusion.

The principle is best illustrated by this short sentence from a melodramatic chapter in Graham Greene's novel *It's a Battlefield*:

> 'Kay Rimmer sat with her head in her hands and her eyes on the floor.'

And her teeth on the mantelpiece? A slip like this will break the spell of a novel for any intelligent reader.

In the following quotation from J. N. W. Sullivan's *The Bases of Modern Science* (1928), the fantastic metaphor in the first sentence is disconcertingly given an appearance of reality in the second and third sentences:

'The principle requires us to believe that, *to an observer mounted on such an electron*, a ray of light would pass the electron with the speed of 186,000 miles per second, whether the electron was moving in the direction of the ray or whether it was moving in the opposite direction. We have said "to an observer", but we do not intend to imply thereby that any merely psychological effect is involved. We may replace the observer by scientific apparatus making the necessary measurements automatically. What is essential is that the apparatus should be mounted on the electron.'

From the Minutes of a Municipal Council:

'The sub-committee have reported that though every avenue has been explored, no street in the central district bounded by Station Road on the North and High Street on the South could be used as a permanent parking-place for cars without incommoding tradesmen and/or impeding traffic.'

There were no avenues in the central district – only narrow streets lined with shops.

PRINCIPLE D

Characteristically poetical expressions should not be used in prose.

Except, of course, in quotations. When Daphne du Maurier writes in a pamphlet:

'All that remained of the gallantry, the courage, the brotherhood and sacrifice, of four years in Flanders, were the graves of the fallen and the blown and scarlet poppies.'

the reader is entitled to make such burlesque variants on 'the blown and scarlet poppies' as 'the infant and chestnut foals', 'the adolescent and Red Indian'.

Our phrase 'poetical expressions' includes such conceits as these from a novel by Dr. A. J. Cronin:

'The force of the hurricane almost bowled him off his feet. The station was deserted. The young poplars planted in line at its entrance bent like bows, whistling and shivering at every blast. Overhead the stars were polished to a high glitter.'

Prose decency demands rather: 'Overhead, the stars glittered with such brilliance that he fancied them burnished by the force of the wind.' These are conceits in the French style. French is a less poetic language than English, since fewer liberties can be taken with it and possible meanings are therefore restricted. If, obeying the traditional rules of French, one attempts to write great poetry, the result, judged by English poetic standards, is at best merely magnificent verse. This is what André Gide meant when, asked who was the greatest French poet, he answered 'Victor Hugo — *hélas*!' Modern poets who are born French have despairingly cultivated an anarchic 'disorientation of the senses', following the example of Rimbaud, a true poet. Such characteristically French movements as impressionism, symbolism, and surrealism all began from disorientation. Impressionism is a hit-or-miss way of describing the general appearance of things without consideration of details; symbolism is a way of describing things with conscious disregard of how one intellectually knows them to be, for the purpose of emphasizing their emotional significance; surrealism is the realistic expression of disturbingly anti-conventional fancies.

Many feelings and scenes are extremely difficult to describe accurately in prose. Here, for example, is a description of a 'damnable room' by Rebecca West, in her novel *Harriet Hume*, as it looked when one Arnold Condorex switched out all the lamps but an alabaster urn on the chimney-piece:

> 'The fluted pilasters, their grooves black with shadow, looked like claw-nails drawn down the walls, and the gold convoluted capitals might have been the claws that traced them. The painted lunettes on the panels and ceiling were black oily smears from which shone only the whiter details of a universe lackadaisically falsified, swan necks bent by angelic meekness to re-entrant curves, profiles so tense with nobility that the breath must rush forth from the nostrils like the shriek of a police whistle, forearms like fins with languishment.'

This reads queerly, but then the room was damnably queer; and when one examines the words in detail there is not one to which one could justly take exception, except 'like claw-nails drawn' for 'as though claw-nails had been drawn': it is as intelligibly expressed as so difficult a scene could be. But in the same novel occurs another passage:

> 'Tenderly he reflected that her little head, which was almost egg-like in its oval blandness, was as full as an egg is of meat with the desire to please. But for that his shrewdness rebuked him. There must be much else besides. She had mastered the shining black leviathan that just behind her proclaimed Bechstein its parent. Like him she had crawled up the dark tunnel which leads from obscurity to the light, and had performed the feat more expeditiously.'

This does not seem written in the same sensitive style as the other passage. Some sort of 'ism' pervades it. The reader feels that Rebecca West is trying to put something over on him, some sort of verbal hypnotism. When he examines the words in detail they do not answer for themselves in a commonsense way. Blandness cannot be oval. 'But for that' is ambiguous. 'Shrewdness' cannot rebuke; though a 'shrewder self' can. Bechstein was not a shining black leviathan who spawned other black leviathans and crawled up dark tunnels rather less expeditiously than Harriet.

Here is an example of impressionism from W. E. Woodward's biography *George Washington*:

> 'Writers, historians, philosophers and men of that tribe have more inner life than they really need. On the other hand, there are many people who could take on a larger amount of inner life without being harmed at all.
>
> McMaster thought that Washington's inner life had never been understood and probably never would be.
>
> From him we get the impression of a great figure, sitting in dusky isolation, like a heroic statute in an empty plain. To reach it we must travel a road that has been worn so deep by McMaster, and Irving, and Sparks, and Wilson, and Lodge – and innumerable others – that we cannot see over its sides. It is cluttered with the prayer tablets of the pilgrims who have preceded us; and we are out of breath from climbing over the hurdles of reverence and fancy. We approach on tiptoe; we utter the sibilant whispers of awe.
>
> No wonder Washington's character appears elusive. Anybody's would under the circumstances. . . .
>
> The background of elusiveness has been painted in the picture by biographers who have looked into Washington's soul for the quivering inner life which they themselves possessed. When they did not find it there they lost their bearings and ran round in circles.
>
> 'Washington's mind was the *business mind.*'

This is a plausible argument and a sensible conclusion; but it would carry far more weight with the ordinary reader if written more soberly. It is not merely that the metaphors are mismated – one does not expect to find hurdles across a well-worn road, or a three-dimensional statue melting into a two-dimensional background; nor merely that the contrast between the crudely facetious 'take on a large amount of inner life' and the rhetorical 'sitting in dusky isolation, like a heroic statue in an empty plain' is shocking. The worst is that the reader feels himself written *at*, not written *for* – especially in the de Quinceyesque: 'We approach on tiptoe; we utter the sibilant whispers of awe.'

Here is an impressionistic passage from a short-story by H. A. Manhood:

> 'They kissed, and happiness was a singing colour in the stillness.

They lay down, and their passion was an exquisite winging of time and beyond reason, a glimpse of harmony at its uttermost source, a moment of immortal growth. And, having raced to rapture and savoured all creation, they came laughing back like guests to sleep where sleep was known, lying close in a gracious half-state that made the final waking less like bruising, gave them time to secure memory for ever. . . .

They never lost the first ecstasy. The richness and marvel of their oneness increased to a deep, sustained over-beat within them, a radiance which seemed larger even than death.'

These are wild words. How can a winging be a glimpse? How can a source be uttermost? How can harmony have even an original source? What is immortal growth? How can a glimpse be a growth? What is the meaning of even so apparently simple a phrase as 'like guests to sleep where sleep was known'? – is the first 'sleep' a verb or a noun? 'Half-smile', 'half-apple', or 'half-century', yes! – but what is a half-state? – does he mean 'intermediate state'? – if so between what extremes? How can an over-beat be a radiance, and how can a radiance seem larger than death?

PRINCIPLE E

Except where the writer is being deliberately facetious, all phrases in a sentence, or sentences in a paragraph, should belong to the same vocabulary or level of language.

Scholars and clergymen are seldom able to keep their language all of a piece.

The following is from a newspaper sermon:

'It is one of the mysteries of that inner life of man (one so replete with mysteries hard to accept or solve) that some of us are clearly, as it were, freeborn citizens of grace, whilst others – alas! many others – can only at great price buy this freedom. Of this there can be no doubt. The Gospel appointed for to-day reports to us, in the words of our Lord Himself, a story at once simple and mystifying, about day-labourers in an Eastern vineyard. Some of them had worked a full day, whilst others had only "clocked in", so to speak, when it was nearly time to go. Yet each received from the employer the same flat rate of remuneration – a Roman penny. Our Lord said that was all right, which must be enough for us.'

It begins with ecclesiastical-scholarly language 'whilst others – alas! many others – can only at great price buy this freedom'; gradually presses through the apologetically modern, 'others had only "clocked in", so to speak, when it was nearly time to go', and the commercial, 'each received from the employer the same flat rate of remuneration'; descends to the downright vulgar, 'Our Lord said that was all right . . .'

Scholars are at their worst in translations, especially when trying to give antique work a modern flavour: over-attention to the Classics has blinded them to the moods of their own language. From Dr. Rouse's translation of Seneca's *Apocolocyntosis*:

> '*Citius mihi verum, ne tibi alogias excutiam.*
> Out with the truth and look sharp, or I'll knock your quips and quiddities out of you.
> *Contentus erit his interim convictoribus.*
> These boon-companions will satisfy him for the nonce.
> *Vosque in primis qui concusso*
> *Magna parastis lucra fritillo.*
> And you, above all, who get rich quick
> By the rattle of dice and the three-card trick.'

This is to dart about confusingly between the seventeenth and twentieth centuries.

The same uncertainty of language-level is found in Michael Heseltine's translation of Petronius's *Satyricon*. Here there is an attempt at brisk modernity:

> ' "*Oro te,*" *inquit Echion centonarius,* "*melius loquere.*"
> "Oh, don't be so gloomy," said Echion, the old-clothes dealer.'

But there are sad lapses into the antique:

> '*In pinacothecam perveni vario genere tabularum mirabilem. Nam et Zeuxidos manus vidi nondum vetustatis injuria victas.*'

Mr. Heseltine's translation is:

> 'I came into a gallery hung with a wonderful collection of various pictures. I saw the works of Zeuxis not yet overcome by the defacement of time.'

This, to match the other quotation, should have read:

> 'I visited the gallery. The exhibition of paintings there was most representative and contained some fine old-masters, among which I even found a few Zeuxises that had kept their original tones surprising well.'

PRINCIPLE F

No reference should be unnecessarily obscure.

If everyone had to write for the stupidest reader, as a regiment on the march accommodates itself to the pace of the slowest soldier, literature would be as tedious as a tenpenny nail,[1] and since the precise degree of literary and historical education with which one's public can be credited varies greatly with its estimated size, this principle is a difficult one to observe.

The Parliamentary Correspondent of a daily paper who writes: 'The "'ouse couldn't but do it" as Bunce remarked on a similar occasion' is expecting too much of even his educated readers. A few of them will have read Trollope's *Phineas Finn,* but of those not all will remember the minor character Bunce and hardly one of those who do will be able to recall the 'similar occasion'.

From a detective novel by Dorothy Sayers:

> ' "I feel," said the lawyer, carefully stirring his coffee, "that . . . Mr. Arbuthnot is right in saying it may involve you in some—er—unpleasant publicity. Er—I . . . cannot feel that our religion demands that we should make ourselves conspicuous—in such very painful circumstances."
>
> Mr. Parker reminded himself of a dictum of Lord Melbourne.
>
> "Well, after all," said Mrs. Marchbanks, "as Helen so rightly says, does it matter? . . ." '

The particular dictum of Lord Melbourne appropriate to this context cannot be unerringly singled out by any of Miss Sayers's readers, who number hundreds of thousands, nor even guessed at by more than a dozen or so Melbourne experts—none of whom is necessarily a reader of Miss Sayers's novels. That Mr. Parker, a police inspector, could recall a dictum of Lord Melbourne's is not an indication, either, that he was an educated person: he might have come across it in a 'Great Thoughts' calendar or in a popular newspaper.

Malcolm Muggeridge writes in his history, *The Thirties*:

> 'In the restless determination to extract ever more material satisfaction from life to compensate for other satisfactions which were lacking, ever heavier drafts were drawn on the future. Expense of shame in a waste of passion . . .'

This crooked reference to the 129th sonnet of Shakespeare's which begins:

> 'Th' expence of spirit in a waste of shame
> Is lust in action . . .'

seems to us indefensible. The line is first inverted, then misquoted, and in its new form does not explain itself as prose.

[1]We use this to exemplify the sort of incidental expression that one should avoid. A 'tenpenny nail' is an old-fashioned school reading-book, but (except in Scotland) the phrase has been a hundred years out of fashion.

PRINCIPLE G

All ideas should be expressed concisely, but without discourteous abruptness.

Circumlocution is one of the few bad habits in writing that have gradually gone out of fashion since the daily newspapers first set an example of snappy reporting of events. Yet there is still plenty of verbosity left over from the leisured days before the First World War when it was often considered a sign not of pomposity but of ingenuity to make five words, without irrelevance or repetition, do the work of one. Pontifical critics, who wish to fill up a column easily, politicians and retired Head Masters who wish to be regarded as men of letters, and officials who wish to be portentous for reasons of policy are, in general, the most verbose writers of to-day.

Victorian readers did not much mind having their time wasted; a few survivors still feel that they are not getting their money's-worth unless, say, an article on modern novels in the leading literary weekly begins in the leisurely expansive style of the following (1940):

> 'Nothing is vainer at the present time, of course, than prediction. But one broad conclusion seems reasonably safe. If, as is most likely, we come out after the war into rather a different sort of world, we shall almost certainly be getting a rather different sort of novel.
>
> English fiction of the past two years throws little light on precisely what differences may be expected. So far, that is, the war has not stimulated any noticeable "new tendencies" in the novel; there is nothing to indicate the birth of either new ideals or new methods. But at the same time there is evidence, admittedly slight and possibly unreliable except in rough outline, of a deepening selectiveness among old ideals and methods. For what it is worth this evidence may supplement certain general deductions from the course of events since the outbreak of war that concern much else besides literature.'

This amounts to no more than:

> 'Though the style of English novels is likely to change after the war is over, it is not safe to prophesy just how it will change. Fiction published during this war has shown signs, not of new ideals and methods, but only of what I, perhaps mistakenly, judge to be a more conscientious choice of old ones. I will relate this judgement to certain general deductions from events of the last two years.'

From the Minutes of a Debating Society:

> 'It was proposed by Mr. J. H. Dix and unanimously carried: that whereas discussions in this Society are not liable to end in the breaking

of furniture or fixtures, so long as they are checked when they become too noisy; and whereas discussions unwisely conducted endanger the peacefulness of this Society; and whereas discussions that go on under the chairmanship of Mr. E. B. Silvoe sometimes end in the breaking of furniture or fixtures; and whereas discussions in this usually peaceful Society are, if wisely conducted, always checked when they become too noisy — Mr. E. B. Silvoe be not again appointed to take the chair at a meeting of this Society.'

This can be reduced simply to:

'It was proposed by Mr. J. H. Dix and unanimously carried: that whereas, when Mr. E. B. Silvoe is appointed chairman, the discussions of this usually peaceful Society are not always checked before furniture or fixtures are broken, he be not again appointed.'

Verbosity, as in the last example, is often due to over-conscientiousness; in the following instance, from a Head Warden's circular, it is due to embarrassment at having to point out something obvious:

'With the coming of the longer periods of darkness the possibility of enemy action is increasing and it is necessary that all steps should be taken by the civilian population to minimize the dangers attendant on the falling of bombs, by organizing themselves into stirrup-pump parties, and so face up to the war.'

This would have been put more simply as:

'As the nights draw out, civilians must face the increased danger of enemy bombing by forming stirrup-pump parties.'

This, from Professor A. N. Whitehead's *Science and the Modern World* (1925), is probably also written in embarrassment with what is obvious.

'The inevitableness of destiny can only be illustrated in terms of human life by incidents which in fact involve unhappiness.'

Since destiny is by definition inevitable, this reduces to:

'Human destiny can be exemplified only with unhappy instances.'

PRINCIPLE H

The descriptive title of a person or thing should not be varied merely for the sake of elegance.

Elegant variation of names and titles is a common French trick, derived from Latin verse. A Latin poet, writing about the God Bacchus, for example, or the God Juppiter, would have thought meanly of himself if he could not present the God under ten or twelve aliases, each recording a part of his legendary history and attributes. The French novelist Balzac, similarly, used as many as six different descriptive identifications of the same person at the beginning of successive sentences. Mr. Philip Guedalla emulates Balzac. Here is a passage from his *Mr. Churchill: a Portrait:*

> '. . . he prepared a discourse, learned it off, and established himself in his father's seat. His predecessor in debate was a Welsh Radical, a few years older than himself, who had been ten years in the House already, and, courageous in his criticism of the war, emulated Winston Churchill's escape from Pretoria in a Dutch pastor's hat by escaping from a hostile audience at Birmingham Town Hall in a policeman's helmet.
>
> The black-haired orator resumed his seat, and Mr. Churchill followed Mr. Lloyd George. It was an unimpressive little speech . . . Though he managed to be loyal to the Government, the new member's tone about the Boers was a shade unusual. . . .
>
> The ordeal was over; and when someone introduced him to Lloyd George, the fervent Welshman told him that he was "standing against the light". The Tory novice answered that his new friend seemed to "take a singularly detached view of the British Empire".'

Anyone who read this passage hurriedly would imagine that a least four or five people, not two, were involved in this historic meeting.

An official leaflet, E D L 66, circulated by the Ministry of Labour to women who registered under the 'Registration for Employment Order, 1941', contains this paragraph:

> 'Women are wanted for the work of supplying the Forces with aeroplanes, guns, shells, and all the munitions and equipment that they need. Large numbers are also required in the Women's Auxiliary Services – the W.R.N.S., the A.T.S., the W.A.A.F., . . . The Nursing Services also require a great many additional recruits. More women are wanted by the Women's Land Army and N.A.A.F.I. There are also many other essential industries and services which must be maintained.'

This constant change of formula is unnecessary, confusing and invidious. The paragraph would have read more persuasively as follows:

> 'Large numbers of women are needed in industry, especially in the factories that supply the Forces with aeroplanes, guns, tanks, ammunition and equipment. Large numbers are needed also in the W.R.N.S., the A.T.S., the W.A.A.F., in the Women's Land Army, in the N.A.A.F.I., in the Nursing Associations – these and many other vital services must be maintained.'

From an historical article on the American War of Independence:

> 'When news of the disaster came, Cornwallis sought to retrieve it by cutting off Morgan, but that general had dropped back with such celerity that the force sent out was too late, the troops being detained by torrents of rain which made the creeks almost impassable.'

'That general', 'that gentleman', 'that worthy' are never either neat or necessary substitutes for 'he'. The author should have written something of this sort:

> 'When news of the disaster came, Cornwallis sought to retrieve his position by cutting General Morgan's line of retreat. But Morgan moved quickly and the force that Cornwallis sent out arrived too late [at the Dan River], having been detained by torrential rain which made the intervening creeks almost impassable.'

Expressions such as 'the former, the latter', 'the first, the second', should be used as seldom as possible: they are invitations to the reader's eye to travel back – and it should be encouraged always to read straight on at an even pace.

An Air Ministry announcement was phrased:

> 'One of our fighters attacked and destroyed three enemy bombers in as many minutes.'

This is a device for avoiding the repetition of 'three'. But why trouble to avoid it? Why ask the reader to work out an equation sum – which is not even amusingly complex?

An American magazine takes this device a stage further into absurdity:

> 'For the second time in as many months the panic was on.'

PRINCIPLE I

Sentences should not be so long that the reader loses his way in them.

A sentence may be as long as the writer pleases, provided that he confines it to a single connected range of ideas, and by careful punctuation prevents the reader from finding it either tedious or confusing. Modern journalists work on the principle that sentences should be as snappy as possible; they seldom, therefore, use colons or semi-colons. Historians and biographers have learned to be snappy too. Here is H. C. Armstrong writing about Mustapha Kemal Ataturk in his *Grey Wolf*:

> 'Enver was always inspired by great ideas, by far-flung schemes. The big idea absorbed him. He cared nothing for details, facts or figures.

Mustafa Kemal was cautious. He was suspicious of brilliancy. Big, vague ideas did not rouse him. His objectives were limited, and undertaken only after long and careful consideration and calculation. He wanted exact facts and figures. He had no sympathy with and no ability at handling Arabs or any foreigners. He was a Turk, and proud of being a Turk. . . .'

A biographer of the old school would have fitted these ten sentences into a single one, connected by a semi-colon at the place where Mr. Armstrong has begun a new paragraph.

Sentences by eighteenth-century authors sometimes continue for a page or more, yet are not allowed to get out of hand. Here, however, are a couple of modern instances where even a seven-line sentence is too long.

From an article by D. R. Gent, the sporting-journalist:

'I spent many hours dipping into Rugby books of all kinds, and two especially suggested lots of subjects that, I think, will interest my readers these days, when we can face up to the strenuous times we are living in, even more bravely when we can refresh ourselves occasionally with memories of great days behind us, and especially days on the Rugby field or watching glorious matches.'

This would have read better if he had broken it up into three sentences, in some such way as this:

'I spent many hours dipping into a variety of books about Rugby, and two especially interested me. I think that they would have interested my readers too, for they concerned great events in the history of the game. In these strenuous times we can face up to our trials and responsibilities more bravely if we occasionally refresh ourselves with memories of the glorious matches which we have witnessed or in which we have been fortunate enough to take part ourselves.'

This is from an article by Ernest Newman, the music critic:

'Berlioz's faults as a composer are obvious, but not more so than those of many other composers who, however, had the good luck to have their misses counted as hits by umpires whose sense of values had been perverted by too long a toleration of bad art so long as it was bad in the orthodox way, whereas Berlioz's directest hits were often debited to him as misses.'

This is too long a sentence only because it is mismanaged. Commas are not enough to separate so many complex ideas into properly related parts of a single argument. We suggest this alternative version:

'Berlioz's faults are obvious to us modern listeners, as are those of many other composers who in their time fared far better with the critics than he did: their misses were often counted as hits, his most direct hits as misses – merely because musical standards had been perverted by a long toleration of work which, though bad, was not eccentrically so.'

This is from an article by Arthur Krock in a New York newspaper (1941):

> 'It is Morava-Varda that is the military stake for which Hitler is playing in his game of high-tension diplomacy with the Yugoslavs. Should he be confined to the Struma because of unwillingness or inability to add to his enemies the Yugoslavs massed against a Salonika front which would be the result if the people and their government fulfil the expectation noted above, Hitler's designs would be obstructed.'

The second sentence is too long only because too many ideas have been tied to one another in a bundle. They should have been separated in this sort of way:

> 'If the people and government of Yugoslavia, fulfilling my expectation of them noted above, decide to forbid Hitler the use of the Morava-Varda valleys, and if he is unwilling or unable to add them to his enemies, he will be unable to approach Salonica except by the Struma valley and his designs will thereby be obstructed.'

PRINCIPLE J

No unnecessary strain should be put on the reader's memory.

Some writers think in far longer stretches than others: they start an essay or article with some unobtrusive point and, after introducing a whole new body of argument, slowly circle round and pick the point up again two or three pages later as if it had only just been made. They should remember that most people, though they may be expected to retain the general sense of any paragraph until the end of the chapter, will forget a particular phrase in it (unless heavily accentuated) after three sentences and a word (unless very remarkable) as soon as they have finished the sentence.

Here are examples, from two leaders by J. A. Spender, of excessive strain put on the reader's memory:

> 'There could, for example, be no better contribution to "Federal Union" than the pooling of resources for mutual defence recently achieved by the United States, Britain and Canada. Here, for the first time, is shown the way to break down the obstacle of "sovereignty" which worked so disastrously before the war to isolate and divide the smaller nations and leave them at the mercy of the Dictators. Lord

Lothian, who has long been a student of this subject, brings back this sheaf with him on his visit to London.'

The phrase 'this subject' in the third sentence presumably refers to 'Federal Union'; and 'this sheaf' to 'the pooling of resources for mutual defence'. But because of the intervening sentence few readers will have been able to identify these references without a quick look-back to the first sentence.

'Our habit of taking the whole world into our confidence about our casualties and the damage done by German raiders to our buildings and property is, I am sure, well justified. A free and self-respecting people needs to be assured that nothing is being concealed from it, and that there will not some day be a sudden shock of discovery when concealment is no longer possible. Yet contrasted with the grim silence of the dictators about what is happening in their countries, it produces a one-sided psychological effect which needs to be corrected by some effort of imagination.'

Here, the 'it' of the third sentence has separated from the subject to which it refers by a longish sentence. Few readers will have been immediately able to identify the 'it' with 'our habit of taking the whole world into our confidence about our casualties and the damage done by German raiders to our buildings and property'.

The Archbishop of Canterbury writes in a pamphlet (1940):

'Especially we must remember that it is very hard to extract justice from strife. The passions evoked by war blind the vision and distort the judgement. We dare not hope to make our victory result in pure justice. We can, indeed, make it result in something far nearer justice than a Nazi domination; that alone would justify our fighting. But we must not ignore the perils inseparable from our enterprise; and we must steadfastly determine that we will resist, so far as by God's help we can, these corrupting influences, so that if He gives us victory we may be found faithful to the principles for which we have striven.'

Here, similarly, the 'corrupting influences' in the last sentence are not easily identified with 'the passions evoked by war' mentioned three sentences previously: most readers will be able to think back only as far as 'a Nazi domination'.

PRINCIPLE K

The same word should not be so often used in the same sentence or paragraph that it becomes tedious.

For emphasis it is legitimate to go on using the same word or phrase time after time:

'The crow has been peculiarly my bird ever since I can remember. Indeed, my earliest recollection of childhood is a crow perched on my nursery window-sill. On my third birthday a crow came to my party and helped himself to my birthday cake. On my first journey to school I was accompanied by a crow. A crow perched on a tree outside the room where I sat for my first successful examination. A crow was the cause of my meeting my first wife; a crow attended our wedding; a crow nested on the chimney of my first freehold house. Finally, a crow gave the alarm when I was drowning in the Regent's Canal in June 1886. It has always been a crow, not lark, robin, blackbird, raven, owl nor lapwing – no other bird but a crow!'

Or:

'Fethi had this tradition from the sage Abdul ibn Rashid, who had it from the sage Daoud ibn Zaki, who had it from his father who was a judge in Homs, who had it from his brother Ali the Copyist, who had it from Mahomed the guardian of the Mosque of Tarjid, who had it from his predecessor of the same name, who had it from [etc. etc.] who had it from Ali, the muezzin of Al Ragga, who had it from his father Akbar, the saddle-maker, who had it from the lips of the blessed Prophet Himself!'

But here are instances where the continued use of the same word becomes tedious. From a 'lay sermon':

'I admire the man who is man enough to go up to a man whom he sees bullying a child or a weaker man and tell him, as man to man, that he must lay off.'

This should read:

'I admire the man who is courageous enough to go up to someone whom he sees bullying a child or a man weaker than himself, and tell him plainly that he must lay off.'

The word 'of' is often a difficulty. From a report on broadcasting by the Committee of Convocation (1931):

'There has been . . . an honest dread on the part of many of the popularization of a form of godliness that lacked its power, of the substitution of an emotional appeal at the fireside for the organized fellowship. . . .'

This should have read:

'Many have honestly dreaded the popularization of a form of godliness that lacked its power, the substitution of an emotional appeal at the fireside for organized fellowship. . . .'

The word 'in' is often a difficulty. From an agricultural report in a newspaper:

> 'In fact, in countless villages in England in this war and in a variety of ways, there has been a most astonishing adaptation of local products to war needs.'

This should have read:

> 'In countless English villages during this war, and in a variety of ways, there has been, indeed,' etc. etc.

PRINCIPLE L

Words which rhyme or form a jingle should not be allowed to come too close together.

Though modern prose is intended to be read silently and two or three times faster than at the ordinary speaking rate, some people read with their mental ear not quite closed. Obtrusive accidental rhymes or jingles are therefore avoided by careful prose writers, as possibly distracting their readers' attention.

The terminations 'otion' and 'ation' are often a difficulty:

> 'The need of registration or re-registration at this station of all workers on probation is to be the subject of examination by the Administration.'

There is usually a way out – here, for example:

> 'The Administration will examine the need of registering or re-registering at this station all probationary workers.'

The termination 'ing' is often a difficulty. This is from a Gossip column (1940):

> 'I have heard something interesting which, anticipating the approaching ending of the Peiping Puppet Government, illustrates popular feeling in Northern China to-day.'

The way out here was:

> 'I have heard an interesting piece of news which illustrates popular feeling in Northern China to-day and anticipates the early collapse of the Puppet Government at Peiping.'

This is from *English Villages*, by Edmund Blunden:

> 'Our great game is cricket; our summer is incomplete without its encounters . . . and however the actual process of play may seem to

the uninitiated visitor, the centre scene . . . with pigeons flying over and cuckoos calling across, and now and then the church clock measuring out the hour with deep and slow notes, cannot but be notable.'

To avoid the jingle with 'notes', 'notable' should have been 'memorable'.

Terminal 'y' is often a difficulty. From an article by Hilaire Belloc on air-superiority:

> 'We have established, and are increasing, our superiority in quality, while time makes steadily for ultimately establishing superiority in quantity as well.'

The way out was:

> 'We have established and are increasing our qualitative superiority, and are making steady progress towards the ultimate establishment of quantitative superiority as well.'

The persistent recurrence of the same vowel-sound is often very ugly. For example, this sentence from an article on the Baconian Theory:

> 'But my main contention is that, though great claims may be made for the name of Bacon, "Shakespeare's plays" remain unchangeably the same.'

Many of these 'a' sounds can be removed:

> 'But my chief contention is that, however strongly it may be urged that Bacon was the author of "Shakespeare's plays", this cannot result in the slightest textual alteration in them.'

Another example, from an article by Herbert Read:

> '. . . Art as we know it now will have disappeared in the flames like so much plush, . . .'

Or like so much crushed, mushy, touchwood.

PRINCIPLE M

Alliteration should be sparingly used.

The use of alliteration need not be altogether discarded. Indeed, when one writes with feeling in English there is a natural tendency for words to well up in a strongly alliterative way; and this should be checked only when the emphasis seems too heavy for the context. The foregoing sentence, for example, has got one 'w' too many in the middle of it: on reading it over we should naturally have changed 'well up' to 'start up', had we not seen that it illustrated our point.

In the following passage from a newspaper article, Mr. J. B. Priestley might well have cut out five of the eight 'w's and two of the four rhymes in *-ore*.

> 'The world before the war produced the war, and we want no more such worlds. But we want . . .'

He could have written:

> 'There must be no more worlds like that which produced this war. Instead, there must be . . .

The B.B.C. news-bulletin editors might well have trimmed off a few 'p's from the following item (1940):

> 'A feature of to-day's news has been important public pronouncements on peace by the Pope and President Roosevelt.'

They could have written:

> 'Important declarations on peace are a feature of to-day's news: they have been made by the Pope and by President Roosevelt.'

PRINCIPLE N

The same word should not be used in different senses in the same passage, unless attention is called to the difference.

If one searches in the kitchen-cupboard for a missing egg-cup and does not find it, though it is there, the chances are that it is doing duty as a mustard-pot—the eye refuses to recognize it as an egg-cup. Similarly, if the same word is used in different senses in a passage, the reader's eye will often fail to recognize the second word—it cannot grasp, as it were, that an egg-cup can also be a mustard-pot.

Here are examples. From a pamphlet by Dr. Hugh Dalton, M.P.:

> 'I have already said that Britain holds the key to this key-problem of Franco-German relations.'

The word 'key' is here used in two different senses. A key-problem is a metaphor derived from the key-stone of an arch; the key to a problem is a metaphor derived from unlocking a chest.

From a newspaper leader (1941):

> 'Roumania must remember that though she has now chosen to take what she believes to be the safest course, namely, to *range* herself with Germany, the *range* of our heavy bombers based on Greek aerodromes constitutes a serious threat to her oil fields.'

From a newspaper report:

'The mob of frightened little children reached the fire-alarm, but were unable to reach it.'

The probable meaning is:

'The mob of frightened little children arrived at the fire-alarm, but none was tall enough to reach the knob.'

From the organ of the International Brigade Association:

'A few letters written in July have reached this country from German and Polish International Brigaders, interned at the concentration camp of Le Vernet. Two hundred prisoners still remain there. All efforts should be concentrated to save them.'

The odium in the word 'concentration camp' should have made the writer avoid using 'concentrated' in a good sense.

PRINCIPLE O

The rhetorical device of pretending to hesitate in a choice between two words or phrases is inappropriate to modern prose.

Many orators have built their reputations on passages such as this:

'Mr. Hacksaw – oh, I beg his pardon, our friend served two whole days in the State militia, so I suppose I ought to call him *Captain* Hacksaw – well, this gallant Captain was born in Clay County getting on for thirty years ago, I reckon. His father was a dishonest, possessed Baptist minister – forgive the slip of the tongue, I should have said "an honest, dispossessed Baptist minister" – from a wretched living near Taunton, Conn. Well, this Rev. Jackstraw – I should say Chop-straw – oh, the devil take it, Hacksaw – was a sheep-stealer, or if that sounds too blackguardly, let us say he was a man who used to rob his fellow-ministers of their flocks and rush them down to the stream to be *dipped*. . . .'

Prose writers, however, are assumed to be able to correct their first inaccurate remarks before publication; so that their play with second thoughts is not amusing, but indicates mere indecision between two ideas.

From an article by Brigadier-General Morgan, K.C.:

'When the great explosion of 1914 occurred, the doctrine was there ready to the hands of the German armies to justify, or rather to excuse, every outrage they committed.'

From an article by Negley Farson:

'This might all be fruitless were it not that, in his self-overhaul, the Englishman has begun to question some of his traditions, or (let us call them correctly) his obsessions.'

From a woman's column in a weekly paper:

> 'Typewriting, from the very beginning, has been a woman's means of earning a livelihood—or, more correctly, a girl's perhaps because women, taking them all round, are nimbler with their fingers than men.'

From Sir Walter Citrine's *My Finnish Diary*:

> 'Below us were masses of trees fringing tracts of snow, which quite possibly were small lakes, or to put it more correctly, perhaps, creeks.'

(Or shall we say 'fjords'?)

In each of these cases, if second thoughts were best, the writer should have expunged the first.

PRINCIPLE P

Even when the natural order of its words is modified for the sake of emphasis, a sentence must not read unnaturally.

The three following examples of inversion suggest too-literal translations from a foreign language:

From a note by 'Atticus', the columnist:

> 'Colonel Bishop became a truly remarkable shot and the higher his score of victims amounted the more his china-blue eyes grew humorously pensive.'

(Here 'amounted' is probably a slip for 'mounted'.)

From an article by Ivor Brown:

> 'News comes of the death of a clown absolute . . . one of a dynasty adored . . . The clown absolute is quite a different person from the actor-droll.'

(Yes, quite a person different.)

From an unsigned book-review:

> 'That till he had installed himself at Ferney never, surely, in his whole life had he been so much of his fate the master, this was the burden, or under-song, of all Voltaire's later writings: . . .'

From an American news magazine:

> 'Unhappily, the Rome radio admitted: "There is a possibility of our having to yield some further points".'

The effect in this last instance is ambiguity. The writer did not mean that he was made unhappy by the admission, but that the Rome radio was unhappy.

PART II

EXAMINATIONS AND FAIR COPIES

★

EXPLANATION

WHILE noting typical errors or shortcomings in English prose-works of the 1918-1941 period we came across numerous short passages, from each of which we could draw examples of several different sorts of error; and were surprised to see what eminent people some of the writers were. We then concentrated on the writings of eminent people, and the frequency of confusion or obscurity in their work supported our original contention: that English has for some time been written with great carelessness not only among the uneducated and semi-educated but also among the educated classes, who once prided themselves as much on their ability to write and speak well as on their lineage, wealth, or administrative capacities.

We do not claim that our system for classifying faults is the only practical one, or even the best one; or that, when we quote a passage, every one of the objections which we raise on behalf of the common reader is justified; or that the fair copies we offer are perfect; or that no faults in plain statement or shortcomings in the graces of prose are to be found in our own writing. But we hope at least that our inquiries will make people more conscious of the reader-writer relationship than they have hitherto been.

★

The quotations we use are chosen 'almost at random': which means that, having decided that so-and-so was eminent in such and such a profession, we took up the first popular book, pamphlet or article by him that came our way and read on at our usual speed until we found ourselves bogged in a difficult passage. This passage became the subject of our analysis. Often we were bogged in the opening paragraph; often we were not bogged at all and mentally apologized to the author — Godfrey Winn is an instance — for having suspected him of writing badly, merely because we did not much like his point of view, or because — Elizabeth Jenkins is an instance — popular reviewers whom we mistrusted had praised his or her work extravagantly.

We have had no intention of pillorying the writers whom we include in our list, or of suggesting that the passages chosen are characteristic of their work. We considered, at first, quoting examples of good prose by the same writers; but decided against this because one cannot profitably compare a straightforward account of one thing with a confused account of another, and because we did not wish to compile an anthology.

Our friend Captain Liddell Hart has suggested as a sub-title to this book 'A Short Cut to Unpopularity'. It is true that many small-minded people would almost rather be told that they have no sense of humour than that they have expressed themselves badly in prose: for every English writer considers himself, like the Emperor Sigismundus, to be 'superior to the grammarians'. But we shall not impute small-mindedness to any of those from whose writings we quote and shall assume that, like ourselves, they are always glad to have their errors pointed out, so long as this is done justly and without malice.

When we began making our comments, always from the reader's point of view, these were at first limited to surface faults or shortcomings; but we were soon reminded that good English is a matter not merely of grammar and syntax and vocabulary, but also of sense: the structure of the sentences must hold together logically. In analysing a passage we have often found ourselves in disagreement with the facts presented in it, but have not tampered with them in our fair copy, unless they seemed too contradictory to support their logical structure. If it is objected 'You really know what the writer means — why shouldn't he put it in his own way? — you can't pass a steam-roller over individuality?', our reply is: 'In some cases we don't know at all what he means and doubt whether he is sure of it himself; in others we have guessed with varying degrees of certainty; in the remainder we have found out after only a slight delay.' Our contention is that each focusing of the reader's mind on an eccentricity or error or ambiguity interrupts the continuity of his reading and distracts him from a clear understanding of what the passage means. Every writer is entitled to make his own mistakes, if he is prepared to stand by the consequences and not expect the reader's gratitude for being given unnecessary work to do. But he must remember that even phrases which can be justified both grammatically and from the point of view of sense may give his reader a wrong first impression, or check his reading speed, tempting him to skip.

We do not attempt to stereotype English. The principles which we suggest, and which if adopted would, we believe, help people to read and understand books far more easily than now, allow full scope for individual style; just as the conventions of legible handwriting do. One cannot bind a lively intelligence to the dull regularity of copperplate script. In each fair copy we have tried to keep as close as possible to the style and spirit of the original.

If it is further objected that many of the points which we raise are so small as to seem hardly worth raising, our reply is that, though a single fly-spot does not make a dirty window-pane, twenty or thirty do. It is strange how insensitive English-speaking people are to faults in their own language, even those who pride themselves on the correctness of their French or Spanish. In our analyses we do not pass any fault or shortcoming however small; but to avoid tediousness we make a few of our more pettifogging points by implication in the fair copy rather than by direct comment in the analysis.

We have included the work of six Americans. British writers, unless they have lived in the United States for some years, which we have not, cannot be judges of American writing; but the work we examine here has been published in Great Britain and therefore seems a legitimate subject of scrutiny. Our impression is that the level of educated American writing as a whole is higher than the British, though when Americans attempt the grand or the quaint style the result is more shocking than when the British do so. Timidity leading to under-statement, irrelevancy, contradiction, repetition, is far rarer in American writing than in English; instead there is over-confidence, leading to dropped threads, faulty connexion of ideas, hasty choice of words, unannounced changes of standpoint.

Only one writer, in giving permission for a passage to be quoted, has asked to see the critical use we make of it. This is Miss Helen Waddell. We are sorry to say that she disagrees strongly with our comments, rejects the fair copy as 'singularly inaccurate, verbose and silly', and maintains that the original context makes the meaning of the passage perfectly clear. We consider it most generous of Miss Waddell to let us use the quotation in spite of her strong feelings. Naturally, she has shaken our confidence in all our examinations and fair copies: we begin to wonder whether they are after all a monument rather to our own stupidity than to the obscurity of the passages examined. Yet we refuse to regard ourselves as more than averagely stupid; and that our two pairs of eyes have checked at particular passages suggests that other eyes have done the same and that therefore our remarks have some pertinence, even if none of our fair copies (in the writing of which we have had the critical assistance of several intelligent friends) is regarded by the author as doing justice to his or her concept. We have here briefed ourselves to represent the reader's point of view, and solemnly protest that we have wrenched no quotation unfairly from its context. Our simple contention is, that a passage which reads clearly enough to its author does not necessarily read clearly enough to his public, not even if it occurs in a book which, like Miss Waddell's, has been worked over for ten or twelve years.

Here is a list of the twenty-five numbered categories which we use for tabulating errors in clear statement, and of the sixteen lettered categories we use for tabulating shortcomings in the graces, or decencies, of prose. With each category goes the principle which rules it.

1. WHO? *It should always be made clear who is addressing whom, and on the subject of whom.*

2. WHICH? *It should always be made clear which of two or more things already mentioned is being discussed.*

3. WHAT? *Every unfamiliar subject or concept should be clearly defined; and neither discussed as if the reader knew all about it already nor stylistically disguised.*

4. WHERE? *There should never be any doubt left as to* where *something happened or is expected to happen.*

5. WHEN? *There should never be any doubt left as to* when.

6. HOW MUCH? *There should never be any doubt left as to* how much *or* how long.

7. HOW MANY? *There should never be any doubt left as to* how many.

8. INAPPROPRIATE WORD OR PHRASE. *Every word or phrase should be appropriate to its context.*

9. AMBIGUOUS WORD OR PHRASE. *No word or phrase should be ambiguous.*

10. MISPLACED WORD OR PHRASE. *Every word or phrase should be in its right place in the sentence.*

11. UNINTENTIONAL CONTRAST. *No unintentional contrast between two ideas should be allowed to suggest itself.*

12. DUPLICATION. *Unless for rhetorical emphasis, or necessary recapitulation, no idea should be presented more than once in the same prose passage.*

13. SELF-EVIDENT STATEMENT. *No statement should be self-evident.*

14. MATERIAL OMISSION. *No important detail should be omitted from any phrase, sentence or paragraph.*

15. UNFULFILLED PROMISE. *No phrase should be allowed to raise expectations that are not fulfilled.*

16. UNDEVELOPED THEME. *No theme should be suddenly abandoned.*

17. FAULTY CONNEXION. *Sentences and paragraphs should be linked together logically and intelligibly.*

18. MISPUNCTUATION. *Punctuation should be consistent and should denote quality of connexion, rather than length of pause, between sentences or parts of sentences.*

19. CONFUSED SEQUENCE OF IDEAS. *The order of ideas in a sentence or paragraph should be such that the reader need not rearrange them in his mind.*

20. IRRELEVANCY. *No unnecessary idea, phrase or word should be included in a sentence.*

21. FALSE CONTRAST. *All antitheses should be true ones.*

22. OVER-EMPHASIS. *Over-emphasis of the illogical sort tolerated in conversation should be avoided in prose.*

23. LOGICAL WEAKNESS. *Ideas should not contradict one another, or otherwise violate logic.*

24. CHANGE OF STANDPOINT. *The writer should not, without clear warning, change his standpoint in the course of a sentence or paragraph.*

25. MIXED CATEGORY. *In each list of people or things all the words used should belong to the same category of ideas.*

A. MISMATING OF METAPHORS. *Metaphors should not be mated in such a way as to confuse or distract the reader.*

B. TOO MANY METAPHORS. *Metaphors should not be piled on top of one another.*

C. METAPHOR CONFUSED WITH REALITY. *Metaphors should not be in such close association with unmetaphorical language as to produce absurdity or confusion.*

D. POETICALITY. *Characteristically poetical expressions should not be used in prose.*

E. MISMATING OF STYLES. *Except where the writer is being deliberately facetious, all phrases in a sentence, or sentences in a paragraph, should belong to the same vocabulary or level of language.*

F. OBSCURE REFERENCE. *No reference should be unnecessarily obscure.*

G. CIRCUMLOCUTION. *All ideas should be expressed concisely, but without discourteous abruptness.*

H. ELEGANT VARIATION. *The descriptive title of a person or thing should not be varied merely for the sake of elegance.*

I. OVERLONG SENTENCE. *Sentences should not be so long that the reader loses his way in them.*

J. MEMORY STRAIN. *No unnecessary strain should be put on the reader's memory.*

K. TOO MUCH OF THE SAME WORD. *The same word should not be so often used in the same sentence or paragraph that it becomes tedious.*

L. JINGLE. *Words which rhyme or form a jingle should not be allowed to come too close together.*

M. TOO MUCH ALLITERATION. *Alliteration should be sparingly used.*

N. SAME WORD IN DIFFERENT SENSES. *The same word should not be used in different senses in the same passage, unless attention is called to the difference.*

O. SECOND THOUGHTS. *The rhetorical device of pretending to hesitate in a choice between two words or phrases is inappropriate to modern prose.*

P. AWKWARD INVERSION. *Even when the natural order of its words is modified for the sake of emphasis, a sentence must not read unnaturally.*

In the texts that we examine, a small letter following a numeral means that we have found more than one example of the same type of error; similarly, a small numeral following a capital letter means that we have found more than one example of the same type of shortcoming. The best way to follow our argument is first to read a text through without regard to numbers and letters; then to read it again, sentence by sentence, looking up each note in the EXAMINATION under the corresponding number or letter; then to read the FAIR COPY, comparing it with the TEXT, and finally the COMMENT.

Sir Norman Angell

from *Why Freedom Matters*, 1940

TEXT

. . . The new inquisitions[23a] and the new Popes assume infallibility. Stalin and Hitler pronounce[14] the true doctrine; decide on[18a] pain of death and torture,[P] that it shall not be questioned; decide what facts the millions[1a]/[H] shall be allowed to know, and what they shall not be allowed to know concerning those[2a] doctrines.[G]

And the new inquisitions[8a] are immensely more powerful, more efficient, more omnipresent[22a] than the old, because they possess instruments so

immeasurably [22b] more efficient[8b] for reaching the mind of the million.[H] It will be[5] easier for the new Popes to crystallize error.[9]

From the day[22c] that a child is born in Germany or Russia, and to a lesser extent in Italy,[10a] it is brought under the influence of the State's doctrine; every teacher teaches it[2b] through the years of childhood and adolescence. In[4] every conscript, whether military or industrial, the process is continued;[18b] every book suggests the prevailing orthodoxy; every paper shouts it; every cinema gives it visual suggestion.[21/10b]

The effect of the process is, of course,[23b] to worsen the quality of the mass mind;[18c] to render it less and less capable of sound judgement.

The protagonist of dictatorship argues[1b] that the quality of the mass mind does not matter[18d] because the dictator rules[23c] and the mass only have to obey. . . .

EXAMINATION

1. WHO?

(*a*) **. . . decide what facts the millions shall be allowed to know . . .**

Who are the millions? Their own nationals or the world at large?

(*b*) **The protagonist of dictatorship argues . . .**

A 'protagonist' is the leading character in a dramatic situation. Is Mussolini, Stalin or Hitler intended? Or does Sir Norman Angell mean merely 'enthusiastic advocates of the dictatorial form of government'?

2. WHICH?

(*a*) **. . . what they shall be allowed to know . . . concerning those doctrines.**

Which doctrines? So far only one, true, doctrine has been mentioned.

(*b*) **From the day that a child is born in Germany or Russia it is brought under the influence of the State's doctrine; every teacher teaches it through the years of childhood and adolescence.**

At first one naturally reads the second 'it' as meaning the child; but this makes poor sense, so one decides that the doctrine is meant. 'The years of childhood and adolescence' are presumably the child's years, not the State's.

4. WHERE?

In every conscript the process is continued . . .

This 'in' conveys no clear location. It is probably short for 'in the case of'; but means literally that the process of education in State-doctrine is carried on by the conscript for himself.

5. WHEN?

It will be easier for the new Popes to crystallize error.

But it is said in the next paragraph that the process of bringing up children and adults in the way that (according to the Democrats) they should not go, is already complete in Germany and Russia.

8. INAPPROPRIATE WORD OR PHRASE

(*a*) **And the new inquisitions are immensely more powerful, more efficient,**

more omnipresent than the old, because they possess instruments so immeasurably more efficient for reaching the mind of the million.

Is not 'inquisitions' too limited a word for the context? The task of the original Inquisitors was to smell out heresy, not to be missionaries of Christian doctrine – that was left to the priests and the friars. The Nazi and Communist parties as orders of priesthood should perhaps have been mentioned; the Inquisitors – Ogpu or Gestapo – not being numerous compared with the mass of the party to which they belonged.

(*b*) **The new inquisitors . . . possess instruments so immeasurably more efficient for reaching the mind of the million.**

The phrase 'efficient instruments' suggests people; 'efficacious', a word reserved for things as opposed to personal agents, would be better – if microphones, the radio, modern newspaper plant and suchlike are meant. Also, 'efficient' has already been used in the sentence.

9. AMBIGUOUS PHRASE

It will be easier for the new Popes to crystallize error.

The argument is not at all clear. Play has been made with the ironical use of 'true doctrine' so that we do not know whether 'error' here is meant seriously or not. Real (as opposed to figurative) Popes may be said to crystallize error by their pronouncements against current heretical tendencies not previously regarded as erroneous. The edicts of these 'new Popes', however, unless Sir Norman is so violent an anti-Papist that he really means his readers to regard every pronouncement from the Vatican City as wilfully fraudulent, have, according to his argument, the effect, not of crystallizing error, but on the contrary of making it flow more freely.

10. MISPLACED PHRASE

(*a*) **From the day that a child is born in Germany or Russia, and to a lesser extent in Italy, . . .**

How can a child be born to a lesser extent in Italy than in Germany or Russia?

(*b*) **Every book suggests the prevailing orthodoxy; every paper shouts it; every cinema gives it visual suggestion.**

These are presumably the more efficient instruments hinted at in the second paragraph; and should have gone in there.

14. MATERIAL OMISSION

Stalin and Hitler pronounce the true doctrine . . .

This reads as though the Nazi and Communist doctrines were identical. They might have been emotionally allied in Sir Norman's mind in 1940, but in fact they were distinct and antagonistic to each other. He meant that Stalin and Hitler pronounced each his own true doctrine.

18. MISPUNCTUATION

(*a*) **Stalin and Hitler . . . decide on pain of death and torture, that it shall not be questioned; . . .**

With punctuation, it is often difficult to know whether the author, the typist, or the printer is responsible for the omission of important commas. The one that has dropped out after 'decide' is an important one, because without it the sentence means that the dictators decide on inflicting pain by death and torture in order that the doctrine may not be questioned; rather than meaning that death and torture are inflicted only in cases where the doctrine is questioned.

(*b*) **In every conscript . . . the process is continued; every book suggests the prevailing orthodoxy; every paper shouts it; every cinema gives it visual suggestion.**

These three semi-colons and the stop suggest that the items which they terminate are parallels. But the first item is of a different order from the rest, which all have to do with the dissemination of orthodox beliefs, and belongs with the previous sentence; the conscript has orthodoxy preached to him as part of his education, but does not necessarily disseminate it. Nor is the first semi-colon a possible misprint for a colon. Not only conscripts but the whole public are subjected to propaganda by books, papers and cinemas.

(*c*) **The effect of the process is, of course, to worsen the quality of the mass mind; to render it less and less capable of sound judgement.**

The semi-colon makes the phrases 'to worsen the quality' and 'to render it less capable' parallel and independent of each other. What is needed is a colon, to show that the second phrase is an interpretative enlargement of the first.

(*d*) **. . . the quality of the mass mind does not matter because the dictator rules . . .**

One should be careful of commas dropping out before the word 'because'. Here the omission makes the sentence mean: 'it is not because of a dictator being in power that the quality of the mass-mind matters' – which is contrary to the argument.

21. FALSE CONTRAST

Every book suggests the prevailing orthodoxy; every paper shouts it; every cinema gives it visual suggestion.

The implied contrast between the different degrees of emphasis used by newspapers as a whole, books as a whole, films as a whole, does not stand. Some Russian and German books shouted their propaganda; in some newspapers, especially scientific and technical ones, it was only suggested. And the implication that Russian and German films restricted their doctrine to visual suggestion, dispensing with the aid of sound, is unfortunate.

22. OVER-EMPHASIS

(*a*) **The new inquisitions are more omnipresent than the old . . .**

There are no degrees in omnipresence: any more than there are in absoluteness, or completeness. A thing is either everywhere, or it is not. Its absence even from a single locality would deny its omnipresence. But a thing can be said to be more nearly omnipresent, absolute or complete than another.

(*b*) **. . . they possess instruments so immeasurably more efficient for reaching the mind of the million.**

'Immeasurably' does not ring true. The Spanish Inquisition managed to inculcate orthodoxy pretty well with the crude instruments at its disposal; and the heretic of those times could not secretly switch on a radio-set and console himself with a free Lutheran broadcast in Spanish.

(*c*) **From the day that a child is born in Germany or Russia it is brought under the influence of the State's doctrine;**

One cannot believe that the German or Russian midwives and doctors exert their doctrinaire influence quite so early.

23. LOGICAL WEAKNESS

(*a*) **The new inquisitions and the new Popes assume infallibility.**

This suggests that the old Inquisition also assumed infallibility, whereas it was merely an instrument of the Pope's and could be censured by him for errors in carrying out its task. Nor did the Russian Ogpu assume infallibility: an Ogpu chief had recently been purged by Stalin for making grave mistakes. Similarly, in Germany Hitler had not delegated his 'infallibility' to the Gestapo.

(*b*) **The effect of the process is, of course, to worsen the quality of the mass mind; to render it less and less capable of sound judgement.**

'Of course' is gratuitous. It is arguable that the effect of Communist or Nazi State-doctrine on the public mind was not to worsen its quality, but only to give it a new set of axioms on which to form its judgements. Either doctrine, whatever might be said against it by democratic moralists, could surely be held by a convert without impairing his faculty of judgement – by the way, can a public mind be said to form spontaneous judgements even in the most favourable circumstances? – so long as he had confidence in the axioms and adhered to them.

(*c*) **. . . the quality of the mass mind does not matter because the dictator rules and the mass only have to obey.**

This argument is not fairly presented. Obedience is demanded from the people in all forms of government.

G. CIRCUMLOCUTION

Stalin and Hitler decide what facts the millions shall be allowed to know, and what they shall not be allowed to know concerning those doctrines.

The rhetorical repetition of 'shall be allowed' would be more effective if it led up to something that stirred the imagination more than the bald 'facts . . . concerning those doctrines'.

H. ELEGANT VARIATION

. . . What facts the millions shall be allowed to know, . . . for reaching the mind of the million.

Is there any justification for reducing the millions from plural to singular?

P. AWKWARD INVERSION

. . . on pain of death and torture; . . .

It is useless to torture a dead man; 'torture' should therefore come first. It is true that in the Middle Ages people were sometimes sentenced to be 'hanged, drawn and quartered and mulcted of 1000 marks', but the mulct was intended as a punishment of the criminal's heirs rather than of the criminal himself.

FAIR COPY

'A modern dictator, or lay-Pope, has his assumption of infallibility maintained by an ubiquitous priesthood of Party-men, which includes an

Inquisition of secret police. Popes Stalin and Hitler have each a political faith to enunciate which nobody in his State may question, under pain of torture or death; they decide just how many of the authentic facts of history and science may safely be taught to their docile millions.

Both the Communist and Nazi priesthoods, because of the superior efficacity of their instruments for controlling the public mind, are immensely more powerful than was the Catholic priesthood in the times of the Inquisition. The new Popes, indeed, find it easy enough to disseminate and perpetuate error: they can ensure that every book and newspaper published in the countries which they control, every cinema-film shown, must at least suggest, if it does not forcibly present, the new faith.

Children in Germany and Russia are introduced to the orthodox doctrine of their State as soon as they begin to talk, and are continuously instructed in it by all their teachers throughout the years of childhood and adolescence, and by their officers when they become military or industrial conscripts; the effect, of course, is to make them incapable of forming judgements on other bases of thought than those thus provided. This is also true of party education in Italy, though there the system is not run so thoroughly.

Those who advocate dictatorship as a practical form of government argue that the capacity of the common people for forming sound judgements does not matter, because the dictator and his staff do all the thinking for them. . . .'

COMMENT

A biographical note to Sir Norman Angell's book explains that he spent his childhood in England, but was educated in France and French Switzerland, and then worked as a cowboy and prospector in America; that subsequently he took to journalism in the United States, France and England; that for the last thirty years his chief interests have been economics and peace agitation. Graces of all the schools of language from which he graduated may be discovered in this passage: French rhetorical tricks, a go-as-you-please Western-American sequence of ideas, journalistic brightness, the insensitivity of the modern economist to the graces of prose, the uncertain emotional emphasis of pacifism. The liberties that we have taken in suggesting an alternative version to the passage chosen are far greater than in most cases; but this is a complicated case.

IRVING BABBITT

from *Rousseau and Romanticism*, 1919

TEXT

Those who have sought to set up a cult of love or beauty or science or humanity or country[25] are open[9a] to the same objections as the votaries[11a]

of nature. However important each of these things[2a] may be in its own place, it[3a] cannot properly be put in the supreme[20a] and central place[3b/18a] for the simple reason[22] that it does not involve any adequate[20b] conversion[8a] or discipline of man's ordinary self[3c] to some ethical centre.[3d] I have tried to show that the sense of solitude[20c] or forlornness that is so striking a feature of romantic melancholy arises not only from a loss of hold on[8b] the traditional centres,[3e] but also from[20d] the failure of these new attempts[3f] at communion[14] to keep their promises.[8c] The number of discomfitures of this kind[2b] in the period that has elapsed since the late eighteenth century, suggests that this period[2c] was[18b] even more than most periods[K] an age[H] of sophistry.[G] Every age has had its false teachers, but possibly no age ever had[24] so many[12] dubious[9b] moralists as this,[11b] an incomparable[10] series of false prophets. . . .

EXAMINATION

2. WHICH?

(*a*) **Those who have sought to set up a cult of love or beauty or science or humanity or country are open to the same objections as the votaries of nature. However important each of these things may be . . .**

The reader's eye has to turn back, past the words 'objections', 'votaries', and 'nature', to remind himself what 'each of these things' means. 'Things' is rather too blank a word of reference.

(*b*) **The number of discomfitures of this kind . . .**

Which kind? Failures merely to achieve romantic communion with nature? Or failures of 'those who have sought to set up a cult of', among other things, 'science, humanity and country'?

(*c*) **The number of discomfitures of this kind in the period that has elapsed since the late eighteenth century, suggests that this period was . . .**

The rest of the paragraph, which refers to Tolstoy and other late nineteenth-century people, makes it clear that 'this period' is the one from, say, 1770 to 1919; but the use of 'was' instead of 'has been' will have misled the reader into thinking that only the late eighteenth century is meant.

3. WHAT?

(*a*) **However important each of these things may be in its own place, it cannot properly be put in the supreme . . . place . . .**

The word 'it' refers to 'each of these things' — which does not make sense in the second half of the sentence. Instead of 'it cannot', 'none of them can' should have been written.

(*b*) **. . . it cannot properly be put in the supreme and central place . . .**

It is not clear what 'properly' means. There have been a great many ancient, honourable and self-sufficient cults of Nature, Country and Love. Perhaps 'in modern North America' is meant.

(*c*) **. . . any adequate conversion or discipline of man's ordinary self to some ethical centre.**

What has 'man's ordinary self' to do with the case? This is a passage about Romantic cranks who set up minor cults. Are they concerned with 'man's ordinary self', as opposed to their own? Or are their own selves really meant?

(*d*) **. . . to some ethical centre.**

What is an 'ethical centre'? Is it an institution, like the Episcopal Church? A place, like Boston? A national code of manners? A local code of manners? Is there a back-reference in the word 'centre' to 'the supreme and central place'?

(*e*) **. . . a loss of hold on the traditional centres . . .**

Are these the same as 'some ethical centre'?

(*f*) **. . . the failure of these new attempts at communion to keep their promises.**

No such attempts have been specified.

8. INAPPROPRIATE WORD OR PHRASE

(*a*) **. . . it does not involve any adequate conversion . . . of man's ordinary self to some ethical centre.**

The word 'conversion' is puzzling. Those who sought to set up these minor cults were once necessarily attached to some 'ethical centre' – if that means a community with a code of manners. Presumably they became apostates, otherwise the question of conversion does not arise; and if so, the word should be 'reconversion'.

(*b*) **. . . a loss of hold on the traditional centres . . .**

A centre is literally a point, though metaphorically it may mean an area, as in 'Manchester is the centre of the Lancashire cotton industry'. But neither a point nor an area may be grasped, or (consequently) 'lost hold of'.

(*c*) **. . . the failure of these new attempts at communion to keep their promises.**

An 'attempt' cannot be said either to keep or break a promise.

9. AMBIGUOUS WORD OR PHRASE

(*a*) **Those who have set up a cult of love . . . are open to the same objections . . .**

In modern usage only arguments, plans, policies, and so on are 'open to objection' in the sense of 'injuriously exposed to objection'. A person who is said to be 'open to objection' is one who welcomes criticism. Is this what is meant here?

(*b*) **. . . so many dubious moralists . . .**

Did they doubt themselves, or did they cause others to doubt them?

10. MISPLACED WORD OR PHRASE

. . . an incomparable series of false prophets. . . .

Since 'incomparable' is usually a word of praise, perhaps what is meant is 'a series of incomparably false prophets'; or perhaps 'an unparalleled series of false prophets . . .'

11. UNINTENTIONAL CONTRAST

(*a*) **Those who have sought to set up a cult of love or beauty . . . are open to the same objections as the votaries of nature.**

Irving Babbitt probably thought of the cult of nature as an exact parallel to the cult of love or of beauty; but 'those who have sought to' seem to be contrasted, as unsuccessful would-be founders of a cult, with the votaries of a cult already successfully founded. The words 'sought to', which have a peculiar fascination for academic writers, should have been omitted.

(*b*) **Every age has had its false teachers, but possibly no age ever had so many dubious moralists as this, an incomparable series of false prophets. . . .**

It is doubtful whether a contrast is here intended between 'false teachers' and 'dubious moralists' (who are also 'false prophets'). Probably what is meant is that there were false prophets and unsound moralists in every age, but never so many as in this.

12. DUPLICATION

. . . even more than most periods an age of sophistry.

. . . possibly no age ever had so many dubious moralists as this, . . .

These are two ways of saying much the same thing; one would have been enough.

14. MATERIAL OMISSION

. . . these new attempts at communion . . .

Communion with what or whom?

18. MISPUNCTUATION

(*a*) **. . . each of these things . . . cannot properly be put in . . . the central place for the simple reason that . . .**

The lack of a comma after 'place' suggests that none of these things may be put in the central place for this simple reason, though they may be put there for other, perhaps more complicated, reasons.

(*b*) **. . . suggests that this period was even more than most periods an age of sophistry.**

Without commas enclosing 'even more than most periods', the phrase 'was even more than' seems at first to mean 'was even greater than'. A comma has also dropped out earlier in the sentence, after 'kind'.

20. IRRELEVANCY

(*a*) **. . . it cannot properly be put in the supreme and central place . . .**

Perhaps this is a compromise between 'supreme position' and 'central place'. 'Supreme' is unnecessary.

(*b*) **. . . it does not involve any adequate conversion . . . of man's ordinary self to some ethical centre.**

The word 'adequate' plays for safety. But conversion (like salvation, or damnation) is not a matter of degree: the 'con' in the word expresses completeness.

(*c*) **I have tried to show that the sense of solitude or forlornness . . .**

The word 'solitude' should have been omitted. The Romantics often found a 'bliss of solitude', and in this context only 'discomfitures' are being discussed.

(*d*) **. . . the sense of solitude or forlornness that is so striking a feature of romantic melancholy arises not only from a loss of hold on the traditional centres, but also from the failure of these new attempts at communion to keep their promises.**

This is like saying: 'The deficiency diseases from which the people of Occupied France suffered were due not only to their inability to buy the butter, veal and eggs to which they were accustomed but also to the poor nutritive value of the turnips, grass and small vermin which they ate in despair. The 'loss of hold of the traditional centres' presumably prompted 'these new attempts at communion' and need not have been mentioned as an immediate cause of 'forlornness'.

22. OVER-EMPHASIS

. . . for the simple reason that it does not involve any adequate conversion or discipline of man's ordinary self to some ethical centre.

It does not seem a very 'simple reason'. This phrase should be reserved for such contexts as: 'Shakespeare could not have written *Colin Cloute*, for the simple reason that it was published before he was born.'

24. CHANGE OF STANDPOINT

Every age has had its false teachers, but possibly no age ever had so many dubious moralists as this, . . .

The change from 'has had' to 'had' is confusing, especially as 'this' age proves to be the one reaching from the late eighteenth century to the time of writing, not the late eighteenth century itself.

25. MIXED CATEGORY

Those who have sought to set up a cult of love or beauty or science or humanity or country. . . .

'Love' is too large a concept for this category, because 'humanity' – unless perhaps this means 'the humanities' – necessarily stands for 'love of humanity', and 'country' for 'love of country'. Perhaps 'love' here should have been expanded to 'love of particular persons'.

G. CIRCUMLOCUTION

The number of discomfitures of this kind in the period that has elapsed since the late eighteenth century, suggests that this period was even more than most periods an age of sophistry.

This amounts to: 'The frequency of such discomfitures since the late eighteenth century suggests that this has been an even more sophistical age than most.'

H. ELEGANT VARIATION

. . . the number of discomfitures . . . in the period . . . suggest that this period was even more than most periods an age of sophistry. Every age has had its false teachers, but possibly no age . . .

Irving Babbitt, growing weary of the word 'period', has here changed to 'age' and used this too to the point of weariness. If he had had occasion to go on writing about periods he would then probably have switched to 'epoch'; 'age', 'period', 'epoch' being synonymous to the academic writer.

K. TOO MUCH OF THE SAME WORD

. . . the period that has elapsed since the late eighteenth century, suggests that this period was even more than most periods . . .

One use of the word 'period' would have sufficed. Indeed, our alternative version shows that neither 'age' nor 'period' needed to be mentioned in the context.

FAIR COPY

'Apostates from ethical tradition who become single-hearted votaries of Beauty, or Science, or Love – whether it be love of particular persons, or of a whole nation, or of humanity in general – expose themselves to the same disappointment as the votaries of Nature. However important these abstractions may be, no single one of them should be made the supreme object of a cult, because the adoption of such a cult neither restores the votary to the major ethical system of his community nor compensates him for the loss of its discipline.

I have tried to show that the sense of forlornness, which is a striking symptom of the condition known as romantic melancholy, can be traced to disappointment at failing to achieve that communion with Nature which the founders of the Romantic cult promised. The unparalleled increase since the late eighteenth century in the number of disappointed people suggests a corresponding increase of sophistical philosophers, of unreliable moralists and especially of false prophets.'

COMMENT

More attention is paid at American than at British universities to text-books in German, French and Italian. This has perhaps had an unsettling effect on the writing of English, which – as we have suggested in the first chapter of this book – is not so formal as most European languages. Besides, most academic writers in the U.S.A. try to keep closer than most of those in Great Britain to the formal style that was common to both countries in the middle of the nineteenth century; and meanwhile colloquial speech in the U.S.A. has developed so luxuriantly that the academic writers there seem to be using a dead language, rather than – as in Great Britain – merely an old-fashioned one. To write a language as if it were dead is to use words as counters: to move them about in verbal computation without considering the imagery latent in each. This practice is consistent with an attempt at academic eloquence, for usually such eloquence is achieved at the expense of logic – the word that seems to suit the rhythm best is taken from the required group in a mental dictionary of synonyms, without thought for the comparative meanings of the words in the group.

EARL BALDWIN OF BEWDLEY

from Address to Leeds Luncheon Club, 1925

TEXT

There is another observation I [22a] would like to make about the war before I pass on.[20] It became evident to me[22b] a long time before the war was over

that the effect[10a] of it, which[8a] would hit this country hardest in the years immediately succeeding,[5/9a] was the tragedy[10b] of the loss of the men[10c] who were just qualifying and getting ready to be[12] the leaders of our younger men[11a] – the men[1a] who had already been at work[11b] in[14] the factory and the mill,[25] in all kinds of business and in the professions, who were just beginning to be masters[9b] of their own[11b] work – men[1b] of about thirty years of age[7] who by now would have been qualified to be leaders[11a] in their respective[8b] spheres.

There is nothing[10c] in the first twenty years[23] after the war that can make good to this country the loss of so many[10d] men of that age.[G]

EXAMINATION

1. WHO?

. . . the loss of the men who were . . . getting ready to be the leaders of our younger men – the men who had already been at work in the factory, . . . who were just beginning to be masters of their own work – men of about thirty years of age who would by now have been qualified to be leaders in their respective spheres.

(*a*) It is not clear who are the men mentioned in the phrase between the dashes. Are they the older or are they the younger men?

(*b*) The 'men of about thirty years of age' should, by the conventions of punctuation, mean 'the younger men', as being the last group mentioned before the interpolation. But is this intended?

5. WHEN?

It became evident to me long before the war was over that the effect of it, which would hit this country hardest in the years immediately succeeding . . .

Succeeding the war? Or succeeding his realization of something, long before the war was over?

7. HOW MANY?

– men of about thirty years of age . . .

How many years are intended by this phrase? 'About thirty' is a small age-group to particularize so tragically, unless it covers the ages of at least twenty-five to thirty-five.

8. INAPPROPRIATE WORD OR PHRASE

(*a*) **. . . the effect of it, which would hit this country hardest in the years immediately succeeding, . . .**

This 'which' should have been 'that' ('that' particularizes less sharply) and the comma should be omitted. Otherwise, the sentence means that the writer foresaw what the total effect of the war would be: the killing off of men of about thirty years old.

(*b*) **. . . men who had already been at work in the factory and in the mill, in all kinds of business and in the professions . . . who by now would have been qualified to be leaders in their respective spheres.**

'Respective' probably stands for 'various'. 'Respective' could be used if certain sorts of people were particularized as engaged in certain jobs. For example: 'Welsh miners, Scottish engineers, Sheffield steel-workers, Lancashire mill-hands, who would by now have been qualified to be leaders in their respective spheres.'

9. AMBIGUOUS WORD OR PHRASE

(*a*) **. . . that the effect of it, which would hit this country hardest in the years immediately succeeding . . .**

It is not clear whether he means merely that the blow would be hardest in those years, or that it would be hardest of any blows resulting from war-losses.

(*b*) **masters of their own work. . . .**

Does this mean experts or proprietors?

10. MISPLACED WORD OR PHRASE

(*a*) **. . . that the effect of it, which would hit the country hardest . . .**

The word 'effect' is out of place. The tragic loss of men was a result, not an effect. What is probably meant is 'the result of the war which would have the worst effect'.

(*b*) **. . . the effect of it, which would hit this country hardest . . . was the tragedy of the loss of the men . . .**

The 'tragedy' has been inserted in generous emotion; but does not help the sentence. It was not the sense of tragedy, but the actual loss, that might be expected to cause so ruinous an effect.

(*c*) **. . . the tragedy of the loss of the men . . . who were just qualifying to be leaders . . . men of about thirty years of age. . . . There is nothing in the first twenty years after the war that can make good to this country the loss of so many men of that age.**

Since the 'so many' does not appear in the first of these sentences, one is encouraged to believe that the entire age-group, rather than every second or third member of it, was killed or incapacitated in the war.

(*d*) **There is nothing in the first twenty years that can make good . . . the loss.**

This is an upside-down way of saying 'there can be nothing in the first twenty years to make good'. One could not speak in 1925 about the next fourteen years as if they had already passed.

11. UNINTENTIONAL CONTRAST

(*a*) **. . . men who were . . . getting ready to be the leaders of our younger men – men . . . who would by now have been qualified to be leaders in their respective spheres.**

It is improbable that the two sorts of leadership, that of 'our younger men' and that of 'their respective spheres' are intentionally contrasted; but the whole passage is very obscure. It is not, for a start, clear whether the lost young leaders would have led men of their own generation, or of a younger one still.

(*b*) **. . . men who had already been at work in the factory and in the mill . . . who were just beginning to be masters of their own work.**

This contrast between factory or mill work and the men's own work is probably not intended.

12. DUPLICATION

. . . qualifying and getting ready to be the leaders of our younger men . . .

In this context 'getting ready to be' is included in 'qualifying'.

14. MATERIAL OMISSION

— the men who had already been at work in the factory and the mill, in all kinds of business, . . .

'Already at work in the factory and the mill' suggests men who have only just started — the twenty-year-olds rather than the thirty-year-olds, who are more probably meant. Some such phrase as 'for some years' should have been inserted.

20. IRRELEVANCY

There is another observation I would like to make about the war before I pass on.

A remark of this sort does not seem worth making. Lord Baldwin did not intend to pause here until his audience gave him permission to proceed; nor did he tell them to what he intended to pass on; and they would know that the observation was about the war as soon as he made it.

22. OVER-EMPHASIS

(*a*) **There is another observation I would like to make . . .**

Normally one says 'should' in such a context. The form 'would' is emphatic and suggests that there is likely to be opposition to the observation.

(*b*) **It became evident to me**

There seems no reason why instead of this phrase, which suggests a judge's note in the course of an important trial, he should not have used, 'I realized' or 'I foresaw.' 'It became evident' implies that he was setting this view against others that were being put forward — such as, perhaps, that the worst effect of the war was the loss of the men 'of about twenty' whose minds would have been more adaptable than those of 'about thirty' to post-war conditions.

23. LOGICAL WEAKNESS

There is nothing in the first twenty years after the war that can make good to this country the loss of so many men of that age.

To specify a period of twenty years, or any period at all, is to suggest that when it has lapsed the loss will somehow be restored. But by the end of the twenty years the thirty-year-old men, had they survived, would have been fifty, and, in many trades and professions, would have been at the peak of their usefulness. In 1939, it is true, their loss would not be so tragically felt by their friends and former dependants as in 1925, the date of this speech, but its effects would remain; just as French history was permanently changed by the expulsion of the Huguenots in the seventeenth century. If Lord Baldwin meant that there would be no complete group of thirty-year-olds before 1939, he miscalculated.

25. MIXED CATEGORY

. . . at work in the factory and the mill, in all kinds of business and in the professions, . . .

The factory and the mill are merely two examples of an industrial centre. A great many more could be instanced, such as the shipyard and the coal-mine. They do not belong in the same category as 'all kinds of business', or 'the professions'. One would have to say either 'in factory and mill, on 'Change and in the cotton market (etc.)' or 'in trades, businesses and professions'.

G. CIRCUMLOCUTION

There is nothing in the first twenty years after the war that can make good to this country the loss of so many men of that age.

When everything is removed from this sentence that has already been said, it boils down to the platitudinous thought: 'these men were irreplaceable'; and even this has been suggested by the phrase 'the effect of it, which would hit this country hardest was the tragedy of the loss . . .' But the whole passage is circumlocutory: as will be seen by comparing it with the alternative version we offer, which contains all its essentials at half the length.

FAIR COPY

'I realized long before the war was over that its most damaging effect on the peace-time life of this country would be that very many capable workers between the ages of twenty-five and thirty-five had been killed or crippled — men who had already spent several years in their trades, businesses, and professions, qualifying to become the leaders of the nation: it would be twenty years before the loss of these irreplaceable men was no longer tragically felt.'

COMMENT

The emotions here expressed are generous; but Earl Baldwin, who announced in 1924 that, like Froude, he regarded rhetoric as 'the harlot of the arts', was tempted by his preference for blunt, rugged language — a supposed proof of British integrity in politics and business — to confuse the tricks of rhetoric with the decencies of oratory. (He used the words 'rhetoric' and 'oratory' interchangeably, and even confused 'talking too much' with 'eloquence'.) As a result, he stumbled unnecessarily in his speech, like a cripple on the way to Lourdes who has prematurely cast away his crutches. Nor did his 'positive horror of rhetoric' prevent him, a year later, from addressing the University of Edinburgh in the following terms:

> There is much that is profoundly wrong and remediable in our civilization, but let us not lightly discard the gains so hardly won from the savagery which so readily besets us. In stretching forth our hands to the further shore, let us realize that civilization itself is but the ice formed in process of ages on the turbulent stream of unbridled human passions, and while this ice seemed to our fathers secure and permanent, it has rotted and cracked during the agony of the Great War, and in places the submerged torrent has broken through, leaving fragments in constant collision threatening by their attrition to diminish and ultimately disappear. The more need for you, the lamp-bearers of

your generation, to guide your own steps by the truth, and to light the way for the wandering people of the world.

CLIVE BELL

from *Civilization*, 1928

TEXT

... [One may compare the claims of the Renaissance and Roman philosophers to be regarded as of civilized intelligence] ...
To play the Renaissance off[9a] against the middle ages is to deal oneself[5] too strong a hand. But if you[24a] have the courage[8a] to examine the philosophic syncretisms[8b/13] of the Medicean Platonists you will find that, silly[9b] as they are, they conceal beneath their mountainous quilts of metaphysical goose-down an infantile clutching at truth[4] which distinguishes them from the lucubrations[22] of Roman philosophers[18] who merely restate familiar fallacies[14a] with the complacent and cumbrous[10] air of one[24b] who discharges a moral obligation.[1] Lucretius himself[1] was not original,[14b] but he was exceptional.[9c]

EXAMINATION

1. WHO?

Lucretius himself was not original, ...

The uninstructed reader would not know from the context that Lucretius was a Roman, since the 'but he was exceptional' seems to identify him with the Medicean Platonists who have just been described as original in their silly way.

4. WHERE?

... they conceal beneath their mountainous quilts of metaphysical goose-down an infantile clutching at truth ...

In this metaphor, are the philosophers themselves the infants under the coverlet; or are they the shamefaced parents? 'Their' has been misplaced; they conceal their clutching beneath mountainous quilts.

5. WHEN?

(*a*) **To play the Renaissance off against the middle ages is to deal oneself too strong a hand.**

Surely this should read: 'is to have dealt oneself too strong a hand.' One cannot play cards before they are dealt.

(*b*) **... the lucubrations of Roman philosophers ...**

Does this mean Romans of the Classical age? Or are the Medicean Platonists, as Florentines, being played off against a contemporary Roman school?

8. INAPPROPRIATE WORD OR PHRASE

(*a*) **... if you have the courage to examine the philosophic syncretisms of the Medicean Platonists ...**

The need for courage is not explained. Surely it is rather patience, energy, curiosity and a knowledge both of the language in which they wrote and of the systems they 'syncretized'.

(*b*) **. . . the philosophic syncretisms of the Medicean Platonists . . .**

The word 'syncretisms' is unfortunate as suggesting that it was in use in the fifteenth century. It was first coined by the religious philosopher George Calixtus early in the seventeenth. The Platonists synthesized, rather than syncretized.

9. AMBIGUOUS PHRASE

(*a*) **To play the Renaissance off against the middle ages . . .**

'To play off' can mean 'to show in a disadvantageous light'. Addison wrote in *The Guardian*: 'He would now and then play them off and expose them a little unmercifully'. Here, however, the sense of the passage demands the contrary meaning: to give the advantage to the Renaissance, not to the middle ages.

The most familiar sense of 'play off' is to 'pit one party against another for one's own advantage'. Here, this would mean that one paraded one's own civilized intelligence by a comparison between the mediaeval and Renaissance philosophies which equally discredited both.

Perhaps what is meant is 'an all-trump hand of Renaissance philosophers is easily played out against a hand of mediaeval ones'; but it is not clearly stated what makes trumps.

(*b*) **. . . you will find that, silly as they are . . .**

It is not clear how this silliness is manifested: whether in argumentative inexpertness, or in wanton playfulness.

(*c*) **Lucretius himself was not original, but he was exceptional.**

Does this mean that he was exceptional in his unoriginality; or that he was exceptionally gifted in other, unspecified, respects?

10. MISPLACED WORD

. . . restate familiar fallacies with the complacent and cumbrous air of one who discharges a moral obligation.

'Cumbrous' means 'awkward to handle'. An 'air' may be 'clumsy' or 'awkward', but hardly 'cumbrous'. It is perhaps the moral obligation that is cumbrous; perhaps the restatement.

13. SELF-EVIDENT STATEMENT

. . . philosophic syncretisms . . .

Syncretisms are, by definition, philosophic, whatever the axioms (religious or non-religious) used in the divergent systems syncretized.

14. MATERIAL OMISSION

(*a*) **. . . Roman philosophers who merely restate familiar fallacies . . .**

This does not give them the credit for also restating familiar truths.

(*b*) **Lucretius himself was not original, . . .**

Is originality a characteristic of civilized intelligence? If so, this should be said. Otherwise it might be thought that the Roman philosophers' crime was less that they restated philosophical conclusions than that these conclusions were fallacious ones.

18. MISPUNCTUATION

. . . which distinguishes them from the lucubrations of Roman philosophers who merely restate familiar fallacies . . .

Has a comma been missed out after 'philosophers'? Without one, the sentence means that some, perhaps not many, Roman philosophers restated popular fallacies. This weakens the argument against the Romans. Those Roman philosophers who refrained from fallacious lucubration may have been sound thinkers – not so silly as all the Medicean Platonists are here stated to be.

22. OVER-EMPHASIS

. . . an infantile clutching at truth which distinguishes them from the lucubrations of the Roman philosophers . . .

It seems going a little far, in a comparison of philosophies, to praise the silly baby beneath its own mountainous quilt at the expense of the industrious philosopher who lucubrates – that is, burns the midnight oil.

24 CHANGE OF STANDPOINT

(*a*) **. . . to deal oneself too strong a hand. But if you have the courage to examine . . .**

The 'you' seems to be not a particular person to whom the book is addressed, but the vague 'one' of the previous sentence. No reason for this sudden variation appears.

(*b*) **. . . Roman philosophers . . . with the . . . cumbrous air of one who discharges . . .**

It would be less confusing if Clive Bell had either written of 'the Roman philosopher' as a type, so that 'one who' would be parallel; or, writing of Roman philosophers in the plural, as he has done, had continued 'with the air of men discharging a moral obligation'.

I. OVERLONG SENTENCE

But if you have the courage to examine the philosophic syncretisms of the Medicean Platonists you will find that, silly as they are, they conceal beneath their mountainous quilts of metaphysical goose-down an infantile clutching at truth which distinguishes them from the lucubrations of Roman philosophers who merely restate familiar fallacies with the complacent and cumbrous air of one who discharges a moral obligation.

'There is no point of rest in the sentence after 'silly as they are'; and the last 'who' clause depends on another 'who' clause, which depends on a 'which' clause. This causes fatigue.

FAIR COPY

'In a game of deciding which age showed the more civilized intelligence, with originality as trumps, it would be easy to play out a hand of Renaissance philosophers against one of mediaeval philosophers, and win every trick. Moreover, one could score almost as heavily against a hand of Classical Romans. '[*Or, more soberly:* It takes little skill to prove that the Renaissance philosophers were of a far more civilized intelligence than their mediaeval predecessors. Moreover, since civilized intelligence implies originality of thought, they can also be shown to have outshone the Classical Romans.']

Students who trouble to examine the reconciliations of rival philosophical systems attempted by the Medicean Platonists will find that all of them, though playful and highly verbose—suggesting huge, prettily quilted goose-down coverlets—reveal a certain groping instinct for the truth; whereas most Classical Roman philosophers of all schools had been content always to restate the same threadbare, often fallacious, platitudes with the complacent air of men discharging a cumbrous moral obligation. Even the exceptionally gifted Lucretius was less concerned with thinking for himself than with transcribing Epicurean doctrine into Latin hexameter verse.'

COMMENT

This passage is in the table-talk tradition, and has the hit-or-miss charm of the dessert course, when all the diners feel self-confident, knowledgeable and uncritical. It was written during the most prosperous and care-free period between the two World Wars.

VISCOUNT CASTLEROSSE (now the Earl of Kenmare)
from *The Londoner's Log* (December 1940)

TEXT

The history of the times[12a] of the century before one[9] I find to be deeply interesting,[12b] for the reason that there[G] are so many incidents and situations which coincide[8] with[14a] the present day.[16] There are also[4] odd bits of interesting information.[12b]

Few people know that Napoleon was a British subject. But nevertheless, it is the truth anyway.[12c] He was thus placed technically[20a] and for a period.[14b]

It happened like this. A few months after Napoleon had distinguished himself at the taking of Toulon, Corsica[14c] proclaimed herself to be a monarchy under the sovereignty[23] of King George III, who once[5] addressed a most august assembly[3] as 'My dear Lords and Turkey Cocks.'[20b]

EXAMINATION

3. WHAT?

. . . a most august assembly . . .

The House of Lords? A convocation of spiritual peers at Lambeth Palace? The Lords of the Admiralty?

4. WHERE?

There are also odd bits of interesting information.

This perhaps refers to some book he has been reading, but he does not mention it.

5. WHEN?

. . . George III, who once addressed a most august assembly . . .

Was this before or after Corsica put herself under the King's sovereignty?

8. INAPPROPRIATE WORD OR PHRASE

. . . many incidents and situations which coincide with the present day . . .

Incidents and situations of 1790 cannot coincide with those of 1940; though historical parallels may be drawn.

9. AMBIGUOUS WORD OR PHRASE

The history of the times of the century before one I find to be deeply interesting, . . .

'The century before one' may mean the century that lies ahead of one; or the century that one is examining; or (from the point of view of the reader of 1940) the nineteenth century. The only event here particularized took place in the 1790's. 'The century before one' therefore probably means 'one hundred years before my birth'.

12. DUPLICATION

(*a*) **. . . history of the times of the century . . .**

All histories of a century are necessarily histories of its times.

(*b*) **. . . the history of the times of the century before one I find to be deeply interesting, . . .**

There are also odd bits of . . . information.

All history is composed of odd bits of interesting information, sometimes strung together on threads of argument, sometimes merely juxtaposed.

(*c*) **But, nevertheless, it is the truth anyway.**

It would have been enough to write either:

'But it is the truth',

or: 'Nevertheless it is the truth,'

or: 'Anyway, it is the truth.'

Duplication has here been enlarged to triplication.

14. MATERIAL OMISSION

(*a*) **. . . so many incidents and situations which coincide with the present day.**

An incident or situation cannot coincide with a day, but only with another incident or situation

(*b*) **. . . Napoleon was a British subject. He was thus placed technically and for a period.**

For a period should read: 'only for a short period'. A subject's technical subjection to the King lasts normally for the period of his life.

(*c*) **A few months after Napoleon had distinguished himself at the taking of Toulon, Corsica proclaimed herself to be a monarchy . . .**

It should have been explained to the millions of Sunday paper readers who knew no history that Napoleon was born in Corsica, and that it was as a citizen of France that he assisted in the re-capture of Toulon from the British.

16. UNDEVELOPED THEME

The history of the century before one I find to be deeply interesting, for the reason . . . that so many incidents . . . coincide with the present day.

This generalization that so many incidents are always duplicated a hundred years later falls to the ground. When the next paragraph begins with the statement that Napoleon was British, one expects to read that Adolf Hitler was once British too; but one is disappointed.

20. IRRELEVANCY

(*a*) **. . . Napoleon was a British subject. He was thus placed technically . . .**

Every Briton's subjection to the King has been 'technical' since at least 1688: the King has no power over his life or property.

(*b*) **It happened like this. A few months after Napoleon had distinguished himself . . . at Toulon, Corsica proclaimed herself to be . . . under the sovereignty of George III, who once addressed a most august assembly as 'My dear Lords and Turkey Cocks.'**

The eccentricity of George III does not clarify the reasons for Napoleon's temporary subjection to him.

23. LOGICAL WEAKNESS

. . . Corsica proclaimed herself to be a monarchy under the sovereignty of King George III, . . .

A monarchy cannot be under a sovereignty. What is meant is 'proclaimed her independence and put herself under the sovereignty of King George III.'

G. CIRCUMLOCUTION

. . . for the reason that there are . . .

'Because there are' would surely have been simpler and more suitable to the context?

FAIR COPY

'Recently, I read a history of the 1790's and was deeply interested to find so many incidents and situations of the time – just a century before I was born – reminding me of 1940. I also came across some odd bits of unfamiliar information. Did you know that Napoleon was once a British subject? Few do. But he was, though only for a short period and without residing in this country.

It happened like this. A few months after Napoleon had distinguished himself at the recapture of Toulon from us, his native island of Corsica repudiated her allegiance to the French Republic. She proclaimed herself a kingdom under the rule of our George III. This was the George who later went mad and addressed the House of Lords [?] in august assembly as 'My dear Lords and Turkey-cocks'!

COMMENT

This writing is deliberately conversational, and Lord Castlerosse perhaps does not greatly care whether or not his readers understand just what he is trying to say. And perhaps they do not care, either; much can be forgiven a peer who consents to gossip with commoners in this genial way.

Bishop of Chichester

from *Christianity and World Order*, 1940

TEXT

Christianity[8a] sets a standard.[16a] Nothing that I have said[8b] about principles governing human relationships, or about the social implications[9a] of the Gospel, should be permitted for a moment to obscure the crucial[9b] importance of personal character.[8c] Life[14a] has been described as a perpetual offensive against the repetitive mechanism of the universe![18/A1] This is profoundly true of moral life,[14a] which is the overcoming and transforming[14b] of hostile or unfavourable conditions and temptations[10a] continually recurring.[10a/23] The Christian faith[H] demands integrity of conduct, uprightness, truth,[25] sincerity[12a] and a vigorous initiative. The Christian religion[H] reinforces man's resistance to the struggle. It does not deny it.[9c/19a] It[2/K] is neither[10b] quietism in social matters, nor is it 'socialism' or 'social reform' without[9d] the energy of faith, and the vitality of personal effort rightly[I] directed.[12b/16b] Christianity[H] is not a fugitive and cloistered[8d] religion. It does not slink out of the race. It endures dust and heat. It sallies out and seeks its adversaries.[A2] It is exercised and fully breathed.[9e/19b]

EXAMINATION

2. WHICH?

The Christian religion reinforces man's resistance to the struggle. It does not deny it. It is neither quietism in social matters, nor is it 'socialism' . . .

Which of these concepts is 'neither quietism nor "socialism"'? The Christian religion, man's resistance, or the struggle? In formal grammar it would be the one referred to by the preceding 'it' — which is probably, but not necessarily, 'the struggle'.

8. INAPPROPRIATE WORD OR PHRASE

(*a*) **Christianity sets a standard.**

Christianity is too large a word for the ensuing context, which concerns not the standard that Christians of all sorts set for Buddhists, Moslems, and the like, but the standard that the Gospel sets for sincere Christians.

(*b*) **Nothing that I have said . . .**

The word 'written' would have been better than 'said': it would have referred the reader plainly to the early chapters of the book, instead of making him wonder what the Bishop might have been saying in the pulpit.

(*c*) **. . . the importance of personal character.**

This figurative use of 'character' refers to the stamp put on coins as a token of their uniform goodness though the word is sometimes facetiously applied to a thoroughly eccentric person, as *type* is in French. It should have been avoided here, where a distinction is made between man in his social setting and man as exercising free will. 'Character' refers more appropriately to social conformity than to free will exercised.

(*d*) **. . . Christianity is not a . . . cloistered religion.**

Then why has the word 'cloister' in Christian countries an almost purely religious sense?

9. AMBIGUOUS WORD OR PHRASE

(*a*) **. . . the social implications of the Gospel, . . .**

This might well mean 'the implications in the four Gospels as to social life in the Roman Empire in the first and second centuries, A.D.' To hope that it will mean 'the modifications of natural principles governing social behaviour that are implicitly ordered in the Gospels' is to put too great faith in the ordinary reader's understanding.

(*b*) **Nothing that I have said about principles governing human relationships . . . should be permitted to obscure the crucial importance of personal character.**

There are three senses of 'crucial', besides the scientific one of 'in the form of a cross'. 'Crucial' may refer to Francis Bacon's phrase *instantia crucis* and so mean 'pointing the logical course where rival hypotheses are offered'. And if the rival hypotheses are, that men should think and act as individuals, and that they should think and act as loyal members of Christian society, then 'crucial' is properly used here in this sense. 'Crucial' may also mean 'of the nature of a crux, or textual difficulty', and so, loosely, 'testing one's intelligence' — also a possible sense in this context. A third sense was given to the word by Elizabeth Barrett Browning in *Aurora Leigh* in 1856. Apparently she thought it had something to do with the word 'crucible'. 'Crucial importance of personal character' in this sense would mean 'the importance of personal character in purging away the dross of social relationship'.

Since, however, the theme of 'crucial importance' is not developed in the succeeding sentences, we never learn which of these senses was intended.

(*c*) **The Christian religion reinforces man's resistance to the struggle. It does not deny it.**

The second sentence may mean: 'The Christian religion does not deny that the struggle exists.'
Or: 'The Christian religion does not deny that it reinforces resistance.'
Or: 'The Christian religion does not deny (refuse) its help.'
Or: 'The Christian religion does not deny that man resists.'

(*d*) **. . . nor is it 'socialism' or 'social reform' without the energy of faith, . . .**

This may mean: 'Christianity is not "socialism" or "social reform", both of which lack the energy of faith.'
Or: 'Christianity is not "socialism" or "social reform" of a sort that lacks the energy of faith.'
Or: 'Unless Christianity has the energy of faith it is not really "socialism" or "social reform".'

(*e*) **It is exercised and fully breathed.**

Is 'breathed' formed from 'breathe' or from 'breath'? If from 'breathe' the phrase, which is an odd one, means having had full opportunity to breathe after violent exercise; if from 'breath' it means that the lungs have a full capacity for drawing breath.

10. MISPLACED WORD

(*a*) **. . . the overcoming and transforming of hostile or unfavourable conditions and temptations continually recurring.**

The natural order of these words is 'the overcoming of continually recurring temptations and the transforming of continually recurring hostile or unfavourable conditions'. The word 'temptations' has been misplaced. It is difficult to see how one can 'transform an unfavourable temptation'. One can only reject, end, or yield to any temptation. And in what sense is a temptation 'unfavourable'? Does this mean that one cannot readily yield to it? The phrase 'constantly recurring' is also misplaced. It has been put at the end of the sentence probably to avoid a clumsy repetition of '-ings' – 'the overcoming and transforming of continually recurring temptations' – but reads there as though it were an afterthought, rather than an important step in the argument about the 'repetitive mechanism of the universe'.

(*b*) **It is neither quietism . . . nor is it 'socialism' . . .**

This should have read: 'Neither is it quietism, nor is it "socialism".' Or: 'It is neither quietism, nor socialism'. Or: 'It is not quietism, neither is it "socialism".' The two phrases, as they stand, are not parallel.

12. DUPLICATION

(*a*) **The Christian faith demands integrity of conduct, uprightness, truth, sincerity . . .**

'Uprightness' and 'sincerity' are included in 'integrity of conduct'.

(*b*) **. . . nor is it 'socialism' or 'social reform' without the energy of faith and the vitality of personal effort rightly directed.**

'The vitality of personal effort rightly directed' surely includes the 'energy of faith'? 'Rightly', to a Bishop, means 'by the guidance of God sought in faith'.

14. MATERIAL OMISSION

(*a*) **Life has been described as a perpetual offensive against the repetitive mechanism of the universe! This is profoundly true of moral life.**

Since the unnamed natural philosopher expressed himself very loosely, the Bishop might well have restated the phrase in his own words. He could then have qualified 'life' as physical life, and afterwards shown moral life as analogous to it. This would have been far better than quoting the phrase just as he heard it, without commenting on its heretical implications, and drawing a pious conclusion from it which the originator might well have disavowed.

(*b*) **. . . moral life, which is the overcoming and transforming of hostile or unfavourable conditions . . .**

Transforming them into what?

16. UNDEVELOPED THEME

(*a*) **Christianity sets a standard.**

What kind of standard? The next sentence should explain, but does not.

One has to guess from 'the crucial importance of personal character' that a moral standard for personal behaviour is meant.

(*b*) **. . . nor is it 'socialism' or 'social reform' without the energy of faith and the vitality of personal effort rightly directed.**

'Rightly directed' should be expanded. Does it mean 'under ecclesiastical tutelage'?

18. MISPUNCTUATION

Life has been described as a perpetual offensive against the repetitive mechanism of the universe!

An exclamation-mark after a quoted opinion usually denotes surprise that such an opinion has been expressed. Very occasionally it denotes intense admiration for the opinion: e.g. 'Christ said that I should love my neighbour as myself! What a noble ideal!' The opinion quoted by the Bishop does not seem to merit either surprise or intense admiration.

19. CONFUSED SEQUENCE OF IDEAS

(*a*) **The Christian religion reinforces man's resistance to the struggle. It does not deny it.**

'Does not deny it' reads weakly after 'reinforces', which it should perhaps have preceded.

(*b*) **Christianity . . . does not slink out of the race. It endures the heat and dust. It sallies out and seeks its adversaries. It is exercised and fully breathed.**

The last sentence belongs to the racing metaphor and should have introduced it. And it would have been better to attach this brisk metaphorical passage to the strongly alliterative preceding one — about man's resistance to the struggle — from which it is separated by a long-winded sentence in another style.

23. LOGICAL WEAKNESS

Life . . . a perpetual offensive against the repetitive mechanism of the universe! This is profoundly true of moral life, which is the overcoming and transforming of hostile or unfavourable conditions and temptations continually recurring.

'The repetitive mechanism of the universe' is identified by all sects of Christians with the 'immutable laws of God'. Personal morality, by the Bishop's argument, consists in a perpetual offensive against these laws. He surely cannot mean this?

25. MIXED CATEGORY

The Christian faith demands integrity of conduct, uprightness, truth, sincerity and a vigorous initiative.

'Truth' does not fit in with the other qualities here listed: it is one of the prime words, like 'love', 'death', 'God'. What is doubtless meant is 'truthfulness'. Nor does 'a vigorous initiative' belong to the list. 'A vigorous initiative' is an action, like 'a vigorous offensive'; whereas sincerity and uprightness are qualities. The 'a' should be omitted to make initiative into a quality too.

A. MISMATING OF METAPHORS

1. **. . . a perpetual offensive against the repetitive mechanism of the universe!**

One undertakes an 'offensive' only against a living enemy; one attempts to break a mechanism or to throw it out of gear.

2. **Christianity is not a fugitive . . . religion. It does not slink out of the race. It endures the dust and the heat. It sallies out and seeks its adversaries.**

Though Homer and Virgil celebrate one or two very irregular incidents in Classical foot-races, the modern athlete at least would not 'sally out' of his race, struggle and overthrow his adversaries, and then return to the track; if he did so he would be disqualified for going out of bounds and dismissed from his club for disorderly conduct. Moreover, 'religion' is a feminine abstract, like 'the Church'. Translation of this passage into Latin would bring out the singular impropriety of the metaphor. The Christian is an athlete, perhaps, but to picture Mother Church lumbering half-naked round the dusty Stadium, and carrying on a perpetual running-fight with her adversaries on the side-lines – this will never do.

H. ELEGANT VARIATION

Christianity sets a standard. . . . The Christian faith demands integrity of conduct . . . and a vigorous initiative. The Christian religion reinforces man's resistance to the struggle. . . . Christianity is not a fugitive religion . . .

'The Christian faith', 'the Christian religion', 'Christianity', are used indiscriminately in this passage. If more than a single loose concept had been intended, this would have been shown by making Christian *religion* demand integrity of conduct, and Christian *faith* reinforce man's resistance to the struggle against mechanized evil.

K. TOO MUCH OF THE SAME WORD

The Christian religion reinforces man's resistance to the struggle. It does not deny it. It is neither . . .

These three 'its', the second two of which are not clear in their reference, would be avoided if the sense of 'It does not deny it' were given its natural place in the previous sentence.

L. JINGLE

. . . the energy of faith, and the vitality of personal effort rightly directed.

One would not perhaps notice the succession of 'y's' if 'vitality' and 'rightly' were not so similar in sound. The sentence has a far more gracious sound with 'well' substituted for 'rightly'.

FAIR COPY

'The Gospels set a moral standard for the Christian. Nothing that I have here written about the natural principles governing social behaviour, or about the necessary modifications of these implied in the Gospels, should have made my readers forget that man is an individual as well as a social being. Physical life has been described by a natural philosopher in some such terms as "a perpetual reassertion of individual uniqueness against the mechanical repetitiveness of the universe". This is a profound saying, if not read as a disparagement of the wonderful mechanical structure of Creation, and can be applied analogically to moral life also:

Christian morality consists in overcoming, time after time, the same recurrent temptations, and transforming into blessings the same recurrent trials.

The Church does not counsel quietism but demands vigour of action, as well as integrity of conduct, from the Christian; and, without belittling the severity of his struggle against sin, fortifies him to survive it. He must be no fugitive from the world, self-immured in a cloister, but (to adopt St. Paul's imagery) an athlete, well-exercised, with unlabouring breath: one who does not avoid the race or slink from it before he has finished the course, but who endures the dust and heat. He must be no passive defender of the soul's citadel, but sally boldly thence to seek out his adversary. Yet neither does the Church counsel "socialism" or any other secular means of "social reform"—unless the Christian be supported therein by faith in God's guidance of himself personally, rather than by vain partisan enthusiasm.'

COMMENT

It will be seen that whereas some of the alternative versions that we offer — for example, in the cases of G. D. H. Cole and J. N. W. Sullivan — are far shorter than their originals, this one is far longer. The Bishop, in fact, has too much, not too little, to say. In trying here to urge his fellow-Christians to a vigorous moral effort he writes with more succinctness than clarity; and grafts modern concepts ('the offensive', 'a vigorous initiative', 'repetitive mechanism of the universe', 'socialism', 'social reform') on the stock of Church rhetoric, with rather too hurried a hand.

POSTSCRIPT

Since writing these pages of comment, and too late to recast them, we have accidentally come across a passage in Milton's *Areopagitica*:

> 'He that can apprehend and consider vice with all her baits and seeming pleasures, and yet abstain and yet distinguish, and yet prefer that which is truly better, he is the true wayfaring Christian. I cannot praise a fugitive and cloister'd virtue unexercised and unbreath'd, that never sallies out and sees her adversary, but slinks out of the race, where that immortal garland is to be run for, not withstanding dust and heat.'

Milton was pleading that the reading of immoral books helped a Christian to distinguish evil from good.

The Bishop should have looked up the passage, made sure that it was appropriate to his theme, and then either quoted it whole, with acknowledgements to Milton as its author, or translated its substance into modern language. If he had done this he would have avoided several mistakes. He would not have changed the subject of Milton's metaphors from 'a cloister'd virtue' to 'Christianity', which is too large a concept for them; nor would he have run together and confused the two metaphors which Milton kept separate; nor misquoted 'sees' as 'seeks'; nor changed 'unbreath'd' to the ambiguous 'fully breathed'. Milton's original is, admittedly, not very good prose: the metaphors 'wayfaring Christian', 'fugitive virtue', 'sallies out', 'slinks out of the race' are too similar, without being allied, to be safely juxtaposed. We would mark this passage of Milton's with a 'B' to signify 'too many metaphors'. Milton was normally a careful writer; but Parliament had recently been petitioned (August 24th, 1644) by the Stationers' Company to take action against him for publishing two editions of his Divorce pamphlet without Parliamentary licence. Milton, alarmed, worked himself into an angry, bitter mood and because the Divorce pamphlet meant so much to him, dared to hit back with the *Areopagitica*, a plea for the liberty of the Press — a liberty which, by the way, as Assistant Press Censor to the Council of State, he afterwards denied his political opponents. In most of the *Areopagitica* he kept his anger simmering quietly; but here, where he was excited by the dangerousness of his theme, it boiled over in a stream of ill-assorted metaphors.

G. D. H. Cole

from *The Intelligent Man's Guide Through World Chaos*, 1932

TEXT

The economic activities[H1] of mankind[H2] have only one object—the promotion of human happiness.[23/G1/H3] There is no purpose in any economic activity[H1] unless it ministers to [H3] this object.[12a] Economists have indeed[9] often defined the objects[3] of man's[H2] economic activity[H1] in terms somewhat different from these. They have said that the purpose of economic activity[H1] is to secure the maximum production of economic wealth.[16a/H4] But it is necessary both to qualify and to expand[8] this definition.[16b] For in the first place men[H2] may prefer more leisure to more material wealth, and in the second place it is impossible to leave out of account the conditions under which material[20/22a] wealth is created.[H4] The conditions under which men[H2] have to work[12b] may make either for happiness or for unhappiness.[13] Work[H1] is in itself a good and not an evil[G2]; and mankind[H2] would be miserable without it. But some work — some toil, let us say rather[o] — is very definitely[22b] evil; and it should be the object of the economic system[2] not merely to create as much wealth as possible,[23a] but to create it under conditions which will[24] make as much as possible for happiness in the doing of it[23b] and as little for fatigue, disgust and sheer boredom.[19]

EXAMINATION

2. WHICH?

The economic activities of mankind . . .

. . . man's economic activity . . . it should be the object of the economic system . . .

Which 'economic system' of the many that have here been mentioned by implication? 'Capitalism' (if that is the system meant) is by no means equivalent to 'man's economic activity'.

3. WHAT?

The economic activities of mankind have only one object . . . happiness. There is no purpose in any economic activity unless it ministers to this object. Economists have indeed often defined the objects of man's economic activity in terms somewhat different from these. They have said that the purpose of economic activity is to secure the maximum production of economic wealth.

The first view is: economic activity has only one object — happiness, and no purpose but to secure it. Against this is set the economists' view, that economic activity has other objects and also another purpose, that of securing material wealth. What are these other 'objects of man's economic activity'?

8. INAPPROPRIATE WORD OR PHRASE

. . . it is necessary both to qualify and to expand this definition. . . .

To qualify a definition is to expand it to the extent of the qualification. Perhaps what is meant is 'to qualify this definition, and then to apply it to an altogether other concept'.

9. AMBIGUOUS WORD OR PHRASE

The economic activities of mankind have only one object — the promotion of human happiness. Economists have indeed often defined the objects of man's economic activity in terms somewhat different from these.

'Indeed' is usually an emphatic word introducing a confirmation of what has gone before; but it is sometimes used unemphatically and apologetically to mean 'I grant you', when quoting a contrary argument. In speech, the difference is immediately made clear by the tone in which 'indeed' is said. Here it is not at first clear that 'I grant you' is the intended meaning.

12. DUPLICATION

(*a*) **The economic activities of mankind have only one object — the promotion of human happiness. There is no purpose in any economic activity unless it ministers to this object.**

The substitution of 'purpose' for 'object' in the second sentence does not add anything to the sense of the first: for in the fourth sentence 'purpose' and 'object' are by implication shown to mean the same thing to Mr. Cole.

(*b*) **. . . it is impossible to leave out of account the conditions under which material wealth is created. The conditions under which men have to work may make either for happiness or for unhappiness.**

The words 'and these' could be substituted for the repetitive 'conditions under which men have to work', without loss to the argument.

13. SELF-EVIDENT STATEMENT

The conditions under which men have to work may make either for happiness or for unhappiness.

Was this really worth recording, even without the word 'may'?

16. UNDEVELOPED THEME

(*a*) **. . . the purpose of economic activity is to secure the maximum production of economic wealth. But it is necessary both to qualify and to expand this definition. For . . . men may prefer more leisure to more material wealth.**

'Economic wealth' and 'material wealth' are apparently both used as amplifications of 'wealth', in implied contrast with the immaterial (and therefore uneconomic) wealth that may be earned in leisure. It is a pity that this argument by an economist in favour of a kind of wealth which he implicitly defines as uneconomic should not have been brought to its natural conclusion.

(*b*) **Economists have defined the objects of man's economic activity in terms somewhat different from these. They have said that the purpose of economic activity is to secure the maximum production of economic wealth. But it is necessary both to qualify and to expand this definition.**

The 'But' implies 'if this definition is to mean the same thing as I do'. And the necessary work of qualification and expansion here mentioned is not undertaken. The subject is changed, and we are told what *ought to be* the object of a particular economic system, instead of what *is* the common object of all economic activities.

19. CONFUSED SEQUENCE OF IDEAS

The following is the natural sequence of ideas in this passage; it has the advantage of eliminating the constant restatement of the principal subject of the argument, namely 'what is the object of man's economic activity?':—

(1) Economists have defined the object of all economic activity as 'maximum production of wealth'.

(2) But many workers prefer not to attain this maximum—

(3) which shows the faultiness of the definition.

(4) No useful definition, indeed, can be made of any agreed common object in the present economic system.

(5) But, since work is proved by the miseries of idleness to be good

(6) (unless performed in fatiguing or disgusting circumstances),

(7) a definition can be found for what the object of all economic activity *should be*,

(8) namely, 'happiness

(9) experienced both in the performance and the outcome'.

In the original the sequence is

8, 1, 3, 2, 5, 7, 9, 6

with 4 omitted, and the argument is at several points implied rather than expressed.

20. IRRELEVANCY

Economists have often defined the objects of man's economic activity . . . They have said that the purpose of economic activity is to secure the maximum production of economic wealth. But it is necessary both to qualify and to expand this

definition. For in the first place men may prefer more leisure to more material wealth, and in the second place it is impossible to leave out of account the conditions under which material wealth is created.

The second reason here given for qualifying and expanding the definition has nothing to do with the common *purpose* of all economic activity — any more than the common purpose of all people who go to restaurants, namely to eat and drink, is affected by the different conditions obtaining at the tables or in the kitchens of different restaurants. It would, however, have been relevant to the Socialist argument to mention that even those workers who, in order to enjoy greater leisure, choose to produce less than the maximum are often obliged to produce less even than they wish — by those whose economic activity consists in adjusting supply to demand.

22. OVER-EMPHASIS

(*a*) **. . . it is impossible to leave out of account the conditions under which material wealth is created.**

But the economists who defined the object of man's economic activity merely as 'the maximum production of economic wealth' are being scolded for having done this very thing. It is therefore not impossible, but perhaps only stupid.

(*b*) **. . . some work . . . is very definitely evil . . .**

It would have been sufficient to say merely that 'some work is evil'. 'Definitely evil' is emphasis denoting that one was not sure at first, but now has proof. 'Very definitely' is over-emphatic: one cannot have degrees of definiteness.

23. LOGICAL WEAKNESS

(*a*) **The economic activities of mankind have only one object — the promotion of human happiness.**

. . . But some . . . toil is very definitely evil, and it should be the object of the economic system not merely to create as much wealth as possible, but to create it under conditions which will make as much as possible for happiness.

The meaning of the second sentence is that, though the object of the economic activity of mankind *should* be the promotion of human happiness, it is, in fact, only the rather unhappy production of wealth. This contradicts the first sentence.

(*b*) **. . . men may prefer more leisure to more material wealth . . . some toil is evil . . . it should be the object of the economic system not merely to create as much wealth as possible, but to create it under conditions which will make as much as possible for happiness in the doing of it . . .**

If maximum production is incompatible with leisure, and thus with the happiness of the workers, then the object of the economic system should *not* be to create as much wealth as possible with the greatest possible alleviation of the resulting distress: it should be to create wealth in such a way as 'to make as much as possible for happiness in the doing of it'.

24. CHANGE OF STANDPOINT

It should be the object of the economic system . . . to create it under conditions which will make . . .

This is a compromise between:

It should be the object of the economic system to create it under circumstances which would . . .
and
It must be the object of the economic system to create it under circumstances which will . . .

G. CIRCUMLOCUTION

(1) **The economic activities of mankind have only one object — the promotion of human happiness.**

This is a long-winded way of saying: All work has a single object: namely happiness. 'Human happiness' is a phrase which often slips into writing of this sort — as though 'happiness' by itself could be understood to mean the happiness of dogs, cats or angels.

(2) **. . . it is impossible to leave out of account the conditions under which material wealth is created. The conditions under which men have to work make either for happiness or for unhappiness. Work in itself is a good and not an evil; . . .**

This suggests the elaborately over-simplified style of the Scottish parochial sermon. It means no more than: 'One must not forget that though the work of producing wealth is good in itself, working conditions sometimes cause unhappiness.'

H. ELEGANT VARIATION

(1) **The economic activities of mankind**
any economic activity
man's economic activity
economic activity
work

The same subject is here continuously restated under various names. There seems no reason for this.

(2) **mankind**
man's
men
men
mankind

There seems no reason for this variation, either; and when only 'men' are said to work, to the exclusion of women (who form a half of working mankind), it becomes misleading.

(3) **. . . only one object — the promotion of human happiness. . . . unless it ministers to this object.**

There seems no difference in sense intended here between 'promoting' this object and 'ministering' to it.

(4) **. . . the production of economic wealth**
. . . the conditions under which material wealth is created.

These apparently mean the same thing, since economists only write in terms of material as opposed to spiritual wealth, and make no fine distinctions between ordinary 'production' and extraordinary 'creation'.

O. SECOND THOUGHTS

But some work — some toil, let us say, rather — is very definitely evil.

There is no reason for letting the reader see that one has orginally put 'work' and then changed it to 'toil', unless one is not sure that second thoughts are best. Here 'toil' is used to patch up a logical flaw: 'Work in itself is good; yet sometimes work is an evil. Therefore in such circumstances it cannot really be work — let us call it toil.' But the word 'work' has to be kept, because the argument cannot start with 'Toil is good'; and since, in any case, toil is not necessarily an evil and can be enjoyed if undertaken in a good cause, 'some' qualifies 'toil'.

FAIR COPY

'Economists have defined the object of all work whatsoever as "the maximum production of wealth". Many workers, however, choose to produce less than the maximum, in order to enjoy greater leisure—thus disproving the definition. It is, indeed, doubtful whether the multitudinous reasons why people do work have any important common factor. But, since work is proved, by the misery which idleness causes, to be a good thing in itself and to have the appearance of an evil only when attended by avoidable fatigue, disgust or boredom, one can at least define the single object which *ought to be* common to all workers, namely, "happiness, as experienced both in the performance and the result".'

COMMENT

Mr. Cole intends to guide the reader through 'World Chaos' with Socialist doctrine plainly and cheerfully delivered in the style of a Methodist tract. In avoiding the charge of being literary he falls into repetitions, loose phrases, a disorderly sequence of ideas, over-emphasis, dropped threads and other characteristics of the merely conversational style. He also over-simplifies his argument: for example, 'man's economic activity' is apparently limited to Unionizable male-workers directly engaged in the production of wealth under Capitalism.

The use of such grand phrases as 'the economic activity of mankind' and 'the conditions under which material wealth is created', in combination with such ingenuous phrases as 'work is in itself a good and not an evil', is expected to persuade the reader, flattered as an 'intelligent man', that he will soon escape from the Chaos: for his guide, though at home with complicated economic theory, does not despise simple moral truths.

MARQUESS OF CREWE

from an Article in the Sunday Press, 1940

TEXT

Words, like writings,[14a] have their destined fates,[13] and it[15] is often the distressful[8a] fate of coins[14b] in a debased currency. They gradually de-

preciate.[16a] Once 'indifferent' meant 'just' and 'adventurers' were honourable pioneers.[16b] In recent times[5a] Empire and its derivations[8b] have fallen from their high estate.[F1]

Emperors, indeed, as a class[8c] have not fared well in the judgement of history. . . . In the long corridor of the Holy Roman Empire[F2] many noble figures stand out, but many that are petty.[23] . . . In modern times[5a] Napoleon undeniably filled the part of[8d] Emperor, but his nephew's crown was almost pinchbeck.[8e/F3] The later Hapsburgs[1a] could not unite their tessellated pavement of states into a solid foundation.[A/16c] The style of German Emperor was rejected[5b] by Frederick William IV[3/14c/16d] and reluctantly accepted[5c] by William I. [17]The old soldier[1b] thought it a finer thing to be King of Prussia[9a] as heir[9b] of Frederick II.[1c/16e/F4]

EXAMINATION

1. WHO?

(*a*) **The later Hapsburgs could not unite their tessellated pavement of states into a solid foundation.**

Does this refer only to the Hapsburgs of Vienna, or to the Hapsburgs of Madrid as well?

(*b*) **The style of German Emperor was rejected by Frederick William IV and reluctantly accepted by William I. The old soldier thought it a finer thing to be King of Prussia . . .**

Most readers of this article in the Sunday Press will naturally have assumed that the 'old soldier' is the king who rejected the style – namely Frederick William IV. But they will be wrong: it is William I.

(*c*) **The old soldier thought it a finer thing to be King of Prussia as heir of Frederick II.**

Who was Frederick II in relation to Frederick William IV and William I?

3. WHAT?

The style of German Emperor was rejected by Frederick William IV and reluctantly accepted by William I.

Of what was this Frederick king? Prussia is only mentioned in connection with William I – if indeed he is the king intended by the 'old soldier' – and since William I reads like a much earlier character than Frederick William IV, one cannot assume that they were kings of the same country; for it is unlikely that a king would be in a position to refuse a hereditary title that a predecessor had accepted.

5. WHEN?

(*a*) **In recent times**
In modern times

There is no indication when 'modern times' gave place to 'recent times'.

(*b*) **The style of German Emperor was rejected by Frederick William IV . . .**
The appropriate date should surely have been given?

(*c*) . . . and reluctantly accepted by William I.

The appropriate date should have been given here too.

8. INAPPROPRIATE WORD OR PHRASE

(*a*) Words, like writings, have their destined fates, and it is often the distressful fate . . .

'Distressful', though once a respectable word, has been given a comic connotation in English by 'The Wearing of the Green': it is chiefly used when referring in stage-Irish to Ireland's grievances. 'Distressing' sounds more sincere, and has acquired solemnity from its use in medical contexts.

(*b*) . . . Empire and its derivations . . .

The derivations of 'Empire' are the Latin 'imperium' and 'impero' and some Sanskrit word or other. He probably means 'derivatives', such as 'Imperial' and 'Emperor'.

(*c*) 'Emperors, indeed, as a class . . .'

Emperors can hardly be said to form a 'class', as merchants or peasants do. 'Emperors on the whole' would have been better.

(*d*) Napoleon undeniably filled the part of Emperor . . .

So did the least worthy of the forgotten Holy Roman Emperors. What may be meant is that Napoleon restored the lost meaning of the word by being an active commander-in-chief of the forces of his country and its dependencies.

(*e*) . . . his nephew's crown was almost pinchbeck . . . .

This suggests that a crown with less than a certain proportion of gold in it becomes pinchbeck. This is not so: pinchbeck is an alloy of five parts of copper to one of zinc and contains no gold at all. What is probably meant is 'of very low gold'. The metaphor is an unfortunate one, since Napoleon I who restored glory to the word 'Emperor' was crowned with the famous iron crown of Lombardy, not with a golden diadem.

9. AMBIGUOUS WORD OR PHRASE

(*a*) The style of German Emperor was rejected by Frederick William IV and reluctantly accepted by William I. The old soldier thought it a finer thing to be King of Prussia . . .

This suggests that the old soldier could not be German Emperor and King of Prussia at the same time—which is not the case. Some such word as 'simply' is needed.

(*b*) . . . as heir of Frederick II.

This suggests that 'the old soldier' (probably William I) was the immediate successor of Frederick II—which was not the case. Nobody would guess from this passage that the reigns of three Frederick Williams intervened.

13. SELF-EVIDENT STATEMENT

Words . . . have their destined fates . . .

Are not fates always destined?

14. MATERIAL OMISSION

(*a*) Words, like writings, have their destined fates . . . often . . . They gradually depreciate.

What follows is an account, not so much of how the word 'Emperor' has depreciated as of how historians have written unfavourably about dead Emperors who were flattered while alive, and of how two kings of Prussia preferred to be known by an illustrious old title rather than by a high-sounding new one. It would have been appropriate to point out after 'writings' that reputations depreciate too.

(*b*) **... the distressful fate of coins in a debased currency. They gradually depreciate.**

This tendency of coins to depreciate gradually when a currency is debased should have been dated. It is not a modern phenomenon. The 'Khaki shilling' with a low silver content, which resulted from a silver shortage in the First World War, had a far greater purchasing capacity, hence value, a few years after its minting than one year after.

(*c*) **The style of German Emperor was rejected by Frederick William IV ...**

Who offered it to him?

15. UNFULFILLED PROMISE

Words, like writings, have their destined fates, and it is often the distressful fate of coins in a debased currency.

If 'it is often' had been 'they are often', the fates would have been clearly referred to; but, as it is not, one expects the sentence to run: '... the distressful fate of coins in a debased currency to be refused by shopkeepers' – or something of that sort. But it stops suddenly at 'currency'.

16. UNDEVELOPED THEME

(*a*) **Words, like writings, have their destined fates ... They gradually depreciate.**

Nothing more is said about the depreciation of 'writings' – though 'Emperors have not fared well in the judgement of history' perhaps implies a contrast with contemporary eulogies by court orators.

(*b*) **Once 'indifferent' meant 'just' and 'adventurers' were honourable pioneers.**

It should have been further explained that these words retain their original meanings, but are more generally used in others, less reputable.

(*c*) **The later Hapsburgs could not unite their tessellated pavement of states into a solid foundation.**

It should have been further explained, to continue the argument, that they thereby brought the name 'Emperor' into disrepute.

(*d*) **The style of German Emperor was rejected by Frederick William IV ...**

Why was this? Did he dislike the title 'Emperor'? Or were his feelings the same as those of William I?

(*e*) **The old soldier thought it a finer thing to be King of Prussia as heir of Frederick II.**

It should have been explained that the new title would take precedence over the older one, which would therefore fade out of popular memory.

17. FAULTY CONNEXION

The style of German Emperor was rejected by Frederick William IV and reluctantly accepted by William I. The old soldier thought it a finer thing to be King of Prussia ...

It is not clear that the reluctance felt by William I is explained by what the old soldier thought. A 'For' would have helped.

23. LOGICAL WEAKNESS

. . . many noble figures stand out, but many that are petty. . . .

If they are petty, they do not stand out.

A. MISMATING OF METAPHORS

. . . could not unite their tessellated pavement of states into a solid foundation.

This begins with the figure of uniting awkward bits of marble into a tessellated pavement, and ends with the figure of piling up awkward blocks of stone into a solid foundation.

F. OBSCURE REFERENCE

(1) **Empire and its derivations have fallen from their high estate.**

This is perhaps a reference to Dryden's 'Alexander's Feast' in which Darius is mentioned as having 'fallen, fallen, fallen from his high estate'. But Darius fell by ceasing to be an Emperor. Lord Crewe is here writing of Emperors who have kept their high estate but not greatly adorned it.

(2) **. . . the . . . corridor of the Holy Roman Empire . . .**

This is perhaps a reference to the corridor at the British Museum with the statues of the Classical Emperors. Or is there also one somewhere at Vienna, with the statues of the Holy Roman Emperors? There is none at Schönbrunn, where one would expect to find such a thing.

(3) **. . . his nephew's crown was almost pinchbeck.**

Few readers could say offhand who Napoleon's nephew was.

(4) **. . . as heir of Frederick II.**

Few British readers could identify the famous 'Frederick the Great' with this 'Frederick II'—'Frederick the Great' would naturally be assumed to have been Frederick I, whereas Frederick I was his grandfather, a Frederick William having intervened.

FAIR COPY

'It is often the distressing fate of words—and of reputations—gradually to depreciate in value, as the coins of a debased currency did in the days before paper-money. The word "indifferent" used to mean "impartial in judgement" but now seldom means anything except "evincing no interest" or "of poor quality"; "adventurer" used to mean "honourable pioneer", but now usually means "unscrupulous self-seeker". In modern times "Empire" and its derivatives "Emperor" and "Imperial", have similarly lost their original connotations of glory, because Emperors, though flattered while living, have not on the whole earned the approval of historians. In the long corridor at . . . [?] where the Holy Roman Emperors stand in effigy, some are pointed out by the cicerones as noble, but most are dismissed as undistinguished puppets.

Napoleon's military exploits, it is true, restored some glory to the word Emperor, but this faded again when his nephew Napoleon III was likewise crowned Emperor of the French.

The numerous states of the Austro-Hungarian Empire resembled the insecurely mortised pieces of a grandiose tessellated pavement; and the later Hapsburgs, who ruled them, enhanced neither their own glory nor that of the Imperial tradition.

The title "German Emperor" had little attraction for the veteran soldier, King William I of Prussia, when he was offered it in 1871 by a representative assembly of German states. He accepted it only with great reluctance, for it would take precedence over the lesser but more illustrious title, "King of Prussia", which reminded the world that he was descended from Frederick the Great. It had perhaps[1] been a similar sentiment that led his brother and predecessor, Frederick William IV, to reject an identical invitation in 1848.'

COMMENT

This is the writing of a distinguished Liberal statesman, born in 1858, who held various Cabinet appointments between 1905 and 1931 and has published a biography of Lord Rosebery and a book of poems. The shortcomings of his style here seem due rather to colloquial geniality than ignorance or haste; and to his ingenuous assumption that most readers of the Sunday paper for whom he is writing have the same easy familiarity with Continental history as himself.

DR. HUGH DALTON, M.P.

from *Hitler's War*, March, 1940

TEXT

We[1] must do our best[8a] for a new Commonwealth of States and for new strong Federal Unions,[14a] as soon as men[1] will take[8b] them. Meanwhile, even some new Confederacies might be useful.[16] But in the early post-war phase it is the existing Anglo-French Alliance, with such extensions as it can attract,[10] which will be the hard core of World Order.

Let us meditate for a moment longer[20] upon this Alliance, and upon its power of gathering reinforcements. First, in Europe, Britain and France, Poland and Czechoslovakia; then, outside Europe, the British Dominions, India — soon, I hope, to become a Dominion, in spite of present misunderstandings and muddled negotiations — the British Colonies, the French Empire — including a number of territories directly represented in the French Parliament — Egypt, Iraq.[3a/14b] This is already a massive combination. I hazard no guess as to how many States, now neutral, will, either of their own free will,[N] or as victims of Nazi aggression,[21] join this Alliance

[1] The more probable explanation is that Frederick William IV mistrusted the Liberal revolutionaries who offered him the title, and feared to upset the Old Order by accepting it.

before the war ends. But many of the European neutrals I think will surely join it, if not before, then when the war is over.[G] And I hope it will be a term of the Final Settlement that the New Germany[3b] too shall enter it.

EXAMINATION

1. WHO?

We must do our best . . . as soon as men will take them.

Who are 'we' and who are 'men'? This was written when Dr. Dalton was out of office — perhaps 'we' are the Socialists and 'men' are the Tories.

3. WHAT?

(*a*) **Let us meditate for a moment upon this Alliance, and upon its power of gathering reinforcements. First, in Europe, Britain and France, Poland and Czechoslovakia; then, outside Europe, the British Dominions, India — soon, I hope, to become a Dominion, in spite of present misunderstandings and muddled negotiations — the British Colonies, the French Empire . . . Egypt, Iraq.**

The Anglo-French Alliance was made between Great Britain with her dependencies and France with her Empire. New contracting parties were the self-governing Dominions of the British Empire, Poland and the exiled Czech Government. Perhaps Dr. Dalton was instancing Egypt and Iraq as typical potential reinforcements — at the time of writing they were both non-belligerent — and hinting that Turkey, or even Russia, might join the Alliance, though not wishing to mention them by name.

(*b*) **. . . the New Germany . . .**

Is this Hitler's Greater Germany, or a Germany miraculously reconverted by a second defeat to the World Order of which Dr. Dalton writes?

8. INAPPROPRIATE WORD OR PHRASE

(*a*) **We must do our best for a new Commonwealth of States . . .**

One can only do one's best for someone or something already in existence. The 'for' here apparently does duty for 'to bring into existence'.

(*b*) **. . . new strong Federal Unions, as soon as men will take them.**

This final clause perhaps means 'as soon as men will accept the idea of Federal Union'.

10. MISPLACED WORD OR PHRASE

. . . it is the existing Anglo-French Alliance, with such extensions as it can attract, which will be the hard core of World Order.

The Anglo-French Alliance is thought of as the 'hard core'; the extensions are an afterthought and do not belong to it. They are probably the 'new Confederacies' which 'might be useful'.

14. MATERIAL OMISSION

(*a*) **. . . and for new strong Federal Unions, . . .**

He does not state whether these are, or are not, to be included within the proposed Commonwealth of States: for example, would the United States, or the U.S.S.R., enter as a single state or as a Federal Union? The difference between a Commonwealth of States and a Federal Union of States is not defined.

(*b*) **First, in Europe, Britain and France, ... then, outside Europe, the British Colonies, ... the French Empire ... Egypt, Iraq.**

He leaves out British possessions in Europe, and does not mention that, of the British Commonwealth of Nations, South Africa then stood out of the Anglo-French Alliance. That he does not mention the British Commonwealth of Nations by name is probably due to his allocation of the word 'Commonwealth' to his own more grandiose Alliance.

16. UNDEVELOPED THEME

Meanwhile, even some new Confederacies might be useful.

This is soon forgotten in the Anglo-French scheme, which is evidently intended to embrace most of the world.

20. IRRELEVANCY

(*a*) **Let us meditate for a moment longer upon this Alliance, ...**

He forgets that he is writing a book, not addressing a prayer-meeting. Neither he nor his readers pause for silent meditation.

21. FALSE CONTRAST

... how many states, now neutral, will, either of their own free will, or as victims of Nazi aggression, ...

Surely the Nazis would not force European states which they had over-run to join the Anglo-French Alliance against them?

G. CIRCUMLOCUTION

I hazard no guess as to how many States ... will join this Alliance before the war is over. But many of the European neutrals I think will surely join it, if not before, then when the war is over.

He is playing for safety. His anxiety not to be wrong leads him to qualify 'surely' with 'I think' and to put in the unnecessary 'if not before'. 'I hazard no guess as to how many' is longhand for 'who knows how many?'

N. SAME WORD IN DIFFERENT SENSES

... how many states, now neutral, will, either of their own free will, ...

The use of the word 'will' in different senses catches the eye because in both cases a comma comes immediately afterwards.

FAIR COPY

'A Commonwealth of States, with some of its members linked together in Federal Unions, must be formed as soon as possible. But this cannot happen until some time after Germany has been defeated: we shall have to be content meanwhile with extensions of the confederacy known as the Anglo-French Alliance. This was originally formed between Great Britain with her colonies and dependencies, including India, and France with her Empire (some parts of which are represented in the French Chamber of Deputies, some governed by officials appointed by the Colonial Ministry). Most of the self-governing states of the British Empire, together with Poland and the exiled government of Czechoslovakia, have since attached themselves to this already massive combination. They will, perhaps, even while the war is still in progress, be joined by Egypt, Iraq, and many other states at present neutral – some European ones because they have experienced Nazi aggression, some without such an incentive – then, after the war, as soon as this alliance begins to transform itself into the firm nucleus of the desired Commonwealth, by still more. I hope that by that time the negotiations between Great Britain and India – now all muddle and misunderstanding – will have been satisfactorily concluded, so that India may re-enter the Commonwealth as a self-governing member state; and finally that it will be an article in the final peace settlement that Germany, abjuring her Nazi creed, will also be admitted to membership.'

COMMENT

The obscurity of the federal scheme that Dr. Dalton advocates is perhaps due to his not allowing himself time to look up in a Year Book, or other work of reference, the status of the different parts of the British Empire and the political relations, at various dates, between the countries he mentions. Nevertheless an eminent politician, especially one who is commonly regarded by his Party as an expert on foreign affairs, should know these elementary facts; and a Doctor of Philosophy should write with greater composure than this passage displays.

The Fair Copy that we offer may not correspond with his views; but these are difficult to grasp.

DAPHNE DU MAURIER

from *Come Wind, Come Weather*, 1940

TEXT

[The gallant times of Drake, Raleigh, Sir Philip Sidney, the Pilgrim Fathers and Oliver Cromwell's Ironsides.]

I cannot believe that[14a] the men and women of those days[5] said 'How is the war going to affect me?' when[14b] the Spanish Armada put forth from Cadiz Bay. They would have[8a] sworn[8b] in rich Elizabethan words which are not, alas, at my disposal,[9] 'How can I affect[8c] the Spanish Armada?'

I believe that the old English spirit is not dead. It still lurks[8d] in the hearts and minds[7] of every man and woman in this island,[22a] but centuries of soft living and thinking only in the first person[23a] singular have made the spirit[1] a shadow of its former self,[22b] and the door which hides it is not always easy to unlock.[23b]

EXAMINATION

1. WHO?

. . . centuries of soft living . . . have made the spirit a shadow of its former self, ..

It should be made clear that it is people whom the spirit should animate who have made pigs of themselves, not the spirit itself.

5. WHEN?

I cannot believe that the men and women of those days said 'How is the war going to affect me?'

Which days? Cromwell's Ironsides were formed nearly sixty years after the defeat of the Spanish Armada.

7. HOW MANY?

It still lurks in the hearts and minds of every man and woman . . .

How many hearts and how many minds has every man and woman? Whatever the answer, there is only one door to them all, according to the last sentence.

8. INAPPROPRIATE WORD OR PHRASE

(*a*) **They would have sworn . . .**

There is no hypothesis here, because the Armada did 'put forth'. What is meant is: 'They must have sworn'.

(*b*) **They would have sworn . . . 'How can I affect the Spanish Armada?'**

One cannot swear a question; one can only decorate it with blasphemous or obscene terms.

(*c*) **'How can I affect the Spanish Armada?'**

Affect is unsuitably lame for this dashing paragraph. Or is it a joking word?

(*d*) **. . . the old English spirit is not dead. It still lurks in the hearts and minds of every man . . .**

Would so tough and courageous a spirit 'lurk'? 'Lurk' in its modern use always conveys the sense of furtiveness. 'Pines' or 'languishes' would be more understandable in this prison metaphor.

9. AMBIGUOUS WORD OR PHRASE

. . . rich Elizabethan words which are not, alas, at my disposal, . . .

It is not clear whether delicacy or ignorance prevented these words from being reproduced. It should have been easy enough for a novelist like Miss Du Maurier to produce a rich Elizabethan objurgation, such as: 'By God's Body I will serve those rascal Dons as the city wife served the cook-wench's brat.' More likely it was considerations of 'Moral Rearmament' (mentioned in the foreword) that restrained her pen.

14. MATERIAL OMISSION

(*a*) **I cannot believe that the men and women of those days said . . .**

Who has suggested that they did?

(*b*) **. . . when the Spanish Armada put forth from Cadiz Bay.**

Immediate news of foreign events was not available in 1588. 'When they heard that' would have been better than 'when'.

22. OVER-EMPHASIS

(*a*) **. . . the old English spirit still lurks . . . in the hearts and minds of every man and woman in this island, . . .**

This statement, even when its application is restricted to British nationals, is not borne out by common experience.

(*b*) **... centuries of soft living ... have made the spirit a shadow of its former self, ...**

This recalls the Victorian comic verses about the ghost who kept on having fatal accidents and eventually became: 'The ghost of a ghost of a ghost of a ghost, Of a ghost of a ghost of a ghost.'

23. LOGICAL WEAKNESS

(*a*) **... soft living and thinking only in the first person singular have made the spirit a shadow of its former self, ...**

In the only example here given, the Elizabethan heroes and heroines use the first person singular: 'How can I affect the Spanish Armada?' The moderns, on the contrary, use the third person singular: 'How is the war going to affect *me*?' When a person refers to himself with selfish pride, he does not necessarily use the first person singular: for example, 'It seems to me that my own comfort should always come first.' Indeed, the third person singular conveys a coldness which the first person cannot match: 'Lady Proudie-Pontifex's compliments, and she does not wish to be troubled by further charitable appeals.'

(*b*) **... the door which hides it is not always easy to unlock.**

'Lurking' denotes voluntary concealment; the metaphor of unlocking the door suggests that the spirit is an involuntary prisoner.

FAIR COPY

'I should not believe anyone who assured me that, when the men and women of Elizabethan England heard that the Spanish Armada had put forth from Cadiz Bay, they asked one another, as people do now, "How will this war affect *me*?" Rather, they must have sworn with rich objurgations (which would probably be too coarse to print here) to do whatever lay in their power to prosecute the war and destroy the would-be invaders.

I believe that the Elizabethan spirit is not dead: rather it languishes wanly in prison, waiting century-long for the cell-door to be unlocked, while those whose breasts it should inspire have enervated themselves with soft and selfish living.'

COMMENT

Here it is patriotic emotion that has thrown a usually careful writer off her balance, by making her write too fast and throw together such ready-made phrases as 'hearts and minds', 'every man and woman in this island', 'thinking only in the first person singular', 'the old English spirit is not dead', 'a shadow of its former self'.

Sir Arthur Eddington

from *The Expanding Universe*, 1932

TEXT

The position[1a] with regard to[9a] the thermodynamical[H1] running-down of the universe has not materially altered since I discussed it four years ago. The impression has got abroad[G1] that the conclusions[1b] have been shaken by recent work[1c/9b] on cosmic rays. That would be[24] impossible, so far as I am concerned[9c]; for the theory of cosmic rays that is being urged in this connection[G2] happens to be the one I was advocating[H2] at the time of writing,[J1] viz. that the cosmic rays give evidence of the building up of higher elements[3a] out of[K] hydrogen[H3] in distant regions[4] occupied by diffuse matter.[3b] I am not at all sure[G3] that the more recent evidence[14a] should be interpreted as favourable to it[3c]; but if it is favourable, as Dr. Millikan maintains, I have the less reason to change my views.[J2/16/23]

The coming together of electric particles to form a complex[20a] atom,[H3] and the consequent[9d] dispersal[H4] of some of the energy in[9e] cosmic rays, is clearly a step in the same direction as the other energy-dissipating[H4] processes — for example, the coming together of nebulous[9f] matter to form a star, and the consequent[9d] dispersal of energy as radiant heat. It[3d] is one more contributor[8a] to[12] the general[8b] running-down towards an ultimate[20b] state of thermodynamic[H1] equilibrium. Millikan has sometimes called the atom-building process[H3] a 'winding-up'[9g] of the universe; but 'up' and 'down' are relative[9h] terms,[14b] and a transformation of axes may be needed in comparing his descriptions with mine.[8c]

EXAMINATION

1. WHO?

(*a*) **The position with regard to the thermodynamical running-down of the universe has not materially altered since I discussed it four years ago.**

When one has come to realize that Sir Arthur is writing not about the actual running-down of the universe, but about a scientific view of it, one asks oneself, whose 'position' is meant? His own, or that of other scientists?

(*b*) **The impression has got abroad that the conclusions have been shaken by recent work on cosmic rays. . . .**

Whose conclusions? His own? Why not say so?

(*c*) **. . . the conclusions have been shaken by recent work on cosmic rays. . . .**

Whose recent work? If this had been specified, much of the later obscurity caused by 'the more recent evidence' might have been avoided.

3. WHAT?

(*a*) **. . . building up of higher elements . . .**

Does this mean higher in the scale of atomic weight? If so, this should have been explained for the benefit of the ordinary reader.

(*b*) **. . . the building up of higher elements out of hydrogen in distant regions occupied by diffuse matter.**

What is this diffuse matter? Is it hydrogen, restated? Since hydrogen is the lowest element in the scale of atomic weight the reader should be told whether other elements are believed to exist in these distant regions, which might affect the action of the rays on the hydrogen.

(*c*) **I am not at all sure that the more recent evidence should be interpreted as favourable to it . . .**

Does this mean that he has, or has not, examined the more recent evidence?

(*d*) **The coming together of electric particles to form a complex atom . . . is clearly a step in the same direction as . . . the coming together of nebulous matter to form a star, and the consequent dispersal of energy as radiant heat. It is one more contributor to the general running-down . . .**

To what does this 'It' refer? The last subject mentioned was the dispersal of energy as radiant heat. A colon put at 'heat' instead of a full stop would have shown that 'It' meant the 'coming together of electric particles to form an atom and the consequent dispersal of energy . . .'

4. WHERE?

. . . the cosmic rays give evidence of the building up of higher elements out of hydrogen in distant regions occupied by diffuse matter.

Regions distant from what point? From some hypothetic source of the cosmic rays? Or from the earth?

8. INAPPROPRIATE WORD OR PHRASE

(*a*) **It is one more contributor to the general running-down . . .**

'The coming together of electric particles' may be a 'contribution' but cannot decently be personified as a 'contributor'.

(*b*) **. . . one more contributor to the general running-down . . .**

'General' seems too small a word, since it refers only to *genera*: 'universal' or 'cosmic' is surely what is wanted.

(*c*) **It is one more contributor to the general running-down . . . Millikan has sometimes called the atom-building process a 'winding-up' of the universe; but 'up' and 'down' are relative terms and a transformation of axes may be needed in comparing his descriptions with mine.**

Dr Millikan and Sir Arthur seem to be describing the same sort of facts, while using exactly contrary metaphors. What is needed, in turning from one to the other, is not a transformation of axes, but the reversal of a single axis.

9. AMBIGUOUS WORD OR PHRASE

(*a*) **The position with regard to the thermodynamical running-down of the universe has not materially altered since I discussed it four years ago.**

Literally, this means that the universe has not run down much during the past four years. What is probably meant is that scientists have not greatly altered their opinions about this hypothetic phenomenon.

(*b*) **. . . shaken by recent work on cosmic rays. . . .**

This probably means, not that someone has been deflecting or otherwise manipulating cosmic rays, but that someone has published results of research on the subject of these rays.

(*c*) **The impression has got abroad that conclusions have been shaken by recent work on cosmic rays. That would be impossible, so far as I am concerned; . . .**

Since it is not yet clear whose conclusions these are, one reads this second sentence as a denial that recent work of Sir Arthur's could have shaken them.

(*d*) **The coming together of electric particles . . . and the consequent dispersal of some of the energy in cosmic rays, . . .**

'Consequent' might mean that the energy was dispersed not in the confusion of the coming together, but by the atom after its formation. The same ambiguity is repeated later in the sentence.

(*e*) **. . . the consequent dispersal of some of the energy in cosmic rays, . . .**

The later and parallel phrase about the star's 'dispersal of energy as radiant heat' suggests that 'the energy in cosmic rays' means 'energy in the form of cosmic rays', not 'energy resident in cosmic rays', as one understands at first.

(*f*) **. . . the coming together of nebulous matter to form a star . . .**

It would have been safer to use 'nebular' here, as meaning nothing but 'diffused in the form of nebulae'. 'Nebulous' can mean 'misty'; or, metaphorically, 'vague'.

(*g*) **. . . Millikan has sometimes called the atom-building process a 'winding-up' of the universe; . . .**

It should be made clear that Dr. Millikan was using a domestic, not a commercial, metaphor. When a clock runs down, and is wound up, it goes on again; when a business runs down and is wound up, it stops.

(*h*) **. . . 'up' and 'down' are relative terms . . .**

This may mean that 'up' and 'down' express the relation of moving objects to a fixed point; or (by making the word 'relative' refer to 'Einsteinian "relativity" ') that there is neither an absolute 'up' nor an absolute 'down' in this swirling universe.

12. DUPLICATION

. . . the coming together of electric particles to form a complex atom . . . is a step in the same direction as the other energy-dissipating processes — . . . It is one more contributor to the general running-down . . .

There seems no reason for this change of metaphor from 'a step in the same direction as . . .' to 'It is one more contributor to . . .' If a colon or a long dash were put at the end of the first sentence, 'It is one more contributor to' could be omitted.

14. MATERIAL OMISSION

(*a*) **I am not at all sure that the more recent evidence . . .**

It has not yet been said that there *is* any more recent evidence — though perhaps this is obscurely hinted in 'the position with regard to the thermodynamical running-down of the universe has not materially altered . . .' What this evidence is, and who supplied it, should have been briefly stated.

(*b*) **Millikan has sometimes called the atom-building process a 'winding-up' of the universe; but 'up' and 'down' are relative terms . . .**

To an ordinary reader, who thinks in terms of 'winding up' a watch or modern clock – as opposed to a grandfather, or wall, clock – this seems like a wanton play on words. But the phrase originated in the winding-up of the clock-weight on its cord until it could go no higher; the pendulum was then set swinging again and the weight slowly ran down to the full extent of the cord. It is just possible that Sir Arthur had this figure in mind; but if so he should have made it plain why 'up' and 'down' are essential parts of the metaphors 'winding-up' and 'running-down', and not verbal accidents.

16. UNDEVELOPED THEME

I am not at all sure that the more recent evidence should be interpreted as favourable to . . . [a view that I was advocating at the time that I was discussing the thermodynamical running-down of the universe]; **but if it is favourable, as Dr. Millikan maintains, I have the less reason to change my views.**

Here it should be indicated that even if this more recent evidence (which his detractors do not seem to have quoted) is unfavourable, his original conclusions are not affected by it.

20. IRRELEVANCY

(*a*) **The coming together of electric particles to form a complex atom, . . .**

The complexity of this atom is irrelevant, since we are not told what 'higher element' it constitutes. All atoms are complex: Nils Bohr went mad while trying to understand them.

(*b*) **. . . the general running-down towards an ultimate state of thermodynamical equilibrium.**

It would have been enough to say 'towards thermodynamical equilibrium'. 'Ultimate' begs the question of whether the run-down universe may not be wound up again by, for instance, the radiant heat diffused by the stars.

23. LOGICAL WEAKNESS

The impression has got abroad that the conclusions have been shaken by recent work on cosmic rays. That would be impossible, so far as I am concerned; for the theory . . . that is being urged in this connection happens to be the one that I was advocating at the time of writing . . . I am not at all sure that the more recent evidence should be interpreted as favourable to it. But if it is favourable . . . I have the less reason to change my views.

The argument seems to be as follows: 'People are saying that recent conclusions about cosmic rays shake my conclusions about the running-down of the universe. It is impossible that this should be so: because the cosmic ray conclusions which they quote are those of which I approved when writing out my thesis. However, there is fresh evidence on the same subject (of which these people have not heard) which very likely disproves the cosmic ray conclusions. *Ergo*: people are doubly wrong, and I am doubly right.'

The flaws in this argument are:

(1) That though he may have advocated the original cosmic-ray conclusions,

these do not necessarily support his own conclusions about the running-down of the universe;

(2) That the 'more recent' cosmic ray conclusions are not proved, to leave his own conclusions unshaken, merely by the omission of his detractors to 'urge them in this connection'.

24. CHANGE OF STANDPOINT

The impression has got abroad that the conclusions have been shaken by recent work on cosmic rays. That would be impossible . . .

He means, no doubt, 'That is not so'. There is no hypothesis involved. Perhaps 'would be' is intended to correspond with another form of the first sentence: e.g. 'Someone has been pointedly asking whether these conclusions could be shaken by recent work on cosmic rays.'

G. CIRCUMLOCUTION

(1) **The impression has got abroad that the conclusions have been shaken . . .**

A lordly way of saying that perhaps someone has written to that effect in a scientific journal.

(2) **. . . the theory of cosmic rays that is being urged in this connection . . .**

A cumbersome way of saying 'the theory of cosmic rays mentioned'.

(3) **I am not at all sure that the more recent evidence should be interpreted as favourable to it; . . .**

A roundabout way of saying 'I doubt whether the more recent evidence is favourable to it.'

H. ELEGANT VARIATION

(1) **thermodynamical running-down**
thermodynamic equilibrium

It is difficult to justify this variation of word-form on grounds either of sense or of euphony.

(2) **. . . the theory that is being urged happens . . . to be the one that I was advocating . . .**

Unless 'urge' is considered a stronger word than 'advocate' there seems to be no reason for the variation. Moreover, the previous remark 'an impression has got abroad' has suggested that this theory was not urged at all, but only loosely quoted as having shaken the conclusions mentioned in the first sentence.

(3) **. . . the building up of higher elements out of hydrogen . . .**
The coming together of electric particles to form a complex atom . . .
. . . the atom-building process . . .

These are apparently all accounts of the same phenomenon and it would have greatly assisted the reader if the key-word 'building-up' had been used throughout.

(4) **the . . . dispersal of some of the energy in cosmic rays, is clearly a step in the same direction as other energy-dissipating processes — for example, . . . the dispersal of energy as radiant heat.**

The variation between 'energy-dispersal' and 'energy-dissipation' is unnecessary and unfortunate. 'Dissipation' implies that one neither knows nor cares where the things dissipated go; 'dispersal' is often used of an orderly process of decentralization or disbanding – 'the tribesmen dispersed to their villages', 'stocks of food are dispersed as a precaution against warehouse fires'.

J. MEMORY STRAIN

The position with regard to the thermodynamical running-down of the universe has not materially altered since I discussed it four years ago. The impression has got abroad that the conclusions have been shaken by recent work on cosmic rays. That would be impossible, so far as I am concerned; for the theory happens to be the one that I was advocating at the time of writing, viz. that the cosmic rays give evidence of the building up of higher elements out of hydrogen in distant regions occupied by diffuse matter. I am not at all sure that the more recent evdience should be interpreted as favourable to it; but if it is favourable, as Dr. Millikan maintains, I have the less reason to change my views.

1.

The reader cannot readily relate 'the one that I was advocating at the time of writing' to 'since I discussed it four years ago'. If 'at the time of writing' had been 'at the time of my discussion', the word 'discuss' would have stimulated his memory.

2.

'To change my views' is another phrase not readily related to 'since I discussed it four years ago'. The only view of his own that Sir Arthur has admitted expressing is that a cosmic-ray theory (of the truth of which, however, he is no longer sure) supported certain conclusions about the running-down of the universe.

K. TOO MUCH OF THE SAME WORD

. . . evidence of the building up of higher elements out of hydrogen . . .

These three 'of's' are tedious and could have been avoided by 'evidence that higher elements are built up out of hydrogen'.

FAIR COPY

'My theory, published four years ago, about the thermodynamic running-down of the universe has not since been seriously questioned. Some people have written loosely about its having been disproved by Professor X's researches into the action of cosmic rays, which are held to show that in comparatively empty parts of the universe, far distant from the Solar system [?] diffused particles of hydrogen are being built up by these rays into elements of greater weight. The facts are: that at the time of forming my theory I accepted as credible Professor X's account of this particular transformation of elements, and related my conclusions to it; and that Professor Y's more recent researches have given fresh results which, according to Dr. Millikan, corroborate this account, but which I have not yet fully examined. If Dr. Millikan is right, then there is no more to be said; if, however, he is wrong, as I incline to believe, my conclusions are not necessarily disproved, since Professor X's account did not form an integral part of my argument.

It is clear that the concurrence of electric particles, resulting in the building-up of an atom and involving a [?] dissipation of some energy in the form of cosmic rays, is matched by other physical phenomena: for example, by the concurrence of nebular matter resulting in the building-up of a star and involving a dissipation of some energy in the form of radiant heat. Dr. Millikan, writing of such atom-building as illustrative of the universal tendency towards thermodynamic equilibrium, which is my main thesis, has expressed this tendency in terms of the winding-up of a clock – not, as I have done, in terms of its running-down. However, neither metaphor has absolute force: indeed, though opposite in sense, both give equally legitimate descriptions of facts about which he and I are in general agreement. In comparing his descriptions of this process with mine, the reader will need only to remember that, whereas I make it analogous with the running-down of a wall-clock until the clock-weight can fall no lower in the case, Dr. Millikan makes it analogous with the winding-up of this clock until the weight can rise no higher.'

COMMENT

Some phrases used in this passage are borrowed from business or official English:

> 'the position with regard to'
> 'in this connection'
> 'a step in the same direction'

Some are colloquial:

> 'the impression has got abroad'
> 'that would be impossible, so far as I am concerned'
> 'I am not at all sure that the more recent evidence should be regarded'
> 'It is one more contributor to the general running-down towards'

Some are relics of Victorian formality:

> 'the one that I was advocating at the time of writing, viz. that the cosmic rays give evidence'
> 'But if it is favourable, as Dr. Millikan maintains, I have the less reason to change my views.'

Scientists have no fixed scientific English prose style to supplement their large vocabulary of Latin and Greek borrowings – now being supplemented with such Classically incorrect forms as 'psycho-analysis' and 'auto-erotic' and such mule-words as 'television' and 'auto-suggestion'. They are reduced to using the current English of their period, unless they can express all that they have to communicate in mathematical or chemical formulae. Scientists living between Newton's time and Darwin's were luckier in their periods than those of the present day.

In the passage here quoted, which illustrates the modern tendency towards ambiguous and inaccurate expression in scientific writing, it is perhaps Sir Arthur's anger at having his reputation unjustly assailed by ignorant critics that causes much of the confusion. Though wishing to show that they are not only wrong in their contentions but out of date in their scientific reading, he does not deign to mention their names or even to identify, with name and date, the scientific theory that they quote against him. This reticence makes the passage read most mysteriously. After rebuffing his critics in this off-hand way, Sir Arthur deliberately undermines his own position, as a proof of self-confidence; and retires to the company of his one scientific equal with a smiling face and a little joke about the relativity of 'up' and 'down'.

T. S. Eliot

from *Elizabethan Essays*, 1934

TEXT

Massinger has been more fortunately[3a] and more fairly judged[1] than several of his greater[8a] contemporaries. Three critics have done their best by him: the notes of Coleridge exemplify Coleridge's[22a] fine and[17a] fragmentary[10] perceptions;[23a] the essay of Leslie Stephen is a piece of formidable destructive analysis[23b]; and the essay of Swinburne is Swinburne's[22b] criticism at its best.[12a] None of these, probably,[17b] has put Massinger finally and irrefutably into a place.[3b]

English criticism[8b] is inclined to argue[8c] or to persuade[8d] rather than to state[8e]; and, instead of forcing the subject[8f] to expose himself,[8g] these critics have left in their work an undissolved residuum of their own[22c] good taste,[3c] which, however impeccable,[23c] is something that requires our faith.[3d] The principles which animate[8h] this taste remain unexplained.[12b] Canon Cruickshank's book[17c] is a work of scholarship; and the advantage of good[20a] scholarship is that it presents us with evidence which is an invitation to the critical faculty of the reader: it bestows a method[9] rather than a judgement.

It is difficult – it is perhaps the supreme difficulty of criticism – to make the[2] facts generalize[8i] themselves; but Mr. Cruickshank at least presents us[24] with facts which are capable of generalization.[8j/13] This is a service of value; and it is therefore[23d] wholly a compliment[20b] to the author to say that his appendices are as valuable as the essay itself.[3e]

EXAMINATION

1. WHO?

Massinger has been more fortunately and more fairly judged . . .

By whom? Playgoers of his own time? Historians of Elizabethan drama? A few discerning critics?

2. WHICH?

It is difficult — it is perhaps the supreme difficulty of criticism — to make the facts generalize themselves; . . .

Which are 'the facts'? A great many have been introduced into this passage but no particular set is here indicated. Does he perhaps mean just 'facts'?

3. WHAT?

(*a*) **Massinger has been more fortunately and more fairly judged . . .**

'Fortunately' is not parallel with 'fairly'. A writer cannot be judged 'fortunately', though he may have the good fortune to be judged by understanding critics.

(*b*) **None of these, probably, has put Massinger finally and irrefutably into a place.**

Does this perhaps mean 'his place' — an undisputed niche, however humble, in the Hall of Fame?

(*c*) **. . . these critics have left in their work an undissolved residuum of their own good taste . . .**

This is perhaps intended to mean that, when each stage of the critical argument has been examined by the reader, some expression of praise or dispraise unrelated to it will be found to remain, which he will accept as true because he knows the writer to have good taste. But this is not what is said. 'An undissolved residuum left in their work' can only be found after an examination by the reader — who, however, is not mentioned. And to what sort of critical process 'undissolved' refers is not clear. A writer does not *dissolve* his own good taste in criticism: he proves it, or *resolves* it (in the sense of making it clear to others).

(*d*) **. . . an undissolved residuum of their own good taste, which . . . is something that requires our faith.**

The comma after 'taste' plainly shows that it is the residuum, not the taste, which 'requires our faith'. This means merely that 'we' are asked to believe that a residuum exists. Is this what is intended?

(*e*) **. . . it is therefore wholly a compliment to the author to say that his appendices are as valuable as the essay itself.**

This is 'an undissolved residuum' of Mr. Eliot's 'own good taste'. We are given no indication of what sort of facts, or how many, are contained in the essay or in the appendices.

8. INAPPROPRIATE WORD OR PHRASE

(*a*) **. . . than several of his greater contemporaries.**

The words 'great' and 'greater' must always be defined when applied to people; otherwise, this 'leaves a residuum of good taste undissolved'. It would have been enough here to say that these contemporaries were more deserving of critical appreciation than Massinger.

(*b*) **English criticism is inclined to argue . . .**

No: it is the critics who argue; criticism is the argument.

(*c*) **English criticism is inclined to argue . . . rather than to state . . .**

As this seems to be intended as a derogatory remark, perhaps what is meant is 'to wrangle'. Criticism is necessarily argument: that is to say, it is the orderly demonstration of the critic's opinion.

(*d*) **English criticism is inclined to . . . persuade . . .**

Even if 'persuade' is a slip for 'try to persuade', this is surely not the required meaning? All critical writers try to 'persuade'. Mr. Eliot apparently wishes to point out that the difference between effective and ineffective critical writing lies in whether or not the critics' opinions are substantiated by quotation. Perhaps what is meant is 'coax and charm'.

(*e*) **English criticism is inclined to argue or to persuade rather than to state . . .**

An argument, whether persuasive or not, and whether in good taste or bad, is a statement, unless put in the form of a rhetorical question. Perhaps what is meant is 'rather than to substantiate opinions'.

(*f*) **. . . and, instead of forcing the subject to expose himself.**

The 'subject' is not necessarily a person: there can be criticism of, say, a whole body of religious or philosophical opinion, or of national character. If Massinger is here expressly referred to, then 'the subject' is a misleading alias for him.

(*g*) **. . . and, instead of forcing the subject to expose himself, . . .**

Criticism is not necessarily destructive: 'expose himself' should have been 'reveal himself', because exposure implies the revelation of weakness or badness.

(*h*) **The principles which animate this taste remain unexplained.**

Surely they do not 'animate' it? Natural talent, vigour, or appetite may be said to animate taste; but principles 'control' rather than 'animate'.

(*i*) **. . . it is perhaps the supreme difficulty of criticism — to make the facts generalize themselves.**

Anyone who lets the facts do all the work of sorting themselves into generalizations is not a critic, but a literary spectator. A critic makes his own generalizations out of the facts.

(*j*) **. . . facts which are capable of generalization.**

Rather: 'suitable for generalization'. This phrase, too, makes the facts responsible for sorting themselves into generalizations.

9. AMBIGUOUS WORD OR PHRASE

. . . scholarship . . . bestows a method rather than a judgement.

Does this mean a method of delivering judgement? A scholar classifies facts methodically, but the method of delivering a judgement by interpretation of these facts is for the critic to provide.

10. MISPLACED WORD OR PHRASE

. . . the notes of Coleridge exemplify Coleridge's fine and fragmentary perceptions.

Surely 'fragmentary' belongs with 'notes', not with perceptions'? Coleridge's mental eye did not have a cracked retina: more than any other poet of his time he saw things whole, not in fragments (as, say, Milton and Keats may be said to have seen them).

12. DUPLICATION

(*a*) **Three critics have done their best by him . . . the essay of Swinburne is Swinburne's criticism at its best.**

It would have been enough to say: 'Three critics, including Swinburne in an essay, have done their best by him.'

(*b*) **. . . an undissolved residuum of their own good taste, which . . . requires our faith.**

The principles which animate this taste remain unexplained.

If the first sentence had been more clearly expressed, the second would have been unnecessary.

13. SELF-EVIDENT STATEMENT

. . . Mr Cruickshank at least presents us with facts which are capable of generalization.

A generalization of sorts can be made from every collection of facts, though not necessarily an informative or stimulating one.

17. FAULTY CONNEXION

(*a*) **. . . Coleridge's fine and fragmentary perceptions.**

This is like speaking of a 'fine and leaky kettle'. To be fine is good; to be fragmentary is not good. 'But' is the obvious connexion between 'fine' and 'fragmentary'.

(*b*) **Three critics have done their best by him; . . . None of these, probably, has put Massinger finally and irrefutably into a place.**

A 'But' or 'However' is needed to introduce this obscure second sentence.

(*c*) **English criticism is inclined to argue and persuade rather than to state . . . these critics have left in their work an undissolved residuum of their own good taste. The principles which animate this taste remain unexplained. Canon Cruickshank's book is a work of scholarship . . . it bestows a method rather than a judgement.**

The connexion between the first two sentences and the last is obscure, though a close connexion is implied by their inclusion in the same short paragraph. The argument appears to be: 'Some critics deliver a judgement without substantiation; Canon Cruickshank, on the other hand, provides material for forming and substantiating a judgement but does not deliver one'. This should have been made clear.

20. IRRELEVANCY

(*a*) **Canon Cruickshank's book is a work of scholarship; and the advantage of good scholarship is . . .**

The word 'good' is irrelevant unless it carries a suggestion that Canon Cruickshank's book, or essay, does not deserve to be called good.

(*b*) **. . . it is therefore wholly a compliment to the author to say that his appendices . . .**

It is difficult to see what place the ceremonious giving or withholding of compliments has in what purports to be a critical essay. A critic 'bestows a judgement'; a courtier 'bestows a compliment'. Dr. Johnson rightly distinguished 'compliment' from 'praise' as being 'usually understood to mean less than it declares'.

22. OVER-EMPHASIS

(*a*) **... the notes of Coleridge exemplify Coleridge's ... perceptions ...**

No need to repeat Coleridge's name. Why not 'Coleridge's notes exemplify his ... perceptions' ... ?

(*b*) **... the essay of Swinburne is Swinburne's criticism at its best.**

No need to repeat Swinburne's name. 'Swinburne's critical essay shows him at his best'?

(*c*) **... these critics have left in their work an undissolved residuum of their own good taste, ...**

Of whose else could it have been? The word 'own' should have been omitted. It suggests that other people's taste may have been more successfully dissolved.

23. LOGICAL WEAKNESS

(*a*) **Three critics have done their best by him: the notes of Coleridge exemplify Coleridge's fine and fragmentary perceptions. . . .**

This suggests that Coleridge's critical perceptions (or perhaps the records he has left of his critical perceptions) were, even at their best, fragmentary. This is not so: probably Mr. Eliot is thinking only of the fineness of Coleridge's perceptions when he was at his best, not of the fragmentariness.

(*b*) **Massinger has been more fortunately and more fairly judged . . .**

Three critics have done their best by him . . . the essay of Leslie Stephen is a piece of formidable destructive analysis. . . .

It is not clear how Leslie Stephen can be said to have 'done his best by' Massinger in a destructive analysis of his work; or how Massinger can be said to have been 'fortunately judged' by him – unless the analysis was so formidable to its readers that it made them sympathize with Massinger as unjustly treated. If they considered the analysis fair they would have been discouraged from reading his plays.

(*c*) **... their own good taste, which, however impeccable ...**

The word 'however' denotes degree: e.g. 'however hot', 'however cold', 'however bright'. But 'impeccable' does not admit of degrees: one is either impeccable or peccable.

(*d*) **... Mr. Cruickshank at least presents us with facts which are capable of generalization. This is a service of value; and it is therefore wholly a compliment to the author to say that his appendices are as valuable as the essay itself.**

It does not necessarily follow that because it is a service of value to provide facts capable of generalization, it is a compliment to say that Canon Cruickshank's appendices are as valuable as the essay itself.

24. CHANGE OF STANDPOINT

... the advantage of good scholarship is that it presents us ... with ... an

invitation to the critical faculty of the reader . . . Mr. Cruickshank presents us with facts . . . capable of generalization.

First it is 'us', then 'the reader', then 'us' again. Are 'we' not readers?

FAIR COPY

'Celebrated critics, including Coleridge, Stephen and Swinburne, have written more interestingly and passed fairer judgements on Massinger's dramatic work than on that of several of his contemporaries who were more deserving of their attention. However, Coleridge's notes, though characteristically illuminating, are fragmentary; Stephen's impressive analytic essay emphasizes only Massinger's demerits; and not even Swinburne, whose essay deals equally with merits and demerits [?], has passed convincing judgement on his status as a dramatist. Like most English critics, each of these three tries to persuade readers to share his taste without either sufficiently explaining his critical principles or—a supremely difficult task—substantiating his general conclusions with relevant generalizations: his taste may be impeccable, but readers are obliged to take it largely on faith. Canon Cruickshank's valuable book, which consists of an essay and appendices, is free from faults of this sort. Indeed, it is a work of pure scholarship rather than of criticism: by a just and methodical arrangement of the necessary material he invites his readers to pass judgement on Massinger, but abstains from doing so himself.'

COMMENT

Comment on this passage is embarrassing, because T. S. Eliot is now widely regarded as the leading poet and critic of his generation. It will be noticed that no shortcomings in the Graces of Prose appear, but that, by the standards of ordinary intelligible English, his failures to choose the appropriate word and to connect his argument lucidly are more frequent here than in any passage we have examined—even from the works of his fellow-critics. This is due less, perhaps, to a wilfully individualistic vocabulary than to critical nervousness. In his poems Mr. Eliot uses words with 'impeccable taste'; but in prose seems to shrink from the responsibility of 'bestowing judgement' and often slides into a conversational looseness which belies his 'fine perceptions'.

LORD ESHER

(*Chairman of the Society for the Protection of Ancient Buildings*)

from Letter to the Press, January 1941

TEXT

The Society for the Protection of Ancient Buildings has been pressed from several quarters to give its general reactions to the question of the fate of

London's churches[9a] and[17] the principles it would recommend with regard to their final treatment[9b] after serious[24a] destruction.[G1]

The society was formed 63 years ago to combat the fashion, then so prevalent,[G2] for the restoration[9c] of mediaeval buildings,[11] and advocated that repairs, reconstructions, and additions should be made to old[11] buildings, frankly,[10a] in the manner of current work[5] most natural to those concerned,[1] and not in a conjectural[10b] attempt to produce[8a] what was lost.[14a] The society has, however, always contended that each building must, to a very large extent,[20a] be judged individually[14b] on its own merits,[12] and it would be manifestly absurd not to replace fragments of a building which may have been temporarily[20b] dislodged. . . . Since the form of use of[20c] a church has altered less perhaps than that of any other special type of building, the plan forms[8b] used by Wren are equally suitable to-day, and it may well[10c] be that fittings salved from one of his churches might be incorporated in a new church elsewhere planned on the original lines[2] but freely interpreted[9d] in present-day architecture.

The question of finance with which the Church will be confronted is very serious,[K] and the society could not well raise objection if a site on which a church is totally or almost totally demolished has[24b] to be sold to help finance the reconstruction of one less seriously[K] damaged.

EXAMINATION

1. WHO?

. . . additions should be made to old buildings, frankly, in the manner of current work most natural to those concerned . . .

The phrase 'those concerned' is mysterious. Does it mean owners and trustees? Or does it mean architects and workmen? (If it means architects and workmen, then those whom owners and trustees of that date would have engaged as a matter of course would have found the mock-antique style the one most natural to them.)

2. WHICH?

. . . the plan forms used by Wren are equally suitable to-day, and . . . fittings salved from one of his churches might be incorporated in a new church elsewhere planned on the original lines.

It would have been better to make it clear that 'original lines' refers specifically to the damaged church from which the fittings are salved.

5. WHEN?

. . . 63 years ago . . . the society . . . advocated that repairs . . . should be made to old buildings in the manner of current work . . .

Were repairs always to be done in the current manner of 1878, or was progress in styles envisaged as the years went by?

8. INAPPROPRIATE WORD OR PHRASE

(*a*) **A conjectural attempt to produce what was lost.**

This should be 'reproduce', the original work being beyond hope of recovery.

(*b*) **. . . the plan forms used by Wren . . .**

Wren drew plans for the churches he built; each plan was different from the others, but all had common characteristics. He did not use 'plan-forms' in the sense that the speculative builder of the 1930's did – 'Type 17 b, mid-Gothic church, in brick, with spacious tiled chancel, seating 200, carved free-stone font, chestnut rafters, lych-gate in solid oak frame and weather-boarding, etc., etc., contract price £3750; or with oriel window by Messrs. Deacon & Cleaver – £3800.' 'Forms' is probably used here to correspond with 'forms of use', and to make clear that the original plans, if they survive, must not be slavishly followed.

9. AMBIGUOUS WORD OR PHRASE

(*a*) **. . . its reactions to the question of the fate of London's churches . . .**

This means at first sight 'what the society thinks should be done to protect London's churches from air-attack'; after patient reflection one realizes that it means 'whether the society thinks that seriously damaged London churches should be rebuilt, and, if so, where it thinks this should be done, and in what style, or styles'.

(*b*) **. . . the principles it would recommend with regard to their final treatment . . .**

'Final treatment' might mean 'complete structural repair after a period of patching'; or it might mean 'treatment of whatever sort (even the demolition of the remaining walls and the sale of the site) when the war is finally over'.

(*c*) **. . . the fashion, then so prevalent, for the restoration of mediaeval buildings . . .**

The word 'restoration' should have been immediately defined as meaning 'restoration to what was conjectured to have been their original state'. The Society itself recommends restoration in the sense of 'rebuilding what has been damaged'.

(*d*) **. . . a new church planned on the original lines but freely interpreted in present-day architecture.**

'Freely interpreted' seems to give the modernist too wide a scope for his fancy. It might mean inverting the cupola of a new St. Paul's to provide sun-bathing facilities for the Dean, Chapter and choristers. Perhaps all that is meant is that rafters should be cut with a steam-saw, not trimmed with an adze; that steel girders and ferro-concrete should replace stone; that heating, ventilation and sanitation should be modernized; and so on.

10. MISPLACED WORD OR PHRASE

(*a*) **advocated that . . . additions should be made to old buildings, frankly, in the manner of current work.**

Or rather: 'that additions made to old buildings should be frankly in the manner of current work'.

(*b*) **. . . and not in a conjectural attempt to produce what was lost . . .**

It was not the attempt that was conjectural, but the architectural style of what was lost.

(*c*) **. . . it may well be that fittings salved from one of his churches might be incorporated in a new church . . .**

The 'well' has got misplaced. What is meant is that 'fittings salved from one of his churches might well be incorporated in a new church': that is to say, the society would approve this incorporation. 'It may well be' means merely 'perhaps'; and 'might be incorporated' does not clarify the Society's attitude to the action.

11. UNINTENTIONAL CONTRAST

. . . the restoration of mediaeval buildings . . . repairs to old buildings.

The Victorian fashion for 'restoration' extended to late Tudor and Jacobean buildings. The same word, preferably 'ancient', should have been used in both contexts.

12. DUPLICATION

each building must . . . be judged individually on its own merits . . .

Either 'individually' or 'on its own merits' could be omitted without loss of sense.

14. MATERIAL OMISSION

(*a*) **The society . . . advocated that repairs . . . should be made to old buildings . . . in the manner . . . most natural to those concerned. The society has, however, always contended that each building . . . must be judged on its own merits.**

It should have been stated, between these two sentences, that exceptions are made to the principle enunciated in the first one.

(*b*) **each building must . . . be judged individually on its merits.**

Surely it is not the merits of the building that are to be judged, but the merits of a case that could be made out for its 'restoration'?

17. FAULTY CONNEXION

The Society . . . has been pressed from several quarters to give its general reactions to the question of the fate of London's churches and the principles it would recommend with regard to their final treatment.

Lord Esher has strained his memory and (the reader's) by putting four nouns inside one another like Chinese boxes:

The question of
the fate of
London's
churches

and, when he comes to the word 'churches', cannot recall what went before. As the sentence stands, the Society is apparently being pressed 'to give its general reactions' either to 'the principles it would recommend' or to 'the question of the principles it would recommend', or to 'the question of the fate of the principles it would recommend' — and these three alternatives make progressively worse sense. If one finally reads the sentence as meaning: 'pressed to give the principles it would recommend', this is not much better: it is a very clumsy way of saying 'pressed to recommend principles'.

20. IRRELEVANCY

(*a*) **. . . each building must, to a very large extent, be judged individually . . .**

The reservation 'to a very large extent' is too indefinite to justify its inclusion in the sentence.

(*b*) **. . . it would be . . . absurd not to replace fragments of a building which may have been temporarily dislodged.**

If someone replaces them, they will have been 'temporarily dislodged', so the word is unnecessary; if no one replaces them, they will be permanently dislodged, so the word is misleading. It should have been omitted in either case.

(*c*) **. . . since the form of use of a church has altered perhaps less . . .**

'Form of' intended perhaps to make 'use' clearer, merely confuses the reader; 'use of a church' says everything.

24. CHANGE OF STANDPOINT

(*a*) **. . . after serious destruction . . .**

This is perhaps the result of hesitation between two phrases: 'after serious damage' and 'after complete destruction'.

(*b*) **. . . the society could not well raise objection if a site has to be sold . . .**

Either: 'the society will not raise objection if a site has to be sold.'

Or: 'the society could not well raise objection if a site had to be sold.'

G. CIRCUMLOCUTION

(1) **The Society . . . has been pressed from several quarters to give its reactions to the question of the fate of London's churches and the principles it would recommend with regard to their final treatment after serious destruction.**

This is rather a long way of writing that the society is now often pressed to say what ought eventually to be done about badly damaged London churches.

(2) **. . . the fashion then so prevalent . . .**

'A prevalent fashion' is enough: the society could not combat a fashion prevalent at another time than theirs; and 'so prevalent' gives no measure of prevalence.

K. TOO MUCH OF THE SAME WORD

The question of finance is . . . very serious, and the society could not well raise objection if a site on which a church is . . . almost totally demolished has to be sold to help finance the reconstruction of one less seriously damaged.

'Serious' loses its cutting edge by being used in different contexts.

FAIR COPY

'The Society for the Protection of Ancient Buildings has received several demands for general recommendations on the rebuilding of London churches seriously damaged in air raids.

The Society was formed in 1878 to combat a prevalent fashion for restoring dilapidated ancient buildings to what was conjectured to be their original state; and has ever since advocated that all repairs and additions to such buildings should be executed in the contemporary style, other than mock-antique, most natural to the builders set to work on them. The

Society has, however, always made certain exceptions to this rule: considering it absurd, for example, that slight dilapidations should not be made good with the original stones, whenever these can be recovered. . . .

The use made of English churches has altered less since the time of Wren than, perhaps, that of any other sort of private or public building, and the general plan to which all his churches conform is therefore not yet antiquated. The Society does not object to this plan being now used in the erection of new churches, so long as they are not slavish reproductions of demolished ones and are built by modern methods; nor to the incorporation in them of suitable fittings salved from the ruins.

The Anglican Church must soon find itself so short of funds that the Society will not object to the sale of sites where churches have been practically demolished, if the proceeds are devoted to the repair of churches less seriously damaged.'

COMMENT

This must have been a difficult letter to write, because the Society, having no official authority, must assume rather magisterial airs if it is to achieve anything, and must also be careful to violate neither the spirit of its original articles nor that of war-time reasonableness. The style is therefore cold and businesslike. The difficulty of drawing a sharp line, between what is aesthetically barbarous 'restoration' and what is legitimate adherence to an honoured and not yet antiquated architectural tradition, accounts for a good deal of ambiguity and unnecessary qualification of opinion.

ADMIRAL C. J. EYRES

from a Letter to the Press, October 1940

TEXT

The European nations[14a] and the U.S.A., in the last century, meeting in conference in[K] peace time, agreed to renounce, or to lay restrictions on,[23] the use of certain weapons which, they considered, inflicted much human suffering without any appreciable[8a] military effect.[12]

The first of these[3a] – the use[14b] of explosive bullets in small arms – is about the only one which has survived, and it has survived just because the military effect was trifling[8b] and the human suffering involved was great and lasting.[12]

The others,[20] notably the use of[14c] lethal gas, and the obligation on the belligerent[8c] to provide for the safety of crews and passengers of merchant ships sunk[25] by him, have gone by the board just because the use or the practice of them[3b] proved to be effective weapons.

EXAMINATION

3. WHAT?

(*a*) **. . . to lay restrictions on the use of certain weapons . . . The first of these — the use of explosive bullets in small arms — is about the only one which has survived, . . .**

What does 'the first' mean? The first restriction agreed upon? Or the most important?

(*b*) **. . . restrictions on the use of certain weapons . . . The first of these . . . has survived . . . The others, notably the use of lethal gas, and the obligation on the belligerent to provide for the safety of crews and passengers of merchant ships sunk by him, have gone by the board just because the use or the practice of them proved to be effective weapons.**

What is 'them'? 'The use or practice' of 'restrictions' did not prove these restrictions to be effective weapons; and neither 'the use of lethal gas' nor 'the obligation on the belligerent to provide for the safety of crews etc.' can be meant: for there can be no 'use or practice' of 'the use of lethal gas', nor is an 'obligation to provide for the safety of crews' an 'effective weapon'.

8. INAPPROPRIATE WORD OR PHRASE

(*a*) **. . . restrictions on the use of certain weapons which, they considered, inflicted much human suffering without any appreciable military effect.**

Weapons that produced no 'appreciable military effect' would need no such legislation, but would be relinquished in the natural course of events — as maces, chain-shot, calthrops, halberds and spontoons have been. But weapons that 'inflict much human suffering' must surely have 'an appreciable military effect' if used against the enemy's armed forces. This phrase, therefore, probably stands for 'superiority in tactical effect over more humane weapons'.

(*b*) **. . . the use of explosive bullets in small arms . . . the military effect was trifling . . .**

To shoot a man with a well-constructed explosive bullet is more effective, militarily speaking, than shooting him with an ordinary one: it is more likely either to kill him or to put him permanently out of action.

(*c*) **. . . the obligation on the belligerent . . .**

Merchant ships in wartime have belligerent status, too, unless they belong to a neutral nation or are privateers. 'Belligerent' here stands for 'the attacking party'.

12. DUPLICATION

. . . agreed to renounce the use of certain weapons which . . . inflicted much human suffering without any appreciable military effect . . . The first of these . . . has survived just because the military effect was trifling and the human suffering involved was great and lasting.

The restatement of the formula could have been avoided with a little care.

14. MATERIAL OMISSION

(*a*) **The European nations and the U.S.A.**

The leading nations were represented; but some smaller ones sent no delegation.

(*b*) and (*c*) . . . certain restrictions . . . The first of these – the use of explosive bullets in small arms . . . The others, notably the use of lethal gas . . .

Neither the use of explosive bullets nor that of lethal gas were 'restrictions'. The word 'on' has dropped out.

20. IRRELEVANCY

The first of these . . . is about the only one which has survived . . . The others have gone by the board . . .

Unless the first was literally the only one, all the others cannot have gone by the board; 'about the' should be omitted.

23. LOGICAL WEAKNESS

. . . agreed to renounce, or to lay restrictions on, the use of certain weapons . . .

This seems an equivocal sort of agreement. No doubt they agreed to renounce the use of certain weapons, and to restrict the use of others.

25. MIXED CATEGORY

. . . to lay restrictions on the use of certain weapons . . . The first of these is about the only one which has survived, . . . The others, notably the use of lethal gas, and the obligation on the belligerent to provide for the safety of crews and passengers of merchant ships sunk by him, have gone by the board . . .

'Lethal gas' is a 'certain weapon'; the sinking of merchant ships is not a weapon but a practice – for one may sink a vessel by torpedo, mine, bomb or even by old-fashioned ramming.

K. TOO MUCH OF THE SAME WORD

The European nations and the U.S.A., in the last century, meeting in conference in peace time . . .

One at least of these 'ins' could have been avoided.

FAIR COPY

'At a nineteenth-century conference held in peace time between representatives of most European nations and of the United States of America, it was agreed to restrict some, and renounce other, practices of war that caused suffering out of all proportion to their tactical effect. The first on the list [?] of practices then renounced – the use of explosive bullets in small arms – is one of the few that has not since been officially revived. Most of the others, notably the use of lethal gas, and the sinking of merchant ships without provision for the safety of crews and passengers, are again general, because the tactical advantages that they give to the side practising them greatly outweigh the suffering that they cause, and therefore the formula agreed upon at the conference, though still applicable to the use of explosive bullets, no longer applies to them.'

COMMENT

The writer has the argument clear enough in his mind but is careless of his words. He cannot trouble to keep to the full title of the subject under discussion, namely 'renunciation of certain warlike practices and restriction of others', but refers to it in various abbreviated forms until apparently he forgets what it originally was; and gets into a thorough tangle.

NEGLEY FARSON
from an Article in a Weekly Journal, December 1940

TEXT

England[8a] and France, since[14a] the last war, presented no programmes that aroused the faintest national interest[10a] in their young men,[1a] or even flicked their imagination.[12] The United States was even worse[22a] . . .

Well, at the moment, the chief desire in every sensible Englishman's mind is to last out this war without getting killed.[23a] Of course we find marvellous heroism in the R.A.F., Army, Navy, and amongst[14b] the A.R.P.[11a/25]

But I'm not writing about the Englishman's[24a] courage, for that has gone over in all the world's mind[F] (remarkable as it is);[10b/11b] the thing that strikes me as being so remarkable about the British[24a] — rich and poor — is that no one seems to be thinking about any return to 'the good old days!'

Now that is a departure — an attitude vastly more significant[14c] than the feeble reconstructive effort[E] to make this a 'Land Fit for Heroes to Live In' which disgraced the years after 1918.[23b] And, also significant,[17/14d] you will[1B] find this receptiveness[8b] for a new kind of life — perhaps some great co-operative effort — more widely held by[24b] the average Englishman in, say, the countryside, than you will even among London's intellectuals.[G]

The reason for this,[23c] it seems to me, is that everyone's life in England, these days, has been thrown out of gear. In the countryside,[4a] shopkeepers have been evacuated[9]; there are vast segments[8c] of your[1b] seacoast perimeter[8d/21] where they have not been evacuated[4b] — but are without customers[22b] . . . Buildings, such as the long-tolerated London slums,[8e] have been physically[22c] knocked down.[14e] It is as if some great Nihilism[8f] had swept the country, getting ready to rebuild.

EXAMINATION

1. WHO?

(*a*) **England and France . . . presented no programmes that aroused the faintest interest in their young men . . .**

This suggests an Act of Union between England and France which allowed the same programme to be presented to the young men in both countries. What is meant is: 'Neither Britain nor France presented any programmes . . .'

(*b*) **. . . you will find this receptiveness . . . more widely held by the average Englishman . . .**

. . . there are vast segments of your seacoast perimeter . . .

The 'you' in the first case is addressed to an international audience whom

Mr. Farson is telling about the English people and their courage; in the second it seems to be the English people themselves.

4. WHERE?

(*a*) **In the countryside, shopkeepers have been evacuated . . .**

From the countryside to the town, or to the countryside from the town, or in both directions?

(*b*) **. . . there are vast segments of your seacoast perimeter where they have not been evacuated.**

Does 'where' here mean 'from where' or 'to where'?

8. INAPPROPRIATE WORD OR PHRASE

(*a*) **England and France . . . presented no programme that aroused the faintest interest in their young men . . .**

'England' is a geographical, not a political, entity and does not present programmes: that is done, if at all, by the Government of the United Kingdom of Great Britain and Northern Ireland, or (briefly) by 'Britain'.

(*b*) **. . . you will find this receptiveness for a new kind of life . . .**

'Receptiveness' means a capacity for passively absorbing instructions or impressions. 'Some great co-operative effort' does not call for 'receptiveness' but for 'readiness to join in'.

(*c*) **. . . there are vast segments of your seacoast perimeter . . .**

A segment is a piece chopped off the outside of a circular or curvilinear figure. But the danger areas here referred to are reckoned in depth from the coast, not enclosed by lines drawn from one coastal point to another.

(*d*) **. . . there are vast segments of your seacoast perimeter . . .**

A perimeter is the boundary only of a geometrical figure. England does not possess a geometrical coast-line.

(*e*) **Buildings, such as the . . . London slums . . .**

The slums are districts notorious for insanitary houses; not the houses themselves. (Until the recent Slum Clearance Act, a slum was urban or sub-urban, thickly populated, and with a high rate of mortality. It now officially includes any picturesque country district sparsely populated by healthy peasants, some of whom live in cottages built before the Government applied to the country sanitary standards necessary in crowded industrial areas.)

(*f*) **. . . a great Nihilism . . . getting ready to rebuild . . .**

But Nihilism is philosophic repudiation of constructive action.

9. AMBIGUOUS WORD OR PHRASE

In the countryside shopkeepers have been evacuated; there are vast segments of your seacoast perimeter where they have not been evacuated . . .

The only explanation of this mysterious passage which fits the historical facts is that Mr. Farson is using 'evacuated' in a novel way: as meaning not 'forced to evacuate their premises' but 'called upon to deal with evacuees'

10. MISPLACED WORD

(*a*) **England and France . . . presented no programmes that aroused the faintest national interest . . .**

The word 'national' is needed with 'programmes' rather than with 'interest'.

(*b*) **But I'm not writing about the Englishman's courage, for that has gone over in all the world's mind (remarkable as it is);**

'Remarkable as it is' perhaps refers to the Englishman's courage; but its place in the sentence makes it seem to flatter 'the world's mind'.

11. UNINTENTIONAL CONTRAST

(*a*) **. . . the chief desire in every sensible Englishman's mind is to last out this war without getting killed. Of course we find marvellous heroism in the R.A.F., Army, Navy, and amongst the A.R.P.**

'Marvellous heroism' is generally understood to mean having the well-being of others as one's chief consideration and cheerfully risking one's life for them. Does he mean that the English members of the Army, Navy, Air Force, and A.R.P. services are not 'sensible?'

(*b*) **But I'm not writing about the Englishman's courage . . . (remarkable as it is); the thing that strikes me as being so remarkable about the British . . . is that no one seems to be thinking about any return to 'the good old days!'**

The use of 'so remarkable' after 'remarkable' makes a contrast between the Englishman's courage and his readiness for change — to the disadvantage of his courage, which has been already characterized as based on his desire not to get killed. We guess that the contrast is unintentional, because of 'courage that has gone over in all the world's mind', though indeed 'gone over' suggests skilful newspaper advertising of something not necessarily estimable. What is perhaps meant is: 'the thing about the British which has struck me with almost equal force . . .'

12. DUPLICATION

. . . aroused the faintest . . . interest . . . or even flicked their imagination . . .
These phrases are not sufficiently different to justify the inclusion of both.

14. MATERIAL OMISSION

(*a*) **England and France, since the last war, presented . . .**

'Since' means from that time to the time of writing. It needs 'have' before 'presented'.

(*b*) **. . . amongst the A.R.P.**

Not 'amongst the Air Raid Precautions' but amongst the people who enforce their observance.

(*c*) **. . . an attitude vastly more significant . . . And, also significant . . .**
Significant of what?

(*d*) **And, also significant, you will find . . .**

This should have been 'And, what is also significant, you will find . . .'

(*e*) **Buildings, such as the long-tolerated London slums, have been physically knocked down.**

It should have been honestly admitted that though many old and dilapidated houses were destroyed, especially in the neighbourhood of the docks, so were many new and well-built ones there and elsewhere.

17. FAULTY CONNEXION

... that is ... an attitude vastly more significant than the feeble reconstructive effort ... which disgraced the years after 1918. And, also significant, you will find this receptiveness for a new kind of life ... widely held ...

The 1940 attitude is described as vastly more significant than the 1918-1939 attitude. 'And also significant' does not relate itself to 'vastly more significant', since no comparative degree of significance is suggested. Possibly what is meant is: 'Equally significant is the receptiveness'.

21. FALSE CONTRAST

In the countryside shopkeepers have been evacuated; there are vast segments of your seacoast perimeter where they have not been evacuated ...

The contrast is not really between 'seacoast' and 'countryside', but between 'inland' and 'seaboard' districts.

22. OVER-EMPHASIS

(*a*) **England and France presented no programmes that aroused the faintest national interest in their young men ... The United States was even worse ...**

In the only matter of comparison, namely programmes intended to arouse the interest of young men, the United States could not have been 'even worse than England and France', where the young men, we are told, were completely uninterested — not even hostile.

(*b*) **... there are vast segments of your seacoast perimeter where they have not been evacuated but are without customers ...**

This suggests that special regulations had been issued for evacuating from certain coastal districts all civilians but shopkeepers.

(*c*) **Buildings ... have been physically knocked down.**

It would have been difficult to knock them down mentally, or spiritually, or morally.

23. LOGICAL WEAKNESS

(*a*) **... the chief desire in every sensible Englishman's mind is to last out this war without getting killed ...**

One could not last out the war, *with* getting killed.

(*b*) **... no one seems to be thinking about any return to the 'good old days!' Now that is a departure — an attitude vastly more significant than the feeble reconstructive effort to make this a 'Land Fit for Heroes to Live In' which disgraced the years after 1918.**

It seems illogical to contrast everyone's failure during the Second World War to think of a return to 'the good old days', with the 1918-1939 failure to 'build a new Jerusalem': during the First World War there was a strong popular desire never to return to the 'good old days'. Again, the emphatic 'disgraced' is intended perhaps to drown the reader's memory of the opening sentence, which told how no programme in England aroused 'the faintest national interest'. Here the suggestion is that there was a programme and that it met with a response, though a disgracefully feeble one, from the young heroes concerned.

(*c*) **You will find this receptiveness for a new kind of life more widely held by**

the average Englishman in, say, the countryside than you will even among London's intellectuals. The reason for this . . . , is that everyone's life has been thrown out of gear . . .

It does not seem logical to make the general confusion explain why the receptiveness for change among English country-dwellers was greater than that of London's intellectuals – whose lives had on the whole been thrown far more violently out of gear.

24. CHANGE OF STANDPOINT

(*a*) **England and France . . .**

But I'm not writing about the Englishman's courage (remarkable as it is); the thing that strikes me as so remarkable about the British . . .

And later he goes back to 'English' again.

(*b*) **You will find this receptiveness more widely held by the average Englishman than even among . . .**

It should have been either:

'You will find this receptiveness in the average Englishman more frequently than . . .'

Or:

'You will find this view more widely held by the average Englishman than by . . .

25. MIXED CATEGORY

. . . In the R.A.F., Army, Navy, and amongst the A.R.P. . . .

The form R.A.F. does not belong in the same category as 'the Navy': one should write either 'Navy, Army, Air Force' *or* 'Royal Navy, Army, Royal Air Force'. Also, 'amongst the A.R.P.' is not a phrase consistent with 'in the Army, Navy': it should have been 'and the A.R.P. services'.

E. MISMATING OF STYLES

But I'm not writing . . . gone over in all the world's mind . . . vastly more significant than the feeble reconstructive effort . . .

A conversational style mated with a cumbersome literary one.

G. CIRCUMLOCUTION

. . . a new kind of life – perhaps some great co-operative effort – more widely held by the average Englishman in, say, the countryside than you will even among London's intellectuals.

He seems afraid of committing himself. 'A new kind of life' is weakened by its qualification 'perhaps some great co-operative effort'; 'the Englishman' is weakened by 'average'; the 'receptiveness' of the country-dweller as well as the town-dweller is weakened not only by 'say' but by limiting the town-dwellers to 'even London's intellectuals', who are not at all necessarily looking for a new kind of life.

FAIR COPY

'Between the last war and the present one there was no national programme put forward by the Government of either Britain or France that aroused more than very faint interest in the young men of these nations. It was the same in the United States. . . .

Well, at the moment, though every sensible Englishman hopes to survive the war without mutilation, marvellous heroism is of course shown — especially in the Navy, Army, Air Force and the A.R.P. services. But I wish to dwell not on this heroism, since it is already everywhere acknowledged, but on something that has struck me with equal force: that no one in England, whether rich or poor, seems to be thinking about a return to "the good old days". That people began to do so after the last war was what made the response to Lloyd George's call for "A Land fit for Heroes to live in" so disgracefully feeble. I find it significant of the sort of life, in Great Britain, likely to follow this war that the usually unresponsive countryman is on the whole as ready to join in a national effort of social reconstruction as is the town-dweller — even the London intellectual. The reason for this widespread change of heart is that everyone's life has been thrown out of gear. For example, shopkeepers in many inland districts have been hard pressed to satisfy the demands made on them by crowds of evacuees from dangerous areas; while in many long strips of coastland shopkeepers have not only had no evacuees to cater for, but have lost most of their business through the departure of regular customers to safer areas.

Buildings of all sorts have been bombed or burned, including many in the too-long tolerated London slums. There, at least, one might fancy that people in a great surge of enthusiasm had swept away the rows of mean houses, with the object of leaving the sites free for the erection of better ones.'

COMMENT

Mr. Farson is an American journalist with a fertile imagination and a quick, emphatic narrative style. Everything comes tumbling out when he begins to write, and it is apparently the fear of forgetting the next thing to be said that prevents him from revising what he has written. If he cannot find the right word he takes the readiest one, and juxtaposes instances rather than connects ideas.

MAJOR-GENERAL J. F. C. FULLER

from *Pegasus*, 1925

TEXT

The fire of Prometheus is[14] as a rush-light[18a/21a] compared to[8a] the volcano of steam[F] which, like all great world forces, is a mixture of Pandora and her box[23/18b/A]; for it has given us beauty and wealth, and[17] also ugliness and starvation. It revived the world, bled white by the Napoleonic wars,[22] and, in place of conquering[21b] the world as the great Corsican[H] attempted, it recreated it.[B,K]

. . . Nations grew and doubled, trebled and quadrupled[G] their populations, and the wealth of Crœsus is[8b] to-day but the bank balance of Henry Ford. Yet out of all this prosperity,[5] created by steam-power, arose the Great War of 1914-1918, which, in its four years[12] of frenzy, was to show a surfeited[9] civilization the destructive power of steam.

EXAMINATION

5. WHEN?

. . . the wealth of Crœsus is to-day but the bank balance of Henry Ford. Yet out of all this prosperity . . . arose the Great War of 1914-1918 . . .

General Fuller speaks of the size of Henry Ford's bank balance 'to-day' — 1925 — and then goes on to mention the Great War as having arisen destructively out of this prosperity. It would have been better to have mentioned John Rockefeller, who belonged to the Steam Age more obviously than Henry Ford.

8. INAPPROPRIATE WORD OR PHRASE

(*a*) **The fire of Prometheus is as a rush-light compared to the volcano of steam . . .**

The forms 'compared to' and 'compared with' have different meanings. One may compare a girl to a flower, a summer's day, an angel, a harpy or a vampire — but not *with* those things: 'to' is used to express any likeness that is emotionally felt, but 'with' is reserved for comparisons in which judgement is delivered only after critical examination. 'A rush-light compared to the volcano', in fact, will be understood by the reader as meaning: 'though the rush-light gives out only a feeble light and heat, it is as powerful in its way as the volcano'; but this meaning contradicts the theme.

(*b*) **. . . the wealth of Crœsus is to-day but the bank balance of Henry Ford.**

The wealth of King Crœsus of Lydia is no longer in existence: it was taken from him during his life-time by King Cyrus of Persia. 'Is' should therefore be 'would be'.

9. AMBIGUOUS WORD OR PHRASE

. . . out of all this prosperity, created by steam-power, arose the Great War of 1914-1918, which, in its four years of frenzy, was to show a surfeited civilization the destructive power of steam.

With what was civilization 'surfeited'? With the frenzy of war, or with prosperity?

12. DUPLICATION

. . . the Great War of 1914-1918, which, in its four years of frenzy . . .

The reader is capable of doing this sum himself: subtracting 1914 from 1918 and getting the answer 'four'.

14. MATERIAL OMISSION

The fire of Prometheus is as a rush light . . .

Can the reader be expected to know about the fire of Prometheus? Should he not be reminded that this was the fire, stolen from Heaven, that lit the first domestic hearth and thus prepared for steam-power by giving water the heat necessary for making it boil?

17. FAULTY CONNEXION

. . . a mixture of Pandora and her box; for it has given us beauty and wealth and also ugliness and starvation.

Should this not be '*but* also ugliness and starvation' – if only to avoid connecting 'beauty and wealth' with the contrastive pair 'ugliness and starvation' by means of another 'and'?

18. MISPUNCTUATION

(*a*) **The fire of Prometheus is as a rush-light compared to the volcano of steam . . .**

Without a comma at 'rush-light' it is the rush-light, not the fire of Prometheus, which is being compared to the volcano.

(*b*) **The fire of Prometheus is as a rush-light compared to the volcano of steam, which . . . is a mixture of Pandora and her box; for it has given us beauty and wealth, and also ugliness and starvation.**

This suggests that the comparison of the fire of Prometheus to a volcano of steam is justified by the explanation that 'it' (whichever of the two 'it' may be) has given us a mixture of blessings and curses. The mistake lies in not having put a long dash at 'steam' and a comma at 'box'.

21. FALSE CONTRAST

(*a*) **The fire of Prometheus is as a rush-light compared to the volcano of steam . . .**

This suggests that the fire of Prometheus would have seemed of one-rush-light-power when compared with a volcano in eruption, but only when so compared – that it was in reality very much brighter. But, according to the legend, Prometheus stole the merest spark from Heaven, concealed in the pith of a dry fennel stalk – a lighted rush-light would have been detected by Celestial, the porter.

(*b*) **. . . in place of conquering the world as the great Corsican attempted, it recreated it.**

The contrast here is between Napoleon attempting the conquest of the world but failing, and the steam-engine successfully recreating the world. A truer contrast would be between a cannon and a steam-engine, or between Napoleon with his marshals and James Watt with his industrialist successors, each attempting to conquer the world in a different way.

22. OVER-EMPHASIS

It revived the world, bled white by the Napoleonic wars . . .

Only France and Spain were bled white. Many other parts of the world were unaffected.

23. LOGICAL WEAKNESS

The fire of Prometheus is . . . a mixture of Pandora and her box; for it has given us beauty and wealth, and also ugliness and starvation.

The legend of Pandora is that she was the first woman created, and was given a number of presents by her godfathers and godmothers, the Olympian gods. Jove's gift was a box which was to be kept shut until further orders. Pandora's companion, Epimetheus, foolishly opened it and out flew all the Spites – the disasters that afflict mankind. However, Pandora found that Hope had also been shut in the box, and this became her consolation for what she suffered from the Spites. Epimetheus was Prometheus's brother and acted against his advice.

General Fuller in his 'mixture of Pandora and her box' perhaps means 'a mixture of the delightful gifts given by the other gods to Pandora, and the gift, given by Jove, which proved noxious in the main – though it had its compensatory blessing'. But, if he means this, he has not expressed himself clearly; and he has confused Pandora herself with the gifts given her. It would perhaps have been tedious to tell the whole legend at length in order to make this complicated point; but had the contrast of the Spites with Hope been clearly drawn in the steam-power connexion, only the Box would have needed a mention – the other gifts could have been omitted.

A. MISMATING OF METAPHORS

The volcano . . . a mixture of Pandora and her box . . .

Could this figure be intelligibly illustrated, even in a grotesque cartoon? This is a convenient question for testing the legitimacy of metaphors, because a metaphor that does not convey a clear picture has a distracting effect on the reader's attention. The answer here is 'no!'

B. TOO MANY METAPHORS

The fire of Prometheus is as a rush-light compared to the volcano of steam which . . . is a mixture of Pandora and her box. It revived the world, bled white by the Napoleonic wars, and in place of conquering the world . . . recreated it.

Generally speaking, a single metaphor is enough for any short paragraph.

F. OBSCURE REFERENCE

The fire of Prometheus is as a rush-light compared to the volcano of steam, which . . . has given us beauty and wealth, . . . ugliness and starvation.

What is this volcano of steam? The simile is confusing, because volcanoes do blow out steam, in purposeless clouds, but do not emit much *light* while doing so – the light comes with the lava. Perhaps the invention of the steam-engine is meant. If so, the reference to Henry Ford, who made his money by exploiting the steam-engine's rival, the internal combustion engine, is most misleading.

G. CIRCUMLOCUTION

Nations grew and doubled, trebled and quadrupled their populations . . .

'Doubled' and 'trebled' are included in 'quadrupled'.

H. ELEGANT VARIATION

It revived the world, bled white during the Napoleonic wars, and, in place of conquering the world as the great Corsican had attempted . . .

It is probably because he had just used 'Napoleonic' that General Fuller finds it necessary to use 'the great Corsican' instead of 'the Emperor Napoleon'.

K. TOO MUCH OF THE SAME WORD

It revived the world . . . and in place of conquering the world . . . it recreated it.

'It' is repeated three times and 'world' twice. This could have been avoided by: 'it revived and recreated, rather than conquered, the world'.

FAIR COPY

'The spark of fire that the demi-god Prometheus stole from Heaven for man's domestic hearth has never been put to such astounding uses as since James Watt's invention of the steam-engine. The tremendous power of Steam, first introduced into a world impoverished by the futile conquests of Napoleon, brought hope of beauty, wealth and recreation, rather than fear of future wars. The enormous enrichment of the leading nations of Europe and America during the century which followed was shown by the increase of their populations, which in some cases were quadrupled. Industrialists became multi-millionaires: Mr. John Rockefeller habitually kept in his bank-account a sum that cannot have been less than the entire capital of the legendary King Crœsus of Lydia. Yet Watt, like most famous inventors, had opened Pandora's Box: not only Hope was contained in it, but a crowd of Spites, including Ugliness and Starvation. For prosperity brought surfeit, and surfeit brought the frenzy of the Great War of 1914-1918 – when Steam was used to destroy wantonly the very riches it had created.'

COMMENT

This writing is the product of a highly imaginative and impatient mind. Unless the reader thinks at a furious rate, he will find that the word-pictures succeed one another too rapidly for his comfort: the impression of the first will not have faded before the third and fourth are imposed upon it. Since these pictures are not interrelated, the result will be a confusion, like that of a camera-film which has been several times exposed to different objects, but each time under-exposed. First comes Prometheus stealing fire – then a rush-light is compared to a volcano – then out flies a cloud of steam and pushes along as a world force – then Pandora is mixed up with her box.

The faults are those of over-confidence in the reader's intelligence and knowledge: it is dangerous to use such brevity.

Major-General Sir Charles Gwynn

from an Article in the Daily Press, Winter 1940

TEXT

Particularly in the Koritza region,[4a] the Greek victories[3a] have had an immense effect on the strategic position of Jugoslavia[12]. . . .

Germany's strategic objective[8a] would obviously be[14] to secure a passage for her troops down the railway through Nish[4b] and the Vardar Valley towards Salonika and Western Macedonia. That is a route which passes

through many mountain defiles[4c] that are defensible[6] by a resolute army and subject to air attack.[1]

Greece's successes, I should say, have a much wider strategic significance than their effect[H] on operations in Albania[21/12] — a significance which would not have sprung[8b] from mere stubborn resistance within Greek territory.[13] At Koritza an effective wedge[20a] has been driven between possible theatres of operations of the Italian and German armies,[3b] and a connecting link broken[24] which Jugoslavia, acquiescing in Axis demands, might have provided.

Even more important[17] is the fact[20b] that Jugoslavia has been afforded new prospects of effectively[20c] maintaining her independence.[19]

EXAMINATION

1. WHO?

. . . mountain defiles that are defensible by a resolute army and subject to air attack.

Who would do the attacking from the air? The resolute Jugoslav army? Or the Germans?

3. WHAT?

(*a*) **. . . the Greek victories . . .**

Over whom? And what sort of victories? Offensive, defensive, or counter-offensive?

(*b*) **. . . possible theatres of operations of the Italian and German armies . . .**

Only a military expert would know that General Gwynn means 'between the Italian expeditionary force, based on Argyrocastro, and German forces that might succeed in reaching Monastir in South-Western Jugoslavia'.

4. WHERE?

(*a*) **Particularly in the Koritza region . . .**

In what country is Koritza?

(*b*) **Germany's strategic objective would obviously be to secure passage for her troops down the railway through Nish . . . towards Salonika . . .**

In what country is Nish?

(*c*) **That is a route which passes through many mountain defiles . . .**

Are these defiles in Jugoslavia, or also in Greece?

6. HOW MUCH?

. . . mountain defiles that are defensible by a resolute army . . .

Almost any position may be defended by a resolute army; but how much resistance could the Jugoslavs hope to put up against German air-borne and mechanized divisions?

8. INAPPROPRIATE WORD OR PHRASE

(*a*) **Germany's strategic objective would obviously be to secure passage for her troops . . .**

The 'objective' was Salonika, lying at the end of the 'passage'; 'object' is what is meant.

(*b*) **. . . a significance which would not have sprung . . .**

Significances do not 'spring'; they are discovered.

12. DUPLICATION

Particularly in the Koritza region the Greek victories have had an immense effect on the strategic position of Jugoslavia . . .

. . . Greece's successes, I should say, have had a much wider significance than their effect on operations in Albania.

The second sentence is included in the first.

13. SELF-EVIDENT STATEMENT

Greece's successes [in Albania] have had a much wider significance than their effect on operations in Albania, a significance which would not have sprung from mere stubborn resistance within Greek territory.

Certainly, the significance of Greek successes in Albania could not have been that of Greek successes in Greece: they are different countries.

14. MATERIAL OMISSION

Germany's strategic objective would be to secure a passage for her troops down the railway through Nish . . .

He omits to say that the Germans after first passing through Hungary would have to overrun the whole Slavonian plain.

17. FAULTY CONNEXION

Even more important is the fact that Jugoslavia has been afforded new prospects of effectively maintaining her independence.

Even more important than what? The previous sentence suggests that the chief importance of the Greek wedge between Jugoslavia and Albania was that it seemed to afford Jugoslavia these very prospects.

19. CONFUSED SEQUENCE OF IDEAS

The following is the natural sequence of ideas in the argument:

(1) The Greeks' counter-offensive in Albania is of far greater importance

(2) than would have been their static defence of the Greek frontier regions,

(3) for it gives the Jugoslavs new hope of maintaining their independence.

(4) By the Greek capture of Koritza

(5) a wedge has been driven between the Italian army and the Southern Jugoslavian frontier.

(6) Since the Jugoslavs are no longer in immediate danger in this quarter, they may refuse to allow German forces to pass southward through their territory into Greece.

(7) If the Germans try to force the passage

(8) the Jugoslavs will now be able to concentrate their forces and resist them.

(9) The Germans would naturally try to pass, first through Hungary, then through the plains of Northern Jugoslavia,

(10) then southward down the railway from Nish towards Salonika.

(11) But even if they overran Northern Jugoslavia they might be halted in the mountains,

(12) for between Nish and the Greek frontier

(13) the railway passes through several defiles defensible by a resolute army and air force.

(14) Another German army, based on Bulgaria, might attempt to invade South-Western Jugoslavia in order to relieve Greek pressure on the Italians.

The order in the original is:

4, 7, 10, 12, 13, 1, 2, 5, 14, 6, 3. Steps 8, 9, 11 are omitted.

20. IRRELEVANCY

(*a*) **. . . an effective wedge has been driven . . .**

Any wedge, actual or metaphorical, is 'effective'; or it is not a wedge. If General Gwynn meant 'a wedge that the Italians will be unable to dislodge' he should have put this prophecy on record in plainer terms.

(*b*) **Even more important is the fact that Jugoslavia has been afforded . . .**

'The fact that' is irrelevant here, as it is in 99 cases out of every 100 in which it occurs. 'It is even more important that Jugoslavia . . .' is enough.

(*c*) **. . . prospects of effectively maintaining . . .**

Either it would be maintained 'effectively' or not at all.

21. FALSE CONTRAST

Greece's successes have a much wider strategic significance than their effect on operations in Albania . . .

This suggests that they took place elsewhere than in Albania.

24. CHANGE OF STANDPOINT

. . . a connecting link broken which Jugoslavia, acquiescing in Axis demands, might have provided.

All that had happened at the time of writing was that by their capture of Koritza the Greeks had cut the road between the South Albanian coast, which was held by Italy, and Monastir, the principal town of Southern Jugoslavia. The wedge-metaphor gives this sense; the link-metaphor seems to confirm it – but at the end of the sentence the link changes and becomes the whole of Jugoslavia – as lying between Hungary, a junior partner in the Axis, and Italian-occupied Albania. This link was not *broken*: it had not yet been forged. Nor did the capture of Koritza do more than cut the southern land-communications between Albania and Jugoslavia; there was still air-communication, and land-communications in the north remained unbroken.

H. ELEGANT VARIATION

Greece's successes . . . have a much wider strategic significance than their effect on operations in Albania.

General Gwynn perhaps avoided writing 'a much wider strategic effect than their effect on operations in Albania' by changing the first 'effect' into 'significance'. A simple way round would have been 'a much wider strategic effect than on operations in Albania'.

FAIR COPY

'The success of the recent Greek counter-offensive against the Italians in Southern Albania is of far greater strategic importance than would have been a static defence, however stubborn, of the Greek frontier-regions: for it gives the Jugoslavs new hope of maintaining their independence. By the capture of Koritza a strong wedge has been driven between the Italian expeditionary force, based on Argyrocastro, and South-Western Jugoslavia; and since therefore the Jugoslavs are no longer in immediate danger of invasion from this quarter, they may well refuse the expected demand of the Axis for permission to send a German army through their territory against Greece. If the Germans were to disregard such a refusal and attempt to force a passage, the Jugoslavs would now be better able to concentrate their main forces to resist them. The obvious route for the Germans to choose for their principal attack would be through Hungary, which is friendly to the Axis, then across the Northern plains of Jugoslavia, and finally down the railway which runs through the mountains of Southern Jugoslavia by way of Nish and the Vardar valley, and so across the Greek frontier to Salonika and the Aegean Sea. But, even though they succeeded in overrunning Northern Jugoslavia, they might be halted in the mountains: for between Nish and the Greek frontier the railway passes through several defiles which a resolute army, properly supported in the air, could defend for at least a week or two against mechanized and air-borne troops. Another German army, based on Bulgaria, might attempt to invade South-Western Jugoslavia, in the hope of relieving Greek pressure against the Italians.'

COMMENT

It may be objected to the questions of 'where?' and 'who?' which we have here put into the mouth of the reader, that late in 1940, when this war-commentary was written, most educated people knew in what country Koritza lay, and what had happened there. But in articles for the daily press a writer should not assume that more than one in three of his readers has any but the most rudimentary geographical and political knowledge. To have written: 'The Greeks are now fighting the Italians north of Koritza in Southern Albania, a country which lies west of Jugoslavia, at present neutral. . . . They have just captured Koritza . . .' would, we admit, have offended better-informed readers by telling them what they already knew. Yet it is always possible to convey this information to the ignorant with tactful indirectness — we have shown what we mean in the Fair Copy.

The geographical positions of Nish and the Vardar Valley, moreover, were not generally known to the British public at the time — they had been out of the news since the First World War — and because of the haphazard order in which the steps of the argument were given, nobody but an expert could have deduced from it which country was fighting which, or with what allies, and what each wanted. The opening sentence should have explained that the effect of the fall of Koritza had been to give Jugoslavia hope of keeping her independence. This independence is not mentioned until the end; nor does the reader learn, until the last sentence but one, which nations are threatening it. The suggested route that the Germans would take is, therefore, not immediately intelligible to the reader with only vague geographical knowledge: Nish for him might be in Bulgaria just as well as in Jugoslavia — or even in Albania. General Gwynn's flattering but untenable assumption, that his readers were so familiar with the strategical situation of the Balkans that they would understand even an inside-out argument about the military prospects there, was not the only reason for the obscurity of this passage. He had also cramped himself by a reluctance to write in so many words: 'The Germans will invade Jugoslavia if they are not permitted a through passage to Greece.' Perhaps he wished to avoid the charge of bullying Jugoslavia into joining the Anglo-Greek alliance by ascribing dishonourable intentions to Germany, of which he had no proof.

VISCOUNT HALIFAX

from an Address after the German re-occupation of the Rhineland, November 19th, 1936

TEXT

We[1a] have been witnessing[14a] the gradual substitution in Europe of a new order[15] — which in some degree[20a] many have long deemed[E] inevitable[14b] — for the order[N] constituted by the Versailles Treaty. For years the attempt was[5] made to find some simultaneous solution for the twin[8] problems of German equality[3a] and general security[9] and when a simultaneous solution was not found,[22] it was not unnatural that they,[1b] still to some extent under the influence of the earlier order[N] of ideas,[2] should naturally[12] feel[5] that same doubt[3b] whether German equality unilaterally[E] achieved[3a] would not[23] in fact[20b] be found[1c] compatible with security.[19/L]

EXAMINATION

1. WHO?

(*a*) **We have been witnessing the gradual substitution in Europe of a new order . . . for the order constituted by the Versailles Treaty.**

By making the undefined 'we' vague enough to include all Europe, Lord Halifax, speaking as a member of the Government, is hinting that Britain will raise no objection to the Nazi assertion of Germany's right to rearm. (The word 'witness' suggests passive contemplation of a scene.)

(*b*) **. . . it was not unnatural that they, still to some extent under the influence of the earlier order of ideas . . .**

'They' have not been mentioned before. Perhaps 'they' are included in the 'we' who 'have been witnessing the gradual substitution in Europe of a new order'. 'They' are certainly not the 'many' who 'have long deemed inevitable' this new order. Lord Halifax disapproves of these 'they': perhaps this is why he has failed to identify them.

(*c*) **... whether German equality ... would not be found compatible with security.**

By whom? It might even be by the Germans, who had hesitated fearfully before the reoccupation of the Rhineland.

2. WHICH?

... they, still to some extent under the influence of the earlier order of ideas ...

Which order of ideas? Strictly speaking, this cannot refer to the 'order constituted by the Versailles Treaty', which was not an order of ideas, but a political ordering of conquered nations.

3. WHAT?

(*a*) **... German equality and general security ...**

... whether German equality unilaterally achieved ...

The phrase 'German equality', here probably standing for 'the right of Germany to rearm as she pleases, just as other European states do', means literally 'equality of all Germans with one another', an equality which could not be 'unilaterally achieved'.

(*b*) **... should naturally feel that same doubt ...**

The doubt has not been mentioned; perhaps he means 'an old doubt'.

5. WHEN?

We have been witnessing the gradual substitution in Europe of a new order ... for the order constituted by the Versailles Treaty. For years the attempt was made to find some solution for the twin problems of German equality and general security and when a simultaneous solution was not found, it was not unnatural that they ... should feel that same doubt ...

There is a change of tense early in this sentence. The phrase 'we have been witnessing' assumes the old order as already practically succeeded by the new. 'For years the attempt was made', if it refers to the years previous to this change, ought to be 'had been made', and 'it was not unnatural that they should feel' ought to be 'it was not unnatural that they should have felt'; but if the attempt was still being made at the time Lord Halifax was speaking, then it ought to be 'the attempt has been made' followed by 'it is not unnatural that they should feel'.

8. INAPPROPRIATE WORD OR PHRASE

... some simultaneous solution for the twin problems of German equality and general security ...

Twin problems are connected problems closely resembling each other: for example, the problems of how to buy chocolate and how to buy sausages, in the same village, after closing hours, in wartime, during a food-shortage.

The problems hinted at by Lord Halifax were not two problems, but a single one: how to satisfy German military aspirations without danger to Great Britain and France.

9. AMBIGUOUS WORD OR PHRASE

. . . the twin problems of German equality and general security . . .

Does this mean 'general German security' or just 'general security'?

12. DUPLICATION

. . . it was not unnatural that they . . . should naturally feel that same doubt . . .

No, naturally not.

14. MATERIAL OMISSION

(*a*) **We have been witnessing the gradual substitution in Europe of a new order . . .**

This should have been supplemented with an explanation of why no attempt was made to check the process, or at least with a clear confession either of indifference or of impotence.

(*b*) **. . . which . . . many have long deemed inevitable . . .**

If Lord Halifax had wished to be plain he would have identified himself with these 'many' (or spoken against their view); and would have pointed out that the 'New Order' was a Nazi concept, connecting it with the 'unilaterally' that follows; and would have admitted that the 'new order' which 'many deemed inevitable' was not by any means the sort that the Nazis were proclaiming.

15. UNFULFILLED PROMISE

We have been witnessing the gradual substitution in Europe of a new order – which in some degree many have long deemed inevitable –

The reader expects '*by* a still newer order' but finds that the new order is being substituted *for* another.

19. CONFUSED SEQUENCE OF IDEAS

The natural sequence of ideas in this argument is:

(1) Britain and France have watched the rise of Nazidom for some years.

(2) Their problem has been whether or not to concede to Germany the same right to arm which other states enjoy.

(3) Some of their politicians, possessed by the vengeful spirit of Versailles,

(4) have believed that this concession would be incompatible with the security of Europe.

(5) Others have believed that the Treaty is obsolescent

(6) and that a new settlement, in making which Germany will have an equal voice with other states, must supersede it.

(7) Owing to these disagreements, the two governments have not been able to find any common solution to the problem,

(8) though they hoped, until the other day, that Germany would at least not assert her sovereign rights by unilateral action.

The order hesitantly followed in the original is:

1, 6, 5, 2, 4, 7, 3, 8.

20. IRRELEVANCY

(*a*) **. . . a new order which in some degree many have long deemed inevitable . . .**

To what word does 'in some degree' refer?
Not to 'inevitable' — there are no degrees of inevitability.
Not to 'many' — there are no degrees of maniness.
Not to 'deemed' — there are no degrees of deeming.
Not to 'a new order' — there are no degrees of a new order.
The phrase has been slipped in as a general reservation.

(*b*) **... should naturally feel that same doubt whether German equality unilaterally achieved would not in fact be found ...**

'In fact' suggests that there has been a contrast made with 'in theory'; this is not so, and 'would not be found' is quite sufficient.

22. OVER-EMPHASIS

to find some simultaneous solution ... and when a simultaneous solution was not found ...

By this heavy repetition Lord Halifax is making it seem due to a mere technical failure, in synchronizing the solutions to two connected problems, that France and Britain could not decide what to do about Germany. Actually, there was only one problem, and neither in France nor Britain was there any unanimity about its solution between 1919 and 1939. The failure of the two nations to have a 'Be Kind to Germany' party in power at the same time is perhaps what Lord Halifax means; but does he think that this would have been a solution?

23. LOGICAL WEAKNESS

... it was not unnatural that they, still ... under the influence of the earlier order of ideas, should naturally feel that same doubt whether German equality unilaterally achieved would not in fact be found compatible with security.

Lord Halifax has introduced this conclusion in so negative a style, that he has contradicted his theme by putting in one 'not' too many, after 'would'.

E. MISMATING OF STYLES

... which in some degree many have long deemed inevitable ...
... whether German equality unilaterally achieved ...

The 'deemed' is archaic except in school translations from the Classics; but 'equality unilaterally achieved' is Genevan modernism.

L. JINGLE

... should naturally
feel that same doubt whether German equality
unilaterally
achieved would not, in fact, be found compatible with
security.

'Equality' and 'unilaterally' come awkwardly together and call attention to the other two words ending in 'y'.

N. SAME WORD IN DIFFERENT SENSES

... a new order ...

This is a translation of the German 'Ordnung', meaning 'ordering' or 'organization'.

The order constituted by the Versailles Treaty . . .

This is 'order' in the similar sense of (imposed) political harmony.

The earlier order of ideas . . .

This is 'order' in the very different sense of 'class' or 'sort'.

FAIR COPY

'For some years now we British and French have watched, but not ventured to check, a gradual troubling of the European peace by the National Socialists for the furtherance of their "New Order". Our common problem has been whether or not we should restore Germany to equal status with her neighbours, by allowing her to maintain whatever armed force she pleases in any part of her territory. Some politicians, both here and in France, have believed that to do so would be incompatible with the general security of Europe; and have still been possessed by the spirit of revenge which animated the victorious Allies at the time of the Versailles Conference. Others, including myself, have for some years believed that the Versailles Treaty is obsolescent and that a new European settlement, in making which Germany will have an equal voice with all other states concerned, must one day supersede it. Owing to these differences of opinion, the two Governments have found no solution to the problem, though, until only the other day, both hoped that Germany would at least not reassert her sovereign rights by taking action without the formal consent of the League of Nations.'

COMMENT

Lord Halifax in making this speech, as a Minister without portfolio, was restrained by many considerations from saying frankly what he meant. First, whatever he said would be regarded as the mature opinion of the British Cabinet, from whose unanimous decisions and collective responsibility no member could dissociate himself except by resignation. Yet he was also a sincere Christian and did not wish to misrepresent the situation, which was that in both the British and the French governments great difference of opinion existed as to whether or not Germany should be permitted to become a first-class power again — it was not a case of France unanimously approving the Versailles Treaty and of Great Britain unanimously disapproving. The common irresolution encouraged the Nazis to defy both powers.

The large French army of 1936 might have successfully opposed the reoccupation of the Rhineland, which was an overt breach of the Treaty of Versailles, and so have suppressed the Nazi power before it had fully entrenched itself. But the French High Command did not feel strongly enough about the matter to force the issue; and the British Government, believing that the Nazis merely wanted to regain for Germany the sovereign rights forfeited at Versailles, decided to take no action – though annoyed that the Nazis had acted 'unilaterally'. Lord Halifax could not mention the Nazis by name, because their anti-Semitic activities had already made them extremely unpopular to the masses of the French and British people. Indeed, he had to omit every controversial word, since the Government was already committed to a policy of appeasement. It is remarkable that with all these handicaps he managed to convey as much as he did to readers patient enough to unravel his tangled sentences. The Fair Copy that we have given represents what he would no doubt have said, had he been in a less delicate position.

Cicely Hamilton

from 'The Englishwoman', a Semi-Official Propaganda Pamphlet, 1940

TEXT

Another form of club-association[12a] that has become of late years[E] exceedingly popular[12b] is the women's luncheon club[H]; it flourishes[12b] especially in provincial towns and in some of the larger among them its membership will run into hundreds -- with a long waiting list in the background.[20] As the name betokens,[E] the meetings of the club take place at a midday meal[H]; this is held at intervals[13a] (as a rule once a week) when the members assemble[13b] at some local hotel or restaurant with a room large enough to accommodate its numbers[12c] and partake of a fixed-price lunch.[E] When the serious business[21] of the meal is over and the stage of cigarettes and coffee has been reached, the gathering passes on to its intellectual course – it is addressed by a speaker on some topic of general interest.[13c] As many of the audience are business women who will have to return to their work after lunch,[E/H] the address is not overlong.[23] To be present at a meeting of one of these luncheon clubs – in a restaurant dining-room thronged with its members[12c] – is to wonder who started the curious idea, entertained by our fathers,[D] that women dislike each other's[8] company.[22]

EXAMINATION

8. INAPPROPRIATE WORD OR PHRASE

. . . women dislike each other's company . . .

This should be 'one another's'; 'each other' refers to two people only, and such a crowded room would not make one think of a tête-à-tête.

12. DUPLICATION

(*a*) Another form of club-association . . .

A club is necessarily an association.

(*b*) **. . . has become exceedingly popular . . . it flourishes . . .**

With a stricter arrangement of ideas this restatement would be unnecessary.

(*c*) **. . . the members assemble at some local hotel or restaurant with a room large enough to accommodate its numbers . . . a meeting of one of these luncheon clubs — in a restaurant dining-room thronged with its members . . .**

This repetition, too, could be avoided; and why in the second instance is the hotel omitted?

13. SELF-EVIDENT STATEMENT

(*a*) **. . . a midday meal; this is held at intervals . . .**

Naturally.

(*b*) **. . . the members assemble . . .**

Who else?

(*c*) **. . . it is addressed by a speaker on some topic of general interest. . . .**

A topic is, by definition, a subject of general interest to people of a given locality.

20. IRRELEVANCY

. . . with a long waiting list in the background . . .

It is difficult to see the force of 'in the background': it is not usual in any club to post the names of would-be members on the green-baize board in the hall or lobby.

21. FALSE CONTRAST

When the serious business of the meal is over . . . the gathering passes on to its intellectual course . . .

This suggests that the address is always a frivolous one.

22. OVER-EMPHASIS

To be present at a meeting . . . is to wonder who started the curious idea that women dislike each other's company.

It is inconceivable that one necessarily wonders this: indeed, it is hard to imagine anyone raising so unanswerable a question.

23. LOGICAL WEAKNESS

As many of the audience are business women . . . the address is not overlong.

Would it be overlong if there were no business women present?

D. POETICALITY

. . . the curious idea, entertained by our fathers . . .

'Our fathers' is a Biblical reminiscence and misleading. Cicely Hamilton is not of the same generation as her younger readers. Her father was perhaps contemporary with their grandfathers; their *fathers* are unlikely ever to have entertained this idea.

E. MISMATING OF STYLES

. . . of late years . . . to partake of a fixed-price lunch.

'Business women' and 'fixed-price lunch' are modernisms. 'Of late years', 'as the name betokens', 'partake of' are Victorianisms.

H. ELEGANT VARIATION

. . . luncheon club . . . take place at a midday meal . . . return to their work after lunch . . .

These are all aliases of the same meal.

FAIR COPY

'Another form of club that has grown exceedingly popular during recent years, especially in the provinces, is the women's luncheon club: in some of the larger towns a club's membership often runs into hundreds, with a long waiting list. Meetings are held, usually once a week, in a large room at a local hotel or restaurant, where a fixed-price lunch is served for members. When the stage of coffee and cigarettes has been reached, the gathering passes on to its intellectual course: someone gives a topical address. This is short enough to allow the numerous members who are in business to get back punctually to their work when the proceedings are over. A crowded luncheon-club meeting sometimes makes one wonder how men of former generations can have thought that women dislike one another's company.'

COMMENT

This passage shows the chief disability from which the British propaganda writer suffers in wartime: having to combine sobriety with journalistic brightness, and often to equivocate between the view of Britain as gay, careless and unperturbed and that of Britain as struggling grimly and austerely against desperate odds. And another disability: not to have been officially advised what public to address. Here Cicely Hamilton wants to make everything plain to as large a public as possible, but seems embarrassed at having to explain, in consequence, that a luncheon club is so called because that is what it is. Hence the half-ironic heaviness of the words 'betokens' and 'partake'; the elegant variation of 'midday meal' for 'luncheon' or 'lunch'; the information that a midday meal is held at intervals (instead, perhaps, of being continued for weeks like one of Alexander's Persian banquets or the Mad Hatter's Tea Party), and that the members attend. Nor does Miss Hamilton mean that eating and drinking are the 'serious' part of the meeting: she is apologizing that the members have physical as well as intellectual appetites to satisfy in these dark days. Except for the common error of 'each other' for 'one another', the literary shortcomings of this passage all derive from the unnatural attitude of mind that contribution to a *British Life and Thought* series entails.

'IAN HAY'

from *The Battle of Flanders*, October, 1941

TEXT

In all wars the final victory must be won on land.[9a] However irresistible[14a] the armed forces of a country may show themselves by sea or in the air, the naval and aerial arms[12a] can never strike the decisive[22a] blow. They can guard[12b] and protect on the one hand,[9b] devastate, cow, and paralyse on the other, but they cannot break through[22b] the last lines of defence. That task must be left to the tanks[22c] and their supporting infantry.

The importance of an early success or failure cannot therefore[17] be estimated at once; there must be an interval of waiting until it can be fitted into the final pattern — it may be years later.[12c] Of what value were Marengo or Austerlitz to Napoleon the day after Waterloo was fought?[8a/23a]

The British Army, by traditional usage, always seems[10] to be compelled to start a war[14b] from small beginnings, and either play for time or take desperate risks[21] until it has built itself up into an effective striking force. The entire[22d] history of that Army is chequered with tales of early reverses or expensive resistances,[20a] redeemed in the end, as resources and experience accumulated, by the final crown of victory.[22e]

This is partly due to the fact that though we[1] have usually been prepared to maintain a Navy second to none, and came recently to a similar though somewhat tardy conclusion[8b] upon the subject of an Air Force,[23b/G] we have[14c] systematically starved[22f] our Army throughout its history,[12d] both in numbers, equipment, and adequate[20b] means of training . . . and partly because when war does break out the Navy and Air Force are served first.[19]

EXAMINATION

1. WHO?

. . . though we have usually been prepared to maintain a Navy second to none . . . we have systematically starved our Army throughout its history, both in numbers, equipment, and adequate means of training . . .

Who is 'we'? When the reader turns to the back of the pamphlet he finds: 'Issued by the War Office'. Are the heads of the War Office, each in a white sheet, accusing themselves of having always been prepared to maintain the Navy at the expense of the Army, and of having always failed to recruit, train or equip sufficient men for their own purposes? This is unlikely. It seems rather to be a complaint of the War Office against the Government that Army Estimates have always been kept too low for safety; but the public might well retaliate that if the War Office had spent the money allotted to it in recent years on improving its armament and mobility and cutting down its numbers, the Battle of Flanders might have had a less disastrous outcome. By May, 1940, it had sent thirteen infantry divisions to France, but not one armoured division.

8. INAPPROPRIATE WORD OR PHRASE

(*a*) **Of what value were Marengo or Austerlitz to Napoleon the day after Waterloo was fought?**

'The night of Waterloo' would have made the point better. On the day after Waterloo, when Napoleon had time to reflect on his position, they may have seemed to him imperishable glories, entitling him to courteous treatment at the hands both of his defeated countrymen and of the victorious British and Prussians.

(*b*) **. . . we have usually been prepared to maintain a Navy second to none, and came recently to a similar . . . conclusion upon the subject of an Air Force . . .**

To be 'usually prepared to' do something is not a 'conclusion'.

9. AMBIGUOUS WORD OR PHRASE

(*a*) **In all wars the final victory must be won on land.**

This may mean 'In all future wars the final battle must be fought on land', or 'In every war the final battle has always been fought on land'; or both of these meanings may be combined in a timeless generalization. The reader cannot choose between these alternatives unless he has read some military history. If he has, he will know that few major wars end in a complete victory for either side, and that in many of them it has been naval action that has forced one side to sue for peace; he will therefore conclude this sentence to be a simple prophecy, unsupported by historical evidence and derived solely from the 1941 War Office point of view in the Second World War.

(*b*) **They can guard and protect on the one hand, devastate, cow and paralyse on the other . . .**

The phrases 'on the one hand' and 'on the other' are legitimate when a very long and complicated antithesis is being made; here they are too heavy for the sentence. And does 'on the one hand' mean the Navy, and 'on the other' mean the Air Force? Or is 'Ian Hay' contrasting the defensive and offensive rôles sustained by both arms?

10. MISPLACED WORD

The British Army, by traditional usage, always seems to be compelled to start a war from small beginnings . . .

The phrase 'traditional usage' shows that the British Army is, in 'Ian Hay's' opinion, compelled to 'start from small beginnings' and does not merely seem to do so. The 'always seems' has presented itself far ahead of its proper context: 'we have [it always seems] systematically starved . . .'

12. DUPLICATION

(*a*) **However irresistible the armed forces of a country may show themselves by sea or in the air, the naval and aerial arms can never strike the decisive blow.**

By the removal of duplicated ideas, this reduces to:

'However plainly the naval and aerial arms may show their irresistibility, they can never strike the decisive blow.'

(*b*) **They can guard and protect on the one hand . . .**

Here 'guard' clearly does not mean 'blockade', because it is opposed to 'paralyse', and is probably therefore an unnecessary synonym for 'protect', used to balance the sentence elegantly.

(*c*) **The importance of an early success . . . cannot therefore be estimated at once; there must be an interval of waiting until it can be fitted into the final pattern — it may be years later.**

By removal of the duplicated ideas, this reduces to:
'The importance of an early success cannot therefore be correctly estimated for a time — perhaps not for years.'

(*d*) **The entire history of that Army is chequered with . . . early reverses . . . This is partly due to the fact that . . . we have systematically starved our Army throughout its history . . .**

The over-emphatic 'entire history' need have been mentioned only once, if at all.

14. MATERIAL OMISSION

(*a*) **However irresistible the armed forces of a country may show themselves . . .**

There are no degrees in 'irresistibility'. Perhaps what is meant is: 'However plainly the armed forces of a country may show their irresistibility.'

(*b*) **The British Army . . . always seems . . . compelled to start a war from small beginnings . . .**

Here only major wars can be meant: in small Colonial wars the local forces have often proved sufficient to achieve a rapid victory.

(*c*) **we have systematically starved our Army . . . in numbers, equipment and . . . training . . .**

'In peace-time' is probably meant, since later 'Ian Hay' tells how what he describes (wrongly) as 'a fully trained and equipped' army 'went raging into the Battle of the Somme' on July 1st, 1916.

17. FAULTY CONNEXION

. . . The naval and aerial forces can never strike the decisive blow . . . That task must be left to the tanks and their supporting infantry.

The importance of an early success or failure cannot therefore be estimated at once . . . Of what value were Marengo or Austerlitz to Napoleon the day after Waterloo was fought?

The 'therefore' does not follow logically, unless 'early success or failure' is confined to sea and air operations — which here it is not.

19. CONFUSED SEQUENCE OF IDEAS

The natural order of ideas in the argument implicit in this passage is:
(1) A nation at war may show itself irresistible at sea,
(2) as Britain has usually done,
(3) yet not strike such a decisive blow on land
(4) as Britain and its allies eventually struck against Napoleon.
(5) The British Army has always been reduced to modest size
(6) in peace time; and therefore at the outbreak of war,
(7) its expeditionary forces and overseas garrisons have often suffered reverses while waiting for reinforcements.

(8) This phase has sometimes lasted for years
(9) and short-sighted critics
(10) have accused the Government of starving the Army.
(11) Yet the peace has usually favoured Britain.
(12) The tardy realization, at the outbreak of the present war, that the 1923 decision to strengthen the Air Force comparably with the Navy had not been carried into effect,
(13) is said to have hindered the immediate expansion of the Army;
(14) but the War Office are now of opinion that the traditional British strategy must be changed:
(15) the final victory must be won on land.
(16) The Army must be built up for Continental warfare
(17) alongside our Russian allies.
(18) Let us hope that when its spearhead of tanks
(19) pierces Hitler's last defences,
(20) and redeems our early reverses,
(21) the Battle of Flanders will seem to him as Marengo and Austerlitz must have seemed to Napoleon after Waterloo.

The order followed in the original is: 15, 1, 3, 19, 18, 9, 8, 21, 5, 7, 16, 20, 11, 2, 12, 10, 13.

4, 6, 14 and 17 are omitted.

20. IRRELEVANCY

(*a*) **. . . chequered with tales of early reverses, or expensive resistances, redeemed in the end . . .**

Expensive resistances cannot be 'redeemed'; nor, however expensive, do they 'chequer' a history: to 'chequer' is to cast patches of shadow over something bright, and when resistance is offered at great expense to the defenders, there is a blaze of military glory. 'Expensive resistances' is obviously an afterthought, and does not suit the sentence.

(*b*) **starved of . . . adequate means of training . . .**

'Adequate' is unnecessary. To be starved of something means to be given inadequate supplies of it.

21. FALSE CONTRAST

The British Army . . . seems . . . compelled to . . . either play for time or take desperate risks.

These are not true alternatives. An army that plays for time, by fighting delaying actions, may risk annihilation. The true alternatives are: to avoid battle, and to risk battle against superior forces.

22. OVER-EMPHASIS

(*a*) **However irresistible the armed forces of a country may show themselves by sea or in the air, the naval and aerial arms can never strike the decisive blow.**

Were not the sea-battles of Aegospotamoi, Actium and Lepanto decisive blows?

(*b*) **. . . the naval and aerial arms . . . cannot break through the last line of defence.**

This was untrue of 'the aerial arm' when 'Ian Hay' wrote: the Germans had broken through the 'last line' of Dutch defences in 1940 with air-borne troops, and in Crete had shown that a strongly held island could be taken from the air (though at great expense) even when the sea was commanded by the defenders' fleet. It was also untrue of the 'naval arm': if the enemy population were 'cowed' and 'paralysed', the commander of the fleet would have to send only a small, unarmed party ashore to demand their capitulation.

(*c*) **In all wars the final victory must be won on land . . . the naval and aerial arms . . . cannot break through the last line of defence. That task must be left to the tanks and their supporting infantry.**

'In all wars' is an exaggeration. All wars of the past cannot be meant, since the tank was not introduced until September, 1916. In wars of the future, the dive-bomber might replace the tank as a means of breaking down the defenders' resistance sufficiently to allow the attackers' lorry-borne infantry to take a position. It had been demonstrated by 1941 that the dive-bomber caused more alarm than the tank and was more useful than the tank where the enemy had been able to fortify his position strongly.

(*d*) **The entire history of that Army is chequered with tales of early reverses . . .**

Is the history of Marlborough's campaigns in the War of Spanish Succession — to instance the first important European war fought by the British standing army — chequered with tales of early reverses due to the shortage of 'numbers, equipment and adequate means of training'?

(*e*) **The entire history of that Army is chequered with tales of early reverses . . . redeemed . . . by the final crown of victory.**

Marlborough's unbroken series of successes was not crowned by a final decisive victory. In the first two years of the American War of Independence there were very few British reverses; by the sixth two British armies had been forced to capitulate, and the peace treaty signed in the seventh lost Britain half her colonial Empire.

(*f*) **. . . we have systematically starved our Army throughout its history, both in numbers, equipment and adequate means of training . . .**

This seems to be a complaint that it had always been the British Government's policy to give the Army less than it needed for the function assigned to it. The truth was, that since there had been a standing army in Britain its equipment had nearly always compared favourably with that of Continental armies; and that its peacetime establishment and training had been based on the assumption that it would not be needed for European warfare but only for the defence of various key-posts of the British Empire against native assailants or the troops of another maritime power. The Army had hitherto proved adequate to this task. Only when some Continental ally of Britain called for direct military aid did the Army seem to be 'starved'. This was, however, also true: that when it began to be realized, soon after Hitler came to power in Germany, there was a danger of another European war, the Army did not spend nearly enough of the money allotted to it by the Government on the tanks which 'Ian Hay' now seems to consider have *always* been necessary for successful warfare.

23. LOGICAL WEAKNESS

(*a*) **. . . the naval and aerial arms can never strike the decisive blow . . .**

. . . Of what value were Marengo or Austerlitz to Napoleon the day after Waterloo was fought?

This would be logical only if Marengo and Austerlitz had been fought either at sea or in the air. Probably 'Ian Hay' means: 'Trafalgar had to be followed by the Peninsular War, and then by Waterloo, before Napoleon's power could finally be broken.' But that then Marengo and Austerlitz profited him nothing—just as the Battle of Flanders will profit Hitler nothing after British tanks have broken through *his* last defences—is part of another argument.

(*b*) **The entire history of that Army is chequered with tales of early reverses, . . . redeemed in the end . . . by the final crown of victory.**

This is partly due to the fact that though we have usually been prepared to maintain a Navy second to none, and came recently to a similar . . . conclusion upon the subject of an Air Force . . . [and partly because when war does break out, the Navy and Air Force are served first].

This makes the 'recent' conclusion about the size of the Royal Air Force—taken in principle in 1923—partly responsible for early reverses in wars long before the invention of the aeroplane; and 'Ian Hay' should have remembered that there was no Royal Air Force when the First World War broke out—but only air-wings of the Army and the Navy.

G. CIRCUMLOCUTION

This is partly due to the fact that though we have usually been prepared to maintain a Navy second to none, and came recently to a similar though somewhat tardy conclusion upon the subject of an Air Force, we have systematically starved our Army . . .

This reduces to:

'This is partly because our settled policy of maintaining naval supremacy and our rather tardily expressed ambition for air supremacy has starved the Army . . . '

FAIR COPY

'A strong naval power, when it makes war on a strong military power, is usually content to demonstrate its invincibility by protecting its own coasts and sea-ways and by so harassing those of the enemy that he begins to feel cowed and paralysed. Thus Britain, which for the last three centuries has seldom relaxed its policy of maintaining a navy more powerful that any probable combination of enemy navies, has, when involved in war with a strong military power, seldom attempted to strike a decisive blow with its land-forces even after the enemy has begun to feel the pinch of blockade: it has preferred instead to use its Army mainly for defensive purposes, and eventually to sign a 'compromise peace' on terms advantageous to itself. An exception was the last war; but it is clear that the ensuing peace was not secure enough to justify the tremendous expense in lives and treasure that this modification of traditional strategy had cost Britain. It may be suggested that there had been an earlier modification of

British strategy when the Emperor Napoleon so disturbed the balance of power in Europe that Britain, not content with having shattered the French and Spanish fleets at Trafalgar, built up its army and continued to fight until Napoleon's defeat at Waterloo, to which it contributed, permitted the Allied occupation of Paris. But it should be remembered that the British contingent which took part in this campaign formed only a seventh part of the Allied forces engaged, and only a twentieth part of the total Allied forces.

British national economy has kept the peacetime establishment of the Army down to the modest size needed for garrisoning the Empire under naval protection; and when Britain has been involved in a war with another maritime power, its overseas garrisons have often been compelled to play for time – either avoiding battle or risking defeat by engaging the enemy with inadequate forces – while new formations are raised, equipped and trained at home, and hurried to their relief. Sometimes this phase of a war has lasted for years, during which many reverses have been suffered and the Government has been accused by short-sighted critics of "starving the Army"; but very seldom has a peace been signed that did not favour Britain.

In 1923 the British Government decided to strengthen its traditional strategy by giving the Air Force a supremacy comparable to that of the Navy. It is claimed that, at the outbreak of the present war, what hindered the immediate expansion of the Army was the tardy realization that this decision had not been carried into effect: for it was found necessary to concentrate the national industrial effort largely on increased aircraft production. Be that as it may, it is only fair to admit that the Army was not equipped and trained for Continental warfare even after the Germans had shown in 1935 that they intended to upset the European balance of power. When Hitler invaded the Low Countries, the British Expeditionary Force in France consisted of thirteen infantry divisions, and not a single armoured division; and since the French Army had also fallen behind the times in training and equipment, all Europe west of Russia was soon under German domination. The power of the British naval blockade, which had been decisive in the last war, was thus seriously weakened and the traditional British strategy has in consequence been modified, though to what extent is not yet clear. At all events, the Army, under naval and air protection, is being built up into an offensive force which, it is hoped, will be of great assistance to the Russians when, with British and American arms, they mount their promised counter-offensive against Hitler. The Army is confident that it will be a spearhead of British tanks that finally pierces Hitler's last line of defence and avenges our early reverses, and that then even the Battle of Flanders will seem to him as faded a glory as Marengo or Austerlitz must have seemed to Napoleon on the night of Waterloo.'

COMMENT

The official commentary on Lord Gort's despatches, which this passage introduces, is issued by the War Office and published by His Majesty's Stationery Office. 'Ian Hay', the author, was a temporary infantry officer in the First World War but does not seem to have studied the tactics of the Second World War with sufficient attention.

The absurdity of trying to justify an unusual, if perhaps necessary, divergence from the traditional principles of British strategy by misrepresenting military history, and of excusing the Army's own lack of foresight by accusing the Government of having systematically starved it of men, equipment and training facilities, is proved by the tangle into which 'Ian Hay' has here tied himself. The prose is ambiguous, repetitive, over-emphatic, carelessly articulated, and so full of omissions that the Alternative Version, in which we attempt to supply the main points missing from the original, has to be twice as long.

ERNEST HEMINGWAY

from *For Whom the Bell Tolls*, 1940

TEXT

Robert Jordan knew that it was all right again now.[E] Finally she stopped cursing . . . and said calmly, 'Then just shut up about[E] what we are to do afterwards, will you,[E] Inglés?'[E] . . . 'Take thy[E] little cropped headed[8a] whore and go back to the Republic but do not shut the door on others who . . . loved the Republic when[5] thou wert[E] wiping thy mother's milk off thy chin.' . . . 'I am a whore if thee wishes,[8b] Pilar,' Maria said. 'I suppose I am in all case[8c] if you say so. But calm thyself. What passes with thee?'[E]

EXAMINATION

5. WHEN?

. . . who loved the Republic when thou wert wiping thy mother's milk off thy chin. . . .

This action of wiping off milk was, presumably, habitual: it did not happen on one particular occasion which happened to coincide with the love of 'others' for the Republic. A Spaniard would not have said *cuando* ('when') but *mientras aun* ('while yet'). The careless modernism of 'when' does not suit the careful antiqueness of 'thou wert'.

8. INAPPROPRIATE WORD OR PHRASE

(*a*) **Take thy little cropped headed whore . . .**

Either 'cropped' or 'crop-headed'; both are reputable English words.

(*b*) **'I am a whore if thee wishes . . .'**

The English form is either 'if thou wishest' or 'if you wish'. The Spanish from which this is supposedly a translation would be either:

si Usted quiere (literally, 'if your Ladyship wishes')

or:

si tu quieres (literally 'if thou wishest').

No Spaniard, even of the most ignorant sort, ever used *si te quiere* (the literal translation of 'if thee wishes') to mean 'if thou wishest', because the words mean something else: 'if he (or she) loves thee'.

(*c*) **'I suppose I am in all case . . .'**

This is perhaps a translation of

supongo que yo lo soy en todo caso.

But *en todo caso* means either 'in every case' or 'in all cases'. To translate it as 'in all case' is like translating the French '*qu'est-ce que c'est que ça*?' as 'what is it that it is that yonder?'

E. MISMATING OF STYLES

Robert Jordan knew that it was all right again now. . . . 'Just shut up about what we are going to do afterwards, will you?'

. . . 'Take thy little cropped headed whore . . . '

. . . 'I suppose I am . . . if you say so . . . '

. . . 'But calm thyself. What passes with thee?'

This suggests undergraduates in a mock-Shakespearean farce, purposely mixing modern colloquialisms with archaisms. It does not correspond with Spanish usage. The Spanish phrase from which 'What passes with thee?' seems to be translated is *¿que te pasa*? But it has no antique ring. Its English equivalent is 'What's the matter with you?', and once a Spaniard uses the familiar *tu* ('thou') he keeps to it, without switching back to the polite '*usted*' ('your Honour', your Reverence', or 'your Ladyship'), which corresponds with 'you' in English, except where 'you' means more than one person, when *os* is used.

FAIR COPY

'Robert Jordan knew that all was well again. Finally she stopped cursing and said calmly: ''So just keep quiet about what we are going to do afterwards, will you, Englishman? Take your little crop-headed whore and go back to the Republic, but don't shut the door on others who . . . loved the Republic while you were still wiping your mother's milk from your chin. . . .''

''Very well, I *am* a whore, if you like, Pilar,'' Maria said. ''I must be, if you say so. But do calm down! What's the matter with you?'' '

COMMENT

It does not matter much what conventions are adopted for this sort of writing, so long as they explain themselves and are consistently observed.

To translate Spanish conversations in 1936 Revolutionary Spain, Ernest Hemingway was entitled to use Pilgrim Father English, 'thou wert';

or early nineteenth-century Pennsylvania-Quaker English, 'if thee wishes'; or twentieth-century colloquial English, 'I suppose I am, if you say so' – but not all three mixed up together. This confusion of styles suggests, falsely, that peasants in Spain make the same sort of mistake in speaking their native dialects.

Arturo Barea, a Spaniard, has written of *For Whom the Bell Tolls*: 'I resent Spaniards in a serious book speaking like Don Adriano de Armado, the "fantastical Spaniard" of *Love's Labour's Lost*. As a writer, I should be unhappy if Spanish dialogue I had written were to be translated into something as affected and artificial as: "I encounter it to be perfectly normal" when all I had said in Spanish was: *Lo encuentro perfectamente normal* – "I find it perfectly normal"; or into: "You have terminated already?", when I had said *¿Habeis terminado ya*? – "Have you finished already?" . . . The Castilian peasants speak forcefully and simply. When it comes to rendering the dignity and sobriety of their speech, Hemingway invents an artificial and pompous English which contains many un-English words and constructions, most of which cannot even be admitted as literal translations of the original Spanish.'

ALDOUS HUXLEY

from Introduction to J. D. Unwin's *Hopousia*, 1940

TEXT

It has become fashionable to talk, in a rather romantic[3a] way, about the intellectual dangers[3b] of analysis. [24a]If one would understand anything, we are told, one must consider it as a whole. By taking an organism or a process to bits,[8a] we[24b] destroy it, or at least distort it in such a way that it ceases to be itself.[21] To be adequate to reality,[3c] knowledge must be a knowledge of wholes.[1/H1]

All this, of course, is true and obvious.[22a] The entities[H1] which we describe as[20] 'society', 'man', 'cell', 'molecules',[25] 'atom' are other than the sum of their respective parts.[8b/24b] If our study is confined to the parts, we shall not understand the whole. Shall we then confine our study to the whole? No; for experience shows that, if we consider only the whole, we shall never understand the nature of the whole.[G] Knowledge of a whole[K] cannot be adequate[14] unless it is based on a thorough knowledge of parts.[H2] The whole must[23a] be taken to bits; these bits[H2] must be studied: having been studied, they must be recombined and the whole re-examined[23b] in the light of our knowledge of its constituents.[H2] Meanwhile, of course,[17] we must remember that this knowledge of the bits has been obtained by a process which profoundly[22b] modifies

the nature of the whole of which they are the components;[H2] hence the light it throws upon the nature of the unmodified[8c] whole may be[8d] misleading.

EXAMINATION

1. WHO?

If one would understand anything, we are told, one must consider it as a whole. By taking an organism or a process to bits, we destroy it, or at least distort it in such a way that it ceases to be itself. To be adequate to reality, knowledge must be a knowledge of wholes.

It is not clear whether the second and third sentences are Mr. Huxley's own view or a continuation of 'we are told'.

3. WHAT?

(*a*) **It has become fashionable to talk, in a rather romantic way, about the intellectual dangers of analysis.**

What does 'romantic' mean here? Is it opposed to 'classical?' Or to 'Teutonic'? Or to 'rational'?

(*b*) **. . . the intellectual dangers of analysis . . .**

Does this mean the dangers of getting incorrect results? Or does it mean the dangers of injuring one's intellect?

(*c*) **To be adequate to reality . . .**

This is a mysterious phrase. Does it mean simply 'To be real'? Or has a phrase, such as 'for dealing with' or 'for the comprehension of', dropped out before 'reality'?

8. INAPPROPRIATE WORD OR PHRASE

(*a*) **By taking an organism or process to bits, we destroy it . . .**

One cannot take a 'process' to bits. And if 'process' refers forward to 'atom', it is an improper term. An atom is a 'system', not either an 'organism' or a 'process'. Suitable examples of 'process' would be 'fermentation', 'generation', and 'growth'.

(*b*) **To be adequate to reality, knowledge must be a knowledge of wholes. All this . . . is true and obvious. The entities which we describe as 'society', 'man', 'cell' are other than the sum of their . . . parts.**

But 'society' is an entity consisting of men and women. Granted, a whole is something other than the sum of its parts, but in this case the parts (the men and women) are also entities or wholes. A knowledge of these wholes is, however, *not* 'adequate to reality' — if that implies a real understanding of the nature of 'society'. The logical difficulty, however, disappears if 'the whole' is substituted for 'the wholes'.

(*c*) **. . . this knowledge has been obtained by a process which profoundly modifies the nature of the whole; hence the light it throws upon the nature of the unmodified whole may be misleading.**

'Must be', not 'may be'.

(*d*) **. . . this knowledge has been obtained by a process which profoundly modifies the nature of the whole . . . hence the light it throws upon the nature of the unmodified whole may be misleading.**

But there is no longer an 'unmodified' whole. What is meant is 'the nature of the whole before it was thus modified'.

14. MATERIAL OMISSION

Knowledge of a whole cannot be adequate unless it is based on a thorough knowledge of parts.

Adequate for what purpose? Most people in Great Britain who have a clock and a wireless set in their houses are not mechanics or electricians. They find their limited knowledge of the use and manipulation of these complex machines adequate to their limited purposes.

17. FAULTY CONNEXION

Meanwhile, of course, we must remember . . .

The 'of course' should have been 'however' to limit the force of the over-confident statement 'the whole must be taken to bits'.

20. IRRELEVANCY

The entities which we describe as 'society', 'man', 'cell' . . .

The inverted commas make 'which we describe as' unnecessary, since the 'we' is not defined.

21. FALSE CONTRAST

. . . we destroy it, or at least distort it in such a way that it ceases to be itself.

The proper contrast here is not between destruction and distortion, but between different processes of destruction.

22. OVER-EMPHASIS

(*a*) **All this, of course, is true and obvious . . .**

It may be true, but it is not 'of course obvious': it would be disputed by many people and puzzled over by a great many more.

(*b*) **Meanwhile, of course, we must remember that this knowledge has been obtained by a process which profoundly modifies the nature of the whole.**

It is by no means obvious enough for an 'of course' that the process of taking a thing to bits and recombining these will profoundly modify its nature. If a careful mechanic takes a machine-gun or a printing-press to bits and re-assembles them correctly without cleaning or repair, the effect on the performance or appearance of the machine will not be noticeable.

23. LOGICAL WEAKNESS

(*a*) **We are told . . . by taking an organism to pieces, we destroy it. This is true . . . Shall we then confine our study to the whole? No . . . The whole must be taken to bits . . . these must be recombined and the whole re-examined.**

The 'must' is illogical. If the organism is destroyed by being taken to bits, there is no compulsion on 'us' to take it to bits: it will not reward examination.

(*b*) **The whole must be taken to bits; these bits must be studied: having been studied, they must be recombined and the whole re-examined in the light of our knowledge of its constituents.**

Since it is 'obvious and true' that the whole is 'destroyed' by analysis, how can it be re-examined?

24. CHANGE OF STANDPOINT

(*a*) **If one would understand anything, we are told, one must consider it as a whole. By taking an organism . . . to bits, we destroy it . . .**

Since 'we' and 'one' are the same person here, only one term should have been used.

(*b*) **The entities are other than the sum of their respective parts.**

Either: 'Each entity is other than the sum of its respective parts' or:

'The entities are other than the sums of their respective parts.'

25. MIXED CATEGORY

The entities which we describe as 'society', 'man', 'cell', 'molecules', 'atom' are other than the sum of their respective parts.

A 'molecule' is held to be a group of atoms connected in a system. The word should not, therefore, be put in the plural: it is parallel with the others, which are in the singular.

G. CIRCUMLOCUTION

Shall we then confine our study to the whole? No; for experience shows that if we consider only the whole, we shall never understand the nature of the whole.

This amounts to: 'Yet experience shows that if we confine our study to the whole we shall never understand its nature.'

H. ELEGANT VARIATION

(1) **. . . knowledge must be a knowledge of wholes. The entities . . . 'society' 'man', 'cell' . . . are other than the sum of their respective parts.**

Unless the same word is used throughout, whether 'wholes' or 'entities', the argument is liable to be misunderstood.

(2) **Knowledge . . . based on a thorough knowledge of parts.**

The whole must be taken to bits; these bits must be studied.

. . . the whole re-examined in the light of our knowledge of its constituents.

. . . this knowledge of the bits has been obtained by a process which . . , modifies the nature of the whole of which they are the components.

Since 'parts', 'bits', 'constituents', 'components' are not here differentiated in meaning, only one term should have been used.

K. TOO MUCH OF THE SAME WORD

Shall we confine our study to the whole? No; for . . . if we consider the whole we shall never understand the nature of the whole. Knowledge of a whole . . .

Two of these 'wholes' could be omitted, with advantage.

FAIR COPY

'It has become fashionable to say that analysis has its dangers, since perfect understanding of a thing cannot be achieved unless its integrity remains unimpaired. With this view (though many of those who repeat it are expressing merely a sentimental aversion to science) I am in agreement. Since, for example, each of the entities, "society", "man", "cell", "molecule", "atom", is distinguishable from the sum of its constituents, even a perfect understanding of these constituents cannot be equivalent to a perfect understanding of the entity. And, though experience shows that, by studying an entity without a thorough knowledge of its constituents, one cannot achieve a perfect understanding of it, yet if it is analysed, and the constituents studied and then re-combined, what is achieved will be an understanding not of its original nature but of its nature as modified by analysis and reconstruction.'

COMMENT

This is hurried and disdainful writing. 'It has become fashionable to talk in a rather romantic way' ... 'All this, of course, is obvious.' The supposed obviousness of what Dr. W. H. R. Rivers once called 'the synthetic fallacy of Science' does not justify Aldous Huxley's failure to restate it clearly. His constant change of terms has led him into obscurity and repetition: even 'study', 'consider', 'examine' are unnecessary verbal variations. And he has carelessly used the terms 'romantic' and 'reality', which require careful definition in every new context. Again, to use 'take to bits' as a popular equivalent of 'analyse' is to give unnecessarily physical associations to processes that are often wholly metaphysical. Finally, having described as 'true and obvious' the theory that analysis necessarily destroys an entity, he feels the sudden prick of his inherited scientific conscience, and decides that the useless analytical processes must be used after all. So, disingenuously, he tones down 'destroy or at least distort in such a way that it ceases to be itself' into 'profoundly modify' and suggests merely that, 'of course', the light which analysis throws on the nature of the whole before modification *may be*, not *must be*, misleading.

Dr. Julian Huxley

(*Secretary of the Royal Zoological Society*)

from an Article, 'Animal Pests in Wartime', *October* 1941

TEXT

Man's struggle for existence[14a] falls under three heads; his struggle with the forces of the inorganic environment, his struggle with other[14b] species of organisms,[24/G] and his struggle with his own works and his own nature.

It is this last aspect[H1] of the struggle[K] which has come to bulk larger[8a] in recent times; the economic and social forces generated by human systems[3] have taken the bit in their teeth and threaten to pull the fabric of civilization down[A] if not harnessed[23a] and controlled, while at the same time[17] new manifestations of cruelty and lust for power, organized on an unprecedented scale, have arisen[8b] as monsters to be fought and overcome.[1] Meanwhile[5] the struggle with the inorganic world[H2] has become progressively less

important[8c] during history[8d]; indeed, apart from occasional[11a] tornadoes, floods, and earthquakes, the inorganic forces have been mastered,[22] and the old struggle[11b] has been in the main converted into a drive for increased mastery.[8e]

The struggle with other[14c] organisms, however, continues.[21] It changes its character as civilization progresses. Every new advance[8F] in civilization, while it may knock out one set of competitors,[14d/23b] often favours new ones.

EXAMINATION

1. WHO?

Man's struggle for existence . . . new manifestations of cruelty and lust for power . . . have arisen as monsters to be fought and overcome.

These monster-manifestations of cruelty and lust for power are necessarily man's own. Who then is to fight and overcome them?

3. WHAT?

. . . the economic and social forces generated by human systems . . .

This is mysterious. What human systems are meant? In the biological context a 'human system' is understood as being the nervous, or the digestive, or the procreative system, or another of the same order. Perhaps 'economic and social' have lost their way in the sentence and were intended to qualify 'systems'.

5. WHEN?

. . . in recent times . . . new manifestations of cruelty . . . have arisen as monsters to be fought and overcome. Meanwhile the struggle with the inorganic world has become progressively less important during history.

When is 'Meanwhile'? One assumes at first that it lies between 'recent times' and now; but 'during history' contradicts this.

8. INAPPROPRIATE WORD OR PHRASE

(*a*) **It is this last aspect of the struggle which has come to bulk larger . . .**

Since there are three aspects, 'largest' should have been used, not 'larger'.

(*b*) **. . . new manifestations of cruelty have arisen . . .**

Surely manifestations 'appear', though monsters may 'arise'?

(*c*) **. . . the struggle with the inorganic world has become progressively less important during history . . .**

Is 'important' the right word? Perhaps what is meant is that the struggle has passed its most critical stage.

(*d*) **. . . has become progressively less important during history . . .**

Does this mean during the times *about* which history is written? Or during the times *in* which history has been written? There is a difference of thousands of years between these two concepts.

(*e*) **. . . a drive for increased mastery . . .**

One is either the master, or one is not. The area of mastery may be increased, but not the mastery itself.

(*f*) **It changes its character as civilization progresses. Every new advance . . .**

This rather spoils the force of the first sentence in the paragraph, which reported a deterioration in civilization amounting to theatened collapse. It would have been more scientific to write 'at each stage of civilization': this does not commit the writer to the view that civilization is necessarily progressing, in the sense of gradually improving human conditions.

11. UNINTENTIONAL CONTRAST

(*a*) **Meanwhile the struggle with the inorganic world has become progressively less important during history: indeed, apart from occasional tornadoes, floods, and earthquakes, the inorganic forces have been mastered . . .**

'Occasional' suggests that tornadoes and earthquakes, as well as floods, have become less frequent since history began, owing to man's successful engineering feats. This is unwarranted.

(*b*) **Meanwhile the struggle with the inorganic world has become progressively less important . . . and the old struggle has been in the main converted . . .**

The 'old struggle' seems at first to be contrasted with 'the struggle with the inorganic world', but turns out to be identical with it.

14. MATERIAL OMISSION

(*a*) **Man's struggle for existence falls under three heads . . .**

The phrase 'struggle for existence' was first used by Sir Charles Lyell in his *Principles of Geology* (1832) and was popularized, in the times of the Darwinian controversy, to describe the relation between co-existing organic species when the survival of some tends to the extinction of others. Here 'man's struggle with . . . his own nature' confuses the issue. What Dr. Huxley seems to be discussing is not only a struggle for existence by the human species but also a struggle by one part of it for the maintenance of certain social traditions.

(*b*) **. . . his struggle with the forces of the inorganic environment, his struggle with other species of organisms . . .**

One has to read this two or three times before realizing that 'other' means 'other than the human organism'.

(*c*) **The struggle with other organisms, however, continues.**

This is short for 'with other species of organism than man' and does not accurately pick up the second of the 'three heads'.

(*d*) **Every new advance in civilization, while it may knock out one set of competitors . . .**

The word 'competitors' is perhaps intended to mean 'competitors in the struggle for existence', but the hasty reader will take it as meaning 'competitors in civilization'.

17. FAULTY CONNEXION

. . . the economic and social forces generated by human systems . . . threaten to pull the fabric of civilization down, while at the same time new manifestations of cruelty and lust for power organized on an unprecedented scale . . .

The connexion 'while at the same time' makes two parallel phenomena out of what is only one.

21. FALSE CONTRAST

The struggle with other organisms, however, continues.

The struggle with the inorganic world is not yet over, though man has had successes. The only legitimate contrast is between the degree of success that man has attained in this struggle and the degree attained in his struggle against other species than his own.

22. OVER-EMPHASIS

. . . the inorganic forces have been mastered.

This confident assertion implies that man has made himself superior to gravitation, that he can penetrate with impunity the central fires of the Earth, and that he can prolong his life indefinitely by preventing the accretion of inorganic matter which hardens his arteries.

23. LOGICAL WEAKNESS

(*a*) **. . . social forces have taken the bit in their teeth and threaten to pull the fabric of civilization down if not harnessed and controlled.**

But an animal that takes the bit between its teeth and threatens to pull down the fabric of a building must be already harnessed to it.

(*b*) **Every new advance in civilization, while it may knock out one set of competitors, often favours new ones.**

If it 'often' favours new ones, the presumption is that sometimes it does not do so. 'Every new advance' is therefore too inclusive a phrase: it should be 'New advances . . .'

24. CHANGE OF STANDPOINT

. . . his struggle with other species of organisms.

This is a compromise between three concepts:
his struggle with other species,
his struggle with other organisms,
his struggle with other species of organism.

A. MISMATING OF METAPHORS

. . . social forces . . . have taken the bit in their teeth and threaten to pull the fabric of civilization down . . .

It is difficult to imagine a context in which horses or mules taking the bit in their teeth threaten to pull down the fabric of a building. Was Dr. Huxley thinking of Tom Mix's horse in a Western film, hitched to the post of the Sheriffs' rickety office in a mushroom town? But Tom Mix's horse always found it more convenient to bite the rope through.

G. CIRCUMLOCUTION

. . . his struggle with the forces of the inorganic environment, his struggle with other species of organisms . . .

This boils down to: 'his struggle with the elements, and with organic nature'.

H. ELEGANT VARIATION

(1) **Man's struggle for existence falls under three heads . . . It is the last aspect of the struggle which . . .**

It would be less confusing if this had been written as: 'Man's struggle for existence has three aspects . . . It is this last aspect which . . .' There seems to be no justification for changing 'heads' to 'aspects'.

(2) **Man's struggle . . . with the forces of the inorganic environment.**
. . . the struggle with the inorganic world.

When a scientific article starts with 'three heads', each head should be picked up, as the argument proceeds, without alteration in its phrasing.

K. TOO MUCH OF THE SAME WORD

Man's struggle for existence falls under three heads: his struggle with the forces of the inorganic environment, his struggle with other species of organisms, and his struggle with his own works and his own nature.

It is this last aspect of the struggle . . .

The word 'struggle' need have been used only once.

FAIR COPY

Man is fighting three simultaneous campaigns in his struggle for civilized existence: against the elements, against other species than his own, and against the products of his own ingenuity. This last campaign has become the most spectacular of the three, since forces generated by the interaction of new economic, industrial, military and other systems may now disrupt civilization: a few savage renegades with a lust for power are using these forces as it were to animate monsters of unprecedented ferocity, which the rest of mankind must set themselves to vanquish. In his campaign against the elements, man has greatly increased his general physical security by inventing countless devices to protect him from their assaults; and though he remains unable to transcend his organic limitations, and though tornadoes, floods and earthquakes still occasionally cause him losses, he already regards himself as victor in this campaign and is making concerted efforts to consolidate his position. In his campaign against other species than his own, he has also won successes, but the composition of the forces arrayed against him changes continually: each new stage of civilization is likely to discourage some sorts of organic pest, but to encourage others.'

COMMENT

In one of the sessions of the B.B.C. 'Brains Trust', held in the same month as this article was published, Dr. Huxley, a permanent member, cited his grandfather, Thomas Huxley, as a 'nearly faultless writer of English'. The contributions to zoology of both these Huxleys are extensive, and neither could be described as less gifted or industrious than the other. It is therefore significant of the great deterioration in the accepted standard of English prose since 1863, when Thomas Huxley wrote his *Evidence as to Man's Place in Nature*, that Julian Huxley in 1941 could dash off a passage so confused as this. It is the introduction to a well-informed and, on the whole, clearly-written account of new methods of exterminating rats, rabbits, wire-worms, lice and such-like. Thomas Huxley was by no means a faultless writer, but he never published anything for which we should venture to provide a Fair Copy.

PAUL IRWIN

from his Sports Commentary, June 1941

TEXT

Arsenal may have[9a] lost the League Cup replay[3a] by the odd goal of three before a 40,000 Blackburn crowd, but they made the swift moving Preston boys go all the way.[8a]

They[1a] were one down in 94 minutes — [14]little Bob Beattie[4] snapped McLaren's[4] short pass to beat Marks with a left-foot drive — but were square again with a quarter of an hour to go.[H1]

Not so bad, that. Ted Drake, who had been limping on the right wing from the start of the second-half, was off the field and Kirchen[4] had gone into the centre[3b] when the equalizer[H1] arrived.

Kirchen, a one-man attack,[8b] crashed through as[8c] Bernard Joy took a free-kick. . . .

Level![H1] Could Arsenal, struggling since Drake hurt a knee just before the interval,[16] hold out? They couldn't. Straight from the kick-off, Dougal[4] and Bob Beattie switched passes — the final one bringing Beattie his second goal.[9b]

While Arsenal made a scrap of it, all the grandstand experts[22] agree that Preston had the craft.[12]

Not even Ted Drake's early outbursts could really[20] upset the offside trap laid by Tom Smith and Co. Still, George Allison's[1b] long-service star[H2] did bring speed to the attack, a thing that Leslie Compton[1c] never did in the Wembley game.[3c]

As a[17] fact, he came within a 'toucher' of getting a goal just before the interval.[16] A long, loping ball went down[8d] the middle. Drake followed it up, heading past the advancing Fairbrother.[4]

Nothing is a certainty in Soccer, though. Smith dropped out of the clouds to hook the ball away.

Forward, Arsenal were best served by Kirchen and Denis Compton. They made grand individual runs, but the verdict is[1d] that the attack, once disorganized by Drake's injury, never had a chance.[23/19]

EXAMINATION

1. WHO?

(*a*) **Arsenal may have lost the . . . replay . . . but they made the swift-moving Preston boys go all the way. They were one down in 49 minutes.**

The Preston team are so vividly characterized that one naturally takes 'they were one down' as referring to them.

(*b*) **. . . George Allison's long-service star . . .**

Who is George Allison? Until one guesses that the long-service star **is** Ted Drake, it is not clear whether Allison is the Preston or the Arsenal manager.

(*c*) **. . . a thing that Leslie Compton never did in the Wembley game.**

Did Leslie Compton lead the Arsenal attack in the Wembley game?

(*d*) **. . . but the verdict is that the attack . . . never had a chance.**

Is this Paul Irwin's verdict? Or that of the grandstand experts?

3. WHAT?

(*a*) **. . . the League Cup replay . . .**

Was this a Final or Semi-Final match?

(*b*) **Ted Drake, who had been limping on the right wing from the start of the second-half, was off the field and Kirchen had gone into the centre when the equalizer arrived.**

Since Ted Drake, like Leslie Compton in the Wembley game, seems to have led the Arsenal attack, the presumption is that he played centre-forward. That he is here mentioned as limping on the right wing and that 'Kirchen had gone into the centre' suggests that the two changed places: a limping centre-forward slows down an attack more than a limping outside right. But this is guess-work.

(*c*) **. . . a thing that Leslie Compton never did in the Wembley game.**

What was this game? Was it the draw that necessitated the replay? If so, were any goals scored?

4. WHERE?

. . . little Bob Beattie snapped . . .
. . . McLaren's short pass . . .
. . . Kirchen had gone into the centre . . .
. . . Dougal and Bob Beattie switched passes . . .
. . . heading past the advancing Fairbrother . . .
. . . Forward, Arsenal were best served by Kirchen and Denis Compton . . .

It is clear on which side each of these men was playing; yet unless we know what positions in the field they occupied we cannot visualize the game. For instance, was Fairbrother the Preston goal-keeper, or a back?

8. INAPPROPRIATE WORD OR PHRASE

(*a*) **. . . they made the swift-moving Preston boys go all the way.**

This is a metaphor from a paper-chase in which the hares circle back to their starting point. Good hares make the hounds 'go all the way'—i.e. are not caught before they get home. But in this case Arsenal were overtaken nearly a quarter of an hour from the whistle. (Could Arsenal hold out? They couldn't.)

(*b*) **Kirchen, a one-man attack, crashed through . . .**

A man cannot *be* an attack. 'Kirchen crashed through on his own' would have been equally vivid, and also briefer.

(*c*) **. . . as Bernard Joy took a free-kick. . . .**

He did not crash through *as* Bernard Joy took the free-kick, but followed up the ball after Joy had kicked it towards the Preston goal.

(*d*) **A long, loping ball went down the middle.**

'Down' and 'up' are ambiguously used in English. Sometimes they refer to a difference of level, sometimes not. 'Let's go up to Town next week' would be said by someone living in the Cotswolds some hundreds of feet above the level of London. In Tennyson's poem *The Lady Clare*, Lord Burghley 'walking up and pacing down' his apartment was not ascending and descending a slope. 'Up' usually suggests the direction away from one's base, and 'down' the return journey. Here the ball evidently came *up* the field from the Arsenal backs, not *down* towards Drake from the Preston backs.

9. AMBIGUOUS WORD OR PHRASE

(*a*) **Arsenal may have lost the League Cup replay . . .**

This suggests that the result is doubtful. Perhaps Arsenal have appealed against the verdict on some technical ground and demanded a replay?

(*b*) **Dougal and Bob Beattie switched passes, the final one bringing Beattie his second goal.**

Does this mean that Bob Beattie's last pass did not reach Dougal, but went between the posts? Or that Dougal's last pass gave Bob Beattie a chance to score?

12. DUPLICATION

Arsenal may have lost the League Cup replay, . . . but they made the swift-moving Preston boys go all the way.

While Arsenal made a scrap of it . . . Preston had the craft.

These two sentences should have been combined. Both are summings up of the game, and contain the common element that Arsenal kept Preston very busy, though Preston were the quicker team.

14. MATERIAL OMISSION

They were one down in 49 minutes — little Bob Beattie snapped McLaren's short pass to beat Marks with a left-foot drive.

The reader will want to know how McLaren got the ball. Did he and Beattie run up the field together, switching passes? Did one of the outsides make a long burst and centre nearly from the corner-flag? Or what happened? We are given the opening movement in the case of the other two goals.

16. UNDEVELOPED THEME

Drake hurt a knee just before the interval . . .

Drake . . . came within a 'toucher' of getting a goal just before the interval . . .

Was he injured in the course of this incident? The use of the same phrase in both sentences seems to suggest this.

17. FAULTY CONNEXION

Ted Drake did bring speed to the attack . . . As a fact, he came within a 'toucher' of getting a goal . . .

'As a fact' probably stands for 'in fact' and is intended to support what has just been observed about Drake's speed; but more generally the phrase is used, like 'in point of fact', to contradict, not to support, a previous statement. For example, 'The Poles allege that the Czechs oppressed their minority in Teschen; as a fact, that minority controlled the police-force to which the oppression was credited.'

19. CONFUSED SEQUENCE OF IDEAS

The natural sequence of ideas in this passage is:

(1) (Preston 2 – Arsenal 1)
(2) At Blackburn
(3) the replay of the Arsenal-Preston Cup final,
(4) after a draw at Wembley,
(5) drew 40,000.
(6) Arsenal made a tough scrap of it.
(7) But Preston is generally agreed to have played the faster
(8) and trickier game.
(9) It was 49 minues before either side scored.
(10) Then Bob Beattie shot a goal for Preston.
(11) Ted Drake,
(12) George Allison's star,
(13) led the Arsenal attack.
(14) He gave it greater speed than Leslie Compton had done at Wembley.
(15) Though most of his bursts were smothered by Tom Smith's offside trap,
(16) he nearly scored just before the interval.
(17) But Smith robbed him as he made for an open goal.
(18) Drake then unluckily hurt his knee
(19) and went to the right wing, [?]
(20) Kirchen coming into the centre.
(21) Kirchen and Denis Compton made some grand runs.
(22) But the attack was now disorganized by Drake's injury.
(23) However, with a quarter of an hour to go,
(24) and Drake off the field
(25) Arsenal were awarded a free-kick.
(26) Joy took it.
(27) Kirchen scored off it.
(28) All square! Could Arsenal hold out?
(29) No! With Dougal's help, Bob Beattie scored again.

The order in the original is: 3, 1, 5, 2, 7, 9, 10, 23, 11, 19, 24, 20, 27, 26, 25, 28, 18, 29, 6, 8, 15, 12, 13, 14, 4, 16, 17, 21, 22.

20. IRRELEVANCY

Not even Ted Drake's early bursts could really upset the offside trap laid by Tom Smith and Co.

'Really' is unnecessary. The trap was either always effective or only occasionally so.

22. OVER-EMPHASIS

. . . all the grandstand experts agree . . .

It is difficult to believe either that Paul Irwin had the opportunity of canvassing all their opinions, or that they were unanimous.

23. LOGICAL WEAKNESS

Nothing is a certainty in Soccer, though. . . . the attack, once disorganized by Drake's injury, never had a chance.

But it has just been explained that more than half an hour after Drake's injury, the glorious uncertainty of Soccer gave Arsenal a free kick; and that Kirchen, who led the attack, then took the opportunity to score an 'equalizer'.

H. ELEGANT VARIATION

(1) . . . were square again with quarter of an hour to go.
. . . when the equalizer arrived.
. . . Level! Could Arsenal . . . hold out?

Since there is only a limited variety of possible incidents in football, many sports writers jolly up their accounts with amusing synonyms. A player who scores a goal is sometimes described by them as 'propelling the leather into the raspberry-net' or 'ramming the old pill home'. Paul Irwin does not descend to this sort of rhetoric, but might well have avoided the variation 'square', 'level', and 'equal'.

(2) Not even Ted Drake's early bursts . . .
Still, George Allison's long-service star . . .

It is difficult at first to recognize these two characters as identical.

FAIR COPY

(Preston 2 — Arsenal 1)

'At Blackburn the replay of the Arsenal-Preston Cup Final [?] after their goalless [?] game at Wembley, drew a 40,000 crowd. Though Arsenal made a tough scrap of it right to the end, the general verdict of the grandstand seemed to be that Preston played the faster and trickier game.

It was 49 minutes before a goal was scored. Then [after a tussle in mid-field?] little Bob Beattie, the Preston [centre-forward?] snapped up a short pass from McLaren [his right half?] and beat Marks with a left-foot drive.

Ted Drake, George Allison's veteran star, led the Arsenal attack. He gave it greater speed than Leslie Compton had given it at Wembley. And, though most of his bursts were smothered by the offside trap set by "Tom Smith and Co.", the Preston backs, he was within a toucher of scoring just before the interval.

A long, loping ball went up the middle of the field with Drake in pursuit. Catching it on the rise, he headed it past Fairbrother who had come out of goal [?], and rushed on with it. But nothing is certain in Soccer. Tom Smith, dropping from the clouds, hooked the ball away. And [in trying to recover it?] Drake injured a knee and began to limp.

In the second half Drake swapped places with Kirchen [his outside right?] who, like Denis Compton, [the inside left?] then made some grand individual runs. But the attack was disorganized by Drake's injury.

However, with a quarter of an hour to go, and Drake off the field for good, Arsenal were awarded a free kick. Bernard Joy took it, and Kirchen saw his chance. He crashed through on his own.

All square! Could Arsenal hold out until the whistle? They couldn't. Straight from the kick-off Bob Beattie and Dougal [his inside right?] switched passes down the field, Beattie finally pushing the ball through.'

COMMENT

One expects a highly paid report of a football match to be self-explanatory to all readers who know the rules and technical dialect of the game. Since there are constant changes in every team, as players are injured or discarded, only 'grandstand experts' will be able to follow an account of a match that gives no precise indication of who was who on the field – unless a table of the rival sides is supplied elsewhere on the sports-page, with names and positions clearly set out. On the sports-page from which this passage is quoted no such table appears. Should a sports-writer to a paper of two-million circulation write only for fellow experts, even for the sake of giving the football-pool crowd an illusion of being on the grandstand?

There is a new journalistic convention by which the dramatic moment of a newsworthy story is put first, in large print, and the setting tagged on in small print. For example: ' "I did it all with my crutch," announced a lame man at Lambeth police court yesterday. He was charged with setting a lodging-house on fire and tearing seven blankets, valued at 10s. apiece, into strips. It appears that he felt aggrieved with his landlord, to whom he owed a month's rent. The man gave his name as James Marshall and wore the ribbon of the D.C.M. . . .' Here the theory is that the reader's eye is caught by the opening phrase, which vaguely suggests George Washington and the cherry-tree, and is tempted to find out how it came to be used. But a football match treated in this way is robbed of its natural rhythm. If Ted Drake's activities in the first half of the Preston-Arsenal match had been presented as a prologue, rather than an epilogue, to the Arsenal's gallant struggle in the second half, readers would have been better able to appreciate the seriousness of his loss. Again, the grand individual runs of Kirchen and Denis Compton for Arsenal, and Tom Smith's crafty defence, being as important to the football enthusiast as the goals, should have been given their proper place in the sequence of events.

Sir James Jeans

from *The Stars in Their Courses*, 1931

TEXT

[Scientists can weigh stars by calculating the amount of gravitational pull that components of the same stellar system exert on one another.]

The results are interesting. Our[20] sun proves[8a] to be of about average weight, or perhaps somewhat over.[o] Taken as a whole,[23] the stars shew only a small range in weight[12/H1]; if we compare[14a] the sun to a man of average weight, most[10] of the weights of the stars lie[14b] between those of a boy[8b] and a heavy man. Yet a few exceptional stars have quite exceptional weights.[12/16] A colony of four stars,[H2] 27 Canis Majoris, is believed to have a total weight[8c] nearly 1,000 times that of the sun,[H3] although this is not certain. An ordinary binary system,[H2] Plaskett's star, is believed, this time with fair certainty,[8d] to have a total weight of more than 140 suns.[H3] But such great weights are very exceptional.[12] It is very rare[3] to find a star with[14c] ten times the weight of the sun,[H4] and no star yet found[14d] has as little as a tenth of the sun's weight.[H4] Thus on the whole the stars shew only a very moderate range in weight.[H1/12]

EXAMINATION

3. WHAT?

It is very rare to find a star with ten times the weight of the sun, . . .

'Very rare' is hardly admissible as a scientific expression except when applied to occurrences of particular birds, flowers, diseases and other organic phenomena, of which a census is impracticable. Here the reader deserves to be told whether one in fifty, or one in five hundred, or one in five thousand, of the star-weights recorded at reputable observatories is ten times as much as that of the sun.

8. INAPPROPRIATE WORD OR PHRASE

(*a*) **Our sun proves to be of about average weight, or perhaps somewhat over.**

If Sir James really has scientific proof of the stars' comparative weight, then there is no need for a 'perhaps'; but if he doubts the accuracy of the calculation, then the results *suggest* rather than *prove* to him that the sun is a little heavier than the average star.

(*b*) **. . . if we compare the sun to a man of average weight, most of the weights of the stars lie between those of a boy and a heavy man.**

A 'boy' is a term implying sexual immaturity, not weight. Some boys weigh more than an average man; some are infants and weigh only a few pounds. Here 'boy' must be qualified by some phrase suggesting a narrower range of weight than from five pounds to one hundred and fifty.

(*c*) **. . . 27 Canis Majoris, is believed to have a total weight . . .**

An astronomer should avoid the word 'believe' wherever the question is one of reckoning rather than faith.

(*d*) **. . . Plaskett's star, is believed, this time with fair certainty . . .**

An astronomer should also avoid such illogical colloquialisms. A thing is either certain, or it is uncertain. It would be better here to say that the second reckoning is less widely disputed than the first.

10. MISPLACED WORD

. . . most of the weights of the stars . . .

It should be 'the weights of most of the stars'.

12. DUPLICATION

Taken as a whole the stars shew only a small range in weight; . . .
Yet a few exceptional stars have quite exceptional weights. . . .
But such great weights are very exceptional. . . .
Thus on the whole the stars shew only a very moderate range in weight.

Sir James should have remembered that the Bellman in 'The Hunting of the Snark' was considered eccentric because he said things merely three times over, if he wanted them to be true.

14. MATERIAL OMISSION

(*a*) **. . . if we compare the sun to a man of average weight . . .**

The intended comparison is not of the sun to a man, but of the weight of the sun to that of a man of average size.

(*b*) **. . . most of the weights of the stars lie between . . .**

A logical link has been omitted: 'it will be found that, proportionately, . . .'

(*c*) **It is very rare to find a star with ten times the weight of the sun, and no star yet found has as little as a tenth of the sun's weight.**

If it was necessary for the sake of clarity to put 'as little' into the second half of the sentence, then 'as much' should have been put into the first half, before 'ten times the weight of the sun', to show that 'ten times or more' is meant, not merely 'ten times'.

(*d*) **. . . and no star yet found has as little as a tenth of the sun's weight.**

Many stars have been found but not yet examined: 'and weighed' should therefore have been inserted after 'found'.

16. UNDEVELOPED THEME

Yet a few exceptional stars have quite exceptional weights.

Unless they are exceptional in other ways also, which should be briefly summarized, there is no point in repeating 'exceptional'.

20. IRRELEVANCY

Our sun proves to be of about average weight. . . .

'Our' is used perhaps to remind the reader that besides the Solar system there are others that consist of sun and planets; and that 'our' sun is not, as has for centuries been assumed, the Lord of the Visible Universe. But this 'our' is a dangerous irrelevancy in a passage containing the phrase 'a weight of more than 140 suns' – for these 140 then seem to be suns selected from 140 systems, rather than 'our sun' raised to the power of 140.

23. LOGICAL WEAKNESS

Taken as a whole, the stars shew only a small range in weight . . .

He probably means 'most stars show only . . .' But 'taken as whole', they show a very wide range: for 'the whole' includes the exceptionally heavy ones, which are two or three thousand times heavier than the exceptionally light ones.

H. ELEGANT VARIATION

(1) **. . . Only a small range in weight . . .**

. . . a very moderate range in weight . . .

(2) **. . . a colony of four stars . . .**

. . . an ordinary binary system . . .

(The second phrase means a colony of two stars.)

(3) **. . . a total weight nearly 1,000 times that of the sun . . .**

. . . a total weight of more than 140 suns. . . .

(4) **. . . ten times the weight of the sun . . .**

. . . as little as a tenth of the sun's weight . . .

This variation, pardonable in a copy of ornate Latin verses, seems out of place in a scientific exposition.

O. SECOND THOUGHTS

Our sun proves to be of about average weight, or perhaps somewhat over.

It confuses the reader to be told something, and then to have this qualified with a contradiction. What is meant is: 'of perhaps a little more than average weight'.

FAIR COPY

[Scientists can weigh stars by calculating the amount of gravitational pull that components of the same stellar system exert on one another.]

'The results are interesting. They suggest that the sun is a star of little more than average weight. On the whole, stars have only a small range in weight. If the weight of a medium-sized man were to stand for that of the sun, then the weights of most other stars would, in proportion, be found to lie between those of a large man and a ten-year-old boy. Of all the stars that have been weighed, only one in every [so many] has proved to be as much as ten times heavier than the sun; none has yet proved to be as little as ten times lighter. Among the few exceptionally heavy stars are the four components of the system *27 Canis Majoris*: they have been reckoned as being, together, nearly 1,000 times heavier than the sun. The accuracy of this figure is disputed by astronomers; but at least they generally agree that the two components of a system named "Plaskett's Star" are, together, over 140 times heavier than the sun.'

COMMENT

Sir James Jeans has set himself the task of translating the theories of physicists from mathematical formulae into ordinary English. A late Victorian education seems to have taught him to shun a bald style; and his experience at Cambridge and Princeton to have taught him that the best way to make students in the lecture-room remember things is to repeat himself constantly. But such repetition is unnecessary in writing, if the points are clearly made in the first place: a reader can turn back the pages and refresh his memory whenever he wishes. And when repetition is disguised by constant variation of language, with the object of making the passage seem less tedious, the reader becomes confused. He is not quite sure whether the second and third repetitive phrases are the exact equivalent of the first or whether there is meant to be a subtle difference between them.

It is remarkable that nearly all scientists, at the point where they turn from mathematical or chemical language to English, seem to feel relieved of any further obligation to precise terminology. The sentence: 'It is very rare to find a star with ten times the weight of the sun, and no star yet found has as little as a tenth of the sun's weight' would, if the words were translated into a mathematical formula, be found lacking in three necessary elements, and to have an inexplicable variation of symbols in the elements given. A more scientific presentation of the sentence is: 'Of all the stars that have been weighed, only one in every [so many] has proved to be as much as ten times heavier than the sun; and none has yet proved to be as little as ten times lighter.' If the second part of the sentence is thus phrased in the same style as the first, they both become easier to understand and remember.

Professor C. E. M. Joad

from *Guide to Philosophy*, 1936

TEXT

There,[4] spread out in space is nature,[9a] and here,[4] inserting[8a] itself into the bits[8b] of nature, which we[1] call bodies,[9b/23a] is life, producing effects upon bodies,[8c/22] which are other than those which the laws of physics[3] will enable us[1] to predict,[13/G] and introducing an element of arbitrary caprice which we[1] call free will[12] into the apparently[8d] orderly scheme of nature. Such, Whitehead says in effect, is the conventional[23b] pattern of the universe which the scientist[H] takes for granted . . . Unable[P] within its borders[20] to find room for moral and aesthetic experience, for creativity and free will,[23c] Science[H] has had to leave them outside the pattern.[14]

EXAMINATION

1. WHO?

. . . the bits of nature which we call bodies . . .
. . . other than those which the laws of physics will enable us to predict, . . .
. . . which we call free will . . .

Who is 'we'? Whitehead and certain scientists? Or Whitehead and his readers? 'We' is certainly not all English-speaking people, for it clearly excludes Calvinists and 'behaviouristic' scientists.

3. WHAT?

... which the laws of physics will enable us to predict ...

If the word 'bodies' has to be explained as meaning 'bits of nature' and 'free will' as meaning 'arbitrary caprice', surely the reader is entitled to an explanation of 'the laws of physics'?

4. WHERE?

There, spread out in space, is nature, and here, inserting itself into the bits of nature, which we call bodies, is life.

The organic and the inorganic are so mixed up together in nature that one cannot divide them by pointing in any direction to express a 'here' and a 'there'; scientists even hold that occasional 'cosmic accidents' – planets belonging to distant stellar systems but of a physical history similar to that of the earth – may support organic life.

8. INAPPROPRIATE WORD OR PHRASE

(*a*) **... and here, inserting itself into ... bodies, is life.**

This is to give life a physical entity distinguishable from the bodies which it activates. Few scientists think of life as a parasitic entity in this sense.

(*b*) **... inserting itself into the bits of nature ...**

'Bits' are irregular fragments. A body is an organized physical entity.

(*c*) **... producing effects upon bodies, which are often other than those which the laws of physics will enable us to predict.**

The effect is not merely to alter the 'bodies' thus animated: it is also to alter, to an unpredictable extent, the physical surface of the earth.

(*d*) **... introducing an element of ... free will into the apparently orderly scheme of nature.**

The unpredictable effects of life have already been noted, so 'apparently' should be 'otherwise'.

9. AMBIGUOUS WORD OR PHRASE

(*a*) **There, spread out in space is nature ...**

'Nature' is more often used to mean the animated part of the physical universe, or the power which animates it, than to mean the inanimate part – as it seems to do here.

(*b*) **... the bits of nature, which we call bodies ...**

In science, 'bodies' is a term applied to living organisms; to 'celestial bodies'; and to classifiable substances whether 'simple' or 'compound'. The argument leads the reader to suppose that living organisms are meant, since celestial bodies show no caprice, and 'simple or compound bodies' are 'elements' rather than 'bits' of nature; but this, if so, is not immediately clear.

12. DUPLICATION

... an element of arbitrary caprice which we call free will ...

'Caprice' is by definition arbitrary, i.e. expressing an independent will or pleasure. Nor is anything added to this phrase by giving 'free will' as a synonym.

13. SELF-EVIDENT STATEMENT

. . . life, producing effects upon bodies, which are other than those which the laws of physics will enable us to predict, . . .

In modern usage, physics is a department of science which excludes biology. If Professor Joad had remarked that the effects of life were sometimes also biologically unpredictable, that would have been worth while.

14. MATERIAL OMISSION

Unable within its borders to find room for moral and aesthetic experience, for creativity and free will, Science has had to leave them outside the pattern.

Aristotle, who inaugurated formal science, divided his studies into two departments, 'physics' (which included biology) and 'metaphysics'. Modern scientists have divided physics up into 'physics', 'biology' and 'chemistry' — each with sub-departments; they do not entirely rule out moral and aesthetic experiences, but make them a part of metaphysics under the headings 'ethics' and 'aesthetics'. Unless 'Science' means merely 'physics', the place of moral and aesthetic experience in metaphysics should have been noted.

20. IRRELEVANCY

Unable within its borders to find room for . . . creativity and free will, Science has had to leave them outside the pattern.

'Within its borders' is not intelligibly related to 'outside the pattern' and confuses the metaphor without adding anything to the sense.

22. OVER-EMPHASIS

. . . inserting itself into the bits of nature, which we call bodies, is life, producing effects upon bodies. . . .

There seems no reason for repeating 'bodies' instead of writing 'them'.

23. LOGICAL WEAKNESS

(*a*) **. . . inserting itself into the bits of nature which we call bodies. . . .**

Even if life is regarded as a parasitic entity, the bits of nature that it animates by an intrusion into them are not called 'bodies' until animation is apparent.

(*b*) **Such, . . . is the conventional pattern of the universe . . .**

If it includes an element of arbitrary caprice, it is neither conventional nor a pattern.

(*c*) **There, spread out in space is nature, and here, inserting itself into bits of nature . . . is life . . . introducing an element of . . . free will into the apparently orderly scheme of nature. Such . . . is the conventional pattern of the universe which the scientist takes for granted . . . Unable within its borders to find room for . . . creativity and free will, Science has had to leave them outside the pattern.**

i.e. Science leaves outside the conventional pattern of the universe the element of free will which it takes for granted as belonging to it. This is self-contradictory. Perhaps Professor Joad is thinking of two patterns, the universe's pattern and the interpretative pattern of Science. But, if so, he has not expressed himself well.

H. ELEGANT VARIATION

. . . which the scientist takes for granted . . .

Unable . . . to find room for . . . free will, Science has had . . .

'The scientist' and 'Science' are not sufficiently distinguished from each other to warrant the change from one to the other.

P. AWKWARD INVERSION

Unable within its borders to find room for moral and aesthetic experience, for creativity and free will. . . .

'Within its borders' gets an undeserved emphasis by being pushed so far forward in the sentence; it should have gone in after 'to find room'.

G. CIRCUMLOCUTION

. . . effects . . . which are other than those which the laws of physics will enable us to predict, . . .

This means 'effects unpredictable in physics'.

FAIR COPY

'Whitehead's view of the universe which scientists have made a subject for research amounts to this: they have found that by far the greater part of physical nature is spread out in space according to what seems to them an orderly pattern, but that the animizing of certain physical entities, the organic bodies, produces effects which are not consistently deducible from scientific generalizations about cause and effect . . . Deciding that these effects, which include their own moral and aesthetic experiences, and which they ascribe, variously, to creativity, free-will, or caprice, are independent of the principal pattern, they put them by for metaphysical research.'

COMMENT

Professor Joad's self-confidence in his task of making metaphysical problems read simply is reinforced by an unusual rhythmic fluency, which tempts him to a surprising carelessness of expression. This passage reads as if it had been dictated without a pause to his secretary — a magnificent extempore. The logical faults could easily have been amended, the right word easily found for each nearly-right stand-in; then why were the printers never sent a revised draft?

SENATOR HIRAM JOHNSON

from an Address to the People of California, 1940

TEXT

Jefferson established the principle of a two-term limit for President.[8a/E1] Washington set the precedent.[19/L] Madison and Monroe acquiesced in it and Andrew Jackson, who until the Democratic Convention of 1940 was[9a] the second greatest[K1] Democrat of all time,[F] favoured it. All the great[K1] Demo-

crats from that day to this[5a] have been in accord.[14a] None has dissented.[12a] The reasons were[5b] plain.[16] It was a fear[1] of personal power[8b/K2] in one man, the fear of personal power[K2] which would lead that one man to excesses.[23a] Power[K2] is a heady wine. Few human[22a] brains can resist it.[23b] And certainly there has been no evidence,[14b] or[8c] even desire of resistance in the gentleman who seeks it[23c] now.

If your imagination will permit you, go back to the first beginnings[5c] of this country. Can you see Washington and Jefferson and Madison and Monroe and Jackson and all the remaining galaxy[22b] of the great[K1/E1] safe-guarding our precious liberties? We're the last country on earth[9b] to possess them.[23d] Shall one of our own[3] jeopardize them, or[11] shall one of our own be permitted to violate[E2] the sacred tradition built up by these great[K1] men of the past[12b] for the preservation and for the perpetuity[22c/M] of our institutions?

EXAMINATION

1. WHO?

All the great Democrats . . . have been in accord.
None has dissented. The reasons were plain.
It was a fear of personal power in one man, . . .

Who had this fear? Was it the great Democrats who feared the effect of 'personal power' upon themselves; or was it the people who feared and the great Democrats who respected their fear?

3. WHAT?

Shall one of our own jeopardize them, . . . ?

Our own what? Democrats? Americans? Or times?

5. WHEN?

(*a*) **. . . Andrew Jackson, who until the Democratic Convention of 1940 was the second greatest Democrat of all time, favoured it. All the great Democrats from that day to this have been in accord.**

From that day to this? During the three months that had elapsed between the Democratic Convention and this utterance?

(*b*) **All the great Democrats . . . have been in accord.**
The reasons were plain.

When were they plain? And are they plain no longer?

(*c*) **If your imagination will permit you, go back to the first beginnings of this country.**

The first beginnings of America are prehistoric. But the context shows that Senator Johnson means neither these, nor the times of the first European visitor to America, Lief Ericsson, nor even those of the Pilgrim Fathers — but the late eighteenth and early nineteenth centuries. He should have said 'this nation'.

8. INAPPROPRIATE WORD OR PHRASE

(*a*) **... a two-term limit for President.**

This should be 'for the Presidency', except in banner headlines.

(*b*) **... a fear of personal power in one man ... which would lead that one man to excesses.**

This invidious word *personal* is perhaps suggested by George III's 'personal government' at the time of the American War of Independence – the King personally intervening in parliamentary affairs instead of remaining outside politics – which Congress protested against when they framed their Declaration of Independence. But the fear here is not one of personal power, for Washington and others enjoyed great personal power for their two terms of office, but of power prolonged beyond the second term.

(*c*) **... there has been no evidence, or even desire for resistance....**

When it corresponds with a negative, 'or' becomes 'nor'.

9. AMBIGUOUS WORD OR PHRASE

(*a*) **... Andrew Jackson, who until the Democratic Convention of 1940 was the second greatest Democrat of all time ...**

Does this mean that he really ceased in 1940 to be the second greatest? Or only that the Democratic Convention unjustly denied him the title of second greatest and tried to foist it on F. D. Roosevelt?

(*b*) **Can you see Washington and Jefferson and Madison and Monroe and Jackson and all the remaining galaxy of the great safeguarding our precious liberties? We're the last country on earth to possess them.**

'Can you see' might be read ironically (as in the phrase 'Can you see a Scotchman paying sixpence for a cup of tea?'). The word 'precious' seems used disparagingly. And 'We're the last country on earth to possess them' seems to confirm the irony by suggesting that every country in the world will possess liberties before the U.S.A.

11. UNINTENTIONAL CONTRAST

Shall one of our own jeopardize them, or shall one of our own be permitted to violate the sacred tradition....

These are not alternatives, as they appear to be, but variants of the same theme.

12. DUPLICATION

(*a*) **All the great Democrats from that day to this have been in accord. None has dissented.**

The second sentence is unnecessary.

(*b*) **... tradition built up by these great men of the past ...**

A tradition implies a past – though in an American college a notice was recently posted: 'Sophomores are not permitted to bring their dates on the Campus before 5 p.m. This tradition will commence on Thursday next.'

14. MATERIAL OMISSION

(*a*) **All the great Democrats from that day to this have been in accord.**

Only about the two-term question.

(*b*) **And certainly there has been no evidence, or even desire of resistance . . .**

He means 'no evidence of capacity, nor even of desire, to resist'.

6. UNDEVELOPED THEME

The reasons were plain.

Only one reason is then given: 'Fear of personal power'. Perhaps the Senator had in mind the political realism of these Presidents, each of whom, aware of the popular prejudice against running for a third term, prepared to stand down in favour of a candidate of his own Party, rather than make a gift of the Presidency to an opposing candidate.

19. CONFUSED SEQUENCE OF IDEAS

Jefferson established the principle . . . Washington set the precedent.

Washington came first in historical order and should have been mentioned first.

22. OVER-EMPHASIS

(*a*) **Power is a heady wine. Few human brains can resist it.**

Can horses' brains? Or cats' brains?

(*b*) **. . . all the remaining galaxy of the great . . .**

'Galaxy' means thousands of stars. The Senator cannot be referring to more than a dozen or two Democratic great men.

(*c*) **. . . for the preservation and for the perpetuity of our institutions.**

He means 'for the perpetual preservation of our institutions'. There is no obvious reason here for making two nouns out of a noun and an adjective, though this was a cant device of Latin poets — *pateris libamus et oro* ('we pour libations from dishes and from gold', i.e. from gold dishes) — to avoid difficulties of scansion. They called it *endiadis*.

23. LOGICAL WEAKNESS

(*a*) **It was a fear of personal power in one man, the fear of personal power that would lead that one man to excesses.**

Whatever the fear, it was obviously not a fear of 'personal power in one man', since the third term gave him no greater power than the first and second had done.

(*b*) **Power is a heady wine. Few human brains can resist it.**

He has already mentioned several great Democrats who did so, and soon mentions a whole galaxy more.

(*c*) **Power is a heady wine. . . . the gentleman who seeks it now . . .**

This is an attempt to disguise the facts. Franklin Delano Roosevelt had enjoyed Presidential power for nearly eight years and previously was Governor of the State of New York. The Senator here represents him as a political parvenu.

(*d*) **. . . the galaxy of the great safeguarding our precious liberties? We're the last country on earth to possesss them.**

How could other countries possess these peculiarly American liberties?

E. MISMATING OF STYLES

(1) **. . . two-term limit for President.**

. . . all the remaining galaxy of the great . . .

The first is modern journalistic shorthand; the second an imitation of eighteenth-century rhetoric.

(2) **We're the last country on earth to possess them.**

Shall one of our own jeopardize them, or shall one of our own be permitted to violate ...

'We're the last country' is the colloquial equivalent of 'we are the last nation'. 'Shall one of our own ... or shall one of our own' is Old Testament rhetoric.

F. OBSCURE REFERENCE

... Andrew Jackson, who until the Democratic Convention of 1940 was the second greatest Democrat of all time ...

Who then became the second greatest? Surely not President Roosevelt? Or is Senator Johnson being ironical? And who was the first? Pericles, Marius, Robespierre, Cobden, Garibaldi — or what have you? Is the choice perhaps limited to a mere hundred and fifty years of American Presidents? And is 'Democratic' used in the anti-Federal Party sense — which would exclude all the Presidents here mentioned except Jackson? — or in a general sense, as opposed to 'autocratic'?

K. TOO MUCH OF THE SAME WORD

(1) **... Andrew Jackson ... the second greatest Democrat of all time ...**

... all the great Democrats ...

... Monroe and Jackson and all the galaxy of the great ...

... the sacred tradition built up by these great men of the past.

Surely Jackson and his fellow-Presidents might here have been occasionally characterized as 'wise', 'noble' or 'good', rather than as 'great' every time?

(2) **It was a fear of personal power ...**

... the fear of personal power ...

Power is a heady wine.

To mention power twice would have been enough.

L. JINGLE

... a two-term limit for President. Washington set the precedent.

'President' and 'precedent' coming at the end of these sentences have too similar a sound.

M. TOO MUCH ALLITERATION

... by the great men of the past for the preservation and for the perpetuity of our institutions.

Three p's so close together suggest too literal an expression of scorn for Mr. Roosevelt.

FAIR COPY

'Washington, after holding the Presidency for two terms, chose not to stand again. Jefferson, his successor, converted this precedent into a guiding principle for all holders of the office. Presidents Madison and Monroe acquiesced in the principle. President Andrew Jackson clearly proclaimed his adherence to it. Nor from Jackson's day, until the Democratic Convention of 1940 — the Convention which has shamefully denied him his just title as, next to Lincoln [?], the greatest of all American democrats — was there a single dissentient from the principle among the leaders of the Party. It is easy to see why. All respected the popular fear of what might happen to this country, should the Presidential powers remain too long in the hands of one man.

But what of the gentleman who has held these powers for the past two terms and who now seeks to renew them? Can it be said that his record shows him capable, or even desirous, of resisting the temptation to excess into which a third bottle of this heady wine might lead almost any man?

Go back in thought, if you will, to our early national history. Do you not see how Washington, Jefferson, Madison, Monroe, Jackson and all the other great ones, safeguarded our common liberties? Shall any American of to-day be permitted to violate the sacred tradition that they built up? Shall our institutions be jeopardized in which these liberties — the more precious because no other nation on earth still possesses the like — are perennially vested?'

COMMENT

Senator Johnson had just received the nominations of the Republican, Democratic and Progressive Parties of California, for re-election. Not to have a well-trodden party-line to follow is a confusing experience for a politician. Senator Johnson, taking the Anti-Third-Term line, did not make it clear to those millions of Americans who were vague about political history that, in a Party sense, all the United States' Presidents before the Civil War, with the exception of Polk, Van Buren and Jackson, had been anti-Democratic.

Moreover, as a Senator, he had to be careful what he said. He could only hint, however broadly, at the identity and the autocratic aims of 'the gentleman who seeks power now'. For President Roosevelt was the active head of the Federal Government and the Commander-in-Chief of the Army and Navy, as well as being Democratic candidate for re-election.

The style is an uncomfortable compromise between the sonorous rhetoric of Patrick Henry or Jefferson and new-style journalistic brevity.

PROFESSOR J. M. KEYNES (now Lord Keynes)

from *How to Pay for the War*, Spring 1940

TEXT

[How we are to decide on the best use of our productive resources in war time, considering the rival demands of the fighting services, exporters and civilians. We should be producing as much as possible and importing as much as we can afford, using as much as we need for war purposes, exporting as much as we can spare, and leaving a sufficiency for civil consumption.]

It is extraordinarily difficult to secure the right outcome for this resultant[12a] of many separate policies.[8a]

We[1a] can start out either[14a] by fixing the standard of life[3a/8b] of the civilian[H1] and discover what is left over for the service departments and for export; or by adding up the demands of the latter[1b] and[17] discover what is left over for the civilians.[H1/14b] The actual result will be a compromise between the two methods.[23a] At present it is hard to say who, if anyone, settles such matters. In the final outcome[11/22a] there seems to be a larger element of chance than of design.[12b] It is a case of pull devil, pull baker[J] – with the devil so far on top[1c/4]. . . .

On the assumption[15] that our[1a] total output is[5a] as large as we know how to organize,[6a] a definite residual[H2/12c] will be left over which is[5b] available for civilian consumption. The amount of this residue[H2] will certainly be influenced[8c] by the reasonable requirements of the civilian[8d] population.[H1] . . .

[The civilian – the baker – will have to be humoured to some extent.[14c]]

. . . But unless we[1a] are to fall far short of our maximum war effort, we cannot allow[1a] the amount of more money in the pockets of the public[H1] to have a significant influence, unjustified by other considerations,[6b] on the amount which is released to civilians.[H1]

This leads up to our[1a] fundamental proposition.[19] There will be a certain definite[22b] amount[H2] left over for civilian consumption.[12d] This amount may be larger or smaller than what perfect wisdom and foresight[22c] would provide . . . [But this amount will depend far less than in peace time on what people can afford to spend. Before the war they were accustomed to produce less than they were capable of producing.] **In such circumstances if we[1a] have more to spend, more will be produced and there will be more[14d] to buy. Not necessarily in the same proportion.[3b] . . .** [The demand for some sorts of goods may exceed the supply and producing power may thus be reduced.]

. . . Nevertheless, when men were working harder and earning more, they have[5c] been able to increase their consumption in not much less than the same proportion.

In peace time, that is to say, the size of the cake[J] depends on the amount of work done. But in war time the size of the cake is fixed. If we[1a] work harder, we[1a] can fight better. But we must not consume more.[1a/H1]

This is the elementary fact which in a democracy the man in the street[H1] must learn to understand[12e] if the nation is to act wisely – that the size of the civilian's[H1] cake is fixed.[23b]

What follows from this?

It means,[24] broadly speaking, that the public[H1] as a whole cannot increase its consumption by increasing its money earnings.

EXAMINATION

1. WHO?

(*a*) i. **We can start out either by fixing the standard of life of the civilian . . .**
ii. **On the assumption that our total output . . .**
iii. **But unless we are to fall far short of our maximum war effort . . .**
iv. **. . . we cannot allow the amount of mere money in the pockets of the public to have a significant influence . . . on the amount . . . released to civilians.**
v. **This leads up to our fundamental proposition.**
vi. **. . . if we have more to spend, more will be produced.**
vii. **If we work harder, . . .**
viii. **. . . we can fight better.**
ix. **But we must not consume more.**

Readers would welcome a definition of 'the little word we' by Professor Keynes, even a paradoxical one, as in the song:

> 'We', *the little word* 'we':—
> *She said,*
> *She didn't do it;*
> *I said,*
> *I didn't do it.*
> *Who did it?*
> We *did it* —
> We, *my honey and me.*

In i, the 'we' is apparently a group of economic statisticians anxious to assist the puzzled Government.

In ii, it is apparently the united workers of Great Britain.

In iii, it is apparently the workers, fighters and exporters.

In iv, it is an ideally prudent War Cabinet.

In v, it is Professor Keynes.

In vi, it is probably the civil population of Great Britain, including the idle mouths.

In vii, it is the united workers again.

In viii, it is the fighters.

In ix, it is probably the civil population again.

(*b*) **. . . we can discover what is left over for the service departments and for export; or by adding up the demands of the latter . . .**

'The latter' apparently does not mean the export trade, but the service departments and the export trade.

(*c*) **It is a case of pull devil, pull baker — with the devil so far on top.**

It is not made clear until several lines further down that the baker is the civilian. Then is the devil the service departments and the export trade? Or is he only the service departments?

3. WHAT?

(*a*) **We can start out by fixing the standard of life of the civilian . . .**

At a minimum or a maximum rate of consumption?

(*b*) **In such circumstances if we have more to spend, more will be produced, and there will be more to buy. Not necessarily in the same proportion . . .**

This is puzzling. Does he mean perhaps that the ratio between production of goods and purchasing power is not necessarily constant in boom periods?

4. WHERE?

It is a case of pull devil, pull baker — with the devil so far on top. . . .

Since, as subsequently appears, the devil and the baker are tugging for the possession of a cake, neither will be pictured by the reader as on top of the other. Are they perhaps scrambling for the cake, as in the Westminster School pancake scramble? If so, does 'on top' mean 'on top of the cake' or 'on top of the baker who is clutching it'?

5. WHEN?

(*a*) **On the assumption that our total output is as large as we know how to organize . . .**

The most ignorant economist would not have assumed this in the Spring of 1940. What is surely meant is 'will eventually be as large . . .'

(*b*) **A definite residue will be left over which is available . . .**

Is it available now? Or will it be available later?

(*c*) **Nevertheless, when men were working harder, they have been able to increase their consumption . . .**

'Have' suggests that this ability continues, despite the war.

6. HOW MUCH?

(*a*) **. . . is as large as we know how to organize . . .**

'As we know how to organize' is no measure of size. He means perhaps that the maximum power to produce goods will presumably be exerted.

(*b*) **. . . we cannot allow the amount of mere money in the pockets of the public to have a significant influence, unjustified by other considerations, on the amount which is released to civilians.**

'Mere money' is a very loose way of talking about money; 'significant influence' is a vague extension of 'influence'; 'unjustified by other considerations' is a vague qualification of the preceding bold statement. The question here implied, 'What proportion of goods to money available for their purchase should be released to the public?' is not faced.

8. INAPPROPRIATE WORD OR PHRASE

(*a*) **It is extraordinarily difficult to secure the right outcome for this resultant of many separate policies. . . .**

Hardly 'many separate policies'. Already in the Spring of 1940 there was national agreement on a single policy, that of winning the war, though it was found difficult to assess the needs of civilians, fighting services and exporters in the light of this policy.

(*b*) **We can start out . . . by fixing the standard of life . . .**

'Standard of life' is a social, rather than an economic, concept. The normal phrase is 'standard of living'.

(*c*) **The amount of this residue will certainly be influenced by the reasonable requirements of the civilian population.**

An 'amount' can hardly be 'influenced', as an animate or semi-animate thing can be; an 'amount' is 'affected'.

(*d*) **. . . the reasonable requirements of the civilian population.**

Either 'the civil population' or 'civilians'.

11. UNINTENTIONAL CONTRAST

At present it is hard to say who, if anyone, settles such matters.

In the final outcome there seems to be a larger element of chance than of design.

The phrase 'at present' is unnecessary and induces 'In the final outcome' (which does not refer to time but to arithmetic) to become its partner in a contrast between 'now' and 'eventually'.

12. DUPLICATION

(*a*) **It is extraordinarily difficult to secure the right outcome for this resultant of many policies.**

An outcome *is* a resultant.

(*b*) **At present it is hard to say who, if anyone, settles such matters . . . In the final outcome, there seems to be a larger element of chance than of design.**

The second sentence is implied in the first.

(*c*) **. . . a definite residual will be left over. . . .**

A residual *is* what is left over.

(*d*) **. . . a definite residual will be left over for the civilian.**

. . . there will be a certain definite amount left over for civilian consumption.

The second sentence does not add anything material to the argument; it was already clear that the goods were to be consumed.

(*e*) **This elementary fact which . . . the man in the street must learn to understand . . .**

Either 'understand' or 'learn' would have sufficed.

14. MATERIAL OMISSION

(*a*) **We can start out either by fixing the standard of life of the civilian . . .**

The total national production of goods would first have to be assessed.

(*b*) **We can start out either by fixing the standard of life of the civilian and discover what is left over for the service departments and for export; or by adding up the demands of the latter and discover what is left over for the civilians.**

This is too exclusive an alternative. Another method would be to give priority to the service departments, then satisfy the civilians and finally export what goods remained.

(*c*) **[The civilian — the baker — will have to be humoured to some extent.]**

Why? This should be explained at length.

(*d*) **. . . if we have more to spend, more will be produced and there will be more to buy.**

The first 'more' means money, the other two mean goods; this should be made clear.

15. UNFULFILLED PROMISE

On the assumption that our total output is as large as we know how to organize, a definite residual will be left over.

After 'on the assumption', one expects something like 'we can count on'.

17. FAULTY CONNEXION

We can start out either by fixing the standard of life of the civilian and discover what is left over for the service departments and for export; or by adding up the demands of the latter and discover what is left over for the civilians.

In each case 'and discover' should be 'so as to discover'; the 'or' is separated from its 'either' by an idea not relevant to the alternative methods of starting out.

19. CONFUSED SEQUENCE OF IDEAS

This leads up to our fundamental proposition.

The fundamental proposition 'a definite residual will be left over which will be available for civilian consumption' has already been stated. It is now restated: 'There will be a certain definite amount left over for civilian consumption.'

22. OVER-EMPHASIS

(*a*) **In the final outcome there seems to be a larger element of chance than of design.**

This happens, apparently, not merely in the final outcome but at every stage.

(*b*) **There will be a certain definite amount left over. . . .**

'Certain definite' suggests, falsely, that he knows what this amount will be.

(*c*) **This amount may be larger or smaller than what perfect wisdom and foresight would provide.**

'Perfect wisdom and foresight' are too high-sounding conceptions to introduce into so chancy a subject as this.

23. LOGICAL WEAKNESS

(*a*) **The actual result will be a compromise between the two methods.**

Not if 'we' follow one or other of the methods he has sketched out.

(*b*) **. . . when men have been working harder and earning more they have been able to increase their consumption in not much less than the same proportion. In peace time, that is to say, the size of the cake depends on the amount of work done. But in war time the size of the cake is fixed. If we work harder we can fight better. But we must not consume more. This is the elementary fact . . . that the size of the civilian's cake is fixed.**

In peace time this cake apparently represents something different from what it does in war time. In peace time it is the total amount of consumable goods which the public can afford to buy; in war time it is apparently the amount of consumable goods which the Government would be wise to let the public buy, because 'we must not consume more'. To call both these concepts 'cake' con fuses the argument. Moreover, whichever of these concepts is meant, a war does not 'fix' the size of the civilian's cake. The amount of cake may vary not only seasonally but according to military gains and losses.

24. CHANGE OF STANDPOINT

What follows from this? It means, broadly speaking . . .

Either: 'What does this mean? It means, broadly speaking . . .'

Or: 'What follows from this? Broadly speaking, that . . .'

H. ELEGANT VARIATION

(1) **. . . the standard of life of the civilian.**

. . . what is left over for the civilians.

. . . the reasonable requirements of the civilian population.

. . . mere money in the pockets of the public. . . .

. . . the amount which is released to civilians.

. . . men . . . were able to increase their consumption . . .

But we must not consume more.

. . . the man in the street must learn to understand . . .

. . . the public as a whole cannot increase its consumption.

All these are apparently the same character: the civilian-worker-consumer.

(2) **. . . a definite residual will be left over . . .**

The amount of this residue . . .

There will be a certain definite amount left over . . .

These are all the same thing.

J. MEMORY STRAIN

It is a case of pull devil, pull baker. . . .

In peace time, that is to say, the size of the cake depends on the amount of work done.

The reader has to wait all this time before he discovers that the devil and the baker are pulling at a cake

FAIR COPY

[How we are to decide on the best use of our productive resources in war time, considering the rival demands of the fighting services, exporters and civilians. We should be producing as much as possible and importing as much as we can afford, using as much as we need for war purposes, exporting as much as we can spare, and leaving a sufficiency for civilian consumption.]

'It is extraordinarily difficult to coördinate all these different parts of our war policy. One sensible approach to the problem, after first assessing the country's maximum productive power (which will, prosumably, be exerted), would be to fix a strict ration for civilian consumption of goods and then to see what was left for distribution between the fighting services and the exporters. Another sensible approach would be to determine the needs of the fighting services and the exporters and then see what goods were left for civil consumption. But nobody in authority has yet tried either way: it has been a case of "pull devil, pull baker" at the cake of available goods. Demands coming from all sides have been met by manufacturers, or by the Ministries which regulate the production and marketing of goods, without any common formula for reckoning proportionate needs. On the whole, the fighting and exporting devil has had a stronger pull than the civilian baker, who has had to go short of cake. However, when British production is fully organized, there will be quite a large surplus of cake after the devil's immediate needs have been satisfied; the baker will then probably be allowed more than his bare rations. He must be humoured to some extent because it is he who does the baking. Then the harder he works, the better will the devil be fed and so the better will the devil fight and export on the baker's behalf; but since there will not be an unlimited amount of cake the baker must be prevented from eating as much as he would like.

How great a quantity, in fact, of consumable goods the civil population will be allowed to buy during this war – it may be more or less than is prudent – will depend far less than in peace time on what they can afford to spend. Before the war, they were accustomed to produce less than they were capable of producing, which meant that occasional increases in production resulted in higher wages and more goods to spend them on. The ratio between production and purchasing power is not necessarily constant in such boom periods – the demand for some sorts of goods may exceed the supply, and purchasing power may thus be reduced – but in practice there is not much variation. In war time, then, under a democratic system, the civil population should be forced to understand this: that the amount of goods, imported or manufactured, that they are allowed to buy, must be limited in the national interest – that they cannot, as a body, expect increased consumption of goods in proportion to their increased earnings.'

COMMENT

The bright modern way of writing about what is generally regarded as a dry subject seems inseparable from conversational carelessness. A dry subject is one in which one cannot afford to be inaccurate, because it concerns facts and figures. Here, in explaining the principles of prudent wartime expenditure, it would have been well to choose and keep consistently to the recurrent elements in the argument: for it is better to be dull than obscure. No amount of brightness ever made a naturally dry subject less dry, and a neatly developed argument on however dry a subject may convey a certain pleasure even to readers who are not particularly interested in it. Here the happy-go-lucky economic argument is interrupted by omissions, obscurities and even illogicalities. The last six paragraphs could have been compressed into half the space they occupy, without material loss; whereas the whimsical 'it is a case of pull devil, pull baker –

with the devil so far on top' needs explanatory expansion to three or four times its space.

An expert on a dry subject who writes down to inexpert readers is tempted to indulge, and even imitate, their mental confusions. When, for example, scientific hypotheses are put into simple popular language they are removed as far from their originals as Catholic peasant superstitions are from orthodox Patristic theology. It is ridiculous to fob off on the inexpert reader any non-mathematical account of the structure of an atom, brightening it with a diagram of little electric balls whizzing round a solid nucleus, much as the planets whizz round the sun. This (to use a Puritan metaphor) leads to 'mere idolatory'. If the inexpert reader has never even made the step from Euclid to algebraic geometry he cannot begin to understand how an atom works; and it is flattering his vanity to pretend that he can. He will take the little balls literally.

The popular 'interpretation' of poetry and art for the inexpert person is equally open to objection. Either he has the poetic faculty, or he has not; either he has the artistic eye, or he has not. There are no substitutes for direct understanding or vision.

COMMANDER STEPHEN KING-HALL

from *The News Letter*, Autumn 1940

TEXT

I shall catalogue[8a] some of the views I find uppermost[16a] in people's minds.

(a) *We shall gain air-superiority and gradually dislocate the economic life of Germany by dropping explosives on selected points.*[16b]

My comment: I think[11/12] the phrase air-superiority is misleading.[14a] Most people think[11] of it as meaning a superiority in numbers[3a] (and quality)[6] of say two or three[20] or four to one. But the Germans with some inferiority in quality and great superiority in numbers and all the geographical factors[22] in their favour,[23] as well as highly concentrated targets,[3b/9a] could[9b] not knock us out of the war. Real air-superiority[8b/14b] means undisputed control of the air over all vital targets,[3b] such as the Germans achieved in Poland and Holland. I cannot see this happening over[9c] Germany in any period of time related to this war.[5/14c]

(b) [About the war on land]

(c) [About the war at sea]

EXAMINATION

3. WHAT?

(*a*) . . . air-superiority . . . meaning a superiority in numbers (and quality) of say . . . four to one.

Numbers of what? Planes? What sort of planes? Bombers, fighters, dive-bombers, troop-carriers, gliders and training-craft should not all be lumped together. And planes are no use without trained air-crews and ground staff — are these also reckoned in the vague phrase 'numbers'? If 'most people' think in these terms they should be immediately put right.

(*b*) **. . . highly concentrated targets . . .**

. . . vital targets . . .

Are these the same thing? If so, what is it? The aerodromes of the R.A.F. were vital targets, but not highly concentrated (in the sense of being grouped close together in a single district). Commander King-Hall is probably thinking of railway junctions and docks. But the first heavy German attack was on the aerodromes as being the most vital targets.

5. WHEN?

I cannot see this happening over Germany in any period of time related to this war.

'Any period of time related to this war' might mean 'after the war' or 'during the war'. He probably would have liked to admit that he could not see this happening, however long the war lasted, but did not venture to write so brutally, for fear of seeming to be a defeatist. The U.S.S.R. and the U.S.A. were still neutral.

6. HOW MUCH?

. . . a superiority in numbers (and quality) of say . . . four to one.

Does this mean that the superior air force has four times as many planes as the enemy, each a match for any four of his, so that the total superiority is sixteen to one? Or does it mean that the quantitative superiority is, say, two to one, and that the qualitative is the same?

8. INAPPROPRIATE WORD OR PHRASE

(*a*) **I shall catalogue some of the views . . .**

To 'catalogue' is to classify a great number of different items and arrange them in an intelligible list. In this case there are only three items, (*a*), (*b*), and (*c*) — all of the same class and forming a simple list.

(*b*) **Real air-superiority means undisputed control of the air . . .**

Here 'real' suggests a contrast with either 'false' or 'ideal' superiority, neither of which makes sense. To qualify 'superiority' with 'real' does not turn it into 'supremacy', which is the word Commander King-Hall wants. 'Superiority' implies the continued resistance of an inferior enemy force; supremacy, or 'command of the air', implies that resistance has been crushed.

9. AMBIGUOUS WORD OR PHRASE

(*a*) **. . . as well as highly concentrated targets, . . .**

'Highly concentrated targets' may mean either 'a concentration, in one district, of a large number of important ''target-areas'' ' or 'the concentration in one ''target-area'' of many important targets'.

(*b*) **But the Germans . . . could not knock us out of the war.**

Does *could* mean that they would not be able to do so either at the time of writing (November 1940) or at a later stage of the war; or merely that they had not been able to do so in July and August of that year?

(*c*) **I cannot see this happening over Germany . . .**

Does this mean 'I cannot see the R.A.F. getting undisputed control of the air over Germany', or 'I cannot see Britain getting air-superiority over Germany'?

11. UNINTENTIONAL CONTRAST

I think the phrase air-superiority is misleading.
Most people think . . .

If he had left out 'I think', this unintentional contrast would not have occurred.

12. DUPLICATION

My comment: I think the phrase air-superiority misleading.

Either 'My comment' or, 'I think' — or neither, since the act of comment needs no introduction of this sort.

14. MATERIAL OMISSION

(*a*) **I think the phrase air-superiority is misleading.**

There is nothing ambiguous about the phrase: it means having an air-force which the enemy air-force cannot engage on equal terms with a reasonable expectation of victory. What is misleading is its use on occasions when 'supremacy', not 'superiority', is meant; or when 'superiority' over a prospective enemy is ascribed to an air-force, without taking all the relevant factors into consideration.

(*b*) **Real air-superiority means undisputed control of the air over all vital targets . . .**

He does not here differentiate between air-superiority in defence, and air-superiority in attack, and so throws away the key to his argument. Nor does he mention ground defences (which are not usually reckoned in air-force strength, but are important for the help they give to fighter planes in denying supremacy to an invading air-fleet), or the difference in the tasks assigned to bombers and fighters.

(*c*) **I cannot see this happening over Germany in any period of time related to this war.**

Here he has suppressed the expected reference to the comparative rates of improvement in the aircraft and ground-defences of the opposing air-forces.

16. UNDEVELOPED THEME

(*a*) **I shall catalogue some of the views I find uppermost . . .**

This implies a reservation of opinion on the part of his informants, to which, however, he makes no further reference.

(*b*) **We shall gain air-superiority and gradually dislocate the economic life of Germany by dropping explosives on selected points.**

He has not answered the suggestion that the result of bombing raids, spread over months or years, as opposed to a lightning air-attack of the sort that Germany made in Poland and Holland, might be the dislocation of German economic life and an eventual military collapse.

20. IRRELEVANCY

. . . a superiority in numbers (and quality) of say two or three or four to one.

'Two to one' and 'four to one' are such different concepts — the difference, in this case, representing several years of British plane-production — that 'say two, or three or four' is not the view of 'most people', but a variety of views held by different groups of people. If most people favour 'four to one', the other two proportions are irrelevant.

22. OVER-EMPHASIS

But the Germans . . . with all the geographical factors in their favour . . .

Not all: to begin with, the English Channel prevented the Germans from bringing up troops by land and occupying the temporarily abandoned forward aerodromes.

23. LOGICAL WEAKNESS

But the Germans with inferiority in quality and great superiority in numbers and all the geographical factors in their favour, as well as highly concentrated targets . . .

'Inferiority in quality' was *not* in the Germans' favour. The illogic is not wholly due to insufficient commas. This sentence is about the German failure to knock out England in spite of favourable conditions, and the inferiority in quality, if it is to go in at all, should be shown as offset by the accessibility and size of vital British targets.

FAIR COPY

[The argument that we have here used is built up speculatively on the skeleton provided by the original passage. Our version is neither necessarily what Commander King-Hall meant, nor necessarily true, but it is plumped out with the sort of details that ought to have been included.]

'I shall quote and comment on three popular views about the future conduct of the war:

(a) *We shall gain air-superiority and gradually dislocate the economic life of Germany by dropping explosives on selected points.*

Most people use the word "air-superiority" without defining either the standard by which it is to be judged or mentioning the degree of superiority which they expect to be attained. Nor do they consider that an air-force, though superior to its opponent in the number and quality of its bombers and fighters, and also of its crews and ground-staff, may not always be able to achieve local command of the enemy's air. Admittedly, the *Luftwaffe* in their recent attack on Britain had a slight qualitative inferiority to the R.A.F. in planes and crews, but this was offset by the size and accessibility of some of their main bombing-targets — the vital centres of British production, supply and communication; and they had a four-to-one superiority in the number of combat planes that they could bring into action. Yet they failed to paralyse British resistance, because they failed to achieve undisputed command of the air over their targets. Decisive power can be exercised by an air-force only if it has such command of the enemy's air. The *Luftwaffe* had achieved it in their previous campaigns against Poland and Holland.

Thus, though the R.A.F. are likely to remain qualitatively superior to the *Luftwaffe* in planes, crews and ground-staff, and their quantitative inferiority in all these particulars is being fast reduced, I do not see how they will be able to win undisputed command of the German air, however long this war may last — the planes and anti-aircraft batteries that the Germans already possess and those that they will continue to produce (though perhaps on a reduced scale) and find crews for, will be sufficient to prevent this. Nor do I see how the cumulative power of months, or even years, of British bombing raids will be sufficient to dislocate German economic life and bring it to the point of collapse.'

COMMENT

If time and space were too short for Commander King-Hall to comment lucidly in his 'News Letter' on all these three popular views of the progress of the war, he would have been wiser to concentrate on one. Here too many factors are left out of consideration to make his comment immediately intelligible, and 'air-superiority' as a phrase remains 'misleading' to the end. The passage reads as if he were quoting an argument, which he had not had time to make his own, and as if he were prevented by his position at the Ministry of Aircraft Production from writing in any but vague terms about the probable length of the war.

DR. F. R. LEAVIS

from *New Bearings in English Poetry*, 1932

TEXT

The ordinary cultivated reader is ceasing to be able to read poetry.[3a] In self-defence amid the perpetual avalanche of print he has had to acquire reading habits[A] that incapacitate[22a] him when the signals[8a] for unaccustomed and subtle responses present[8b] themselves. He has, moreover, lost the education[3b] that in the past[5a] was provided by tradition and social environment. Even the poetry of simple sensibility,[9] if it is not superficially familiar,[3c] seems incomprehensible to him.[22b] And the more important[3d] poetry of the future is likely to be simple.[5b]

For[17a] not only poetry, but literature and art in general,[20] are becoming[14a] more specialized[3e]: the process is implicit in the process of modern civilization.[22c] The important works of to-day, unlike those of the past,[5c] tend to appeal only at the highest level of response, which only a tiny minority can reach,[12] instead of at a number of levels.[3f] On the other hand,[17b] the final values[3g] are ceasing to be a matter of even conventional concern for any except the minority capable of the highest level.[12] Everywhere below, a process of standardization, mass-production and levelling-down goes forward,[8c] and civilization is coming to mean a solidarity achieved by the exploitation

of the most readily released[8d] responses.[M] So that poetry in the future,[5b] if there is poetry, seems likely to matter even less in the world.[14b/22d]

Those who care about it can only go on caring.[13]

EXAMINATION

3. WHAT?

(*a*) **The ordinary cultivated reader is ceasing to be able to read poetry.**

Does Dr. Leavis mean that the readers he has in mind are becoming unable to read a particular sort of modern poetry? If so, what sort? He cannot mean 'any sort of poetry' because he admits that such readers can still assimilate a sort of poetry 'superficially familiar' to them.

(*b*) **He has, moreover, lost the education that in the past was provided by tradition and social environment.**

What sort of education? The word 'moreover' makes it clear that it was not a sort of education that made him able to respond to 'unaccustomed and subtle signals'. Nor is 'education' defined by 'social environment'. Everyone has *some* sort of social environment.

(*c*) **Even the poetry of simple sensibility, if it is not superficially familiar. . . .**

'Superficially'? Does this perhaps mean 'generally'? For 'superficial' introduces a confusing antithesis between superficial and fundamental familiarity.

(*d*) **And the more important poetry of the future is likely to be simple.**

Important to whom? And judged by what standard?

(*e*) **For not only poetry, but literature and art in general, are becoming more specialized: . . .**

In what respect?

(*f*) **The important works of to-day . . . tend to appeal only at the highest level of response, which only a tiny minority can reach, instead of at a number of levels.**

Are these levels determined by social environment — which is the only clue so far given? It is not clear either in this passage, or elsewhere in the book from which it is quoted, whether or not Dr. Leavis is postulating that some people can 'respond to', or understand, poems which require a high level of intelligence, and that others cannot. And what does he mean by 'response'? Here he is perhaps thinking of poems requiring recognition of their truth, but these he sentimentalizes by introducing the word 'appeal', with its popular associations of murder-cases and sex-glamour.

He writes about appealing 'at a level'. In his own terms he probably means appealing to people whose education has given them a 'high level of response' — that is, appealing to people who can respond to high demands upon their intelligence. The rest of the sentence perhaps means that, formerly, important works had elements in them which appealed to lower levels of intelligence as well as to higher.

(*g*) **On the other hand, the final values are ceasing to be a matter of even conventional concern . . .**

What are the final values? Values finally arrived at by centuries of critical refinement, or values suggested by such final considerations as 'death', 'salvation', 'immortality', 'ultimate truth'?

5. WHEN?

(*a*) **The ordinary cultivated reader . . . has . . . lost the education that in the past was provided by tradition and social environment.**

Is 'the past' the early life of the reader? Or is it the Victorian period?

(*b*) **. . . the more important poetry of the future is likely to be simple.**

. . . So that poetry in the future, if there is any poetry, seems likely to matter even less in the world.

How does Dr. Leavis distinguish, in time, between these irreconcilable futures?

(*c*) **The important works of to-day, unlike those of the past . . .**

What is this past? If one goes far enough back into the past of English literature, say to Caedmon, one finds that only an appalling simplicity of response is required.

8. INAPPROPRIATE WORD OR PHRASE

(*a*) **. . . when the signals for unaccustomed and subtle responses present themselves.**

'Signals' are prearranged. 'Stimuli' is probably the psychological word needed.

(*b*) **. . . when the signals . . . present themselves.**

Signals do not 'present themselves': they are presented.

(*c*) **Everywhere below, a process . . . goes forward, . . .**

People 'go forward'; processes 'continue'.

(*d*) **. . . the most readily released responses.**

A response may be 'elicited' but hardly 'released', as a flood of tears or pent-up laughter may be.

9. AMBIGUOUS WORD OR PHRASE

Even the poetry of simple sensibility . . . seems incomprehensible to him.

Does this mean poems written by people whose sensibilities are simple? Or poems that appeal to people of simple sensibility? Or poems which are 'simple and sensuous' by Matthew Arnold's definition?

12. DUPLICATION

. . . the highest level of response, which only a tiny minority can reach, . . .

. . . any except a minority capable of the highest level.

This restatement could have been avoided.

13. SELF-EVIDENT STATEMENT

Those who care about it can only go on caring.

Since 'those' people are defined only as the ones who care for poetry, they can obviously 'only go on caring' – because they have no other characteristic capacity.

14. MATERIAL OMISSION

(*a*) **The ordinary cultivated reader . . . amid the perpetual avalanche of print . . .**

. . . literature and art in general are becoming more specialized: the process is implicit in the process of modern civilization.

. . . civilization is coming to mean a solidarity achieved by the exploitation of the most readily released responses.

The argument as it stands is illogical:

Literature goes on perpetually.
Its tendency is to become more specialized.
This is part of the process of civilization.
Civilization means standardization,
with a consequent disappearance of specialized literature.

What is needed is a note that the tendency to specialization in literature is a transitional one, affecting only a cultivated public which will eventually be liquidated.

(*b*) **So that poetry in the future, if there is poetry, seems likely to matter even less in the world.**

What has been omitted from the argument is a consideration of the publishing problem. The disappearance of high-class poetry because of the 'avalanche' of non-poetical printed matter should have been made analogous with the disappearance of high-class goods because of the avalanche of mass-produced ones.

17. FAULTY CONNEXION

(*a*) **And the more important poetry of the future is likely to be simple. For not only poetry, but literature and art in general, are becoming more specialized.**

'For' contradicts the preceding sentence.

(*b*) **The important works of to-day, unlike those of the past, tend to appeal only at the highest level of response . . . On the other hand, the final values are ceasing to be a matter of . . . concern for any except the minority capable of the highest level.**

'On the other hand' should be 'and', unless there is a contrast intended between the 'important works of to-day' and 'final values'.

20. IRRELEVANCY

For . . . art in general is becoming more specialized.

This may be true, but what musicians and sculptors do has no obvious relevance to the 'perpetual avalanche of print'.

22. OVER-EMPHASIS

(*a*) **. . . amid the perpetual avalanche of print he has had to acquire reading habits that incapacitate him when the signals for unaccustomed and subtle responses present themselves.**

Hardly 'incapacitate'. Dr. Leavis, like ourselves, has formed self-protective reading habits; but they do not seem to have incapacitated him, as they have not incapacitated us, from responding to difficult poetry, once it is recognized as not unnecessarily difficult. 'Disinclined' is perhaps the word intended.

(*b*) **Even the poetry of simple sensibility . . . seems incomprehensible to him.**

Not 'incomprehensible'; only (perhaps) 'unnecessary'.

(*c*) **. . . the process is implicit in the process of modern civilization.**

Why not 'in that of modern civilization'?

(*d*) **. . . Poetry in the future, . . . seems likely to matter even less in the world.**

Where else than 'in the world'? This is perhaps a slip for 'than now'.

23. LOGICAL WEAKNESS

The ordinary cultivated reader is ceasing to be able to read poetry.

But 'cultivation', according to Dr. Leavis's thesis, includes the ability to read poetry. If, therefore, the ordinary reader ceases to be able to read poetry, he ceases to qualify as 'cultivated'.

A. MISMATING OF METAPHORS

In self-defence amid the perpetual avalanche of print he has had to acquire reading habits . . .

No one can form habits amid an ordinary avalanche, let alone a freakishly perpetual one. Instead, one gets out of its path.

M. TOO MUCH ALLITERATION

. . . most readily released responses . . .

'Round the rugged rocks the ragged rascals rush, running rural races.'

One can usually avoid distractive alliteration without injury to the sense:

'About the rugged rocks the tattered scoundrels pelt, in country steeple-chases.'

Or, here: '. . . readily elicited responses.'

FAIR COPY

'The tradition that everyone of respectable social standing should be a reader of the best contemporary poetry [?] has now lapsed. Indeed, many of those who pass for cultured persons are fast losing their taste for it, perhaps because in their daily business they must struggle through so much reading-material of all sorts that they form a self-protective habit of disregarding whatever does not have immediate intelligibility and pertinence [?]: even the simplest contemporary poem, unless it reminds them vaguely of something that they once enjoyed reading at school, [?] seems to have no excuse for not being written in straightforward prose [?]. Yet the poets whom I regard as important because . . . [?] . . . are not trying, by a simplification of their work, to redeem this vanishing public. (Nor, by the way, are men of letters, artists and musicians, when faced with analogous difficulties.) Instead, they are addressing a public that specializes in poetic intelligence — one that is very small indeed, in comparison with that addressed by, say, poets of the mid-Victorian period, when even the less well educated readers of books professed a polite concern for "final", as opposed to ephemeral, values.

These modern poets are not to blame for the smallness of their available public: almost the whole population of Britain has fallen in with a new development of civilization — the mass-production of commodities, standardized in quality and style below the level of what has hitherto been considered good taste. In the publishing industry this means that the market is supplied largely with ephemeral reading matter, designed for the busy or the ill-educated, and with little poetry upon which anyone could exercise his intelligence. If this process of "levelling-down" continues, all poets who wish to publish their work will gradually be obliged to conform to it; nor can anything be done by people who, like myself, hold that poets should not toady to the commercial publishing system [?]. It may even eventually happen that no more poetry of any sort will be written.'

COMMENT

Dr. Leavis feels himself to be carrying the white man's cultural burden in an increasingly barbarian world. Despair prevents him from making his argument into more than a series of disjointed laments. The subject he professes at Cambridge being English literature, he can himself, in the course of the day's work, 'release his responses' to literature 'at the highest level'. Yet he feels himself almost alone. Besides, he is stunned by the 'avalanche of print' to which his scholastic duties subject him, and has in consequence acquired regrettably careless reading habits for all but specialized literature. His correspondingly careless writing habits are illustrated here: the chief fault being a failure to define any of the principal words used. Literary criticism should consist largely of precise definitions of the terms it employs. To turn such a remark as, for example, 'I regard this biography of Genghis Khan as important' into literary criticism, one would have to add, for example: 'because, though written in a lifeless style, it is the first one published in Europe to contain pertinent extracts from Chinese and Persian historians'. Or: 'because it is the only one which relates Genghis's cavalry tactics to modern theories of mechanized warfare'.

CECIL DAY LEWIS

from *A Hope for Poetry*, 1935

TEXT

A century and a half ago English poetry left those formal gardens brought to perfection by Dryden and Pope, where now[20] their successors seemed able only to raise forced blooms and artificial flowers,[8a] and went into the wilderness for a change of air, a transfusion[8b] of blood.[16] There Blake built a chapel to an unrecognized[1a] god, and Wordsworth heard on his mountain-sides the still, small voice[7] of gods almost forgotten. Coleridge went to sea with an ancient mariner and was made immortal on those[3a] uncharted waters, though[17a] he returned[4a] from them a ghost.[F1] The boy, Keats, like Thomas

the Rhymer, was rapt[8c/14] by a belle dame sans merci; and rode with her across the frontiers of fancy. We[1b] had many a hearty laugh at their antics, their wild-goose chases, but as the years went by we began to see that they had made the wilderness blossom like a rose. So it was roses, roses all the way, for a while[1c]: the full-blooded[8d] frank, romantic rose; till under the strain of constant crossings and variations,[1d] it lost its scent.[23] Yes,[17b] that desert is[5a] populous now. Where the first romantic poets staked their claims,[8e] there are great cities, and many budding townships that follow their style of architecture.[3b] Tennyson, the master-builder of verse, is running up[9] his monumental buildings with one eye on Beauty and the other on Queen Victoria.[3c] But something has been happening.[13] Little rifts and cracks are beginning to appear in the whole, bland, ecclesiastical façade of Victorian England,[4b] and some of the more sensitive occupants are feeling the wind. There are tremors beneath our[1e] feet, and a great din of grouting[8f] fills our ears, through which we can dimly hear[1e] the voice of Matthew Arnold calling upon poetry to save our souls. At this interesting moment a Latin scholar, A. E. Housman,[25] flinging round him a mantle of stoicism, broke[5b] out into a pure, unrivalled burst of song, the last ecstasy we were to hear[8g] for many a long day[1f]; and as suddenly fell silent: while a young Jesuit, Gerard Manley Hopkins,[25] slipped off unnoticed[11] and took a train for an unknown destination.[F2]

EXAMINATION

1. WHO?

(*a*) **. . . Blake built a chapel to an unrecognized god . . .**

Who did not recognize this god? Blake recognized him well enough to build a chapel to him.

(*b*) **We had many a hearty laugh . . .**

Who are 'we', the contemporary spectators of these antics? Mr. Day Lewis himself was not alive at the time, and is not even sympathetic with the sort of people — perhaps he means Samuel Rogers and his associates — who stood for poetic formality in the late eighteenth, and early nineteenth, century.

(*c*) **. . . it was roses, roses all the way for a while . . .**

For whom? For someone travelling somewhere — that is all one learns.

(*d*) **. . . till under the strain of constant crossings and variations . . .**

Who were the gardeners? Not the original Romantic poets?

(*e*) **. . . there are tremors beneath our feet and a great din of grouting fills our ears, through which we can dimly hear . . .**

Who are 'we'? The Victorians of the Eighteen-Nineties?

(*f*) **. . . A. E. Housman . . . broke out into . . . song . . . the last ecstasy we were to hear for many a long day . . .**

Evidently 'we' survived the Victorians and lived on until Housman published his second book of poems about forty years later.

3. WHAT?

(*a*) **Coleridge went to sea, . . . and was made immortal on those uncharted waters . . .**

What waters?

(*b*) **. . . there are great cities, and many budding townships that follow their style of architecture.**

Unless we know in what style the cities are built we cannot guess that of the townships.

(*c*) **Tennyson, . . . is running up his monumental buildings with one eye on Beauty and the other on Queen Victoria.**

Meaning that he not only did not watch what he was doing, but squinted?

4. WHERE?

(*a*) **. . . poetry left those formal gardens . . . and went into the wilderness . . . Coleridge went to sea . . . and was made immortal on those uncharted waters though he returned from them a ghost.**

The general context suggests that Coleridge, along with other romantic poets, went into the wilderness with Poetry and staked a claim there. But did he go to sea from the wilderness, or from the formal garden? And to which did he return?

(*b*) **. . . English poetry . . . went into the wilderness . . .**
. . . Where the first romantic poets staked their claims. . . . there are great cities. . . . But something has been happening. Little rifts and cracks are beginning to appear in the whole bland, ecclesiastical façade of Victorian England, . . . There are tremors beneath our feet, . . .

Where are 'we'? The wilderness metaphor has relevance only in the poetry context; the buildings are presumably poems. Now apparently the breakdown of the social, as opposed to the poetical, structure of Victorian England is being written about: the buildings are institutions and religious or political beliefs. This is in contradiction to the poetical context, because the romantic tradition of Blake, Coleridge, Keats, Shelley, Byron, Darley, was not ecclesiastical – and Wordsworth only wrote his 'Ecclesiastical Sonnets' when he had long repudiated his romanticism.

5. WHEN?

(*a*) **Yes, that desert is populous now . . .**

'Now' must be 1935, since the story started with 'a century and a half ago' and a mention of Blake, Wordsworth and Coleridge. But this is contradicted by 'Tennyson is running up his monumental buildings' . . .

(*b*) **. . . the voice of Matthew Arnold calling upon poetry to save our souls. At this interesting moment . . . A. E. Housman, . . . broke out into . . . song . . . and as suddenly fell silent: . . .**

Housman's *Shropshire Lad* appeared some years after Matthew Arnold's Oxford lectures on poetry. And why has Mr. Lewis put the romantic poets in the past, the mid-Victorians in the present and the more recent Housman and Hopkins again in the past? Does this imply that Housman and Hopkins are less immediate than the Victorians? Is it a subtle device to make readers feel kinship with the Victorians who gallantly carried on, though their facades were cracking?

7. HOW MANY?

. . . Wordsworth heard on his mountain-sides the still, small voice of gods . . .

This reference to Wordsworthian pantheism is intelligible only if more than one voice was heard.

8. INAPPROPRIATE WORD OR PHRASE

(*a*) **. . . where now their successors seemed able to raise only forced blooms and artificial flowers . . .**

Artificial flowers are not 'raised', except perhaps by fakirs and mediums, which the successors of Pope certainly were not.

(*b*) **A century and a half ago . . . poetry . . . went into the wilderness for a change of air, a transfusion of blood.**

Experiments in the transfusion of blood had been carried out since the seventeenth century, but only by skilled surgeons in fully-equipped city hospitals, never in the wilderness. And what blood-donor did Poetry expect to find in the wilderness, even if she was bent on being her own surgeon? The Phœnix and the Unicorn? Perhaps what is meant is 'a cleansing of her blood'.

(*c*) **The boy, Keats, . . . was rapt by a belle dame sans merci, . . .**

Does he mean rapt up? If he means merely 'rapt', in the obsolete sense of 'raped', the word can only be used of the action of a man against a woman, not contrariwise.

(*d*) **. . . full-blooded . . . rose . . .**

In the U.S.A., Red Indians, Yankees and merino sheep can be full-blooded, but neither in the U.S.A. nor in the British Isles can a rose be so.

(*e*) **Where the first romantic poets staked their claims . . .**

But, according to Mr. Lewis, neither Blake, Wordsworth, Coleridge nor Keats went to the wilderness as gold-diggers or oil-drillers. They built chapels, mused on mountain-sides, went sailing or riding, chased geese, planted roses; but did nothing more practical.

(*f*) **. . . a great din of grouting fills our ears . . .**

'Grouting' in Victorian England meant either 'pouring liquid cement into fissures', or (of pigs) 'rooting for food'. In the first sense 'grouting' is noiseless, in the second it is inapplicable to the context. He probably means 'repointing' — a process of scraping away crumbled mortar with a trowel and then making good.

(*g*) **. . . the last ecstasy we were to hear . . .**

Properly, one does not 'hear' an ecstasy, but witnesses it.

9. AMBIGUOUS WORD OR PHRASE

Tennyson, the master-builder of verse, is running up his monumental buildings with one eye on Beauty and the other on Queen Victoria.

Is Tennyson indulging in master-builder antics by running up the buildings as a spider would? Or as a jerry-builder 'runs up' a villa? 'Monumental' does not suggest jerry-building.

11. UNINTENTIONAL CONTRAST

. . . A. E. Housman, . . . broke out into a pure, unrivalled burst of song . . . while a young Jesuit, Gerard Manley Hopkins, slipped off unnoticed . . .

This suggests that Hopkins slipped off unnoticed because he could not rival Housman in purity of song, and that he was younger than Housman at the time. Neither suggestion is warranted.

13. SELF-EVIDENT STATEMENT

But something has been happening.

A great many things seem to have been happening.

14. MATERIAL OMISSION

The boy, Keats, like Thomas the Rhymer, was rapt by a belle dame sans merci . . .

Thomas the Rhymer's fairy was benignant; the difference between his experience and that of the boy Keats should have been made clear.

16. UNDEVELOPED THEME

. . . English poetry left those formal gardens brought to perfection by Dryden and Pope. . . . and went into the wilderness for a change of air, a transfusion of blood.

We hear no more about the Goddess and the success of her mission, but only about her votaries — who seem to have 'gone whoring after other gods in the wilderness', in Hebrew fashion.

17. FAULTY CONNEXION

(*a*) **. . . Coleridge . . . was made immortal on those uncharted waters, though he returned from them a ghost.**

If the form of immortality that Coleridge achieved at sea was to become a ghost — ghosts certainly are said not to die — then 'though' should be 'for'.

(*b*) **. . . they had made the wilderness blossom like a rose. So it was roses, roses all the way . . . the full-blooded, frank, romantic rose; till . . . it lost its scent. Yes, that desert is populous now.**

'Yes' reaffirms a surprising statement (e.g. 'Rosie Flynn lighted her dudheen and drew a few contented puffs. Yes, Rosie was smoking again now, as though she had never been away from her dear old cabin.') Here there has been nothing said about the desert's repopulation: only that four poets visited it on wild-goose chases and that roses (apparently) sprang up where they trod.

20. IRRELEVANCY

A century and a half ago English poetry left those formal gardens brought to perfection by Dryden and Pope, where now their successors seemed able to raise only forced blossoms . . .

'Now' is irrelevant and confusing, since the date has already been given as *circa* 1785.

23. LOGICAL WEAKNESS

. . . it was roses, roses all the way . . . the full-blooded, frank, romantic rose; till under the strain of constant crossings and variations, it lost its scent.

The constant crossings of the frank, romantic rose may have deprived it of its scent, but do not account for its no longer being strewn in quantities on the roads.

25. MIXED CATEGORY

Dryden, Pope, the boy Keats, Coleridge, Wordsworth, Tennyson, A. E. Housman, Gerard Manley Hopkins.

There is perhaps a faint excuse for using initials to distinguish Housman, the poet, from his brother the playwright. 'Matthew Arnold' is also perhaps excusable, because of Sir Edwin Arnold. But if 'Gerard Manley Hopkins' is described in full why not 'Samuel Taylor Coleridge', 'Alfred, Lord Tennyson' and so on? There are no other famous Hopkinses in recent literature.

F. OBSCURE REFERENCE

(1) **Coleridge . . . was made immortal on those uncharted waters, though he returned from them a ghost.**

Perhaps this means that after the year in which he wrote *The Ancient Mariner*, the first part of *Christabel* and *Kubla Khan*, Coleridge faded out as a poet – a false view, but so often quoted that, if one had to guess the meaning of this extremely difficult sentence, it is what one would guess.

(2) **. . . Hopkins took a train for an unknown destination.**

This cannot refer to his taking Holy Orders – he was already a Jesuit. Does it refer to his death? Or to his temporary abandonment of verse? Or to his poems not having been collected until many years after his death? Why a train? A train suggests that he travelled in crowded company. Why not a fiery chariot?

FAIR COPY

'A century and a half ago, English poets began to desert the formal gardens which Dryden and Pope had brought to perfection and where their successors seemed able to raise only forced and hot-house blooms, and went out, singly, into the wilderness. There one of them, Blake, built a chapel to a god not known before, and another, Wordsworth, heard on mountain-sides the still small voices of gods almost forgotten. A third, Coleridge, came to an inland sea [?], an uncharted waste of waters, which he crossed, and recrossed, in the company of an ancient mariner; stepping ashore at last a sadder and a wiser man. Then the boy Keats, like Thomas the Rhymer, was rapt away by a fairy and rode with her across the frontiers of Fancy; but she proved to be *La Belle Dame Sans Merci*.

There was laughter from the gardens when news came of these antics and wild-goose chases, but as the years went by it was learned that the pioneers had "made the wilderness to blossom like the rose". An army of settlers went out to the new country, and it was roses, roses all the way – blooms from the sturdy tree of romance. But the settlers crossed these roses with the effete varieties that they had brought with them, and bred away the scent.

The desert soon became populous. Where the first romantic poets had camped, great cities rose, and many budding townships, all in the same pseudo-Gothic literary style. Tennyson, the master-builder of verse, erected monumental buildings to a design which proved his double loyalty — to Beauty and to Queen Victoria. But soon little rifts and cracks appeared in the façades of the newer buildings, and some of the more sensitive occupants felt the wind. There were tremors beneath their feet, and through a great clatter of trowels, as masons repointed the walls, came dimly the voice of one Matthew Arnold calling upon Poetry for salvation. Presently, Housman, a young Latin scholar, flung round him the stoic's mantle, broke into a pure burst of song, and fell silent again — while a young Jesuit, Hopkins, thrusting a paper of verses into a coffer, slipped off before it might be discovered and applauded.'

COMMENT

This is not a parable, but literary history written in imitation of dream language, with the incidents strung together on a thread of quotations and popular clichés. It is a legitimate way of telling a story, but the ordinary principles of prose apply here just as much as, for example, in the composition of military despatches or blue-books on agriculture. Once Mr. Lewis has started his account with 'A century and a half ago English poetry left those formal gardens . . .' he is committed to a narrative of events from the standpoint of the year in which he is writing. But if he wishes to use the historic present: 'Tennyson . . . is running up his monumental buildings . . . There are tremors beneath our feet . . . We can dimly hear the voice of Matthew Arnold,' then he should start off with, say: 'Poetry, heaving a sigh, lifts her swathed and anaemic limbs from an ottoman by the carp-pool. . . .' He should then keep to the historic present, not changing back to 'A. E. Housman *broke* out into a pure, unrivalled burst of song.'

DESMOND MACARTHY

from his Weekly Column of Literary Criticism, 1940

TEXT

Of latter-day[9a] poets I like Louis MacNeice as well as any. His muse attracts me,[12] and I like the balance that he keeps as a poet between his body and his mind.[9b]

Such expressions of personal preference are not, I know, criticism, and they have the disadvantage of drawing more attention to the critic[22] than to the author he is writing about.[23] But I have written often enough on[8] this page for them to suggest something, even if it is only a negative,[3] about any poet I am about to[5] discuss.

EXAMINATION

3. WHAT?

Such expressions of personal preference are not, I know, criticism . . .

But I have written often enough on this page for them to suggest something, even if it is only a negative, about any poet I am about to discuss.

Are we to understand this as meaning that his personal preferences have no positive value as criticism, but may lead his readers to some critical conclusion – though, indeed, as in a photographic negative, the conclusion may be exactly the wrong way round, and with all its blacks and whites interchanged? Or does 'a negative about any poet . . .' mean 'a warning against reading any poet'?

5. WHEN?

Such expressions of personal preference . . . I have written often enough on this page for them to suggest something about any poet I am about to discuss.

Here the expression of personal preference does begin the article, but this is not an invariable rule with Mr. Macarthy.

8. INAPPROPRIATE WORD OR PHRASE

. . . I have written often enough on this page . . .

He does not write *on* this page, but *for* it.

9. AMBIGUOUS WORD OR PHRASE

(*a*) **Of latter-day poets I like Louis MacNeice as well as any.**

The adjective 'latter-day' has a definite meaning only when used by the Mormons (who first coined it): 'of the new religious dispensation consigned to Joseph Smith Junior'. But Louis MacNeice is not a Mormon. Wherever 'latter-day' is a playful word for 'modern', one must be told at what point the former days ended and the latter days began. Here, did the dividing line come between Homer and Aeschylus or between, say, Aubrey de Vere and T. S. Eliot?

(*b*) **. . . I like the balance that he keeps as a poet between his body and his mind.**

Does this mean that Mr. Macarthy knows of Louis MacNeice's way of living, and approves of it, or merely that he approves of his way of writing?

12. DUPLICATION

Of latter-day poets I like Louis MacNeice as well as any. His muse attracts me.

If it can be assumed that the first sentence means that Mr. Macarthy likes at least some of these poets, then the second sentence is unnecessary.

22. OVER-EMPHASIS

I like Louis MacNeice . . . His muse attracts me . . . Such expressions of personal preference . . . have the disadvantage of drawing more attention to the critic than to the author . . .

This is not the case, except perhaps where the author's work is so well known that a critic is judged by his opinion of it. In this case, far more people had read Desmond Macarthy than had read Louis MacNeice, and public attention therefore would focus on MacNeice – a latter-day poet with an attractive Muse, awarded two columns of praise on the most important Sunday literary page.

23. LOGICAL WEAKNESS

Such expressions of personal preference are not, I know, criticism, and they have the disadvantage of drawing more attention to the critic than to the author he is writing about.

But since what he writes is not criticism, he is not a critic.

FAIR COPY

'Of the younger contemporary poets, I like Louis MacNeice as well as any, perhaps because of the balance he keeps in his work between physical and spiritual interests [?]. That I cannot account more critically than this for my preference is a pity, since I profess to write here as a critic – a critic should not divert the attention of his readers from the work which he is examining to his own appetites and prejudices. However, readers of this page will by now have learned to do some of my critical work for me. If I happen to say that I like a poet, this must suggest some positive critical judgement to them – even perhaps that he is below their notice!'

COMMENT

Mr. Desmond Macarthy seems to have few fixed critical values to which he can refer in his weekly column, and has to rely on conversational fluency to fill it. Occasionally, as here, he realizes the anomaly of being regarded as a critic when all that he can conscientiously offer is amusing literary journalism; the embarrassment makes him write with less readability than he usually does.

It may amuse our readers to analyse a paragraph from another conversational book-review by Mr. Macarthy:

> 'I salute cleverness in young or old: but it was not that which made me mourn [Nigel Weir] while I read as if I had known him well; nor was I regretting the loss of a fine poet-to-be. He might have become one, but do not expect to find in these pages poetry of high excellence. But value, if you can see it still through a telescope, the eager, beautiful sincerity of youth, which does not necessarily show itself in celebrating joys, but while the capacity to feel them is keenest, wonders and worries which are best.'

We suggest that this would have read more clearly as follows:

> 'I admire cleverness in the young as I do in the old – and Nigel Weir was very clever; but when I read this book it was not merely the loss of a clever young writer that made me mourn as deeply as if I had known him personally; nor was it the loss of a poet – he might have become one, but I cannot honestly credit him with high poetic achievement. Rather, it was the loss of a young man who was both eager and sincere. Elderly people who, like myself, can still recognize

the beauty of such sincerity (descried as it were through a telescope) should always salute and prize it, even where it does not show itself in the celebration of youthful joys, but — while the senses are at their keenest — in anxious debate as to which joys are the best.'

BRIGADIER-GENERAL J. H. MORGAN, K.C.[1]

from a Newspaper Article, 1940

TEXT

During the years 1920-1923,[5a] when the Disarmament Commission in Berlin had Hitler and his furtive[8a] activities 'under observation'[3a] in Bavaria, we all[1] knew that Ludendorff's political foundling[8b/H1] had been put out[4] to nurse[3b/5b] by the Reichswehr officers quartered in Bavaria, who taught him all he knew.[22a]

He learnt from them to lisp[8c] the teaching of the German War Book [a Clausewitzian handbook for Army officers] and palmed off its doctrines[5b/H2] on a credulous German public[A] in an illiterate paraphrase[22b] known as 'Mein Kampf'.[24] In him Prussian militarism has, as it were,[20] touched bottom.[14] It has sunk to its lowest depths.[12]

EXAMINATION

1. WHO?

During the years 1920-1923, when the Disarmament Commission in Berlin had Hitler and his furtive activities 'under observation' in Bavaria, we all knew that . . .

Was General Morgan a member of the Commission? He does not say so.

3. WHAT?

(*a*) **. . . the Disarmanment Commission had Hitler and his furtive activities 'under observation' . . .**

Why the inverted commas? Did the Allied Commission detail agents to shadow Hitler, or did they not?

(*b*) **Ludendorff's political foundling had been put out to nurse by the Reichswehr officers . . . who taught him all he knew.**

What does this mean? That he was sent by these officers for political instruction to some school? If so, what did he imbibe from his 'nurse', since it was apparently the officers themselves who taught him all he knew? Was it just wind?

4. WHERE?

We all knew that Ludendorff's political foundling had been put out to nurse by the Reichswehr officers quartered in Bavaria, . . .

Where was he put out to nurse? Elsewhere than in Bavaria?

[1] Vice-Chairman, Government Committee of Inquiry into Breaches of the Laws of War, 1919.

5. WHEN?

(*a*) **During the years 1920-1923 . . . we all knew that Ludendorff's political foundling . . .**

Hitler did not get into touch with Ludendorff until the middle of 1923.

(*b*) **During the years 1920-1923, we all knew that Ludendorff's political foundling had been put out to nurse by the Reichswehr officers quartered in Bavaria. . . .**

He learned from them to lisp the teaching of the German War Book and palmed off its doctrines . . . in an illiterate paraphrase known as 'Mein Kampf'.

It is not made clear that Hitler published *Mein Kampf* after, not during, the 1920-1923 period.

8. INAPPROPRIATE WORD OR PHRASE

(*a*) **. . . the Disarmament Commission had Hitler and his furtive activities 'under observation' . . .**

Perhaps he means 'sinister' activities. Hitler had ceased to act furtively by 1920. Towards the end of 1922 'he would engage the fourteen largest halls in Munich for a single night and dash from one Party meeting to the other in a powerful car' (Harold Nicolson, M.P.).

(*b*) **. . . we all knew that Ludendorff's political foundling . . .**

When Hitler became General Ludendorff's ally about the middle of 1923 he brought with him a large and well-organized party. If either of the two was the other's political foundling, it was Ludendorff who was Hitler's.

(*c*) **He learned from them to lisp the teaching of the German War Book. . . .**

Hitler never lisped. He had always been phenomenally eloquent and clear-toned.

12. DUPLICATION

In him Prussian militarism has, as it were, touched bottom. It has sunk to its lowest depths.

Where one touches bottom it is clear that one can sink no lower. The second sentence is therefore unnecessary.

14. MATERIAL OMISSION

In him Prussian militarism has, as it were, touched bottom.

Hitler was an Austrian and had served in the Bavarian Army only. It should be made clear that he derived his Prussian militarism from 'the German War Book', and from the Reichswehr officers who had been trained on it.

20. IRRELEVANCY

In him Prussian militarism has, as it were, touched bottom.

Since 'touched bottom' is an accepted phrase there seems to be no need to apologize for it with 'as it were'.

22. OVER-EMPHASIS

(*a*) **. . . the Reichswehr officers . . . who taught him all he knew.**

They did not teach him how to sway public meetings and build up a party; it was these self-taught arts that made him valuable to them.

(*b*) **. . . in an illiterate paraphrase known as 'Mein Kampf' . . .**

Mein Kampf is Hitler's autobiography, not a mere paraphrase of a military handbook and it is not 'known as' *Mein Kampf* (as *Genesis, Exodus, Leviticus, Numbers,* and *Deuteronomy* are known as *The Pentateuch*): that was its title when first published, and still is.

24. CHANGE OF STANDPOINT

. . . 'Mein Kampf' . . .

. . . the German War Book . . .

Either: 'My Struggle' . . . 'The German War Book'

Or: *Mein Kampf . . . Das Deutsches Kriegsbuch.*

A. MISMATING OF METAPHORS

. . . we all knew that Ludendorff's political foundling had been put out to nurse by the Reichswehr officers. . . .

He learned from them to lisp . . . and palmed . . . off . . . on a credulous public . . .

This illiterate foundling, with his foster-nurse's milk still wet on his lips, learns to do successful conjuring tricks in public. General Morgan thus makes a god out of Hitler by ascribing the same sort of prodigies to him as are ascribed to Jesus Christ in the pseudo-Matthew, or to Hermes in the Homeric hymn.

H. ELEGANT VARIATION

(1) **. . . Hitler and his furtive activities . . .**

. . . Ludendorff's political foundling . . .

It is not clear that these two characters are the same; 'who had become Ludendorff's political protégé' would have been a better way of putting it.

(2) **. . . the teaching of the German War Book . . .**

. . . and palmed off its doctrines . . .

There does not seem to be any reason for this variation.

FAIR COPY

'When Hitler made his successful *putsch* towards the end of 1923, in alliance with General Ludendorff, this did not surprise the Allied Disarmament Commission, or myself. Since the beginning of 1920, we had been kept informed, at Berlin, of his sinister activities in Bavaria and were well aware that he had become the protégé of certain Reichswehr officers quartered there. How much of their political theory he had imbibed was shown in the following year when he published his autobiography, *Mein Kampf*. Though this was presented as original to the credulous German public, much of it consisted of a loose paraphrase of passages from the Clausewitzian handbook for Army officers, *Das Deutsches Kriegsbuch*.

Never had the Prussian militaristic faith found so base a proselyte.'

COMMENT

Mentions of Napoleon, Lenin and Hitler have the effect of tempting most writers to insobriety of language. Here General Morgan's passionate resentment of the alliance between Prussian militarists and the Nazi party has led him into an insobriety of language which amounts to a distortion of historical facts.

J. MIDDLETON MURRY

from *Keats and Shakespeare,* 1925

TEXT

The history of the souls of those men whose writings[8a] are thus passionately remembered[9] is to me,[20a] by the very fact of that passionate remembrance,[12a/K] not indeed the outward and visible but the inward and spiritual[20b] history of the human soul. For these are the men who have uttered a truth[7a] so mysterious[3a] that it cannot be wrenched apart[22a] from the words in which they uttered it; it cannot be made current or passed from lips to lips save in that living flesh of speech with which they clothed it.[A/12b] Not this abstraction nor that commonplace can contain their wisdom[3b]; it is what it is and cannot be translated.[12c] Through their words[1a] men have touched what they[1b] do not understand, yet cannot[8b] forgo.[8c]

Shall we[1c] take our courage in both[7b] hands and say mysteriously[22b] that they[2] have touched[8d] their own souls?[16] There is nothing men understand less than their own souls, or[8e] more passionately desire to remember.[11/K]

EXAMINATION

1. WHO?

(*a*) **Through their words men have touched what they do not understand . . .**

Are 'their words' the words of the men who touch, or of the men who utter a mysterious truth?

(*b*) **. . . men have touched what they do not understand . . .**

If 'their words' are those of the men who utter a mysterious truth, are 'they' the men who utter or the men who touch?

(*c*) **Shall we take our courage in both hands and say mysteriously . . .** ?

Who is 'we'? Mr. Murry has used 'to me' so it seems unlikely that 'we' is an editorial 'we'. Is he here identifying himself with the men who have already uttered one truth?

2. WHICH?

Shall we take our courage in both hands and say mysteriously that they have touched their own souls?

Are 'they' the hands which are mystically clasping our courage?

3. WHAT?

(*a*) **For . . . they have uttered a truth so mysterious that it cannot be wrenched apart from the words . . .**

Is the mysteriousness of the truth the reason why it cannot be wrenched apart from its words? Surely it is its lucidity?

(*b*) **Not this abstraction nor that commonplace can contain their wisdom; . . .**

This is, apparently, to deny that any abstraction can be a truth: e.g. "God is love" is not a truth. Nor is it clear whose 'their wisdom' is: 'their' may refer either to 'the words', some distance back, or to the men who utter them. Also, 'this' and 'that' make a contrast which does not explain itself: for some abstractions are extremely commonplace. It may be that by 'abstraction' he means 'abstract', in the sense of a brief summary.

7. HOW MANY?

(*a*) **. . . men who have uttered a truth so mysterious that it cannot be wrenched apart from the words in which they uttered it . . .**

Not '*a* truth'. A truth is a single incontrovertible statement, such as 'A thing of beauty is a joy for ever', or 'Th' expence of spirit in a waste of shame, Is lust in action'. Men utter either 'truths' or 'truth'.

(*b*) **Shall we take our courage in both hands?**

Surely 'we' would use more than two hands? Perhaps the word 'each' has dropped out.

8. INAPPROPRIATE WORD OR PHRASE

(*a*) **. . . those men whose writings are thus passionately remembered . . .**

He means, specifically, poems; spiritual prose-writings can often be translated without loss of inward truth. The Sermon on the Mount, for example, in the version 'passionately remembered' by Mr. Murry, is a translation from Aramaic into Greek and then from Greek into English.

(*b*) **. . . they have touched what they do not understand, yet cannot forgo . . . their souls. There is nothing men understand less or more passionately desire to remember.**

'Cannot' should surely be 'do not wish to'. 'Cannot' suggests that they try to forgo their souls, but find it impossible.

(*c*) **. . . men have touched what they do not understand, yet cannot forgo.**

This turns out to be 'their own souls'. One can be said to forgo (i.e. refrain from) glory; or flesh in Lent; or revenge; or the pleasures of poetry — but not any integral part of oneself.

(*d*) **. . . men have touched what they do not understand . . . their souls . . .**

In poetic experience one's soul is touched, and one is aware that it stirs; but one does not touch it oneself.

(*e*) **There is nothing men understand less . . . or more passionately desire to remember.**

After 'nothing', 'or' should be 'nor'.

9. AMBIGUOUS WORD OR PHRASE

. . . writings . . . passionately remembered . . .

Does this mean that the act of remembering has caused passion? Or that former passions have been re-awakened when things that roused them are remembered? Or that Mr. Murry himself is passionately eager to remember these writings?

12. DUPLICATION

(*a*) **The history of the souls of those men whose writings are thus passionately remembered is to me, by the very fact of that passionate remembrance . . . the inward . . . history of the human soul.**

No need to pile 'passionate remembrance' on 'thus passionately remembered'. Once the peculiarity of the history has been defined — that it is passionately remembered — the argument can proceed.

(*b*) **. . . truth so mysterious that it cannot be wrenched apart from the words in which they uttered it; . . . it cannot be made current . . . save in that living flesh of speech with which they clothed it.**

The second part of the sentence adds nothing to the first.

(*c*) **. . . it is what it is and cannot be translated.**

The same thing again.

14. MATERIAL OMISSION

There is nothing men understand less than their own souls, or more passionately desire to remember.

What men passionately desire to remember is the circumstances in which they have been reassured that they possess souls, not the souls themselves.

16. UNDEVELOPED THEME

Shall we take our courage in both hands and say mysteriously that they have touched their own souls?

Shall we? Or would it sound rather silly?

20. IRRELEVANCY

(*a*) **The history of the souls of those men . . . is to me . . . the spiritual history of the human soul.**

The phrase 'to me' should be reserved for cases where other people's opinions have been quoted and the writer then modestly gives his own. Here the eccentricity of the writing proves it to be all Mr. Murry's own work; 'to me' is unnecessarily modest.

(*b*) **. . . not indeed the outward and visible but the inward and spiritual history of the human soul.**

A reminiscence from the Church Catechism has been dragged in here: 'outward and visible sign of an inward and spiritual grace'. 'Outward' and 'inward' are the only two words that apply, but they trail 'visible' and 'spiritual' along with them. 'Visible' makes no sense, because the spiritual history of the human soul could not be visible; 'spiritual' is unnecessary, because a history of the human soul could only be spiritual.

22. OVER-EMPHASIS

(*a*) **. . . a truth . . . that . . . cannot be wrenched apart from the words in which they uttered it; . . .**

'Wrench' denotes violence: a thief may wrench a handbag from a shopper's hands; a critic may wrench a quotation from its context. But a paraphrase is not an act of violence unless it is intended to supersede the original.

(*b*) **Shall we take our courage in both hands and say mysteriously . . . ?**

It needs no great courage to write mysteriously; it is frank writing that is often shirked.

A. MISMATING OF METAPHORS

. . . passed from lips to lips . . . in that living flesh . . . with which they clothed it.

To pass living flesh from lips to lips is considered rather disgusting in civilized countries, especially where there are skeletons underneath – which is the usual meaning of 'clothed in flesh'.

K. TOO MUCH OF THE SAME WORD

. . . whose writings are thus passionately remembered . . .
. . . the very fact of that passionate remembrance . . .
. . . or more passionately desire to remember . . .

The first two acts of passionate remembrance concern 'writings'; the third concerns something very different – people's souls. Both 'passionate' and 'remember' are becoming tedious.

FAIR COPY

'A memorable poem is not merely the record of one man's spiritual experience, but an epitome of the spiritual history of mankind. And it is made memorable by its inward truth, not by its outward sense. This sense may be given currency in philosophical or colloquial paraphrases, or in foreign translations, whereas the truth is inseparable from the original words which embody it. Though the readers of the poem may be unable to explain why they feel stirred, they never regret the experience: for they have been touched in that part of themselves which they understand less than any other, and of the existence of which they most passionately desire to be reassured – their souls.'

COMMENT

Mr. Murry has often apologized to his readers for the confusion of his thought, but ascribed it to the difficulty of conveying novel and important intuitions of spiritual truth. The confusion is due rather to the mystical ecstasy which overtakes him and blunts his critical sense of what he is writing. Many truths that mystical prose-writers have uttered become less mysterious and therefore more convincing when (as in our Fair Copy of the passage under examination) they are 'wrenched apart from the living flesh of speech' in which they are clothed, and given a sober suit of paraphrase.

SIR CYRIL NORWOOD

(then Headmaster of Harrow School)

from *The English Tradition of Education*, 1929

TEXT

The practical man[8a] who theorizes[14a] is seldom accounted wise by his own generation, or, for that matter, by any other,[8b] and the Headmaster who theorizes may be[8c] a conspicuous example of the saying.[3] Thring is remembered as the creator of Uppingham,[14b] but not as the author[H1] of *Education and School*, which no one would buy,[14c/22a] nor yet as the writer[H1] of the *Theory and Practice of Teaching*, for which he did indeed receive fifty pounds.[14d] Headmasters cannot[8d] even write novels[14e] about school life,[23a] for it is generally agreed that to this poor branch of literature their contributions have been the worst.[8e] They are men of action who should forswear the pen.[22b] If then I venture to tread where many predecessors have fallen, I do so because, like all authors,[22c] I have something which I want at this present time[23b] to say,[H2] and, since it belongs neither to the realms[11] of imagination[8f] nor to the province[11] of pure theory,[23c] I hope that even an active Headmaster[14f] may not be wholly ineffective[G] in stating[H2] it.

EXAMINATION

3. WHAT?

The practical man who theorizes is seldom accounted wise by his own generation, or, for that matter, by any other, and the Headmaster who theorizes may be a conspicuous example of the truth of the saying.

What saying? 'Don't-care was made to care', 'Republicans are always the worst masters', 'Of every ten men eleven have the itch' are typical sayings. There may be a saying 'Men of action should forswear the pen' (though it is not a familiar one), but there certainly is no saying cast in the form: 'The practical man who theorizes is seldom accounted wise by his own generation, or, for that matter, by any other.' Is Sir Cyril trying to give proverbial force to a generalization of his own?

8. INAPPROPRIATE WORD OR PHRASE

(*a*) **The practical man who theorizes is seldom accounted wise by his own generation, or . . . by any other, . . .**

The statement is so patently untrue that one naturally questions whether the word 'practical' is the one meant. A later sentence ' . . . men of action should forswear the pen' suggests that what is meant is: 'men engaged in responsible executive jobs are seldom . . .'

(*b*) **. . . by his own generation, or, for that matter, by any other . . .**

'Or by any other' would have been the right phrase to tag on to a generalization about a theorist not being honoured by his own *country*. Here 'by any later generation' is what is meant.

(*c*) **The practical man who theorizes is seldom accounted wise . . . the Headmaster who theorizes may be a conspicuous example of the truth of the saying.**

'May be' adds an unnecessary qualification to a remark that has already been sufficiently qualified with 'seldom'. What is meant is: . . . 'the Headmaster who theorizes is a conspicuous example of this'.

(*d*) **Headmasters cannot even write novels about school life . . .**

He means 'should not'. They both can and do write them.

(*e*) **. . . to this poor branch of literature their contributions have been the worst.**

The 'worst' suggests that they have been morally the worst, as well as exceedingly dull and ill-constructed. Their badness should be more accurately defined.

(*f*) **. . . Since it belongs neither to the realms of imagination nor to the province of pure theory, . . .**

'Imagination' perhaps refers to the novels about school life, and therefore should have been 'fiction'. He surely does not consider that his own work lacks imagination?

11. UNINTENTIONAL CONTRAST

. . . neither to the realms of imagination nor to the province of pure theory, . . .

It is unlikely that the contrast between 'realms' and 'province' is intended. Of what realm is pure theory a province?

14. MATERIAL OMISSION

(*a*) **The practical man who theorizes is seldom accounted wise . . .**

This perhaps means that, like the proverbial water-beetle who skates easily on the surface of the water 'But if he ever stopped to think just how he did it, he would sink', the executive who stops to think about the general theory of his own profession is unwise: that where tradition does not help him he should trust to instinct and deal with problems empirically. Here 'theorizes' is not enough, since nobody can be practical who does not form theories. For example, even a practical plumber must have a theory as to where a drain is clogged before he sets to work on it. Also, 'or by any other generation' suggests that 'theorizes' is restricted to literary expression; it should be made clear whether this is intended.

(*b*) **Thring is remembered as the creator of Uppingham . . .**

It should have been explained that Uppingham had been, and was, considered a very fine public school; otherwise ignorant readers might take it for the name of a character in a play or novel by a more literary Thring than the Headmaster.

(*c*) **. . .** ***Education and School*****, which no one would buy . . .**

'No one' would buy Shakespeare's *Sonnets* in 1609 or for two centuries later; but this did not mean that Shakespeare, as a practical actor-manager, should have forsworn the pen. It should be indicated here that Thring's theoretical works were on a par with the school-novels, written by Headmasters, which are mentioned in the next sentence.

(*d*) **. . .** ***Theory and Practice of Teaching*****, for which he did indeed receive fifty pounds.**

On the strength of Thring's scholastic reputation some publisher may have bought the book outright for fifty pounds — and may then have sold a great many copies, or very few. The argument suggests that the book did not do much better than the first, but this is not specifically stated.

(*e*) **Headmasters cannot even write novels about school life . . .**

This is an irrelevant remark, unless such novels are cloaks for the unwise theorization which is the subject of this passage.

(*f*) **I hope that even an active Headmaster . . .**

'Such as I am', should have been inserted.

22. OVER-EMPHASIS

(*a*) . . . *Education and School,* **which no one would buy . . .**

Perhaps it only sold two hundred copies, perhaps only fifty; that nobody at all bought it is unbelievable.

(*b*) **They are men of action who should forswear the pen.**

What is meant is perhaps 'the pen with which they record their general theories'. It would be very awkward for a Headmaster to go without a pen altogether.

(*c*) **I do so because, like all authors, I have something which I want at this present time to say.**

Many authors feel no such incentive — as Sir Cyril ought to know from class-room observation of boys composing Latin verses or English essays.

23. LOGICAL WEAKNESS

(*a*) **Headmasters cannot even write novels about school life, for it is generally agreed that to this poor branch of literature their contributions have been the worst.**

That Headmasters have written bad school novels may be a reason for not expecting a good school novel from a Headmaster, but not for pronouncing such a thing to be impossible.

(*b*) **. . . like all authors, I have something which I want at this present time to say.**

'All authors' do not want to say something 'at this present time'. Many are taking a rest, or waiting for an idea.

(*c*) **They are men of action who should forswear the pen.**

If then I venture to tread where many predecessors have fallen, I do so because . . . something which I want to say belongs neither to the realms of imagination nor to the province of pure theory . . .

Unless he literally means that men of action, as such, should not write books of any sort — which would rule out many of the best English writers from Chaucer to the present day — and that therefore he, too, should not write books, then 'if I venture to tread where many predecessors have fallen' must refer to Headmasters who have 'fallen' when writing directly or indirectly about educational theory. Yet unless he also is writing about educational theory, they are not his predecessors; and if he is not, then this excuse for authorship breaks down.

G. CIRCUMLOCUTION

If then I venture to tread where many predecessors have fallen, I do so because, like all authors, I have something which I want at this present time to say . . . and . . . I hope that even an active Headmaster . . . may not be wholly ineffective in stating it.

This means only, 'Undeterred by the literary failures of many other active Headmasters, I am writing because I have something to say.'

H. ELEGANT VARIATION

(1) **. . . as the author of *Education and School* . . .**

. . . as the writer of the *Theory and Practice of Teaching* . . .

There seems to be no reason for this variation.

(2) **. . . something which I want . . . to say . . .**

. . . even an active Headmaster may not be wholly ineffective in stating it.

Nor any reason for this.

FAIR COPY

'Books written about the general theory of a profession by one of its executive members, however able as such he may be, are seldom admired either by his own or by a later generation. Books written by Headmasters about the theory of education are a case in point. Thring is famous for having made Uppingham one of the best public schools in England, not for having written either *Education and School*, which sold wretchedly, or *The Theory and Practice of Teaching*, which did little better – though indeed a publisher paid him fifty pounds for the rights and probably just recovered his outlay [?]. Nor, frankly, did these books deserve a kinder reception. Perhaps Headmasters who are not content merely to follow tradition should restrict themselves to the empiric practice of education: they should avoid theorizing upon it generally, even under the cloak of novels about school-life. (Certainly the dullest and most artificial contributions to that poor branch of literature have, it will be agreed, been written by Headmasters.)

However, though myself an active Headmaster, I remain undeterred by the literary failures of so many of my predecessors, and have here ventured to write about education. I have two excuses: that the impulse to authorship has been irresistible, and that this is a work neither of general theory, nor of theory disguised as fiction, but of school history – and with a direct bearing on present-day problems in education.'

COMMENT

This is the first paragraph of a first book by an eminent Headmaster. He is not sure how to break into his subject, and tries to hide his embarrassment by alternations of pride and humility – ranging himself beside the famous Thring of Uppingham as a man of action – and at the same time hinting that Thring could not write for toffee! (Perhaps he is not so great a Headmaster as Thring, but at least he hopes to be more successful as an author.)

This embarrassment leads him to write in block-phrases, borrowed from the grand oratorical tradition, like those that Headmasters memorize for delivery on school Speech Days:–

... seldom accounted wise by his own generation.

... men of action who should forswear the pen.

If then I venture to tread where many predecessors have fallen ...

It is generally agreed that to this poor branch of literature their contributions have been the worst.

... and, since it belongs neither to the realms of imagination nor to the province of pure theory, I hope that, etc.

The block-phrase system ensures the continuity, but not the logical articulation, of an argument. As a speech this passage would doubtless have carried conviction, the heaviness of the style being relieved by playful intonations; the omission of important links in the argument, and the conversational looseness, would not have been noticed.

Headmasters, like bishops, suffer from an occupational disability: it is very seldom that people venture to criticize their literary style. The headmaster style is usually an uneasy mixture of semi-ecclesiastical oratory, Government Department English, and colloquialisms intended to disarm the natural hostility of schoolboys.

'Observator'

from his Weekly Column in the Sunday Press, 1940

TEXT

The repercussions of the war go into very far corners.[8a] The derangement of the pigeon population[4a] was to be expected — for the bird[H] may be classed as a combatant[3a] — but who would have thought that the casualties on the way home[4b] (through the depredations of the peregrine[9] breed[8b]) would be so heavy that it has[24] been found necessary to enlarge by a depth of ten miles the coastal strip in which the destruction of the peregrine (or[14] its eggs) is permitted? The ornithological gain-and-loss problem[3b] must be very complicated.

EXAMINATION

3. WHAT?

(*a*) **... for the bird may be classed as a combatant ...**

How can pigeons be so classed? Only the carrier-pigeon, a particular breed, is used for military purposes, and even so in a non-combatant capacity. Wood-pigeons, white fantails, pouters, and so on, are not only non-combatant but non-belligerent.

(*b*) **The ornithological gain-and-loss problem must be very complicated.**

Does this mean that it is not clear whether the protection of pigeons, at the expense of the peregrine breed, will or will not be a gain to ornithology, since, though the peregrine is a rare and interesting wild bird, there are many varieties of pigeon which also repay scientific study? Or does it mean that the peregrine preys on other birds besides pigeons, many of them rare and interesting varieties; and that it may therefore be a good plan to keep the peregrine down?

4. WHERE?

(*a*) **The derangement of the pigeon population was to be expected . . .**

Is the pigeon population of London, or of England in general, meant? This was written before other cities had been seriously damaged from the air.

(*b*) **. . . but who would have thought that the casualties on the way home . . .**

Where is 'home' and from where do they start flying?

8. INAPPROPRIATE WORD OR PHRASE

(*a*) **The repercussions of the war go into very far corners.**

A repercussion is the recoil of an explosion, or similar disturbance, against the area of its origin. Whereas ripples caused by a disturbance may be described as going into very far corners of a pool or swimming-bath, a repercussion should be measured in strength, not in extent.

(*b*) **. . . through the depredations of the peregrine breed . . .**

The peregrine falcon is a species, not a breed. Even when it was used for hawking it was not hatched in the mews – the peregrine will not breed in captivity – but taken from the eyrie when an 'eyas'.

9. AMBIGUOUS WORD OR PHRASE

. . . through the depredations of the peregrine breed . . .

'Peregrine' means 'imported from abroad, extraneous'. This suggests that a foreign breed of pigeon (the pigeon being the only sort of bird so far mentioned) has been preying on the domestic breeds. But what is probably meant is 'the peregrine falcon'.

14. MATERIAL OMISSION

. . . the destruction of the peregrine (or its eggs) . . .

One destroys a peregrine, but normally 'takes' its eggs to sell, or give, to oologists. 'Take' is the word usually used in Orders about birds' eggs.

24. CHANGE OF STANDPOINT

. . . who would have thought that the casualties would be so heavy that it has been found . . .

Either: 'who would have thought that the casualties would be so heavy that it would be found . . .'

Or: 'Who would have thought that the casualties would be so heavy? For it has been found . . .'

H. ELEGANT VARIATION

The derangement of the pigeon population was to be expected – for the bird . . .

It would have been better to write 'the pigeon', because 'the pigeon population' means a certain number of pigeons in a given locality, whereas 'the bird' means the pigeon as a kind of bird, and does not correspond with 'the pigeon population'.

FAIR COPY

'The indirect effects of this war are seen in very unexpected places: for example, in an Order deepening by ten miles the coastal strip in which the destruction of the peregrine falcon and the taking of its eggs are permitted. It is not surprising that the pigeon population of London has been thinned by German bombs [?] — for carrier-pigeons at least are employed by the fighting services and are thus legitimate objects of attack, and nobody could expect the Germans to discriminate between one breed and another. But who would have thought that carrier-pigeons flying across the coast on duty would have been killed by peregrines in large enough numbers to justify this Order? Perhaps it will not displease the ornithologists, when they consider that the peregrine preys also upon many birds as rare and interesting as itself.'

COMMENT

The difficulty of understanding this passage is caused by the wilfully jocose hit-or-miss use of words, recalling someone's Uncle Ernest officiating as Father Christmas at a children's party. A hearty laugh or two would ease the tension; but laughs are not recordable in print.

An Editor of the Oxford English Dictionary

from the Historical Introduction

TEXT

[Three lists of works were compiled by the Dictionary Committee, one for the period 1250-1526, another for 1526-1674, the third for 1674-1858.]

This division of the literature into three periods, which originated with Coleridge[9] and was maintained for some time as a basis of collecting,[3a] has a real foundation[A] in fact.[20a/22a] Although the dates 1526 and 1674 were chosen because the former was that of the first printed English New Testament, and the latter[H] the year of Milton's death, they correspond very closely with significant[20b] epochs in the development of the English vocabulary.[14a] If arrived at by accident,[23a] they[14b] at the same time[10a] show a sound instinct for detecting the periods of essential[8a] change[12/16] . . .

At this point it will be well, both[10b] for the sake of greater clearness and of giving credit where credit is due, to give[K] some account[22b] of the method of collecting the material for the Dictionary and of the work done by the voluntary readers and sub-editors.[11] Each member of these two classes stood to the final editors[1] in a relation[14c] similar to that which Socrates in the *Ion* compares to the magnet and the suspended rings, each depending on and

operating through the other, although in the case of the Dictionary the order of their sequence was reversed[3b] . . .

In May 1884 Dr. Murray thought[8b] that with six good assistants 'it might be possible to produce two parts in a year and thus finish the work in eleven years from next March'. This suggestion[8c] was no doubt justified by the facts as they were at the time. That it failed to work out was certainly due in great part to the fact that A was not a good letter[14d] on which to base the calculation, and to a steady increase in the material[14e] which could not at that time be foreseen[23b]. . .

If[8d] various [scientific] errors to be found in standard works are not repeated in the Dictionary, it is frequently because someone with a practical knowledge of the subject[3c] had been[24] specially consulted on the point[3d] and had freely[14f] given the information desired.

EXAMINATION

1. WHO?

. . . the final editors . . .

Who are these? The 'final editors' should mean Drs. Craigie and Onions, since they outlived Drs. Murray and Bradley who had begun the work. But this is not borne out by the context, which suggests that the 'final editors' were those whose decision was final: that is, the editors-in-chief.

3. WHAT?

(*a*) **This division . . . was maintained for some time as a basis of collecting . . .**

The division was not a basis of collecting. The basis was the principle of allotting voluntary collectors certain books to read through in search of illuminating quotations. The division was merely a convenience to the editors in observing this principle.

(*b*) **Each member of these two classes stood to the final editors in a relation similar to that which Socrates in the *Ion* compares to the magnet and the suspended rings, each depending on and operating through the other, although in the case of the Dictionary the order of their sequence was reversed.**

This is a hard problem to solve. We are told that each reader and each sub-editor stood to the 'final editors' (whoever these may have been) as Socrates's magnet and suspended rings all stood to one another, each depending and operating through another of a pair; but that in the case of the Dictionary the order in which the readers and sub-editors and final editors were arranged was the reverse order to that in which the magnet and the various suspended rings were arranged (whatever that may have been). We offer a solution in the Fair Copy; but without much confidence that it is the correct one.

(*c*) **. . . someone with a practical knowledge of the subject . . .**

No subject has been indicated.

(*d*) **. . . had been consulted on the point . . .**

No point has been indicated.

8. INAPPROPRIATE WORD OR PHRASE

(*a*) **. . . a sound instinct for selecting the periods of essential change . . .**

All changes in English are 'essential' in the sense that it is in the nature of English to change. 'Radical' would be too strong a word for what is meant, because an Englishman returning to London in 1536 or 1684 from a ten-year residence abroad would have been able to understand any ordinary conversation; 'remarkable' is perhaps the word needed.

(*b*) **In May 1884 Dr. Murray thought that 'it might be possible . . . '**

The quotation marks make it clear that he translated his thought into writing.

(*c*) **This suggestion was no doubt justified . . .**

Dr. Murray expressed an opinion, but made no suggestion, so far as we know.

(*d*) **If various errors to be found in standard works are not repeated in the Dictionary . . .**

Why 'if'? There is no point in stating as a hypothesis what is known to be a fact.

9. AMBIGUOUS WORD OR PHRASE

This division . . . which originated with Coleridge . . . has a real foundation in fact.

What does 'originated with' mean? H. Coleridge has been mentioned as the Secretary of the Dictionary Committee, but it is not clear whether he himself made the division or whether it was made during his secretaryship by someone else.

10. MISPLACED WORD OR PHRASE

(*a*) **If arrived at by accident, they at the same time show a sound instinct . . .**

The writer means: 'If we admit that they were arrived at by accident, at the same time we must insist that they show . . .' 'At the same time' must therefore come before 'they'; otherwise 'show' should be 'showed'.

(*b*) **. . . it will be well, both for the sake of greater clearness and of giving credit . . .**

Unless 'both' goes after 'sake', one does not recognize 'and of giving' as the expected parallel to 'of greater clearness'.

11. UNINTENTIONAL CONTRAST

. . . of the method of collecting the material for the Dictionary, and of the work done by the voluntary readers and sub-editors.

It was the readers and sub-editors who did the collecting. The form of the sentence makes it seem as though there were other collectors at work.

12. DUPLICATION

. . . they correspond very closely with significant epochs.

. . . they at the same time show a sound instinct for detecting the periods . . . of . . . change.

Much the same thing.

14. MATERIAL OMISSION

(*a*) **. . . development of the English vocabulary . . .**

The word 'vocabulary', where it does not mean 'the range of language commanded by a particular person or class of people', means the 'sum or aggregate of words in a language'. A sum or aggregate cannot develop, it can only be increased or decreased. What is meant is: 'a development of the English language by an increase in the vocabulary'.

(*b*) **... the dates 1526 and 1674 ... show a sound instinct for detecting the periods of essential change.**

The choice of the dates may show a sound instinct for detecting the periods of change; but not the dates themselves, which are uninformative.

(*c*) **... a relation which Socrates in the *Ion* compares to the magnet and the suspended rings. ...**

No: not to the magnet and the suspended rings but to the relation between them.

(*d*) **... A was not a good letter ...**

Had A been completed, or nearly completed, at the time of calculation?

(*e*) **... a steady increase in the material ...**

The increase in the amount of material might be offset by an increase in the speed with which it could be edited and published. This element in the computation should not be slurred over.

(*f*) **If various errors are not repeated ... it is ... because someone has freely given the information.**

The connexion between the avoidance of the error and the gratuitousness of the information is not given.

16. UNDEVELOPED THEME

... the dates 1526 and 1674 correspond very closely with significant epochs in the development of the English vocabulary ... periods of essential change.

Why these dates were significant, and of what, is not explained. Something more should have been said, perhaps about the Renascence and the Restoration.

20. IRRELEVANCY

(*a*) **... a real foundation in fact.**

'Foundation in fact' is a synonym for reality; 'real' is therefore unnecessary.

(*b*) **... significant epochs ...**

An 'epoch' in the sense of a new thing happening is always 'significant' – that is, it illuminates the succeeding age.

22. OVER-EMPHASIS

(*a*) **This division of the literature into three periods ... has a real foundation in fact.**

English literature did not stop for a while in 1526 and 1674 and on each occasion start again in a different style. The most that one should say about the division is that it has advantages over others that might have been suggested.

(*b*) **At this point it will be well, both for the sake of greater clearness and of giving credit where credit is due to give some account ...**

The phrase 'it will be well for the sake of greater clearness to give some account of' means no more than 'we intend to describe'. And 'giving credit where credit is due' is so emphatic as to suggest that credit has been unfairly awarded elsewhere.

23. LOGICAL WEAKNESS

(*a*) **Although the dates 1526 and 1674 were chosen because the former was that of the first printed English New Testament, and the latter the year of Milton's death, they correspond very closely with significant epochs in the development of the English vocabulary. If arrived at by accident, they at the same time show . . .**

It has just been explained that the dates were *not* arrived at by accident, but chosen for their literary associations.

(*b*) **This suggestion was no doubt justified by the facts as they were at the time. That it failed to work out was certainly due in great part to the fact that A was not a good letter on which to base the calculation, and to a steady increase in the material which could not at that time be foreseen.**

The writer sets out to show that Dr. Murray's computation was founded on a misconception, but that the misconception was unavoidable. He asserts this unavoidability, with the qualifications 'no doubt' and 'as they [the facts] were at the time'. The 'no doubt' is perhaps intended to convey 'there is a grave doubt', and 'as they were at the time' is an attempt to furturize the facts of 1884. Yet 'A' was as unfortunate a letter for computative purposes in 1884 as in 1924, and though the increase in the post-1884 vocabulary could not have been accurately forecast, it would have taken Dr. Murray with his six good assistants at least a hundred years, not eleven, to edit the pre-1884 vocabulary. The defiant 'certainly due in great part' clangs the front door of argument shut; but the draught opens a back door of escape – 'in small part'. The failure, the writer is tacitly admitting, may be attributed by ill-natured persons to Dr. Murray's optimism or stupidity.

24. CHANGE OF STANDPOINT

If various errors . . . are not repeated . . . it is . . . because someone . . . had been specially consulted on the point.

Either: 'if an error is not repeated, it is because someone has been specially consulted on the point . . .'

Or: 'if various errors were not repeated, it was because people had been specially consulted on the points.'

A. MISMATING OF METAPHORS

This division . . . maintained . . . as a basis . . . has a real foundation in fact.

It is difficult to think of a division as being a 'basis'; and a basis cannot have a foundation, any more than a foundation can have a basis.

H. ELEGANT VARIATION

Although the dates 1526 and 1674 were chosen because the former was that of the first printed English New Testament and the latter the year of Milton's death . . .

'The former' and 'the latter' should be used only when it would be tedious to restate at length the subjects to which they refer – for example, rival points of view, arguments or formulae. Here there was no need to restate the dates (as we show in the Fair Copy); and, if there had been, plain restatement would have been better than restatement under an alias which compels the eye to travel back.

K. TOO MUCH OF THE SAME WORD

... giving credit where credit is due, to give some account ...

Either of these 'gives' could have been changed without spoiling the sense.

FAIR COPY

'This division of English literature into three periods was first made by the Secretary, H. Coleridge, and was retained by the editors for some years as a convenience for their task of allotting books to the word-collectors. Coleridge chose 1526 as the opening year of the second period, because that was when the New Testatment was first printed in English translation; and 1674 as its close, because that was the year of Milton's death. Though the two dates seem at first sight to have been somewhat arbitrarily chosen, a remarkable change in the vocabulary of English did occur at, or near, each of them; which suggests that Coleridge had sound philological sense. The change of 1526 was principally due to new sources of reading made available by the Renascence, [?] that of 1674 to the increasing strength of the French literary influences which had accompanied the Restoration. [?] ...

We now intend, by describing the method used in collecting and arranging material for the Dictionary, to show how much credit is due to the voluntary word-collectors and to the sub-editors. In Plato's *Ion*, Socrates explains some relationship by the metaphor of a magnet with a number of rings suspended from it in the form of a chain, each of the rings, except the one next to the magnet, drawing its power from the ring immediately above it. The relationship between the magnet and the rings and that between the editors-in-chief and their chain of helpers would have been analogous, had the current of dictionary material flowed in the reverse direction – downwards from the editors-in-chief, not upwards to them from the word-collectors by way of the sub-editors' assistants, the sub-editors themselves, and the sectional editors....

In May 1884, Dr. Murray wrote that with six good assistants "it might be possible to produce two parts in the year and thus finish the work in eleven years from next March". Though this calculation, based on the amount of time so far spent on the letter A, which seemed to be near completion, may have looked reasonable enough then, it proved to be most inaccurate: not only was A an easier letter to treat than most others, but Dr. Murray had not foreseen that the amount of material sent in by the collectors would steadily increase without a compensatory increase in the speed with which it could be edited for the Press....

In many cases where a technical term, incorrectly used in other standard works of reference, has been correctly defined in the Dictionary, this has been due to the editors having found someone with a practical knowledge of the subject concerned who would freely give them the required information – for which they could not have afforded to pay.'

COMMENT

The writer has evidently accustomed himself in his reading to note and identify unfamiliar usages of words, without much regard for the general sense of the passages in which they occur. He has written this passage in the same uncritical frame of mind as regards sense, and has not examined his own novel usages of words. The confusion of the later sentences seems to be due to embarrassment: he wishes to exculpate Dr. Murray from a charge of stupidity, but finds this difficult, and he also becomes self-conscious about the help which the editors were obliged to ask from experts who had not volunteered their services and to whom they could not afford to offer a fee.

ERIC PARTRIDGE

from *The Teaching of English in His Majesty's Forces*, 1941

TEXT

... everybody needs to learn at least part of his own[8a] language,[12a] however much one[11] may assimilate[21]; moreover, much of the English one assimilates is bad, or at best,[8b] inferior English. Men nurtured in good[8c] homes are often astonishingly inarticulate[22a]; although they are not classified as illiterate (nor are they illiterate),[G] they are,[14] when they try to instruct others,[9a] as difficult to understand[H] as those men whom we[1] should classify as illiterate[G/K]: many an officer is as hard to follow[H] as the N.C.O. that[8d] the officer[12b] would condemn[8e] as ignorant.[23a] Indeed,[17] an illiterate may be an effective instructor if he has the gift of vivid presentation,[9b] but it must be admitted that illiteracy usually makes for imprecision.[12a/19]

Clarity is essential in peace time: in war, it is doubly necessary,[22b] for men's lives are at stake.[8f/23b]

EXAMINATION

1. WHO?

Men nurtured in good homes ... often ... are ... as difficult to understand as those men whom we should classify ...

Who is 'we'? Mr. Partridge and his fellow-lexicographers? The Army Educational Corps, to which he belonged at the time of writing? Or merely himself and his readers? Whatever the answer, he makes a clear distinction between the literate 'we' and the almost illiterate 'men nurtured in good homes'. 'We' therefore, by implication, were nurtured in 'bad or, at best, inferior' homes.

8. INAPPROPRIATE WORD OR PHRASE

(*a*) **... everybody needs to learn at least part of his own language, ...**

His 'national language' is meant; if it is his own domestic language he does not need to learn it in this sense.

(*b*) **... much of the English one assimilates is bad, or, at best, inferior English.**

He probably means 'at least' not 'at best': at best, obviously, much of the English one assimilates is the best English.

(*c*) **Men nurtured in good homes are often astonishingly inarticulate: ...**

By 'good homes' he doubtless means the homes of the well-to-do, whose sons naturally become officers. The contrast made between these officers and their N.C.O.s suggests that the N.C.O.s do not come from good homes. This is invidious; and untrue. Moreover, 'nurtured' means 'cherished and educated'. These men are shown by the colon which comes later in the sentence to belong to the officer-class, and so to have seldom been cherished and educated at home, but in general to have been away as boarders at preparatory and public schools for more than half the year, from the age of eight to that of eighteen.

(*d*) **... those men whom we should classify as illiterate: many an officer is as hard to follow as the N.C.O. that the officer ...**

Why not 'whom the officer'? An N.C.O. is not a thing but a person, like 'the men *whom* we should classify as illiterate'.

(*e*) **... as the N.C.O. that the officer would condemn as ignorant.**

Not 'condemn'. Perhaps 'look down on'. More likely: 'whose shortcomings the officer would ascribe to an incomplete education'.

(*f*) **... in war ... men's lives are at stake.**

'In peril' rather than 'at stake'. What is at stake in the game of war is usually military honour or a political principle, rarely national independence – but not the lives of soldiers. Soldiers are the pawns or superior pieces in the game for which these stakes are put up by either side. Each side expects its soldiers to be killed in large numbers before it wins, or before it forfeits its own stakes.

9. AMBIGUOUS WORD OR PHRASE

(*a*) **Men nurtured in good homes ... are ... when they try to instruct others ...**

Does 'others' mean 'other men from the same environment as themselves'? Or 'men other than those from good homes'? Or is the word irrelevant?

(*b*) **... the gift of vivid presentation, ...**

It would have been wise to write 'power', not 'gift': the words 'gift' and 'presentation' are too closely associated in the reader's mind.

11. UNINTENTIONAL CONTRAST

... everybody needs to learn at least part of his own language, however much one may assimilate; ...

The unintentional contrast between 'everybody' and 'one' would not have arisen had the word 'he' been used instead of 'one' – or 'some people', if 'everybody' was thought too large a concept.

12. DUPLICATION

(*a*) **... everybody needs to learn at least part of his own language ... much of the English one assimilates is bad, or, at best, inferior English.**

... Illiteracy usually makes for imprecision.

To be illiterate is to have assimilated, not formally learned, one's native language; 'bad or inferior English' in this context means imprecise English. So the second statement repeats the first.

(*b*) **. . . many an officer is as hard to follow as the N.C.O. that the officer would condemn as ignorant.**

There seems no reason for repeating the word 'officer'. 'He' would be clear enough and indeed clearer than 'the officer', which suggests a broader category than 'many an officer'.

14. MATERIAL OMISSION

Men nurtured in good homes are often astonishingly inarticulate; they are, when they try to instruct others . . . difficult to understand . . .

'Often' should have been repeated in the second statement; without it the implication is that men from good homes are always hard to understand.

17. FAULTY CONNEXION

. . . many an officer is as hard to follow as the N.C.O. that the officer would condemn as ignorant. Indeed, an illiterate may be an effective instructor . . .

The 'indeed' suggests, very improperly, that in 1941 there were illiterate N.C.O.s in the Army, who instructed troops. No man who could not read or write was given a stripe.

19. CONFUSED SEQUENCE

Men nurtured in good homes are often astonishingly inarticulate . . . they are not . . . illiterate . . . they are, when they try to instruct others, as difficult to understand as those whom we should classify as illiterate: . . . an illiterate may be an effective instructor if he has the gift of vivid presentation, but it must be admitted that illiteracy usually makes for imprecision.

The natural order of points in this argument is:

(1) Illiteracy makes for imprecision.

(2) But an illiterate may be an effective instructor, if he has a gift of vivid presentation.

(3) Officers are not illiterate,

(4) but they are often inarticulate,

(5) and make no better instructors than the illiterate.

But the order of points as Mr. Partridge gives them is:

4, 3, 5, 2, 1.

21. FALSE CONTRAST

. . . everybody needs to learn at least part of his own language, however much one may assimilate; . . .

'Assimilation' is a form of learning; the true contrast is between language learned consciously and language learned unconsciously.

22. OVER-EMPHASIS

(*a*) **Men nurtured in good homes are often astonishingly inarticulate: . . .**

'Inarticulate' means incapable of articulated speech. (Thackeray in *The Newcomes*: 'She was found in the morning, inarticulate but still alive'.) Men from good (i.e. well-to-do) homes are seldom in this paralytic condition, though they often speak incoherently when called upon to express themselves on unfamiliar themes, or in embarrassing circumstances.

(*b*) **Clarity is essential in peace time: in war, it is doubly necessary. . . .**

The necessity for clear verbal expression in war is contrasted with that in peace. But instead of writing 'clarity is necessary in peace time; in war, it is doubly necessary', he has changed the first 'necessary' to 'essential', probably for extra emphasis. This has upset the antithesis; for he could not write 'doubly essential' — 'essential' being as absolute a word as 'perfect', 'non-existent' or 'omnipresent'.

23. LOGICAL WEAKNESS

(*a*) **Men nurtured in good homes . . . are often . . . inarticulate . . . not illiterate; they are, when they try to instruct others, as difficult to understand as those men whom we should classify as illiterate: many an officer is as hard to follow as the N.C.O. that the officer would condemn as ignorant.**

A colon means that what follows is an explanation or fulfilment of the idea just recorded. But illiteracy and ignorance are by no means synonymous (as is admitted in the last sentence), therefore the colon here is misleading — that is to say: 'men from good homes are often as difficult to understand as illiterates' is not illustrated by 'many an officer is as hard to follow as the N.C.O. he condemns as ignorant'. One would judge the colon to be a misprint for a semicolon (which would make the second idea parallel to, not explanatory of, the first) if it were not for the 'Indeed' sentence which reaffirms the colon and identifies the plainly ignorant N.C.O. with 'the men whom we should classify as illiterate'.

(*b*) **Clarity is essential in peace time: in war it is doubly necessary, for men's lives are at stake.**

This logically implies that in peace time no lives are ever 'at stake' when orders are given; but that when they are given in war time lives are always at stake. This is untrue. In peace time lives are at stake when, for example, orders are given to engine-drivers, guards and signalmen, and to workers in explosives factories; whereas in war time a great many orders, given to troops not in contact with the enemy, may be disregarded without fatal consequences.

G. CIRCUMLOCUTION

. . . although they are not classified as illiterate (nor are they illiterate), they are, when they try to instruct others, as difficult to understand as those men whom we should classify as illiterate.

The classification idea seems unnecessary and even if it were retained there would be no need to bring it into the sentence twice. All that, perhaps, is relevant is: 'although they are not illiterate, their incoherence as instructors makes them seem so'.

H. ELEGANT VARIATION

Men nurtured in good homes are often as difficult to understand . . .
. . . many an officer is as hard to follow as the N.C.O. . . .

There seems no reason for this change of phrase, which is unfortunate because to 'follow' an officer or N.C.O. also has the sense of accepting his leadership in battle.

K. TOO MUCH OF THE SAME WORD

. . . although they are not classified as illiterate (nor are they illiterate), they are, when they try to instruct others, as difficult to understand as those men whom we should classify as illiterate.

If this sentence had been more closely articulated, the word 'illiterate' need not have been used more than once.

FAIR COPY

'Everyone, however fluent, who has assimilated his national language without consciously learning any part of it, is imprecise in expression. In English-speaking countries, where current speech is particularly slipshod, much schooling in the niceties of expression is everywhere needed. However, an ill-educated person, if he has the power of vivid presentation, is not necessarily an ineffective instructor. And it must be admitted that men from well-to-do homes and expensive schools often speak with astonishing incoherence: for example, some Army officers, when giving instructions, are as difficult to understand as the N.C.O.s whose shortcomings in the same field they usually ascribe to an inferior education.'

COMMENT

Mr. Partridge, who has done valuable lexicographical work on English slang, writes sensibly, in the pamphlet from which this passage is quoted, about the need for clear thinking in war time and so for close attention to the principles of English prose. But he has evidently not found time to read through his own sentences to make them illustrate his point.

'PETERBOROUGH'

from his Daily Column, 1940

TEXT

Mr. de Valera, I hear, is considered[8a] in Dublin to have claimed from the Vatican the preponderating[8b] voice in the appointment of the new Archbishop of Dublin.

Pundits point out that the Pope[M] delayed nine months over his choice,[22] and then his candidate,[8c] Dr. John McQuaid, proved to be one of Mr. de Valera's closest friends. All his[1] sons were[5] educated under Dr. McQuaid at Blackrock.

To appoint Dr. McQuaid[14a] Pope or Premier[9] went outside the eligible 369 secular parish priests of the diocese[14b] and picked on a 'regular'. Dr. McQuaid is a member[8d] of the French-originating[8e] Holy Ghost Fathers. He is only the fifth non-secular priest to be Archbishop of Dublin in 10 centuries.[10a]

Though no one had tipped Dr. McQuaid for the Dublin vacancy, at least

one forecast about the new prelate[H] has immediately gained some credence.[E/24] Cardinal MacRory of Armagh is now in his 80th year, and the question of his successor in the Irish Roman Catholic Church is frequently canvassed.[8f]

Tradition has it[8g] that the Armagh Archbishopric goes to a priest of the Ulster province. That tradition may be changed[8h] by Dr. McQuaid's translation later on[3] to Armagh.

The break would be softened because he was actually[10b] born in Cavan, though he has spent most of his life in Dublin.

I need hardly say how important[20] it would be if Mr. de Valera had such a friend and confidant north of the border at Armagh.[10c]

EXAMINATION

1. WHO?

. . . the Pope delayed nine months . . . and then his candidate, Dr. John McQuaid, proved to be one of Mr. de Valera's closest friends. All his sons were educated under Dr. McQuaid at Blackrock.

The Pope is the most important person in the first sentence; Dr. McQuaid is the next most important; Mr. de Valera is only mentioned indirectly. Everyone knows that Popes have no sons 'according to the flesh', and even in Renaissance times had only nephews; but the reader has to check for a moment before hitting on Mr. de Valera as the father of Dr. McQuaid's pupils.

3. WHAT?

Cardinal MacRory of Armagh is now in his 80th year and the question of his successor in the headship of the Irish Roman Catholic Church is frequently canvassed. . . .

. . . Dr. McQuaid's translation later on to Armagh.

'Peterborough' was shy of saying outright that the Cardinal was not expected to live long. This makes it difficult for the reader to understand whether the Cardinal would be allowed to retire, as an Archbishop of Canterbury had recently done, or whether only his death could create a vacancy.

5. WHEN?

. . . Dr. John McQuaid, proved to be one of Mr. de Valera's closest friends. All his sons were educated under Dr. McQuaid at Blackrock.

Surely 'had been educated'? The words 'were educated' suggest that they were educated subsequently to Dr. McQuaid's appointment.

8. INAPPROPRIATE WORD OR PHRASE

(*a*) **Mr. de Valera . . . is considered . . . to have claimed . . .**

One might write 'Mr. de Valera is considered to have erred', or 'considered to have made a shrewd political stroke'. But not 'considered to have claimed'. 'Consider' is a critical word, not one which can be used, like 'think', 'conjecture' or 'guess', about actions which may or may not have taken place.

(*b*) **. . . the preponderating voice . . .**

A Prime Minister cannot claim a right which the Catholic Church holds is exclusively the Pope's, and a gift of the Holy Spirit. Nor can one voice of two be 'preponderating': the word needed is 'stronger' or 'more insistent'. Two voices might preponderate in a council of three, but only two are here mentioned.

(*c*) **... the Pope delayed ... and then his candidate ...**

Whether Dr. McQuaid's name was suggested by Mr. de Valera or by some one else, the Pope did not offer a 'candidate': he appointed an Archbishop.

(*d*) **... a member of the French-originating Holy Ghost Fathers.**

He may have been 'one of the Fathers', or 'a member of the Fatherhood', but not a 'member of the Fathers'.

(*e*) **... the French-originating Holy Ghost Fathers.**

These did not originate the French language, but were of French origin.

(*f*) **... the question of his successor ... is frequently canvassed.**

The word 'canvassed' is misleading: it suggests that prominent clerics went round asking parish priests for their opinion on this embarrassing subject. 'Canvassed' can legitimately be used in the sense of 'discussing' a meal or summarizing a character, but it should have been avoided in this context.

(*g*) **Tradition has it that the Armagh Archbishopric goes to a priest of the Ulster province.**

'Tradition has it' is a phrase used when one is scoffing gently at some popular legend: 'Tradition has it that Joseph of Arimathea brought to Glastonbury a thorn that flowered only on Christmas Day.' Here 'It is a tradition that the Armagh Archbishopric should go' would have been a more suitable phrase.

(*h*) **That tradition may be changed ...**

A tradition of this sort can only be broken: to change it would imply that the Armagh Archbishopric thereafter always went to a non-secular schoolmaster who had taught the Premier's sons.

9. AMBIGUOUS WORD OR PHRASE

To appoint Dr. McQuaid Pope or Premier ...

This reads at first glance as though Dr. McQuaid might have been appointed to either of these high offices.

10. MISPLACED WORD OR PHRASE

(*a*) **He is only the fifth non-secular priest to be Archbishop of Dublin in 10 centuries.**

This should be: 'only the fifth non-secular priest in ten centuries to be Archbishop of Dublin'.

(*b*) **... he was actually born ...**

'Actually, he was born' is meant. As it stands, 'actually' emphasizes the fact of his birth, ruling out other, perhaps more spiritual, ways of entering the world.

(*c*) **... a friend and confidant north of the border at Armagh.**

There is no border at Armagh. What is probably meant is 'at Armagh, north of the border'.

14. MATERIAL OMISSION

(*a*) **To appoint Dr. McQuaid Pope or Premier went outside ...**

Only the Pope can have made the appointment; though the wishes of the Premier may have assisted him in his choice.

(*b*) **... Pope or Premier went outside the 369 eligible parish priests ... and picked on a 'regular'.**

Surely the Pope might alternatively have chosen a bishop or chaplain?

20. IRRELEVANCY

I need hardly say how important it would be ...

He does say it, however.

22. OVER-EMPHASIS

Pundits point out that the Pope delayed nine months over his choice.

It would not need a pundit to point out what most good Catholics in the Dublin Diocese must have known.

24. CHANGE OF STANDPOINT

Though no one had tipped Dr. McQuaid for the Dublin vacancy, at least one forecast about the new prelate has immediately gained some credence.

The word 'has' should be omitted, as not matching 'had tipped'.

E. MISMATING OF STYLES

Though no one had tipped Dr. McQuaid for the Dublin vacancy, at least one forecast about the new prelate has immediately gained some credence.

'Gained some credence' is the language of the Close; 'tipped' that of the street-corner.

H. ELEGANT VARIATION

Though no one had tipped Dr. McQuaid for the Dublin vacancy, at least one forecast about the new prelate ...

The 'new prelate' is Dr. McQuaid. The alias, which gives no fresh information about him, is confusing and unnecessary.

M. TOO MUCH ALLITERATION

Pundits point out that the Pope ...

This could easily have been avoided.

FAIR COPY

'It is conjectured in Dublin, I am told, that early this year [?] Mr. de Valera informed the Vatican authorities that he expected to be consulted before any final decision was made in the choice of an Archbishop for the vacancy at Dublin. He may even have put forward his own candidate. At all events, there was a delay of nine months before the name of the new Archbishop was announced, and then it proved to be that of Dr. John McQuaid, who as principal of Blackrock College [?] had educated all Mr. de Valera's sons and was one of his closest friends.

Nobody expected Dr. McQuaid to be appointed, since he was not a bishop nor even one of the 369 eligible parish priests of the Dublin Diocese, but a member of the Holy Ghost Fatherhood — an Order of French origin

— and only five times in a thousand years has a "regular", as opposed to a secular, priest been given this appointment.

Now that he is elevated to the Archbishopric of Dublin he may achieve yet higher Church dignity. Cardinal MacRory, who as Archbishop of Armagh is the Primate of the Roman Catholic Church in Ireland, has reached his eightieth year and the question of his probable successor has long been privately discussed. To-day people are prophesying that on the Cardinal's decease Dr. McQuaid will be translated from Dublin to Armagh, even though it is a tradition that the Archbishop of Armagh should be chosen from the Ulster priesthood — to which Dr. McQuaid (who has spent most of his life in Dublin) cannot claim to belong. The resentment that such a break in the tradition might cause would be allayed, however, by Dr. McQuaid's having at least been born in the province — in County Cavan.

It is easy to see how important for Mr. de Valera it would be to have a confidant exercising spiritual authority at Armagh, across the Northern Irish frontier.'

COMMENT

The difficulty of writing a daily column of social events in London during the second part of 1940 was increased by constant air-raids. It seems to have been further increased on this occasion by an embarrassing problem: how to write, without offence, of a rumoured understanding on ecclesiastical appointments between the Pope and a Premier — as a result of which the Premier has got an Archbishopric for an obscure schoolmaster, who is his personal friend — and of a rumour that this same friend is likely to be given a Cardinal's hat, in defiance of tradition, as soon as the present aged wearer is dead. That 'Peterborough' did not succeed in writing as lucidly as usual is understandable.

EZRA POUND

from an Article in a Quarterly Review, January 1939

TEXT

It may[20a] (doubtless will) be objected by those who have[14a] the cult of criticism as such,[3a] but have forgotten its (criticism's[20b]) scope and original purposes,[5a/16a] that I have not much discussed the 'art' of R. Crevel. Technically,[8a] I should have spent more words on his 'how',[16b] and the condemned reviewer[1a] for his weekly rent[D] would[16c] furnish MM. les lecteurs with 'the faded[14b] and stuffy atmosphere of the bourgeois home'[9a] etc. etc., my position being that the novel (as such)[3b] was carried to its[14c] development by Flaubert and H. James (with parenthesis[2] already indicated[9b] in other notes[3c] by the present expositor[H]) that *since*[F1] (underlined)[20c] Mr. Joyce carried on from Bouvard[F2]

there has been probably no development. I don't mean no[15] good novels, no particular[3d] cases,[17] Rodker's *Adolph* as a delicate variant,[3e/25] Cumming's [sic] *Eimi* as a masterwork,[3f] dealing with a particular subject matter,[3g] masterwork because its author recognized that that matter could not adequately be presented in the idiom of James or Flaubert, [23]but outside these specific examples one can only say of a given novel that it is a fine (or other[8b]) specimen of a known category. I mean[11] that is all one[1b] would say in speaking of the book to one's most intelligent friends.

EXAMINATION

1. WHO?

(*a*) **. . . and the condemned reviewer for his weekly rent would furnish . . .**

A reviewer refers to himself often as 'the reviewer' instead of 'I'. *Is* this condemned reviewer Ezra Pound?

(*b*) **. . . one can only say of a given novel . . . I mean that is all one would say in speaking of the book to one's most intelligent friends.**

The word 'one' means either 'everyone' or 'an ordinary person'. The 'one' here is limited, however, to a person who has so peculiar a view of 'the novel' that he includes non-fictional works in the category, and regards novel-writing as having stood still since the very early Twenties.

2. WHICH?

. . . the novel (as such) was carried to its development by Flaubert and H. James (with parenthesis already indicated in other notes by the present expositor) that *since* **(underlined) . . .**

Which parenthesis? There have already been three of them in this paragraph, and now here are a fourth and a fifth.

3. WHAT?

(*a*) **. . . the cult of criticism as such . . .**

This use of 'as such' is not clear. The phrase correctly distinguishes the professed function of a person or thing from the extraneous qualities of that person or thing. For example: 'The priest, as such, was useless to the parish, but he was the most reliable authority on bees in the county.' Here 'the scope and original purposes' are obviously part of the function of criticism 'as such', and cannot be contrasted with it. Perhaps what is meant is 'so-called criticism', rather than 'criticism as such'.

(*b*) **. . . the novel (as such) was carried to its development . . .**

The reader wonders what 'the novel (as such)' means. The phrase had a derogatory sense when used in the previous sentence.

(*c*) **. . . the novel (as such) was carried to its development by Flaubert and H. James (with parenthesis already indicated in other notes by the present expositor) . . .**

What are these other notes and how do they indicate a parenthesis? Perhaps what is meant is that the reasons for putting 'as such' into a parenthesis after 'the novel' have been indicated in other critical work by Ezra Pound, and that he cannot be bothered to redefine the novel.

(*d*) **... there has probably been no development ... I don't mean no good novels, no particular cases ...**

What sort of particular cases? Does this mean that there *have* been particular cases in which there has been a marked development of the novel?

(*e*) **... I don't mean no good novels, no particular cases, Rodker's *Adolph* as a delicate variant ...**

A variant of what? The Flaubert, the Joyce, or the James type of novel?

(*f*) **... I don't mean no good novels ... Cumming's** [sic] ***Eimi* as a masterwork ...**

Cummings's *Eimi* is not a novel, but a factual account of a visit to the U.S.S.R. Perhaps Ezra Pound's 'other notes' on the novel widen its scope to include all travel books, whether fictional or not.

(*g*) **... a masterwork dealing with a particular subject matter ...**

Most books, except unused note-books and ledgers, have a particular subject-matter.

5. WHEN?

... its (criticism's) original scope and purposes ...

When did criticism start?

8. INAPPROPRIATE WORD OR PHRASE

(*a*) **Technically, I should have spent more words on his 'how' ...**

'Technically' is probably not intended to mean 'in a way suited to "the scope and original purposes" of criticism', but 'according to the technical standards of bourgeois critics'.

(*b*) **... a fine (or other) specimen ...**

Perhaps 'or otherwise' is meant.

9. AMBIGUOUS WORD OR PHRASE

(*a*) **... would furnish MM les lecteurs with 'the faded and stuffy atmosphere of the bourgeois home' etc. etc., ...**

The 'etc. etc.' do not sufficiently explain whether Crevel's or the condemned reviewer's home-atmosphere was faded and stuffy.

(*b*) **... (with parenthesis already indicated ...)**

Was the parenthetical remark indicated? Or was it the need for putting the remark in parenthesis?

11. UNINTENTIONAL CONTRAST

I don't mean no good novels ... I mean that is all one would say ...

'I don't mean' and 'I mean' do not here make a contrastive pair.

14. MATERIAL OMISSION

(*a*) **... those who have the cult of criticism ...**

Something has been left out which would have explained that 'to have the cult of criticism' means to Ezra Pound something 'bourgeois' and (to use his favourite adjective of reproach) 'usurious'.

(*b*) Technically I should have spent more words on his 'how', and the condemned reviewer . . . would furnish . . . 'the faded and stuffy atmosphere of the bourgeois home' etc. etc., my position being that the novel . . .

After the 'etc. etc.' something has been left out: possibly 'but I have not done so because I have not thought it worth while'.

(*c*) . . . the novel was carried to its development . . .

The novel had been developing for several centuries before Flaubert's day. Perhaps some adjective like 'supreme' has been omitted before 'development'.

15. UNFULFILLED PROMISE

I don't mean no good novels . . . but outside these specific examples one can only say . . .

The reader's expectation of 'but I do mean that . . .' is disappointed.

16. UNDEVELOPED THEME

(*a*) . . . its (criticism's) original scope and purposes . . .

What these are, the reader will expect to be told.

(*b*) Technically, I should have spent more words on his 'how'.

As opposed to what? To his 'why'? Or to his 'when'? Or to his 'what'?

(*c*) . . . the condemned reviewer for his weekly rent would furnish . . .

In what circumstances?

17. FAULTY CONNEXION

. . . there has been probably no development. I don't mean no good novels, no particular cases, Rodker's *Adolph* as a delightful variant . . .

The syntax of this sentence is very loose. Probably 'I don't mean' is not intended to refer to more than the phrases 'no good novels' and 'no particular cases'; after which one must understand the words 'For example, I regard'.

20. IRRELEVANCY

(*a*) It may (doubtless will) be objected . . .

The phrase 'doubtless will' in conversational English has little more force than 'may': 'may' should have been left out.

(*b*) . . . but have forgotten its (criticism's) scope . . .

It is never necessary, except when quoting, to restate a word, after 'its' or 'his', by putting it into a parenthesis. If one finds that it is not clear to whom the 'its' or 'his' refers, the sentence can always be rewritten to make it clear.

(*c*) . . . that *since* (underlined) . . .

The underlining of *since* has been taken care of by the printer, who has put it into italics. The word 'underlined' could have been omitted.

23. LOGICAL WEAKNESS

. . . there has been probably no development . . . Cumming's *Eimi* as a masterwork dealing with a particular subject matter, masterwork because its author recognized that that matter could not adequately be presented in the idiom of James or Flaubert . . .

In other words, if *Eimi* is to be reckoned as a novel, there has been development. It could have been equally said of Flaubert and James that their novels were master-works because the subject matter dealt with in them could not have been adequately presented in the idiom of the Abbé Prevost or Dickens.

25. MIXED CATEGORY

R. Crevel, Flaubert, H. James, Mr. Joyce, Rodker's, Cumming's . . .

Mr. Joyce is probably called 'Mr.' because he was alive when Ezra Pound wrote this, whereas Crevel, Flaubert and James were all dead: but Mr. Cummings (not 'Cumming') was also alive and was entitled to the 'Mr.' So was Mr. Rodker.

D. POETICALITY

. . . the condemned reviewer for his weekly rent . . .

This reads so queerly that it may be a quotation from a poem, with the word 'condemned', or 'reviewer', changed at the expense of the metre.

F. OBSCURE REFERENCE

(1) . . . that *since* (underlined) Mr. Joyce carried on from Bouvard there has been probably no development.

The underlining of *since* is evidently intended to convey something important. Perhaps the reference is to James Joyce's having ceased to be a novelist in the sense 'indicated by the present expositor' – but whether this was before or after he wrote *Ulysses* is not clear.

(2) . . . that the novel . . . was carried to its development by Flaubert and H. James . . . that *since* (underlined) Mr. Joyce carried on from Bouvard there has probably been no development.

Anybody who had not studied French literature would guess that Bouvard was the name of a French novelist intervening between Flaubert and James Joyce. But it is a familiar way of referring to Flaubert's novel, *Bouvard et Pécuchet*.

H. ELEGANT VARIATION

. . . my position being . . .

. . . by the present expositor . . .

The 'present expositor' is perhaps a joking way of writing 'me'.

FAIR COPY

'Professional critics who have forgotten that the true scope and purpose of criticism is [. . .] will doubtless object that I have not written enough here, by their standards, about the "art" of R. Crevel – *how* he wrote, as distinguished from *what* he wrote. But though, if put into my position, "the condemned scribbler for his weekly rent"[?] would doubtless have furnished his readers with "the faded and stuffy atmosphere of the bourgeois home" in which Crevel worked, I have not thought his work important enough for so pious a treatment. [?] I hold that the novel (as defined by me elsewhere – and I can't be bothered to repeat myself) was brought to maturity by Flaubert in his *Bouvard et Pécuchet*, and by James, and further developed by Joyce; but that since Joyce faded out as a novelist [?] it has stood practically still. I admit that Rodker in his *Adolph* has achieved a new delicacy of expression and that Cummings's *Eimi* which, though not advertised as a novel, comes within my definition of one, is a master-work. But Rodker's theme is not a new one, and *Eimi* is a master-work only because Cummings recognized that his particular subject — the negativeness of Russian life under the Soviet system — could not be adequately presented in the idiom of James or of Flaubert. In fact: all recent novels, with very few exceptions, can be dismissed by intelligent people merely as specimens, fine, fair, or dull — of one of several familiar categories.'

COMMENT

Ezra Pound's writing is wilfully loose — not a natural half-apologetic 'barbaric yawp' like Walt Whitman's, but yawp for yawp's sake — and offered with the ironical glare of a Classical *grand maître*. Perhaps in 1939 his public was large and pious enough for him to be able to dispense with ordinary literary precautions against misunderstanding, and in this passage he apparently distinguishes himself from the professional reviewer forced to write for cash. But it seems unlikely that, after reading this passage, even his 'most intelligent friends' were able to supply the missing links in the argument, or that intelligent strangers when they had decoded it, so far as it went, found the information that it conveyed sufficiently fresh to justify their effort. It lacks even rhetorical grace and resonance.

J. B. PRIESTLEY

from an Article in the Sunday Press, 1941

TEXT

The Government will have to come out into the open and choose a road.

There are two roads. One is the nationalist-imperialist-big-business-and-privilege road.[22a] Hitler is to be defeated not because[14a] his very existence challenges[8a] any attempt to bring into being the good life,[3/12a] but because his lust for power conflicts with other people's lust for power. He wants what 'we' have got. He must be put out of the way so that 'we' can get on with the old job,[12b] and, indeed, perhaps with more power to our elbow. . . .

The other road, the mere thought of which must give Goebbels a head-ache, is international instead of nationalist[21]; is truly and sharply[22b] demo-cratic, and proclaims its faith[8b] in every value that Hitler's existence challenges.[12a/22c] It is the road of peoples[N] really on their way to a genuine freedom[22d]. . . .

Every move we[1a] made along that road would create hope and faith in the people[N] here and elsewhere. . . .

'A grand life if we don't weaken'.[14b] It is not a grand life. It is a filthy life, with most of the things that raise us above the level of fearful cowering savages rapidly disappearing. But on that true road, where the decent ordinary folk[11] who are suffering most for our past[1b] idiocies can look for a recompense, we[1c] shall not weaken. Men can endure toil and sweat and tears[1d] and the pointing finger of death[8c] if they know that one day their children can come running out[4] into a cleaner world.

EXAMINATION

1. WHO?

(*a*) **Every move we made along that road would create hope and faith in the people here and elsewhere.**

Who is the 'we'? It cannot logically be 'the people here'. The only previous 'we' mentioned is the wicked capitalist 'we', hoping to get on with 'our old job': perhaps this 'we' is now reformed by its change of road.

(*b*) **. . . our past idiocies . . .**

Who committed 'our past idiocies'? Apparently not the decent ordinary folk, but the fearful, cowering savages who, however, now shall not weaken. It is suggested, by 'men' in the next sentence, that they include no women. Perhaps the women *will* weaken.

(*c*) **. . . on that true road where the decent ordinary people . . . can look for a recompense, we shall not weaken.**

Who is the 'we' here? It is apparently not the decent, ordinary folk, but the 'we' who are in a fair way to becoming fearful cowering savages.

(*d*) **. . . men can endure . . . tears. . . .**

Whose tears? The women's and the children's? One cannot 'endure' one's own tears; they are, indeed, a relief to suffering.

3. WHAT?

. . . his very existence challenges any attempt to bring into being the good life . . .

The virtue of this good life is not indicated. Yet 'the' implies that it is a good life of a particular sort. Is it perhaps 'the good life' of Plato or some other philosopher?

4. WHERE?

. . . on that true road . . . men can endure toil and sweat . . . if they know that one day their children can come running out into a cleaner world.

Where will the children run? Along the road or into the road?

8. INAPPROPRIATE WORD OR PHRASE

(*a*) **. . . Hitler . . . his very existence challenges any attempt . . .**

An existence cannot 'challenge' an attempt: it can only hinder or prevent.

(*b*) **The other road . . . proclaims its faith . . .**

Roads do not proclaim faiths: this is done by the people on them.

(*c*) **. . . men can endure . . . the pointing finger of death . . .**

Death's pointing finger may be bravely disregarded; or the distress it causes may be endured; but the finger itself cannot be said to be 'endured'.

11. UNINTENTIONAL CONTRAST

It is a filthy life, with most of the things that raise us above the level of fearful, cowering savages rapidly disappearing. But on that true road, where the decent ordinary folk . . .

Are the 'decent ordinary folk' on the road being intentionally contrasted with 'us', the cowering savages? Or are they the same people seen in different aspects?

12. DUPLICATION

(*a*) **Hitler . . . his very existence challenges any attempt to bring into being 'the good life' . . .**

The other road . . . proclaims its faith in every value that Hitler's existence challenges . . .

The phrase about Hitler's very existence challenging this or that need not have been repeated.

(*b*) **Hitler is to be defeated . . . because . . . he wants what 'we' have got. He must be put out of the way so that 'we' can get on with the old job.**

These two nearly equivalent statements should have been combined into one.

14. MATERIAL OMISSION

(*a*) **Hitler is to be defeated not because . . .**

The reader may be slow to grasp that this is not Mr. Priestley's view, but that of the wicked politicians.

(*b*) **'A grand life if we don't weaken'. It is not a grand life, it is a filthy life, with most of the things that raise us above the level of fearful cowering savages rapidly disappearing.**

Mr. Priestley hesitates to say outright either that the Prime Minister is talking nonsense; or that the British people is weakening. But in the phrase 'fearful cowering savages' he hints at both these things.

21. FALSE CONTRAST

The other road . . . is international instead of nationalist . . .

Why not 'internationalist'? Or 'national'?

22. OVER-EMPHASIS

(*a*) **The Government will have to come out into the open and choose a road. There are two roads . . .**

Mr. Priestley asserts that the Government will be forced to declare which road it intends to follow. He knows perfectly well that the Government could never declare openly that Hitler's lust for power conflicted with that of British business-men and imperialists; that the most it could say would be that it intended to continue on traditional lines. He is concealing his view that the Government is already tacitly committed to the nationalist-imperialist-big-business-and-privilege road, which is certainly not one to which a government would change in war-time; but admits it later in the phrase 'the old job'.

(*b*) **The other road, . . . is truly and sharply democratic . . .**

It is difficult to see the force of 'sharply'. 'Truly democratic' is as democratic as anyone can be without overstrain, just as a musical note cannot be sung more than 'truly'. When a tremendous effort to attain true pitch is made by a singer who usually sings flat, the chances are that he will overshoot the mark and sing sharp.

(*c*) **. . . proclaims its faith in every value that Hitler's existence challenges.**

Hitler's existence also 'challenges' the pluto-democracy which is here being arraigned.

(*d*) **. . . peoples really on their way to a genuine freedom . . .**

Could peoples be really on their way to an illusory freedom?

N. SAME WORD IN DIFFERENT SENSES

. . . of peoples on their way to freedom . . .

Every move . . . would create hope . . . in the people here and elsewhere.

Peoples in the first sentence means *nation.*

People in the second is the plural of person.

FAIR COPY

'The Government will have to come out into the open and announce its intention either of maintaining its traditional policy or of making a sharp change of course. The traditional policy amounts to working for Hitler's defeat only because his lust for power conflicts with that of British nationalists, imperialists, big business men and members of the privileged classes in general—in other words, because he wants what "we" have already got and prevents "us" from grabbing still more. The new course would be to proclaim Britain's faith in internationalism, democracy and all the other noble ideals which cannot co-exist with Hitler — the course of a people on its way to true freedom at last, inspiring faith and hope in all others. And if it were taken, what a headache that would give Dr. Goebbels!

The Prime Minister has offered Britain a watchword: "It's a grand life if we don't weaken!" It is not a grand life yet, but a filthy one, and growing rapidly filthier as so many of the amenities disappear that can raise the civilized person above the crouching savage. But if the Government takes this nobler course, from which decent, ordinary folk may expect an eventual recompense for their sufferings, none of these will weaken. It is they who are paying the dearest price for all the idiocies of former governments; yet they will endure toil, sweat, sorrow and will not quail at the pointing finger of Death, so long as they know that, when all is over, their children will be able to run out for play into a cleaner world than this.'

COMMENT

J. B. Priestley is conscious of the extreme difficulty of forcing a fundamentally Conservative Government, during a party-truce and at a critical stage in a world-war, to change its domestic policy; and of the danger of seeming to interfere with 'the war effort'. He apparently has no plan worked out in detail for the betterment of social conditions, but only a burning sense of indignation that ordinary decent people should suffer for the idiocy of previous governments, and that the present government consists largely of the same idiots as before. Caution and doubt therefore combine to keep his remarks extremely vague; but the genuine indignation will not be denied and boils up in over-emphatic phrases.

D. N. PRITT, K.C., M.P.

from *Light on Moscow*, 1939

TEXT

On balance, both before and after the advent[5a] of Hitler, Germany is entitled to more good marks for friendly conduct towards the U.S.S.R. than we[24a] are; and it is not even more than partly true[6] to say that she should also be given more bad marks for unfriendly conduct. If one includes[15] the very early[11] days,[5b] when we were financing one semi-piratical[3] invasion after another[7] against the Soviet Republic,[2a] the score[2b] is heavily against us[14]; if one looks at the more recent[11] years,[5c/15/16] it is true that the leaders of Germany have fulminated[24b] against her[1] more vilely and more officially[22] than our leaders ever did, but is that not perhaps only[10] a difference of technique and manners?

EXAMINATION

1. WHO?

. . . against the Soviet Republic . . . It is true that the leaders of Germany have fulminated against her . . .

If 'Russia' had been used instead of 'the Soviet Republic' it would have been clear that 'her' does not mean Germany.

2. WHICH?

(*a*) **. . . friendly conduct towards the U.S.S.R . . .**
. . . against the Soviet Republic . . .

The U.S.S.R. is a Union of Socialist Soviet Republics. Were these invasions directed against only one of these? If so, against which?

(*b*) **. . . Germany is entitled to more good marks for friendly conduct . . . and . . . not . . . more bad marks for unfriendly conduct . . . If one includes the very early days, . . . the score is heavily against us.**

Which score? The good mark score, or the bad mark one? The notion of a single score, with good marks cancelling bad, has not been suggested.

3. WHAT?

. . . when we were financing one semi-piratical invasion after another . . .

What does semi-piratical mean? Great Britain had not yet diplomatically recognized the U.S.S.R. as existing, and the invasions were made by forces of the exiled Tsarist Government in an attempt to restore it to power. A 'piratical' invasion means one by an army with no accredited diplomatic representatives. 'Semi-piratical' means nothing at all.

5. WHEN?

(*a*) On balance, both before and after the advent of Hitler, . . .

When did this advent take place? The Advent of Jesus Christ is dated from the year of His birth, but Hitler's advent, in this sense, preceded 1917, the foundation-year of the U.S.S.R. A likely date is 1923 when Hitler first achieved European fame in the Munich *putsch*. But perhaps 1933 is meant, which was when he became Chancellor.

(*b*) If one includes the very early days, . . .

Which are these? The U.S.S.R. was founded in 1917, when the representatives of the German Second Reich behaved with conspicuous unfriendliness, both at the Brest-Litovsk meeting and afterwards. The Tsarist invasions of Russia took place some time after the collapse, a year later, of the Second Reich.

(*c*) If one looks at the more recent years . . .

Which are these? Tsarist invasions of U.S.S.R. territory, financed by Britain, ceased in the very early 'Twenties. Did the leaders of the German Weimar Republic ever fulminate vilely against the U.S.S.R.? Or was it only the leaders of the Third Reich in 1933 and later?

6. HOW MUCH?

. . . and it is not even more than partly true . . .

How much truth does this indicate? The question which Mr. Pritt has asked himself is a simple one: 'Is it true that Germany should be given more bad marks for unfriendly conduct towards the U.S.S.R. than Britain?' The answer cannot be either 'Partly' or 'More than partly' or 'Not more than partly': it must be either 'Yes', or 'No', or 'I don't know'.

7. HOW MANY?

. . . one semi-piratical invasion after another . . .

This suggests at least half-a-dozen. How many were there?

10. MISPLACED WORD

. . . is that not perhaps only a difference in technique and manners?

Rather: '. . . a difference only of technique and manners'.

11. UNINTENTIONAL CONTRAST

If one includes the very early days . . .

. . . if one looks at the more recent years . . .

This suggests a misleading contrast between the first week or two after the October Revolution of 1917 and later years.

14. MATERIAL OMISSION

If one includes the very early days, the score is heavily against us; if one looks at the more recent years . . .

In a discussion of comparative national scores over a period of twenty-two years, the eleven middle years should not be left out of the account so brusquely as this.

15. UNFULFILLED PROMISE

If one includes the very early days . . .

. . . if one looks at the more recent years . . .

In both cases the reader expects 'one finds that . . .'

16. UNDEVELOPED THEME

If one includes the very early days . . . the score is heavily against us; if one looks at the more recent years, it is true that the leaders of Germany have fulminated against her more vilely . . . than our leaders, but is that not perhaps only a difference of technique and manners?

The total score from 1917 to 1939 is here computed to be heavily against Britain; and even if one reckons only from – (from when? Perhaps from 1933?) – well, what? Mr. Pritt withholds the required information about the comparative scores in good marks and bad achieved by Britain and Germany in 'the more recent years'.

22. OVER-EMPHASIS

. . . the leaders of Germany have fulminated against her more vilely and more officially . . .

When a leader of one state fulminates against another state, he does so either in his official capacity, or unofficially. In such cases there are no degrees to 'officially', though 'semi-officially' is loosely used of news-reports to mean that though unofficial they are issued by people in close contact with the government concerned.

24. CHANGE OF STANDPOINT

***(a)* . . . Germany is entitled to** more **good marks . . . than we are; . . .**

Either: 'Germany is entitled to more good marks . . . than Britain . . .'

Or: 'the Germans are entitled to more good marks . . . than we are . . .'

***(b)* On balance, both before and after the advent of Hitler . . . if one looks at the more recent years, it is true that the leaders of Germany have fulminated . . .**

The word 'after' implies that the period under review has since ended; but 'the more recent years' and 'have fulminated' makes it clear that it has not. This 'after' should be 'since'.

FAIR COPY

'Though the Government of the German Second Reich had imposed harsh peace-terms on the U.S.S.R. in 1917 and sponsored separatist movements in Soviet territory, the Allied victory of 1918 changed German policy in the East. The Weimar Republic showed an increasing friendliness to the U.S.S.R., which was substantiated in several treaties and agreements. On the other hand, the British Coalition Government financed three [?] Tsarist invasions of Soviet territory between 1919 and 1921, and almost every succeeding Government, though abstaining from further warlike action, has treated the U.S.S.R. with suspicion and high-handedness. It is true that the leaders of the Third Reich have fulminated against the U.S.S.R; but if one compares the British political record as a whole with the German, awarding bad marks for unfriendliness and good ones for friendliness,

Britain makes by far the worse showing on both counts. She hardly makes the better one if the comparison is limited to the years since 1933: for, though public abuse of the U.S.S.R. has been official in Germany, and in Britain both unofficial and less vilely phrased, these are perhaps unimportant differences of technique and manners, and the Government of neither nation has earned any good marks during this period for acts of positive friendship [?].'

COMMENT

D. N. Pritt felt very strongly that the hostile policy of Britain to the U.S.S.R. had been indefensible, and did not hesitate to say so. But his book was published when Britain was already at war with Germany and not yet allied with the U.S.S.R. To say any good word for Hitlerite Germany at the expense of the British Government was dangerous.

This limitation has cramped his style. He has carried into prose the forensic habits of emphasising the dramatic points of his case at the expense of the less dramatic; of purposeful vagueness in assessing degree; of sly innuendo.

HERBERT READ

from *English Prose Style*, 1928

TEXT

Words are the units of composition,[13a] and the art of Prose[9a] must begin with a close attention to their quality.[3a] It may be said[15] that[14a] most base[9b] styles are to be traced to a neglect of this consideration[8 '13b]; and certainly if style[3b] is reduced in the last analysis[22] to a selective instinct,[14b] this instinct manifests itself most obviously in the use of words.[13c]

EXAMINATION

3. WHAT?

(*a*) **Words are the units of composition, and the art of Prose must begin with a close attention to their quality. . . .**

Herbert Read has an italicized note, on the page opposite this passage, explaining that prose may be studied from two points of view: composition and rhetoric. This perhaps gives a clue to the intended meaning of 'quality': the quality of words as used rhetorically—perhaps their persuasive force when spoken, as opposed to their prose logic. But, though the most important word in the passage, 'quality' is not defined.

(*b*) **. . . the art of Prose must begin . . . and certainly if style is reduced to the last analysis . . .**

What is the connexion or difference between these two concepts? 'The art of Prose' is here said to depend on a close attention to words; and 'style' on an instinctive use of words. Yet they are logically united by the phrase 'a neglect of this consideration'.

8. INAPPROPRIATE WORD OR PHRASE

. . . most base styles are to be traced to a neglect of this consideration.

'The art of Prose must begin' is not a 'consideration' but an instruction.

9. AMBIGUOUS WORD OR PHRASE

(*a*) **. . . the art of Prose must begin with a close attention . . .**

This may mean either the art of prose composition, or the artful power exercised by prose.

(*b*) **. . . most base styles . . .**

This may mean either 'basest styles' or 'most examples of base style'.

13. SELF-EVIDENT STATEMENT

(*a*) **Words are the units of composition . . .**

The word 'composition' means putting words together as units.

(*b*) **Words . . . the art of Prose must begin with a close attention to their quality. It may be said that most base styles are to be traced to a neglect of this consideration.**

It is a platitude that 'all base styles are due to the writer's failure to choose the right sort of words'. That 'most' base styles are due to this failure is an even grosser platitude. That '*it may be said* that *most* base styles are due to this failure' is so obvious as to be almost an irrelevancy.

(*c*) **If (prose) style is reduced to a selective instinct, this instinct manifests itself most obviously in the use of words.**

Since a prose style is a characteristic way of using words, it is hard to guess how the selective instinct could manifest itself otherwise.

14. MATERIAL OMISSION

(*a*) **. . . most base styles are to be traced . . .**

He means the causes of most base styles.

(*b*) **. . . if style is reduced in the last analysis to . . . instinct . . .**

When a product of many constituents is analysed by the method of reduction — the successive removal, by chemical action, of the less doubtful ones — the last stage of the analysis reveals the nature of the constituent that provoked the analysis. 'In the last analysis' therefore means, if anything, 'in the last stage of an analysis'.

15. UNFULFILLED PROMISE

It may be said that most base styles are due . . .

When 'it may be said' is used, followed by the concession 'and certainly' one expects: 'But this view cannot be maintained when one considers' . . . This expectation is disappointed. 'It may be said' is here used by Mr. Read apparently to avoid personal responsibility for a platitude.

22. OVER-EMPHASIS

. . . if style is reduced in the last analysis . . .

This hypothetic investigation by literary chemists is perhaps intended to conceal the painful obviousness of what he has to say.

FAIR COPY

'Every prose writer should learn to weigh instinctively the rhetorical persuasiveness, as well as the logic, of each word that he intends to use. It can be shown that a prose style generally regarded as base is one in which this rule has been neglected.'

COMMENT

Written at full length, the preceding argument would read as follows:

(*a*) Composition is the logical putting together of ideas in prose.

(*b*) Words are the units used in this composition.

(*c*) A study of how to write prose should start with an examination of a particular quality of words.

(*d*) This is their rhetorical quality.

(*e*) The practise of prose writing results in a personal style.

(*f*) Styles may be analysed.

(*g*) It will be found on analysis that styles generally regarded as base show a neglect of this rhetorical quality of words.

(*h*) The neglect is due to a failure of the writer's selective instinct.

But Herbert Read has chosen the wrong terms for definition and compromised between the long version and the short. This appears to be due to a failure of imagination: he should have realized that a reader who can understand the terms 'unit' and 'composition' must necessarily know that words are units of composition, and that if introductory platitudes are unavoidable in a book about prose they should at least be given with honest directness. It is curious how he fails by his own standards. The unrhetorical quality of the words 'most base styles are to be traced' proves a temporary failure of his 'selective instinct'—perhaps due to the embarrassment of breaking into his subject. Most critical writers begin with a sort of stammer; few manage to correct the stammer when they come to rewrite the passage. Plato showed a good example by working over the first paragraph of *The Republic* about a dozen times.

I. A. RICHARDS

from *Principles of Literary Criticism*, 1926

The arts[3a] are our storehouse of recorded values.[3b/12a] They[2] spring from and perpetuate hours in the lives of exceptional[14a] people,[12b] when their control and command[12c] of experience is[24a] at its highest, hours when the varying possibilities of existence are most clearly seen and the different

activities which may arise[3c] are most exquisitely reconciled,[12d] hours when habitual narrowness of interests[23a] or confused bewilderment[12e] are replaced by an intricately wrought composure.[3d] Both in the genesis of a work of art, in the creative moment,[9] and in its aspect[8a] as a vehicle of communication, reasons can be found for giving to the arts[G1] a very important place in the theory of Value.[3e] They record the most important[K] judgements we possess as to[8b] the values of experience.[12a] They form a body of evidence which, for lack of a serviceable psychology by which to interpret it, and through the desiccating influence of abstract[12f] Ethics, has been left almost untouched by professed students of value.[3f] An odd omission,[23b] for without the assistance of the arts we[1a] could compare very few of our experiences and without such comparison we could hardly hope to agree as to which are[24b] to be preferred.[22] Very simple experiences — [14b] a cold bath in an enamelled tin,[14c] or running for a train — may to some extent[20a] be compared without elaborate vehicles[8c]; and friends exceptionally well acquainted with one another may manage some rough comparisons in ordinary conversation.[12g] But subtle or recondite experiences are for most men incommunicable and indescribable,[12h] though social conventions or terror of the loneliness of the human situation[3g] may make us[1b] pretend the contrary. In the arts we find the record in the only form in which these things[P] can be recorded[18] of the experiences which have seemed worth having to the most sensitive and discriminating persons.[12b/G2] Through the obscure[8d] perception[1c] of this fact[20b] the poet has been regarded as a seer and the artist as a priest, suffering from usurpations.[1d] The arts, if rightly approached, supply the best data available for deciding what[8e] experiences are more valuable than others. The qualifying clause is all-important, however.[H] Happily[8f] there is no lack of glaring examples to remind us of the difficulty of approaching them rightly.

EXAMINATION

1. WHO?

(*a*) **Without the existence of the arts we could compare . . .**

Who is 'we'? Unless this is explained, the argument is not complete.

(*b*) **But subtle . . . experiences are for most men incommunicable . . . though . . . terror of the loneliness of the human situation may make us pretend the contrary.**

Does 'us' refer to 'most men'? Does I. A. Richards, despite his long study of the arts, admit himself at the same disadvantage as the uneducated mass?

(*c*) **Through the obscure perception of this fact . . .**

By whom?

(*d*) **. . . the poet has been regarded as a seer and the artist as a priest, suffering from usurpations.**

Who have usurped their places?

2. WHICH?

The arts are our storehouse of recorded values. They spring from and perpetuate hours . . .

Is it the arts or the values that spring from the hours? Values do not spring from hours but from the works of art that perpetuate them; if the arts are meant, then these are not a storehouse but the fruits stored inside.

3. WHAT?

(*a*) **The arts are our storehouse of recorded values.**

'The arts'? Which are these? Traditionally the phrase means either Grammar, Logic, Rhetoric, Arithmetic, Geometry, Music, and Astronomy or else 'The Fine Arts' – Painting, Sculpture and Architecture. Elsewhere in the book, I. A. Richards writes of 'Literature and the Arts', but here the Arts apparently include Literature, because 'the poet' though distinguished from 'the artist' is mentioned as recording experience by means of 'the arts'.

(*b*) **The arts are our storehouse of recorded values.**

The modern habit of lumping poetry, music and the graphic arts together as 'the arts' has been one of the chief causes of critical confusion in writing about them separately. In literature one can define, but in painting only record, and in music only suggest, valuable experience. What are these 'recorded values'? Does he mean 'recorded experience'?

(*c*) **. . . hours when the different activities which may arise are most exquisitely reconciled . . .**

It is difficult to understand how activities which have not yet arisen and have not therefore clashed can be reconciled to one another. Perhaps 'may arise' should 'have arisen'.

(*d*) **. . . hours when habitual narrowness of interests or confused bewilderment are replaced by an intricately wrought composure.**

Possibly what is meant: is 'hours when habitual narrowness of interests is replaced by intricacy; habitual agitation by composure'. Our suggestion is perhaps too bold a reading of the original; but how 'composure' can be intricately wrought, or how it can replace 'narrowness of interests', which usually denotes composure, puzzles us.

(*e*) **. . . giving to the arts a very important place in the theory of Value . . .**

What is this particular theory of Value?

(*f*) **. . . a very important place in the theory of Value . . .**

. . . left almost untouched by students of value.

Are 'Value' and 'value' the same thing? If so why is only the first one capitalized?

(*g*) **. . . terror of the loneliness of the human situation.**

What is this human situation? Man's position on the earth? Or some person's particular situation?

8. INAPPROPRIATE WORD OR PHRASE

(*a*) **Both in the genesis of a work of art . . . and in its aspect as a vehicle of communication reasons can be found for giving to the arts a very important place.**

The reasons are to be found, if at all, not in the work of art's 'aspect' as a vehicle, but in its quality as a vehicle: that is, not in what it seems; but in what it is.

(*b*) **... the most important judgements ... as to the values of experience ...**

The words 'as to' introduce a vagueness into what should be simple judgements upon the values of experience.

(*c*) **... a cold bath in an enamelled tin, or running for a train – may ... be compared without elaborate vehicles.**

The word 'vehicles' should have been avoided because it recalls the train.

(*d*) **Through the obscure perception of this fact ...**

The perception is 'dim'; the thing seen is 'obscure'.

(*e*) **... for deciding what experiences are more valuable than others.**

Since 'experiences' are mentioned, not 'experience', the 'what' should be 'which'.

(*f*) **Happily, there is no lack of glaring examples to remind us of the difficulty of approaching them rightly.**

'Unhappily', if one is more interested in critical successes than in failures.

9. AMBIGUOUS WORD OR PHRASE

Both in the genesis of a work of art, in the creative moment, and in its aspect as a vehicle of communication ...

Is 'in the creative moment' an explanation of 'the genesis', or is it a separate occasion? 'Both' suggests that it is an explanation: if so, it is not a helpful one. No work of art is created in a moment.

12. DUPLICATION

(*a*) **The arts are our storehouse of recorded values ... They record the most important judgements we possess as to the value of experience.**

If the first sentence had been more lucid the second could have been omitted.

(*b*) **... they perpetuate hours in the lives of exceptional people ...**

the record ... of the experiences which have seemed worth having to the most sensitive and discriminating persons.

The first sentence seems to be contained in the second.

(*c*) **... when their control and command of experience ...**

The distinction between control and command is not obvious enough to warrant the use of both words.

(*d*) **... hours when the varying possibilities of existence are ... most clearly seen, and the different activities which may arise are most exquisitely reconciled ...**

There does not seem to be any difference between the 'varying possibilities of existence' and the 'different activities which may arise', existence being proved by activity, whether mechanical or volitional.

(*e*) **... confused bewilderment ...**

One cannot be bewildered unless one is confused.

(*f*) **... the desiccating influence of abstract Ethics.**

'Ethics' necessarily deal with abstractions; but 'ethology', 'ethnology' and 'anthropology' with concrete instances of human behaviour.

(*g*) **... may to some extent be compared without elaborate vehicles.**
... may manage some rough comparisons in ordinary conversation.

Surely these two phrases mean the same thing?

(*h*) **But subtle . . . experiences are for most men incommunicable and indescribable.**

Description is communication; 'incommunicable and' could therefore have been omitted.

14. MATERIAL OMISSION

(*a*) **... they ... perpetuate hours in the lives of exceptional people ... hours when habitual narrowness of interests or confused bewilderment are replaced by ... composure.**

In what way are these people exceptional? Their range of interests is habitually narrow and their minds are habitually confused and bewildered.

(*b*) **... a cold bath in an enamelled tin, or running for a train ...**

These experiences are not parallel unless something is inserted before 'a cold bath': either 'taking' or 'making up one's mind to take'...

(*c*) **Very simple experiences – a cold bath in an enamelled tin ...**

Perhaps 'tin bath' was originally written, and 'bath' then struck out because the word has just been used in another sense. But 'a tin' means a small tin container for biscuits, cocoa, or the like. And the circumstances of the bath are not sufficiently indicated: the season at least should have been mentioned.

18. MISPUNCTUATION

In the arts we find the record in the only form in which these things can be recorded of experiences which have seemed worth having to the most sensitive and discriminating persons.

The commas omitted after 'record' and 'recorded' make it difficult for the reader to find his way about this sentence.

20. IRRELEVANCY

(*a*) **Very simple experiences . . . may to some extent be compared without elaborate vehicles . . .**

Since 'to some extent' suggests no measure of comparison it should have been omitted.

(*b*) **Through the obscure perception of this fact, the poet has been regarded . . .**

Here, as practically always in modern English, the word 'fact' can be omitted.

22. OVER-EMPHASIS

... without the arts we could compare very few of our experiences, and without such comparison we could hardly hope to agree as to which are to be preferred.

If 'the arts' mean the Fine Arts, or even the Fine Arts and Literature, this is an over-statement. Most people manage well enough to explain their preference for countless different sorts of experience without recourse either to Literature or the Arts. Moreover, there is more disagreement about the goodness or badness of works of art than there is about the goodness or badness of food, drink or the weather. 'Our' preference, since 'we' is left undefined, is not necessarily the popular preference. And popular preference is not synonymous with greater value. Most people prefer Murillo to El Greco; educated taste and the art-market at present favour El Greco.

23. LOGICAL WEAKNESS

(*a*) **. . . hours in the lives of exceptional people . . . when habitual narrowness of interests . . .**

If, as seems clear, these exceptional people are the same as the 'most sensitive and discriminating persons' mentioned later it seems odd that they should be restricted to a habitual 'narrowness' of interests which leaves them little opportunity for discrimination.

(*b*) **. . . a body of evidence which, for lack of a serviceable psychology by which to interpret it, and through the desiccating influence of abstract Ethics, has been left almost untouched by professed students of value. An odd omission . . .**

The omission is not odd: it has just been plausibly explained.

24. CHANGE OF STANDPOINT

(*a*) **. . . when their control and command of experience is at its highest . . .**

Either: '. . . when their control of experience is . . .' Or: 'when their control and command of experience are at their highest.'

(*b*) **. . . without such comparison we could hardly hope to agree as to which are to be preferred . . .**

Either: 'without such comparison we could hardly hope to agree as to which should be preferred . . .'

Or: 'without such comparison we can hardly hope to agree as to which are to be preferred . . .'

G. CIRCUMLOCUTION

(1) **Both in the genesis of a work of art, in the creative moment, and in its aspect as a vehicle of communication, reasons can be found for giving to the arts . . .**

This means no more than: 'Both the creation and the communicative power of a work of art suggest that the arts should be given . . .'

(2) **In the arts we find the record in the only possible form in which these things can be recorded of the experiences which have seemed worth having to the most sensitive and discriminating persons.**

This could have been written more clearly, in fourteen words instead of twenty-four: 'The arts provide the only possible record of the worthwhile experiences of discriminating persons'.

H. ELEGANT VARIATION

The arts, if rightly approached, supply the best data available for deciding what experiences are more valuable than others. The qualifying clause is all-important, however.

Better to have repeated the clause than to have forced the reader to look back and identify it.

K. TOO MUCH OF THE SAME WORD

. . . giving the arts a very important place in the theory of Value. They record the most important judgements we possess as to the values of experience.

The word 'important' can be justified in either of these two sentences, but to use it in both is careless: the two occasions are not parallel.

P. AWKWARD INVERSION

(1) In the arts we find the record in the only form in which these things can be recorded of the experiences which have seemed worth while . . .

It is not immediately clear to what 'these things' refers; it proves to be 'the experiences', which have not yet been mentioned.

FAIR COPY

'Though good manners or a sense of loneliness may make ordinary people pretend that every experience, however elaborate or recondite, can readily be communicated in conversation, and even compared in value with analogous experiences, yet in fact only the simplest ones – for example, that of taking a cold bath in winter in an enamelled tin hip-bath, or running to catch the morning train to business – can be so communicated and compared even between close friends.

The working out of a theory by which to reckon, account for, and compare the intrinsic values of spiritual [?] experience, implies the study of poems and works of art – no other evidence being so helpful – in an investigation both of the circumstances in which they were produced and of the communicative power which they exercise. Poems and works of art are accurate and lasting records of certain tranquil hours in the lives of exceptionally sensitive people, when their vision has been keener, their range of observation wider, their faculty for co-ordinating intricate facts and possibilities stronger, and their power of expression more felicitous than usual.

That philosophers and scientists have done little towards preparing the ground for such a theory is at first sight surprising, but can readily be explained: philosophers are restricted to the vocabulary of ethics, too dry for the purpose; scientists to the vocabulary of psychology, as yet not fully formulated. The popular view that the poet's divinatory function has been usurped by the scientist, and the artist's priestly function by the philosopher, shows a vague understanding that, when properly consulted, poems and works of art yield the right answer to many questions about the comparative value of experiences, which have baffled professors both of ethics and psychology. But alas, how improper have the methods of consultation usually been!'

COMMENT

If I. A. Richards really finds the communication of simple experiences so much more difficult than most people do, this is probably because he avoids defining the terms he uses: here, for example, he does not explain what 'the arts' are, what 'values' are, who it is who decides about 'values', or who is thought to have usurped the functions of the artist and the poet.

Also, the argument is incomplete, repetitive and disordered, and the language an uneasy mixture of Victorian literary incantation:

> — hours when the varying possibilities of existence are most clearly seen and the different activities which may arise are most exquisitely reconciled, hours when habitual narrowness of interests or confused bewilderment are replaced by an intricately wrought composure.

and bald modern laboratory exposition:

> The arts, if rightly approached, supply the best data available for deciding what experiences are more valuable than others.

Our alternative version may not represent exactly what I. A. Richards had in mind; but it is the nearest that we can get to a coherent statement, with the materials supplied by him.

BERTRAND RUSSELL

from *On Education*, 1926

TEXT

[Education must be democratic.] **This matter of democracy and education is one as to which[8a] clarity is important. It would be disastrous to insist upon a dead level of uniformity.[3a/12a] Some boys and girls are cleverer[14a] than others, and can derive more benefit from higher education. Some teachers[14b] have been better trained or have more native[20a] aptitude than others, but it is impossible that everybody[9] should be taught by the few best[7] teachers.[12b] Even if the highest education[3b] were desirable for all, which I doubt,[20b] it is[24] impossible that all should have it[12b] at present,[22a] and therefore a crude application of democratic principles[3c] might lead to the conclusion that none should have it. Such a view, if adopted,[8b/22b] would be fatal[8c] to scientific[20c] progress, and would make the general level of education a hundred years hence[22c] needlessly low.[12a/13] Progress should not be sacrificed to a mechanical quality[3d] at the present moment[15]; we must approach educational democracy[8d] carefully, so as to destroy[8e/10] in the process[3e] as little[8f] as possible of the valuable products that happen to have been associated with social injustice.[3f/14c]**

EXAMINATION

3. WHAT?

(*a*) **It would be disastrous to insist upon a dead level of uniformity.**

Uniformity in what? In democracy, in educational method, in the educational attainment of teachers, or in the educational standard reached by their pupils?

(*b*) **Even if the highest education were desirable for all . . .**

Is this 'highest education' what would be given if the few 'best teachers' were reduced to fewer and better, and finally to the single paragon?

(*c*) **. . . a crude application of democratic principles . . .**

Define! Define!

(*d*) **Progress should not be sacrificed to a mechanical quality at the present moment . . .**

What is this 'mechanical quality'? Is it equivalent to 'a crude application of democratic principles'? Or to 'a dead level of uniformity'?

(*e*) **We must approach educational democracy carefully, so as to destroy in the process . . .**

The 'process' of an 'approach' to 'democracy' can cause no destruction; but only the action taken when one reaches it.

(*f*) **. . . as little as possible of the valuable products that happen to have been associated with social injustice.**

This is perhaps an embarrassed way of admitting that although the present social system is unjust in giving the governing class privileges denied to the working class, it has produced some very gifted educationalists (including Bertrand Russell himself) whom it would be absurd to throw on the scrap-heap. 'That happen to' suggests that the Cambridge Mathematical School, for example, an incidental product of capitalism, is politically blameless.

7. HOW MANY?

. . . it is impossible that everybody should be taught by the few best teachers.

How many are 'the few best'? (How long is a piece of elastic?) 'The few good teachers' is a sober concept, so is 'a few of the best teachers'. But 'the few best' is a capricious one, there being always fewer, better, teachers, until a single paragon is left.

8. INAPPROPRIATE WORD OR PHRASE

(*a*) **This matter of democracy and education is one as to which clarity is important.**

Clarity cannot be called important 'as to this matter of democracy and education'; but 'clarity about the relation of democracy to education' can be.

(*b*) **. . . the conclusion that more should have it. Such a view, if adopted, . . .**

Rather: 'Such a conclusion, if translated into action . . .'

(*c*) **Such a view . . . would be fatal . . .**

'Disastrous', perhaps; but no element of fate seems to enter into this hypothesis.

(*d*) **. . . we must approach educational democracy carefully . . .**

This should be 'democratic education' – a very different concept.

(*e*) **. . . we must approach educational democracy carefully, so as to destroy in the process as little as possible of the valuable products . . .**

The question of destroying University laboratories and professors does not arise; the question is whether they should, or should not, be allowed to fade away.

(*f*) **. . . as little as possible of the valuable products . . .**

Rather: 'as few as possible . . .'

9. AMBIGUOUS WORD OR PHRASE

Some teachers have been better trained . . . than others, but it is impossible that everybody should be taught by the few best teachers.

Does this refer to a course in pedagogy by the 'few best teachers', which the other teachers cannot all attend because they are too numerous? Or does it refer to the general 'higher education' of children? The use of 'everybody', instead of 'all children', suggests that a course in pedagogy is meant.

10. MISPLACED WORD

. . . we must approach educational democracy carefully, so as to destroy in the process as little as possible of the valuable products . . .

If the word 'destroy' had been put later in the sentence, the idea of destruction would not have time to register itself violently in a reader's mind, before being cancelled by 'as little as possible'. Thus: 'We must approach democratic education carefully, so that as few as possible of the valuable products . . . may be destroyed'.

12. DUPLICATION

(*a*) **It would be disastrous to insist upon a dead level of uniformity . . .**

Such a view, if adopted, would make the general level of education a hundred years hence needlessly low.

The first instance is not introduced by any explanatory argument, as the second is, and should have been omitted because it contains nothing that the second does not.

(*b*) **. . . it is impossible that everybody should be taught by the few best teachers.**

. . . highest education . . . it is impossible that all should have it . . .

The second statement is repetitive.

13. SELF-EVIDENT STATEMENT

. . . the highest education . . . the conclusion that none should have it . . . would make the general level of education a hundred years hence needlessly low.

Since 'the highest education' here apparently means no more than 'higher education', it is obvious that to deny this to all children would needlessly reduce the level of education.

14. MATERIAL OMISSION

(*a*) **Some boys and girls are cleverer than others, and can derive more benefit from higher education.**

'Cleverness' is not the only consideration: some clever children cannot, or do not wish to, concentrate on school subjects, and some are lacking in moral sense.

(*b*) **Some teachers have been better trained or have more native aptitude than others . . .**

It should be made clear that these are the teachers required for higher education, not those, however well qualified, who work in elementary schools.

(*c*) **. . . we must approach educational democracy carefully, so as to destroy**

as little as possible of the valuable products that happen to have been associated with social injustice.

The simple solution, namely, to make higher education the privilege of intelligent children, rather than of children with moneyed or intellectual parents, should surely have been indicated?

15. UNFULFILLED PROMISE

Progress should not be sacrificed to mechanical quality at the present moment...

This suggests: 'but in a few years we shall be able to do so'.

20. IRRELEVANCY

(*a*) **Some teachers have more native aptitude than others . . .**

Aptitude is necessarily 'native': 'native' could have been omitted.

(*b*) **Even if the highest education were desirable for all, which I doubt . . .**

'Which I doubt' is unnecessary, the word 'even' has already indicated his doubt.

(*c*) **Such a view, if adopted, would be fatal to scientific progress . . .**

Why is 'scientific' progress mentioned? If education were, absurdly, limited to an elementary course, *all* intellectual progress would be disastrously affected.

22. OVER-EMPHASIS

(*a*) **Even if the highest education were desirable for all, . . . it is impossible that all should have it at present.**

The phrase 'at present' shows that what is suggested in the 'if' clause is something that might conceivably come about one day; this in turn shows that what is really meant is '*higher* education for all children, with degrees of height corresponding with the capacities both of teachers and children', not '*the highest* education'.

(*b*) **Such a view, if adopted, would be fatal . . .**

It should have been made clear that this argument is a *reductio ad absurdum* and that the view could not possibly be adopted.

(*c*) **. . . would make the general level of education a hundred years hence needlessly low.**

Immediately, not merely a hundred years hence. 'A hundred years hence' is a familiar conversational phrase used often to intensify a statement emotionally rather than to be taken literally.

24. CHANGE OF STANDPOINT

Even if the highest education were desirable . . . it is impossible . . .

Either: 'Even if the highest education were desirable . . . it would be impossible . . .'

Or: 'Even if the highest education is desirable, . . . it is impossible . . .'

FAIR COPY

'It is important to decide how far the crude democratic formula "equal opportunities for social advancement must be given to all" can, and should, be applied to education.

Since there are far fewer trained and gifted teachers available for higher education than could cope with all the boys and girls now completing their elementary schooling, a strict application of the formula would mean that no child at all would be allowed to pass the elementary stage; which would be absurd, as entailing a sacrifice of intellectual progress to political dogma and as further depressing the standard even of elementary education. But once it is admitted that some boys and girls can derive more benefit than others from higher education because they have greater intelligence or power of concentration, and that by no means all of these are children of the well-to-do families who form the greater part of the present "governing class", then the formula can be modified without loss of principle. Since, therefore, higher education for all children is at present impossible, even if it were desirable, and since it would be both foolish and disastrous to discard valuable products of the present social system merely on the ground that it is founded on injustices, the obvious course is to restrict equal educational opportunities for social advancement to those who are likely to make the best use of them: those children of well-to-do families who show little aptitude for higher education should be given only elementary schooling, and the resultant vacancies filled with promising children of the wage-earning, or "governed", class.'

COMMENT

Professor (now Earl) Russell's mind is reputedly exact and brilliant when it deals with problems of mathematics; when it deals with politics and education it tends to relax. Here he has omitted to define or even stabilize his terms. One moment the subject is 'democratic education'; then without warning it becomes 'educational democracy'. Similarly, 'higher education' becomes 'the highest education'; and what 'democracy', 'democratic principles' and 'social injustice' mean, the reader is left to guess. It should have been made clear that 'democracy' means government by a majority of the people, as opposed to 'aristocracy', which means government by the best people, or to 'oligarchy', which means government by a few people. Higher education is supposedly a way of teaching children to be 'the best' for governmental and similar functions. The paradox here is that Professor Russell upholds majority government against government by people who call themselves 'the best', but are not; but also upholds government by the best against majority government if the majority prove to be unscientific and dogmatic. He does not wish to own up to this paradox, perhaps for fear he should be mistaken for an aristocrat by principle as well as by birth. It therefore remains unresolved.

VISCOUNT SAMUEL

from *Belief and Action*, 1937

TEXT

Another ingredient[14a] in the seething cauldron of our times is the conflict that has arisen[8] on liberty.[H] At the beginning of this[2] century it seemed as though that[3a] were among the settled questions. There might be exceptions[3b] here and there[18]; some countries might be laggards in the march to freedom,[H] but all enlightened men[21] everywhere sought the same ultimate goal.[13/14b/A]

Nations should[9a] be free from alien[14c] domination[L]; the nineteenth century had seen the overthrow of Napoleon's empire over[N] Europe,[14d] the birth of the republics of South and Central America, the Italian *risorgimento*, the liberation of the Balkan peoples.[14e] These were illustrious examples of a rule[9b] destined[9c] to become universal.

EXAMINATION

2. WHICH?

At the beginning of this century . . .

It is not immediately clear that Viscount Samuel is contrasting the beginning of the Twentieth Century (when he was himself already a Member of Parliament) with 'our times': that is to say, with Hitlerian times. 'This' is therefore not recognizable as meaning 'the present century'.

3. WHAT?

(*a*) **. . . it seemed as though that were among the settled questions . . .**

'That' may refer to 'ingredient' or 'the conflict that has arisen on liberty'. Neither makes sense, however.

(*b*) **There might be exceptions here and there . . .**

Exceptions to what rule? To one of seeming-as-though? Or to one of conflict on liberty?

8. INAPPROPRIATE WORD OR PHRASE

Another ingredient in the seething cauldron of our times is the conflict that has arisen on liberty.

If a cartoon were drawn, showing witches brewing their 1937 hell-broth, the ugly bone or piece of offal that the First Witch was casting in would certainly not be labelled 'The Conflict that has Arisen on Liberty'. 'A conflict on liberty' implies that someone at least is in active support of the principle of liberty, and therefore 'Denial of Liberty' or simply 'Slavery' would be the cartoonist's label.

9. AMBIGUOUS WORD OR PHRASE

(*a*) **Nations should be free from alien domination . . .**

Since a new paragraph starts here, it is not clear whether this is the reported assertion of the enlightened men, 'Nations shall be free', or an opinion of Lord Samuel's own: 'Nations should be free'.

(*b*) **These were illustrious examples of a rule . . .**

Perhaps the 'rule' intended is 'Nations shall be free from alien domination . . .' but 'a rule' can be read as meaning not 'a law' but a 'form of government'.

(*c*) **. . . destined to become universal . . .**

Again, it is not clear whether the 'enlightened men' regarded this rule as destined to be come universal, or whether this view is Lord Samuel's own.

13. SELF-EVIDENT STATEMENT

. . . sought the same ultimate goal . . .

A goal is necessarily ultimate. One may have intermediate mile-stones, cross-roads, turning-points, hurdles and so on in this well-worn marathon-race metaphor. But (except for the stupid Swede in the American football story who, not having been given clear directions as to what he was to do after carrying the ball between the goal-posts, ran on with it across country for twenty miles or more), players always stop when they reach the goal.

14. MATERIAL OMISSION

(*a*) **Another ingredient in the seething cauldron of our times . . .**

An ingredient is added to broth, stew, pottage or other contents of a cauldron — not to the cauldron itself.

(*b*) **There might be exceptions here and there; some countries might be laggards in the march to freedom, but all enlightened men everywhere sought the same ultimate goal.**

There is a good deal omitted here, the gaps filled with Liberal metaphor. Viscount Samuel, who had been High Commissioner for Palestine and, also, Home Secretary, was shy of mentioning the hundreds of millions of coloured British subjects described by Rudyard Kipling as the 'lesser breeds without the law'.

(*c*) **Nations should be free from alien domination . . .**

The argument demands the inclusion of native domination too. The Italian *risorgimento* was directed against the Italian nobility as well as against foreign princes, and in Central and South America not all the revolutionaries could regard their Spanish or Portuguese overlords as aliens.

(*d*) **. . . the overthrow of Napoleon's empire over Europe . . .**

Napoleon did not retain his overseas Empire, either.

(*e*) **. . . the birth of the republics of South and Central America . . . the liberation of the Balkan peoples.**

Who were the alien oppressors?

18. MISPUNCTUATION

There might be exceptions here and there; some countries might be laggards in the march to freedom, but all enlightened men everywhere sought the same ultimate goal.

The middle part of this sentence, which amplifies the first part, should be closely attached to it (perhaps as a parenthesis followed by a comma)—not forced by a semi-colon to unite with the last part as a parallel to the first.

21. FALSE CONTRAST

. . . some countries might be laggards in the march to freedom; but all enlightened men everywhere sought the same ultimate goal.

The opposition between 'some countries' and 'all enlightened men everywhere' does not work out very well. Though laggards in the march, these countries were at least making *some* progress in the same direction as 'all enlightened men everywhere'; and these, if the word 'ultimate' means anything at all, were not making forced marches, either.

A. MISMATING OF METAPHORS

. . . some countries might be laggards in the march to freedom, but all enlightened men everywhere sought the same ultimate goal.

St Paul used the metaphor of a runner racing for the goal; he was himself the runner. And: 'Those that run in the race run all, but one receiveth the prize.' It is an obscure literary question: where the curious ecclesiastical metaphor originated in which masses of enlightened men and women march fearlessly shoulder to shoulder, or clasping hands, through the cold and darkness in an Easterly direction. How this metaphor happened to combine with the runner-and-goal one into a sort of Arctic football is a still more obscure question.

H. ELEGANT VARIATION

. . . the conflict that has arisen on liberty . . .

. . . laggards in the march to freedom . . .

'Liberty' and 'freedom' are not synonyms, but are here used as if they were. There is a challenging ring in 'liberty', a quiet assurance in 'freedom'.

L. JINGLE

Nations should be free from alien domination . . .

A jingle is especially noticeable when it is formed by the first and last words of a short sentence.

N. SAME WORD IN DIFFERENT SENSES

. . . the overthrow of Napoleon's empire over Europe.

The 'over' in 'overthrow' has a different force from the one in 'over Europe' and comes dangerously near it. The sentence suggests at first sight that Napoleon's Empire was metaphorically sent crashing right across Europe.

FAIR COPY

'Another ingredient in the hell-broth seething in the cauldron of to-day is slavery. Forty years ago, though the Great Powers of Europe were reluctant to admit the coloured races of their empires to full citizenship, and though here and there, even in Europe, the lower classes lived in traditional serfdom, the eventual liberty of all mankind seemed assured. During the previous century, illustrious examples had been seen of oppressed populations gaining their liberty: the overthrow of Napoleon's empire, the rebirth as independent republics of the revolted Spanish and

Portuguese colonies in Central and South America, the *risorgimento* in Italy, the gradual liberation of all the Balkan peoples from Turkish oppression.'

COMMENT

This is the writing of a busy and progressive administrator who has been tempted to cultivate oratory. Though with no gift for phrase-making, he has at least a rhythmic sense and a retentive memory. At the end of the short book from which we take this extract is an index of the two or three hundred quotations which occur in it: beads in the necklace of argument. The intervening rhetorical links, though not assignable quotations, are all borrowed from the common Parliamentary stock. Viscount Samuel had learned from his political career to use idealistic generalities as a cover for embarrassing facts; his technique may be compared with that of Lord Halifax. He was President of the British Institute of Philosophy, but as a patron rather than as a practising philosopher.

GEORGE BERNARD SHAW

from a Letter to a Weekly Journal, June, 1941

TEXT

[Because the Führer had proved that he could get all he wanted without fighting, I said that there would be no war] **. . . I was wrong. I am always making mistakes by imagining that other people are as clever as I am myself.[23a] The Führer was not the first statesman to take me in[8a] and is unlikely to be the last.** [There was a war, Hitler wiped the floor with us, and Mr. Churchill then told him that he was fighting with a rope round his neck. I blundered again about Russia: I could not believe the Führer would make Germany commit military suicide by attacking Russia in the middle of a very tough war.]

. . . Can it be that he is as blind as all our own Tories and Clericals[16] who persist in believing what they have been telling themselves[8b] for twenty years: that Stalin is a vulgar brigand and assassin whose rabble of tatterdemalions[5a] must scatter before the Nazi legions[5b] like autumn[20a] leaves before October winds? If so, he is lost; for[17] if he is as far behind the times and as obsolete politically as our Old School Ties,[22a] we[1] shall not be able to put the rope round his neck[23b] when Churchill, Roosevelt and Stalin have him finally by the collar. We shall have to send him to Broadmoor.[8c, 22b] But he is not as mad as that. The only sane[20h] explanation possible[22c] is that when Russia refused to join the Axis he concluded that[14] Stalin was waiting to attack him in the rear when[8d] he was fully engaged on the west[21] with Britain and

America, and that his only chance was to smash the Red army first.[24] The gambler's last throw: double or quits.[23c]

EXAMINATION

1. WHO?

. . . we shall not be able to put the rope round his neck when Churchill, Roosevelt and Stalin have him finally by the collar.

Who are we, as opposed to 'Churchill, Roosevelt and Stalin' who presumably represent the governments and fighting services of Great Britain and the Dominions, the U.S.A., and the U.S.S.R.?

5. WHEN?

(*a*) **. . . our own Tories and Clericals who persist in believing what they have been telling themselves for twenty years: that Stalin is a vulgar brigand . . . whose rabble of tatterdemalions must scatter before the Nazi legions . . .**

For several of these twenty years, Stalin was neither a combatant Red Army officer nor executive head of the U.S.S.R.

(*b*) **. . . whose rabble of tatterdemalions must scatter before the Nazi legions.**

In 1921 the Nazi legions were not in existence. Bernard Shaw is perhaps thinking of the Tsarist counter-revolutionary armies financed by Britain.

8. INAPPROPRIATE WORD OR PHRASE

(*a*) **The Führer was not the first statesman to take me in and is unlikely to be the last.**

This suggests that the Führer deliberately hoodwinked Bernard Shaw; but it is unlikely that he considered him a person of sufficient political importance to hoodwink.

(*b*) **. . . who persist in believing what they have been telling themselves . . .**

Rather: 'in telling one another'. The word 'themselves' suggests that they all independently fell under the same obsession.

(*c*) **We shall have to send him to Broadmoor.**

Rather 'a criminal asylum'. If Churchill, Roosevelt and Stalin were to be all equally responsible for his arrest, would he necessarily be committed to an English asylum?

(*d*) **. . . he concluded that Stalin was waiting to attack him in the rear when he was fully engaged on the west with Britain and America . . .**

The 'when' should surely be 'if'. Stalin could not have been sure that the U.S.A. would enter the war, or that Britain and the U.S.A. together would ever be able to bring sufficient forces into action in the west to engage the Führer fully.

14. MATERIAL OMISSION

. . . he concluded that Stalin was waiting to attack him in the rear when he was fully engaged in the west with Britain and America, and that his only chance was to smash the Red army first.

If Bernard Shaw believed that the Führer expected to be 'fully engaged on the west with Britain and America,' he should have said so; here the word 'first' suggests that the Führer believed that the U.S.A. would enter the war, whether or not he attacked the U.S.S.R., and in June, 1941, this was doubtful.

16. UNDEVELOPED THEME

Can it be that he is as blind as all our own Tories and Clericals . . .

A comparison between the British and German Tory-Clerical blocs is suggested by 'our own'; but whether the German Tories and Clericals influenced Nazi political thought is not discussed.

17. FAULTY CONNEXION

Can it be that he is as blind as all our own Tories and Clericals . . .? If so, he is lost; for . . . we shall not be able to put the rope round his neck. We shall have to send him to Broadmoor.

It is not clear why the Führer is described as 'lost' because his life will be eventually spared when he pleads 'guilty but insane'.

20. IRRELEVANCY

(*a*) **. . . must scatter like autumn leaves before the October winds?**

Since October is an autumn month, 'autumn' could have been omitted.

(*b*) **But he is not as mad as that. The only sane explanation possible is that when Russia refused to join the Axis he concluded . . .**

The word 'sane' has been introduced perhaps as a contrast to 'he is not as mad as that'. But whether the Führer is or is not mad is one thing, and whether political experts who debate the point are mad is another thing, and the two should not have been confused.

21. FALSE CONTRAST

. . . to attack him in the rear when he was fully engaged on the west . . .

This suggests that all the German armies, including the Eastern frontier guards, would automatically face west if engaged on the Atlantic sea-board. The proper contrast is 'attack him from the east when he was fully engaged on the west'.

22. OVER-EMPHASIS

(*a*) **. . . if he is as . . . obsolete politically as our Old School Ties . . .**

It was absurd to suggest in June 1941 that the 'Old School Ties' (if this means members of the British governing class with a public-school education and a clannish spirit) were politically obsolete. If by 'Old School Ties' is meant merely: 'our own Tories and Clericals who persist etc.' this should have been made clear.

(*b*) **. . . if he is as far behind the times and as obsolete politically as our Old School Ties we shall not be able to put the rope round his neck . . . We shall have to send him to Broadmoor.**

This suggests that 'our Old School Ties' deserve hanging but are, instead, usually sent to Broadmoor. Perhaps Mr. Shaw is referring to the popular outcry in the early 'Twenties when Ronald True, who wore an old-school-tie, was spared the rope and sent to Broadmoor; but True's crime was murder, not being politically obsolete.

(*c*) **The only sane explanation possible is that . . .**

There are many other sane, though not necessarily correct, explanations, such as that the Führer needed Russian oil, grain, factories, labour; that he counted on the Old School Ties and the American Isolationists to welcome the attack; that he wished to give his army something to do, since an immediate invasion of Britain was not practicable; that he hoped, by a further demonstration of military power, to discourage the U.S.A. from entering the war and from sending further help to Britain.

23. LOGICAL WEAKNESS

(*a*) **I am always making mistakes by imagining that other people are as clever as I am myself.**

He always imagines that other people are as clever as he is; this is a mistake; therefore, they are not so clever as he is; therefore, it is perhaps a sign of cleverness to be always mistaken; therefore, since they are not so clever as he is, they are perhaps less often mistaken than he; therefore, the German invasion of Russia is perhaps after all not a mistake; therefore, the Führer is perhaps clever after all; therefore, Bernard Shaw is not mistaken; therefore . . . etc.

(*b*) **[Mr. Churchill then told him that he was fighting with a rope round his neck] . . . we shall not be able to put the rope round his neck.**

Since it is 'the rope' and not 'a rope', the reference is clearly to the figurative rope which Mr. Churchill put there. How can it be put there again, if already in position?

(*c*) **. . . his only chance was to smash the Red army first. The gambler's last throw: double or quits.**

When the desperate gambler calls for 'double or quits', it means that he has had several serious losses but hopes to recoup them and return to the *status quo ante ludum* by staking all his remaining cash on a last throw. This metaphor does not correspond with the known facts. The Führer, so far, had been almost uniformly successful in his gambles. If 'winner take or lose all' is the phrase meant, it should have been made clear that a German victory over Russia would either discourage or make hopeless the feared Anglo-American invasion of Western Europe.

24. CHANGE OF STANDPOINT

When Churchill, Roosevelt and Stalin have him . . . by the collar. . . . When Russia refused to join the Axis he concluded that Stalin was waiting to attack him in the rear when he was fully engaged in the West with Britain and America, and that his only chance was to smash the Red army first.

Since it is clear that Churchill, Roosevelt and Stalin could not literally take Hitler by the collar, these men must be understood as representing their nations. To switch from 'Stalin' to 'Russia', then back to 'Stalin' again, and from Stalin to the Red Army, and from 'Churchill and Roosevelt' to 'Britain and America' is confusing for the reader.

FAIR COPY

['Because the Führer had proved that he could get all he wanted without fighting, I said that there would be no war.] I was wrong, as I frequently am when I over-estimate people's intelligence: he was not the first statesman I had gone wrong about and is unlikely to be the last. [There was a war, Hitler wiped the floor with us, and Mr. Churchill told him that he was fighting with a rope round his neck. I blundered again about Russia: I could not believe that the Führer would make Germany commit military suicide by attacking Russia in the middle of a very tough war.] Can it be that he is as far behind the times as those British Old School Ties and Clericals who for more than twenty years have blindly persisted in lying to one another about the military and political strength of Russia? Does he perhaps believe that Stalin is a vulgar brigand and assassin whose rabble of tatterdemalions must scatter before the Nazi legions like leaves before October winds? If so, he is lost. To invade Russia in reliance on such a misconception must inevitably lead to defeat; and when he is eventually dragged before an Anglo-Russo-American court of justice the verdict can only be "guilty but insane"; so that the other end of the rope will not, after all, be hitched to a beam. But I do not think him mad.

The only reasonable explanation of his attack on Russia, that I can suggest, is that he does not trust Stalin, fears an Anglo-American invasion of Western Europe, and has decided to forestall this by smashing the Russian army which, by a diversion in the East when he was fully engaged with the invaders, could alone give these a reasonable hope of success. Hitler's is a bold gamble: "winner take or lose all".'

COMMENT

Age, self-confidence, excitement at the Russian news, and, perhaps a slight annoyance at having made two wrong guesses, here combine to make Bernard Shaw write with unusual carelessness. Much of the passage is humorously intended, and was perhaps written with smothered guffaws and ogre-like grimaces; but a writer should be particularly careful when he is being humorous or ironical, because vocal inflections are not communicable in ordinary printed prose.

STEPHEN SPENDER

from *Books and the War*, 1941

TEXT

... Political beliefs and events play a part[8a] in the lives of contemporaries[1a] which religious and spectacular warnings[9] of the working out of doom amongst the great[21a] used to play in the past.[20a] Problems of social organization[3a] are so crucially important that any religious mind which ignores them, instead of providing an example to the world, like[3b] the teaching of Christ,[16] has shrunk into a shelter from the world. [17]The destruction which one nation can inflict on another has dwarfed even terrible natural events[3c] and examples of happiness or unhappiness in private life made public.[3d]

For the poets to ignore this tendency[8b] of every smaller issue to be swept up in the ever-widening stream of the vast issues that threaten to engulf[8c] the

whole world, would be to abandon the main tradition[3e] of a culture which has always been at the centre of the life of the time.[4a] However limited its[2] audience may have been, or, rather,[o] however indirectly its lessons may have seeped through the select audience of the genuinely[20b] initiated to the vast surrounding life outside,[3f/12] poetry has been a clearing house[^] of the deepest emotional life of the people in the past.[10] There has been no act of abdication by which[8d] poets have decided to abandon their interpretations of these passionate forces, for the transplanted[4b] alpine flowers of a rock garden.[21b] There have certainly always been gardens of retreat for poetry,[1b] but these have implied the existence of a greater life of literature outside.[21c]

EXAMINATION

1. WHO?

(*a*) **Political beliefs . . . play a part in the lives of contemporaries . . .**

Whose contemporaries?

(*b*) **There have certainly always been gardens of retreat for poetry . . .**

It is not poetry, but the poets, who retreat to gardens.

2. WHICH?

. . . would be to abandon the main tradition of a culture which has always been at the centre of the life of the time. However limited its audience may have been . . .

Is this the audience of the 'tradition'? Or of the 'culture'? Or of the 'life of the time'?

3. WHAT?

(*a*) **Problems of social organization are so crucially important . . .**

By no means all problems of this sort are crucial. Does Mr. Spender mean 'reorganization'? If the relation between Labour and Capital is particularly referred to, this should be indicated.

(*b*) **. . . any religious mind which ignores them, instead of providing an example to the world, like the teaching of Christ, . . .**

Is this intended to mean 'an example to the world resembling the teaching of Christ'? If so, this seems to be asking too much of the religious mind. Or is it intended to mean: 'an example to the world like that enjoined by Christ in the text: "Let your light so shine before men, etc.,"?' If so, some words are omitted. Or is it intended to mean 'providing an example to the world, as the teaching of Christ did'? If so, it is very loosely expressed. Literally (because of the commas) it means either: 'which ignores them, as it does the teaching of Christ . . .', or: 'which ignores them, as does the teaching of Christ'.

(*c*) **The destruction which one nation can inflict on another has dwarfed even terrible natural events . . .**

Are these events the same as 'spectacular warnings of the working out of doom amongst the great'? Or what else are they?

(*d*) **. . . and examples of happiness or unhappiness in private life made public.**

This reads mysteriously. Perhaps it means 'published records of happiness or unhappiness in private life'.

(*e*) **For the poets to ignore . . . the ever-widening stream of the vast issues that threaten to engulf the whole world, would be to abandon the main tradition of a culture . . .**

What tradition is this? The word 'tradition' suggests that these vast issues have always threatened to engulf the whole world.

(*f*) **. . . the vast surrounding life outside . . .**

Does this life comprise all nature, or only all occasional readers of poetry?

4. WHERE?

(*a*) **. . . a culture which has always been at the centre of the life of the time.**

Where is the centre of the life of the time? In peace-time England, for example, was it in Bermondsey or in Bloomsbury?

(*b*) **. . . transplanted alpine flowers of a rock garden.**

Transplanted from, or to, the rock garden?

8. INAPPROPRIATE WORD OR PHRASE

(*a*) **Political beliefs and events play a part . . . which spectacular warnings of the working out of doom among the great used to play in the past.**

People or dramatizable abstractions may be said to 'play parts' but not beliefs, events or warnings. If 'spectacular warnings of the working out of doom among the great' refers to Greek tragedy and its mediaeval and early modern derivatives, then 'play a part' is a particularly inappropriate phrase. Actors play parts, but not the warnings which they may have to deliver.

(*b*) **. . . this tendency of every smaller issue to be swept up in the ever-widening stream of the vast issues.**

The tendency is for the stream to sweep up obstacles, not for the obstacles to be swept up.

(*c*) **. . . stream of the vast issues that threaten to engulf the whole world.**

Perhaps a stream of disasters that threatens to engulf the whole world; but 'issues' cannot 'engulf' anything.

(*d*) **There has been no act of abdication by which poets have decided . . .**

Not 'by which'. An act of abdication puts into effect a decision already taken.

9. AMBIGUOUS WORD OR PHRASE

. . . religious and spectacular warnings of the working out of doom . . .

Does this mean warnings given in the course of a religious drama about the working out of doom? Or does it mean 'warnings from the pulpit, and also warnings inferred from natural catastrophes'?

10. MISPLACED WORD OR PHRASE

However limited its audience may have been . . . poetry has been a clearing house of the deepest emotional life of the people in the past.

This should be: '. . . poetry in the past has been a clearing house of the deepest emotional life of the people'. Otherwise, it suggests that poetry takes its subjects only from antiquity.

12. DUPLICATION

. . . the vast surrounding life outside.

Anything that surrounds anything else is necessarily outside it.

16. UNDEVELOPED THEME

Problems of social organization are so crucially important that any religious mind which ignores them, instead of providing an example to the world, like the teaching of Christ . . .

It should have been shown in what way Jesus Christ, though living some nineteen hundred years previously, was interested in crucial modern problems of social organization.

17. FAULTY CONNEXION

Problems of social organization are so crucially important that any religious mind which ignores them . . . has shrunk into a shelter from the world. The destruction which one nation can inflict on another has dwarfed even terrible natural events. . . .

The connexion between a nation's domestic problems and its foreign wars is not shown.

20. IRRELEVANCY

(*a*) **. . . used to play in the past.**

Unless 'the past' is characterized as 'recent' or 'distant' it is irrelevant, since 'used' conveys the past.

(*b*) **. . . the select audience of the genuinely initiated.**

An audience of people initiated into the mysteries of poetry is 'select' indeed. The words 'select' and 'genuinely' need not have been used.

21. FALSE CONTRAST

(*a*) **Political beliefs . . . play a part in the lives of contemporaries which religious and spectacular warnings of the working out of doom among the great used to play in the past.**

In 1941, when this was written, popular dramatic interest in Great Britain had been drawn to the impending doom of Mussolini and Hitler; in Classical times political beliefs had been strongly held, especially whenever there was a conflict between the rival principles of monarchy, aristocracy and democracy. Modern doom-interest and modern political belief could therefore each be contrasted with its past manifestations; but a contrast between modern political belief and ancient doom-interest seems unjustified.

(*b*) **. . . to abandon their interpretations of these passionate forces, for the transplanted alpine flowers of a rock garden.**

One might conceivably abandon an interpretation of emotions, in favour of a contemplation of flowers; but 'interpretations' and 'flowers' are concepts too dissimilar to be decently contrasted.

(*c*) **. . . gardens of retreat for poetry, but these have always implied the existence of a greater life of literature outside.**

Surely the intended contrast is not between poetry and literature but between poetry and 'crucially important problems of social organization'.

A. MISMATING OF METAPHORS

However limited its audience . . . however indirectly its lessons may have seeped . . . poetry has been a clearing-house . . .

Clearing-houses neither have audiences, nor teach lessons which seep through them.

O. SECOND THOUGHTS

However limited its audience may have been, or, rather, however indirectly its lessons may have seeped through the select audience of the genuinely initiated to the vast surrounding life outside . . .

Perhaps, after all, he means: 'however mystical it may seem to suggest that poetry written for a carefully chosen audience has had any influence at all on the masses of the people, who neither read it nor could understand it if they did. . . .' 'Or rather' always shows indecision in the writer.

FAIR COPY

'Since political creeds have largely superseded religious ones, popular dramatic interest is no longer concentrated on natural catastrophes or on the supernatural doom which overtakes the ambitious Great. It has turned instead to the prolonged conflict between the working-classes and their exploiters, which is now complicated by the hideous destructiveness of international warfare. How the conflict can best be resolved is a question of such crucial importance that to make formal Christianity an excuse for ignoring it would be more than cowardice: it would be a rejection of the example set by Jesus Christ, who actively championed the poor and oppressed in an age not yet consciously committed to the class-struggle.

Nor should the practice of poetry be made an excuse for ignoring this conflict, which threatens to sweep away all non-political issues. If poets did so, they would be abandoning their main cultural tradition, which is so to interpret every passionately-held popular obsession that, even when the initiates of poetry are few, the unpoetical masses become dimly, but gratefully, aware that the interpretation has been truly made. We poets of to-day have not abandoned this tradition, nor abdicated our title as prime arbiters of popular conflict. Poets have always had gardens for their retreat and refreshment between periods of active participation in worldly affairs; but we have not now permanently retired to them, to cultivate in pretty rockeries the blooms we once culled on perilous Alpine slopes.'

COMMENT

The difficulties of this passage are perhaps due to Stephen Spender's discovery of himself in unexpected transition from Marxism to Christianity during a World war. He seems to have been more conscious of the rhythm of his sentences than of the meaning of the words contained in them. All that he is sure about is that, whether Marxist or Christian, he is a poet, and as such has a public responsibility, which he must face at all costs, of interpreting popular emotions rather than expressing his own thoughts. He resolves the uncomfortable paradox, that the masses are not really capable of appreciating how he interprets their emotions, by crediting them with a mystical trust in their spiritual betters, a small circle of poetical initiates.

J. W. N. SULLIVAN

from *The Bases of Science*, 1928

TEXT

The mediaevalist's[9] chief criterion was teleological.[12a] Phenomena[E] were ordered[14] in accordance with their bearing on human[23a] purposes. . . .

. . . The central and dominating fact[12b] was man and his immortal destiny. The 'material universe' was merely a setting[23b] within which a moment of this destiny was being worked out . . . As a natural consequence of this point of view phenomena were explained in terms of their supposed purposes.[12a] The 'why' of phenomena, not the 'how'[21a] of phenomena, was the question that interested the mediaeval mind.[12a] The mediaeval universe was informed through and through with *purpose*.[12a/22/E] Men did not interpret the temporal passage of Nature as a bare[8a] succession of events, but as the passage from potentiality to actuality. All things conspired together towards some divine end.[23a/12a/E] The merely spatial and temporal connections of phenomena were not considered to be of importance compared with their logical connections.[21b] Phenomena were regarded as exemplifying certain general logical principles and as serving a universal purpose.[12a] The general mediaeval outlook made[3] the assumption that Nature was rational a reasonable one.[8b] Since both Nature and man had the same author, and Nature was designed to forward man's destiny,[12a/23b] it was not unreasonable to suppose that the workings of Nature should proceed in a manner intelligible to the human mind.

EXAMINATION

3. WHAT?

. . . the general outlook made the assumption . . . reasonable . . .

Can the 'outlook' be said to have made the assumption? Or was the assumption part of the outlook?

8. INAPPROPRIATE WORD OR PHRASE

(*a*) **. . . bare succession of events . . .**

What is perhaps meant is 'scientifically observable'. The bareness or richness of the succession is immaterial.

(*b*) **The mediaeval outlook made the assumption that Nature was rational a reasonable one.**

The word 'reasonable' has been used here probably in order to avoid repetition of 'rational'. The words needed were perhaps 'a logical necessity'—following on the premiss that Nature exemplifies logical principles.

9. AMBIGUOUS WORD OR PHRASE

The mediaevalist's chief criterion was teleological.

The word 'mediaevalist' means 'someone who studies mediaeval history', more often than 'someone living in the Middle Ages'.

12. DUPLICATION

(*a*) **The mediaevalist's chief criterion was teleological.**

. . . phenomena were explained in terms of their supposed purposes.

The 'why' of phenomena . . . was the question that interested the mediaeval mind.

The mediaeval universe was informed through and through with ***purpose.***

All things conspired together towards some divine end.

Phenomena were regarded as . . . serving a universal purpose.

Nature was designed to forward man's destiny . . .

The same point is here made over and over again: that people in the Middle Ages were more interested in Nature as revealing God's intentions for man than in examining her spatial and temporal aspects. The passage quoted is only a part of an argument which batters away at the same point for several pages. The Fair Copy which we offer shows how these seven sentences could have been compressed into one.

(*b*) **. . . the central and dominating fact . . .**

The centrality of a fact (for example, that potatoes are cultivated principally for human consumption) necessarily makes it dominate all outlying facts (for example, that potatoes are also used for pig-food and that potato-haulms can be used for paper-making). Either 'central' or 'dominating' could have been omitted.

14. MATERIAL OMISSION

Phenomena were ordered in accordance with their bearing on human purposes.

It should have been made clear that this was 'the mediaevalist's' view, not J. W. N. Sullivan's.

21. FALSE CONTRAST

(*a*) **The 'why' of phenomena, not the 'how' of phenomena, was the question that interested the mediaeval mind.**

No: 'how' the phenomena exemplified God's purpose was also of interest to them, as the rest of the passage makes clear.

(*b*) **The merely spatial and temporal connections of phenomena were not considered to be of importance compared with their logical connections.**

'Merely spatial and temporal connections' are also logical connections, though some logical connections transcend space and time.

22. OVER-EMPHASIS

The mediaeval universe was informed through and through with ***purpose.***

The 'through and through' and the italicising of *purpose* suggest that

J. W. N. Sullivan realized that he was over-stating his case. 'Hap', 'luck', 'fortune', 'adventure', 'sort', and 'case' were all common mediaeval English words that expressed seemingly accidental, or purposeless, happening.

23. LOGICAL WEAKNESS

(*a*) **Phenomena were ordered in accordance with their bearing on human purposes. . . .**

All things conspired together towards some divine end.

Though in the course of the argument it is explained that the *final* end of man was held to be union with God, these sentences contradict each other. In mediaeval Christian philosophy 'the divine end' was very sharply distinguished from temporal and foolish 'human purposes'.

(*b*) **The 'material universe' was merely a setting within which a moment of this destiny was being worked out.**

. . . the assumption that Nature was rational . . .

Nature was designed to forward man's destiny.

If, as seems probable, 'Nature' and 'the material universe' are identical, it is not clear how a 'mere setting' could rationally 'forward man's destiny'.

E. MISMATING OF STYLES

The mediaevalist's chief criterion was teleological.

Phenomena were regarded . . .

The mediaeval universe was informed through and through with *purpose*.

All things conspired together towards some divine end.

The words 'teleological' and 'phenomena' are scientific ones. 'The universe was informed with' is a poetical phrase; and so is 'All things conspired together'.

FAIR COPY

'Mediaeval people believed that all natural events happened purposefully in fulfilment of God's plan for the redemption of the human soul. How the causal relation between these events exemplified the principles of God's logic was considered more worthy of study than how they were related in terms of time and space. The assumption that God had created both the human race and Nature, whose sole function, apparently, was to conduct human souls through a short stage of their destined journey, led to the further assumption that the purpose of each of Nature's processes was intelligible to the human mind.'

COMMENT

In popular interpretations of scientific or theological thought it is usually found convenient to use first technical, and then untechnical, language in pressing each point. J. W. N. Sullivan's interpretative method, of presenting a point over and over again in much the same language – he hopes, perhaps, that one way at least will be intelligible to every reader – is not only a tedious but a confusing one. The slight differences between the various presentations assume too much importance; and his zeal to burn some message into his readers' minds leads him to over-emphasis and illogic.

HELEN WADDELL

from *The Wandering Scholars*, 1927

TEXT

It is[K] not to say[24a] that satire upon woman is not a distinct[G] branch of mediaeval clerical literature.[15a] It[15b/K] is to this day the *fonds*[8a] of most[22a] music-hall jokes,[E] thanks to[8b] that obscure instinct[1a] for which 'woman, in herself and without any effort on her part, is always News'.[F1] But the bourgeois[21a/J] is a far richer[8c] vein than the clerical. Bernard of Morlaix is rough-tongued[21b] enough in the *De Contemptu Mundi*: **[18]and Golias in his[11]** *De Conjuge Non Ducenda* **is profoundly grateful to the three angels who come to dissuade him from matrimony. But there is nothing in Latin[9a] to touch the sheer brutality[21b] of the vernacular.[9b] 'I always bless God', said William Morris, 'for making anything so strong as an onion'[P]; it is[8d/K] the ideal temper in which to approach the grosser half[3a] of mediaeval literature. It is[K] true that Jean de Meung, the mediaeval Diogenes,[F2] is a clerk[5] but he is too often[8e/22b] taken as the representative of his order,[9c] his** *Roman*[3b] **as the outrage of clerical prejudice[3c] on the chivalrous Dream of the Rose.[F3] But[17] the author of the first** *Roman*[2] **seems himself to have been a clerk[E]: his successor[1b] wrote . . . at the end of the thirteenth century, in the first blast of the east wind that blows[24b] for nearly two centuries.**

EXAMINATION

1. WHO?

(*a*) **. . . the *fonds* of most music-hall jokes, thanks to that obscure instinct for which, 'woman, . . . is always News'.**

Since the instinct is described as 'obscure', the reader will expect to be told whose it is.

(*b*) **But the author of the first *Roman* seems himself to have been a clerk: his successor wrote at the end of the thirteenth century . . .**

It is not easy to grasp that 'his successor' is Jean de Meung.

2. WHICH?

But the author of the first *Roman* seems to have been a clerk . . .

Which *Roman* was this? Only Jean de Meung's has been clearly mentioned. Was it the first?

3. WHAT?

(*a*) **. . . the grosser half of mediaeval literature . . .**

What is this? Vernacular as opposed to Latin literature? Does it include vernacular work by clerics? And courtly romances as well as bourgeois brutalities?

(*b*) **. . . his *Roman* as the outrage of clerical prejudice on the chivalrous Dream of the Rose.**

If Jean de Meung was a 'clerk', why did he write in the French vernacular?

(*c*) . . . his *Roman* as the outrage of clerical prejudice on the chivalrous Dream of the Rose.

It is not clear whether the Dream of the Rose outraged de Meung's clerical prejudice, or whether de Meung's *Roman* outraged chivalrous admirers of the Dream of the Rose.

5. WHEN?

It is true that Jean de Meung, . . . is a clerk . . .

It is customary to say, for example: 'Shakespeare writes prettily of Spring' or 'Demosthenes speaks resentfully of his guardian's avarice'. But to refer in the present tense to other actions of literary men than speaking or writing — 'Shakespeare is managing-director of the Globe Theatre', 'Demosthenes speaks with his mouth full of stones in order to cure a stammer' — is bizarre.

8. INAPPROPRIATE WORD OR PHRASE

(*a*) It is to this day the *fonds* of most music-hall jokes . . .

There seems no reason for using a French word in so British a context. Why not 'basis'?

(*b*) It is to this day the *fonds* of most music-hall jokes, thanks to that obscure instinct . . .

This is a forced use of 'thanks to', which normally expresses real or ironic gratitude in personal contexts: 'I fell and broke my arm, thanks to Mrs. Elmslie who had left the coal-scuttle on the dark stairs.' 'Because of' is appropriate to impersonal contexts, as here.

(*c*) But the bourgeois is a far richer vein than the clerical.

'Not richer'. *De Contemptu Mundi* is written in far richer language than the bourgeois satires. (The luscious hymn 'Jerusalem the Golden' is a faithful translation of one part of it.) Probably the word that first occurred to Miss Waddell was 'coarser'; but she did not wish to seem squeamish.

(*d*) 'I always bless God,' said William Morris, 'for making anything so strong as an onion'; it is the ideal temper in which to approach the grosser half of mediaeval literature.

The reader does not immediately grasp to what 'it is' refers, especially since there has been a semi-colon, not a colon. It should have been: 'This is . . .'

(*e*) . . . he is too often taken as the representative . . .

Even once would be bad enough. What is meant is . . . 'he is often wrongly taken as representative'.

9. AMBIGUOUS WORD OR PHRASE

(*a*) But there is nothing in Latin to touch the sheer brutality of the vernacular.

Is this a general reflection on the suavity of the Latin language, or does it refer only to clerical and lay satire?

(*b*) . . . nothing in Latin to touch the sheer brutality of the vernacular.

Many vernaculars were spoken in Christendom during this period. But since all the persons mentioned in this passage were French either by birth or adoption, does 'the vernacular' refer to French or to vernaculars in general?

(*c*) **. . . he is too often taken as the representative of his order . . .**

Does 'his order' mean all clerics? Or does it mean some particular fraternity to which Jean de Meung belonged?

11. UNINTENTIONAL CONTRAST

Bernard of Morlaix is rough-tongued enough in the *De Contemptu Mundi*: **and Golias in his** *De Conjuge Non Ducenda* **. . .**

The change from 'the' to 'his' suggests that St Bernard was not the sole author of *De Contemptu Mundi* as Golias was of *De Conjuge Non Ducenda.*

15. UNFULFILLED PROMISE

(*a*) **It is not to say that satire upon woman is not a distinct branch of mediaeval clerical literature. It is to this day the** *fonds* **of most music-hall jokes . . .**

That jokes about women are still prevalent in British music-halls is not the expected amplification of the statement that satire on women was a distinct literary form in mediaeval clerical literature.

(*b*) **It is not to say that satire upon woman is not a distinct branch of mediaeval literature. It is to this day the** *fonds* **of most music-hall jokes, thanks to that obscure instinct . . .**

One reads the second 'It is' as parallel with the first, and therefore expects the sentence to run something like this: 'It is to this day the *fonds* of most music-hall jokes . . . that woman is a depraved and contrary creature.'

17. FAULTY CONNEXION

It is true that Jean de Meung . . . is a clerk but he is too often taken as the representative of his order, his *Roman* **as the outrage of clerical prejudice on the chivalrous Dream of the Rose. But the author of the first** *Roman* **seems himself to have been a clerk . . .**

Even readers who realize that what is meant is that 'Jean de Meung was a cleric, yet did not, in his sequel to the *Roman de la Rose,* express the prejudice of all clerics', will be puzzled by 'But the author . . .' After 'he is too often taken' the appropriate connexion is not 'But', which expresses an objection, but 'Indeed', which affirms.

18. MISPUNCTATION

Bernard is rough-tongued enough in the *De Contemptu Mundi*: **and Golias in his** *De Conjuge Non Ducenda* **is profoundly grateful to the three angels. . .**

It is not immediately clear that Golias is an author, like St Bernard, not a character in a piece of St Bernard's entitled *De Conjuge Non Ducenda.* The fault lies in the colon, which should have been a semi-colon.

21. FALSE CONTRAST

(*a*) **But the bourgeois is a far richer vein than the clerical.**

The contrast should be surely between the 'clerical' and the 'lay'? A mediaeval 'bourgeois' would be more properly contrasted with a peasant or with a gentleman.

(*b*) **But the bourgeois is a far richer vein than the clerical. Bernard of**

Morlaix is rough-tongued enough in the *De Contemptu Mundi* . . . But there is nothing in Latin to touch the sheer brutality of the vernacular.

The contrast should be between roughness and brutality, or between poorness and richness. Here the identification of richness with brutality confuses the argument.

22. OVER-EMPHASIS

(*a*) **It is to this day the *fonds* of most music-hall jokes . . .**

In the music-hall (and in the variety-theatre which had superseded it by 1927, when this was published) jokes about cheese, kippers, tripe, the pawnshop, the lunatic asylum, the Government, racing, betting, beer, babies, policemen, landlords, fishermen, Scotsmen, Channel-swimmers, and so forth, together greatly outweighed jokes about the peculiarities of wives and mothers-in-law.

(*b*) **. . . he is too often taken as the representative of his order . . .**

It would have been more sober to write: 'he is too often taken as representative of his order'. The word 'the' suggests that critics believe him to have been briefed by his clerical colleagues to satirize woman for them.

24. CHANGE OF STANDPOINT

(*a*) **It is not to say that satire upon woman . . .**

This is probably a compromise between 'This is not to say that satire . . .' and 'It is not right to say that satire . . .'

(*b*) **. . . his successor wrote . . . in the first blast of the east wind that blows for two centuries.**

Either: '. . . his successor writes in the first blast of the east wind that blows . . .'

Or: '. . . his successor wrote in the first blast of the east wind that blew . . .'

E. MISMATING OF STYLES

. . . most music-hall jokes . . .

. . . Jean de Meung is a clerk . . .

The mediaeval meaning of 'clerk' was 'one who has been educated by the Church, can read and write Latin and thus comes under the jurisdiction of ecclesiastical courts'. By the time of music-halls a 'clerk' was an accountant or secretary, usually in commercial employment, with no knowledge of Latin and without 'benefit of clergy'. 'Cleric' would have been a more appropriate word here.

F. OBSCURE REFERENCE

(1) **. . . 'woman, in herself and without any effort on her part, is always News'.**

Who wrote this? Bernard of Morlaix? Golias? Jean de Meung? Randolph Hearst? Lord Northcliffe? Helen Waddell?

(2) **. . . Jean de Meung, the mediaeval Diogenes . . .**

Does this mean that Jean de Meung was as surly as Diogenes? That he lived in a tub? That he was a cynic philosopher?

(3) **. . . his *Roman* as the outrage of clerical prejudice on the chivalrous Dream of the Rose.**

The forgetful reader would not guess from this passage that Jean de Meung had written a sequel to an existing poem called the *Roman de la Rose*.

G. CIRCUMLOCUTION

It is not to say that satire upon woman is not . . .

This amounts to: 'Satire upon woman is, I grant . . .'

J. MEMORY STRAIN

It is not to say that satire upon woman is not a distinct branch of mediaeval literature. It is to this day the *fonds* of most music-hall jokes, thanks to that obscure instinct for which 'woman, in herself and without any effort on her part, is always News'. But the bourgeois is a far richer vein than the clerical.

The reader, after the distracting interpolation of the second sentence, will probably be unable to supply the word 'satire' after 'bourgeois' in the third sentence.

K. TOO MUCH OF THE SAME WORD

It is not to say that . . .
It is to this day the *fonds* . . .
. . . it is the ideal temper . . .
It is true that Jean de Meung . . .

The 'it is' repetition catches the eye, and the various occasions are not even parallel. In the first and the fourth cases the 'it' has no particular back-reference, as it has in the second and third.

P. AWKWARD INVERSION

But there is nothing in Latin to touch the brutality of the vernacular. 'I always bless God,' said William Morris, 'for making anything so strong as an onion;' it is the ideal temper in which to approach the grosser half of mediaeval literature.

The sudden transition from St Bernard and Golias to the nineteenth-century William Morris is disconcerting to the reader. It would have been better if the applicability of William Morris's remark to the context had been explained first.

FAIR COPY

'It is difficult to understand why women should be so constant a subject for vaudeville jokes, or why — as Lord Northcliffe [?] once remarked — "woman in herself, and without any effort on her part, is always news". Whatever the explanation may be, this popular obsession was, I grant, already noticeable in the Middle Ages, when satires on the behaviour of women formed a distinct branch of Latin Clerical literature as well as of literature written in the various vernaculars of the time.

St Bernard of Morlaix in his ecstatic poem *De Contemptu Mundi*[1] roughly castigates the sinful folly of women;[2] Golias in his *De Conjuge*

[1] Of Contempt for the World.

[2] Miss Waddell, who considers that the passage is self-explanatory in its original context, writes to us that 'neither St Bernard nor Golias has this prejudice' against women. But if the passage is, as seems to be implied by the three first sentences, about clerical and bourgeois satire on women, and if neither St Bernard nor Golias is an instance of the clerical satirist, the reader is entitled to wonder why they are brought in? Should a new paragraph perhaps have begun with 'But the bourgeois . . .'?

Non Ducenda[1] a verse dialogue, [?] expresses profound gratitude to three angels who, it appears, have come to dissuade him from matrimony. A third cleric, Jean de Meung, satirizes the *Roman de la Rose* in an outrageous sequel which has been held to prove an inveterate prejudice among all clerics against the ideal of chivalrous love embodied in the *Roman*. This is a mistaken view, however: for the author of the original *Roman* seems to have been a cleric himself; and no general deduction about clerics can be made from the case of Jean de Meung, who was surly, ill-conditioned and idiosyncratic and who wrote (in French, not Latin) at the end of thirteenth century under the first blasts of that east wind which was to blow through Europe for the next two centuries. Certainly, neither St Bernard nor Golias shows any prejudice against chivalrous love.

Vernacular satire was far grosser, more brutal, and more humorous than the Latin, and is best approached nowadays in the mood of William Morris's: "I always bless God for making anything so strong as an onion".'

COMMENT

The general meaning of this highly stylized passage is not clear to ordinary readers even if they have followed the wandering argument of the book with close attention; the precise meaning is clear only to the very few who have the same intimate knowledge of mediaeval literature as Miss Waddell herself. The book was written as a University thesis and not sufficiently modified for popular publication.

The popular Turkish story of 'The Khoja' is to the point here. 'One day at the Mosque, the Khoja addressed his university class with the words: "My Children, do you know the moral story of the Prophet Balaam and his Ass?" They all answered proudly and expectantly: "Yes, learned Khoja! We do!" "Good", said the Khoja, "then I need not expound it to you, since you are so wise." He rose and left them. The next day he asked the class: "My Children, do you know the moral story of the Prophet Jonah and the Gourd?" They all answered humbly and prudently: "No, learned Khoja! We know nothing!" "That is bad", said the Khoja, "for you come to me as a class of initiates, not of ignorant men. If you do not know even the bare story, it is not worth my while explaining its moral implications to you." He rose and left them, and by this act is held to have ridiculed his colleagues at the Mosque who preached either above the heads of the ignorant, or below those of the initiates.'

[1] Of a Man's Not Marrying.

Sir Hugh Walpole

from his Weekly Review Column, March 1940

TEXT

. . . There has just been published[P] Eric Linklater's autobiography: 'The Man on My Back'. It is a most readable book, and,[17] finally,[9a] as I found[5a] every work of Mr. Linklater,[24a] except 'Juan in America' and 'Ben Jonson',[16] unsatisfactory.

Why is it unsatisfactory? Because Mr. Linklater himself is not there.[4]

I do not know why he is so elusive — whether it is by intention or by some perverseness[21] of his own.[20a] I thought I had caught him[9b] in 'Juan in America', which[2] is a consistent piece of brilliant nonsense.[3a/23] Now I am not sure.[3b]

He can describe beautifully. The picture[7] of Compton Mackenzie in[9c] Barra, Panama,[9d/25] trains in America, a Scottish election, all these things are word pieces[20b] strung like little sparkling jewels[A] — on what? Practically nothing at all.[9e]

The point of autobiography, I imagine,[20c] is that it should be about[24b] somebody,[8] but I believe[10] that Mr. Linklater is so fundamentally[20d] modest that he was[24c] compelled to leave out of his book the only thing that really mattered,[5b/22] namely, himself.

EXAMINATION

2. WHICH?

I thought I had caught him in 'Juan in America', which is a consistent piece of brilliant nonsense.

The comma suggests that 'I thought I had caught him' is the piece of nonsense, not 'Juan in America'.

3. WHAT?

(*a*) **. . . a consistent piece of brilliant nonsense.**

This might mean almost anything. The reader should at least have been told that 'Juan in America' is a novel.

(*b*) **Now I am not sure.**

Of what?

4. WHERE?

Why is it unsatisfactory? Because Mr. Linklater himself is not there.

Where? Mr. Linklater has written the book most readably and is therefore, metaphorically, between its covers, even if it is not the autobiography it purports to be.

5. WHEN?

(*a*) **. . . as I found every work of Mr. Linklater except . . .**

If this were 'as I have found' it would be clear; but 'as I found' suggests that Sir Hugh read the whole of Eric Linklater's works through on a single occasion. When was that?

(*b*) **. . . to leave out . . . the only thing that really mattered . . .**

Since this is a book review, 'that really mattered' should have been 'that really matters', unless Sir Hugh is referring to a particular occasion.

7. HOW MANY?

The picture of Compton Mackenzie in Barra, Panama, trains in America, a Scottish election, all these things are . . .

Unless a portrait of Compton Mackenzie, hanging in a Barra house, is meant, the words 'The picture of' are either unnecessary or should have been altered to 'The pictures of' to cover all the items in the category.

8. INAPPROPRIATE WORD OR PHRASE

The point of autobiography, I imagine, is that it should be about somebody.

The point of autobiography is: not that it is about somebody (which is the point of biography), but that it is about the writer himself.

9. AMBIGUOUS WORD OR PHRASE

(*a*) **. . . and, finally, . . . unsatisfactory.**

Does 'finally' express lapse of time? Or evaluative degree?

(*b*) **I thought I had caught him in 'Juan in America', which is a consistent piece of brilliant nonsense.**

How can an elusive author be 'caught'? Does this mean that, except by mistake, he never commits himself to any opinion, but contents himself with making his characters give opinions which are not necessarily his own? Or does it mean that, except by mistake, he gives no self-portrait?

(*c*) **The picture of Compton Mackenzie in Barra, Panama, trains in America, a Scottish election . . .**

Readers who associated Compton Mackenzie with the Hebridean island of Barra, and with adventurous travel, and who also knew that he had stood for election as a Scottish Nationalist, might be doubtful whether the word 'in' covered not only Barra but 'Panama', 'trains in America', and 'a Scottish election'.

(*d*) **The picture of Compton Mackenzie in Barra, Panama . . .**

A cable sent to Compton Mackenzie at 'Barra, Panama, Central America', would have been returned to the sender with the explanation: 'place unknown'. For Barra is an island in the Hebrides; and Eric Linklater saw Panama and Compton Mackenzie on separate occasions.

(*e*) **He can describe beautifully . . . all these things are . . . strung like little sparkling jewels on — what? Practically nothing at all.**

It is not clear whether 'Practically nothing at all' is an answer to the question 'on — what?', or whether it is a general comment on the poverty of the material so beautifully treated by Eric Linklater.

10. MISPLACED WORD OR PHRASE

The point of autobiography, I imagine, is that it should be about somebody, but I believe that Mr. Linklater is so fundamentally modest . . .

What he perhaps means is that he *believes* that the point of an autobiography to be that it is about its writer, but that he *imagines* Mr. Linklater to have been too modest to stick to this point.

16. UNDEVELOPED THEME

. . . and, finally, as I found every work of Mr. Linklater except 'Juan in America' and 'Ben Jonson', unsatisfactory.

'Juan in America' is subsequently written about, but there is no further mention of 'Ben Jonson'.

17. FAULTY CONNEXION

It is a most readable book, and, finally . . . unsatisfactory.

Since a 'most readable book' usually satisfies the reader, a 'but' not an 'and' seems called for after 'book'.

20. IRRELEVANCY

(*a*) **. . . — whether it is by intention or by some perverseness of his own.**

There is no secondary contrast between his own perverseness and that of other people; so 'of his own' should not have appeared.

(*b*) **The picture of Compton Mackenzie, Barra, Panama, trains in America, a Scottish election, all these things are word pieces strung like little sparkling jewels . . .**

It would have been enough, after going through the list of things described, to continue: 'all these are strung like little sparkling jewels . . .', leaving out the unnecessary words 'things' and 'word pieces.'

(*c*) **The point of autobiography, I imagine, is that it should be . . .**

'I imagine' is perhaps an apology for a self-evident statement. It should have been omitted.

(*d*) **. . . but I believe that Mr. Linklater is so fundamentally modest . . .**

Unless this is to suggest that his work is superficially modest, the word 'fundamentally' should have been omitted.

21. FALSE CONTRAST

— whether it is by intention or by some perverseness of his own.

The contrast should either have been between intention and involuntary action; or between perverseness and right-mindedness, with a reservation that right-minded people often move in a way that seems perverse.

22. OVER-EMPHASIS

. . . to leave out of his book the only thing that really mattered . . .

Obviously, Eric Linklater has not left himself out entirely. And obviously in an autobiography other things than the writer 'really matter': if he has existed in a vacuum there is no story.

23. LOGICAL WEAKNESS

. . . 'Juan in America', which is a consistent piece of brilliant nonsense.

Brilliant nonsense is utterly inconsistent.

24. CHANGE OF STANDPOINT

(*a*) **. . . and, finally, as I found every work of Mr. Linklater . . .**

Either: 'every work by Mr. Linklater'.
Or: 'all the works of Mr. Linklater'.
Or: 'every work of Mr. Linklater's'.
In the third case the word 'works' is understood but not written.

(*b*) **The point of autobiography . . . is that it should be about . . .**

Either: 'Autobiography should be about . . .'
Or: 'The point of autobiography is that it is about . . .'

(*c*) **. . . Mr. Linklater is so fundamentally modest that he was compelled . . .**

What he is now does not necessarily account for what he did then. It should have been: 'that he has been compelled'.

25. MIXED CATEGORY

. . . Compton Mackenzie in Barra, Panama, trains in America, a Scottish election . . .

To make 'Panama' fit this category something more should have been recorded as happening in it: 'Life in Panama', 'Drinks in Panama', 'The Canal at Panama'.

A MISMATING OF METAPHORS

The picture of Compton Mackenzie . . . trains in America, a Scottish election, all these things are word pieces strung like little sparkling jewels . . .

Can a picture be a little sparkling jewel?

P. AWKWARD INVERSION

. . . There has just been published Eric Linklater's autobiography . . .

Since the newness of the book is not contrasted with the oldness of other books mentioned in the review, there seems no justification for not putting the name of the book first.

FAIR COPY

'Eric Linklater's "autobiography", "The Man on My Back", has just been published. His talent for description makes it most readable. Here are beautiful accounts, for example, of Compton Mackenzie in the Hebridean island of Barra, of life in Panama, of American trains, of a Scottish election. They are strung sparklingly together, like little gems, on a thread of – what?

Yes, there lies the difficulty, in the elusive quality of the thread. The feeling with which I am left on laying down this book is one of dissatisfaction: dissatisfaction that either from perverseness, or, more probably, from excessive modesty, Mr. Linklater has failed to delineate what should be the most important character in everyone's autobiography – his own The same impersonality spoilt all his previous books for me as I read them, except "Juan in America," a consistently brilliant humorous novel, and "Ben Jonson and King James" [. . . ? . . .]. In both of these I fancied that Mr. Linklater allowed a hint of his own appetites and prejudices [?] to appear; but after reading "The Man on My Back" I am not sure whether I was right.'

COMMENT

The strain of having to write weekly book-reviews for an illustrated daily, when in ill-health, and the knowledge that his public was not a very literate one, made Sir Hugh grow more and more careless as his death approached. Perhaps also the terse conversational style demanded by the editor did not come easily to him. Moreover, Sir Hugh, being very sensitive about reviews of his own work, did not like writing unkindly about his fellow-authors, though their books were bad. Here his attempt to reprove Eric Linklater for not 'coming clean' about himself in an autobiography, and yet to make the reproof read like a Balaam's blessing, has had a particularly disorderly effect on his sentences.

H. G. WELLS

from *The Common Sense of War and Peace*, February 1940

TEXT

For the greater part of my life I have given most of my working time to[12] the problem of the human future,[5a/20a] studying the possibility of a world-wide re-organization of human society,[H1] that might avert[3a] the menace[14a] of defeat[3b] and extinction[20b] that hangs over our species.[E/H1] That has been my leading[20c] pre-occupation since I[5b] published 'The Time Machine' in 1893.[12] I have never thought, much less[6] have I asserted,[H2] that progress[3c] was[24a] inevitable, though numerous people chose[5c] to fancy that about me.[8a] I have always maintained[H2] that by a strenuous effort mankind[H1] *might* defeat the impartial destructiveness[14b] of nature,[23] but I have always insisted[20d/H2] that only by incessant hard thinking and a better co-ordination of man's[H1] immense but dispersed[8b] powers of self-sacrifice and heroism[E] was such[24b] a victory possible.[20d]

EXAMINATION

3. WHAT?

(*a*) **. . . that might avert the menace of defeat and extinction that hangs over our species.**

Does this mean that individual man might become physically immortal?

(*b*) **. . . that might avert the menace of defeat and extinction . . .**

A 'menace of defeat' by what? Flood? Fire? Disease? Exhaustion of food and fuel supplies? Moral degeneration?

(*c*) **I have never thought, . . . that progress was inevitable . . .**

Does this mean progress in his own studies? Or progress in the re-organization of human society? Or Progress, in the late-Victorian sense of the continuous betterment of mankind by civilization?

5. WHEN?

(*a*) **. . . the problem of the human future . . .**

H. G. Wells gives no clue as to whether he is speaking in terms of a few months, a few generations, or millions of years.

(*b*) **That has been my leading preoccupation since I published 'The Time Machine' in 1893.**

Did the publication of *The Time Machine* have anything to do with his studies? He is probably referring to the writing, not to the publication. Was that all done in 1893? We should guess 1892 as the date of his first preoccupation, if he means that the writing marked the end of some earlier preoccupation.

(*c*) **I have never thought . . . that progress was inevitable, though numerous people chose to fancy that about me.**

On what particular occasion did they make this choice?

6. HOW MUCH?

I have never thought, much less have I asserted . . .

How much is less than never? He means: 'I have never asserted, nor even thought'.

8. INAPPROPRIATE WORD OR PHRASE

(*a*) **I have never thought . . . that progress was inevitable, though numerous people chose to fancy that about me.**

Why not: 'though numerous people chose to fancy that I did'.

(*b*) **. . . a better co-ordination of man's immense but dispersed . . .**

The sense of 'dispersed' is already contained in 'world wide'. He perhaps means 'dissipated'.

12. DUPLICATION

For the greater part of my life I have given most of my working time to the problem of the human future . . . That has been my leading pre-occupation since I published 'The Time Machine' in 1893.

Unless H. G. Wells was a centenarian when he wrote this, and had started his literary career in early childhood, it would have been enough for him to write: 'I have given most of my working time to the problem of the human future since I published "The Time Machine" in 1893.'

14. MATERIAL OMISSION

(*a*) **. . . the possibility . . . of a . . . re-organization . . . that might avert the menace . . .**

Two subjects of study are concealed in this doubled contingency: what the nature of the menace is, and what social reforms will best avoid it. Both of these subjects should have been clearly stated.

(*b*) **. . . the impartial destructiveness of nature . . .**

This, as H. G. Wells knew, is offset by Nature's equally impartial constructiveness, e.g. the creation of fertile islands by cooperation between the coral insect, sea-birds, tides and currents.

20. IRRELEVANCY

(*a*) **. . . I have given most of my working time to the problem of the human future, studying the possibility of a world-wide reorganization . . . that might avert the menace . . . that hangs over our species.**

Since 'the problem of the human future' is set out at length in the remainder of the sentence, there seems no reason for this anticipatory mention of it.

(*b*) **. . . the menace of defeat and extinction that hangs over our species.**

The concept 'extinction' contains 'defeat', which could have been omitted.

(*c*) **. . . my leading pre-occupation since I published 'The Time Machine'.**

Any 'preoccupation' is a leading one: the 'pre' in the word denotes priority.

(*d*) **I have always maintained that by a strenuous effort mankind *might* defeat the impartial destructiveness of nature, but I have always insisted that only by incessant hard thinking . . . was such a victory possible.**

The phrases 'I have always insisted that' and 'was such a victory possible' could have been omitted without loss to the sense.

23. LOGICAL WEAKNESS

. . . our species.

. . . mankind might defeat the impartial destructiveness of nature . . .

H. G. Wells regards man as a species: and a species is a department of Nature. He wants man to survive as long as possible. Therefore he wishes Nature well. Yet he urges Natural Man not to co-operate with Nature, but to defeat her; and promises him survival as a reward. Nature's impartial destructiveness, also characteristic of Natural Man, is the poor excuse offered for his waging war against her.

24. CHANGE OF STANDPOINT

(*a*) **I have never thought that progress was inevitable . . .**

Either: 'I never thought that progress was inevitable . . .'

Or: 'I have never thought that progress is inevitable . . .'

(*b*) **. . . I have always insisted that only by . . . hard thinking . . . was such a victory possible.**

Either: 'I have always insisted that only by . . . hard thinking is such a victory possible.'

Or: 'I always insisted that only by . . . hard thinking was such a victory possible.'

E. MISMATING OF STYLES

. . . the menace of defeat . . . that hangs over our species.

. . . man's immense . . . powers of . . . heroism . . .

The word 'heroism' is used only in idealistic contexts; 'our species' in materialistic ones.

H. ELEGANT VARIATION

(1) **. . . human society . . .**
. . . our species . . .
. . . mankind . . .
. . . man's immense powers . . .

The same word, probably 'mankind', would have served in all these four contexts.

(2) **I have never thought, much less have I asserted, . . .**
I have always maintained . . .
I have always insisted . . .

There seems no reason for the variation between 'asserted', 'maintained', 'insisted', which has a contrastive effect.

FAIR COPY

'Ever since 1892 [?], when I began to write "The Time Machine", the two chief subjects of my literary studies have been the process of moral and physical degeneration [?] that now threatens to make mankind extinct in a few hundred years [?], and the various theories of world-wide social reorganization that have been designed to arrest this process. Many people fancy me to have asserted, at some time or other, that nothing can prevent the beneficent progress of civilization from continuing indefinitely. They are wrong: on the contrary, I have often asserted that mankind's survival for thousands, rather than hundreds, of years [?] depends on whether it will make a strenuous effort to coördinate its immense but dissipated powers of thought, and on whether each individual will always be prepared to sacrifice himself intrepidly for the common good.'

COMMENT

This passage, which opens the book from which it is taken, seems to have been hurriedly dictated, and not afterwards revised. The resonance of the sentences suggests that H. G. Wells is proud of the immense effect that his novels and other works have had on contemporary imaginative thought. But the passage is not, perhaps, intended to be more than a clearing of the throat, a signal for attentive silence. He does not trouble to define the meanings of his words, confident that most of his readers will have read at least one or two of his important works and be able to make the definitions for themselves. Possibly the phrase 'though numerous people chose to fancy that about me' conceals a slight pique – pique almost always has a destructive effect on the orderly progress of prose.

Most readers will sum up vaguely: 'Oh, yes, H. G. Wells is reminding us that ever since 1893 he has been warning us of the danger that mankind will one day become extinct, by some means or other, if we don't do something about it.' And perhaps this is how they are intended to sum up.

Professor A. N. Whitehead

from *Science and the Modern World*, 1926

TEXT

If we attend[24a] to what actually has happened in the past,[14/15a] and disregard romantic visions[8a/9a] of democracies, aristocracies, kings, generals, armies, and merchants,[25a] material power[9b] has generally been wielded with blindness, obstinacy, and selfishness, often with brutal malignancy. And yet mankind has progressed.[5a/16a] Even if you take[24a] a tiny oasis of peculiar excellence,[2a/15b] the type[12] of modern man who would have most chance of happiness in ancient Greece at its best[3] period is probably (as now[4]) an average professional heavyweight boxer,[23a] and not an average Greek scholar from Oxford or Germany.[25b] Indeed,[17] the main[23b] use of the Oxford scholar[16b] would have been[5b] his capability[8b] of writing an ode in glorification of the boxer.[16c/23b] Nothing does more harm[22] in unnerving men for[24b] their duties[16d] in the present than the attention devoted to the points[2b] of excellence in the past as compared[8c] with[G] the average failure[9c] of the present day.[H]

EXAMINATION

2. WHICH?

(*a*) **Even if you take a tiny oasis of peculiar excellence, the type of man who would have most chance of happiness in ancient Greece at its best period . . . is . . . an average professional heavyweight boxer, and not an average Greek scholar from Oxford or Germany.**

It is not immediately obvious whether the tiny oasis of peculiar excellence is the Greek faculty of Oxford (or of Heidelberg) University, the modern heavyweight boxing ring, or 'ancient Greece at its best period'. Ancient Greece at its best period seems quite a large oasis: ancient Greece, with its colonies, stretched from Spain to the Caucasus, and from Marseilles to Alexandria.

(*b*) **. . . devoted to the points of excellence in the past . . .**

These points have not yet been specified, so 'points of excellence' is enough.

3. WHAT?

. . . ancient Greece at its best period . . .

There are divergent views as to which this 'best period' was. It may well have been the Homeric age; or the Sixth Century B.C.; or even the age of Alexander and Aristotle. However, the view that Pericles's Athens was Greece at its best is held by most University professors who are Professor Whitehead's contemporaries.

4. WHERE?

. . . the modern men who would have most chance of happiness in ancient Greece at its best period is probably (as now) an average professional heavyweight boxer . . .

Does this really mean, as it seems, that only in modern Greece is an average professional heavyweight boxer the happiest man – happier even than a visiting scholar from Oxford or Germany? Or does 'as now' cover all Europe and America too?

5. WHEN?

(*a*) **And yet mankind has progressed.**

Since when?

(*b*) **The type of modern man who would have most chance of happiness in ancient Greece at its best period . . .**

Indeed, the main use of the Oxford scholar would have been . . .

The change from 'would have' to 'would have been' throws the date back behind 'the best period of ancient Greece' to an archaic second-best one.

8. INAPPROPRIATE WORD OR PHRASE

(*a*) **. . . and disregard romantic visions . . .**

Surely 'versions' is meant? 'Visions' are of the future, as ghostly apparitions are of the past.

(*b*) **. . . the main use of the Oxford scholar would have been his capability of writing an ode . . .**

Capabilities are put to uses, but are not themselves uses.

(*c*) **. . . the points of excellence in the past as compared with the average failure . . .**

This is surely a case of contrast rather than comparison? One compares like with like; one contrasts dissimilars.

9. AMBIGUOUS WORD OR PHRASE

(*a*) **. . . disregard romantic visions of democracies, aristocracies . . .**

Does 'of' here mean that the democracies, aristocracies and so forth had the visions; or that the visions were had of them?

(*b*) **. . . material power has generally been wielded . . .**

Does 'material power' in this context mean 'power that matters'? Or is it an implied contrast with spiritual, or with intellectual, power?

(*c*) **. . . compared with the average failure of the present day . . .**

Does this mean that, on an average, people of the present day are failures? Or that the comparison is with an average case of failure – failures not necessarily being common?

12. DUPLICATION

. . . the type of . . . man . . . is . . . an average professional heavyweight boxer, . . .

'Type' here means 'an average representative of a class' and can be omitted; unless perhaps what is meant is that such people as dirt-track racers, rodeo-performers and caber-tossers would have been equally happy at Athens – which is historically doubtful.

14. MATERIAL OMISSION

. . . what actually has happened in the past . . .

To say 'has happened' implies 'the past', which need not be mentioned unless to distinguish it as a 'recent past' or a 'far past'. What past is this?

15. UNFULFILLED PROMISE

(*a*) **If we attend to what actually has happened in the past . . . material power has generally been wielded with blindness . . .**

The expected conclusion to 'if we attend' is 'we shall discover'; but this is not provided.

(*b*) **Even if you take a tiny oasis of excellence, the type of modern man who would have most chance of happiness in ancient Greece at its best period is . . .**

The expected conclusion to 'if you take' is 'you will find'; but this is not provided.

16. UNDEVELOPED THEME

(*a*) **And yet mankind has progressed.**

The form that this progress has taken is not indicated. The hypothesis of the scholar and boxer, intended perhaps to bear out the statement, only confuses it. Apparently, the heavyweight boxer is still the happiest man, though nowadays the scholar no longer glorifies his happiness for him.

(*b*) **. . . the main use of the Oxford scholar would have been . . .**

What would the use of the German one have been?

(*c*) **. . . his capability of writing an ode in glorification of the boxer.**

More than this is needed to make the point clearly. Average heavyweight boxers in Greece did not have odes addressed to them; only a champion who managed to win a laurel, ivy or parsley crown for his city-state was so rewarded.

(*d*) **. . . his capability of writing an ode in glorification of the boxer. Nothing does more harm in unnerving men for their duties . . .**

The present position of the average scholar is left undefined; but 'mankind has progressed' suggests that, though the boxer nowadays is still the happier man, the scholar is the more highly honoured by the enlightened authorities.

17. FAULTY CONNEXION

. . . the . . . man who would have most chance of happiness in ancient Greece is probably (as now) an average professional heavyweight boxer, and not an average Greek scholar from Oxford or Germany. Indeed, the main use of the Oxford scholar would have been his capability of writing an ode in glorification of the boxer.

'Indeed' always emphasizes a point made in the preceding sentence. But here not a word has been said about happiness; nor can it be assumed that an Oxford scholar would *not* be as happy to write a graceful ode in glorification of a boxer as Pindar was.

22. OVER-EMPHASIS

Nothing does more harm in unnerving men for their duties in the present than the attention devoted to the points of excellence in the past . . .

A great many things obviously do more harm: such as domestic worries, fear of death, boredom, the tyranny of employers or the apathy of fellow-workers.

23. LOGICAL WEAKNESS

(*a*) **. . . the type of modern man who would have most chance of happiness in ancient Greece at its best period is probably (as now) an average professional heavyweight boxer.**

A professional boxer, unlike an amateur, would probably be disappointed at getting a perishable crown rather than a cartload of *minae* for his splendid victories; and an *average* professional heavyweight boxer would be less likely than a leading one to win any victories worth eulogizing by the Oxford (or German) scholar. And any modern boxer, whatever his status or skill, would be disgusted at the persistent fouling which characterized the Greek ring.

(*b*) **. . . an average Greek scholar from Oxford or Germany. Indeed, the main use of the Oxford scholar would have been his capability of writing an ode in glorification of the boxer.**

The *main* use of the Oxford scholar would no doubt have been his Homeric commentary and philosophic argument in the Schools. Odes were written by poets, not scholars.

24. CHANGE OF STANDPOINT

(*a*) **If we attend . . .**

Even if you take . . .

The change from 'we' to 'you' seems arbitrary. (Nor are 'we' and 'you' defined.)

(*b*) **Nothing does more harm in unnerving men for their duties . . .**

The sentence starts with the idea of 'unnerving men *in* their duties' and changes to that of 'incapacitating men *for* their duties'.

25. MIXED CATEGORY

(*a*) **. . . romantic visions of democracies, aristocracies, kings, generals, armies, and merchants . . .**

This catalogue begins with forms of government, and then suddenly switches to kinds of people. There seems no reason why it should stop here, or anywhere, once it has thus changed its theme: it might continue with a list of trusts, trade-unions, and courts of law.

(*b*) **. . . Greek scholar from Oxford or Germany . . .**

'Oxford' and 'Germany' are not parallel. It should be: 'Oxford or Bonn', 'Oxford or Heidelberg' or 'an English or German university'.

G. CIRCUMLOCUTION

. . . attention devoted to the points of excellence in the past as compared with . . .

Why not 'the greater attention devoted to past excellences'?

H. ELEGANT VARIATION

. . . their duties in the present . . .

. . . the average failure of the present day . . .

There seems no need for 'present day' to become 'present' in the same sentence.

FAIR COPY

'Those who study the authentic records, disregarding idealistic misrepresentations of the past, will discover that in democracies, aristocracies, monarchies, plutocracies and military dictatorships, alike, temporal power has usually been wielded with blindness, obstinacy and selfishness, often with brutal malignance. Yet, despite all this, mankind has slowly progressed during the last thousand years, at least in gradually adopting a more respectful attitude towards literary culture. If two moderns, a good Greek scholar, say, from Oxford or Heidelberg, and a good professional heavyweight boxer, were to be carried back in time to Pericles's Athens – often described as a small oasis of enlightenment in the desert of that semi-barbaric age – the boxer would be the one likely to receive the more handsome civic honours; though the scholar, if his literary capacities permitted, and if the boxer carried off the prize at some important festival, might perhaps win the approval of the authorities by an ode written in the boxer's honour. (Nowadays boxers, though still popular heroes, are never officially honoured with titles and orders, as scholars sometimes are.) It unnerves the modern worker to hear the successes of the past constantly cried up at the expense of the failures of his own day: as though the past had never had failures, nor modern times successes.'

COMMENT

Professor Whitehead is generally acknowledged to be the most thorough, acute and original of contemporary British philosophers. It is strange to find him unbending in this popular work: becoming as conversationally loose as any feather-headed undergraduate.

SIR LEONARD WOOLLEY

from *Ur of the Chaldees*, 1929

TEXT

Excavating the site, we found Ennatum's building standing on the stumps[8a] of the older walls which had been used by the new bricklayers[1] as a foundation, and so recovered at one time[8b] the ground-plan of both temples.

The building was a rectangle measuring 240 feet either way,[3a] and was surrounded by an enormously heavy[8c] wall[3b] through the heart of which[3c] a narrow paved corridor ran round three sides of it,[3d] leading from a gate-tower over the main[16] entrance to two fortified towers at the far corners[4]; a similar corridor cut straight across the building, dividing it into two unequal parts[3e] and affording quick access from one tower to the other.

EXAMINATION

1. WHO?

. . . we found Ennatum's building standing on the stumps of the older walls which had been used by the new bricklayers as a foundation . . .

Who were these new bricklayers? If Ennatum's, why not 'his'?

3. WHAT?

(*a*) **The building was a rectangle measuring 240 feet either way . . .**

Does he mean that the elevation was rectangular? – if so, what were the lateral dimensions? For though a square *is* a rectangle, it is usually called a square; 'rectangle' is reserved for a figure with two equal sides longer than the two other equal sides.

(*b*) **. . . and was surrounded by an enormously heavy wall . . .**

At what distance? Or was the heavy wall part of the structure?

(*c*) **. . . through the heart of which a narrow paved corridor ran round three sides of it . . .**

Usually 'through the heart of' means 'direct through the middle of an object, from a point outside and in front of it'. Here it apparently means 'transversely inside'. And at what height did the corridor run?

(*d*) **. . . ran round three sides of it . . .**

Which three sides?

(*e*) **. . . a similar corridor cut straight across the building, dividing it into two unequal parts . . .**

In which direction? Which part was the larger? How was this corridor similar to the other? Was it also enclosed in an enormously heavy wall? At what height did it run?

4. WHERE?

. . . two fortified towers at the far corners . . .

Does this mean the rear angles?

8. INAPPROPRIATE WORD OR PHRASE

(*a*) **. . . the stumps of the older walls . . .**

It is easy to imagine the stumps of pillars, columns, posts, or piles: but what are the 'stumps' of walls?

(*b*) **. . . and so recovered at one time . . .**

The phrase he wants is either 'At one and the same time' or 'at once'. 'At one time' means 'formerly'.

(*c*) **. . . an enormously heavy wall . . .**

Surely it is the massiveness of the wall that is being stressed, not the weight. If it had been built of stone it would have been far heavier.

16. UNDEVELOPED THEME

. . . a gate-tower over the main entrance . . .

Were there other entrances?

FAIR COPY

'When we excavated the site we solved two problems at the same time: for we found that Fnnatum's bricklayers had used the broken lower courses of the original walls as foundations for the new temple, so that the ground plan, the outline of which was a square with a 240-foot side, had remained unaltered.

Fifty [?] feet above ground level along the interior of each of the massive main walls, except the rear one, ran a narrow paved passage, connecting a tower over the front gateway with two fortified towers at the rear angles. Easy communication between these two was provided at ground level [?] by a similar passage contained in an equally massive [?] inner wall standing parallel with the rear wall, fifty feet [?] from it.'

COMMENT

The failure to explain clearly the lay-out of a situation is due sometimes to uncertainty about one or more of the elements, sometimes to haste or emotion, sometimes to caring little whether or not the reader forms an accurate mental picture. Here the failure does not seem to be due to any of these causes. Probably Sir Leonard Woolley has himself so clear a memory of the temple that he forgets that his readers know only as much as he cares to tell them about it.

In the Fair Copy we have guessed at the heights and distances which the reader will want to be given; the correct ones are not to be found in the original.